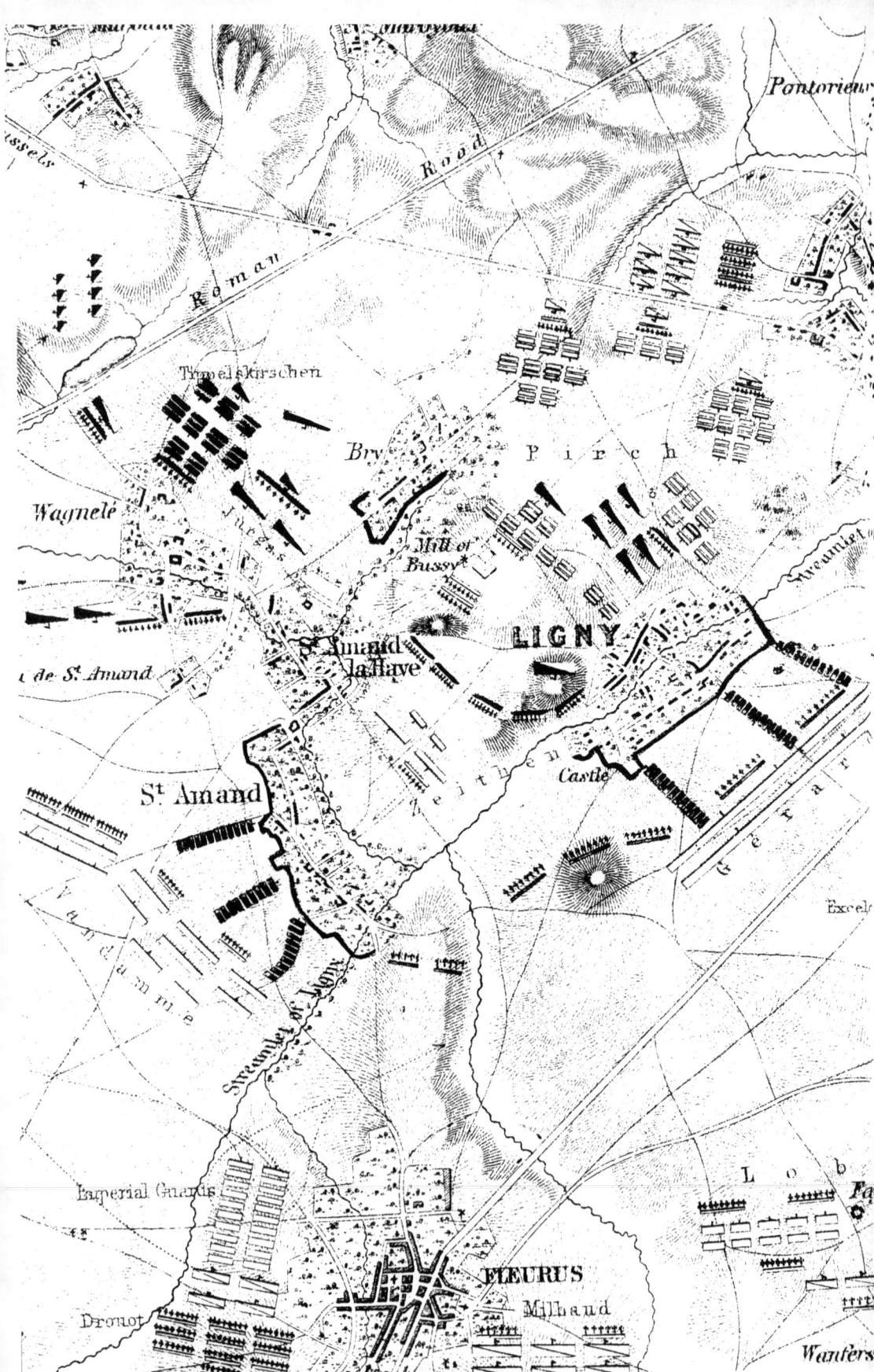

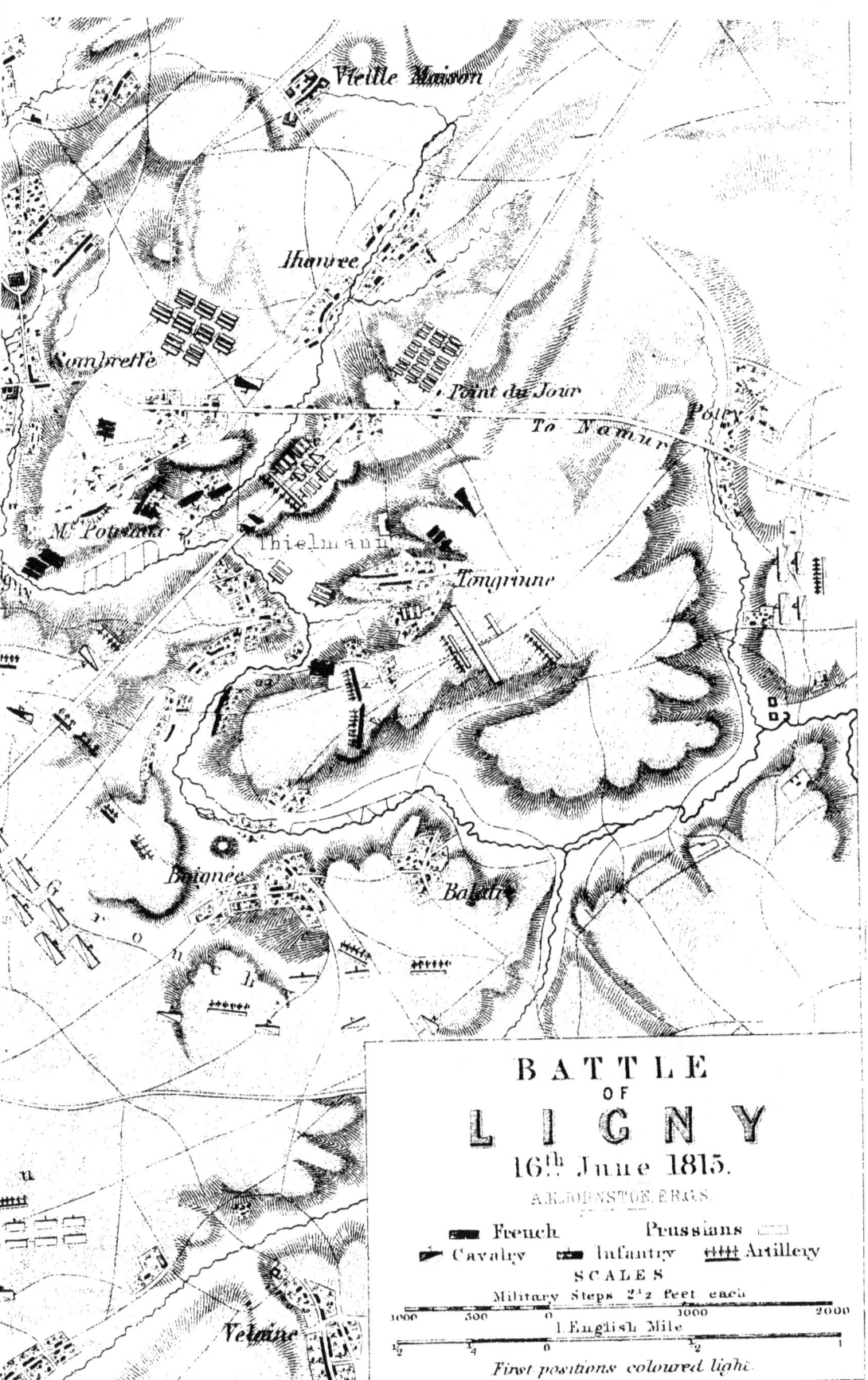

NAPOLEON
AND THE CAMPAIGN OF
1815
WATERLOO

HENRY HOUSSAYE

The Naval & Military Press Ltd

Published by
The Naval & Military Press Ltd
Unit 10, Ridgewood Industrial Park,
Uckfield, East Sussex,
TN22 5QE England
Tel: +44 (0) 1825 749494
Fax: +44 (0) 1825 765701
www.naval-military-press.com
© The Naval & Military Press Ltd 2004

In reprinting in facsimile from the original, any imperfections are inevitably reproduced and the quality may fall short of modern type and cartographic standards.

CONTENTS

BOOK I

COMMENCEMENT OF THE CAMPAIGN

CHAPTER I

THE LAST ARMY OF THE EMPIRE

		PAGE
I.	Change from a Peace footing to that of War—Recall of men on leave—Mobilisation of the National Guards—The Conscription of 1815	3
II.	Arming and equipping—Supplies—Military strongholds and forts—The War Budget	11
III.	First and second re-division of the troops into Army Corps—Strength of the Army of the first line and of the Auxiliary Army on 15th June 1815	19
IV.	Dismissals and promotions	22
V.	Leaders: The Marshals of France	26
VI.	Leaders: The Chief of the Staff	32
VII.	Leaders: The Generals	35
VIII.	The spirit of the Army	40

CHAPTER II

THE PLANS FOR THE CAMPAIGN

I.	Project for an invasion of Belgium in the early part of April	49
II.	The plan of campaign formed of the Allies	51
III.	Napoleon's plan of campaign	54

IV. Concentration of the French Army (8th to 14th June)—Arrival of the Emperor at Beaumont—Strength and positions of the armies on the 14th of June. . . 57

CHAPTER III

THE FIRST ENGAGEMENTS

I. Passage of the Belgian frontier (15th June)—The desertion of General de Bourmont 60
II. Taking of Charleroi 63
III. The interview between Napoleon and Ney—Battle at Gilly with the right wing 65
IV. Ney's operations on 15th of June—Battle of Gosselies—Battle of Frasnes—Quatre-Bras 70

BOOK II

LIGNY AND QUATRE-BRAS

CHAPTER I

THE MORNING OF THE 16TH OF JUNE

I. Plans and orders of Napoleon (from five o'clock to eight) . 75
II. Departure of Napoleon for Fleurus (half-past nine o'clock) 77
III. Concentration of the Prussian Army on the north of the brook of Ligny — Immobility of the English Army throughout the 15th of June—The Duchess of Richmond's ball (night of the 15th to the 16th of June) . 79
IV. Wellington's arrival at Quatre-Bras (16th June, ten o'clock)—Interview between Wellington and Blücher at the mill of Bussy, near Ligny (one P.M.) 84

CHAPTER II

THE BATTLE OF LIGNY

I. The field of battle — Dispositions of Blücher and Napoleon 88

CONTENTS

	PAGE
II. From three to four o'clock—Attacks on Saint-Amand by Vandamme, and on Ligny by Gérard	93
III. From four o'clock to half-past seven: Counter-attack by Blücher—Appearance on the French flank of a column recognised as belonging to the enemy—Grouchy's demonstration against the Prussian left—Fierce contest at Saint-Amand and at Ligny	96
IV. From half-past seven to half-past nine o'clock—Final assault—Capture of Ligny—Engagements on the hills —Retreat of the Prussians	103

CHAPTER III

THE BATTLE OF QUATRE-BRAS

I. Inaction of Marshal Ney during the morning of the 16th of June—Repeated orders from the Emperor . .	108
II. Attack on Quatre-Bras by Reille's corps (two o'clock P.M.)—Wellington's return to Quatre-Bras and arrival of the first English reinforcements (three o'clock)—Death of the Duke of Brunswick (half-past four o'clock) . .	112
III. The false move of Count d'Erlon	116
IV. Charge of Kellermann's cuirassiers (six o'clock)—Offensive action of Wellington (seven o'clock)—The French driven back on their original positions (from eight to nine o'clock)	119

CHAPTER IV

THE RETREAT OF THE PRUSSIAN ARMY

I. First plans of Napoleon for 17th June	125
II. The Emperor's orders to Grouchy (between eleven o'clock and half-past eleven)	128
III. Retreat of the Prussian Army on Wavre . . .	132
IV. Movements of Pajol towards Namur and of Exelmans on Gembloux in pursuit of the Prussian columns . .	134
V. March of Grouchy's army — Bivouac at Gembloux — Grouchy's letter to the Emperor (ten o'clock P.M.) .	137

CHAPTER V

THE RETREAT OF THE ENGLISH ARMY

I. Exchange of despatches between Blücher and Wellington (morning of the 17th of June)—Retreat of the English (ten o'clock) 143
II. Arrival of Napoleon at Quatre-Bras, still held by the English cavalry (two o'clock) 145
III. Keen pursuit of the English rearguard personally led by Napoleon — Engagement at Genappe—Cannonade at Mont-Saint-Jean (seven o'clock) 149
IV. Night in camp 151
V. Indecision of Napoleon—Letter from Blücher to Wellington —Orders of Napoleon (night of the 17th to the 18th of June) 153

BOOK III

WATERLOO

CHAPTER I

BLÜCHER AND GROUCHY

I. Dispositions and movements of the Prussian Army on the morning of the 18th of June—Departure from Wavre of Field-Marshal Blücher (eleven o'clock) . . . 161
II. Dispositions of Grouchy 164
III. Discussion between Gérard and Grouchy at Walhain (mid-day) 167

CHAPTER II

THE BATTLE OF WATERLOO

The Morning

I. Topography of the field of battle 171
II. Positions of the Anglo-Netherland Army . . . 173

CONTENTS

		PAGE
III.	Napoleon's breakfast at Le Caillou—Letter to Grouchy	177
IV.	The last review (ten o'clock)—Order of battle for the French Army—Napoleon's plan of attack (eleven o'clock)	182

CHAPTER III

THE BATTLE OF WATERLOO (*continued*)

From half-past eleven to three o'clock

I.	Attack on Hougoumont by the division of Jérôme Bonaparte of Reille's corps	187
II.	Appearance of Bülow's corps on the heights of Chapelle-Saint-Lambert— New despatch from Napoleon to Grouchy	189
III.	Attack on La Haye-Sainte and on the plateau of Mont-Saint-Jean by Count d'Erlon's corps	193
IV.	Counter-attack of the English under Picton—Charge of Lord Somerset's horse-guards—The press of the cuirassiers in the hollow road	195
V.	Charge of Ponsonby's dragoons—Rout of d'Erlon's infantry—Counter-charge of Jacquinot's lancers and Farine's cuirassiers—Conflagration of Hougoumont	197

CHAPTER IV

THE BATTLE OF WATERLOO (*continued*)

From three to seven o'clock

I.	Second attack on La Haye-Sainte—The order from Ney to Milhaud	201
II.	First and second charges of Milhaud's cuirassiers and the light cavalry of the Guard—Order of the Emperor to Kellermann's cuirassiers and the cavalry under Guyot	205
III.	Bülow's corps enters in line—Lobau's defence—Capture and recapture of Plancenoit	208
IV.	Third and fourth charges of Milhaud's cuirassiers, supported by those of Kellermann, the dragoons, and the mounted grenadiers of the Guard	211

V. General attack on the plateau by the infantry under Reille and d'Erlon, and by the remainder of the cavalry—Storming of La Haye-Sainte—The English line shaken—New struggle at Plancenoit 214

CHAPTER V

THE BATTLE OF WATERLOO (*continued*)

From seven to nine o'clock

I. Dispositions for the final attack—Strengthening of the English line—Approach of Zieten's corps 220
II. Assault on the plateau of Mont-Saint-Jean by the "Middle" Guard 223
III. "The Guard falls back!"—General forward movement of the English Army—Irruption of the Prussians under Zieten—The panic 228
IV. The squares of Christiani, of Roguet, of Cambronne . . 230
V. Arrival of Pirch's corps to the assistance of Bülow—Slaughter at Plancenoit—The struggle on the plateau of La Belle Alliance—The last squares of the Old Guard . 233

CHAPTER VI

THE ROUT

I. Meeting between Wellington and Blücher in front of the inn of La Belle Alliance (a quarter past nine o'clock)—The rout of the French 237
II. Attempt to resist at Genappe (eleven o'clock) . . . 240
III. Pursuit by the Prussian cavalry (night of the 18th to the 19th of June) 242
IV. Halt of the Emperor at Quatre-Bras—Passage of the army at Charleroi (morning of the 19th of June) . . . 244
V. Retreat on Laon—Departure of the Emperor for Paris (20th June) 248

CHAPTER VII

THE ACTIONS AT WAVRE AND GROUCHY'S RETREAT

I. Grouchy marches on Wavre—Battle at La Baraque—Attack on Wavre (afternoon of 18th June) . . . 253
II. Soult's second despatch—Renewed assaults upon Wavre and Bierges—Passage of the Dyle at Limale and battle in the night 258
III. Renewal of the fight and defeat of Thielmann (morning of the 19th of June)—News of the disaster (half-past ten, morning of the 19th of June)—Retreat of Grouchy (afternoon and evening of the 19th of June) . . . 126
IV. Actions at La Falise and Le Boquet (morning of the 20th of June) — Defence of Namur (from three to nine o'clock at night)—Rallying of Grouchy's army at Givet (21st June) 265

CHAPTER VIII

THE CAMPAIGN OF 1815

I. The operations of the 15th of June—The battles of Ligny and of Quatre-Bras 269
II. Napoleon's mistake 276
III. Marshal Grouchy 280
IV. Waterloo 288

NOTE ON THE MAPS

I

GENERAL MAP OF THE CAMPAIGN OF 1815

II

MAP OF THE MILITARY OPERATIONS FROM THE 15TH TO THE 20TH OF JUNE

I have drawn these maps after two models of those by Ferrari and Capitaine, which were used by the Emperor during the campaign.

I have corrected their inaccuracies (with regard to the positions of certain villages and the direction of the watercourses) by means of the Map of the Military Engineers published in 1825, and the map of 40,000E of the Military Cartographical Institute of Belgium, published in 1892. It is on the latter, on account of the dimensions of the scale, that I have calculated throughout all the distances, when writing *Waterloo*.

Map I. should be consulted for the cantonments of the different armies during the first fortnight of June 1815, and for the passage of the Belgian frontier.

Map II. will be useful for the military operations from the 15th to the 20th of June, and principally for the route followed by Grouchy, as also for that he ought to have taken.

III

PLAN OF THE BATTLE OF WATERLOO

I have reproduced, at half its original size, the plan drawn out in 1816 by Craan, the surveying engineer of Brabant. This plan, which is now extremely rare, is the oldest topographical document. It is, at the same time, the most correct and the most valuable with regard to certain essential details, such as the position and form of the woods, the situation of the farms and of the sandpit, the roads of communication, also the hedges and banks of the Ohain Road. I must also point out, that Craan having made use of an oblique illustration, has by it given undue relief to the undulations of the ground on which the battle was fought. The edges are too sharply defined. The hollows, like the plains, seem to be equalised by the plane. The gradation of the slopes is not sufficiently marked. Thus, on this plan, one would never realise that from La Haye-Sainte the ground continues to ascend to the road of Ohain, which formed the crest of the English position.

Craan has traced all the movements of the troops from eleven o'clock till night. On a reduced plan, the multiplicity of the interlacing lines would have created confusion. I have therefore merely indicated the position of the divisions and of the brigades at the outset of the battle, rectifying at the same time the occasionally incorrect diagrams drawn by Craan.

I have also made use of the plans of Siborne, those in Napoleon's Commentaries and in the *Waterloo Letters*, and also of the information to be gathered from the numerous accounts of the combatants themselves.

H. H.

5th *December* 1898.

BOOK I
COMMENCEMENT OF THE CAMPAIGN

WATERLOO

BOOK I CHAPTER I

THE LAST ARMY OF THE EMPIRE

I. Change from a peace footing to a war footing.—Recall of men on leave.—Mobilisation of National Guards.—Conscription of 1815.
II. Arming and outfitting.—Supplies.—Military strongholds and forts.—War Budget.
III. First and second re-division of the troops into Army Corps.—Strength of the Army of the first line and of the Auxiliary Army on 15th June 1815.
IV. Dismissals and promotions.
V. Leaders: the Marshals of France.
VI. Leaders: the Chief of the Headquarters Staff.
VII. Leaders: the Generals.
VIII. The spirit of the Army.

Section I

On his return from Elba the Emperor found scarcely 200,000 men under arms.[1] Had he felt himself in possession of his former unlimited power, he might have doubled his forces by calling for an extraordinary levy on the lists dating from 1806 to 1814, also on those of 1815, and by anticipating a call on those on the list for 1816. But having just resumed the crown, he hesitated to resort to such an unpopular measure as the re-establishment of conscription, which Louis XVIII. had recently abolished. His only resource lay, therefore, in re-incorporating the men who were on leave for an unlimited or a limited space of time, and in recalling numerous deserters, entered on the reports as "absent without leave." The number of men on six months' leave of absence amounted to

32,800,[2] the deserters to 85,000. It was possible to rely on[3] the vast majority of the former; and already three or four thousand of them had rejoined their depôts in obedience to the Royal decree of 9th March.[4] But amongst the 85,000 men "absent without leave" there would undoubtedly be many refractory ones; there would also be a number liable, on presenting themselves, to be finally dismissed on the ground of their being either invalids or fathers of families. The Minister of War, Marshal Davoût, reckoned that the recall of soldiers of every description would hardly muster a total of 59,000 men.[5]

The proclamation calling out the troops, prepared on 28th March,[6] was not published until April 9th. This delay was owing to political reasons. The Emperor, who was then striving by every possible means to open negotiations with the European powers for the maintenance of peace,[7] was afraid that the placing of the Army on a war footing would seem a flat contradiction of his pacific declarations. With regard to the people of France, who were ardently longing for peace, he felt bound to act with the greatest discretion. The western provinces were in a state of agitation, the south was taking up arms. In the rest of France, the Royalists were labouring to undermine the Emperor's popularity, by prophesying war. This was not a time to alarm and alienate the whole country, by calling out the reserve forces. Moreover, Napoleon still retained a glimmer of hope that a rupture with Europe might be avoided.[8] As this illusive hope grew fainter and fainter every hour, he boldly determined to publish the decree in the *Moniteur* of April 9th. As he had foreseen, this proclamation came as a shock to the whole country. In a few days the funds went down 8 francs. Gloom and depression prevailed among the rural populations. On the whole, the peasants, well satisfied to be exempt from the exactions of their landlords, and from the re-establishment of the rights of their emigrant noblesse, yet felt their loyalty towards the Emperor quickly decline at the thought that his return might produce, probably a second invasion, or at least an endless war.[9]

Owing to the time necessary for the transmission of orders, for the posting of placards, and the legal delays, the muster only began on 25th April.[10] Public opinion was so hostile to the idea of war, that even amongst the men themselves, all of them former soldiers of Napoleon, numbers responded to the call merely to urge reasons for their exemption or disqualification. It is true that, though a great number of these men had deserted in 1814 to avoid wearing the white cockade, a greater number had left the ranks through sheer weariness of war. During the last year they had resumed their labours in the field and workshop; many of them had married, and these were all the less disposed to serve. In the departments where Royalist tendencies prevailed, the recalled men, feeling sure of public sympathy, behaved in a most disorderly way at the recruiting stations. They shouted: "We will not go! Long live the King!"[11] Fearing an insurrection in the west, the Emperor authorised several of the prefects in that region to apply the Act with great discretion, and if need be, to suspend its execution entirely.[12] In spite of all opposition, however, the levy produced 17,000 men more than Davout, little inclined to optimistic views, had predicted.[13] In the early days of June 82,446 recalled men had been enrolled, and 23,448 were on their way to join.[14]

The number of volunteers, so scarce during the campaign of France,[15] amounted approximately to 15,000.[16] A Royal decree issued on 30th December had granted every volunteer a bounty of 50 francs. This premium was suppressed by the Emperor. "Such methods," he said, "are not worthy of the sentiments which should inspire the French to defend their own independence."[17] In order to encourage recruiting, he ordered the call to arms to be read by officers of the Guard, with the accompaniment of drums, on all public squares, and outside all workshops and in the villages. But Davout having pointed out to him that this might cause useless disturbances, he gave up this expedient, adopted from the recruiting sergeants of the eighteenth century.[18]

Reduced to a very few seaworthy ships, which had neither ammunition[19] nor crews (two-thirds of the sailors being on leave), the fleet was useless save for cruising in the Mediterranean.[20] Taking into account the men available in the seaports and those entered on the naval lists, the Emperor hoped to raise from fifty to sixty battalions of sailors.[21] With great difficulty twenty only were formed,[22] and by the middle of June only one had been started,[23] to garrison Calais. The three regiments of naval artillery, which amounted actually to 5284 men under the Restoration, were increased to about 6000 men by the addition of a new battalion.[24] Six battalions remained to defend the seaports of France; two were detached and sent to Paris, another to Lyons, and another fought in Brittany in the flying column of General Bigarré.[25]

Of the three foreign regiments existing under Louis XVIII., the Emperor kept the second (Isenberg) and the third (Irish), mustering together a force of 875 bayonets; the first (La Tour d'Auvergne) was disbanded, having remained faithful to the "Duc d'Angoulême" during the short campaign of the south.[26] The Emperor wished to retain the four Swiss regiments, but the determined refusal of the officers to wear the "tricolor cocade" compelled him to disband these troops.[27] He then turned his attention to the organisation of five new foreign regiments: one of Polish recruits rapidly amounted to the number of 800, thanks to the admission into its ranks of soldiers belonging to the former Vistula Legion, and who, though discharged in 1814, had not yet returned home; one of Swiss, numbering 502 men, from the four Swiss regiments suppressed on 2nd April; one of Italians, one of Germans, one of Dutch and Belgians. The three latter were formed of deserters from the troops of Blücher, Frimont, and the Prince of Orange. In the beginning of June the Dutch and Belgian regiment numbered 378 bayonets. Lastly, in the department of Gironde, a battalion of coloured men was raised, as well as a few companies of Spanish refugees.[28]

The Fatherland itself being in danger, the laws and decrees of 1791, 1792, 1805, and 1813, which had not been abrogated, gave the Emperor the right to increase the Army by mobilising the National Guards. A few days after his return to the Palace of the Tuileries, he with Carnot and Davout set about the reorganisation of the National Guard.[29] At that time there were in the whole of France 200,000 National Guards, or thereabouts, aged from twenty to sixty; Carnot deemed it possible to raise their number to two millions and a half.[30] A decree issued on 10th April provided that all citizens liable to service in the National Guards, should be entered on the rolls, so as to be formed into battalions.[31] The Emperor did not propose organising such an immense multitude; but he intended forming a large number of battalions of the mobilised Guards, composed solely of men from twenty to forty years of age. He remembered that at Fère-Champenoise, in 1814, the National Guards had fought like veterans. By fresh decrees, he ordered the mobilisation of 326 battalions, each 720 men strong, which were to be immediately despatched to the frontier strongholds and to intrenched camps.[32] This amounted to an application of the Legislative Assembly's edict of 11th July 1792, with this amendment, that in the war battalions, paid substitution was permissible. The substitution tax was fixed at the small sum of 120 francs.[33]

In some twenty departments the levy took place without a hitch, viz., in Ain, Aisne, Ardèche, the Ardennes, Aube, Côte-d'Or, Isère, Jura, Marne, Meurthe, Meuse, Mont Blanc, Haut Rhin, Bas Rhin, Rhône, Haute Saône, Saône-et-Loire, Seine-et-Marne, Seine-et-Oise, Vosges, and Yonne; the battalions were soon complete; the recruits left their families and their homes with cries of " Vive l'Empereur," [34] with the same enthusiasm as in 1791. Those of the Guards who could afford it, bought their own arms and uniforms.[35] But the same patriotism and the same zeal did not animate the whole of France. In half the country, only one-quarter of the estimated contingents was raised, spite of the lavish use of flying columns and recruiting sergeants. By the end of May the department of Orne had raised 107 Guards, out of the 2,160 required, Pas-de-Calais 437 instead of 7,440, Gers 90 out of 1,440.[36] At Amiens the following placard was posted up: " Who recalled Buonaparte? The Army. Well, let the Army defend him. It is not for us to carry arms in the defence of a man cast up by hell itself." [37] In Vendée and in Brittany, where an insurrection was feared, the National Guards were never called out; but when civil war broke out, some thousands of citizens spontaneously took up arms, and helped the regulars to fight the Royalist troops, remaining, nevertheless, within the confines of their own department.[38]

On June 15th, out of the 234,720 National Guards

summoned to active service by the proclamations of 10th April and 15th May, about 150,000 had assembled at the various depôts, or were marching to join them.[39] The battalions were composed, in the proportion of one-third, of half-pay officers, and the rest of civilians. The Emperor would not allow these to be elected to posts in their regiments. The officers were appointed from lists made up in each department by a committee formed of the prefect, a "conseiller général," two generals, and one staff officer.[40] Most of the National Guards seemed resigned not only to do their duty, but to do it cheerfully. In the manœuvres they did their very best; they submitted to discipline willingly, marched into the cities with branches of lilac in the barrels of their muskets, singing the Marseillaise and ending each verse with shouts of: "Long live the Emperor! Long live the Nation!" If now and then complaints were uttered, it was by those who, being neither armed nor clothed, clamoured for muskets, greatcoats, and shoes. Mortier, Jourdan, Leclerc des Essarts, Rouyer, Lanusse, Berckheim, all the general officers who commanded or reviewed these mobilised National Guards, praised the fine spirit and martial bearing of these improvised soldiers. On the 5th of June Gérard wrote thus to Vandamme: "The ten battalions of the National Guard of the Nancy reserve are superb. In three weeks there will be no difference between them and the regulars."[41]

If the war lasted, the Emperor could be certain that the number of men from twenty to forty, forming the first corps of the National Guards would amount to 150,000 at least, for a large number of malcontents in the central and southern departments were bound to submit in the long run.[42] In the event of the pacification of La Vendée, which was imminent, the acts of mobilisation might even be applied, in course of time, to the western departments, and it would even be possible to raise fresh levies in the patriotic departments of the east.[43] As for the second militia corps, there was no need to hurry on its formation, except in Paris and at Lyons. Now that time and arms were lacking for the mobilised battalions,[44] it was not expedient to multiply the stationary battalions, which were numerous enough,[45] seeing the services likely to be required of them were of a most peaceful nature.

In the remaining mass of citizens from forty to sixty years of age, there were many able-bodied men, fit to be employed against the enemy, at least in the defence of fortified places. There were the old officers, subalterns, and privates who had retired after a minimum period of twenty-four years' service. As early as April, several retired officers had asked leave to re-enter the Army; but there were more half-pay officers than could be utilised. Davout proposed to form the retired officers and soldiers, into companies of veterans for the fortified places. "They will be an example to the National Guards," he wrote to the Emperor, "and will inspire them with the true soldier spirit." Napoleon did not hesitate to adopt this proposal. On May 18th he issued an edict inviting all retired military men to resume service temporarily, that they might be formed into battalions and garrisons of fortresses. These veterans, numbering 94,000, of which scarcely half seemed capable of serving, hastened to report themselves. Fifty-six battalions and twenty-five companies of artillery, numbering about 25,000 men, were selected from the fittest of their muster.[46]

In Paris the stationary National Guard was raised to 36,518 men.[47] Workmen from the "faubourgs" had spontaneously asked to take part in the defence; they formed twenty-four battalions of sharpshooters. These troops, numbering 18,000 men and commanded by half-pay officers, were destined to occupy the advanced posts and works of the front line.[48] At Lyons 4,000 stationary National Guards were ready on the 12th June, and Mouton-Duvernet was busy forming from these fifteen battalions of sharpshooters.[49] If the worst happened, and France were invaded, in Aisne, in the Ardennes, and in all the eastern departments the general levies could be relied upon. Composed of forest rangers, of gendarmes, of custom-house officers, of stationary National Guards, in a word of all able-bodied citizens, these levies would, upon receiving orders from the military authorities, assemble at the sound of the alarm and occupy the mountains and the passes.[50]

With 150,000 mobilised troops, 25,000 pensioners, 26,000 federated troops from Paris, Lyons, Toulouse, and Nancy, with the rural and city National Guards, the free corps, and the general levies, it seemed that all the strongholds, large towns, passes [51] and bridges were amply supplied with defenders. But notwithstanding that numerous volunteers had enlisted, and two-thirds of the men on leave had rejoined their regiments, the active forces were still far below the mark. After much hesitation the Emperor therefore decided to call out the reserves of 1815.[52] Conscription had been abolished by Article XII. of the Royal Charter; this Article had been interpreted as applying retroactively to the conscripts of 1815,[53] although a "Senatus-consulte" had summoned them to the standard as early as 9th October 1813: the summoning of these conscripts now, would, it was feared, seem an abuse of power. Davout himself, usually so resolute, pointed out to the Emperor that it would be prudent to avoid using the vexatious word "conscription." "Merely give the thing another name," he said, "and declare that all young men in their twentieth year from the 1st of January last are to be enrolled into the National Guard and sent to the military depôts, under the understanding they shall be discharged at the close of the war."[54] The proposed decree regarding the conscription of 1815 was then submitted to the Council of State during the session of 23rd May, and rejected on the ground that "the right of levying men belonged to the legislative power."[55]

To await the meeting of the Chambers! To wait! But would the enemy wait before they invaded France? Now, the conscription of 1815 ought to furnish 120,000 soldiers, 20,000 of whom had fought in the last campaign.[56] The Emperor overcame the scruples of the Council of State by proposing that the conscripts of 1815 should be assimilated with the soldiers on leave. To recall them, an edict was no longer necessary; a simple measure of administration would suffice. The Council of State gave a favourable opinion. From the early part of June Davout was free to send out instructions for levying the class of 1815.[57] The country was now resigned to war. The departure of the conscripts was effected without the resistance and rebellion which the recall of the men on leave, and even the mobilisation of the National Guard, had provoked in so many provinces. On June 11th, only a week after the proclamation had been issued,

46,419 conscripts were assembled and ready to start, in the various headquarters of each department.[58] From Alsace, Lorraine, Champagne, Franche-Comté, Burgundy, and even several provinces of the centre, reports were received of positive eagerness on the part of the men. "The conscripts of 1815," writes the prefect of Seine-et-Oise, "have joined in three days with amazing readiness." The prefect of Mont Blanc remarks that his department has provided the ranks with more combatants than at any period during the Revolution.[59] The Aisne, which from 1st April to 12th June had furnished 18,200 men—volunteers, reserves, conscripts, National Guards, "Francs-Tireurs," and retired soldiers (some of the latter men of seventy-three years of age)—deserves this verdict of Napoleon: "In that department will be found as many men as there are muskets to give them."[60]

Section II

There was a great scarcity of muskets, ammunition, provisions, shoes, and horses: while large supplies were needed, few were forthcoming. War material in every branch was lacking. Though the artillery had 13,947 guns, it had neither horses nor harness, and 600,000 shells were required.[61] The regular regiments of infantry and cavalry, both far beneath their effective strength, were completely equipped; but on the arming of newly formed regiments—the volunteers, the marines, the mobilised National Guards, the sharp-shooters, the conscripts of 1815—which were expected to yield a total of 500,000 men by the middle of September, no sufficient supply existed, the arsenals and the storehouses only furnishing 195,000 muskets, 74,000 of which needed repair.[62]

"The salvation of the country," wrote the Emperor, "depends on the number of muskets we can shoulder.[63] In the Imperial factories all the armourers exempted from former conscriptions, dating from the year VIII, were recalled by an edict,[64] and orders were given for 235,000 muskets and musketoons, and 15,000 brace of pistols. Bayonets were made in the Langres and Moulins cutleries, 10,000 fowling-pieces and 4,000 "short muskets" were dealt out amongst the peasants of Alsace,

Lorraine, Champagne, and Burgundy, that they might be ready for the general levy.[65] The task of repairing the worn-out muskets was left to private industry. In the principal towns, workshops were formed of gunsmiths, armourers, cabinet-makers, and brass-workers; there were six of these in Paris, employing 2000 workmen. Attempts were also made to buy muskets in England, and several thousands were conveyed surreptitiously in coal barges from Belgium and the Rhenish provinces. Others were brought in by the peasants, a premium of 12 francs being offered for every gun recovered; others were raised amongst the merchants and shipbuilders, who were ordered, by means of placards, to declare all the implements of war they might happen to have in their possession.[66]

In spite of the activity displayed, in spite of all the means employed, the men arrived at their depôts far quicker than did their arms at the various magazines. The factories and the workshops could not provide monthly more than 20,000 new rifles, and about as many repaired ones.[67] In the early days of June, scarcely half the mobilised National Guards were provided with muskets.[68] As for sabres, the manufacture of which had been postponed, as bayonets had to be made first, it was decided that even in the line the Grenadiers only should be provided with them. Cuirasses too were lacking: "Never mind cuirasses, send the men off," wrote Napoleon; "cuirasses are not indispensable in warfare."[69] Everywhere the manufacture of cartridges was pressed on so as to allow 100 to each man—fifty in the pouch and fifty in the ammunition waggons. At Vincennes 12,000,000 cartridges were turned out in two months. On the 1st of June the reserve supply for the Army of the North amounted to 5,500,000 cartridges, and in all the regiments of the first line the men—with a few trifling exceptions—had their stock of fifty cartridges per man complete.[70]

The Government of the Restoration had not only neglected to restock the clothing department, which the gigantic armaments of 1812 and 1813 had exhausted, but it had not even provided for the outfit of the troops actually under arms. From May 1814 to February 1815 the war department had allowed 4,000,000f. only for clothing expenses, and of this

1,000,000 alone had been spent.[71] The uniforms were in tatters. In more than twenty regiments the men were without shoes; even in the *élite* corps, such as the Royal Chasseurs, the horsemen had neither boots nor shirts. In the 14th Light Infantry the men had been wearing for the last two years, winter and summer, their canvas trousers. In the 29th Regiment of line 30,000 francs were due for the first outfit of the prisoners sent home previous to the 1st of January 1815: these men served through the campaign with policemen's caps on their heads.[72] The Emperor was forced to raise the credit for equipment of his men to 30,000,000f., and the War Office estimated that it would be necessary to increase that sum to 51,000,000f. in the course of the year.[73] Workshops opened in Paris, turned out 1,250 suits a day. Work meanwhile proceeded briskly at the depôts, to which manufacturers were requested to make an advance of material under guarantee of the several cities. Blue cloth being scarce, greatcoats of various hues were made.[74]

On March 20th the cavalry had only 27,864 horses,[75] the artillery and the auxiliary corps 7,765. 5,000 out of these 35,629 horses had been let out to farmers in order to save their keep; they were hastily reclaimed for the use of the corps.[76] The departments were put under requisition to furnish 8,000 horses, to be paid for on arrival. At the same time horses spontaneously offered by breeders and farmers were purchased at the central remount depôt at Versailles. The horses of the King's bodyguard and those of the Royal volunteers were reserved for the Guard. The depôt centres of every corps were authorised to make purchases on the spot. Finally, the Emperor hit on the excellent idea of appropriating half the horses of the "gendarmerie." Each gendarme received a compensation of 600 francs and was bound to find another horse for himself within a fortnight, and this was an easy task, considering his position in the country. Thanks to this expedient, 4,250 horses, strong and ready trained, were immediately allotted to the cuirassiers and the dragoons.[77] The requisition in the departments yielded more than was expected,[78] but at the central depôt at Versailles the remounting progressed very slowly. It seemed that General Préval was the very man to resume the command of this department, where he had worked miracles in 1814. Justly or unjustly, he was, however, suspected of Royalist opinions. The Emperor sent him, or rather exiled him, to the depôt at Beauvais, and General Bourcier was appointed to Versailles. The latter was a pedant, a slave to rules, quibbling over the smallest trifles. He would refuse any horse over eight years of age, and any which happened to be half an inch under the regulation height. In the midst of the war, within the month of March alone, Préval had collected more than 7,000 horses;[79] in the space of two months, in time of peace, Bourcier could only raise 2,579![80] In spite of this mismanagement at the beginning of the campaign, there was a fine body of horses in the field. The cavalry mustered 40,000 horses at the depôts[81] and with the troops; the artillery and the Army Service Corps amounted to 16,500.[82]

Threatened by the whole of Europe, Napoleon was well aware that he could not guard against invasion at every point of his territory. He might even be compelled at the outset, as in the preceding year, to confine his operations on this side of the Oise, the Aisne, and the Marne. Even under the most favourable circumstances his campaign must be at the same time an offensive and defensive one. Necessary and urgent as the reorganisation of the Army was, it was equally needful to place all the fortified places in a state of defence. As early as the 27th of March the Emperor had issued orders for these preparations, but they were not carried out till between the 15th and 25th April. It was necessary to wait for the reports on the condition of the various fortresses, for instructions from the engineering committees, the opening credit accounts, and the creation of workshops.[83] At Metz 700 workmen were employed daily; at Rocroi, 500; at Toul, 700; at Landrecies, 400; at Dunkerque, 1000; at Huningue, 500; at Grenoble, 400; at Cherbourg, 500; at Bayonne, 400; at Bordeaux, 200; at Perpignan, 150; in the intrenched camp at Maubeuge, 1,000. By June 15th the valleys of the Vosges and the passes of the Argonne, were bristling with redoubts, masked batteries, and stockades. The northern districts could be flooded at a moment's notice, and in more than eighty towns the works were either completely finished or on the high road to being so. Besides, in most of the fortresses there were no breaches in the ramparts; nothing was needed but to raise the slopes of the counterscarps, to set up batteries, to repair the embrasures, the "banquettes," and the glacis, and to add a few necessary defences, and some exterior outworks.[84]

More important by far were the works required at Lyons and in Paris. At Lyons 4,000 workmen were hired. The old walls of Fourvière were repaired, as well as the walls connecting the Rhône with the Saône; "têtes de pont" were built at Le Guillotière and Les Brotteaux, redoubts at Pierre Scise, at Saint-Jean, and at Croix-Rousse.[85] Owing to his fear of estranging the Parisians by bringing them face to face with danger, Napoleon, though he knew the need of fortifying Paris to be paramount, only issued the necessary orders for this on May 1st.[86] It was a serious loss of time, especially as he needed a vast system of fortifications with uninterrupted lines, with works in the shape of "cornes and couronnes," with redoubts and forts crossing their fire.[87] General Haxo and General Rognet designed the plans. But not before the middle of May were these works undertaken seriously. 1,500 men were employed, then 2,000, then 4,000, to say nothing of numerous bodies of volunteers from the Guards, the line, the National Guard, and the sharpshooters.[88] When Napoleon started to join the army, the entrenchments and all the works on the right bank of the Seine, undertaken first because they covered the points most likely to be attacked, were partially finished; the works on the left bank were hardly begun.[89] At the same time that the work of fortification was proceeding, the strongholds were being armed and provisioned. The arsenals of Metz, Douai, Lille, Grenoble, and Toulouse furnished cannon and powder to those towns where the supply of artillery necessaries was insufficient. Furnaces also were established for the casting of projectiles. The naval department sent from Toulon to Lyons, *via* Arles and the Rhône, 100 24-pounders, 12-pounders, and 6-pounders, and 300 pieces from Brest and Cherbourg, *via* Havre and the Seine, to Paris. The armament of Paris also included 300 field guns, 100 of which were sent out to the flying batteries. "Turn out as much cannon as possible," wrote the Emperor; "you must fight with cannon as you would fight with your fists."[90]

In order to gain time Davout directed the commanders of Army Corps to attend personally to the supply of fortified places, with the assistance of the prefects and the other officials.[91] This system was not unsuccessful, but it had a dangerous tendency to develop into the practice of exactions and extortion. There was in existence a contract concluded between the Government of Louis XVIII. and the contractor Doumèrc. This contract was still in force. But Doumèrc, brother of the general of cavalry, was only acting really in the interest of Ouvrard, who was a man who made light of his engagements. Complaints poured in from all sides. It became necessary to draw on the reserve supplies, in order to feed both men and horses. Ouvrard was accused of using the money advanced by the Treasury for speculations on the Bourse. For the maintenance of the forces Davout was obliged to authorise the prefects to buy at any cost, at contractors' prices. This measure, if put into force universally, would have cost Ouvrard dear. He therefore proposed a new contract through the medium of Doumèrc, which was accepted on May 24th by Davout and Daru; it stipulated that the supply was to be completed within thirty days, in exchange for payment in advance of 4,000,000 francs.[92] By the middle of June the fortified places of the first and second lines were supplied for an average period of four months, and the convoys following the Army of the North carried reserve provisions for one week.[93]

More time and more money were needed to effect such immense operations with any degree of success. The Royal War Budget for 1815, which was to have been presented to the Chambers during the April session, amounted to 298,000,000f., including 25,000,000f. for the Royal household troops, the Swiss regiments, and pensions granted to the Emigrés and the Vendéens.[94] Even though he deducted all expenses on these latter items, the Emperor immediately realised that the War Budget would have to be increased by 100,000,000f.,[95] and this was probably too low an estimate. If war lasted, the expenses would greatly exceed this total. Napoleon was averse to loans, because, as he said, "he did not like feeding on the future"; he had besides but small faith in credit.[96] In 1815 he refused to increase the taxes because of his dread of unpopularity. Far from seeking to increase his resources by fresh taxation, he suppressed the tax on the transmission of liquor,[97] the tax on home consumption, and the dues of entry on drinkables, in communes of less than 4,000 inhabitants. This reform, which history has failed to record in the midst of so many greater events, did not fail to influence public opinion at the time. The Bourbons, who had solemnly promised to suppress these duties, had taken good care not to change them one whit; whereas Napoleon, who had promised nothing, abolished all those impositions which were reckoned the most vexatious and unbearable. Among the peasants, among small proprietors, in the comparatively influential circles of innkeepers and wine merchants, this reduction of taxes rallied more people to the Emperor than those who had been alienated by the "Additional Act"; this Act was specially attacked by the wits of society and professional politicians.[98]

An unexpected source of supply was discovered by Napoleon on March 20th in a reserve sum of 50,000,000 francs at the Treasury.[99] The Minister of Finance, Baron Louis, made free use of a part of these funds, by speculating on the Bourse with the Royal bonds; he scrupled, however, to carry them away with him to Ghent.[100] It was fortunate for the Imperial Government that the overthrow of Louis XVIII. had happened when it did; for on 20th March the tax-payers had paid down but a small proportion of the three first monthly instalments of the current year. On this account, a great influx of money came into the receivers' offices during the months of April and May; on the whole the taxes came in in a very satisfactory manner.[101] But the regular receipts and the money in hand were still inadequate to meet the current expenses; Gaudin, by order of the Emperor, then negotiated 3,600,000 francs' worth of bonds from the sinking fund, which were covered by the same amount on credit in the national securities. This transaction, effected with the help of Ouvrard, produced 40,000,000f. in cash, clear of all discount.[102]

The arming, outfitting, and clothing expenses for the

mobilised National Guards, rated at 24,000,000f.,[103] were not included in the War Budget. They were charged to the account of the departments, which had to settle them out of funds for the providing of substitutes (fixed at 120f. per man), by the deduction of one-tenth of the communal revenues and the sale of one-quarter of the wood reserves.[104] The total amount of freewill offerings and a reserve amounting to 6,000,000f., to be drawn on the sinking fund, were devoted to the expenses of the National Guard.[105]

Thanks to these resources and expedients, it became possible at last to place France on a complete war footing. But in how many of the strongholds work had been interrupted for lack of money! how many of the soldiers were still wearing worn-out clothing! How many of the National Guards were waiting in the ranks, useless and discontented, to receive their muskets![106] In May, in spite of delays and difficulties, the men had at last received their pay.[107] On 12th June not more than 1000 pairs of spare shoes [108] were forthcoming for the use of the Army of the North; the bonus usually distributed on taking the field was unpaid;[109] and whilst the total sum required for the pay of the men amounted to 5,000,000f. a month, the strong rooms of the Treasury only contained 670,000f.[110]

The extraordinary resources (viz., the balance left by Baron Louis and the sum derived from the appropriation of 3,600,000 francs' worth of bonds) were exhausted;[111] the regular receipts were already on the decrease. However adverse the Emperor and his advisers were to enforce exceptional measures,[112] they were compelled to adopt them, for the amount demanded by Davout for the month of July alone was computed at the sum of 72,000,000f.[113] Consequently, in the Budget submitted to the Chambers on 19th June a national loan of 150,000,000f. was proposed on the guarantee of the forests of the State. All tax-payers were to subscribe a sum equal to the total of their land and personal taxes.[114] It was, in fact, a compulsory loan.

Section III

The Emperor did not even wait till mobilisation had begun, to organise the Army Corps. Thanks to the body of troops concentrated round Paris by order of Louis XVIII.,[115] the numerous regiments which, from Grenoble onward, had joined the battalion of Elba, the strong garrisons of the northern and eastern frontier towns, Napoleon had scarcely returned to the Tuileries when he found ready to his hand, a great part of the elements of all necessary for forming a mighty army. As early as March 26th, in order to provide against all emergencies, he speedily ordered the formation of eight Corps of Observation. The 1st was to assemble at Lille, the 2nd at Valenciennes, the 3rd at Mézières, the 4th at Thionville, the 5th at Strasburg, the 6th at Chambéry, the 7th at the foot of the Pyrenees, the 8th (or Corps of Reserve) in Paris.[116] The regiments forming these Army Corps were temporarily fixed at two battalions each. The cadres of the 3rd battalions, and of the depôts, would be concentrated under the military government of Paris, and in the towns of the interior, until such time when the calling out of reserves would allow of the forming of the 4th and 5th battalions, which would then immediately join the Army. In the fortresses and depôts the National Guards were to take the place of the troops of the line.[117]

The light cavalry was distributed in the proportion of one division to each Army Corps. Of the surplus of this body of cavalry, and the dragoons, the cuirassiers, and the carabineers, eight reserve divisions were formed, to each of which was attached a battery of mounted artillery.[118]

On 20th March the Imperial Guard only included the two regiments of grenadiers and the two chasseurs regiments of the Old Guard and four cavalry regiments.[119] The Emperor increased the effective strength of the cavalry regiments, created a 3rd and 4th regiment of grenadiers, a 3rd and 4th regiment of chasseurs (Middle Guard), eight regiments of voltigeurs (light troops), and eight of sharpshooters (the Young Guard), and a second regiment of mounted chasseurs.

He reconstituted the regiment of horse artillery, the unmounted artillery regiment of the Old Guard, as well as the Army Service regiment, a squadron of picked gendarmes, the Marine Corps, and the companies of sappers and miners.[120] The Young Guard was formed of volunteers and of men who had formerly served in the corps, and they had special pay—a sou per day. The men of the Elba battalion were incorporated into the Old Guard. For the artillery and cavalry of the Middle Guard, the "gendarmerie" and the line were put in requisition; of these the gendarmerie gave 500 men. Each regiment of the line was to furnish thirty picked men, tall and healthy, with a minimum record of service of four years in the infantry and eight in the cavalry or artillery.[121]

At the end of May, when the reserves, the mobilised National Guards, and the volunteers had swelled the numbers of the Army, the Emperor made a new distribution of his forces. The 1st Corps (under Drouet d'Erlon), the 2nd Corps (under Reille), the 3rd Corps (under Vandamme), the Army of the Moselle, formerly the 4th Corps (under Gérard), the 6th, formerly the 8th Corps, (under Lobau), the Cavalry Reserve (under Grouchy), and the Imperial Guard, formed the Army of the North, 124,139 men strong, and under the personal command of the Emperor himself.[122] The 5th Corps became the Army of the Rhine (23,097 men, including 3,000 mobiles, under Rapp);[123] the 6th Corps became the Army of the Alps (23,617 men, including 13,000 mobiles, under Suchet).[124] The 7th Corps was divided into two parts: one took the name of the Corps of the Western Pyrénées (6,820 men, including 3,300 mobiles, under Clausel);[125] the other that of the Eastern Pyrenees Corps (7,633 men, including 3,300 mobiles, under Decaen).[126] Three new Army Corps were added to the above by the Emperor: the Army of the West (about 10,000 men, under Lamarque),[127] which was told off to repress the insurrection in La Vendée; the Var Corps (5,544 men, under Brune);[128] and the Jura Corps (8,420 men, including 5,500 mobiles, under Lecourbe),[129] who were to support Suchet's Army in defending the Alps.

Four divisions of the select National Guards, altogether 17,466 men strong, were encamped by Avesnes, Sainte

Ménéhould, Colmar, and Nancy;[130] 90,000 mobiles and 25,000 veterans were assembled in the fortified towns and in the depôts;[131] 11,223 gunners of the line,[132] and 6,000 marine artillery[133] to act with 2,071 veteran gunners,[134] and 6,000 garrison artillery.[135] 13,934 soldiers of every branch of the service were marching in detachments to join the active troops;[136] there were 59,559 qualified and disqualified of the line,[137] 5,559 in the depôts of the Guards[138] (which had already been put under contribution). To these must be added 4,700 men from the battalions stationed in the Island of Elba[139] and in the colonies,[140] 8,162 men in the hospitals,[141] 10,000 marine fusiliers,[142] 5,129 veteran fusiliers,[143] 14,521 gendarmes, on horse or on foot,[144] 12,000 custom-house officers enrolled as soldiers,[145] and 6,000 "partisans."[146] Thus the Emperor had raised the active Army from a total of 200,000 men[147] to 284,000, and he had formed an auxiliary army of 222,000 men.[148]

One month later, these two armies would receive an increase of, first, 19,000 re-enlisted men who had received marching orders before 10th June, but had not yet joined their posts;[149] second, of several thousand re-enlisted men who had not yet reported themselves at the depôt centres of the various departments[150] by 15th June; third, of 46,500 conscripts of 1815 who at that date were assembled in the chief towns of departments;[151] fourth, of 15,000 mobilised Guards who were already on their way to the mustering points[152] by the middle of June. In addition to these, from 15th July to 25th September, there would be 74,000 men, completing the contingent of 1815,[153] and 84,000 men, forming the complement of the mobilised National Guards.[154] 60,000 or 70,000 more National Guards could be mobilised at any time by applying to the departments of the west, where it had been postponed, the call to arms, and by issuing orders for a new summons to the field throughout the whole extent of France.[155] Napoleon was not far from the truth when he said the Army would amount to 800,000 men[156] by 1st October!

Section IV

In conformity with the Edicts of Lyons, all officers who, having emigrated, or retired from the service during the Revolution, had returned to the Army since 1st April 1814,[157] were struck off the rolls.[158] But as many of these officers had held commissions, mainly in the household troops and on the staff, this wholesale dismissal created but few vacancies in the Army at large. The officers whose names came next in order were enough to complete the lists. All half-pay officers were placed in the numerous newly-formed battalions, squadrons, and batteries, in the Young Guard, and in the federated sharpshooters. 2500 officers in this category were still available in the middle of May. Napoleon paid them in full for the time they were out of employment and despatched them to the frontier strongholds to command the mobilised National Guards.[159]

Certain of the devotion of those officers who were in direct touch with the troops, there were still many colonels and many generals whom Napoleon had good reason to distrust. In 1814, amongst the officers of high rank many had been the cases of weakness and treachery, of hesitation and disobedience. Numerous changes in the upper ranks of the Army were inevitable. But it was in the interests of the Army itself far more than from motives of personal dislike or sympathy that the Emperor acted in dismissing or promoting his followers. Whilst he was pitiless towards officers who, like Augereau and Oudinot, had shown their incapacity during the French campaign, or their treachery, like Marmont and Souham, he knew how to forget his grievances against those who had from the 1st to the 20th of March striven to change his triumphal march into a miserable fiasco. Colonel Cuneo d'Ornano, who had imprisoned twenty-five grenadiers of the Guard in the citadel of Antibes, was appointed general.[160] General Miollis, who had led the garrison of Marseilles in pursuit of the small Imperial column, was appointed commander of the stronghold of Metz. Colonel Roussille had stubbornly defended the gates of Grenoble; he was allowed to remain in command of the 5th of the line. Colonel Dubalen, of the 64th, had publicly given in his resignation to Ney on the "Place d'Armes" of Lons-le-Saunier; he was recalled to his regiment.[161] General Marchand might have returned to favour, had he not refused, as he said, to "figure on the list of traitors."[162] Foy had been faithful to republicanism under the Empire; he became a convert to constitutional monarchy under Louis XVIII.; in Nantes he did not place himself at the head of the Bonapartist movement till he had done his utmost to thwart it; nevertheless, he was given the command of a fine division in the Army of the North. Several officers of the 10th of the line had been promoted by the Duc d'Angoulême during the campaign of the south; their promotions were confirmed.[163] Harispe and Heudelet were deeply implicated in Bourbonist demonstrations; nevertheless they both received a command. The Emperor employed Rapp, Belliard, Ruty, Haxo, the younger Kellermann, Gourgaud, as though he utterly ignored the fact that they had ever served under the Duke de Berry with the troops assembled at Villejuif. "Would you have dared to fire upon me?" Napoleon inquired of Rapp. "Most certainly, Sire, it would have been my duty." And Napoleon gave him the Army of the Rhine.[164]

On the other hand, Napoleon dismissed or relegated to the retired list a hundred officers of all ranks:[165] Dupont, whose dishonour at Baylen was not effaced by the favours Louis XVIII. had conferred on him; Dessolles, who had so well seconded Talleyrand in April 1814; Beurnonville, Donnadieu, and Bordessoulle, who had emigrated to Belgium; Maison, another *emigré*, who on being invited by the Imperial Government to return to France, replied that he would come back, but with 500,000 bayonets at his back;[166] Curto, whose furious utterances against the Emperor had brought about the mutiny of the garrison at Thionville; the Generals d'Aultanne, Monnier, Ernouf, Loverdo, and Briche; the colonels of the 10th Regiment of the line and the 14th Chasseurs, who were still fighting in the south under the Duc d'Angoulême, a week after the Empire had been acknowledged by two-thirds of France. In no wise conscience-stricken on the score of his complicity with Marmont in the disloyalty of D'Essonnes,

Souham had good hopes of retaining his command at Perigueux. When dismissed, however, he appeared at the Tuileries at a public reception and attempted to move Napoleon. "What more do you want of me?" said Napoleon, turning aside. "Can't you see that I do not know you any more."[167]

At the suggestion of Davoût and the commanders of the Corps d'Armée, several colonels, majors, captains, and lieutenants were struck off the rolls on the charge of persistent hostility. It is more difficult to account for the disgrace of Colonels Moncey, Oudinot, and Zoppfell: Moncey had merely tried to keep the 3rd Hussars faithful to the King, and this only up to 3rd March. In many similar cases the Emperor had shown himself lenient.[168] Against Oudinot nothing could be alleged save that he bore his father's name, whilst Zoppfell was merely guilty of being a *protégé* of the Duke de Feltre. Bugeaud, denounced as a Royalist, was placed on the retired list during the month of April; but Suchet, Grouchy, Gérard, and Bertrand hastened to plead earnestly on behalf of "the best colonel in the Army." He was restored and placed at the head of the 14th of the line, and the rank of Commander of the Legion of Honour was bestowed on him as a compensation for his temporary disgrace.[169]

General de Bourmont was left without employment for some length of time. He had rushed to Paris from Lons-le-Saunier to be with Louis XVIII. At Ney's request the Emperor gave orders for his arrest; but Ney reconsidered the matter, and was the first to petition Napoleon to restore him to his command. Bourmont had served under Gérard during the campaigns of 1812 and 1814, and Gérard requested he might command one of the divisions in his corps. The Emperor consented to this after much hesitation; he had great difficulty in convincing Davout, who only yielded to formal orders from the Emperor. "Gérard answers for Bourmont with his head," said the Emperor. "Gérard is wrong," replied the Prince of Eckmuhl; "I never answer for anybody, I only answer for myself."[170]

The Emperor, as may be seen, was lenient towards men who had wished to fight against him, but at the same time he did not lavishly shower rewards on those who had compromised themselves for his sake from the very first. While he appointed Major-General Labédoyère brigadier, already destined for that rank during the campaign of France, and Mallet, commandant of the battalion of the Island of Elba; while he promoted Simmer, who had brought over to Napoleon two regiments at Lyons, as lieutenant-general, and raised Brayer to the French peerage; still, men like Dessaix, Girard, Allix, Amiel, Mouton-Duvernet, Gilly, Piré, Proteau, Chartran, received no privileges whatever; they were employed in strict accordance with the rights belonging to their rank. Yet Dessaix had accepted the government of Lyons a week before the Emperor's return to the Tuileries; Girard had commanded the Imperial vanguard from Avallon; Allix had proclaimed the Empire at Nevers; Amiel had been arrested at Auxerre as an emissary of Napoleon; Chartran paid with his life for his loyalty to the Emperor's cause; Mouton-Duvernet, Piré, Proteau, had ardently and efficiently helped Grouchy in the southern campaign against the Duc d'Angoulême. General Porret de Morvan, who had led the Infantry Chasseurs of the Old Guard at Sens, indulged the flattering hope of taking Curial's place as principal colonel in the same corps; Curial was disgraced, but the command of the Chasseurs passed on to Morand.[171] Prince Jérôme, Imperial Highness as he was, only obtained an infantry division. Merlin received the three stars for having compelled the Governor of Vincennes to capitulate, while Sebastiani, who had brought about the disbandment of the Duke de Berry's army, was entrusted with a mission utterly unworthy—as he rightly felt—of his merit and his services,[172] namely, the organisation of the National Guard in the 16th military division. Exelmans, who was the first to enter the Tuileries on the 20th of March, was given a cavalry corps, but Kellermann was given one also, though he had been employed in the army of Villejuif. The elder Lallemand, one of the principal chiefs of the northern conspiracy, became a lieutenant-general, while his younger namesake, Lallemand junior, and Lefebvre Desnoettes were merely restored to the command of the mounted Chasseurs and of the unmounted Artillery of the Old Guard. After the skirmish at Compiègne

Colonel Marin, who had galloped off at full speed to join Napoleon at Auxerre,[173] doubtless hoped for the command of the Horse Artillery of the Old Guard, in which he had served as major. Instead of this Colonel Duchand of the Line Artillery was appointed.

Section V

THREE of the twenty Marshals of France, Berthier, Marmont, and Victor, had accompanied or joined Louis XVIII. in Belgium. The Emperor gave orders for their names be to struck off.[174] Pérignon, who had stupidly compromised himself with Vitrolles at Toulouse, and Augereau, whose recent recantation could not efface the stain of his disgraceful conduct while commanding the Army of Lyons in 1814, were both subjected to the same punishment.[175] Napoleon wished also to dismiss Gouvion-Saint-Cyr for having disobeyed his orders after the 20th of March, and having ordered the troops of the 22nd division to resume the white cockade, and Kellermann the elder, Duke of Valmy, for having voted for the Emperor's deposition on 1st April 1814.[176] Madame Gouvion-Saint-Cyr wrote Davout a letter which pacified the Emperor, and the Marshal escaped with no worse punishment than a compulsory exile to his castle at Reverseaux.[177] Napoleon did not even persist in his first decision with regard to the Duke of Valmy.[178] Sérurier, who had also voted for the act of forfeiture in his capacity as senator, was yet allowed to retain his post as governor of the Invalides: Napoleon, however, refrained from including him in the Chamber of Peers, and this lesson was well deserved.[179]

Like Gouvion-Saint-Cyr, Oudinot had refused to comply with the Emperor's orders after the 20th of March. He had refused to proclaim the Empire in Metz until a rising of the garrison and people forced him to do so. Relieved from his command he did all he could to regain the favour of Napoleon. He wrote himself to the Emperor; he besought Davout, Suchet, Jacqueminot, to intercede for him. "Go at once to the Emperor," he wrote to Suchet; "tell him your opinion of me; accuse yourself, say you did not send me your letter or Ney's until the evening of the 27th. Say that Oudinot has never forgotten what he owes to Napoleon, that if Oudinot has done wrong his faults are no sooner pointed out to him but he will do all in his power to expiate and atone for them. I sorely need this intercession of yours for the sake of my wife and my children, who will share in my crushing misfortune." [180] The Emperor revoked the order he had signed for Oudinot's exile to Lorraine, and even consented to see him in the Tuileries, but he left him without employment.[181] Napoleon doubtless would not have remained obdurate had there been nothing against Oudinot except his conduct at Metz. He was more probably influenced by the recollection that the year before the Duke de Reggio had been beaten at Bar-sur-Aube owing to the unskilful marshalling of his troops on the eve of the contest, and his fatal indecision during the battle itself.[182]

Although Macdonald had shown himself a zealous Royalist, and had spared no efforts to organise the opposition at Lyons and Villejuif, the Emperor yet wished to give him a command. But the Marshal, who had returned to Paris after escorting Louis XVIII. to the frontier, was firmly resolved not to serve under the new Government. In vain did General Maurice Mathieu, his former chief on the staff of the Army of the Grisons, beg him to come to the Tuileries, where the Emperor was expecting him. In vain did Davout force himself on him to induce him to yield; he was inexorable. Weary of the struggle, the Emperor granted him the only favour he had deigned to ask, the permission to go and live as a "bon bourgeois" on his estate of Courcelle, near Gien.[183]

After publishing a violent order of the day against Napoleon, Moncey had left Paris on the 20th of March. Two days later he wrote to the Emperor that he intended to retire to the country. Napoleon had already appointed Rovigo in his stead as general inspector of the gendarmerie.[184] But ought not the Emperor to have remembered all Moncey had done in 1814 at the head of the Paris National Guard, and restored him to his command? He was content to raise him to the Chamber of Peers, together with Lefebvre, who had held no command during the campaign in France, and had had no employment under Louis XVIII.[185] It is fair to say

Lefebvre was sixty-seven, and the Emperor naturally preferred younger leaders for the Army Corps.

Masséna had assisted the Duc d'Angoulême during the short campaign on the Rhône, but with evident reluctance, and immediately after the capitulation of La Pallud, he had hastened to proclaim the Empire. On 14th April he gave his reasons for so doing in a report addressed to Napoleon, which concluded thus: "I cannot conceal from Your Majesty how anxious I am for the honour of serving you again and of assuring you of my boundless devotion."[186] The Emperor congratulated the Prince d'Essling in a letter; he summoned him to Paris and received him with great demonstrations of friendship; but notwithstanding his half promise, he decided not to restore him to the command of the 9th military division. To humour the Royalists at Marseilles it was necessary to appoint a man who had *not* already commanded them under Louis XVIII. Masséna, who was too infirm to serve efficiently with the armies in the field, was then offered the government of the 4th and 5th military divisions, including the Moselle, the Meurthe, and the Vosges. The Marshal refused this post and remained in Paris, where he showed himself most zealous in attending all the sessions of the Chamber of Peers.[187]

Although Mortier, Governor of Lilles, Suchet, Governor of Strasburg, and Jourdan, Governor of Rouen, had held out for the King two or three days after the 20th of March, they had not compromised themselves to the extent Oudinot and Gouvion-Saint-Cyr had done, and the Emperor could have no ill-feeling against them; nevertheless he did not wish to retain them in the posts they held under Louis XVIII. To his mind this was a question of principle.[188] Appointed at first to the post of inspector of the fortresses of the northeast stations, then to the command of the cavalry of the Guard, Mortier was finally placed at the head of the Young Guard.[189] Suchet received the command of the Army of the Alps,[190] Jourdan the government of Besançon, a fortified town in the first line of defence, where Davout felt the presence of a Marshal of France was needed.[191]

Brune had been in disgrace since 1807, on account, it was rumoured, of his toleration of De Bourrienne's extortion and peculation in the towns of the Hanseatic league; he had vainly applied for a new post in the early part of the campaign of France.[192] He was still unemployed under the Restoration. On the Emperor's return, Brune again offered his services. His abilities as administrator, which had been tested in Belgium, Gironde, La Vendée, and Tuscany, qualified him for the government of any province which remained persistently hostile. He was sent to Marseilles as governor of the 9th military division; to his duties as governor were added those of the organisation and command of the Army Corps of the Var.[193]

On 23rd March Ney reached Paris with his troops; that same day he started on a mission to the departments of the north and the east. The acknowledged object of his mission was to inspect the fortresses and strongholds, its secret object to ascertain the state of public opinion, to report on the officers and officials, to propose, if need be, fresh dismissals and charges.[194] Ney discharged this mission with zeal, but he had the bad taste to manifest feelings of unheard-of violence against the Bourbons. At the officers' gatherings he would shower abuse on King and princes. "They are a corrupt family,"[195] he would say. Such language was not calculated to pacify the hostility with which he was regarded by popular opinion at large. Even among Bonapartists, even in the Imperial circle, his conduct at Lons-le-Saunier was condemned. In Paris a wretched pun on his name was in every mouth: "Il fallait être né (Ney) pour cela." His sudden change of party did not shield him from suspicion. "If Ney is employed during the campaign," wrote an anonymous correspondent to the Emperor, "he must have a trustworthy staff." Many reminded Napoleon of the memorable scene at Fontainebleau, and possibly some may have repeated to him Ney's remark as he passed through Dijon: "I was congratulating myself on having compelled the Emperor to abdicate, and lo! now I must serve him!"[196] The climax of all was the Marshal's huge blunder when on his return from his tour of inspection towards the 15th of April,[197] he apologised to the Emperor for his speech respecting the iron cage. "The remark is correct," he said, "for I had already made up my mind and there was nothing better I could say to conceal my plans." Not a word did Napoleon answer, but the Marshal saw an ominous flash in his eyes.[198]

Stung with despair, confusion, and remorse, accusing himself and every one else, Ney retired to his estate of Les Coudreaux. For six weeks nothing more was heard of him. People said he was in disgrace; a report was even spread that he had been arrested.[199] He returned to Paris for the ceremony of the Champ-de-Mai. Created Peer of France on June 2nd, he went to the Elysée four days later to obtain a grant of 37,000 francs, which sum was due in arrear on his pay and his travelling expenses.[200] "You here!" said Napoleon; "I thought you had emigrated!" "I ought to have emigrated long ago," replied the Marshal bitterly.[201] On 11th June he called at the Tuileries again, but in neither of these two meetings was any mention made of a command for him with the Army of the North.[202] Ney no doubt knew that Napoleon called him his "bête noire,"[203] and he dared not present his request. As he left Paris on 11th June, a scruple crossed the Emperor's mind. Had he the right to doom the hero of so many battles to degrading inaction? Could he afford to deprive France and himself of such a soldier in the hour of peril? He wrote to the Minister of War: "Recall Marshal Ney. Tell him that if he wants to take part in the first engagements he must be at Avesnes by the 14th; I shall have my headquarters there."[204] Napoleon thought thus to promote the interests of the Army and his own, which were identical, and he was also prompted by feelings of pity, as is evident by the tone of this message. It is not an order, it is merely a piece of advice which left Ney free to choose his course. But could Ney choose any other course than to be present at the opening engagements,[205] if only in the hope of being killed?[206] He left Paris on the 12th of June, reached Avesnes on the 13th, where he dined with the Emperor; but not until the afternoon of the 15th, after the action had begun, did he receive the command of the 1st and 2nd Army Corps.[207]

Since he had "passed over to the King," according to the expression then used in the Army, Murat's name was no longer on the list of Marshals. Three weeks before the beginning of the campaign, deprived of throne and title, Joachim had taken refuge in the suburbs of Toulon. He had not even retained his sword, and he entreated the Emperor to give him one. "I desire," he wrote, "to shed the last drop of my blood for you." Napoleon refused. He felt it was impossible to give a command in the French Army to a Frenchman who had fought against it only twelve months before. He was also irritated with his brother-in-law because the latter, in spite of his positive instructions, had begun the war with Austria before the proper time; above all, he had allowed himself to be beaten.[208] Later, in his musings at Saint Helena, Napoleon would regret his decision concerning this "great leader of cavalry charges." "At Waterloo," he would say, " the victory might have been ours had we had Murat. What was needed? Only a matter of breaking through three or four English squares. Murat was the very man to do this."[209] And, indeed, with his twofold gift of inspiring his men to desperate deeds of valour and of terrorising the enemy might Murat not have ridden down the English?

The name of Grouchy is for ever irrevocably bound up with the accursed memory of Waterloo, so much so that the splendid services and the marvellous feats of this brilliant officer are forgotten. If he could not rival Murat's irresistible dash, like Murat, he could handle skilfully masses of cavalry. Second commander of the Irish expedition of the year V., Governor of Madrid in 1808, Colonel-General of chasseurs and light cavalry in 1809, chief of the sacred squadron during the Russian retreat, he had contributed to the victories of Hohenlinden, Eylau, Friedland, Wagram, and La Moskowa. After Vauchamps, the Emperor had thought of appointing him Marshal of the Empire. In disgrace under Louis XVIII., Grouchy on March 31st was sent to Lyons to fight against the Duc d'Angoulême. Promoted at last to be Marshal, at the close of that short and easy campaign, he was placed at the head of the Army of the Alps, then recalled to Paris on May 8th. The Emperor proposed giving him the four corps of cavalry of the Army of the North, and it was in the capacity of chief commander of the cavalry that he entered Belgium on 15th June. To his own great misfortune the very next day he was entrusted with a post of still greater importance.

Section VI

A MATTER of great moment with Napoleon was the choice of the Chief of the Staff. Who should take Berthier's place? The Prince of Wagram was neither a great soldier, a great organiser, nor a high-minded man. But he possessed extensive technical knowledge, and had shown that he possessed also in the highest degree the gifts of a first-rate agent. Indefatigable, conscientious, diligent, prompt in grasping the most complicated orders, executing them in every detail with admirable minuteness, clearness, and precision, ever punctual in transmitting them at the appointed time, he had been a perfect instrument in Napoleon's hands.[210] With him the Emperor's mind was at rest. The orders were always so worded as to admit of no possibility of doubt or hesitation as to the manner of their execution. These orders always arrived safely, for Berthier would despatch them, if need be, by eight different officers[211] on eight different routes. Many said Berthier had become feeble in body and in mind. Yet his correspondence in 1815 gives evidence that his pen was still active and had lost none of its luminous precision. The Emperor missed him sadly: he could not forget the Prince of Wagram's services during the late campaign, and he never gave up the hope of seeing him return to France. "That brute Berthier!" he would say to Rapp, "he will come back to us, we will forgive him everything provided he wears his uniform of " garde-du-corps " when he appears before me."[212]

Indeed, Berthier was willing enough to return to France, where he had left his wife, the Princess of Wagram, with his son and two daughters. After a short stay at Ghent, he had gone to the Castle of Bamberg, the property of the King of Bavaria, his uncle by marriage. Early in May he started for the French frontier by Basle, but he could not go farther than Stockach, where the Prince of Hohenzollern [213] had his headquarters. The Allies would doubtless have preferred to keep Berthier in their own hands as a semi-prisoner, than to see him on Napoleon's staff. Much dejected, he returned to Bamberg. In the afternoon of June 1st, as a regiment of Russian dragoons on its way to France marched past the castle, Berthier, according to eye-witnesses, disappeared abruptly from a window on the first floor, reappeared on the third floor, and threw himself from the window there, on to the pavement beneath.[214] He was picked up dead, with his skull fractured.

For three weeks previously the Emperor had decided to appoint Marshal Soult as head of the staff. Soult, it seems, had himself applied for the post.[215]

Suspected by the friends of the King, hated by Bonapartists and by Liberals, execrated by the entire body of officers, Soult had retired to Villeneuve l'Etang.[216] This retreat being conveniently near Paris, he presented himself at the Tuileries as early as 26th March.[217] He certainly did not do so, to remind the Emperor that he had spoken of him as a fool and adventurer in his very last "order of the day"; [218] but after this interview, of which nothing has transpired, Soult exchanged several letters with Davout, who liked him. But in spite of the Duke d'Eckmühl's promise to take the thing in hand, the Emperor's decision was delayed for some time. "I hope," wrote Soult on April 11th to the Minister of War, "that your Excellency will be so kind as to answer the letter I had the honour of addressing to you two days ago, in order that I may be prepared for his Majesty's ultimate decision concerning me." [219] A few days later, Soult, who had sent in his written oath of allegiance, was invited to renew it solemnly before the Emperor.[220] The Duke of Dalmatia could now consider his disgrace a thing of the past. On May 9th he was appointed chief of the headquarters staff.

Soult was as much Berthier's superior, as a man of thought and action is the superior of a good clerk. But he had never filled the office of chief of the staff in *any* army corps.[221] He was unaccustomed to the practical workings of the service; he was deficient in the necessary qualities of industry and accuracy. Bailly de Menthyon, who had been always considered Berthier's right hand, who was chief of the general staff from 1812 to 1814, and who had twice filled Berthier's post during the latter's absence; Drouot, deputy-head of the general staff of the Imperial Guard; Belliard, chief of Murat's staff from 1805 to 1808, and deputy-head of the general staff during the two campaigns of Saxony and of France; Reille and Drouet d'Erlon, both former heads of the staff of Lannes; Bertrand, so long aide-de-camp to the Emperor, accustomed as field-marshal to receive and transmit orders; Gérard, ex-chief of Bernadotte's staff; Ruty, chief of the artillery staff in the "Grande Armée" of 1813; also a number of other generals, would have been far more fitted to replace the Prince of Wagram. But from considerations of rank or etiquette, the Emperor desired to have a marshal of France for chief of the headquarters staff. Now, not one among the marshals was more qualified for the post than Soult himself, save Davout and Suchet. At the moment when France was busily engaged in military organisation, on the eve of a war which would include so wide a range as La Vendée, the northern frontier and the Pyrenees, when a political crisis might occur at any moment, it was of the highest necessity to keep Davout as Minister of War and Governor of Paris.[222] But there was Suchet, who had been formerly chief of the staff under Joubert and Masséna. Merely with regard to the moral effect on public opinion, it would have been a happy inspiration on the part of the Emperor, had he given Suchet the preference over Soult—Suchet, who was above mistrust and suspicion; while Soult might without any risk have replaced the Duke d'Albuféra as commander of the Army of the Alps, as this post was far less conspicuous and would not have attracted the attention of the public. Had this been done, the great scandal might have been avoided of having for the highest military personage after the Emperor and the Minister of War, the one man among all the generals who had made himself the most detested by the Army at large, under the Royalist regime.[223]

Soult, before his appointment had been officially announced, sent an order to Vandamme; that irascible general retorted by writing to Davout the following letter, remarkable for its delicate sarcasm: " I have received a letter from the Duke of Dalmatia in which he announces himself as chief of the headquarters staff. I think it my duty to send it to your Excellency before replying to it. As the Duke of Ragusa might send me the same announcement, I must consider this as not having taken place, until informed of the appointment by your Excellency or by an Imperial decree." [224]

Section VII

Before he dealt with the marshals, the Emperor had already appointed to the highest posts, many generals who might aspire to the marshal's bâton, and whom he had mentally promoted long ago. He reckoned on finding amongst those men, " who had still their way to make for themselves," as he said, more zeal and devotion than in his former comrades who were already laden with glory and honour. Therefore he gave the 1st Army Corps to Drouet d'Erlon, commanding a division in 1805, who had fought at Jena and Friedland, and who had proved one of Soult's and Masséna's best lieutenants in the Spanish wars. Reille obtained the 2nd Corps; he was a veteran of the Italian campaigns, commander of a division in 1807, then head of a division of the Guard at Wagram, and commander-in-chief of the Army of Portugal at the end of 1812. Gérard had the 4th Corps; he had been colonel at Austerlitz, brigadier at Jena, lieutenant-general at the Moskva; one of the heroes with Ney, who fought in the long-drawn struggles of the Rear Guard in the retreat from Russia, and the only officer of his rank who had led an army corps during the campaign of France. The 5th Corps, ultimately the Army of the Rhine, was entrusted to Rapp, a man of twenty-two wounds, the celebrated defender of Dantzig; commander of a division in 1805, he had acted as aide-de-camp to Napoleon for twelve years. Mouton, count of Lobau, second to none in the art of handling troops, commanding a division in 1807, received the command of the 6th Corps, which was then being formed in Paris. Charles Lebrun, son of the Duke de Plaisance, and a distinguished cavalry general, was placed for the time being at the head of the 3rd Corps. The Emperor proposed to give his place in course of time to a more "able man,"[225] and by the middle of April he gave this Corps to Vandamme. Napoleon disliked this rough soldier, as disagreeable a man as could be found; but his great soldierly qualities, his claims in seniority of rank (he had commanded a division at the age of twenty-seven in 1799), marked him out above all others, for a command. This command he discharged, so long as he was his own master, with supreme conscientiousness, firmness, and zeal, careful of all details of organisation, equipment, and military instruction, prompt to check all tamperers and alarmists, ardent in kindling the spirit of the soldiers, of the mobilised, and the inhabitants of the Meuse and the Ardennes. Davout's eulogy on Vandamme was well merited: "You have infused your own ardour into the whole country where you are."[226]

Sent to Bordeaux to proclaim the Imperial Government, Clausel, who had distinguished himself in Italy and Spain, remained there as governor of the 11th military division. He also received the command of the Corps of the Western Pyrenees. General Decaen, veteran of the Rhine and Vendéen campaigns, for six years governor of the Ile-de-France and the Ile Bourbon, had sincerely endeavoured to keep Bordeaux faithful to the King; like the Duchess of Angoulême herself, he had been compelled to yield to the force of circumstances. He returned to Paris and started again at the end of May for Toulouse. The Emperor had entrusted to him the command of the 8th and 10th military divisions and the Corps of the Eastern Pyrenees; Decaen would have been wiser had he applied for a corps in the Northern Army instead of accepting this post, which was political as well as military. Owing to his previous attitude at Bordeaux, he was doomed either to incur the suspicion of the Emperor, if he did not show sufficient zeal, or to become an object of intensified hatred to the Royalists, if he acted with the sternness demanded by circumstances. He chose the latter course, as he was bound by duty to do, and the name of Decaen was soon abhorred throughout the length and breadth of Languedoc.[227]

Lecourbe had been struck off the lists in 1804, for having

in full court, expressed his indignation with regard to the trial of his comrade Moreau, but was restored to his rank by Louis XVIII. At Lons-le-Saunier he had striven hard to prevent the desertion of Marshal Ney; but on the report of the latter, Napoleon gave orders for Lecourbe's arrest. However, he presented himself at the Tuileries, to protest his devotion to the Emperor. Only too delighted to attach to his cause, this experienced officer, who passed as a republican, and whose name was still popular among the veterans of the armies of Sambre-et-Meuse, Rhine, and Switzerland, the Emperor gave him the command of the Corps of the Jura.[228]

On the 20th of March, Lamarque had assumed on his own account, the command of the fortress of Paris. Supplanted two days later by General Hullin, who had filled the post from 1807 to 1814, he was appointed to a division in the Corps of Reille; then he was sent to La Vendée as general-in-chief of the Army of the West. He had formerly fought against the troops of the Abruzzi and the guerillas of the Sierras of Aragon. His knowledge of irregular warfare marked him out to operate against the Vendéens.[229]

General Durosnel, formerly aide-de-camp to the Emperor, received the post of second in command of the National Guard in Paris—Napoleon being nominally the first. Durosnel could boast of eminent services in the cavalry; but while Moncey, Ornano, Hullin, D'Hériot, Lespinasse had been present in Paris during the campaign of 1814, he was a prisoner in Dresden, and only returned to France after the war was over. This accounts for his ignorance of what the National Guard had done, and above all, of what it was capable of doing; thus he was ill qualified for its command. He might have made up for his inexperience by zeal and energy, but he was thwarted by his staff, which was composed of secret Royalists and bigoted Liberals.[230] Far from infusing a spirit of patriotism and self-sacrifice into the National Guard, he soon fell a prey to the same feelings of selfish caution, which animated the most influential leaders of this mercenary militia. Entrusted with the revision of the officers of the staff[231] he set about his task with studied carelessness, as if he wished merely to give satisfaction to the Emperor. He could not avoid striking off the names of officers who were too notoriously implicated, such as Decazes and Rémusat; but he retained men like Major Billing, the intimate friend of Comte, editor of the *Censeur*, and Acloque, commander of the "Legion" who forbade the band to play the popular air "Let us watch over the Empire" under pretext that it was an incendiary tune. Warm supporters of the Emperor were dismissed, notably Major Beck, the only superior officer of the 6th Legion who had fought at the Buttes Chaumont in 1814, Captain Albert, who had made the voyage to the island of Elba, and Captain Olivier, who had equipped half his company at his own expense.[232]

Added to this, Durosnel left no stone unturned, first to prevent the creation of the federate sharpshooters, then to delay their organisation. "To arm such men," he said, "would be to create uneasiness and discontent among the National Guards." The truth was that, had they been under the exclusive command of half-pay officers, with a leader who was the exact opposite of Durosnel, such as the enthusiastic and high-spirited General Darricau, a man who had won his steps at Toulon, in Egypt, with the Grande Armée, and in Spain, the National Guards would have effectually contributed to the defence of Paris. As Carnot and Davout justly remarked, the creation of these battalions of workmen could be criticised unfavourably, by none save cowards or enemies.[233]

The appointments in the Army were made by the Emperor *motu proprio*, or on the suggestion of Davout. In a few instances appointments were made directly by the Minister of War.[234] Davout was not infallible, any more than Napoleon himself. Of these a few were unfortunate, some were pitiable. Berkheim and Millet, who had never served but in the cavalry, and Molitor, commanding a division in 1809 (at the age of thirty-two), whose eminent military gifts fitted them to be with the armies in the field, were appointed to command the National Guards; while Marcognet, a second-rate man, and Donzelot, who had lost all his military habits during the seven years he was governor at Corfu, obtained each a division in the 1st Corps of the Army of the North. A few days after being relieved of his command, the colonel of the 14th Chasseurs, one of the most devoted officers of the Duke d'Angoulême, was proposed for a mobilised regiment. Another colonel, who had proved such a coward under fire that he had to be relegated to the retired list, was proposed for a line regiment.[235] Finally, General Moreau, the pusillanimous commander of Soissons in 1814, who only escaped capital punishment through the fall of Napoleon, was given the command of a brigade on active service.[236] The Emperor might well say: "It seems to me that among the general officers, there are many young men who are more clever than those who have been proposed to me." [237]

Overworked, and a prey to the gravest anxieties, the Emperor would often ratify Davout's proposals without examining them. He would then lay all the blame on his minister; for Davout, the Minister of War, was, it appears, little liked at the Tuileries, on account of the stiff and severe manner in which he discharged his duties. The Imperial circle never failed to criticise severely any doings of his, which were in any way censurable.[238] As an additional guarantee for the military staff, the Emperor entrusted to his aide-de-camp, Flahaut, the revision of the propositions of the Minister of War. "Collect as far as you possibly can," he wrote, "all the information obtainable, respecting the generals and officers, for if I make any unfortunate choice, I shall hold you responsible."[239] Flahaut was an excellent staff officer, remarkably brave, and had shown himself as brilliant a rider at Friedland and Moskva, as he was a skilful diplomatist at Neumark and Lusigny. And yet it was believed he owed his extraordinary success to favouritism alone. Indeed, he had been appointed a general of division at twenty-eight, though up to that time (1813) he had only commanded a squadron. For so young a lieutenant-general, it might have been better to decline the mission entrusted to his care, a most delicate one to fulfil in conjunction with such a man as Davout.[240] At all events, he might have performed it with more discretion and with no less zeal. He spent several hours a day at the War Office, overturning the dossiers, examining the accounts, striking out on his own authority the names of candidates entered on the rolls, and even giving orders which flatly contradicted those of Davout. Nor were his selections any better;[241] in spite of his loyalty and intelligence, the aide-de-camp of the Emperor could not judge more wisely than Davout himself. The Prince of Eckmühl deeply resented this inquisition, from which, however, he was soon delivered.[242] He expostulated with the Emperor himself, telling him he would not remain an hour longer at the War Office, did he not deem it cowardly to resign at such a time.[243]

To conclude, among the officers provided with commissions, some were incapable, some were prematurely worn-out, others were disloyal at heart; yet the leaders of the last Imperial Army formed an admirable body as a whole. We may even say that, unless a repetition of such revolutions and wars as occurred between 1789 and 1814 were to arise, the French Army will never again have such chiefs. Independently of their innate military qualities, they possessed the strength of experience and the virtue of youth. They had all fought for more than twenty years, yet they were all under fifty. Napoleon was forty-six; Davout, forty-five; Soult, forty-six; Ney, forty-six; Grouchy, forty-nine; Drouet d'Erlon, forty-nine; Lobau, forty-five; Lamarque, forty-five; Kellermann, forty-five; Reille, forty-four; Vandamme, forty-four; Rapp, forty-three; Clausel, forty-three; Suchet, forty-three; Pajol, forty-three; Gérard, forty-two; Drouot, forty-one; Exelmans, forty. All of these were commanders of army corps or of cavalry corps. Among the generals of division several, such as Alten, Piré, Flahaut, Berckheim, Teste, were under forty. The youngest brigade-general was La Bédoyère; he was twenty-nine.

Section VIII

These men, who had so often led the French to victory, were, unfortunately, more conspicuous for their physical strength and military talents, than for their confidence in the triumph of their cause. They knew only too well the magnitude of the preparations of Europe, and the comparatively small resources of France in point of men and material; they realised that but for a series of lucky accidents of fate, such as are of course always possible in war, the Emperor with his small army could never long resist the overwhelming strength of the coalition. On 10th June, as he passed through La Fère, General Ruty, commander-in-chief of the artillery, said to Colonel Pion des Loches: "Bonaparte is doomed without greater resources. The King will return before long. What is to become of us?—this miserable army that did not want to fire a shot three months ago!" In a gathering of officers, the day before crossing the Sambre, another general spoke in such a discouraging tone that Major Négrier, in spite of the rules of discipline, stopped him sharply: "It is not for you," he said, "to express such feelings. Our bed is made, we must lie on it. Do not try to demoralise us." Confidence was at a low ebb even among the general officers who were among the first to declare themselves for Napoleon, urged to do so by their sympathies or the force of events, and who, deeply compromised as they were, ought to have understood that it was their best policy to raise the spirits of their comrades. But they were all anxious, when they realised that their lives were at stake in this desperate game.[244]

Discord reigned in the general staffs. The generals who, without being ardent Royalists, would yet have preferred to end their career peacefully under the Bourbons, scowled on the conspirators of 20th March, who had plunged their country into a perilous venture and provoked a frightful war. These men were suspected by the others and denounced as officers without energy, lukewarm patriots, shameless Royalists. Fiercer than ever grew the competitions, rivalries, jealousies, respecting promotion. However cautious the Emperor had been in granting rewards to his true adherents, the other generals found that after the first battle these alone would win promotion and rewards. On the other hand, those who had first rallied to the Emperor's standard, were amazed to see men like Soult, Durutte, Bruny, Bourmont, Dumonceau, still in the Army. General Piré objected to the insufficiency of the bonus on taking the field first: "Such flagrant neglect of private interests," he said, "often ruins the general cause." General Mathieu insisted on retiring, to avoid serving under Clausel, who was his junior. Duhesme, placed at first in the

3rd Corps, was sent into the Young Guard. "He cannot possibly," wrote Davout, "serve under Vandamme." General Bonnet accused General Ornano of having prejudiced the Emperor against him; he challenged him and shot him through the lungs. Vandamme, who had a corps of 18,000 men under him, complained to the Minister of War that generals who were his juniors had commands of far greater importance. Gressot wrote to Soult that the generals of the Rhine Army, were unanimous in expressing their regret at being led by Rapp, "Rapp being an utter nonentity." If it had not been the actual day for beginning the campaign, many a general would have refused to serve under the Prince of "la Moskva"; only with the greatest reluctance did Vandamme and even Gérard serve under the command of Grouchy. An officer of the Emperor's staff wrote to Davout: "Each one of us regards his neighbour as a crusader involved in the same adventure, but towards whom he has no duties."[245]

As to the good fellowship and loyalty to each other between the generals of 1815, we need only refer to the noble words pronounced by Cambronne before the court-martial: "I refused the rank of lieutenant-general, because there were so many who were jealous. You saw what happened at Waterloo; we had a leader of great repute. Very well, he was powerless to put everything in order. They would have said *my* appointment was by favour and that I was too young. They might have left me in the lurch, and I did not care to run the risk of endangering the safety of the whole Army."[246]

On the other hand, the soldiers, and nearly all the subalterns, were filled with enthusiasm and confidence. While the generals saw things as they really were, the soldiers were once more dreaming the dream of glory from which they had been awakened by the invasion, but which they could not believe had ended. The Emperor's return had been prophesied for a whole year in all the barrack-room ballads and marching songs—lo! had he not returned at last? In the opinion of the soldiers, Napoleon was invincible. If he were defeated in 1812, it was by the snow and the cold; in 1814, because he was betrayed. This belief, always encouraged by the Emperor, was well adapted to keep up the spirit of the

Army; unfortunately, as an anti-climax, it led to distrust and disbelief in all but Napoleon himself. Defeat was only possible in case of treachery, but then the soldiers imagined traitors to exist everywhere. "Do not employ the marshals during the campaign," somebody wrote to Napoleon. Complaints and denunciations poured into the War Office and to the officials at the Tuileries, concerning officers who had shown leanings towards the Bourbons or Orleanists under the preceding reign, or who were merely guilty of having a handle to their name.[247]

At the advanced posts of the Army of the Rhine, a sentinel fired on a man who was trying to swim across to the German side. A rumour spread among the troops, that on his dead body a note was found, indicating the existence of a plot to blow up the powder magazine of Strasburg.[248] The commander of Condé, Colonel Taubin, pleaded as an excuse for certain delays in provisioning the place that " he could not make himself obeyed," and maddened by the reply of the deputy-chief of the 1st Staff Corps, who wrote sternly that "an officer who cannot make his men obey is not fit to command," Taubin instantly blew out his brains. The garrison believed that the colonel had killed himself for fear of being called before a court-martial as accomplice in some conspiracy.[249] While the minds of the men were filled with fears of treachery, it is easy to imagine the feelings produced in the 1st Regiment by the distribution of defective cartridges. This certainly was no trifling matter, for the artillery authorities at Lille had distributed to the 19th and 42nd Regiments of the line, ball cartridges containing, not gun-powder but bran, clay, and iron filings. The director of the artillery was kept under surveillance by Drouet d'Erlon, who had long suspected him; the latter reported to Davout " that for some time he had suspicions of the man's opinions." Davout ordered an inquiry, which, like most inquiries, led to no results. No one could ever discover why, or how, or when, these extraordinary cartridges found their way to the magazine.[250]

Discipline, which even in the armies of Austerlitz and Wagram had not been nearly as strict as might be imagined, was still further impaired by this universal mistrust coupled with the impression caused by the events of the past year. The soldiers were not inclined to obey chiefs who were capable (they suspected) of treason, or "ragusade" as they expressed it, or to respect their chiefs who, only three months previously, were leading them against the Emperor, and who now professed ardent feelings of loyalty towards him. Only those officers who by word or deed had incited and urged their men to rebel, during the period from 5th March to 20th March, only those retained their authority, and even they could not always do so. Six officers of the 1st Cuirassiers, who had been promoted one rank higher by the Emperor for having gained over the regiment, were regularly installed in presence of the troops. The Cuirassiers received them with groans and shouts, crying, "We have done as much as you, and we have received neither promotion nor reward." In more than one brigade, it was hoped that most of the officers would make way for their subordinates. In many addresses from the regiments to the Emperor they petitioned for the dismissal of their colonel. "We claim," wrote the dragoons of the 12th Regiment, "the dismissal of our colonel, whose ardour in the cause of your Majesty is not by any means equal to our own devotion." "We are convinced," wrote the officers and soldiers of the 75th Regiment of the line, "that it is your Majesty's intention not to keep a single traitor at the head of a French regiment." [251]

There was yet another reason for the decline of discipline. Deceived by appearances, as almost all the world was at that time, the soldiers imagined that the revolution which had brought back the Emperor to the Tuileries, was entirely their work.[252] Napoleon was indebted to them for the throne; and consequently they imagined the cry of "Vive l'Empereur!" entitled them to any license. Had not Davout declared that the desertions of the soldiers which took place during the recent events, amounted to proofs of devotion towards the Emperor? Did not the wise Drouot himself advise the reincorporation into the ranks of the Old Guard, of all those sub-officers who had been cashiered in 1814, for deserting their colours owing to their "grief at the departure of his Majesty"?[253] What examples for an army!

On March 26th the dragoons of the Guard arrived from

Tours. They learnt on the quays that the Emperor was in person, reviewing the troops. It was a year since they had seen their idol! They got beyond the control of their officers, filed through the gateway of the Louvre, and burst in upon the Place du Carrousel at quick trot, bespattered with mud on their smoking horses, with cries of "Vive l'Empereur!" A few days later, during an inspection with open ranks, the dragoons of the line followed their own cue; suddenly the first rank faced right about, and both ranks raised their swords and crossed them over the head of Napoleon. The Emperor bent his head laughingly and finished the inspection under this canopy of steel.[254] This frenzy of devotion towards Napoleon might excuse such breaches of discipline and unsoldierly freaks, but there were faults of a far graver character. At Orgon, on their march from Pont-Saint-Esprit to Marseilles after the capitulation of La Pallud, Grouchy's troops committed the greatest excesses, under the pretext that the previous year, when Napoleon passed through the town on his way to exile, the inhabitants threatened to hang him.[255] At Aire (Pas-de-Calais) the 105th Regiment of the line on its way to the frontier, began pulling down a newly-built house because its frontage was decorated with the royalist *fleurs de lis;* the commander of the garrison had no other means of quieting the soldiers than to put the unfortunate owner of the house into prison. At Aix the artillery, offended by the sight of young Royalists walking about with huge white roses in their buttonholes, rushed upon them with drawn swords and dispersed them.[256] At Saint-Germain the sharpshooters of the Young Guard mutinied and refused to enter their barracks, because there was no tricolor flag over the entrance door. In the theatres the soldiers maltreated those spectators who did not cheer the Marseillaise. In the cafés they beat those who refused to shout "Vive l'Empereur!"[257] In Belgium, where they had just arrived, every man plundered right and left. "Marauding and pillage are rampant in the Army now," wrote Radet, general of gendarmes, to Soult on the 17th; "the Guard itself sets the example. Forage magazines have been plundered, horses have been stolen. Plunder has been going on all night in the homes of Belgians who gave us everything willingly and nursed our wounded. The men flatly defy the authority of the gendarmerie. I beg to tender my resignation as Provost-Marshal of the Army." [258]

Several regiments refused the biscuit-bread. Friant complained that the grenadiers of the Guard were taking women in their train. A voltigeur of the 96th threw down his arms to go and see his parents; on his return after a week's absence the captain merely gave him a trifling disciplinary punishment.[259] 292 soldiers of the 39th and 59th Regiments of the line declared they would desert, if they were not passed on into the Guards. The men of the Transport Corps who had followed the Emperor from Grenoble got incorporated into the 1st Hussars, and the Hussars from the same regiment, had themselves enrolled with the Guards.[260] General Barrois, under whose command a division of the Young Guard was being formed, received this singular petition: "Monsieur le comte, there are 1374 of us of the 1st and 2nd infantry of the line who have always served with honour. We think it our duty to warn you, that we do not intend to stay any longer in our present regiments. Although we have nothing to complain of, we have served in the Guard, and to the Guard we intend to return. It would not be wise to stop us, for our minds are made up irrevocably. You can prevent the error we contemplate, by obtaining our return into the Guard. We will wait four days, but no longer. Our colonels are warned." [261]

Rivalries between the corps led to brawls and duels. The Emperor was compelled to countermand a mere detail of dress viz. the white shoulder-knots hitherto worn by the five cavalry regiments bearing the No. 1, as they provoked the jealousy of all the other regiments.[262] The soldiers from Elba were quartered in the "Hôtel des Cent Suisses" on the Place du Carrousel, and some few enthusiasts had put over the entrance a new inscription, "Quarters of the Heroes." The other heroes of the Army, Bonapartists though they were, took umbrage at this. The old soldiers of the 1st Empire were quizzed by their comrades of the line, and even by the Old Guard. Swords were drawn, and the inscription had to be effaced.[263]

But if the Army was weakened by its lack of discipline, it was filled with eagerness to fight, resolution to conquer, idolatry of the Emperor, and hatred of foreigners. A spy wrote from Paris to Wellington in the middle of the month of May: "To convey an accurate idea of the enthusiasm of the Army, I need merely point a parallel between the period of 1792 and the present year. The balance still would certainly be in favour of Bonaparte, for now it is no longer a question of mere enthusiasm, but of positive frenzy. The cause of the soldiers, who have nothing to hope, after the fall of their chief, is inseparably linked with his own. For this reason I must not conceal from your Excellency that, in spite of all the Bourbonists may say, the struggle will be a bloody one, and will last to the bitter end." "The excitement of the troops," according to General Hulot, "was at its highest pitch, their ardour amounting to fanaticism." On June 15th General Foy writes in his diary that "the moment for taking the field has been admirably chosen. The troops are thrilled, not with patriotism or enthusiasm, but with positive frenzy on behalf of the Emperor and against his enemies." It was in all sincerity that Adjutant-Major Gordon, himself a deserter and traitor, sent the following information to Clarke: "The King on his return will have to disband the Army and to create a new one. The soldiers are infuriated; their temper is frightful!"[264]

"The temper of the soldiers is frightful," meaning that all the soldiers were clamouring to be reviewed by the Emperor himself. They hailed the new eagles with enthusiastic cheers and threatening oaths. They answered the cries of "Vive l'Armée!" with shouts of "Vive l'Empereur!" They put little tricolor flags in the barrels of their muskets. They swore with swords crossed over flaming punch-bowls, that they would conquer or die. "He will be with us,"[265] they said, pointing to the bust of the Emperor. They erected at their own expense a monument at the Gulf of Jouan. They had medals struck to commemorate Napoleon's return. They gave up their pay for one, two, or five days, in order to contribute to the expenses of the war. They left their garrisons and marched through towns and villages shouting, "Vive l'Empereur!" and singing "Le Père la Violette." They tore to shreds, the white flags of the Royalists and put them to the vilest uses. They took it upon themselves to arrest all traitors, and they beat them with the butt-ends of their muskets. They snatched deserters from the hands of the gendarmes and degraded them on the spot, without further ceremony. They would fain have doubled their marches to take part in the first battles. They declared they needed no cartridges, as they meant to rush on the enemy with fixed bayonets. They said "they did not care a rap for their skins provided the Emperor thrashed the Allies!"[266]

Such was the Army of 1815—impressionable, critical, without discipline, and without confidence in its leaders, haunted by the dread of treason, and on that account, perhaps, liable to sudden fits of panic; it was, nevertheless, instinct with warlike aspirations and loving war for its own sake, fired with a thirst for vengeance; it was capable of heroic efforts and furious impulses; it was more impetuous, more excited, more eager for the fray than any other Republican or Imperial Army after or before it. Napoleon had never before handled an instrument of war, which was at once so formidable, and so fragile.

BOOK I CHAPTER II

THE PLANS OF CAMPAIGN

I. Project for the invasion of Belgium in the early part of April.
II. Plan of campaign of the Allies.
III. Napoleon's plan of campaign.
IV. Concentration of the French Army (8th to 14th June)—Arrival of the Emperor at Beaumont—Strength and positions of the armies on the 14th of June.

SECTION I

ON the 25th of March 1815, when the sovereigns at Vienna were forming a seventh coalition against France, the forces they could bring into the field to meet any sudden attack of Napoleon on Belgium, amounted to 80,000 soldiers at the most — 30,000 Prussians, 14,000 Saxons, 23,000 Anglo-Hanoverians, and about 10,000 Dutch and Belgians.[1]

The Saxons were still inclined to mutiny,[2] and defections amongst the Dutch and Belgians were to be expected. Most of the latter had served under Napoleon; and in Brussels, throughout the "Walloon" country, specially the provinces of Namur and Liège, which had suffered most during the stern Prussian occupation, there was a strong French party.[3]

Posted all the way from Trèves and Coblentz to Courtrai and Antwerp, over an extent of seventy miles, the allied troops had begun to concentrate[4] as early as the 15th of March; but this would not have prevented Napoleon from crossing the Belgian frontier with 50,000 men on the 1st of April,[5] and from entering Brussels three days later with perfect ease. Wellington was in Vienna, Blücher in Berlin. The French would not have met with the slightest resistance, for the Prince of Orange and General Kleist, who commanded the Prussian

Army in the Rhenish provinces, had decided, in case of attack, to operate with combined forces on Tirlemont, eleven leagues to the east of Brussels.[6]

Would this easy success have been sufficient to bring about an insurrection in Belgium, as the Emperor hoped? In any case, without deceiving the military authorities, the occupation of Brussels would have created a profound impression in France and abroad. The Prussian generals, the Prince of Orange, Wellington himself, dreaded this sudden attack. "Brussels must be protected," Müffling wrote to the King of the Netherlands, "lest this city should become the focus of the Revolution." "It would be of the greatest importance to Bonaparte," Wellington wrote to Gneisenau, "if he could make us withdraw behind Brussels, drive back the King of France, and overthrow the government established here by the King of the Netherlands. This would have a terrible effect on public opinion."[7] But this bold stroke which had suggested itself to Napoleon, was abandoned as soon as conceived,[8] though he knew it might be executed with ease and certainty. He realised perfectly that a defeat inflicted on the tenth part only of the forces of the coalition, would be considered by the Allies as a mere brush with the advanced guards,[9] and that such a victory, even though it might result in a rising in Belgium, would by no means terminate the war. By crossing the Sambre on the 1st of April, he would endanger his future for the sake of a fleeting success; for the ex-royal army, though able to furnish at a moment's notice 50,000 excellent troops, was in no condition to bear the brunt of a campaign of any length. Men, arms, horses, supplies, all were lacking, and the Emperor could not conduct operations in Belgium and reorganise the Army at the same time. Besides, a corps of 50,000 men could not be formed without drawing on the garrisons of the departments of the north, where the population was hostile to the Empire, and without employing the men of the Paris reserves, which were intended, in case of pressing necessity, to act in the west, where the Vendéen chiefs were still disturbed, and in the south, where Bordeaux, Toulouse, Marseilles still acknowledged the authority of the Duc d'Angoulême, who was preparing to march upon Lyons.[10]

If the military condition of France made it impossible for Napoleon, as a leader, to enter the field hastily, he was also hampered, as a sovereign, by the political situation. A week only having passed since he had resumed the sceptre, it was impossible for him to leave the seat of government to go and fight, unless imperative circumstances compelled him to do so. It was much more needful to reorganise the administration, to fill the treasury, to pacify the country. To win the hearts of the French, who were all so eager for peace, would it not be a questionable stroke of policy to invade Belgium! Would not the taking of Brussels be counterbalanced by the terror of seeing Napoleon, who had only just come back to France, step once more into his seven-league boots and rush to win fresh conquests? The Emperor had another reason, which outweighed all the others, for not beginning the war till he had exhausted all means of conciliation: like his people, he desired to preserve peace, if only for the time being.[11]

For more than a month the Emperor persisted in believing peace was possible. "*If* we have war [12] . . ." he still wrote to Davout on the 30th of April, and with Davout he had no need to dissemble. But, however obstinately he clung to his illusions, he did not fail at the same time to take every measure for defence. He had called out the reserves, he had mobilised the National Guards; he had given orders for the collection of all kinds of warlike supplies, and it was not till the middle of June, when he had almost given up all hope of avoiding war,[13] that he drew out his plan of campaign.[14]

SECTION II

From the beginning of April the Allies were making their preparations. There were several schemes under consideration. Knesebecke actually proposed to deceive Napoleon by putting him in possession of a false plan. "We will make the enemy," he said, "imagine that we mean to operate by Bâsle, that he has nothing to fear from the English Army, which will be engaged at the siege of Dunkerque, nor from the Prussian Army, which will remain on the defensive. We will thus draw

Bonaparte between the Marne and the Upper Rhine against the Austrian, Bavarian, and Russian armies, while the English and the Prussians will easily advance upon Paris." [15]

Schwarzenberg renovated the science of war by gravely declaring that the Allies should neither "divide their forces too much, lest they weakened their strength, nor march in large masses, lest they might not find sufficient for their sustenance." He concluded they ought to march on Paris in three strong columns, "leaving details of the operations to the individual lights and experience of the Generals-in-Chief." [16]

The plan devised by Gneisenau, which was formidable and crushing, was founded on the enormous numerical superiority of the Allies. Gneisenau said: "Four great operating armies, the fourth of which (the Russian Army) will form the Reserve, will enter France simultaneously and march straight on to Paris. Whatever happens to one of the three armies of the first line, whether it be beaten or not, the two others will continue to advance, leaving detachments in their rear to watch the fortresses. The mission of the Russian or reserve army, is to retrieve any misfortune which may overtake either of the armies of the first line. To that end, it will bear down at once to the help of the retreating army, or harass the enemy's flank. Supposing Napoleon beats one of the armies of the first line, the other two, still marching forward, will gain ground and draw nearer Paris, while the army of Reserve will succour the defeated army. If Napoleon, instead of pursuing the defeated army, bears down on the flank of another army of the first line, the Reserve will join the latter, in such a way that the battle must turn to the enemy's disadvantage. Meanwhile the third army will continue to advance, and the troops which received a check at first will recover themselves and start anew on their offensive march." [17]

Wellington wished to begin hostilities without waiting for the arrival of the Russian Army, and even before the three armies had completed their concentration. He wrote on the 10th of April: "It will suffice to bring between the Sambre and the Meuse 60,000 Anglo-Dutch, 60,000 Prussians, and 140,000 Austrians and Bavarians, to find ourselves in

France with forces far superior to those of the enemy, and free to manœuvre in the direction of Paris." Earnestly anxious to protect the interests of Louis XVIII., Wellington felt that every day the truce lasted only made Napoleon's power the firmer; and convinced of the importance of the Royalist operations in the south, he desired to second them by prompt action on the northern frontiers.[18]

At Vienna no such haste was desired. They meant to make war indeed, but war without risks. The idea was to be at least three to one in each battle, and to win "according to mechanical rules and the laws of gravitation."[19] The Council of War held on the 19th of April, under the presidency of the Czar, decided that to give sufficient time for the various armies to concentrate their forces, the campaign should not begin before the 1st of June.[20] This was one month wasted, in the opinion of Wellington and Blücher; one month gained, according to Knesebeck and Schwarzenberg. The latter even hoped to gain another month when the strategical plans were discussed.

In fact, on the 10th of June, when Blücher, although he had had the distraction of a rebellion of the Saxons,[21] was becoming "enraged" at his enforced inaction, and was telling his soldiers of his impatience to go and fetch the pipe he had left in Paris,[22] Schwarzenberg had induced the sovereigns to accept his final plan, the execution of which was deferred till the 27th of June or the 1st of July.[23]

According to these new dispositions, six armies were to cross the French frontier simultaneously: the Army of the Netherlands (93,000 English, Hanoverians, Brunswickers, and Dutch-Belgians[24] under Wellington) between Maubeuge and Beaumont; the Prussian Army (117,000 men under Blücher[25]) between Philippeville and Givet; the Russian Army (150,000 men[26] under Barclay de Tolly) by Saarlouis and Saarbrück; the Army of the Upper Rhine (210,000 Austrians, Bavarians, Würtembergians, and Hessians[27] under Schwarzenberg), the right wing by Sarreguemines, the bulk by Bâsle. These four great armies would march on Paris concentrically, the English by Péronne, the Prussians by Laon, the Russians by Nancy, the Austrians by Langres.

On the extreme left, the army of Upper Italy (38,000

Austrians [28] and 12,000 Piemontese [29] under Frimont) and the Austrian Army of Naples (25,000 men [30] under Bianchi) were to pass the Alps, the former advancing on Lyons, the latter making for Provence, where the English squadron of the Mediterranean would second their operations.

Section III

Through secret reports from Vienna and Brussels, and through the foreign newspapers (the press was most incautious [31] at that time), Napoleon was tolerably well informed of the strength and projects of the enemy. Two plans of campaign presented themselves to his mind.[32]

The first plan consisted in massing round Paris the 1st, 2nd, 3rd, 4th, and 6th Corps, the Guard, the Cavalry Reserve, and the Army of the Rhine (or 5th Corps); in concentrating by Lyons the Army of the Alps and the Corps of the Jura; and in allowing the enemy to fight within this network of military strongholds, which were all well supplied and defended by about 150,000 men—mobilised national guards, pensioners, gunners of the line, veterans, custom-house officials, gendarmes, and the city national guards.[33] The allied armies, which were not to cross the border till the 1st of July, could not arrive within the radius of Lyons before the 15th or the 18th, and the radius of Paris before the 25th.[34] By the 25th of July the intrenchments of Paris would be finished, and the garrison would muster 30,000 regulars, 18,000 sharpshooters, and 36,000 national guards. The army concentrated round Paris would number 200,000 men;[35] and there would be left about 80,000 men at the depôt centres,[36] and 158,000 men learning their drill or under training.[37]

Of the 645,000 allies entering France, 75,000 would have to operate in Lyonnais and Provence. 150,000,[38] owing to his innumerable lines of operation, must perforce be left by the enemy in his rear to guard his communications and to besiege or cover the strongholds. The four great armies, on arrival between the Oise and the Seine, would have dwindled to 420,000 men. Against these 420,000, Napoleon would oppose 200,000 mobilised troops and the intrenched camp of Paris. He would repeat the campaign of 1814, but with 200,000 soldiers instead of 90,000,[39] and with Paris strongly fortified, defended by 80,000 men, under the government of no less a man than Davout, the able captain of Auerstaëdt and Eckmühl, the stern defender of Hamburg.

The second plan, which was bolder, more worthy of the genius of Napoleon, of the French temperament, and even of the principles of *la grande guerre*, though it was infinitely more hazardous, was to attack the enemy without giving him time to concentrate his forces. By the 15th of June the Emperor would be able to assemble an army of 125,000 men on the northern frontier. He would enter Belgium; he would beat in turn, or separately, the English and the Prussians; then, as soon as new reinforcements had arrived from the depôt centres, he would effect a junction with the 23,000 men under Rapp, and would bear down upon the Austro-Russians.

If the military question had been the only one to consider, doubtless the Emperor would have adopted the first plan, the success of which seemed certain.[40] But he was not free to act, as he had been in 1805, or even in 1812. Chief of the Army as he was, he had to reckon with public opinion. What an impression would be produced in the country were he to leave defenceless, a third of his territory—those very provinces, too, which were most patriotic, most devoted to the Imperial cause![41] Would he not provoke universal despondency and disaffection? would he not excite the ill feeling of the Chamber to the pitch of open hostility? would he not spread through the west, and rekindle in the south, fresh sparks of insurrection? The Emperor felt that, in order to raise the spirits of all, to silence the discontented and the factious, he must win a glorious victory on the very outset of the war. With his usual illusions, he imagined such a victory would be conclusive—enough to break up the coalition. The Belgians, he thought, will rally to the French flag, and the destruction of Wellington's army, will lead to the downfall of the Tory cabinet and the advent of a peace ministry in England. If circumstances turned out differently, then the

Army, victorious in Belgium over the Prussians and English, could not fail to be victorious also in France over the Russians and Austrians.[42] At the worst, granting a check on the Belgian frontier, it would be possible to fall back on Paris and to operate on the defensive plan.[43] But the Emperor, nevertheless, did not hide from himself that, in the event of a defeat in Belgium, his first plan, to which he would have to return, would have greatly diminished chances of success. He would have suffered severe losses, the *morale* of the army and the country at large would be lowered, he would provoke the Allies to march into France a fortnight earlier, and decidedly, through the impossibility of attending to everything at once, he would be compelled to neglect in some degree the organisation for defence.[44]

The Emperor pondered lengthily over these schemes.[45] When he had made up his mind to act on the offensive, he still hesitated for several days, before deciding at which point he would strike his first blows.[46] To ensure the success of his plan, which was to beat, one after the other, the two armies occupying Belgium, he would have to attack Wellington or Blücher, before they could effect the junction of their forces. If he directed his line of operations against Brussels through Ath, and debouched from Lille or Condé against Wellington's right, he would merely drive the English Army towards the Prussian Army, and two days later he would find himself face to face with their united forces. If, on the contrary, he marched against Blücher's left through Givet and the valley of the Meuse, in the same way he would still hasten the union of the hostile forces by driving the Prussians to the English. Inspired by one of his finest strategical conceptions, the Emperor resolved to break boldly into the very centre of the enemy's cantonments, at the very point where the English and Prussians would probably concentrate. The road from Charleroi to Brussels forming the line of contact between the two armies, Napoleon, passing through Beaumont and Philippeville, resolved by this road, to fall like a thunderbolt on his foe.

Section IV

The orders for concentration were issued early in June. The 1st Corps proceeded from Valenciennes to Avesnes; the 2nd from Avesnes to Maubeuge; the 3rd from Rocroi to Chimay; the 4th from Thionville to Rocroi; the 6th from Soissons to Avesnes; the Imperial Guard from Paris to Avesnes,[47] viâ Soissons.

Communications between Belgium and the Rhine provinces were intercepted; in the sea-ports all vessels were laid under an embargo, even the fishing-boats; and for fear of giving any hint to the enemy's advanced posts, bodies of volunteers and divisions from the National Guard were posted along the frontiers of the north and the east, to replace troops which were summoned to the various meeting-places.[48] When Napoleon, who had left Paris by night, arrived at Laon at twelve on the 12th of June, all the troops were still on the march. Grouchy's troops were an exception; they had not yet stirred, though Grouchy's headquarters were in Laon itself. Summoned to the Emperor's presence, Grouchy stated that he had received no orders.[49] This was the truth, for not till that very day (12th June) did the chief of the staff at headquarters send him Napoleon's instructions[50] from Avesnes! But immediately after seeing the Emperor, Grouchy issued orders to the four cavalry corps that they were to make for the frontier by forced marches; and he himself started off to Avesnes without losing an hour's time. In this way the concentration was not delayed, since the whole Cavalry Reserve were beyond Avesnes on the night of the 13th; but several regiments had been compelled to ride for 20 leagues without drawing rein,—wretched preparation indeed for horses at the opening of a campaign![51] The misfortune was that this incident, which foreboded evil, failed to arouse the attention of Napoleon to the negligence of the chief of the staff at headquarters.

On the 13th of June the Emperor slept at Avesnes; on the evening of the 14th he moved his headquarters to Beaumont, the centre of his army.[52] That night, in spite of bad weather, all the troops bivouacked in order to keep well together.[53] At the sound of the *réveil* the Emperor's order of the day was read out to them: "Soldiers, to-day is the anniversary of Marengo and Friedland, which twice decided the fate of Europe. We were too generous then, as we were too generous after Austerlitz and Wagram. And now, banded together against us, the sovereigns we left on their thrones, conspire against the independence and the most sacred rights of France. They have begun by the most iniquitous aggression. Let us march to meet them; are we not the men we were then?"[54]

The positions of the Army were as follows:—The 1st Corps (20,731 men under Drouet d'Erlon[55]), forming the extreme left, between the road from Avesnes to Maubeuge and Solre-sur-Sambre; the 2nd Corps (25,179 men under Reille[56]), between Solre-sùr-Sambre and Leers; the 3rd Corps (18,105 men under Vandamme[57]); and the 6th Corps (10,821 men under Lobau[58]) between Beaumont and the frontier; the 4th Corps (15,404 men under Gérard[59]) between Philippeville and Florenne; the Cavalry Reserve (13,144 men under Grouchy[60]) at Valcourt, at Bossus, and at Gayolle; the Imperial Guard (20,755 men[61]) before and behind Beaumont.[62] This army had 370 pieces of heavy artillery.[63] The ground covered by the bivouacks did not exceed 8 leagues in breadth by 10 kilometres in length.

In ten days 124,000 men, separated by distances varying from 10 to 70 leagues, had assembled on the frontier, within easy cannon range of the enemy's advanced posts, before the Allies had taken a single defensive measure. Never was a concentration march better planned or better carried out, save for trifling delays quickly remedied.

While the French Army had massed in such imposing numbers, the English and Prussians were still scattered over a front line extending over more than 35 leagues, and of an average breadth of 12 leagues. On the 14th of June, Blücher's headquarters were at Namur. The 1st Corps (30,800 men under Zieten[64]), which formed the right of the Prussian Army, occupied Thuin, Fontaine-L'Evêque, Marchienne, Charleroi, Moustiers, Fleurus, Sombreffe, and Gembloux; the 2nd Corps (31,000 men under Pirch I.[65]), Namur,

Héron, and Hannut; the 3rd Corps (23,900 men under Thielmann [66]), Ciney, Dinant, and Huy; and the 4th Corps (30,300 men under Bulow [67]), Liège and Tongres.[68]

The cantonments of the army of Wellington, who had established his headquarters at Brussels, extended from the Lys and the Scheldt to the little river of La Haine. The 2nd Corps (27,321 men under Lord Hill [69]) occupied Leuze, Ath, Audenarde, Ghent, and Alost; the 1st Corps (30,246 men under the Prince of Orange [70]), Mons, Rœulx, Frasnes, Seneffe, Nivelles, Genappe, Soignies, Enghien, and Braine-le-Comte; the Cavalry Corps (9913 men under Lord Uxbridge [71]) was encamped along the Dender, between Ninove and Grammont; and the Reserve (25,597 men under the direct command of Wellington [72]) in Brussels and its neighbourhood.

In the positions which they occupied, three days were necessary for each of the two armies to concentrate on the line of contact, and double that time to concentrate, as the case might be, on the right wing of the English troops or the left wing of the Prussians.[73] This unusual extension of the cantonments, so perilous with an adversary like Napoleon, and so favourable to the success of his boldly conceived plan, has been criticised by nearly all military writers. Wellington sought to justify these dispositions, by pointing out the difficulty of keeping the troops supplied with food and the necessity of protecting all points.[74] The truth is, that though they admitted the possibility of an attack from Napoleon, and though they had made arrangements to parry it eventually, they believed such an attack to be more than improbable. On the 15th of June, at the time when the Emperor had already set foot on the Belgian territory, Wellington was calmly expounding, in a long letter to the Czar, his intention of taking the offensive at the end of the month.[75] A few days before, Blücher had written to his wife: "We shall soon enter France. We might remain here another year, for Bonaparte will never attack us."[76]

BOOK I CHAPTER III

THE FIRST ENGAGEMENTS

I. Passage of the Belgian frontier (15th June)—Desertion of General de Bourmont.
II. Taking of Charleroi.
III. Interview between Napoleon and Ney—Battle at Gilly with the right wing.
IV. Ney's operations on 15th June—Battle at Gosselies—Battle of Frasnes—Quatre-Bras.

Section I

At half-past three in the morning of the 15th of June, advanced posts of the French crossed the frontier at Leers, Cour-sur-Heure, and Thy.[1] Carrying out the marching orders issued from Imperial headquarters the evening before, the Army marched on Charleroi in three principal columns: the left column (Corps of Reille and Corps of Erlon by Thuin and Marchienne); the central column (Corps of Vandamme, Corps of Lobau, Imperial Guard, and Grouchy's Cavalry Reserve) by Ham-sur-Heure, Jamioulx, and Marcinelle; the right column (Corps of Gérard) by Florenne and Gerpinnes.[2]

The Emperor had arranged everything from a proégetic point of view, to effect a rapid transport of these masses, and to spare his men the enervating fatigue of aimless tramping to and fro; his dispositions from a tactical point of view were all designed to facilitate, in case of any serious resistance from the enemy, the prompt deployment of the columns, and their mutual assistance. The breaking up of the bivouacs took place at intervals of half an hour, the troops nearest the frontier starting on their way at three o'clock in the morning, those farthest off at eight o'clock. Only twelve regiments of cavalry led the way. The other mounted troops had directions to advance on the left of the infantry. The sappers of each army corps were to keep together, and to march in each division, behind the first regiment of light infantry. Three companies of pontoniers with fifteen pontoons and fifteen boats, were appointed to follow immediately after Vandamme's corps; the ambulances were to start in the rear of the Imperial staff. Orders were given to burn any vehicle that might try to slip in with the columns, and not to allow the baggage waggons or ammunition waggons, to approach the Army within a distance of three leagues, till further notice. The generals who commanded the advanced guards were ordered to regulate their march so as to remain always on a line with one another; they were to send out scouts in every direction, to question the natives about the enemy's position, to seize all letters in the post-offices, and to communicate their information in frequent reports to the Emperor, who would be in person at the head of the central column. The bulk of the Army must have crossed the Sambre before noon.[3]

These orders are justly considered as perfect. Napoleon had never issued marching orders which were more carefully studied or better thought out, even in the happy days of Austerlitz and Friedland. Never had his genius been more brilliant, never had he exhibited to such perfection, his attention to detail, his broad grasp of the whole, his clearness, and his mastery of the science of war.

Unfortunately his orders were not faithfully executed. Drouet d'Erlon preferred to take his own course and started at half-past four,[4] instead of breaking up his camp at three, as he had been ordered. Vandamme, who should have started at three, was at five, still awaiting instructions from the Imperial headquarters; during the night, the officer who had been sent with his marching orders, had fallen from his horse and broken his leg, and had lain all night alone and helpless in the open field. Vandamme was warned of the Army's march only by the arrival of Lobau's corps from the rear of his camp.[5] Finally, the troops of Gérard, which should have been on their way at three, did not meet at the gathering-point, which was on the heights at Florenne, till seven o'clock.[6]

Great agitation reigned in the 4th Corps. They had just heard that General de Bourmont, who commanded the head division, had passed over to the enemy's ranks. This desertion confirmed in the most untimely manner, the fears of treachery, the mistrust of their generals, which had been tormenting the minds of the soldiers for the last three months. Murmurs and imprecations arose from the ranks. One of the brigadiers of Bourmont, General Hulot, "judging the moment was critical," harangued the two regiments under his orders; sword in hand, he gave them his solemn oath "he would fight with them against the enemies of France to his last breath."[7] Gérard in his turn passed along, in front of his troops and addressed a few words to them; they answered him by loud cheers.[8] Gérard was personally very much distressed by the desertion of his protégé Bourmont, all the details of which were related to him later by Hulot.

Shortly after five o'clock in the morning, at Florenne, Bourmont had mounted on horseback with his whole staff, Colonel Clouet, chief of the Villoutreys squadrons, Captains d'Andigné, de Trélan, and Sourda, and an escort of five lancers. Once beyond the French outposts, he had given the corporal of the chasseurs, a letter for Gérard written in Florenne, and had dismissed him with the rest of the escort, and with the other officers had galloped off in the direction of the frontier.[9] In his letter to Gérard he wrote: "I refuse to join in establishing in France, a sanguinary despotism which would ruin my country. . . . I would have resigned and returned home had I thought I should be left free to do so. This seemed so unlikely, that I am obliged to ensure my liberty by other means. . . . I shall never be seen fighting in the ranks of the foreigner. . . . They will get no information from me which could injure the French Army, composed of men whom I love and shall ever continue to regard with deep affection."[10]

Two hours after having written this protest that he was a deserter but not a traitor, Bourmont revealed to Colonel von Schutter, commander of the Prussian advanced posts on the Sambre, that the French would attack Charleroi in the course of the afternoon.[11] Shortly after, he told Colonel von Reiche, aide-de-camp to Zieten, that the French Army amounted to 120,000 men.[12] Finally, at three o'clock, when he met Blücher at Sombreffe, he would doubtless have shown the same eagerness in answering all questions the latter could ask. But the old warrior, indignant that a man wearing the uniform of a general of division, could desert on the morning of a battle, hardly condescended to speak to him. An officer of the Prussian staff having pointed out to the old Field-Marshal that he should not treat Bourmont so rudely, since the latter wore a white cockade, Blücher, little caring whether he was understood or not by the traitor, who probably knew German, said out loud, "Cockade be hanged! a cur must always be a cur!"[13]

Section II

The enemy could afford to dispense with Count de Bourmont's information. As early as the 9th of June, Zieten and General Dörnberg, who commanded the light cavalry brigade detached before Mons, were perfectly well informed on all the great movements of the troops towards the frontier. On the 12th, General Dörnberg had sent to Wellington, who in turn had forwarded it on to Blücher, the news that 100,000 French were concentrating between Avesnes and Philippeville. On the 13th, the same Dörnberg, who had numerous spies on the frontier, wrote directly to Blücher that an attack seemed imminent. On the 17th, Pirch II. announced from Marchiennes, that the French would attack on the following day. In the evening the Prussian outposts were thoroughly well-informed respecting the proximity of the Imperial troops. In vain had they taken the precaution of making their bivouac fires in the hollows of the ground, for the glow of these innumerable fires was reflected on the sky, which glowed with a great white radiance.[14]

Though they did not believe Napoleon would take the offensive,[15] Wellington and Blücher had agreed to provide for such an emergency as early as the 3rd of May, in an interview at Tirlemont.[16] Had they specially decided that day, as many historians declare, that they would concentrate on the line of Sombreffe-les-Quatre-Bras? This is doubtful, as they did not know whether the French Army would debouch by Philippeville, Maubeuge, Condé, or Lille. More probably the two Commanders-in-Chief had merely arranged for a junction before Brussels, without specifying any precise spot, which circumstances alone could decide.[17] The day after the conference at Tirlemont, Blücher, ever zealous for the common cause, ordered a general movement of his troops to their right, that they might be nearer the English Army. The 1st Corps concentrated at Fleurus; the 2nd at Namur; the 3rd Corps marched from Trèves to Arlon, then on to Dinant and Huy; the 4th came from Coblentz to Malmédy, and shortly after to Liège. Blücher transferred his headquarters from Liège to Namur.[18] Zieten, who commanded the 1st Army Corps, which was nearest the English cantonments, received instructions to keep in close contact with the army under Wellington. "In case of attack," Blücher wrote him on the 5th of May, "you will await at Fleurus the development of the enemy's manœuvres, and you will send the news to Wellington, and to me with the greatest possible dispatch."[19] Wellington, relying on the promise made him by Blücher at Tirlemont, to cover the left flank of the English Army, had drawn up his forces in *échelons* in such a manner as to protect specially the roads of Ath, Mons, and Nivelles;[20] he would thus be prepared to meet any attack from Charleroi. Before noon on the 14th of June, the Field-Marshal, warned by reports from Pirch II. and Dörnberg, began taking measures towards a concentration of the whole of his army on Fleurus.[21]

All through the night of the 14th, the outposts of Pirch II., which covered the van of Zieten's corps, expected to be attacked at dawn. They received the French tirailleurs with a volley of musketry; then, fearing lest they should be outnumbered, they retreated step by step, from position to position, to the Sambre. In these various engagements, at Thuin, at Ham, in the woods of Montigny, at "La Tombe" farm, the Prussians lost about 500 men, killed, wounded, or taken prisoners.[22] Still driving their enemy before them, the heads of the French columns reached the banks of the Sambre, between nine and ten o'clock; Bachelu's division, from Reille's corps, in front of Marchienne; Pajol's cavalry in front of Charleroi. The bridges were barricaded and defended by infantry and cannon. The attack of Marchienne, too elaborately prepared, lasted two hours. It was nearly twelve before the 2nd Light Infantry succeeded in clearing the bridge with fixed bayonets. Reille immediately sent up the 2nd Corps; but the bridge being very narrow, the four divisions and the cavalry could not come to the front, till the middle of the afternoon. The 1st Corps, which was following Reille's, did not begin to cross the Sambre till half-past four.[23]

Pajol was also detained for a long time at the entrance of the bridge of Charleroi. Between nine and ten, the 1st Hussars attempted a hurrah, which was at once silenced by the continued firing of the sharpshooters, who lay in ambush in the houses, and behind the barricade. Infantry were needed to carry this position. Pajol resigned himself to wait for Vandamme, who was, he thought, following at a short distance. It must be remembered that Vandamme's corps had broken up its camp, four hours after the time appointed. Towards eleven Pajol, to his surprise, beheld not Vandamme, but the Emperor himself, arriving with the marines, the sappers of the Guard, and the Young Guard of Duhesme. On learning Vandamme's delay, Napoleon instantly ordered Duhesme's division to leave its place in the central column, and to proceed with the greatest haste towards Charleroi by a cross-road. The sappers and the marines made a rush on the bridge, and swept away the barricade, clearing the way for Pajol's squadrons. The Prussians were already in retreat. The horsemen at full trot, mounted the steep and winding street which traverses Charleroi from south to north, and pursued them to the point where the two roads diverged. Pajol dispatched the 1st Hussars to the road to Brussels, to reconnoitre on the left and, with the bulk of his cavalry, dashed up the Fleurus road, in the wake of the retreating Prussians whom he had dislodged from Charleroi."[24]

Section III

It was now a little past noon.[25] The Emperor, amid the cheers of the inhabitants,[26] passed through Charleroi and halted at the foot of the crumbling glacis, some few hundred yards before the branching off of the Brussels and Fleurus roads, near a little public-house called La Belle-Vue. From thence the whole valley of the Sambre could be plainly seen. He got off his horse, sent for a chair from the Belle-Vue, and sat down by the side of the road. The troops defiled past him. As soon as they saw him, the infantry and the cavalry cheered lustily, the sound of their voices completely deadening the roll of the drums and the shrill calls of the bugles. The enthusiasm bordered on frenzy; soldiers broke from the ranks "to embrace the horse of their Emperor."[27] According to an eye-witness, Napoleon soon fell into a doze and the uproarious cheering was powerless to rouse him.[28] This singular fact does not seem impossible, if we remember that during April and May 1815, in Paris, the Emperor was constantly subject to these sudden attacks of drowsiness;[29] and that day at noon, he had been seven or eight hours in the saddle.

Gourgaud, who had accompanied the 1st Hussars on the road to Brussels, came back towards two o'clock with the news that the Prussians were appearing in great force at Gosselies. The Emperor dispatched him instantly to Marchienne, with orders to General Reille to march on Gosselies. Uneasy, nevertheless, about his left flank until this movement had been executed, he posted, at a distance of two kilometres from Charleroi, on the road to Brussels, one of Duhesme's regiments of the Young Guard, and a battery of horse artillery. Shortly after, he commanded Lefebvre-Desnoëttes to hurry off to the assistance of the 1st Hussars with the light cavalry of the Guard (lancers and chasseurs), and he dictated to Soult a letter for d'Erlon, enjoining the latter to march on Gosselies, and second Reille.[30] This letter had just been dispatched—it was then a little after three o'clock—when Ney appeared on the scene.[31]

Ney had arrived at Avesnes on the 13th of June in a post-chaise, without his chargers and with a single aide-de-camp; he found next day he could get no conveyance to take him to Beaumont, save a peasant's cart. At Beaumont, in the morning of the 15th, he had bought two chargers belonging to General Mortier, who was disabled by a sudden attack of sciatica, and he had ridden to Charleroi on the outskirts of the columns.

The soldiers recognised him; they seemed pleased to see him again. "All will go well now," they cried, "there is 'Redhead!'"[32]

The Emperor, who was also desirous that "all should go well," said to the Marshal, "How are you, Ney? I am very pleased to see you. You will take the command of the 1st and 2nd Army Corps. I give you, besides, the light cavalry of my Guard, but do not make use of it. To-morrow you will be joined by Kellermann's cuirassiers. Now you can go; drive the enemy on to the Brussels road, and take up your position at Quatre-Bras."[33]

On the ground, in presence of the enemy, the grand strategical plan conceived in Paris by Napoleon, grew into shape and developed. He had only expected on this, the first day, to bear down towards the supposed point of junction of the allied armies, and if possible to get in advance of it. But now, since his adversaries gave him time, he would extend his field of action, and make it impossible for them to unite at all. As the bulk of the English forces was coming from Brussels, and that of the Prussians from Namur, the two armies must necessarily effect their junction by the high-road from Namur to Nivelles which runs to Sombreffe, and crosses the road from Charleroi to Brussels at Quatre-Bras. The Emperor desired, therefore, to post his left wing at Quatre-Bras, and his right at Sombreffe.[34] He himself would establish his quarters at Fleurus, the summit of the triangle formed by these three points, and on the following day, he would swoop down with his Reserve on that portion of the enemy's forces which should first come up. If both of them retreated, he would gain Brussels without firing a cannon-shot.

Grouchy arrived just as the Emperor had finished giving his instructions to Marshal Ney, who started immediately. An hour before, Grouchy, with the dragoons of Exelmans, had penetrated to the bridge of Charleroi, over which the Young Guard was still defiling. Impatient to join his first cavalry corps, which he supposed was in action, he had outdistanced the column and galloped off to Gilly. After having reconnoitred this position, he came to the Emperor to await his orders. The latter immediately got on horseback, anxious to judge for himself. It was now past three o'clock; the dragoons of Exelmans had finished defiling through, in the rear of the Guard, and now the head of Vandamme's column appeared at Charleroi.[35]

General Pirch II. had posted his division behind Gilly, his front being covered by the muddy stream of Le Grand-Rieux. Four battalions and one battery occupied the slopes of the wooded heights which overlooked the valley from the abbey of Soleillemont as far as Chatelineau; three other battalions were in reserve near Lambusart; and a regiment of dragoons kept watch on the Sambre, from Chatelet to Farciennes.[36] Deceived by the length of their line of battle, an extension which was precisely intended to mislead the French, Grouchy roughly estimated the enemy's forces at 20,000 men.[37] At the first glance the Emperor declared there were not more than 10,000 at the outside. He arranged the plan of attack with Grouchy, whom he invested verbally with the command of the right wing.[38] One of the divisions under Vandamme, seconded by Pajol's cavalry, would attack the enemy in front; Grouchy was ordered to ford the stream with Exelmans' dragoons near the mill of Delhatte, and take the enemy in flank. The Prussians might then be pursued as far as Sombreffe, and there Grouchy was to halt and take up his position.[39]

Having given these orders, the Emperor returned to Charleroi in order to hasten the march of Vandamme's corps.[40] It would have been wiser far had he remained at Gilly. In his absence, Vandamme and Grouchy took two hours to arrange their plan of attack. Towards half-past five the Emperor, surprised at not hearing the sound of cannon, returned to the field and commanded Vandamme to make a headlong rush against the enemy instantly.[41]

After a short cannonade which silenced the fire of Pirch's guns, three columns, two battalions each, dashed up with crossed bayonets. The Prussians of the first line did not wait to receive the shock. On an order from Zieten, Pirch made them retreat without losing a second. Enraged at seeing these battalions retire without any loss, the Emperor ordered one of his aides-de-camp, General Letort, " to charge and crush the Prussian infantry" with the squadrons under his command. Letort did not even take the time to assemble his four squadrons. He dashed off with the dragoons only, trusting the others to follow as soon as they were ready! He passed the stream to the north of the road, by that part of the gorge which was the least steep, recrossed the road of Sart-Allet in front of Vandamme's columns, and fell upon the retreating Prussians. Two out of the four battalions of the enemy succeeded in gaining the cover of the woods of Soleillemont; but the two others, formed in squares, were broken and cut down. Those men who escaped took refuge in the woods, the outskirts of which were occupied by the 1st Regiment of Western Prussia. During the pursuit, a bullet struck Letort in the stomach, and he fell from his horse mortally wounded. He was a kind and fearless leader and the dragoons worshipped him; and they avenged his death by slaughtering all who came within reach of their long swords.[42]

During this engagement Exelmans' dragoons, with the Burthe and Vincent brigades at their head, debouched above Chatelineau; they overthrew Colonel Moïsky's regiment of dragoons, drove a battalion from the Pironchamp woods, and threw them back on Lambusart. Here all the troops of Pirch had rallied and made a stand against the enemy. Attacked simultaneously by Exelmans' dragoons and the light cavalry of Pajol, who had preceded the columns of Vandamme, the enemy retreated beyond Fleurus.[43] Grouchy had personally directed the attack on the right. Though the day was waning, he was anxious to carry Fleurus, which he knew was defended by only two battalions,[44] and to drive the Prussians as far as Sombreffe, in accordance with the Emperor's orders.

But Vandamme, who had already begun to form his camp between Winage and the Soleillemont woods, distinctly refused to go any farther, saying his troops were too tired, and that, at any rate, "he would take no orders from the commandant of the cavalry."[45] Grouchy, who could not attack Fleurus without infantry, remained near the village at a distance of two cannon-shots. The corps of Exelmans and Pajol bivouacked in the first line, covering Vandamme's infantry, between Lambusart and Campinaire.[46]

Section IV

The left wing did not advance as far as Napoleon wished. Towards half-past one the 1st Hussars, sent from Charleroi on the Brussels [47] road, had met, a short distance beyond Jumet, Lützow's cavalry and the sharpshooters of the 29th Regiment, who were covering the concentration of Steinmetz's division at Gosselies. The enemies watched each other for some time, then the two bodies of cavalry began the struggle. The uhlans vigorously drove back the hussars when they were charged, and were repulsed in their turn by Piré's lancers, who formed the vanguard of Reille's corps.[48] Reille hastened the march of his infantry, and within three hours came within cannon-shot of Gosselies, and immediately opened fire on the village. At the moment when the attacking columns were commencing their manœuvre, Marshal Ney arrived [49] with the light cavalry of the Guard, which he had overtaken on the way. Gosselies, defended by the 29th Prussian Regiment, was carried after a slight skirmish. But this was not the end of the matter. The largest portion of Steinmetz's division were still marching to the west of Gosselies; by the occupation of Gosselies their direct road to Heppignies and Fleurus was blocked. Without any hesitation, Steinmetz sent out a few battalions against the French, who were beginning to debouch from Gosselies, drove them back into the village, and under protection of a strong detachment posted in the houses at the north of the town, he continued his retreat upon Heppignies.[50]

The road to Brussels was now free, and daylight would last four hours longer. But Marshal Ney probably felt, that, notwithstanding the Emperor's orders to press the enemy closely, he had already advanced too far from the right of the army. Instead, therefore, of continuing his march with the whole body of his troops, he posted the divisions under Foy, Girard, and Jérôme round Gosselies, sent Bachelu's division to Mellet with Piré's light cavalry, and told off only the lancers and the chasseurs of the Guard [51] towards Quatre-Bras.

The lancers of the Guard got in sight of Frasnes [52] towards half-past five, and their arrival was hailed by a burst of cannon-shot. The village was occupied by the Nassau battalion and a battery of horse artillery under the command of Major Normann. This officer had been left without any instructions, but on hearing the sound of the cannonade towards Gosselies, he had immediately taken steps for a desperate defence of his post. Lefebvre-Desnoëttes instantly applied for a body of infantry. A battalion of the 2nd Light Infantry, the head of the column of Bachelu's division, had already gained the heights of Mellet, and quickening their steps they pressed on towards Frasnes. The sharpshooters opened fire on the Nassau regiments. While waiting for this reinforcement, Lefebvre-Desnoëttes had directed a portion of his lancers to the right of Frasnes, so as to turn the enemy's line.[53] The squadron from Elba (Poles), commanded by General Edouard de Colbert in person, pushed on as far as Quatre-Bras, which was not then occupied. But Colbert, finding himself there without support, and at a great distance from the main body of his division, returned to Frasnes.[54] During this interval, Major Normann's battalion had been retreating down the road, continuing to keep the French well within reach of the cannon. It took up its position on the borders of the woods of Bossu, two kilometres before Quatre-Bras, where, at that very moment, Prince Bernard of Saxe-Weimar arrived with four of the Nassau battalions.[55] Learning accidentally at Gennappe that the French had crossed the Sambre, the young prince, on his own responsibility, marched his troops forward in order to seize and occupy this important strategical post.[56]

At the sound of the cannon Marshal Ney joined his vanguard. He reconnoitred the position. Although the Nassau force only amounted to 4,500 men with six guns,[57] they were strong enough to defend Quatre-Bras against the 1,700 lancers and chasseurs of Lefebvre-Desnoëttes,[58] who were backed by a single battalion. Ney was content to direct a few desultory charges against the Nassau infantry posted before Quatre-Bras, and to send eastwards in the direction of Sart-Dame-Aveline a reconnaissance which did not even come within shot of the enemy's outposts.[59] Then, a little before eight o'clock, he rallied at Frasnes, Lefebvre-Desnoëttes division, which encamped there, while Ney himself returned to Gosselies for the night.[60]

Colonel Heymès, Ney's aide-de-camp during this campaign, has urged as a possible explanation of the Marshal's conduct, that " there was not one chance in ten of seizing Quatre-Bras." [61] And certainly, when they arrived within sight of Quatre-Bras, not at ten in the evening, as asserted by Heymès, but at seven at the latest, he could hardly hope to carry this position with two regiments of cavalry and a single battalion. But if at five o'clock, while at Gosselies, he had dispatched on the road to Brussels, a mere quarter of the troops entrusted to him by the Emperor,—let us say, two divisions of infantry, two of cavalry, and four batteries of artillery,[62]—by nine o'clock, with the help of this force of 14,000 men, he might have annihilated Prince Bernard of Saxe-Weimar's 4,500 infantry, most of whom had only ten cartridges in their belts.[63] In halting Reille's corps at Gosselies, Ney, for the first time in his life, yielded to motives of prudence. He had given up all thoughts of occupying Quatre-Bras, unless as a cavalry post in case this point were not defended. In his opinion it would be endangering his army to transfer it at a distance of four leagues from the right wing, to a position where it might come in contact with the whole body of Wellington's forces. Authorities on strategy have declared that Ney acted according to the strict principles of the art of war. This may possibly be true. But had Prince Bernard adhered as strictly to these principles, he would never have acted on his inspiration of marching on Quatre-Bras, with four battalions, at the risk of being utterly crushed by the whole French Army.

BOOK II
LIGNY AND QUATRE-BRAS

BOOK II CHAPTER I

THE MORNING OF THE 16TH OF JUNE

I. Plans and orders of Napoleon (from five o'clock to eight).
II. Departure of Napoleon for Fleurus (half-past nine).
III. Concentration of the Prussian Army on the north of the brook of Ligny—Inmovableness of the English Army on the 15th of June—The Duchess of Richmond's ball (night of the 15th to the 16th of June).
IV. Arrival of Wellington at Quatre-Bras (16th June, 10 o'clock)—Interview between Wellington and Blücher at the mill of Bussy, near Ligny (one P.M.).

Section I

THE occupation of Sombreffe and Quatre-Bras, on the evening of the 15th of June, was only the necessary sequel to the grand strategical plan conceived by Napoleon. That Grouchy and Ney should have failed to take possession of these two points, was a mere contretemps. The chief aim of the French Army's manœuvre was attained, namely, to bear at once on the point of junction between the English and the Prussians. Almost without striking a blow, and in spite of various delays in the march of several of the columns, the Emperor had crossed the Sambre, penetrated seven miles into the enemy's territory, and encamped his army in the very centre of the Allies' cantonments. He had 124,000 men bivouacked within a triangle of three leagues on each of its sides.[1]

The enemy appeared to be thrown into disorder. In the course of the day not a single English uniform had been seen, neither had the Prussians appeared in any great numbers; they had feebly contested the passages of the Sambre, and their lack of perseverance in the defence of Gilly and Gosselies, skilful and courageous though it was, favoured the assumption that their object was rather to protect a retreat, than to cover a concentration.

Therefore, when the Emperor, who returned to Charleroi for the night,[2] examined the reports sent him by Grouchy and Ney[3] he concluded that the Allies were disconcerted by his unexpected aggression, and had resolved to fall back on the base of their operations, the Prussians in the direction of Liège and Maëstricht, the English and Belgians towards Ostend and Antwerp. The route taken by the Prussian outposts, from Thuin to Marchienne, from Fontaine-L'Evêque and Marchienne to Gosselies, from Charleroi and Gosselies to Fleurus, tended to confirm this presumption. If the Prussians had manœuvred with the design of immediately joining the English, they would have withdrawn towards the north, whereas they had retreated towards the north-east, thus leaving the road to Brussels unprotected. This resolution, which, judging from appearances, Napoleon attributed to Wellington and Blücher, seemed to ensure the victory to him. The further the allied armies were separated from one another, the easier it would be to beat them in detail. It was one thing to attack the English when the Prussians were within a single march of them, and another to do so when Wellington and Blücher were separated by fifteen or twenty leagues.

The Emperor drew out his plan of action on the morning of the 16th of June, probably about six o'clock or a little earlier.[4] With Grouchy and the right wing[5] he meant to march towards Sombreffe and Gembloux. Should a Prussian corps happen to be in either of these two positions, he would attack it. Having reconnoitred and cleared the ground to the east, he would call up the Reserve, temporarily stationed at Fleurus, and with it, he would join Ney and the left wing at Quatre-Bras. From thence he would march on Brussels by a forced night-march. He calculated that the head of the column would reach Brussels on the 17th of June at seven o'clock in the morning.[6]

The orders for the execution of this double movement were dispatched by the chief of the staff between seven and eight in the morning: orders to Kellermann to proceed on Gosselies and place himself at the disposal of Marshal Ney; orders to Drouot to start the Guard on its road towards Fleurus; orders to Lobau to push on the 6th Corps midway between Charleroi and Fleurus; orders to Vandamme and Gérard to march on Sombreffe with the 3rd and 4th Corps, and then to carry out the instructions of Marshal Grouchy, commanding the right wing. Soult wrote to Ney to take up his position at Quatre-Bras, with six divisions of infantry and Kellermann's cuirassiers, and to lead his two other infantry divisions, one to Genappe (five kilometres beyond Quatre-Bras) with Piré's cavalry, and the other to Marbais with the cavalry of Lefebvre-Desnoëttes, in order eventually to support the movements of the right wing. Lastly, Ney was to push his reconnoitring bodies, as far as possible on the Nivelles and Brussels roads. As for Grouchy, he received the order to take possession of Sombreffe, whence he was to send an advanced guard to Gembloux and scouts in every direction.[7]

Section II

At the Imperial headquarters, all were busied with the dispatch of these orders, when the Emperor received a letter from Grouchy, notifying that strong columns of the enemy, which had apparently come up by the Namur road, were proceeding towards Brye and Saint-Amand.[8] Though he believed the Prussians were retreating, Napoleon had recognised the possibility of a collision with them at Sombreffe;[9] but he had not the remotest idea that they would come and take up positions at the entrance of the approach to Fleurus. This movement indicated that, far from withdrawing his troops and forsaking the English Army, as might have been inferred the night before from the direction taken in retreat by his outposts, Blücher was manœuvring to give battle together with Wellington on that very day. Instead of the French having merely to dislodge from Sombreffe or Gembloux, the rearguard or an isolated corps, it was evident they had to encounter on the north of Fleurus the entire Prussian Army, and, as Blücher and Wellington evidently meant to operate in concert, the English would probably be encountered in force on the road to Brussels.

This meant the complete ruin of the plan conceived by the Emperor. He could not possibly beat Blücher's army to his right during the day, destroy Wellington's army to his left in the evening, and then march on Brussels that same night. However, Napoleon was in no wise disconcerted. With him, presumptions quickly changed into certainties. When he had once imagined a thing, that thing had to be as he fancied. Indeed, how many times had not fortune justified his previsions! On the morning of the 16th of June he believed that Blücher was retreating and that the road to Brussels was clear; therefore Blücher must be retreating and the road to Brussels *was* clear. The manœuvres notified by Grouchy were merely demonstrations intended to put him on the wrong scent. It would be mere child's play to settle this handful of Prussian regiments, which was only as it were a screen, to mask the retreat of the bulk of their army.[10] Besides, these views were evidently shared by Grouchy himself; for in the letter in which he mentioned the appearance of the enemy's columns towards Saint-Amand, he also announced that he was mustering his own troops to march on to Sombreffe, in accordance with the orders of the preceding night.[11]

If at five that morning, Grouchy had suspected that the whole of Blücher's army was concentrating to the west of Sombreffe, he would not have prepared for a movement on this village, at the risk of sustaining a disastrous flank attack.

The Emperor did not modify his orders in any way. Far from changing anything, he wrote to Ney and Grouchy towards eight o'clock to reiterate his commands and to hasten their execution. Knowing that his own aides-de-camp were better mounted than the officers of the chief of the staff, he entrusted one of the letters to La Bédoyère, the other to Flahaut, hoping that in this manner, his two lieutenants would receive his reiterated instructions even before those he had just dispatched through Soult. In these duplicates, the Emperor insisted on certain executive details, and disclosed, what Soult had concealed, that the object of this double movement on Sombreffe and on Quatre-Bras, was a night march to Brussels.[12]

Between nine and ten in the morning,[13] as Napoleon was about to start for Fleurus, an officer of lancers arrived from the left wing, to announce that the enemy was massing in great force in the direction of Quatre-Bras.[14] Fearing lest the presence of these supposed masses should cause Ney to hesitate, as on the previous evening, the Emperor thought it necessary to reassure him and to repeat his orders once more. He directed the chief of the staff to write to him immediately to this effect: "As Blücher was in Namur yesterday, it is not likely he has marched his troops towards Quatre-Bras. Therefore you need only attend to what comes from Brussels. Unite together the divisions of Counts Reille and d'Erlon, as well as the corps of Count de Valmy; with these forces you are to beat and to destroy all the enemy's corps which may happen to come in your way."[15] In case of any eventuality occurring, the Emperor commanded Lobau to remain for the time being at Charleroi, so as to march the 6th Corps to the assistance of Ney, if necessary. In pursuance of these orders Adjutant-Commandant Janin, deputy commander on Lobau's staff, was sent to Frasnes to ascertain the position of matters.[16]

The Emperor arrived at Fleurus shortly before eleven o'clock. Here he found Grouchy, and this was no small surprise, as he imagined him to be already marching towards Sombreffe.[17] The Marshal easily explained, that in presence of the hostile masses which were taking up their positions to the north of Fleurus, he had been obliged to confine himself to the occupation of this village, which had been evacuated by the Prussians towards dawn.[18] Napoleon passed along the line of outposts. At the end of Fleurus stood a brick mill, built in the shape of a tower and commanding the whole plain. He ordered his sappers to open a breach in its circular roof and to contrive a kind of *loggia* or balcony, which he ascended to inspect the positions of the enemy.[19]

Section III

At the first alarm, Blücher had hurriedly left Namur, and by four o'clock on the afternoon of the 15th of June he was at Sombreffe.[20] He was confident he could get his four army corps drawn up behind the little stream of Ligny, by the early morning of the 16th;[21] his attention had been directed to this position two months before by Major von Gröben, and from that time he had resolved he would fight the French at that very place, should they cross the Sambre at Charleroi.[22] He was full of ardour and deemed himself invincible. "With my 120,000 Prussians," he wrote to his wife, "I would engage to take Tripoli, Tunis, and Algiers, if there were not the sea to cross!"[23] However, on account of the inordinate extension of his cantonments, the Field-Marshal experienced some disappointments. At eleven A.M. on the 16th, Zieten's corps, which was reduced to 28,000 men by the losses of the previous evening, was the only one in line. The corps of Pirch I. (31,000 men) did not arrive at Sombreffe before noon; it was followed at a short distance by the corps of Thielmann[24] (24,000 men). As for the 4th Corps, a letter from Bülow reached the general headquarters in the night, announcing that this corps could not possibly muster at Hannut (42 kilometres from Sombreffe) before the middle of the day.[25] This meant a difference to Blücher of 30,000 bayonets. Nevertheless, he was determined to accept battle, especially as he counted on the co-operation, more or less effective, of the Anglo-Dutch army.[26] Had not the two Commanders-in-Chief, at the interview of the 3rd of May at Tirlemont, agreed to lend each other mutual support, were Napoleon to take the offensive?[27] And in the evening of the 13th June, had not Wellington himself said to Blücher's emissary, Colonel von Pfüell: "My army will be concentrated at Nivelles or Quatre-Bras, according to circumstances, twenty-two hours after the first cannon-shot"?[28]

There was something of diplomacy in these promises given by Wellington. The effect of Blücher's retreat on Liège would be to leave the English Army alone before Napoleon; in this case there would be no alternative for it but to accept battle, with vastly inferior forces, or to fall back on its base of operation, leaving Brussels unprotected. It was therefore most important that Blücher should remain in his position, and as an inducement to that end, Wellington could not but promise him his support. This promise of support he certainly hoped to give,[29] but, practical Englishman as he was, Wellington

CHAP. I *THE MORNING OF THE 16TH OF JUNE* 81

meant to do so at his own time, and his own convenience, without imperilling in the least, the safety of his own army for the common cause. But might not the offensive movement of the French towards Charleroi be a mere demonstration calculated to draw off in that direction the masses of the Anglo-Prussians ? Might not the Emperor, at the same time, bear down on Brussels with the bulk of his army, either by Maubeuge, Mons, and Hal, or by Lille, Tournay, and Ath ? Such were Wellington's apprehensions, and fearing he might be decoyed into a false manœuvre, he was determined not to move horse or man before he knew on which precise spot Napoleon would direct his principal attack.[30]

Although on the 12th, 13th, and 14th of June numerous warnings respecting the concentration of the French Army on the frontier had reached the headquarters at Brussels;[31] although on the 15th, as early as eight in the morning, Wellington had been informed through a letter from Zieten, that the Prussian outposts had been attacked at daybreak,[32] at three in the afternoon that same day he had not issued a single order.

Müffling, the Prussian commissary attached to the English headquarters, having received a private letter from Zieten confirming these previous warnings, hastened to communicate it to the Duke. "If all is as Zieten thinks," replied Wellington, "I will concentrate on my left wing so as to act in concert with the Prussian Army; but should a portion of the enemy's forces march on Mons, I shall be compelled to concentrate on my centre. Therefore, before coming to any decision or taking any step, I must await news from my outposts at Mons. However, as the destination of my troops remains uncertain, while their departure is certain, I will give orders that they should be in readiness to march at any moment." [33]

After such orders, which were not issued till the 15th of June, between six and seven in the evening,[34] the troops had merely to assemble by divisions at Ninove, Ath, Grammont, Brussels, Braine-le-Comte, Nivelles, and to hold themselves in readiness to march at daybreak on the following day.[35] The result was that when the French left wing had already gone beyond Gosselies, and its right had arrived within sight of

Fleurus, Wellington, instead of directing his troops to the threatened point, was content to assemble them in isolated divisions within a parallelogram of ten leagues by nine. It seemed indeed as if he were bewildered and paralysed by the vision of Napoleon attacking in person at all points at once. At twelve o'clock, Blücher wrote to Müffling to say that Pirch's division was retiring on the left bank of the Sambre, and that he was going to concentrate at Sombreffe, where he intended to accept battle from the enemy. He added: "I am awaiting early news of the Duke of Wellington's concentration." This letter, which arrived about seven in the morning, was immediately laid before Wellington; it had no more power to influence him than the two previous despatches from Zieten. "The dispositions of the Field-Marshal are excellent," he said, "but I cannot decide anything till I know what is going on in the direction of Mons."[36] At last he received the desired assurance that all was quiet there. A letter of General Dörnberg, delivered between nine and ten o'clock, set his mind at rest on that score.[37] He then determined on a partial concentration towards Nivelles, and not, as is claimed by his apologists, on a movement of the whole army upon Quatre-Bras.[38]

After giving these orders, which could not possibly be executed before daybreak,[39] owing to the lateness of the hour and the immense distance between the various cantonments, Wellington said to Müffling: "My troops are on the point of marching. But here in Brussels the partisans of Napoleon are beginning to agitate. We must reassure *our* friends. Therefore let us show ourselves at the Duchess of Richmond's ball, and we will be in the saddle by five to-morrow morning."[40]

In Brussels, though there had been entertainments every night, this long-expected ball was as much a topic of interest as the impending campaign. It was known that the Duchess of Richmond had made great preparations, that a vast barn which adjoined her palace or villa had been transformed into a sumptuous hall, where the guests were to dance to the sound of military music, and to which the *élite* of the British staff and of the cosmopolitan society in Brussels—Russian and German diplomatists, English peers, French *émigrés*—had been invited. There the Duchess of Richmond did the honours with her eldest daughter, who became later Lady de Ros, and was then seventeen years old.[41] All manner of schemes, entreaties, and intrigues had been used to obtain the coveted invitations to this ball. There were hardly more than two hundred present: the Prince of Orange, Prince Frederick of the Netherlands, the Duke of Brunswick, the Prince of Nassau, the Duke of Wellington, the burgomaster of Brussels, Princes Auguste and Pierre d'Arenberg, Duke and Duchess de Beaufort with their daughter, Duke and Duchess d'Ursel, Count and Countess Mercy Argenteau, Count de la Tour-Dupin (French Ambassador at the Hague) and Countess de la Tour-Dupin, Marquis and Marchioness d'Assche, Count de la Rochefoucauld, Dowager Countess d'Oultremont and the Misses d'Oultremont, Lady Fitz-Roy Somerset, Count de Cayla (without his wife), Sir Charles Stewart, Lord and Lady Seymour and their daughter, Count Pozzo di Borgo and Baron de Vincent (Ambassadors of Russia and Austria at the Court of His Majesty the King of France at Ghent), General Alava (Spanish commissary attached to Wellington's staff), General von Müffling, Lord Uxbridge (commander-in-chief of the British Cavalry), Lord Saltoun (colonel of the Foot Guards), Lord Somerset (commander of the Horseguard Brigade), Lord Hill (commander of the 2nd English Corps), Generals Clinton, Ponsonby, Picton, Vivian, Byng, Pack, Cooke, Kempt, Maitland, and a great number of colonels, majors, young captains, lieutenants, and ensigns.[42] When Wellington made his appearance at the Duchess's towards midnight, the ball was in full swing.[43] In the flush of life's happiness, lovely girls and handsome officers were intoxicated with the music and the movement. But as in the "dance of death" of the old frescoes, Death led the dance.

The passage of the Sambre by the French Army was not yet known. Wellington disclosed to the Duke of Brunswick that Bonaparte had entered Belgium, and that there might be fighting that very day. Brunswick, through a sort of presentiment, felt the shudder of death. Turning very pale, he sprang up, and through his abrupt movement, the little Prince de Ligne, whom he had had in his lap, fell to the ground.

Wellington called all the general officers aside and gave them by word of mouth their marching orders, which were the same as the written ones he had dispatched a short time before. They instantly took their leave. In the midst of the ball, towards one o'clock, the Prince of Orange was informed by a despatch from Constant Rebecque, that the French had appeared at Quatre-Bras, and he at once also started for Genappe. By degrees, the rumour spread through the assembly that the Army was on the eve of marching. But the young officers could not tear themselves away from that night of pleasure, little knowing, as Byron says, that—

> Upon night so sweet, such awful morn could rise !

At last, when they heard the trumpets and the bugles sound the assembly, they darted off in their silk stockings and buckled shoes, to join their regiments. The Duchess of Richmond, deeply moved, would fain have stopped the ball, but the young ladies and a few young men who did not belong to the Army, continued to dance till dawn.

Wellington took leave at three o'clock, after supper. The Duchess woke up her youngest little girl, a typical " Reynolds' baby," and the child fastened on the sword of the Commander-in-Chief with her little rosy fingers.[44]

Section IV

Müffling remarks that during the ball Wellington was in high spirits. He had no occasion for being so. All day he had obstinately left his troops in their scattered camps at distances of eight, ten, fifteen leagues from each other; and the orders of the evening, by which he trusted to atone entirely for his mistake, were lamentable. His last plan amounted to nothing less than leaving the road from Charleroi to Brussels exposed in order to protect the road to Mons, which was not threatened. Had Wellington's orders been executed, a gap four leagues wide would have been opened between Brussels and Basse Dyle, and through this gap Ney could have advanced half-way to Brussels without firing a shot, and also, according to Gneisenau, he could have "fallen back upon the rear of the Prussian Army and annihilated it." [45]

Fortunately for the Allies, several of Wellington's officers had deliberately acted without waiting for his orders; others, with great discrimination, had disobeyed the commands which after so much time lost he had issued. In the course of the preceding day Major Normann had defended Frasnes, the Prince of Saxe-Weimar had marched his brigade from Genappe to Quatre-Bras,[46] General Chassé had concentrated his division at Fay.[47] Shortly after, in the absence of the Prince of Orange, Constant Rebecque, the chief of his staff, ordered General Collaert to collect his cavalry behind the Haine, and Perponcher to prepare to march on Quatre-Bras. At eleven in the evening, Rebecque found it impossible to avoid giving the generals of division Wellington's order to concentrate the entire Netherland corps on Nivelles, which would leave the Brussels road unguarded; but at the same time he sent them *verbal* instructions which left them free to comply with this order or not as they judged best. "It is impossible in Brussels," he said, "to know the exact state of things here." Perponcher did not hesitate for an instant. Instead of keeping the Bylandt brigade at Nivelles and summoning the brigade of Saxe-Weimar to take its place, as was enjoined by Wellington, he marched with Bylandt to Quatre-Bras in order to assist Prince Bernard.[48]

Ah! would that Napoleon had been seconded by such a leader of his staff as Constant Rebecque, and such lieutenants as Perponcher and Bernard of Saxe-Weimar! And, on the other hand, what a splendid opportunity for strategists like Charras to denounce the fatal indecision, the mental torpor, the moral weakness of the Emperor, if on the eve of a battle Napoleon had delayed ten hours before concentrating his troops, if he had then ordered a movement in the opposite direction to the enemy's forces, and had passed the night at a ball!

But in war as in cards, nothing prevails against fortune or luck. When Wellington, starting from Brussels at six in the morning, arrived at Quatre-Bras towards ten, he found Perponcher's division intrenched there instead of the advanced guard of Marshal Ney. His Grace apparently forgot that this was in direct contradiction to his own orders, and he condescended to congratulate General Perponcher on the step he had taken, as well as the Prince of Orange, who had had no hand in the matter.[49] Then, after advancing near enough to Frasnes for a thorough inspection of the French outposts,[50] he dispatched orders to Picton's division and the Brunswick corps, posted at Waterloo,[51] to resume their march,[52] and he wrote to Blücher that Quatre-Bras was occupied by a division of the Prince of Orange, and that the English Army was making for that point. The letter ended with these words: "I do not see many of the enemy in our front, and I await news from Your Excellency to decide my operations."[53]

Wellington very soon changed his views. Thinking, justly or unjustly, that ere several hours had elapsed he would be attacked at Quatre-Bras, he concluded that, instead of waiting for news which he could not control, he had better go and see things for himself, and arrange with Blücher by word of mouth. Towards one o'clock he joined the Field-Marshal on the heights of Brye.[54] Together they went up into the mill of Bussy,[55] situated before this village; the whole field lay before them, better even than from the Fleurus mill, where Napoleon had established his observatory.[56] They could now see the French columns debouching, and with the field-glass could even discern the Emperor in the midst of his staff. It appeared evident they would have to contend with the entire Imperial Army, of which the detachment occupying Frasnes was a mere fraction, not worth consideration.[57]

"What do you wish me to do?" said Wellington abruptly in French, for he knew no German. Gneisenau suggested that the Duke should immediately march all his troops behind Brye so as to act as a reserve to the Prussian Army. This plan, based on an incorrect estimate of the redistribution of Napoleon's forces, was opposed by Müffling. He said in substance that the English should manœuvre so as to outflank the French left wing. "Exactly so," exclaimed Wellington. "I will overthrow all before me on my way to

Frasnes, and I will march on Gosselies." Gneisenau objected that this movement would be most eccentric and its success more than doubtful, whereas the concentration on Brye could not fail to be attended by certain and conclusive results. As the discussion continued for some time, Wellington closed it, saying, "Very well! I will come, if I am not attacked myself." Having said these words, which had not in the slightest degree the character of a formal engagement, the Duke returned to Quatre-Bras, while Blücher proceeded to make his final arrangements.[58]

BOOK II CHAPTER II

THE BATTLE OF LIGNY

I. The battlefield—Dispositions of Blücher and Napoleon.
II. From three to four: Attacks on Saint-Amand by Vandamme, and on Ligny by Gérard.
III. From four to half-past seven: Counter-attack by Blücher—Appearance on the French flank of a column recognised as belonging to the enemy—Grouchy's demonstration against the Prussian left—Fierce contest at Saint-Amand and Ligny.
IV. From half-past seven to half-past nine: Final assault—Capture of Ligny—Engagements on the hills—Retreat of the Prussians.

Section I

Opposite the hill of Fleurus, rises in a gentle slope above an undulating plain, a line of ridges of no very great height; in their midst are situated the village of Brye to the west, the village of Tongrinne to the east, in the centre and slightly in the rear, the town of Sombreffe. In themselves, these positions are easy of access. But in the hollow at their foot winds the Ligne,[1] a little stream four or five yards in width, intrenched between vertical banks, from three to four feet deep, bordered with willows, alder trees, and thickets of brambles. This brook, and the broken ground which leads down to it, form a deep trench, flanking to the right the village of Wagnelée, the hamlets of La Haye and Petit Saint-Amand, and the village of Saint-Amand; on the left, the hamlets of Potriaux and Tongrinelle, and the villages of Tongrinne, Boignée, and Balâtre. In the centre, is the village of Ligny, with its two large farms, its old castle,[2] and its church surrounded by a cemetery, stretching upwards and surrounded by walls. The front of the position is thus formed by an uninterrupted ditch and ten bastions, some in front of this fossé, as Petit Saint-Amand, La Haye, Grand Saint-Amand, Tongrinelle, Boignée, Balâtre; others in the rear, such as Potriaux and Tongrinne. The ninth, the most important of all, Ligny, is traversed its entire length by the stream.

From Napoleon's observatory in the mill at Fleurus, the Prussian positions did not appear nearly as strong as they really were. The Emperor could not form an exact idea of the depth of the hollows. The ravine through which the Ligne flowed, was quite hidden from view. Before him lay what appeared to be merely a vast plain covered with corn, slightly depressed to its centre and rising in a gentle slope to the extreme of the horizon—a landscape of the true Beauce type. He sent for the land-surveyor of the town, a certain Simon, who gave him all the information in his power.[3] At twelve o'clock Zieten's four divisions were the only ones drawn up in line of battle, with Röder's cavalry; the corps of Pirch II. and of Thielmann were only just commencing to muster behind Sombreffe and Tongrinne.[4] The Emperor justly concluded that he had only a single army corps before him.[5] But he did not deceive himself as to Blücher's intentions. "The old fox will not stir out," he said. He conjectured that the Field-Marshal had taken up a waiting position, and that Blücher hoped to overawe the French long enough to give his other army corps, and possibly Wellington's army also, time to join him.[6] If Blücher, in short, had had no other object than to defend his lines of communication with his own forces alone, he would have taken up his position perpendicularly to the Fleurus road. The extension of his right towards Wagnelée, indicated the existence of a design to unite with the English army on their march from Brussels.

As he was resolved to attack immediately, the Emperor was much perturbed to learn that Gérard's corps was not even in sight.[7] He waited. Doubtless at the time, he believed that he had only a single army corps to deal with, and he had at his disposal Vandamme's corps, the 1st and 2nd Cavalry Corps, and in the second line, behind Fleurus, the Imperial Guard. He feared, reasonably enough, that during the course of the battle, they might be interrupted by the arrival of the bulk of the Prussian Army, which was then probably marching on Sombreffe.

Shortly after twelve, Gérard, who had preceded his army corps, reached the line of outposts with a small escort. Whilst seeking the Emperor, he came within musket-range of the enemy's cavalry. The Prussians charged; Gérard, thrown from his horse, was in imminent danger of being captured; he was saved by one of his aides-de-camp. Having found the Emperor at the mill, he felt bound to say a few words about the desertion of Bourmont, whose command had been obtained principally through Gérard's pressing entreaties. Napoleon cut him short, saying, "It was just as I told you, General; what is blue is blue, and what is white is always white!"[8]

Not before one o'clock did the head of Gérard's column appear.[9] Their marching orders had been dispatched before eight o'clock,[10] and from Le Châtelet to Fleurus the distance is ten kilometres. Yet, in consequence of the neglect of the Emperor's instructions during the preceding afternoon, ordering the 4th Corps to take up their position on the left bank of the Sambre in the morning, Gérard had to get the greatest part of his troops across the river on a single bridge. Hence arose the long delay in the march of the 4th Corps.[11]

It appears the Emperor had thought at first of attacking by Wagnelée and Saint-Amand, so as to throw the Prussians back on Sombreffe.[12] But the position of their right suggested the idea of surrounding them, instead of driving them back. On this account he modified his previous orders to Ney. According to the instructions forwarded in the morning, the Marshal should have planted his men at Quatre-Bras and beyond it, and awaited the order to march on Brussels.[13] At two o'clock Soult was commanded to write to him thus: "The Emperor bids me warn you that the enemy has assembled a body of troops between Sombreffe and Brye, and that Marshal Grouchy with the 3rd and 4th Corps will attack them at half-past two. His Majesty's desire is that you should also attack the forces in *your* front, press them closely and with great vigour, then draw back in our direction to help us to surround the corps I have just alluded to."[14]

Vandamme's and Gérard's corps, with Grouchy's cavalry, were spread out before Fleurus, and perpendicularly to the road. The Emperor ordered the front to wheel round, the right in the first rank. Through this manœuvre, Vandamme drew nearer Saint-Amand, Gérard advanced within a distance of 1,000 yards from Ligny parallel to the road, and Grouchy posted his men in the form of a T opposite Boignée. The Guard and the cuirassiers under Milhaud, stationed behind Fleurus until two o'clock, came forward and formed the second line.[15]

From the mill at Bussy, where at two o'clock he was still with Wellington, Blücher had been able to watch this movement being carried out. He hastened to complete his own order of battle. Zieten's corps, of which a few detachments only occupied the front, up to that time in the line of defence, now took up their positions: four battalions of Steinmetz's division at La Haye and at Le Hameau (or Petit Saint-Amand), the remaining six supporting the first; three battalions of Jagow's division at Saint-Amand, and the remaining seven under the Bussy mill; Henckel's division at Ligny, with two battalions slightly in the rear, and the division of Pirch II. drawn out between Brye and the mill at Bussy. Röder's cavalry was massed in a hollow to the north of the road from Ligny to Sombreffe, excepting the 1st Silesian Hussars, who, with a light battery to the extreme right, were detached on the Roman way, to reconnoitre on the flank of the Army. The artillery was posted between the villages, on the lower portion of the slopes. Saint-Amand, La Haye, Ligny had all been hastily fortified; but none of the bridges over the Ligne had been cut, as Blücher desired to preserve these outlets, in case he should decide to take the offensive.

Behind this first line, the corps of Pirch I. (divisions Tippelskirch, Krafft, Brause, and Langen, and Jürgass's cavalry), was held in reserve to the north of Brye, along the Nivelles road. As for Thielmann's corps, which formed the Prussian left, the divisions of Luck and Kempter were posted at Potriaux, Tongrinne, Tongrinelle, and Balâtre, and Hobes's cavalry formed the reserve at Sombreffe and behind Tongrinne.[16]

This vast display did not escape Napoleon's vigilant

glance. Until past two o'clock, and until Blücher's own manœuvres compelled the Field-Marshal to reveal the total amount of his forces, the Emperor believed he had to deal with 30,000 men at the most.[17] The extension of the enemy's front, the masses which he saw in motion, now revealed the presence of an entire army. What happy fortune for him! The fight would doubtless be a stubborn one, but he might now settle accounts with Blücher in a single day. In a few hours Blücher would be in his clutches! For Ney had but to storm the position of Brye from the rear, with his cannon to sound the death-knell of the Prussian Army. "It is possible that three hours hence, the fate of the war may be decided," the Emperor said to Gérard. "If Ney executes orders properly, not a single piece of artillery of this army can escape him!"[18] At a quarter past three, a second order was sent to Ney; it was more peremptory, more imperative than the first. "An hour ago," said Soult, "I wrote to you that the Emperor was about to attack the enemy in the position he has taken up between Saint-Amand and Brye, and now the engagement has become very decided. His Majesty charges me to say to you, that you are to manœuvre immediately, so as to surround the enemy's right, and fall on his rear with might and main. This army is lost if you act vigorously. The fate of France is in your hands. Therefore do not hesitate one instant to execute the manœuvre enjoined on you by the Emperor, and make for the heights of Saint-Amand and Brye."[19]

As Soult was dispatching this order, Napoleon received a letter from Lobau informing him that, according to Colonel Janin's report, Ney had about 20,000 enemies before him at Quatre-Bras.[20] The Emperor reflected that were these 20,000 men to defend themselves obstinately, it might prevent the Prince of La Moscow from executing the desired movement against the Prussian Army at the proper time. Evidently his grand tactical combination might prove abortive. He did not flatter himself, as he has been unjustly accused of doing, that he could win two battles in the same day. The important point for him, was not to win a partial victory over Blücher and a partial victory over Wellington, but to hold the English in check, while he annihilated the Prussians. The Emperor thought that Reille's corps was all that Ney needed to overawe the English, and that d'Erlon's corps was amply sufficient to turn the Prussian right. He resolved to entrust to d'Erlon, the charge of executing the movement which he had previously entrusted to Ney, and from which he expected such momentous results. There was not an instant to lose. He sent directly to Count d'Erlon, the order to march with his army corps to the rear of the Prussian Army's right. Colonel de Forbin-Janson, who was told to transmit this order to him, was also directed to communicate it to Ney.[21]

At the same time the Emperor, wishing to have all his forces well in hand, sent a message to Lobau, who was temporarily stationed at Charleroi, ordering him to march on Fleurus.[22]

Section II

The battle was now in full force. Towards three o'clock, three cannon-shots fired at regular intervals by the battery of the Guard, gave the signal for attack.[23] Vandamme did not even deign to prepare the way for the assault with his artillery, but hurled Lefol's division on Saint-Amand. To the tune of "*La victoire en chantant*," played by the band of the 23rd, the division marched forward in three columns, each of which was preceded by a swarm of tirailleurs. The ground in front of the enemy had been swept of every tree and hedge, and was now a sheet of ripening corn four or five feet high. The march through this surging mass was slow and difficult, and though the ears of wheat afforded cover to the tirailleurs, the columns were perfectly visible. It was on the latter, therefore, that the batteries directed their fire: cannon-balls ploughed down files of men eight deep. The Prussians were well under cover, ambushed in the houses or behind the embankments, and the dense hedges which surrounded the orchards. Fifty yards from the village, Lefol's soldiers sprang up to the first enclosures. Even point-blank discharges failed to check their rush; in less than a quarter of an hour's furious fighting, the enemy was driven from the orchards, the houses, the cemetery, and the church. But Jagow's Prussians rallied on the left bank of the brook, and soon after, supported by four battalions under Steinmetz, they prepared for a counter-attack. The battery of Steinmetz's division turned its fire upon Saint-Amand, where several buildings were seen, bursting into flames, and the 24th Regiment crossed the stream at La Haye to take the French in flank. Vandamme ordered Berthézène's division to deploy to Lefol's left, and in accordance with the Emperor's previous instructions, he ordered Gérard's division, stationed on the north of Wangenies, to attack Le Hameau and La Haye.[24]

Whilst Lefol had been working towards Saint-Amand, Pécheux's division had advanced on Ligny in three attacking columns, under the fire of the Prussian batteries. The left and central column carried the hedges and the fences at the entrance to the village; then they were repulsed, their ranks being terribly thinned by the fusillade which poured thick and fast, from the old castle and the nearest houses. The right column of the 30th of the line pushed forward. They fought up the hollow road, at the end of which rose the farm of La Tour, a building with walls like those of a fort, from which poured a perfect hailstorm of bullets; it penetrated as far as the square of the church. Here the regiment, literally surrounded by the enemy, concealed in the houses, in the cemetery, and behind the clumps of willows by the brookside, found itself the centre of a square of crossing fires. In a second the whole head of the column was overwhelmed, 20 officers and nearly 500 men fell, killed or wounded. Those who survived retired in disorder and strove to regain their original positions.[25]

Two fresh attacks proved equally unsuccessful. Batteries from the 12th of the Guard came to reinforce Gérard's artillery, which until that time had merely answered the artillery of the enemy. They opened fire on Ligny. Cannon-balls shattered the houses and ricochetted in the streets, the thatched roofs took fire and fell in; the conflagration burst out in ten different points at once. For the fourth time Pécheux's division, seconded now by a brigade from Vichery, marched against the Prussians. After an obstinate struggle and a succession of assaults on each several house, the French gained possession of nearly the whole upper portion of the village.²⁶

Ligny was formed of two streets which ran parallel to the Ligne, and were separated by it: the " rue d'En-Haut to the south, the rue d'En-Bas to the north." Between the two streets there were a few straggling cottages, the square of the church, and a vast common which sloped down to the Ligne in the form of a glacis. Expelled from the farm of La Tour and the rue d'En-Haut, the Prussians resumed their positions in the cemetery, in the church, in the houses, and on the square. Pécheux's soldiers advanced valiantly under crossing fires. Some dashed into the houses, others climbed the embankment around the cemetery. Thereupon a great body of the enemy which had rallied under shelter of the church, charged the French, who were thrown into great disorder owing to these repeated assaults. The little square, too narrow for such a number of combatants, became the scene of a terrific contest, a hand-to-hand struggle with no quarter given or sought, a frightful carnage! They shot at one another point-blank, they charged with their bayonets, with the butt ends of their muskets, and even fought with their fists. "The men," says a Prussian officer, "slaughtered one another as if they were impelled by personal hatred. It seemed as if each of them felt he was struggling with his own mortal enemy, and rejoiced that he had at last met with an opportunity of avenging himself. No man thought of flight or of asking for quarter." ²⁷

The Prussians at last gave way. They abandoned the houses, the church, and the cemetery, and retired in disorder across the two bridges of the Ligne, and were pursued at the point of the bayonet. More than one was thrown into the muddy bed of the brook beneath. Still, on the left bank, the enemy, reinforced by the two last battalions of Henckel's division, re-formed and made a determined stand. The Prussians fired from the hedges and the fringe of willows that bordered the brook, whilst others fired over the heads of their comrades from the houses of the Rue d'En-Bas, and from loopholes opened in the walls of the large farm on the left bank. In spite of this terrible ladder of fires, the soldiers of the 30th and the 96th crossed the bridges and forced back the tirailleurs on to the houses. But Jagow brought up four battalions to the help of Henckel. The Prussians repulsed their assailants on to the right bank; they even attempted to cross to the other side by the two bridges. It was now the turn of the French to defend the brook. From either bank, the soldiers shot at each other at a distance of only four yards, through dense clouds of smoke. A threatening storm hung heavy in the air, and its sultry heat increased that of the continuous firing and of the flames kindled by the falling shells. Ligny became a fiery furnace. Amid the roar of the battle rose the piercing cries of the wounded who were being burnt alive beneath the flaming ruins.[28]

Grouchy, on his side, had commenced his attack against the Prussian left. His cavalry had driven the enemy's posts from Boignée; and Hulot's division from Gérard's corps, which had passed under his direct command, threatened Tongrinelle and exchanged shots in front of Potriaux with Luck's Prussians.[29]

On all points new batteries were being brought into action, and the firing waxed hotter and hotter. From La Haye to Tongrinelle, the fight waged on both banks of the Ligne, from which rose a curtain of fire and smoke, as if from a river in hell itself.

Section III

Towards four o'clock the battle extended to the west. Girard had marched his division against Le Hameau and La Haye. The assault was so prompt, so resolute, and so spirited, that the terrified Prussians yielded the ground, scarcely striking a blow.[30] Blücher, whose centre was solid, and whose left was intact, saw that his right wing was being overpowered. He knew that it must be relieved by a vigorous counter-attack. Cost what it might, he must clear the way at that point, for there he intended later on to make a joint advance with the English, whose assistance he still expected. The Field-Marshal did not hesitate to diminish his reserve. The division of Pirch II., the only one of Zieten's corps which had not yet been under fire, was ordered to march from Brye against La

Haye and Saint-Amand, whilst Jürgass's cavalry, from the corps of Pirch I., and Tippelskirch's division, from the same corps, 47 squadrons[31] and 9 battalions in all, were to push on to Wagnelée, whence they would fall like a thunderbolt on the French flank.[32]

Formed in battalion columns, the infantry of Pirch II. made a bayonet charge upon Girard's troops, who had already advanced from La Haye to turn the enemy's position at Saint-Amand, where Steinmetz's Prussians had returned in force, reoccupying several points. Girard's division gave way under the attack of these fresh troops, and took refuge in La Haye, and after a stubborn resistance abandoned half of this hamlet. With such a leader as Girard, this state of things did not last long. In the street, swept by shells and bullets, he re-formed his decimated battalions and hurled them once more against the enemy. He led them himself, with sword drawn, and fell mortally wounded; but before his death he saw his soldiers repulse the Prussians from La Haye, on to the left bank of the brook for the second time.[33]

The flank movement attempted by Jagow and Tippelskirch, proved more unsuccessful than the counter-attack of Pirch II. Habert's division and Domon's cavalry, which Vandamme had until then kept in reserve, were deployed opposite Wagnelée with two battalions as skirmishers concealed in the corn. The head of Tippelskirch's column advancing on it in marching order, without reconnoitring, was taken utterly by surprise, by a sustained and well-directed volley from the corn. It fell back in disorder, carrying confusion amid the battalions which were coming up behind it, amongst which were numerous recruits. Without hesitating, Habert charged these disunited troops with the bayonet, and forced them back into Wagnelée. Awkwardly placed, intimidated moreover by the manœuvres of General Domon's mounted chasseurs, Jürgass's cavalry took scarcely any part in the action.[34]

During these struggles Blücher had come down from the mill at Bussy, in order to direct personally further developments of the manœuvre, from which he anticipated such brilliant results. He arrived within easy range of the guns of La Haye, at the precise moment when Pirch II.'s division was being expelled from it by the dying efforts of the intrepid Girard. Without even allowing the men time to recover their breath, Blücher ordered Pirch II. to lead them back under fire and to retake La Haye at all costs. Encouraged by the presence of old " Forwärtz " (Forwards), the soldiers shouted " Hurrah " again and again, leapt across the brook, and with crossed bayonets penetrated into La Haye.[35] Girard's division, reduced from 5,000 to 2,500 men, with its chief mortally wounded, its two brigadier-generals disabled (Colonel Matis of the 82nd of the line was in command at the time), made a desperate resistance. Completely outnumbered, however, it retreated from house to house, from orchard to orchard, from hedge to hedge, till it reached Le Hameau, where it mustered its scattered men and awaited the assault. The enemy was compelled to pause for a moment, for the French had beaten back Tippelskirch into Wagnelée; moreover, at Saint-Amand they stood their ground, and at Ligny they still occupied half the village. Blücher was forced therefore to relieve Steinmetz's division in front of Saint-Amand, as it had lost half its effective strength; he had also to send reinforcements to Henckel in Ligny, and give Tippelskirch time to re-form and rally at Wagnelée, and to forward the manœuvre he then contemplated, he had to move the corps of Pirch I. to the south of Brye.[36]

The Emperor on his part now took measures for the great movement which had been his fixed object, since the outset of the battle. It was now half-past five; at two o'clock he had written to Ney; at six he calculated he would hear the deep roar of the Marshal's cannon, thundering in the rear of the Prussian Army. Then he would hurl his reserves, which were still intact, against the enemy's centre; he would break through it, cut off its retreat towards Sombreffe, and at the point of the sword would thrust it between the murderous fire and steel of Vandamme and Ney. Of the 60,000 Prussians of Zieten and Pirch, not one should escape.[37]

The Guards on foot and on horseback, with Milhaud's cuirassiers, were already preparing for the attack, when an aide-de-camp from Vandamme arrived with grave tidings. A league to the left, a column of the enemy's forces, numbering from twenty to thirty thousand men, had been sighted; they appeared to be proceeding towards Fleurus with the intention of turning the Army's flank. Vandamme added that, on discovering these troops were hostile, Girard's troops had abandoned La Haye, and that he himself would be forced to evacuate Saint-Amand and to beat a retreat, unless the Reserve arrived in time to arrest this column.[38]

Napoleon was much embarrassed. At first the idea struck him, as it had done Vandamme, that this column might be the French division, which according to his orders, dispatched at eight that morning, should have been led by Ney to Marbais. But no division contains twenty or thirty thousand men, and troops appearing to the south of Villers-Perwin could not possibly come from Marbais.[39] Could it be Ney arriving with all his forces, in pursuance of the new orders sent out at two and repeated at three? or was it d'Erlon arriving with the 1st Corps in accordance with the despatch forwarded at half-past three? But d'Erlon like Ney had orders to fall on the enemy's rear from the heights of Saint-Amand, not to come to Fleurus.

To march on Fleurus would be to wreck the Emperor's plan. Neither Marshal Ney nor Count d'Erlon were capable of such a blunder! Besides, Vandamme said positively that the column had been recognised as the enemy.[40] They must therefore be in the presence of an English corps which had passed by Ney's right, or a Prussian corps which had accomplished a wide turning movement by Villers-Perwin and the Roman way.[41] The Emperor lost no time in sending one of his aides-de-camp to reconnoitre the force and intentions of the hostile column. Meanwhile he suspended the movement of the Guard against Ligny, and ordered it to resume its previous position before the mill at Fleurus, with its regiments deployed. Duhesme's division of the Young Guard and the 2nd, 3rd, 4th Unmounted Chasseurs of the Guard, detached from this reserve, advanced by quick steps to the assistance of Vandamme.[42]

It was high time that these reinforcements should arrive. Vandamme's corps had scarcely yet recovered from the panic which had been caused by the approach of the hostile forces, and General Lefol was obliged to arrest the flight of his men by turning his cannons against the fugitives;[43] and this corps had now to receive an attack of nearly the whole Prussian right. A little before six, the batteries in the Reserve formed in line and prepared for the assault. Tippelskirch debouched from Wagnelée and marched on Le Hameau, supported on his right by Jürgass's numerous squadrons. The tirailleurs of the 1st Pomeranians opened fire, and so fiercely and so fast, that in a few seconds they had not a single cartridge left in their pouches; the hussars on their flank supplied them with theirs. The division of Pirch II., seconded by fresh troops from Brause's division and by a portion of Krafft's division, assaulted Saint-Amand at three several points. The French now gave way. The remnants of Girard's division abandoned Le Hameau; Lefol and Berthézène surrendered the entire northern part of Saint-Amand; Habert fell back on his first position to the left of that village. From the mill at Bussy to which he had returned, Blücher watched the success of his troops with keen interest. He had reason to believe he was already master of the road to Fleurus, and that he would soon be at liberty to attack the French reserve in flank, a manœuvre which he had long been meditating.[44]

But Duhesme's Young Guard advanced at quick steps; it rushed past Habert's division and met Tippelskirch's Prussians with superb *élan*. The latter suffered severely, and took refuge, some in Wagnelée, the rest in Le Hameau. The cavalry of Jürgass, held in check by Domon's chasseurs and the lancers under Alphonse de Colbert, which the Emperor had just brought up from the right to the left of the battlefield, were able merely to protect Tippelskirch's retreat and were powerless to make any move against the Young Guard. The indefatigable division of Girard, whose four intrepid regiments, the 11th and 12th Light Infantry and the 4th and 82nd of line, deserve special mention, made a new rush on Le Hameau and drove out from thence the Prussians for the third time. Lefol and Berthézène turned Pirch II. out of Saint-Amand. The French were once more masters of the ground as far as the first houses of La Haye.[45] "What soldiers!" writes a royalist *emigré* who was present at the battle. "These are no longer the spiritless wrecks of Arcis-sur-Aube. They are either a legion of heroes or of devils."[46]

On the right wing, Grouchy's cavalry had occupied Tongrinelle and Hulot's infantry attacked Potriaux vigorously.[47] In the furnace at Ligny, battalions of brave men had melted away like gold in the crucible. Gérard had thrown himself into it with his last reserve, the second brigade of Vichery. Blücher had increased Henckel's division by the largest part of Krafft's corps. The fury of the struggle continued with unabated force; Prussians and French crossed and recrossed the brook in turn, contesting the possession of the church, the cemetery, the farm of "En-Bas," and the château of the Counts de Looz, where two companies of Silesian tirailleurs still held their own valiantly, in spite of the advancing flames of the conflagration which surrounded them. Men fell to the ground from sheer exhaustion. Krafft lost all hope of carrying on the resistance much longer; he sent a message to Gneisenau telling him that he and Jagow were on the point of being hemmed in at Ligny. "Hold on for one half-hour longer," Gneisenau answered, "the English army is drawing near."[48] A delusion or a falsehood! For Blücher was about to receive, if he had not already received, a despatch from Müffling informing him that Wellington was himself contending with a whole army corps, and could not spare him a single squadron.[49]

Nothing, however, could daunt the intrepid soul of Blücher. If Müffling's letter did bring "unpleasant news," as Grolemann mildly put it, at any rate it showed him that Napoleon had not his entire army with him, as he imagined; it gave him the assurance he could not be attacked in the rear, since the French corps detached on the Brussels road, was being held in check by Wellington. Simultaneously he received two messages, one from Pirch II., the other from Thielmann, both announcing that the attack of the French appeared to be slackening towards La Haye and Potriaux. After their forward movement, the Old Guard had resumed their previous positions. This counter-march, which had been noticed from the mill at Bussy, seemed to indicate at least hesitation on the part of the Emperor. The time to act had now come, unless they wished the victory to escape them. Blücher still believed it was possible. He clung to the idea of winning the battle unassisted, if he could only force the French on their centre. This could easily be done if his lieutenants only retained their hold on Ligny. He would take charge of the rest himself. He called up his last reserves, with the exception of two battalions, which he posted at Brye and near the mill. To reinforce Jagow and Krafft, he sent a portion of Langen's division to Ligny, and ordered Thielmann to proceed there also with Stülpnagel's division. Then, taking with him the last battalions of Langen and the remains of Steinmetz's division which had retired to the second line, towards five in the afternoon, this valiant old warrior of seventy-three led them towards Saint-Amand.[50]

On his way he gathered round him all the crowds of soldiers who had left the field: here a company, there a section, farther on a group of fugitives. With these seven or eight battalions he re-formed the exhausted divisions of Brause, Pirch II., and Tippelskirch, and ordered a new attack. "My men have fired off all their cartridges and also emptied the pouches of the dead," Pirch said to him; "they cannot fire a single shot more." "Fix bayonets and forward!" Blücher cried in reply; and brandishing his sword, spurring on his magnificent white horse, a gift of the Prince Regent of England, he swept onward with his electrified soldiers. . . . It was the expiring effort of brave men, but their strength was spent. They retook Le Hameau, but their ranks dashed in vain against the wall of steel formed by the 2nd, 3rd, and 4th Chasseurs of the Guard, who were drawn up in regiments to the left of Saint-Amand.[51]

The Prussians retired in disorder to La Haye. Blücher still entertained the forlorn hope of spending the night in his intrenchments. He considered the battle was over, for it was growing dark.[52] But the darkness was not of the night, for during the solstice of June, at half-past seven the sun is still high above the horizon. It was a storm. Great black clouds rose and massed themselves in the sky, covering the whole battlefield with a vault of inky blackness. Large drops of rain began to fall. Peal after peal of thunder crashed overhead, but the din of the thunder was soon drowned by the roar of the frightful cannonade which suddenly burst out towards Ligny.[53]

Section IV

Towards half-past six [54] the aide-de-camp, sent to reconnoitre the strength of the hostile column marching towards Vandamme's flank from the woods of Villers-Perwin,[55] returned to tell the Emperor that this presumed English column was in reality the corps of Count d'Erlon.[56] Napoleon might have guessed as much. A false manœuvre, a confusion of orders, a cross-march are not such unlikely events in war, as to preclude their being seriously considered as possible. Disconcerted to such a degree that his spirit had sunk, by the threatening direction of this column, he had never thought of d'Erlon's corps, though he had himself summoned it to the battlefield. Had not his usual presence of mind failed him then, the frustrated movement might still have been executed. Its success depended merely on Napoleon's sending to d'Erlon the very aide-de-camp who went to reconnoitre the unknown column, with pressing orders to manœuvre so as to turn the Prussian right. Napoleon never even thought of this; and when the aide-de-camp returned to him, he wisely judged that the delay had made the movement useless. Two full hours would have been required to carry out this march and surround the foe.[57] The Emperor, besides, learned probably from his aide-de-camp, that the 1st Corps was retiring.[58] Had Ney, feeling himself in peril, called it back? Or had d'Erlon discovered his direction was the wrong one, and resolved to bear westwards of Wagnelée, in order to manœuvre on the rear of the Prussian lines, according to the order brought to him by Forbin-Janson?

The Emperor made up his mind at once. If the misunderstanding of his orders, or their non-execution, seemed to him to preclude his relying any longer on the co-operation of a portion of his left, at any rate he was relieved from his anxiety respecting the presence of a supposed column of the enemy on his flank. He was once more free to act. The conclusive victory he had dreamed of the whole afternoon had escaped him; but for all that he might still win the battle and separate

Blücher far from Wellington. He gave his orders for the final assault.[59]

The reserve batteries opened fire upon the little hills above Ligny; the Old Guard deployed in columns; the squadrons of service, the 2nd Cavalry Division of the Guard, and Milhaud's cuirassiers prepared for the attack; Lobau's corps poured out of Fleurus. The cannonade ceased, the drums beat the charge, the seething mass moved off under the warm rain of the storm, with cries of "Vive l'Empereur!" The first column of the Guard (2nd, 3rd, and 4th Grenadiers) penetrated to the west of Ligny; the second (1st Chasseurs and 1st Grenadiers) attacked the village to the east. Led on by Gérard, the soldiers of Pécheux and Vichery crossed the brook of La Ligne; and at last wrested from the Prussians, the farm of En-Bas and all the houses on the left bank. The fragments of Jagow's and Krafft's divisions attempted to re-form on the nearest slopes above the ravine. But Pécheux rushed from the midst of Ligny followed by Vichery and the first column of the Guard; from the right of the village deployed the 1st Grenadiers and the 1st Chasseurs, followed by Milhaud's cuirassiers; while up from the left with the Emperor himself, advanced the service squadrons and the heavy cavalry of the Guard. The Prussians gave way at every point. Describing the rapidity and the effect of this irresistible attack, Soult wrote to Davout, "It was like a scene on the stage."[60]

Blücher arrived at full gallop from La Haye. The rain had ceased and the wind was dispersing the straggling clouds.[61] In the last rays of the setting sun, as they lit up for a minute the hills of Brye, he watched the disastrous retreat of his troops; and in the wide breach made in his line of battle, he saw the shaggy helmets of the Old Guard, the mounted dragoons towering above the rest, the dragoons turning round for a fresh charge, and in a glittering mass, Milhaud's 3,000 cuirassiers.

The veteran Blücher, as Major von Grolemann aptly said, "never considers himself vanquished, so long as he can continue the fight." He counted on Röder's cavalry, in reserve between Brye and Sombreffe; on the remnants of Henckel's division, which had been relieved at Ligny at six; on the Stülpnagel and Borcke divisions, which Thielmann ought to have detached from his army corps, to hold the French in check. But his orders had been misinterpreted; Henckel was already very close to Sombreffe, while Stülpnagel was still far from Ligny. As for Borcke's troops, Thielmann could not afford to diminish this his last reserve, so closely was he pressed in front by Grouchy; Hulot's division had carried Potriaux and was threatening Sombreffe; Exelmans' dragoons (Burthe's brigade) had routed Lottum's cavalry, had taken its cannon, and were advancing towards the Namur road.[62] Röder's 32 squadrons alone were at his disposal. Blücher rode up to them and commanded them to charge. Lützow, the celebrated "partizan" leader in the war of 1813, hurled the 6th Uhlans against a square which he believed to be composed of national mobilised guard, on account of the disparity of the uniforms worn by the men.[63] It was the 4th Grenadiers of the Guard. The uhlans were received by a line of fire at close quarters, and 83 of their men fell to the earth. Lützow was thrown from his horse and made prisoner. A charge of the 1st Dragoons and of the 2nd Landwher of Courmache, then a charge of the Brandeburg uhlans and of the Queen's dragoons, then a fourth one in which all the squadrons took part, were equally unsuccessful. The first were repulsed by the Old Guard, which had come to the first line to relieve Gérard's divisions; the others were sternly flung back by the dragoons of the Guard and Milhaud's cuirassiers.[64] Till nightfall, the intermingled French and Prussian squadrons, surged and struggled on the slopes of the hills, before the squares of the Guard, which continued their slow but steady advance towards the mill at Bussy.

Blücher's horse was struck by a bullet and fell upon its rider. The Field-Marshal's aide-de-camp, Nostiz, who rode beside him, saw him fall and sprang to the ground to assist him. They found themselves in the very centre of the cuirassiers of the 9th Regiment, who were driving back the Prussians, but in the increasing gloom, these passed by without distinguishing the two officers. A few seconds later it was the fate of the cuirassiers to be themselves forced back; for a second time they passed by them, almost over them, without noticing them. Nostiz hailed the Prussian dragoons.

Bruised all over and half-unconscious, Blücher was dragged out from under his horse; bruised and almost fainting, he was helped into the saddle of a charger belonging to a subaltern and led far from the battlefield amid the stream of fugitives, who were innumerable.[65] The next day 8,000 of them were arrested at Liège and Aix-la-Chapelle.[66]

The Prussian centre was shattered and broken, with the exception of a few battalions which retired in good order and bravely resisted Delort's cuirassiers, who were unfortunately not backed up by the second division of Milhaud's corps.[67] The whole infantry fled helter-skelter. Thanks to the desperate charges of Röder's cavalry, they in some degree arrested the impetus of the French march, thus enabling Krafft, Jagow, and Langen to save part of their artillery[68] and to rally the remains of their divisions between Sombreffe and the Roman way. But though the enemy's centre had been cut in two, they regained their former positions on both wings. Zieten and Thielmann only commenced to beat a retreat when they heard of the surrender of Ligny. The Prussians massed around La Haye, and regained with steady steps the higher summits of the hills, harassing by sudden charges from time to time, Vandamme's infantry when it pressed too closely; their rearguard held their own at Brye till daybreak. Thielmann withdrew his corps to the rear of Sombreffe, which he occupied all night with a strong detachment. The sharpshooters again opened fire on the Brye-Sombreffe line about half-past nine.[69]

Towards eleven the Emperor returned to Fleurus, where the 2nd, 3rd, and 4th Chasseurs were assembled from Saint-Amand.[70] With the exception of these three regiments and the reserve batteries, the whole army bivouacked on the left bank of the brook: Lobau's corps, which had not taken part in the action, in the front line near the mill at Bussy: Vandamme's corps before La Haye; Gérard's corps, the Old Guard, and the Guard's cavalry in front of Ligny; Milhaud's cuirassiers to the right of this village; Hulot's division and Grouchy's cavalry between Tongrinne, Potriaux, and Sombreffe. Opposite Brye and facing Sombreffe the French Great Guards found themselves within easy range of the Prussian guards. So vivid was the impression of the enemy's proximity, that the grenadiers of the Guard, though they were on the second line, bivouacked without any fires, with their battalions formed into squares.[71]

During the night the task of removing the wounded commenced; but the ambulances were so few in number, and so imperfectly organised, that they were hopelessly unfitted for the work.[72] In the plain and in the villages, which were veritable charnel-houses, lay 12,000 Prussians[73] and 8,500 French, killed or wounded.[74]

BOOK II CHAPTER III

THE BATTLE OF QUATRE-BRAS

I. Inaction of Marshal Ney during the morning of the 16th of June—Repeated orders from the Emperor.
II. Attack on Quatre-Bras by Reille's corps (two P.M.)—Return of Wellington to Quatre-Bras and arrival of the first English reinforcements (three o'clock)—Death of the Duke of Brunswick (half-past four).
III. The false move of Count d'Erlon.
IV. The charge of Kellermann's cuirassiers (six o'clock) — Offensive action by Wellington (seven o'clock)—The French driven back on their original positions (from eight till nine).

Section I

In the course of the day the Emperor had sent no less than nine despatches to Marshal Ney.[1] But as he said long after at Saint Helena, "Ney was no longer the man he had been."[2] Ney, once the most ardent of Napoleon's lieutenants, he who in so many battles, notably at Jéna and Craonne, had attacked the enemy before the appointed time, had now grown temporising and circumspect, even to moral inertness.

On the previous evening, a prey to strategical scruples, the Marshal had dispatched towards Quatre-Bras only one detachment, which was far too weak to carry that position. On the morning of the 16th of June he did nothing to regain the lost time. Even admitting that he considered it necessary to await fresh orders from the Emperor before attacking,[3] he should at least have so disposed his forces, that he might be ready to act at the first command. His troops were échelonned from Frasnes to Thuin over a distance of seven leagues. At daybreak he should have concentrated at Frasnes the divisions of Jérôme Bonaparte,

Bachelu, and Foy, with the whole of the cavalry, and called up the corps of d'Erlon to Gosselies. This movement might have been completed before nine o'clock in the morning, without including the division of Allix, which could not possibly join till two hours later. Thus by nine o'clock Ney would have been in a position to attack Quatre-Bras, at the first order, with 19,000 bayonets, 3,500 sabres, 64 cannons, and a reserve of 20,500 men.[4] But the Marshal took no steps in preparation for such a move. He left his divisions scattered, his soldiers in camp, while he himself awaited inertly the Emperor's orders.

Towards half-past six the Marshal received Soult's first letter. It was not, strictly speaking, an order to march, but a warning that his troops might be called on to march ere long. Soult also announced the approaching arrival of Kellermann's cuirassiers at Gosselies, and asked Ney whether the 1st Corps had effected a move in that direction.[5] The point was always the same, that Ney's duty was to march straight before him on the Brussels road. Had the Emperor's intention been to summon the Marshal to his left, he would not have sent him a reinforcement of eight regiments of heavy cavalry. Ney, however, remained sunk in apathy. He contented himself with requesting Soult to give him the information he required.[6] Then, towards seven o'clock, he started off for Frasnes without even directing Reille to place the troops under arms.[7] He limited himself to remarking, "If orders from the Emperor should arrive during my absence, you will execute them immediately and communicate them also to Count d'Erlon."[8]

At Frasnes, Ney continued to be as inactive and careless as at Gosselies. He did not even think of examining on the spot, the enemy's positions, or of urging toward Quatre-Bras offensive reconnaissances, in order to compel the enemy to unmask. It even seemed as if he neglected to question his generals, the commanders of his outposts, or that he paid no attention whatever to their reports. Lefebvre-Desnoëttes or Colbert certainly warned him that the Netherlanders appeared to have received reinforcements, that since the morning they had extended and advanced their front, that at six o'clock their skirmishers had driven back the French outposts to the borders of the wood at La Hutte.[9] After these skirmishes, it is true, the firing had degenerated into spasmodic shooting; nevertheless the general aspect of the enemy's dispositions gave reason to conclude, that they meant to remain at Quatre-Bras. All this Ney refused to believe. These were but vain demonstrations made to impose on the French, and to mask a retreat. At the most there would be "but a handful of Germans to deal with, who were cut to pieces yesterday."[10]

The Marshal was so convinced of this, that towards eleven o'clock, when Flahaut brought him the Emperor's letter directing him to take up his position at Quatre-Bras,[11] and in front of Quatre-Bras, he dictated the following orders without any hesitation: "The 2nd Corps is to march immediately and take its place: the 5th division behind Genappe on the heights; the 9th division in the second line to the right and left of Bauterlez; the 6th and 7th divisions at the branch roads of Quatre-Bras. The three first divisions of Count d'Erlon are to take up their positions at Frasnes. The right division will establish itself at Marbais with the 2nd cavalry division. The 1st cavalry division will cover our march and clear our way in the direction of Brussels, and on our flanks. The two divisions of Count de Valmy will place themselves at Frasnes and Liberchies. The cavalry division of the Guard is to remain in its present position at Frasnes."[12] These were not the preparations for a battle; they amounted to a simple order of march. Ney's intentions were now clearly revealed by them. He counted on seizing Quatre-Bras without striking a blow, or at the worst after a very feeble resistance.[13] His instructions were a literal transcription of the Emperor's orders.[14] Like Napoleon himself, he believed the road to Brussels to be clear. And he was on the ground!

As a climax Ney, who seconded the Emperor so badly, was himself badly seconded by Reille. He had enjoined this general instantly to obey any orders he might receive from Napoleon.[15] But when Flahaut passed through Gosselies at ten o'clock, and communicated to Reille the instructions of which he was the bearer, the latter, disturbed by a report from General Girard, considered it his duty to await positive orders from Ney before starting with his troops. "General Flahaut," he writes to the Marshal, "has shown me the orders he is bearing to you. I meant to commence my movement on Frasnes as soon as my divisions were under arms; but after receiving a report from General Girard informing me that two large bodies of the enemy, each six battalions strong, were advancing by the Namur road, their front being at Saint-Amand, I will keep my troops ready to march until I receive your orders. As these can reach me quickly, there will be but very little time lost."[16]

This "very little time lost" meant a delay of two hours. Reille set his troops in motion, only after he had received Ney's order, that is to say, towards noon at the earliest. His vanguard did not arrive at Frasnes before half-past one.[17] In vain, during this interval, Ney had received a fresh letter from the chief of the staff reiterating the previous instructions.[18] With merely a single battalion under his command at that moment, and the mounted chasseurs of the Guard, he could do nothing but wait for Reille's infantry before commencing the attack. Besides, he persisted in believing he had ample time before him, to intrench himself at Quatre-Bras, and he still clung to his delusion that the enemy were in small force and would offer no serious resistance.[19]

As yet, it is true, the Prince of Orange had only the division of Perponcher at his disposal — 7,800 bayonets and 14 cannons.[20] But being firmly convinced of the strategical importance of Quatre-Bras, he was determined to hold his own at any cost, until the arrival of the English Army.

The position was one that lent itself to a sustained defence. The hamlet of Quatre-Bras, formed by a group of three large farms and two houses situated at the point where the roads crossed from Charleroi to Brussels, and from Namur to Nivelles, commanded the numerous undulations of the ground. To the east, the embankment of the Namur road formed a natural intrenchment, in front of which the Piraumont farm rose in the form of a redoubt. To the south-west, the approach to Quatre-Bras was protected by the Pierrepont farm and the thickets of the Bossu woods, which covered a surface of 2,000 yards to the left of the Charleroi road.[21] Lastly, half a mile to the south of the hamlet, in a hollow, stood the large farm of Gémioncourt, built by the roadside and constituting another advanced work.

Although a division which did not amount to 8,000 men was insufficient to guard this front, which was more than three kilometres in length, and to occupy efficiently all its positions, yet Perponcher, in order to impose upon the French and to postpone for a time, the attack on Quatre-Bras, boldly scattered his men. Two battalions with three pieces of artillery were stationed in reserve at Quatre-Bras and on the Namur road; the rest were distributed as follows: to the left, a battalion with five cannon in front of Gémioncourt and another battalion occupying that farm; to the right, four battalions and the mounted battery, on the eastern borders of the Bossu wood and in front of Pierrepont.[22]

Section II

Towards half-past one Reille, who was marching with the vanguard of Bachelu's division, joined Ney. "There is hardly any one in the wood of Bossu," said the Marshal; "we must take it at once." Reille, however, was in no enterprising mood that day. He answered, "It may turn out to be one of these Spanish battles, in which the English never appear till their own time has come. It is prudent to defer our attack until all our troops have mustered here." Ney answered impatiently, "Nonsense! the companies of voltigeurs can manage it alone!" Nevertheless, Reille's remark made him ponder, and he too delayed the attack till the arrival of Bachelu's second brigade and Foy's division.[23]

At two o'clock these troops appeared from Frasnes, and their battalions drew up into columns, Bachelu to the right of the road, Foy to the left, and on the road itself; Piré's chasseurs flanked the right of Bachelu's division, the lancers being posted in the rear of the interval between the two divisions. On the second line, the cavalry of the Guard were stationed in columns on the highway, and the first brigade of

Kellermann's cuirassiers was deployed to the left. Jérôme Bonaparte's division was still on the move between Gosselies and Frasnes, and the three other brigades led by Kellermann, had taken up their positions at Liberchies in accordance with the orders received from Ney.[24]

The Marshal was anxious no longer to delay the attack; but troubled by Reille's speech, he considered that the troops he had in hand, were insufficient to assault the position in front of him. He therefore decided to direct all his efforts against the enemy's left.[25] (He had grounds for hoping that the defenders of Pierrepont and of the wood at Bossu, would draw back as soon as they saw themselves outflanked; but Prince Bernard, having secured his line of retreat on Houtain-le-Val, ran no risk of being cut off from Quatre-Bras.) After a short cannonade, the Marshal hurled the division of Bachelu, the cavalry of Piré, with the Jamin brigade from Foy's division, against the foe in the direction of Piraumont. Foy's second division (General Gauthier) was to act as a temporary reserve. Between the wood of La Hutte and the highroad, Bachelu's division and Piré's cavalry advanced towards Piraumont. The Netherlanders posted on the first line, were not sufficiently numerous to sustain this attack. Bachelu had no difficulty in forcing back the 27th Chasseurs on Piraumont. When they reached the heights by the Lairalle farm, Jamin's brigade, led by Foy, made head against the left column; it forced back the 2nd Nassau battalion, routed the 5th battalion of the militia from Gémioncourt, the remnant of which had re-formed on the west of the road, and then retreated toward the Bossu wood. Ney ordered Piré's lancers to charge and they completely routed them. The Prince of Orange was so closely pressed that he owed his safety merely to the speed of his horse; one of his aides-de-camp was wounded and captured. Excepting to the right, where Prince Bernard of Saxe-Weimar's battalions had not yet been molested, the French were masters of all the enemy's advanced positions.[26]

It was about three o'clock. Wellington, returned from the Bussy mill,[27] saw that the situation was critical, almost desperate.[28] A few minutes more and Quatre-Bras would be carried by Foy and Bachelu; Foy was already marching on the hamlet to attack it from the south, and Bachelu would soon be in a position to attack it from the east. Reinforcements, however, arrived: the brigade of van Merlen (Dutch hussars and Belgian dragoons) by the Nivelles road; Picton's division (eight English battalions and four Hanoverian) by the Brussels road.[29] Wellington was specially uneasy about the left of his line; it was almost denuded of troops and was threatened by Bachelu, who held the Piraumont farm with its dependencies. Picton's division, by a rapid movement, bore down upon the Namur road: the brigades of Kempt and Pack formed the first line, kneeling in the corn, while the Hanoverian brigade, sheltered behind the embankments of the road, formed the second line of fire.[30]

During the deployment of the English, the Prince of Orange made a rush, first with his hussars, then his dragoons against Foy's column, the tirailleurs of which were nearing Quatre-Bras. Before getting a chance of attacking the enemy's squadrons, the infantry were in their turn broken by Piré's lancers, who drove them back sharply to the other side of the cross-roads. Wellington was jostled and swept away in the flight as far as the Brussels highroad. Marching off to the right toward Gémioncourt, Piré's lancers again routed a battalion of militia, and seized eight cannon.[31]

The action had also commenced to the south of the Bossu wood. At three o'clock Prince Jérôme's division debouched from Frasnes, and Ney immediately turned it against the Pierrepont farm, whilst Gauthier's brigade proceeded to join General Foy. Dislodged from Pierrepont, the enemy fell back on the wood, into which the tirailleurs followed on their steps quickly. Here the advance was very slow indeed; not only was the wood well defended, but the underwood was so dense that the men had to cut their way through the thickets with their swords.[32]

At this period of the struggle, shortly before four o'clock, the Marshal received Soult's letter written at two o'clock, which ordered him to press the enemy vigorously and to close round the Prussian corps in its position at Brye, so as to envelop it.[33] Ney had now fully grasped the object of the

Emperor's schemes and the supreme importance of the possession of Quatre-Bras; he at once ordered a general movement forward. Bachelu proceeded to Piraumont toward the enemy's left; Foy marched from the low-lying ground of Gémioncourt toward Quatre-Bras, one column on the road, the other to the right of the road; Jérôme flung Soye's brigade into the Bossu wood and with the brigade of Bauduin marched between the road and the wood, in order to meet the Brunswick corps, which had just arrived to reinforce Wellington. Such was the impetus of this combined attack, that the Allies' right and their centre recoiled before it. Soye's brigade got good hold of nearly the whole of the Bossu wood and drove back its defenders as far as Houtain-le-Val, with the exception of one battalion which still held its own at the northern corner, near Quatre-Bras. Foy's division with Bauduin's brigade marching on its left, repulsed the black battalions of Brunswick. A charge of the Brunswick cavalry conducted by the Duke in person, broke on the steel wall of the bayonets of the 1st Light Infantry. Frederick William of Brunswick received a bullet in the stomach; he was carried into a house at Quatre-Bras, where he died that very evening.[34] His father, the author of the famous manifesto of 1792, had met with his death at Auerstadt. Both were violent enemies of France.

To the right, Bachelu's column had crossed the little valley between the Gémioncourt heights and the hill which commanded the Namur road; it was ascending this slope, when it encountered an almost point-blank fire from Picton's first line ambushed in the corn. The column halted and wavered. Picton, seeing the hesitation of the French, ordered a bayonet charge by Kempt's brigade, which did not stop to take breath, till it had driven them as far back as the vicinity of Piraumont. Here, however, the batteries of Bachelu and the rifles of the 108th, which had been posted as a reserve, commenced mowing down the English battalions as they advanced; and before this murderous fire they were forced to stop and regain their first positions as quickly as possible. As they retreated, they were charged by the 1st and 6th Chasseurs (Piré's division) and their sharpshooters were cut down, but the battalions, quickly forming into squares, presented a firm front to their assailants. The square of the 28th, being attacked on both sides, seemed on the point of giving way, when Picton restored the courage of his men by shouting "28th, remember Egypt!"[35]

The 42nd (Highlanders) and the 44th which formed Pack's right were less fortunate. Piré's lancers, who were galloping in pursuit of the Brunswickers, caught sight of the red-coats who were fighting at the angle of the two roads; they spurred their horses right upon them and scattered them, without, however, routing them. Bayonets against lances clashed together in a furious melée; the flag of the 44th was lost and retaken again and again. Colonel de Gallois with the 6th Lancers managed to pierce through as far as the Namur road, where he cut a battalion of Hanoverians to pieces.[36]

Section III

In order to second his attack, Ney relied on the 20,000 men under Count d'Erlon, who was bound to debouch from Frasnes ere long. But by a chain of fatalities, or rather through the logical consequence of delays in his preparatory arrangements, orders which had been misunderstood or wrongly executed, and inopportune counter-orders, this corps d'armée was destined to fail him, as completely as he had himself failed Napoleon.

In the morning, d'Erlon had concentrated his five divisions at Jumet (half a league in the rear of Gosselies), where he remained in person, from the previous evening, with the divisions of Durutte and Donzelot.[37] As the corps of Reille, the corps with which he was to join his own, did not stir from Gosselies, he waited for instructions. Shortly before eleven, he received word from Reille to prepare to follow the movements of the 2nd Corps, Reille informing him also that he himself would remain in his present position till further orders.[38] D'Erlon therefore could only follow his example. Towards a quarter past twelve, Ney's order to proceed to Frasnes was transmitted to him, either directly or through the medium of Reille;[39] but even then, he did not consider it necessary to start until the whole 2nd Corps, which preceded his own, had marched ahead. Besides, at one o'clock,[40] the division of Prince Jérôme had not broken up their camp on the south of the Lombuc wood, so the vanguard of the 2nd Corps could not possibly reach Gosselies before half-past one or two. There d'Erlon halted his troops, until the return of a strong reconnaissance which he had sent from Jumet, in the direction of Chapelle-Herlaymont. A false account given by the peasants led him to believe he would find a corps of Anglo-Belgians threatening his left at the latter village.[41] In spite of Ney's order of eleven o'clock, dictated in accordance with the instructions the Emperor had issued at eight,[42] he neglected, or he deferred sending either of his divisions to Marbais. Probably his intention was to detach the aforesaid division toward this village as soon as he should have reached Frasnes.[43] Be this as it may, it was three o'clock when he started on his march again.

Between four and a quarter past four, one-half of the column had gone beyond the Roman way, when d'Erlon was joined by Colonel de Forbin-Janson, of the Imperial staff.[44] Forbin-Janson had left Fleurus a quarter of an hour later than the officer entrusted with Soult's despatch,[45] but in taking a short cut through Mellet he had outdistanced the latter and gained almost an hour in advance.[46] He brought an order from the Emperor, commanding Count d'Erlon to march the 1st Corps to the heights of Saint-Amand in order to storm Ligny.[47]

Eager to forward the Emperor's views, General d'Erlon immediately ordered the column to make head against the right.[48] Unfortunately he read the order incorrectly; it was a mere pencil scrawl, and Forbin-Janson, who owed his appointment to favour, and was without any experience in military combinations, could not explain it.[49] The order ran thus: *On the height of Saint-Amand;* d'Erlon read or understood: At the height of Saint-Amand.[50] Consequently, instead of taking the direction of Brye-Ligny, to attack the Prussians cross-wise, he took the direction of Saint-Amand-Fleurus,[51] so as to extend the Emperor's left. This movement was in direct opposition to the instructions issued by Napoleon. It is easy to understand why the Emperor, on being informed that a column was advancing and threatening his left, never thought of d'Erlon, whom he did not expect would be at that point, and why he mistook this column, as Vandamme himself had done, for a body of English or Prussians.[52]

It was an imprudence on the part of the Emperor to entrust an order of such vital importance to an inexperienced staff-officer, such as Count de Forbin-Janson. Up to the year 1814, when he raised a corps of partisans in the Nièvre, Forbin-Janson had hardly been in action at all, save in a few trifling skirmishes. Until that time, Forbin-Janson had never served at all. In 1815 the Emperor admitted him to the army with the rank of colonel, and attached him to his staff. He had no knowledge whatever of staff-officers' duties. In the present instance, he could throw no light on the meaning of the Emperor's command to d'Erlon, and when he did give the order for the proposed movement, he either forgot to give, or misunderstood the subsidiary instructions of the Emperor, or for some other unknown reason he neglected to communicate this order to Marshal Ney, but rejoined the Imperial staff, with the same speed, as in justice to him, we must acknowledge he had shown in delivering his orders.[53]

The Prince of La Moscow only heard of d'Erlon's movement through General Delcambre, chief of the staff of the 1st Corps. As he was marching along the Roman way, d'Erlon, seized with misgivings, had dispatched that officer to the Marshal to inform him of his march toward the other field of battle.[54] Ney flew into a violent passion.[55] His fury increased when a few minutes later there arrived an officer bearing Soult's order, dated a quarter past three: " You must manœuvre immediately so as to surround the enemy's right, and grapple with him at close quarters on his rear. His army is lost if you act vigorously. The fate of France is in your hands. Therefore do not hesitate a second to execute the manœuvre the Emperor orders, and make for the heights of Saint-Amand and Brye."[56] Seeing the enemy's masses rapidly increasing (the vanguard of Alten's division had debouched from Quatre-Bras),[57] Ney perceived more keenly than ever, that he would have to oppose them with all his forces. Moreover, at the very moment when the Emperor's letter suggested to his mind, the grand manœuvre which would have annihilated the Prussian Army, he recognised the utter impossibility of accomplishing it. Ney found himself in the line of fire of an English battery; projectiles ploughed up the ground and ricochetted around him. He was heard to exclaim, "Ah! those English shells; I wish they would all bury themselves in my body!"[58]

Maddened and blinded with rage, Ney did not reflect that the 1st Corps could not possibly arrive at Frasnes in time to be of any use; he forgot that to call it back would be to thwart Napoleon's plans and to contravene his will in the most serious way:[59] he sent back General Delcambre with imperative orders to d'Erlon to march back his troops to the left wing.[60]

Section IV

And yet the words of the letter of Napoleon, "The fate of France is in your hands," troubled and fascinated the Marshal. The very movement which he had exhorted d'Erlon to suspend, he still entertained a lingering hope of executing himself! What if he were still able by a desperate effort, and in spite of the disproportion between the rival forces, to drive back the English beyond Quatre-Bras? and once master of that point, with d'Erlon, who would be back by that time, to effect the decisive manœuvre against the Prussian Army which the Emperor expected? All the troops had been engaged, except the cuirassiers of Kellermann and the cavalry of the Guard. He called for Kellermann.

"My dear General," he said in a broken voice, "the safety of France is at stake! We must make an extraordinary effort. Take your cavalry, throw yourself in the midst of the English. Crush them, trample them under your feet!"

The intrepid Kellermann had never yet discussed an order to charge. Still he could not refrain from representing to Ney that the Dutch and English forces amounted apparently to 25,000 men; and he had at his disposal only a single brigade of cuirassiers, his three other brigades having remained behind, in accordance with the orders of the Marshal himself.

"What does that signify!" cried Ney. "Charge with what you have. Crush them under your feet. I will send after you all the cavalry I can muster. . . . Go, I tell you, go on!"[61]

Kellermann had nothing left but to obey. He rejoined Guiton's brigade (8th and 11th Cuirassiers), formed it into a column by squadron columns, each squadron being separated by an interval double its own front, and led it at full trot to the summit of the eminence which rises between Gémioncourt and Quatre-Bras. There he cried out the command, which was instantly repeated from the head to the foot of the column: "Charge—at full gallop!—Forward—march!" "I used great haste," he said in his report to Ney, "so as not to allow my men time to shrink, or to perceive the whole extent of the danger in front of them."

The trumpets sounded the charge. With a flash of glittering steel and a shower of turf-clods torn up by the hoofs of the chargers, the cuirassiers swept down like an avalanche. At every step their speed increased. The ground trembled and crumbled into clouds of dust. The men in the first rank bent low on their horses' necks, with their lances lowered, point forward; the others flourished their flashing spears. Kellermann, sword unsheathed, charged twenty paces in advance of the leading squadron.

In the valley, the four battalions of Colin Halkett's fresh brigade were drawn up in line of battle or formed into squares. Motionless, resolute, so calm that they were terrible to behold, the English waited and reserved their fire. The 69th Regiment posted in the first line between Bossu and the road, only fired when the French were within thirty paces. The cuirassiers dashed through the hail of bullets, and through the smoke like lightning through a cloud. They swept down on the 69th, broke through, trampling down its ranks, and seized its standard. They then charged the square of the 30th and overthrew the 33rd. Then, without even breathing their horses, they swept up the opposite slope, cutting down the gunners of a battery as they passed, breaking through a square of Brunswickers, and penetrated as far as Quatre-Bras.[62]

The first and second lines of the enemy were divided, and a bloody breach left in their ranks. Unfortunately, the cuirassiers of this gallant charge were not supported. Offended by Ney, who appeared to doubt his resolution, Kellermann had made his charge prematurely. With his mind still filled with rage against d'Erlon, Ney had managed this supreme attack most unwisely; he had delayed sending his orders and had quite forgotten the cavalry of the Guard which was held in reserve near Frasnes.[63] Piré's columns of infantry, his lancers, and his chasseurs were merely beginning to move,[64] while the two regiments of cuirassiers, now reduced to 500 men, broken by the very impetuosity of their charge, with their horses breathless, found themselves alone in the very heart of Wellington's troops. They were at the very apex of a triangle of fire, and were fired on from the Bossu wood by the Dutch, from the embankments of the Namur road by the English, from the houses of Quatre-Bras by the Brunswick sharpshooters, and from the Brussels road shelled by Major Kulmann's batteries which spread death through their ranks. The Count de Valmy fell to the ground under his dying horse.[65] This gave the signal for a general stampede. In vain did he scramble to his feet and strive to rally his squadrons, the cuirassiers were now deaf to his commands. They wheeled round, put spurs to their horses, and in small disorderly groups, but still with their lances threatening their foes, they plunged through a perfect hailstorm of bullets from the enemy's lines, carrying off with them as a trophy, the standard of the English 69th.[66]

These horsemen, perfectly maddened, rode on at breakneck speed, hustling and dragging after them in their headlong flight, several battalions of Foy's division and Bauduin's brigade. From afar, Bachelu, who was advancing toward Piraumont, saw the rout, and also halted in his movement. Alone, Piré's cavalry pressed on against the enemy. At full gallop, they rushed upon Kempt's battalions. They were met by the bayonets of the English battalions and their flanking fires. Again and again did lancers and chasseurs return to the charge—they were utterly powerless.[67]

At this moment Major Baudus, sent by the Emperor, came up to Marshal Ney, who had lost two horses under him and was now standing on foot "at the most threatened point." Baudus acquainted him with the words of Napoleon: "The order delivered to Count d'Erlon must absolutely be executed, no matter in what situation Marshal Ney may be placed. I do not attach any great importance to any event that may occur in his direction, the whole interest centres where I am myself, for I mean to settle matters with the Prussian Army. As for the Prince of La Moscow, he must, if he cannot do better, be content with holding the English Army in check."[68] Ney, maddened and his face crimson, brandished his sword like a madman.[69] He scarcely listened to the words of Baudus, and shouted out that he had just sent to d'Erlon the order to regain Frasnes. Baudus vainly strove to induce him[70] to reconsider this determination. The Marshal left him abruptly, to throw himself into the midst of his routed infantry. He quickly rallied it and led it against Pack's brigade, which was marching to the attack.[70]

From six to seven o'clock, Wellington had been receiving fresh reinforcements: Brunswick's artillery, the brigades under Maitland, and Byng's English guards, Kruse's Nassau brigade.[71] It was now his turn to attack,—and to attack with certainty of success, as was his wont. Maitland and Byng took possession of the Bossu wood; Halkett and Pack, supported by the corps of Brunswick and of Nassau, marched to the right and left of the road leading to Gémioncourt; the English under Kempt, and the Hanoverians with Kielmansegge converged toward Piraumont. The French only yielded the ground which they had conquered but inch by inch, and under repeated attacks. It took more than an hour to drive Jérôme out of the Bossu wood. Foy, repulsed from one position after another as far as Gémioncourt, succeeded in holding his own at this farm for a considerable time. Bachelu only abandoned Piraumont after a severe struggle. When eight o'clock had passed, a battalion under Maitland, sallied forth from the south-western extremity of the wood to recover Pierrepont; the battery of Foy's division arrested its progress with a heavy fire, and Piré's indefatigable lancers charged it, then drove it back in disorder and pursued it to the edge of the Gémioncourt brook; it escaped, however, to the cover of the wood. At the same time the cuirassiers routed the 7th Belgian battalion to the north-west of Pierrepont.[72] Everywhere, heaps of dead bodies and crowds of wounded, bore witness to the fury of the struggle—4,300 French[73] and 4,700 English and Netherlanders.[74]

At nine, with the battle lost, or rather ended without any definite result, since both armies had retaken the same positions they had held in the morning,[75] the 1st Corps appeared from Frasnes.[76]

Having been joined by General Delcambre towards six o'clock, within cannon range from Saint-Amand,[77] d'Erlon had hesitated between obeying the first instructions of the Emperor, or the imperative order of Ney.[78] In spite of the advice of Generals de Salle and Garbé, and to the great discontent of the soldiers, who saw the Prussians, and burned to come to blows with them,[79] he finally resolved on a counter-march. "I decided," he said, "that as he summoned me back, in direct opposition to Napoleon's will, the Marshal must be in extreme peril."[80] But d'Erlon did not reflect that, being only three kilometres from Fleurus, and three leagues from Quatre-Bras, he might have assisted the Emperor most effectually, whereas it was not possible for him to arrive in time to succour Ney. And in fact when he reached Frasnes at nightfall, with his troops "irritated and ashamed at having done nothing during the day,"[81] the Marshal had no longer any need of them.

Count d'Erlon only brought back with him, three of his divisions. The idea having occurred to his mind in the beginning of the counter-march, that the gap between the right wing and the left must be filled, he had left Durutte in sight of Wagnelée with the 4th Infantry division and Jacquinot's cavalry. Having been unable to obtain any definite orders from d'Erlon, excepting the advice "to be prudent," Durutte proceeded slowly between Villers-Perwin and Wagnelée. To the north-west of the latter point, Jacquinot had been skirmishing towards eight o'clock with General de Marwitz's cavalry, which covered Blücher's right. Shortly after, Durutte fell back upon Wagnelée, which he occupied after ousting a feeble rearguard. These positions against the Prussians' flank, were effected in a manner which was neither timely enough, nor thorough enough, to hamper in any way the retreat of the defeated army.[82] And yet at Wagnelée, Durutte could see the Prussians distinctly, as they retired from Le Hameau and La Haye to the heights of Brye. Stolid and unmoved, he allowed them to defile within easy range of his guns. He was paralysed by d'Erlon's instructions as to the necessity of prudence. This inaction of Durutte's so exasperated one of his brigadiers, General Brue, that he cried: "It is unheard of, that we should stand here with folded arms, and witness the retreat of a beaten army, when everything shows we had but to attack, to destroy it." "It is lucky for you," answered Durutte, "that you are not responsible." "Would to God that I were!" retorted Brue. "We should be fighting at this moment."[83]

BOOK II   CHAPTER IV

THE RETREAT OF THE PRUSSIAN ARMY

I. First plans of Napoleon for the day of the 17th of June.
II. The Emperor's orders to Grouchy (between eleven o'clock and half-past eleven).
III. Retreat of the Prussian Army on Wavre.
IV. Movements of Pajol towards Namur, and of Exelmans on Gembloux in pursuit of the Prussian columns.
V. March of Grouchy's army—Bivouac at Gembloux—Grouchy's letter to the Emperor (ten o'clock P.M.).

Section I

On the evening of the battle of Ligny, the Emperor had not thought it possible to pursue the enemy any farther than the Brye-Sombreffe line. The Prussian Army, the right and left wings of which were withdrawing in fairly good order, and which continued to occupy these two villages by detachments, seemed still capable of a serious resistance. The arrival of a reserve corps debouching by the Namur road, was to be feared. And Napoleon was without news from his left. Through the whole of that day, the Prince of La Moscow had not sent him a single despatch.[1] The Emperor knew from indirect information that there had been a battle at Quatre-Bras. But had Marshal Ney been victorious? The presumptions were rather that he had been held in check, if not repulsed, for the orders prescribing a movement on the rear of the Prussian Army had not been executed. There were many reasons against running the risk of a pursuit by night.[2]

The Emperor therefore contented himself with directing Grouchy, who, according to his orders, had come to Fleurus about eleven o'clock, to pursue the enemy at daybreak by the cavalry corps under Pajol and d'Exelmans.[3]

On the 17th of June, toward seven o'clock A.M., Flahaut came back from Frasnes, and brought the account of the battle of Quatre-Bras to the Emperor, who was then at breakfast.[4] At about the same hour, a despatch from Pajol was also received at Imperial headquarters; it was dated from Balâtre, four o'clock A.M., and announced that Pajol was pursuing the enemy, who were in full retreat toward Liège and Namur. He added that he had already made numerous prisoners.[5]

Thus, between seven and eight at the latest, the Emperor was as well-informed with regard to the Prussians, as he was in regard to the English. The former were withdrawing toward Liège and Namur; the latter still held their positions at Quatre-Bras. But was this intelligence sufficiently complete and precise? Was it the bulk of the Prussian Army, or was it merely an isolated corps which was retreating toward Namur? Was it a rearguard which occupied Quatre-Bras, or was it Wellington's whole army? Napoleon considered that he was not sufficiently well-informed to allow of his taking any decided step. Grouchy had come for orders: he was told to wait, and accompany the Emperor to the battlefield of Ligny,[6] where the latter proposed to inspect the troops. At the same time he commanded Soult to write to Ney: "The Emperor is going to the mill of Brye, where the highway leading from Namur to Quatre-Bras, passes. This makes it impossible that the English Army should act in front of you. In the latter event, the Emperor would march directly on it by the Quatre-Bras road, while you would attack it from the front, and this army would be destroyed in an instant. Therefore keep His Majesty informed of whatever takes place in front of you. . . . His Majesty's wishes are, that you should take up your position at Quatre-Bras; but if this is impossible and cannot be accomplished, send information immediately with full details, and the Emperor will act there as I have told you. If, on the contrary, there is only a rearguard, attack it and seize the position. To-day it is absolutely necessary to end this operation, and complete the military stores, to rally scattered soldiers and summon back all detachments."[7]

CHAP. IV *THE RETREAT OF THE PRUSSIAN ARMY* 127

The Emperor's plans for the 17th were therefore limited to the occupation of Quatre-Bras by Ney, and the revictualling of the Army. Undoubtedly, if he had heard that Wellington was still unsupported at Quatre-Bras, he would have taken advantage of this stroke of luck, to march on the English and annihilate them; but he greatly doubted that his wily adversary would commit so great a blunder. Ney would easily drive from Quatre-Bras, the rearguard which still held its own there, and the French Army would remain all day without stirring from its bivouacs.

The morrow of a victory might have been better employed. Nor did Napoleon persist very long in the idea of allowing so long a rest to his troops, and such a respite to the enemy. It may have been his intention up to eight o'clock, as is shown by Soult's letter to Marshal Ney; but at half-past eight, before stepping into his carriage, he was meditating other schemes. He sent an order to Lobau to march the infantry division of Teste, with its battery, on to the Namur road to the assistance of Pajol;[8] he sent a cavalry reconnaissance scouring toward Quatre-Bras to make sure that the English were still occupying that position in force;[9] and left the château de Fleurus himself, resolved not to set his foot there again. Already in the Imperial circle, it was rumoured that the French were about to pursue the Prussians towards Namur, and the English towards Brussels.[10] The Emperor had in fact conceived this double manœuvre, but had not yet settled on the means of executing it. He desired further intelligence. He would wait for it on the battlefield of the day before, and in the midst of his soldiers, to whom he knew he could never show himself too much, or too often.

Shortly before nine, the Emperor drove away.[11] His heavy coach moved at a snail's pace across the furrows, jolting violently. Tired as he was, he alighted, says Grouchy, and mounted his horse. He visited Ligny, Saint-Amand, and the vicinity of La Haye. Innumerable Prussian wounded had remained lying pell-mell among the dead bodies. The Emperor spoke to them, caused money and brandy to be distributed among them, and gave, in their presence, most emphatic orders that they were to be raised from the ground without delay and their wounds dressed with as much care as the French. A Prussian field-officer, horribly mangled, was lying in the same spot where he had fallen the day before. The Emperor hailed a peasant who happened to be close by, and said to him in a solemn voice—" Do you believe in hell ? " The Belgian, terribly overawed, muttered an assent. " Well, if you do not wish to go to hell, take care of this wounded man whom I entrust to you; otherwise God will make you burn; He desires us to be charitable." The injunction, concludes a witness of this scene, was not needless, for, eager as the Belgians were to nurse the French wounded, they were quite as averse to assist the Prussians, who had made themselves hated.[12]

Having arrived at the height of the Bussy mill, the Emperor passed in front of his troops, which were standing in line, unarmed, at the head of their bivouacs. He stopped to congratulate the heads of the corps, the officers, and the men. So tremendous was the cheering on the part of the latter when they saw their Emperor, that the sound was heard at more than three kilometres' distance by General von Gröben, who was in observation before Tilly.[13] Having completed his round, the Emperor dismounted and conversed at some length with Grouchy, and several other generals on the state of public opinion in Paris, on the legislative assembly, and Fouché and the Jacobins. Some among his hearers admired the freedom of mind which he preserved under such grave circumstances, but others were slightly disturbed at seeing him waste his time talking politics, allowing his thoughts to wander on irrelevant topics, instead of on those which should have completely absorbed him. Grouchy did not, however, dare to question the Emperor on the operations he had designed for the day. Already, as they were starting from Fleurus, he had asked for his orders, and Napoleon had answered with some temper— " I will give them to you when I see fit." [14]

Section II

The Emperor was not so absorbed by the intrigues of the liberals in the Chambers, as to forget the enemy. He had received fresh information. First, there was a letter from Ney announcing that the English, posted in front of Quatre-Bras, held the wood of Bossu, Gémioncourt, Piraumont, and numbered eight regiments of infantry and two thousand horses.[15] These masses, the Emperor could no longer doubt, were not a rearguard, but the first line of Wellington, who must be in command there with his army. Shortly after, between ten and eleven o'clock, the officer in command of the reconnaissance sent to Quatre-Bras, returned with tidings that the English still held that point, their left being covered by a force of cavalry, with which he had had an engagement.[16] Information regarding the Prussian retreat also arrived. A despatch from Pajol, announced that in front of Le Mazy on the Namur road, he had captured eight cannon and numerous waggons;[17] a despatch from Exelmans declared that he was marching with his two divisions of dragoons and his mounted batteries on Gembloux, "where the enemy had massed themselves."[18]

It was then about eleven o'clock. The Emperor at last made his final arrangements. He dispatched Lobau to lead the 6th Corps[19] to Marbais, so as to support the attack of Marshal Ney on Quatre-Bras by overpowering the left flank of the English. Drouot received orders to follow up the manœuvre with the whole of the Guard.[20]

The Emperor then said to Marshal Grouchy: "Whilst I am engaged in marching on the English, you must devote your energies to the pursuit of the Prussians. You will have under your orders the corps of Vandamme and of Gérard, the division of Teste, the cavalry corps of Pajol, of Exelmans, and of Milhaud."[21]

From the very first, Grouchy realised the burden, rather than the honour of this mission. In the whole course of his long career he had never held so important a command. He had performed his splendid feats of arms, and won his renown in the capacity of a cavalry general. He had the master-glance of a great leader on the battlefield; he was endowed with a lucid and prompt perception of every weak point, and a power of conceiving sudden and decisive movements. But he was the man of a single hour, a single manœuvre, a single effort. He was a tactician, but only on the spur of the moment, a tactician who was local and special, and he was not fitted for the management and the responsibilities of great strategical operations. What was worse, he was conscious of his inferiority as an army commander, of whom independent action was expected. This feeling naturally paralysed him. Moreover, he knew, or he suspected, that Gérard, and especially Vandamme, whose unbending character he well knew, were both annoyed at being placed under his orders. What authority could he have over lieutenants who lacked confidence in him? Nevertheless, as Marshal of France, he could not decline, nor could he desire to decline, this mission through sheer self-respect, plainly as he foresaw its difficulties and its perils. His secret wish was to refuse it, but he dared not give utterance to this wish.[22]

If, as he asserts, he had observed to the Emperor that the Prussians having commenced their retreat in the night or at daybreak, it would be very difficult to find traces of them and frustrate their designs,[23] Napoleon would not have failed to reply in some such words as these: "Pajol[24] has been marching on the trail of the enemy since three o'clock this morning; as early as five or six on the Namur road, he has captured from them men, baggage, and cannon. Exelmans,[25] who has followed the Prussian infantry mustered at Gembloux, has certainly by this time come into touch with them again. Therefore, even should the vanguards of Blücher's columns have the start of eight or ten hours over you, your cavalry is on the heels of its rearguard." It is even very possible that the Emperor would have added, as Grouchy affirms he did: "All the probabilities lead me to believe that it is on the Meuse that Blücher means to effect his retreat; therefore proceed in that direction."[26] Indeed the reports of Pajol and Exelmans seemed to confirm the assumption that, in accordance with the rules of strategy, the Prussians were withdrawing towards their base of operations.

Grouchy having departed to give his orders, the Emperor reflected that more cavalry were required with the principal part of the army. He determined to take back from his lieutenant the division of Domon, of Vandamme's corps, and Milhaud's corps of cuirassiers. In the absence of the chief of the

CHAP. IV RETREAT OF THE PRUSSIAN ARMY

staff, who was still at the Imperial headquarters in Fleurus,[27] he dictated to Bertrand an order to Grouchy, enjoining the latter to direct these three cavalry divisions on Marbais without delay.[28]

A few minutes later (it might have been half-past eleven or a quarter to twelve) the Emperor resolved to develop, and emphasise in writing, the verbal instructions he had just given to Marshal Grouchy.[29] Soult had not yet arrived. Bertrand again took up his pen and wrote at the dictation of the Emperor: "Repair to Gembloux with the cavalry corps of Generals Pajol and Exelmans, the light cavalry of the 4th Corps, the division of Teste, and the 3rd and 4th Corps of infantry. You will send out scouts in the direction of Namur and Maëstricht, and you will pursue the enemy. Reconnoitre his march and tell me of his movements, that I may penetrate his intentions. I shall move my headquarters to Quatre-Chemins, where the English still were this morning; our communication will then be direct by the Namur road. Should the enemy have evacuated Namur, write to the general in command of the 2nd Miltary Division at Charlemont, to occupy this town by a few battalions of national guards. It is important to discover what Wellington and Blücher mean to do, and whether they meditate uniting their armies to cover Brussels and Liège, by risking the fate of a battle. At all events keep your two infantry corps continually together within the limits of a mile, reserving several outlets for retreat; place cavalry detachments between, so as to be able to communicate with headquarters."[30]

According to this letter, Marshal Grouchy was, first, to concentrate all his forces at Gembloux, the intermediate point between Namur, Liège, and Wavre; second, to reconnoitre by the roads leading to Namur and Maëstricht, the roads by which the enemy would probably retreat, though this was uncertain; third, to follow the traces of the Prussians and to penetrate their designs while pursuing them; fourth, to ascertain whether Blücher's object was to unite with the English. No doubt the Emperor did not indicate as definitely as he ought to have done, the conduct his lieutenant was to adopt in all emergencies; but he could not suspect that Grouchy, who was plainly meant, by his very position on the flank of the army, to cover it against an offensive movement, would not manœuvre so as to act as its shield.

Napoleon had provided for Blücher. He had now to settle with Wellington. He ordered Soult, who had just joined the Imperial staff, to write to Ney that he was to attack the English immediately, while he would himself march to support him.[31] It was now noon. By this time the heads of the columns should have reached Marbais. The Emperor remounted his horse and took the road to Quatre-Bras, upon which were marching, filled with ardour for the fight, Lobau's soldiers, the whole of the Guard, the Domon and Subervie divisions, and Milhaud's cuirassiers.

Section III

Napoleon, Soult, Grouchy, all the staff, believed that the Prussians were retreating toward the Meuse; in point of fact it was toward La Dyle. The night before, at dusk, while the troops were rallying between the Namur road and the Roman way, Zieten, Pirch I., and the other generals, receiving no orders, had hurried to Brye, where they expected to find Blücher. At that very moment the dragoons who had picked up the Field-Marshal on the field of battle, were carrying him into a cottage of Mellery, bruised all over from his fall, and half fainting. His staff had no news of him; they did not know whether he was captive or free, dead or alive. Consternation prevailed; the looks of all eyes were anxiously turned towards Gneisenau, to whom the command fell in the absence of Blücher, through seniority of rank. What course would he adopt? Would he be willing to abandon his lines of communication with Namur, and make a fresh attempt to join the English by a parallel march? Would he resign himself to falling back on his base of operations, thus leaving Wellington alone, face to face with the French army, and overthrowing the plan of campaign settled two months ago? Gneisenau was on horseback in the middle of the road which runs northward of Brye to the Namur road; in the moonlight

CHAP. IV   *RETREAT OF THE PRUSSIAN ARMY*   133

he had some difficulty in studying his map. After a short examination he cried: "Retreat on Tilly and Wavre."[32]

A few days after this, Wellington wrote emphatically to the King of the Netherlands: "It was the decisive moment of the century."[33] In the same strain, German military historians have extolled the retreat on Wavre, and placed it on an equality with the finest conceptions of strategy. This opinion must be discounted in some degree. The decision manifests Gneisenau's firmness under disaster and his comprehensive grasp of the necessities of war; but at the time when he decided on this movement, he certainly did not foresee the tremendous consequences it would bring about. As yet, he had not formed the scheme of joining the English Army to cover Brussels. If he thought that at Wavre the Prussians might once more be in touch with the English, he was by no means certain that this desirable circumstance would come to pass, for everything depended on the line of retreat Wellington might choose, and on many other eventualities besides. At any rate he never expected to be resuming offensive operations again, thirty-six hours after his defeat.[34] It was specially as a position of waiting, as a point of concentration, that he had decided on Wavre, the defence of which was rendered easy by the Dyle. The movement was not so daring as the Germans assert. If Gneisenau did abandon his lines of communication on Namur and Liège, he was about to open fresh ones through Tirlemont and Louvain, on Maëstricht, Cologne, Wezel, Münster, Aix-la-Chapelle. From the morning of the 17th of June, estafettes were dispatched to these various places to order military stores, and a command was transmitted to Liège to bring up the siege artillery to Maëstricht.[35] Gneisenau had therefore not " broken down his bridges behind him," as General von Ollech puts it:[36] rather he had broken them down, but with the certainty of being able to build new ones the very next day.

The corps of Zieten and Pirch I. encamped between Mellery, Tilly, and Gentinnes; three of Jagow's battalions remained as a mainguard at Brye, under the command of Quartermaster-General Grolemann. Notice of the retreat on Wavre was forwarded to Thielmann, who had fallen back with his troops to the north of Sombreffe, and was still continuing to occupy this position with a strong detachment, and to Bülow, who knew already that the battle had been lost, and had halted his army corps on the Roman highway, its head at Baudeset. On his arrival at Mellery, Gneisenau found Blücher lying on a bed of straw in a solitary cottage, sipping a few mouthfuls of milk from time to time.[37]

On the 17th at daybreak the whole Army broke up camp. The corps of Zieten and of Pirch, which had just rallied the three battalions of the mainguard at Brye, reached Wavre by Gentinnes, Villeroux, and Mont-Saint-Guibert; Colonel von Sohr was left temporarily behind Tilly, with two regiments of cavalry. Zieten, who arrived in front of Wavre between eleven and twelve, moved his troops across the left bank of the Dyle and posted them at Bierges and its neighbourhood. Pirch halted his on the right bank; they bivouacked between Aisemont and Sainte-Anne.[38]

From Sombreffe, Thielmann proceeded first to Gembloux. Knowing that his troops were very tired, he took up his position a little beyond this village, and very imprudently remained there without moving, from seven o'clock in the morning till two in the afternoon. At last he resumed his march, passed by Corbais, but did not cross the bridge of Wavre till eight, and then encamped at La Bavette (half a league north of Wavre). The cavalry of Lottum and the division of Borke, which formed the rearguard of this corps, did not arrive in sight of Wavre till long after midnight; they were obliged to bivouac on the right bank of the Dyle.[39]

Bülow, whose troops were drawn up in column on the Roman way, had orders to take up his quarters at Dion-le-Mont (a league to the south-east of Wavre). His progress was very slow. At ten o'clock that night his movement was not yet completed.[40]

Section IV

The retreat of the Prussian Great Guard stationed at Brye, and with them the corps of Pirch and Zieten, completely escaped the notice of the vedettes on watch before the mill at Bussy.

Throughout the morning not a single movement was made by the cavalry outposts, not a reconnaissance, not even a patrol sent out.[41] On the French right toward Tongrinne, the hussars of Pajol showed themselves more vigilant. As early as half-past two in the morning, they had warned their General that the enemy were leaving their positions. Pajol immediately ordered both the regiments which he had kept under his immediate command [42] to saddle and mount, and they dashed up the Namur road in pursuit of the Prussians. Unfortunately he took the wrong direction. He had imagined he was on the track of Thielmann's corps, but he was merely following a few stragglers, a park convoy and a battery which had lost its way.[43] This column he caught up a little beyond Mazy, toward five or six o'clock in the morning; he cut down a squadron of the 7th Uhlans which had joined it, and took both their cannon and their waggons. He did not, however, push on farther up the Namur road than Les Isnes, for he saw nothing more. Very undecided as to what he should do, he sent out reconnaissances in various directions, and halted in person at the junction of the highway and the road to Saint-Denis. Only at midday, misled by false reports and believing that the enemy was retreating, not upon Namur, but on Saint-Denis, to take the road to Louvain, did he start in that direction. Owing to the arrival of the 1st Hussars, who had joined him about nine, and Teste's division, which the Emperor had just sent to him, his forces amounted then to three regiments of cavalry, four regiments of infantry, and two batteries.[44]

The brigade of Berton's dragoons from the corps of Exelmans, had begun to move shortly after Thielmann's rearguard had evacuated Sombreffe. But instead of entering this village and taking the road to Gembloux, Berton struck up the Namur road behind Pajol. However, he marched no farther than the Orneau brook, some peasants having told him that the Prussian army was retreating by Gembloux, and that there were still numbers of troops there. Berton lost no time in acquainting General Exelmans with this news, and he awaited fresh instructions. He should also have informed Pajol, who was 1,500 yards in advance of him. Berton soon received the order to proceed to Gembloux. Accordingly he resumed his march, and arrived before the village at nine o'clock. Prussian vedettes were posted on the left bank of the Orneau; beyond Gembloux the enemy's masses could be perceived, resting.[45]

Soon after, Exelmans, bringing with him three other brigades of cavalry, rejoined Berton. He correctly estimated the Prussians bivouacked behind Gembloux at 20,000. He had himself more than 3,000 mounted dragoons and two mounted batteries; Pajol, at a distance of six kilometres to the right, had 1,400 hussars, 3,000 infantry, and two batteries. But Exelmans never thought of informing him that the Prussians were occupying Gembloux, though this knowledge would have spared his colleague a round-about march of twenty kilometres (there and back) in the direction of Leez.[46] Nor did he make any demonstration to compel the Prussians to reveal their plans. Not a cannon did he fire on these masses, nor even a musket shot against the vedettes. He contented himself with observing the enemy,[47] very half-heartedly, as will be seen later. With unpardonable carelessness, he omitted giving immediate notice to Grouchy, or the Emperor, that he was in presence of one of Blücher's corps.[48]

In spite of all these mistakes, matters were not yet seriously compromised. At midday, at the very moment when the Emperor was reiterating to Grouchy in writing, his orders to pursue the Prussians, the latter found themselves divided and separated. The corps of Zieten and of Pirch were concentrated at Wavre; the corps of Bülow, marching from Baudeset, had not yet passed Walhain;[49] the corps of Thielmann was halting near Gembloux, within range of Exelmans' guns. The inattention of the French vedettes, the carelessness of the officers in command of the mainguard, the time that had been wasted that morning, the false information respecting the line of retreat of the Prussians, all might have been retrieved, if Exelmans had been but vigilant and active, and if Grouchy had hastened the march and had thoroughly understood his mission.

Section V

After leaving the Emperor about half-past eleven [50] near the mill at Bussy, Grouchy sent orders through Colonel de Blocqueville to General Vandamme at Saint-Amand, to dispatch the 3rd Corps promptly to Point-du-Jour, at the intersection of the Namur and Gembloux roads. At the same time he dispatched to Exelmans, in the direction of Gembloux, another aide-de-camp, Captain Bella, with a view to gaining news from him.[51] He then proceeded to Ligny, wishing to give his instructions to Gérard himself. On the way, he came upon Marshal Soult, who was hastening to rejoin the Imperial staff. A short conversation ensued between the two men, which touched merely on the divisions of cavalry which Grouchy was to detach from his army, and direct on Marbais[52] in accordance with the first of Bertrand's orders, which he had just received. When Grouchy had taken his departure, Soult said to one of his aides-de-camp: "It is a mistake to divert so considerable a force from the army which is going to march against the English. Considering the plight into which their defeat has thrown the Prussians, a slight infantry corps, with the cavalry of Exelmans and Pajol, would be quite sufficient to follow the Prussians and observe them."[53] It is true that Soult, who was mistaken as to the extent of the Prussian Army's disorder, censured the too great strength of the detachment placed under Grouchy's orders; but he did not criticise the direction, which had been given for the pursuit of the enemy.

At Ligny Grouchy found Gérard fuming. It seems he was very indignant at not having been awarded the marshal's baton at the close of the battle; and doubtless he was the reverse of delighted at seeing himself placed under the orders of Grouchy.[54] In obedience to the second despatch from Bertrand which had reached him, the Marshal ordered Gérard to follow the 3rd Corps to Gembloux.[55] It is hardly probable, in spite of all that Grouchy may say, that his irritation should have prompted Gérard to postpone the expected movement with any evil design.[56] In order to start his own troops on the march, he was bound to wait until the whole corps of Vandamme had finished defiling. And in those days, the passage of an army corps, which included three infantry divisions, with artillery, engineer and transport corps, would last at least an hour, though the intervals between the various component parts of the column, were less than they are at the present time. If delays arose in the departure of the 4th Corps, the responsibility rested with Grouchy himself. As the 3rd and the 4th Corps were both to follow the same road, and as Vandamme's corps was stationed at Saint-Amand-La-Haye, 2,000 yards in a straight line to the left of Ligny, where the corps of Gérard was encamped, Grouchy should have started Gérard on the march first, not Vandamme. More than an hour would thus have been gained. It has been said that Grouchy desired to humour the pride of Vandamme, whose bad temper he dreaded. What a fine reason to give! Grouchy must then have felt his authority to be feeble indeed! Moreover, for the last two days, on the left wing the 2nd Corps had formed the head of the column instead of the 1st; and in the Guard it was customary for the left to march always in front, nor did the grenadiers ever feel themselves humiliated by this.

The corps of Vandamme plodded on with incredible slowness. From Saint-Amand to Point-du-Jour *via* Ligny and Sombreffe there is a distance of 6,300 yards. Yet the advanced guard of the 3rd Corps, which had broken up camp from Saint-Amand before noon, did not reach Point-du-Jour before three o'clock at the earliest. It would seem from this, that they had marched at the rate of two kilometres an hour.[57]

Grouchy arrived at Point-du-Jour at about the same time as the head of Vandamme's column.[58] What he had been doing from the time he left Gérard at Ligny, less than one league's distance from Point-du-Jour, it is impossible to explain. At any rate it had not occurred to him to send a few squadrons in reconnaissance toward Gentinnes,[59] though the Emperor had said to him, "It is for you to discover the traces of the enemy."[60]

At Point-du-Jour or at Sombreffe, the aide-de-camp Bella returned from his mission to Exelmans and rejoined Grouchy.[61] At Gembloux, between one and two o'clock, Exelmans had entrusted him with a letter to the Marshal, which notified that he was observing the enemy's army collected on the left bank of the Orneau, and that he would follow the Prussians as soon as ever they should begin to march.[62] News of such importance, he should have taken advantage of instantly. Grouchy should have set spurs to his horse and galloped to Gembloux; he should have seen with his own eyes what was going on there, and directed in person, he who was so skilful in handling masses of cavalry, the movements of the four brigades of dragoons. He contented himself with proceeding there at a leisurely pace with the whole of Vandamme's corps, followed by Gérard's men.[63] The troops continued to advance very slowly. There are seven kilometres between Point-du-Jour and Gembloux. Vandamme only arrived there at seven o'clock,[64] Gérard at nine.[65] Notwithstanding the leisurely march of these army corps, they might have reached Gembloux two hours earlier, and, had Grouchy so willed it, they might have simultaneously attacked this village in two separate columns. Gérard should have taken the road to Point-du-Jour, Vandamme might have reached the Roman way above Sombreffe.

Thielmann's corps had departed long ago, and Exelmans, whose vedettes were only separated from the enemy's by the Orneau brook,[66] had allowed the Prussians to escape on his left, without noticing their retreat till it was too late.[67] At two o'clock Thielmann had left his camp at the north of Gembloux; at three only, Exelmans entered the village with his dragoons.[68] The Prussians were not yet very far off. Contact with them, which had been lost through his fault, might yet have been regained. But even now he failed to repair his criminal want of vigilance. Instead of sending out scouts in every direction and with the bulk of his forces following those who should happen first to discover traces of the enemy, he merely marched to take up his position at Sauvenière, a short league to the north of Gembloux, satisfied with having captured near by, a herd of four hundred oxen.[69]

During the afternoon Grouchy displayed but little activity; Exelmans' inertness had completely paralysed him. He put off the pursuit of the Prussians to the following day. Vandamme's corps had hardly accomplished thirteen kilometres, Gérard's barely ten. But though he had two hours of daylight still at his disposal, Grouchy ordered his troops to halt. He ordered Vandamme's infantry to encamp around Gembloux, and Gérard's in the rear of the same village.[70] As an excuse, the Marshal has urged the wretched condition of the roads, and the rain, which fell in torrents.[71] But on the side of Wavre and Dion-le-Mont the roads were no better, yet this did not prevent the Prussians from marching on steadily in the pelting rain.

On the other hand, toward six o'clock, Exelmans had resolved to send Bonnemains' brigade exploring towards Sart-à-Walhain, and the 15th dragoons towards Perwez.[72] Bonnemains advanced beyond Sart-à-Walhain, and sent out scouts toward Nil-Saint-Vincent and Tourinnes. Tourinnes was still held by a Prussian rearguard. After spending an hour in observing this body of infantry, which did not move, the dragoons retraced their steps; they bivouacked at Ernage. Here towards ten o'clock, a peasant informed Bonnemains that the enemy had evacuated Tourinnes and were proceeding towards Wavre. This fact Bonnemains reported. On his return from Perwez, the Colonel of the 15th Dragoons also brought the news, that the retreating Prussian troops were marching on Wavre.[73]

It was late in the night when these reports reached Grouchy. But ever since six o'clock he knew, through a letter from Pajol, that the enemy's column, which seemed at first to be proceeding to Namur, was really marching toward Louvain.[74] Then between seven and eight o'clock he had himself collected much important information at Gembloux. If this information did not agree on every point, if, according to some, the Prussians were marching on Liège or Maëstricht by Perwez, the greater part indicated that they were proceeding by Wavre to join Wellington near Brussels.[75]

Therefore from Pajol's despatch, and from the information afforded by the inhabitants of Gembloux, it seemed clear, in the first place, that the enemy were not retreating on Namur, as had been believed in the morning; in the second, that they were marching either on Louvain, Maëstricht, Liège, or

CHAP. IV RETREAT OF THE PRUSSIAN ARMY   141

Wavre, most likely on the latter point, with the intention of joining the English Army.

Under these circumstances it was in the highest degree advisable to proceed to Wavre, for if the Prussians retreated on Liège, Maëstricht, or Louvain, they would be prevented through their own fault, from taking any part in the proceedings for two days at least, whilst if they succeeded in rallying at Wavre with a view to union with Wellington's army, imminent danger to the Emperor would ensue. Consequently Grouchy's duty, a duty he could have easily accomplished, was at [76] eight o'clock to transfer Exelmans' cavalry to Walhain and Sart-à-Walhain, Vandamme's corps to Ernage, and Gérard's corps to Saint-Géry. By means of this movement, not only would he have established his army a mile nearer Wavre that same evening, but by immediately doubling back the 4th Corps on to the 3rd in order to move it to Saint-Géry, he would have made it possible to march on the next day, without any loss of time, in two parallel columns. Moreover, at Saint-Géry, the 4th Corps would have found itself ready placed to reach rapidly Mont-Saint-Guibert and the bridges of Mousty and Ottignies, and if Grouchy should so decide, at sunrise, to march on Wavre by the left bank of the Dyle.

Grouchy did not grasp the fact that Wavre should be his first aim, and that he ought to sacrifice the doubtful hope of overtaking the Prussians should they prove to be retreating on Liège, to the urgent necessity of covering the flank of the Imperial army, if the former manœuvred to join the English. At ten o'clock P.M. he wrote to the Emperor: "It seems, from all the reports, that on their arrival at Sauvenière, the Prussians divided into two columns; the one must have taken the road to Wavre, the other column seems to have headed towards Perwez. We may therefore, perhaps, infer that one portion is going to join Wellington, and that the centre, which is Blücher's army, is retiring on Liège, another column, with artillery, having effected its retreat on Namur. General Exelmans has orders to push on six squadrons this evening towards Sart-à-Walhain, and three squadrons on Perwez. After their reports, if the bulk of the Prussians retire on Wavre, I shall follow them in that direction, in order that they may not reach Brussels, and in order to separate them from Wellington. If, on the contrary, my information shows that the principal Prussian force has marched upon Perwez, I will proceed by this town in pursuit of the enemy." [77]

Although in this letter, Grouchy declares he is preparing to march either on Wavre or toward Liège, in accordance with the night's news, he takes no steps to further the first of these two movements. His orders for the next day—orders to Exelmans and Vandamme to proceed to Sart-à-Walhain; orders to Pajol to march from Le Mazy to Grand-Leez; orders to Gérard to follow the 3rd Corps to Sart-à-Walhain and to send his cavalry to Grand-Leez, "the enemy retreating on Perwez" [78]—testify that, unmindful of Wellington and neglecting Wavre, it was in the direction of Liège, that he persisted in seeking the enemy.

BOOK II CHAPTER V

THE RETREAT OF THE ENGLISH ARMY

I. Exchange of despatches between Wellington and Blücher (morning of the 17th of June)—Retreat of the English (ten o'clock).
II. Arrival of Napoleon at Quatre-Bras — still occupied by the English cavalry (two o'clock).
III. Brisk pursuit of the English rearguard personally conducted by Napoleon —Engagement at Genappe—Cannonade at Mont-Saint-Jean (seven o'clock).
IV. Night in camp.
V. Napoleon's indecision—Letter from Blücher to Wellington—Orders of Napoleon (night of the 17th to the 18th of June).

Section I

In the direction of Quatre-Bras, the French and English remained motionless in their respective positions during the morning of the 17th of June.[1] Not till past nine, did Ney learn the result of the battle of Ligny.[2] As for Wellington, he had remained all night without news from his allies. The last message which he had received from Blücher the evening before, announced that the Field-Marshal had resumed the offensive and that "all was well."[3] A little later Gneisenau had dispatched an officer to inform him of the retreat; but this officer, seriously wounded on the way by French skirmishers, had not been able to fulfil his mission.[4] Wellington thought that the action, undecided as it had been at Ligny, would be resumed the next day along the whole line;[5] he encamped his troops at Quatre-Bras and summoned up fresh reinforcements. The cavalry of Lord Uxbridge arrived in the evening and during the night; on the morning of the 17th the brigade of Ompteda, the divisions of Clinton and Colville, and the artillery reserve also marched off to join[6] Wellington, who, having slept that night at Genappe, returned to Quatre-Bras at daybreak. Anxious to receive news from Blücher, for a rumour had reached Genappe that the Prussians were beaten,[7] he sent his aide-de-camp, Colonel Gordon, to his left, with a detachment of the 10th Hussars. Gordon, avoiding the French vedettes of Marbais, pushed on as far as Tilly, where he had the good fortune still to find General Zieten with the rearguard of the 1st Corps. He learnt from him that the Prussian Army was retreating on Wavre. Returning to Quatre-Bras at half-past seven, he delivered this intelligence to Wellington, who, in order to relieve his impatience, was pacing with long strides up and down the Charleroi road in front of Quatre-Bras.[8] This indeed was a sudden turn of events! Wellington could no longer remain at Quatre-Bras, where he was exposed to a combined attack of Ney on his front, and Napoleon on his left. Much perturbed, he at first thought of retreating then and there: "Old Blücher," he said, " has had a damned good licking and gone back to Wavre, eighteen miles. We must follow his example. I suppose they will say in England we have been thrashed too! I cannot help it."[9]

Müffling observed that the situation did not seem so desperate: "The Prussian Army," he said, "having marched on Wavre, you can easily resume your connection with it and concert operations together. Fall back on some point parallel to Wavre; there you will have news from the Field-Marshal, and information as to the state of his troops, and you can then take steps according to circumstances."[10]

Wellington determined to occupy the eminence of Mont-Saint-Jean, a strong defensive position which he had examined the year before, when on his journey to Brussels.[11] But ought he to decamp immediately, or should he wait till his troops had taken some food, at the risk of a hot engagement in his rear? From time to time there were a few shots between the outposts, but Ney's troops did not show the slightest sign of moving: "I know the French," said Müffling. "They won't attack before they have made their soup." Wellington decided the retreat should not commence before ten o'clock. To Lord Hill, he sent orders to lead back to

Waterloo, the divisions which were marching on Quatre-Bras. Then, after looking through his mail which had just arrived from Brussels, he wrapped himself in his cloak and fell asleep. When he awoke towards nine o'clock, he threw a glance over the French positions. Seeing that Ney made no preparations for attack, he said: "Are the French retreating? It is not at all impossible."[12]

At this moment a Prussian officer, Lieutenant von Massow, arrived from Mellery. He had been dispatched by Gneisenau to inform Wellington of the intended concentration of the whole Prussian Army on Wavre, and to inquire what he meant to do. In presence of Müffling, the Duke answered to this effect: I am going to take up my position at Mont-Saint-Jean. There I will wait for Napoleon and give him battle, if I may hope to be supported even by a single Prussian corps. But if this support is denied me, I shall be compelled to sacrifice Brussels and take up my position behind the Scheldt. Massow set off immediately for the Prussian headquarters.[13]

The English commenced their movement. The Divisions of Cook and Picton, the Dutch-Belgians under Perponcher, the Division of Alten, finally the corps of Brunswick, passed in succession up the Brussels road. The numerous squadrons of Lord Uxbridge had deployed on the first line so as to conceal, then cover this retreat. By one o'clock this cavalry corps was alone still in position.[14] As Ney allowed plenty of leisure to Lord Uxbridge, the latter seated himself with his aide-de-camp on the edge of the road. To Uxbridge's remark that the French were curiously slow in attacking, the aide-de-camp retorted laughingly, "They are eating."[15] Shortly after, Uxbridge was advised that masses were perceived marching toward the left. The Imperial advanced guard was approaching by the Namur road.

Section II

From the Bussy mill near Ligny, the Emperor, with Domon's light cavalry and Milhaud's cuirassiers, had proceeded to Marbais, whither he had previously dispatched the corps of Lobau, the cavalry division of Subervie, and the Guard.[16]

Having arrived there shortly before one o'clock, he rested a few minutes, expecting news from Ney or the sound of cannon.[17] Becoming impatient, he determined to march himself on Quatre-Bras. About half a league from this point the scouts of the 7th Hussars,[18] who were scouring the country in front of the army, fell back before the English vedettes. The Emperor drew up his troops in order of battle, the artillery in the centre, the infantry in the second line, Milhaud's cuirassiers to the right, the light cavalry of Jacquinot, Subervie, and Domon to the left.[19] In the meantime he detached toward Frasnes, in order to communicate with Ney, the 7th Hussars, who began firing on the red lancers of the Guard, mistaking them for the English. The scouts had captured an English vivandière. Ushered into the presence of the Emperor, the woman declared that Lord Uxbridge's cavalry only, was still at Quatre-Bras, being charged to cover the retreat of the army. As for the French who had fought the day before, she knew nothing about them; she thought they had recrossed the Sambre.[20] Very much provoked that Wellington should thus have evaded his grasp, the Emperor determined at any rate to get as many of the fine English cavalry as possible. The cuirassiers, the chasseurs, the lancers, the mounted batteries dashed off at full trot. He himself in his impatient haste, out-distanced them with the service squadrons.[21]

Lord Uxbridge at the first notice had hurried up to the Namur road. He found Wellington there. The French were still very far distant, and only a glitter of steel could be perceived. "Those are their bayonets," said Wellington. But with the help of General Vivian's field-glass, he recognised the cuirassiers. After exchanging a few words with Lord Uxbridge, he decided to beat a retreat. He entrusted Uxbridge with the command of the rearguard and set off.[22] Whilst the brigades of English dragoons filed on behind him up the Brussels road, Vivian's and Grant's hussars deployed perpendicularly towards the Namur road, the mounted batteries being posted on their front.[23]

It was a little after two o'clock.[24] Great black clouds, driven by a furious wind, were covering the sky. As the storm came from the north-west, Quatre-Bras was already plunged in shadow while it was still fine at Marbais. Lord Uxbridge rode on horseback near the light battery of Captain Mercer, whose guns were winding up the Namur road. Suddenly from a dip of the ground, a horseman was seen to emerge, followed by a small escort. His face, his figure, his horse, lit up from behind, stood out in black relief—a statue of bronze set on a background illuminated with floods of sunlight. From the mere silhouette, Lord Uxbridge at once recognised Napoleon. "Fire! fire!" he said, "and aim well."[25] The cannon thundered; the Emperor called forward a mounted battery of the Guard. The English, considering they were in too great danger to continue this artillery duel, limbered up. The horsemen of Jacquinot and Subervie made a rush forward. Both the hussars and gunners of the enemy fled in disorder, through blinding flashes of lightning and the rain of the storm which now began to fall. "It seemed," said Mercer, "as if the first cannon-shot had burst open the clouds."[26]

Marshal Ney had not yet given the slightest sign of life. The Emperor sent orders direct, to the commanders of the corps in position before Frasnes. D'Erlon appeared at last with the head of his column of infantry.[27] As the Emperor reproached him for having arrested his movement against the Prussian right on the previous evening, he answered that, being under the direct command of Marshal Ney, he had been obliged to obey the orders of his immediate chief. The Emperor, feeling time was too precious to be wasted in idle discussion, ordered Count d'Erlon to take the 1st Corps and instantly follow the cavalry on the Brussels road.[28] Shortly after this, Ney arrived. In his letter of eight o'clock, Napoleon had already expressed his displeasure at Ney's extremely unskilful operations of the previous day.[29] He did not return to the subject, but he very drily expressed his surprise that the orders he had forwarded to him that very morning, relative to the occupation of Quatre-Bras had not yet been executed. Ney excused himself on the ground that he believed Wellington's entire army was before him.[30] In that case the Marshal might at least have ascertained the fact, by sending out a vigorous offensive reconnaissance. Now he had not pushed forward a single squadron beyond his lines. He had proved as negligent, as heedless, as apathetic as on the morning of the 16th and the evening of the 17th.

It is true that Marshal Ney, through the carelessness of the chief of the staff, had remained all night in complete ignorance of the battle of Ligny. He could not have taken the offensive, until he had received the order of eight o'clock in the morning. Moreover, this order was conditional. Even had Ney attacked then, it was likely the English would have effected their retreat with no more confusion than before, thanks to the masses of their cavalry. They would merely have started an hour sooner, and Ney would have occupied Quatre-Bras at noon: a sterile result, indeed. All the same, there would have been the chance, that Wellington, under a vigorous assault, might have decided to fight in his positions. And this action Marshal Ney had done nothing whatever to bring about. For this the Emperor reproved him. Far more bitterly, no doubt, did he reproach himself for not having transferred, as early as seven o'clock that morning, the Guard and Lobau's corps from Ligny to Quatre-Bras. He had thus let slip the opportunity of annihilating the English Army. Wellington, with nearly all his troops still in position, with his line of retreat on Genappe endangered, his left overpowered by Napoleon, his front attacked by Ney, would have been forced to accept a battle which he would have virtually lost before it began.[31]

Whilst speaking to Ney at Quatre-Bras, the Emperor had the vision of this lost victory before his eyes. He wished to seize it still. He imagined that by hastening his march, he might be able to join Wellington and compel him to make a stand. Finally, he gave orders that Reille, then Lobau, then the Guard should rapidly follow the 1st Corps and the light cavalry up the Brussels road; they were to be flanked by the chasseurs of Domon and the cuirassiers. He himself, with the service squadrons and the mounted battery of the Guard, galloped to the head of the column to kindle fresh vigour in the pursuit.[32]

Section III

This pursuit was carried on at the pace of a "fox-hunt," as Captain Mercer terms it. The English rearguard fled in the greatest disorder: hussars and gunners galloped pell-mell, "going like mad," blinded by the flashes of lightning and lashed by the rain, which was falling so thick and so fast that the colour of the uniforms could not be distinguished at a distance of five or six paces. Lord Uxbridge acted as cornet. He galloped along the column, crying to his men: "Faster, faster! for God's sake gallop, or you will be taken." The lancers of Alphonse de Colbert were at times so close on the heels of the English hussars, that through the trampling of the horses and the roar of the thunder, their laughter and their jeers reached the ears of the fugitives.[33]

The English crossed the Dyle[34] by the bridge of Genappe and by another bridge higher up; a few of them by the ford. North of Genappe a curtain of hills slopes gently upward. In order to arrest in some slight degree, the mad pace of the pursuit, half-way up, in two lines, Lord Uxbridge posted the bulk of his cavalry and two batteries. When the 1st Lancers debouched from the village close on the heels of Vivian's brigade, they were saluted by a volley of grape shot, then charged in turn by the 7th English Hussars and the 1st Regiment of *Life Guards*. The lancers had no difficulty in breaking through the hussars; but they were repulsed as far as Genappe by the Guards, who streamed in behind them. Uxbridge himself led this charge. In the narrow, winding street, which at that time formed nearly the whole of the village, a hand-to-hand struggle began, man to man, and the lancers thus lost all the advantage of their long arms. Up in the midst of Genappe the 2nd Lancers, debouching in groups, or rather lines four deep, from the cross lanes, fell upon the Guards and forced them back beyond the first houses. On the Brussels road, the English suffered another charge on the part of Marbot's hussars, who had turned the village on the right. Thrown into disorder, they regained the heights under the protection of their artillery.[35]

At this moment the Emperor appeared from Genappe, with his service squadrons and a mounted battery. Mounted on "Désirée," a very swift white mare, he had galloped from Quatre-Bras to join the head of the column. His gray coat, of very thin cloth, a sort of dust-coat, was soaked. Water was streaming on to his boots. The clasps of his hat snapped under the violence of the rain, the flaps had fallen over in front and behind; he appeared with the same head-gear, as Basile wears in the *Barbier de Séville*. He superintended the placing of the guns in the batteries himself, crying to the gunners in tones of anger and hatred: "Fire! fire! these are the English!"[36]

In the street of Genappe, Colonel Sourd of the 2nd Lancers, surrounded by several Life Guardsmen, had had his right arm hacked by six sabre strokes. Larrey amputated it on the spot. During the operation, Sourd dictated this letter to the Emperor who had just created him general: "The greatest favour you could grant me is to allow me to remain colonel of my regiment of lancers, which I hope to lead again to victory. I refuse the rank of general. May the great Napoleon forgive me! The rank of colonel is everything to me." Then with the fresh bandages on his bleeding stump, he remounted his horse and galloped all along the column to join his beloved regiment.[37] In the armies of the Republic and the Empire there were many men of the same stamp.[38]

After Genappe, the march slackened considerably. The English were in quite as great haste, and the French had not lost their ardour, but under the continuous action of the pouring rain, the ground was becoming more and more difficult. On the road reserved for the artillery and the infantry, the water rushed like a torrent: in the fields, the horses sank up to their knees.[39]

Towards half-past six,[40] Napoleon reached the heights of La Belle Alliance with the head of the column.[41] Brunswick's infantry in the most hideous disorder, and the rearguard of the English cavalry, crossed the valley which separates these heights from the plateau of Mont-Saint-Jean. Marbot's hussars followed them. They were beginning to blaze away again, when from the edge of the plateau a battery of the enemy began cannonading the bulk of the cavalry which had halted near "La Belle Alliance." The rain had ceased, but the atmosphere was still saturated with damp. Through the veil of mist, the Emperor thought he distinguished a host of cavalry and infantry. Was this the whole of Wellington's army, ready to fight a battle, or was it merely a strong rearguard which had taken up its position in order to protect the retreat? The Emperor determined to ascertain the truth. Under his orders, four field batteries opened fire while Milhaud's cuirassiers deployed as if to charge. The enemy's cannon thundered back with increased violence; and the English unmasked. The whole of their army was there.[42]

Section IV

Night drew on, and nearly the whole of the infantry was still very far behind.[43] The Emperor put a stop to the firing.[44] During the cannonade he had remained near La Belle Alliance, exposed to the cannon-balls which Captain Mercer, who had recognised him, was directing on the staff.[45] He himself indicated to the troops, the different positions on which they were to bivouac.[46] D'Erlon's corps (excepting Durutte's division, which joined the next morning) posted itself between Plancenoit and the Monplaisir farm, its front and its right flank being covered by Jacquinot's cavalry. Milhaud's cuirassiers, the light cavalry of Domon and of Subervie, and the cavalry of the Guard, bivouacked in the second line on the height of Rossomme. The corps of Reille and Lobau and Kellermann's cuirassiers, drew up at Genappe and in the vicinity.[47] After crossing this village at sunset, the mounted Guard left the highway, which was encumbered with artillery and transport trains, and struck across country in an attempt to reach the Imperial headquarters. Only two or three regiments arrived near by, in the village of Glabais between eleven o'clock and twelve. The other regiments having gone astray, the men broke from their ranks and wandered all over the country in quest of farms and isolated houses. They did not rejoin their colours till the next morning.[48]

A wretched night for a bivouac! The troops arrived in

the darkness, exhausted with fatigue, streaming with water, and "not a man among them but carried two or three pounds of mud clinging to his boots." Some were walking barefoot, for their shoes had stuck in the greasy earth of the ploughed fields. Now they were to lie down amid stalks of rye, a yard and a half in height and drenched with rain. "It was like stepping into a bath." To erect any shelter was out of the question; the wood which had been cut in the thickets of Vardre, Le Chantelet, Le Caillou, was needed for making the camp fires, which were lighted with great difficulty, kept going out continually, and gave out more smoke than flame in the end. Only now and then was there any pause in the rain. For the sake of receiving a little less water and obtaining a little more warmth, soldiers gathered into groups of ten or twelve and slept standing, closely huddled against one another. Others, more stoical or more exhausted, lay down flat in the mud. There are times in war when one could sleep on bayonets. After picketing their horses, a number of men got back into the saddle and fell asleep, wrapped in their big cloaks, bending down over their horses' necks. The four days' rations of bread carried in each knapsack were consumed. Men were suffering from tortures of hunger. In most of the regiments, the distributions were only made in the middle of the night and even in the morning. The discontent of the soldiers may be imagined, as well as the unrestrained plunder which the Belgian peasants suffered at their hands.[49]

The Guard, which had spent part of the night wandering through the fields and through the lanes, was specially furious. Never had the "grumblers" grumbled so loudly. Murmurs and oaths were coupled with imprecations on the generals; the men accused them of having wilfully led them astray and stranded them in these unknown ways. And under the spell of their recollections of 1814, these old warriors would declare, "This smacks of treason." But neither in the Guard nor in the line was there a sign of demoralisation or even discouragement; they cherished in their hearts still the hope of vengeance and faith in victory. In spite of all and above all, it was on the English, the red-coats, the "goddams," that all the blame fell, on account of this night's misery in the rain, without bread and without fire. And many were the vows made to make them pay dear for this on the morrow.[50]

The English did not fare much better on the plateau of Mont-Saint-Jean. However, the infantry which had begun its retreat as early as four, had reached its positions while it was still light. The head divisions had even arrived before the storm. The soldiers settled down on ground which was still dry, made themselves comfortable straw beds out of the long stalks of rye which they beat down, and proceeded to light the fires; the commissariat having been well managed, they were able to prepare their meal in peace. The cavalry of Lord Uxbridge, which did not take to its bivouacs before night, alone had to suffer severely from the inclemency of the weather.[51]

Section V

The Emperor having retraced his footsteps, put up for the night in the pretty little farm of "Le Caillou," situated by the side of the road, 2,700 yards from "La Belle Alliance."[52] The farmer Boucqueau and his people had fled to avoid the doings of the Brunswickers, who, as they passed on their retreat, had fired shots at the windows, broken in the door, and finally plundered the house. The Emperor had a large fire lit; while he waited for his baggage he dried himself as best he might in the glow of the hearth.[53]

Towards nine o'clock, General Milhaud advised him verbally, that in his march from Marbais to Quatre-Bras, his right flank had recognised a column of Prussian infantry which from Tilly, had withdrawn toward Wavre.[54] It is possible that the Emperor may have written immediately to Grouchy, from whom he had not yet received any news, to warn him of the direction of this column, and enjoin him to march to Wavre so as to be nearer the Imperial Army. But whether the order was sent on or not, it certainly did not reach its destination. The officer who carried the order did not reach the Marshal, either on account of his being captured or killed on the way by the Prussian scouts, or for some other reason.[55]

Be this as it may, it does not seem that the Emperor was alarmed by Milhaud's report. Ever since noon he had manœuvred, on the assumption that Blücher's army was either retreating on Namur or Maëstricht, or withdrawing northward to join the English Army in front of Brussels.[56] Therefore the march of a Prussian column on Wavre would only confirm one of his previsions. Of course this column might be nothing more than a wandering troop cut off from its line of retreat. But if things came to the worst, and all the Prussian corps sought to concentrate on Wavre, Grouchy could get up to them in time to fight them. Should they make straight for Brussels up the road from Wavre to this town, there was nothing to be feared from them for the present. As for supposing that Blücher, thirty-six hours after a defeat and with 33,000 French at his heels, would risk a flank march from Wavre on Plancenoit or Ohain, such a hypothesis never entered the Emperor's mind.[57]

On the evening of the 17th of June, he was far less concerned with the movements of the Prussians, than with the schemes of the English. He feared that Wellington would merely halt at Mont-Saint-Jean, and manage to slip away in the night to take up, before Brussels, a position where the Prussians could join him easily. If such was the enemy's aim, the Emperor considered the game greatly endangered, for, sure as he was of exterminating the English Army at Mont-Saint-Jean, he was quite as keenly conscious of the great peril he ran, in debouching from the forest of Soignes in front of both armies together.[58] However, all this was mere conjecture for the Emperor, as he was still uncertain as to whether the bulk of the Prussians were withdrawing toward Brussels or toward Liège.[59] And amid the tide of conflicting thoughts which surged through his brain, dominated the hope that, even in the event of Blücher's manœuvring so as to get nearer Wellington, the Prussian Army, ruined, cut up, demoralised by the defeat of Ligny, would be in no condition to fight again for several days.[60]

The Emperor's doubts concerning the schemes of Wellington were most justifiable, for, until a late hour of the night, the Duke himself did not yet know what course to adopt.[61] It depended on Blücher. As he had said that morning to Lieutenant von Massow, Gneisenau's orderly officer, he would accept battle at Mont-Saint-Jean, provided he had the assurance of being supported by at least one of the four Prussian Corps. Otherwise he would continue his retreat.[62]

But during the last twelve hours, Wellington was without any news whatever from Prussian headquarters. Blücher, it is true, had been informed through Massow (who returned to him by noon) of the eventual plan of the English General, and he was burning to co-operate with him.[63] But before formally undertaking to second Wellington on the morrow, Blücher was obliged to wait, till his army was concentrated and revictualled.[64] Things do not proceed so quickly. In the afternoon of the 17th of June, only the 1st and the 2nd Corps were mustered at Wavre; and they still lacked ammunition and food. The main park of artillery had been sent by Gembloux to Wavre; but could it avoid the French cavalry? As for the 3rd and 4th Corps they might be followed so closely by the French, that they might be forced to stand and fight.[65]

Towards five o'clock, as the noise of the Genappe cannonade was growing fainter, the main park arrived. Three hours later, the 3rd Corps passed through Wavre on its way to La Bavette. Finally, at eleven o'clock, a report from Bülow announced that he was at Dion-le-Mont with the head of the 4th Corps.[66] Blücher received at the same moment a despatch from Müffling, confirming the news that Wellington had finally taken up his line of battle at Mont-Saint-Jean.[67] Gneisenau still hesitated. "If the English should be defeated," he objected judiciously enough, "they themselves would be utterly destroyed." Blücher succeeded at last in convincing his all-powerful chief of the staff. "Gneisenau has given in!" he said with a triumphant expression to Colonel Hardinge,[68] the English military attaché. "We are going to join the Duke." To Wellington he wrote: "Bülow's corps will set off marching to-morrow at daybreak in your direction. It will be immediately followed by the corps of Pirch. The 1st and 3rd Corps will also hold themselves in readiness to proceed towards you. The exhaustion of the troops, part of which have not yet arrived, does not allow of my commencing my movement earlier."[69]

This letter reached Wellington toward two o'clock in the morning,[70] at his headquarters at Waterloo, a village situated a league in the rear of the first English lines. Now that he could rely on the assistance of the Prussians, Wellington determined to accept battle.[71] Fortune had once more favoured him, but he had not the less remained too long expectant. The failure of news from Blücher ought to have made him conclude, that the Prussians would not be able to second his army, and though he would fight only if he had their support, at one o'clock in the morning, he had not yet made any arrangements for retreating.[72]

At the very moment when Wellington had formed his resolutions, Napoleon divined them. He had retired to bed rather late at Le Caillou. But first, with the probability of a great battle on the morrow, he had dictated the order of battle.[73] The mail from Paris had also been read to him, and he had dictated several letters, " necessitated," says Davout, "by the annoyances and difficulties resulting from the intrigues of the Chambers of Representatives." [74] And when he had hardly slept at all, the Emperor rose about one o'clock in the morning, to make the entire round of his outposts. His only companion was General Bertrand. Rain had set in again, and was falling in torrents. When Napoleon had gained the crest of La Belle Alliance, the English bivouacs appeared before him within easy cannon range. Complete silence reigned, the allied army seemed wrapped in slumber. On the horizon the forest of Soignes, upon which, through a veil of rain and smoke, the innumerable camp fires lit by the soldiers cast their reflections, was glowing red as if it were burning. The Emperor decided that the English would keep to these positions. Had they contemplated retreating in the night, or even at sunrise as he feared, their camp would already have been astir with preparations for the start. The Emperor returned to Le Caillou just as the first streaks of dawn appeared.[75]

There he found the letter which Grouchy had written him at Gembloux the day before, at ten o'clock in the evening. The estafette had arrived at Le Caillou about two o'clock.[76] This despatch announced that the Prussians seemed to be withdrawing in two columns, the one toward Ligny, the other toward Wavre, and that, should the march of these masses be confirmed by the night reports, Grouchy "would follow them so as to separate them from Wellington."[77] Trusting to his lieutenant's word, the Emperor did not think it necessary, for the present, to send any fresh instructions.[78] It does not follow, however, that he was right.

Shortly after, spies, then the officers he had sent off reconnoitring, and some Belgian deserters, came in and confirmed by their various accounts the Emperor's previsions. The English did not stir. The battle would take place at Mont-Saint-Jean.[79]

The Emperor believed he had the victory in his grasp. The pale sun which pierced through the mists "was to shine on the ruin of the English Army."[80] However, Napoleon was filled with anxiety, at being unable to attack as soon as he wished, and as he ought to do.[81] The day before, in the doubtful hope that Wellington would wait for him at Mont-Saint-Jean, he had indicated the position in battle of the various army corps, so as to be able to commence the action at an early hour.[82] Unfortunately, the storm had soaked the ground to a degree, that in the opinion of the artillery generals made it impossible to manœuvre the guns. The rain, it is true, had just ceased; but several hours would be needed to dry and harden the ground.[83] Towards five o'clock the Emperor, judging, no doubt, that it was no longer necessary to occupy the positions for the battle so early, and that it was better to allow the troops time to rally, to clean their arms and make their soup, determined to wait till nine before beginning the attack. He dictated to Soult this order, which modified that of the evening before: "The Emperor orders the army to be ready to attack at nine o'clock in the morning. The commanders of each army corps will rally their troops, will see that their arms are put in order, and will allow their soldiers to make their soup. They will also make the men eat, so that at nine o'clock precisely each man may be ready and standing in battle array, each with his own artillery and his own ambulances, in the same position of battle which the Emperor indicated in his order of last night."[84]

BOOK III
WATERLOO

BOOK III CHAPTER I

BLÜCHER AND GROUCHY

I. Dispositions and movements of the Prussian Army on the morning of the 18th of June—Field-Marshal Blücher leaves Wavre (eleven o'clock).
II. Dispositions of Grouchy.
III. Discussion between Gérard and Grouchy at Walhain (midday).

Section I

FAITHFUL to his promise,[1] Blücher had made his arrangements to second his allies vigorously. Orders dispatched in the night, enjoined Bülow to march at daybreak on Chapelle-Saint-Lambert, at a distance of seven kilometres in a straight line from Mont-Saint-Jean, and Pirch I. to follow this movement of Bülow's corps. Once at Chapelle-Saint-Lambert the generals would act according to circumstances. Should the action not seem to have commenced seriously, they would remain in position, concealing their presence; in the contrary event, they were to attack the right flank of the French army.[2] As for the corps of Zieten and of Thielmann, they were to remain in their cantonments on the left bank of the Dyle, till further notice. Blücher intended to lead them also to the support of the English; but before taking such a determination he must wait for the morning's reports.[3] He could not completely strip the line of the Dyle, without having positive information as to the march, and the forces of the French corps signalled at Gembloux.

Well-planned as this project was, it had one radical defect. As Bülow's corps had not been in the action at Ligny, Blücher wished to use it first. To this design, which was to a certain extent legitimate, he sacrificed the rapidity of his movements. The corps of Zieten and Thielmann were bivouacking at Bierges and La Bavette (eight or nine kilometres from Chapelle-Saint-Lambert); the corps of Pirch and of Bülow were at Aisemont and Dion-Le-Mont (ten and fourteen kilometres from Chapelle-Saint-Lambert). Manifestly the troops which were nearest to the battlefield should have been moved there first, and meanwhile those which were more distant might have come up and occupied the line of the Dyle temporarily. At any rate it was the duty of the staff to have foreseen that Pirch's corps would have to remain without moving, until Bülow's corps had defiled. Therefore it was for Pirch to form the head of the column. Had this course been taken, half the Prussian Army would have found itself concentrated at Chapelle-Saint-Lambert long before midday.

The issue was very different indeed. The Losthin division, Bülow's vanguard, only arrived before Wavre at seven o'clock in the morning. Much time was lost in crossing the bridges, and climbing the main street of the village, which was narrow and very steep. As it debouched, a violent fire unexpectedly broke out in the street and blocked the passage. The bulk of Bülow's corps was compelled to wait till the fire was extinguished. In this way the march of the 4th Corps was delayed for more than two hours; the rearguard division did not reach the vicinity of Chapelle-Saint-Lambert till towards three o'clock.[4] The 2nd Corps (Pirch) was under arms by five, but as they had to let the troops of the 4th Corps defile first, the troops remained at the head of their bivouacs, stamping on the ground where they stood, until past midday. At two o'clock the half of Pirch's corps was still on the farther side of the Dyle.[5]

Between seven and eight o'clock in the morning, Count Gröben, returning from the outposts, had reported that the French stationed at Gembloux had not yet begun to move, and that their forces, in his estimation, did not amount to more than 15,000 men, or thereabouts. "I cannot affirm positively," he added, " that the French are not more numerous, but, were there 30,000 of them, a single one of our army corps would suffice to guard the line of the Dyle. It is at Mont-Saint-Jean that the fate of the battle will be decided. We must send as many men there as possible." Blücher was of the same opinion; but Gneisenau and Grolemann were still averse to stripping the Dyle too much. "The question," said Grolemann, with the formal approval of Gneisenau, "will be settled at noon; if by that time, the enemy has not appeared before Wavre in too great force, the 1st Corps will follow the 2nd and the 4th Corps, and perhaps the 3rd Corps will march as well."[6] Meanwhile Blücher wrote to Müffling: "I request you to say in my name to the Duke of Wellington that, ill as I am, I will put myself at the head of my troops and fall on the right wing of the enemy, as soon as Napoleon begins the battle. Should the day go by without an attack on the part of the French, I propose that we should both attack them together to-morrow."[7]

Before dispatching this letter, which had been dictated to him by Blücher, the aide-de-camp, Nostiz, showed it to Gneisenau. The day before, and on the morning of the battle of Ligny, the latter was doubtful of the promises of Wellington, whom he regarded as a "master knave."[8] The day of the 16th of June, when the Duke had sent to Brye, neither a man nor a cannon, had confirmed and increased these suspicions of Gneisenau. He was afraid lest the English should fall back on Brussels without fighting. In that case the Prussian Army would find itself exposed to a disaster, liable to be surprised in the very act of marching, and attacked by Napoleon in the front, by Grouchy's corps[9] on the flank, or in the rear. To Blücher's letter Gneisenau added this postscript: "General von Gneisenau is of one mind with the Field-Marshal; but he begs Your Excellency to penetrate to the innermost thoughts of Wellington, and to ascertain whether he really entertains the firm resolution of fighting in his present positions, or whether he intends making mere demonstrations, which may involve our army in the greatest peril."[10]

Time drew on; Blücher, ever eager, wished to be on the spot for the first cannon shot. Leaving Gneisenau free to decide on the movements of the remaining army corps, he left Wavre at eleven o'clock to join Bülow near Chapelle-Saint-Lambert. "In spite of all I was suffering from my fall," he said later, "I would rather have been tied to my horse than have missed the battle!"[11]

Section II

If Grouchy, on the evening of the 17th of June, had still been able to preserve any doubts as to the concentration of the Prussian Army on Wavre,[12] the intelligence which reached him during the night was of a nature to dissipate them completely. Between eleven o'clock and midnight, he received a report from General Bonnemains, and another from the colonel of the 15th dragoons, both announcing that the Prussians were marching on Wavre.[13] Towards three o'clock in the morning news from Walhain or Sartà-Walhain advised him that, in the course of the preceding day, three army corps had been perceived passing by in the direction of Wavre, and that, according to what both officers and men were reported to have said, these troops were going to mass themselves near Brussels to give battle.[14]

All these informations, which confirmed those of the previous evening, only threw a confused light upon Grouchy's mind; he no longer doubted that the enemy had marched to Wavre, but, rashly taking the words of the Prussians literally, he imagined their army was merely halting there, not carrying out a strategical concentration, and that it was going to file on towards Brussels by the main road.[15] He was aware that the Emperor had expected a battle against the English, before the forest of Soignes,[16] yet it did not occur to him that, instead of gaining Brussels, the Prussians might join their allies directly by a short lateral march. He did not see that, in order to prevent this junction, it was necessary not to follow the Prussians by Walhain or Corbais, but to pursue them in flank by Saint-Géry and Mousty. There was everything to gain and no peril to incur, by crossing the Dyle at the nearest point, and manœuvring along the left bank of this little river. Should the Prussians have remained at Wavre, which is on the left bank of the Dyle, this position would be much easier to attack from the left bank than from the right. If they proceeded toward Brussels it would be possible to follow them after reaching Wavre. Should they march straight to the English, the appearance of 33,000 men on their flank would stop, or at any rate delay, their movement. Finally, if they had effected their junction with the English and threatened to crush the French Imperial Army under their united masses, the French on the left bank of the Dyle would be near enough to the Emperor to bring him effectual aid in the thick of the battle.

Grouchy had no idea of all this; not a single item did he modify in his order of the previous day. Though he had by that time resolved to march himself to Wavre, he allowed Pajol's corps and Vallin's cavalry to carry out the excentric movement which he had directed, on Grand-Leez.[17] He wrote to the Emperor that, as all information confirmed the news that the Prussians were marching on Brussels *via* Wavre "so as to concentrate there or to give battle after joining Wellington, he was starting immediately for Wavre himself."[18]

Grouchy had at his disposal 33,000 men and 96 pieces of artillery.[19] His servile persistence in keeping in the tracks of the Prussian rearguard, instead of manœuvring from the morning of the 18th of June along the left bank of the Dyle, was a huge strategical blunder. By leaving his troops in bivouac part of the morning, under circumstances so pressing and so grave, he was guilty of an irreparable mistake. At that season, on the 18th of June, the sun rises at half-past two; at three it is quite light enough to march. And yet Grouchy directed Vandamme and Gérard to begin marching, one at six o'clock, the other at eight.[20] Unhappy man!

Owing to delays in the distribution of food, the troops did not even start off at the appointed time.[21] Exelmans' dragoons, who had spent the night at Sauvenière and were to form the head of the column, only mounted their horses about six o'clock.[22] Vandamme's corps only set out on its way from Gembloux between seven and eight o'clock,[23] and Gérard's corps left camp on the right bank of the Orneau at the same hour.[24] Another cause for the delay was, that these troops all took the same route. Had they marched in two separate columns, the one by Sauvenière and Walhain, the other by Ernage and Nil-Pierreux, the two army corps would have mustered at Corbais at the same time.[25]

Grouchy, it appears, did not leave Gembloux before eight or nine.[26] He proceeded slowly and joined the head of the 3rd Corps a little way before Walhain.[27] Having reached the first houses of this village at about ten o'clock, he allowed the infantry column to file on, and entered the house of the notary Hollërt to write to the Emperor.[28] His aide-de-camp, Pontbellanger, sent out to reconnoitre on the banks of the Dyle toward Mousty, had returned and reported—it appears—that no hostile troops were to be found in this region;[29] and a resident, a former officer of the French Army, or said to be such, came to furnish him with new and important information.[30] He declared that the bulk of the Prussians who had passed by Wavre, were encamped in the plain of the Chyse, near the road from Namur to Louvain (three leagues as the crow flies, north-east of Wavre).[31]

This false intelligence, which the ancient officer "gave as positive," more than satisfied Grouchy. Not only was there no attempt on the part of Blücher's army to effect its junction with Wellington by a side march, but it had made a long circuit to concentrate first in the direction of Louvain. Thus the enemy were, for a time, placing themselves out of the proceedings. Grouchy could congratulate himself on having manœuvred so successfully. Though he had not overtaken the Prussians, he was on their traces, and he had separated them from the English, which was the principal aim of his movement. That evening all his troops would find themselves concentrated at Wavre in positions between the two armies of the enemy. The day after, he would be free either to go and fight the Prussians in the plains of La Chyse, or to attack them in their flank march, if they were marching towards Brussels, or to proceed to that town himself and join the bulk of the French forces. The Marshal lost no time, in writing to convey this news to Napoleon. The end of the letter ran thus: "This evening I shall have massed my troops at Wavre, and shall thus find myself between Wellington, who is, I presume, retreating before Your Majesty, and the Prussian Army. I need further instructions as to what Your Majesty desires me to do next. The country between Wavre and the plain of La Chyse is rough and broken and in some parts marshy. I shall easily get to Brussels before the troops, who have halted at La Chyse. Deign, sire, to transmit me your orders; I can receive them before commencing my movement to-morrow." [32]

To-morrow! What would not to-morrow bring forth!

Grouchy gave this letter to Major la Fresnaye, ex-page to Napoleon, who started immediately.[33] As for the Marshal, now freed from all anxiety and believing he still had a whole day before him to make his final decision, he quietly sat down to breakfast.

Section III

He had got as far as his strawberries (eating strawberries, even on the morning of a battle, is not in itself a hanging matter) when Gérard, who had outdistanced the head of the 4th Corps by two or four kilometres, entered the room where he was breakfasting.[34] Shortly after, Colonel Simon Lorière, head of Gérard's staff, was introduced. Whilst walking in the garden of the notary Hollërt, he had heard the roar of cannon in the distance; he hastened to inform his chiefs. It was a little after half-past eleven. Grouchy and Gérard went down into the garden. General Baltus, commander of the artillery of the 4th Corps, General Valazé, commander of the Engineering Corps, the review inspector, Dennić, met there with several other staff-officers, all eagerly listening to the noise of the cannonade. Several of them knelt down with their ears to the ground to ascertain the direction.[35] Gérard listened a few minutes and said, "I think we ought to march to the cannon." [36]

Grouchy objected that more likely than not, it was merely a rearguard affair.[37] But the fire grew quicker and more sustained. "The ground trembled under us," reports Simon Lorière. It was no longer possible to doubt that the two armies were engaged. Toward the west, clouds of smoke arose on the horizon.

"The battle is at Mont-Saint-Jean," said a peasant whom Valazé had taken as guide. "You could get there in four or five hours' march."

Notary Hollërt, called by Gérard, confirmed the opinion of the guide.

"It is on the edge of the forest of Soignes," he said. "The distance from here, is about three leagues and a half."

"We must march to the cannon," repeated Gérard.

"We must march to the cannon," said General Valazé in his turn.[38]

Grouchy has admitted that he was "vexed" to hear his subordinates give him advice publicly.[39] This was one reason for not paying any attention to it. There was another, namely, the fear of incurring any responsibility. Rather than follow the hazardous advice of his generals, was it not better to keep blindly to the letter of the Emperor's instructions, which would cover him, whatever happened. Accordingly he said:

"The Emperor informed me yesterday that his intention was to attack the English Army, should Wellington accept battle. Therefore I am in no wise surprised at the engagement that is taking place at this moment. If the Emperor had wished me to take part in it, he would not have sent me away from him, at the very moment that he was himself bearing down upon the English. Besides, if I took the rough crossroads which are now drenched with the rain of yesterday and this morning, I would not arrive on the field of battle in time to be of any use."[40]

General Baltus came to the same conclusion as Grouchy.

"The roads would be very difficult. The artillery would never be able to extricate itself."[41]

"With my three companies of sappers," retorted General Valazé, "I undertake to settle every difficulty."[42]

"At any rate, I would arrive with the chests!" cried Gérard.[43]

Valazé having again questioned the guide, who gave his word that the march would not be difficult, replied:

"The sappers can make any number of passages." [44]

Gérard grew more and more excited. "*Monsieur le Maréchal*," he said, "it is your duty to march towards the cannon." [45]

Offended that Gérard should take the liberty of rebuking him audibly in the presence of twenty officers, Grouchy retorted in a stern tone, in such a way as to end the discussion: [46]

"My duty is to execute the Emperor's orders, which direct me to follow the Prussians; it would be infringing his commands to follow your advice." [47]

At this moment arrived an aide-de-camp from Exelmans, Major d'Estourmel. He announced that a strong Prussian rearguard was posted before Wavre. This officer was also charged to say that, according to all indications, the enemy's army had passed the bridge of Wavre during the night and morning, in order to get nearer the English Army, and, consequently, that General Exelmans contemplated proceeding to the left bank of the Dyle *vià* Ottignies. This fresh information and the opinion expressed by Exelmans, furnished additional reasons in favour of Gérard's opinions. However, to Grouchy, who was as convinced as ever that the Prussians had gained Wavre in order to retreat towards the Chyse, the presence of their rearguard in this town only confirmed him in his presumptions. He congratulated himself that he had resisted Gérard, because the Emperor's orders were to follow the Prussian Army, and that at last he seemed on the point of reaching this army that had hitherto baffled him. He told d'Estourmel that he would himself give orders to General Exelmans and called for his horses. [48]

As he set foot in the stirrup, Gérard risked a last attempt.

"If you do not wish to march toward the forest of Soignes with all your troops, allow me, at any rate, to effect this movement with my army corps and General Vallin's cavalry. I am certain of arriving, and arriving in time to be useful." [49]

"No," answered Grouchy, "it would be an unpardonable military mistake to separate my troops and make them act on both banks of the Dyle. I should be exposing one or other of these two bodies, which would not be able to support each other, to annihilation by forces twice or thrice their superior."[50]

He set his horse at a gallop.[51] Those among the officers of his staff who had followed the discussion from afar, and who heard the cannon, thought a manœuvre was about to take place with a view to drawing nearer the Imperial Army.[52]

BOOK III CHAPTER II

THE BATTLE OF WATERLOO

The Morning

I. Topography of the battlefield.
II. Positions of the Anglo-Netherlander Army.
III. Napoleon's breakfast at "Le Caillou"—Letter to Grouchy.
IV. The last review (ten o'clock)—Order of battle of the French Army—Napoleon's plan of attack (eleven o'clock).

SECTION I

THE plateau of La Belle Alliance and of Mont-Saint-Jean, each with an average elevation of 132 yards, run nearly parallel to each other from west to east. They are separated by two twin valleys, which the main road from Charleroi to Brussels crosses perpendicularly from south to north. These two valleys are narrow and not very deep; from La Belle Alliance inn to the ridge of Mont-Saint-Jean there is only the distance of 1300 yards as the crow flies, and the lowest levels of the valley are computed at 110. East of the main road, lies the valley of Smohain, which is very broken and grows continually narrower until it becomes a ravine and is lost in the bed of the brook of Ohain; the other valley, that of Braine-L'Alleud, stretches to the west with numerous undulations, and crosses the Nivelles road, cutting it obliquely. This second road runs from S.S.W. to N.N.E. Having gained the plateau of Mont-Saint-Jean, it branches off at an acute angle to the hamlet of the same name on the main road, which, a league farther up, passes through the village of Waterloo, built in a hollow of the forest of Soignes; then it continues towards Brussels, through the wood.[1]

Seen from La Belle Alliance, the main road to Brussels, which goes down and up again in a straight line, seems very steep. But this is an illusion of perspective. In reality the inclination of the slope is not great. A horseman can ascend it at an even gallop, without straining his horse or putting it out of breath.[2] However, to the right as well as to the left of the road, the ground is extremely uneven, and, in many places, becomes steep. It is an infinite succession of mounds and hollows, of depressions and banks, of furrows and hillocks. Nevertheless, when viewed from a height, the double valley has the aspect of a plain extending without any marked depressions between two low hills. It is necessary to walk over the ground, to perceive the constantly undulating formation of the ground, similar to the billows of a swelling sea.

The road from Ohain to Braine-L'Alleud, which skirts the ridge of the plateau of Mont-Saint-Jean where it cuts the Brussels road at a right angle, covers with a line of natural obstacles, nearly the entire line of the English positions. To the east of the main road, this road is on a level with the ground, but a double border of high, thick hedges renders it inaccessible to cavalry. To the west the ground rises sharply, the Ohain road winding between two embankments of from five to seven feet in height; it forms thus, for a distance of 400 yards, a formidable covering trench. Then it regains its level and continues its course without presenting any further obstacles save a few scattered hedges.[3] Behind the ridge, which forms a screen, the ground inclines northward, a tendency favourable to its defence. The troops of the second line and the reserves were thus hidden from the telescopes of the enemy and were partly sheltered from their fire.

Scattered over a radius of 3,500 yards, half-way up the hill and in the levels beneath—the chateau of Hougoumont with its chapel and its vast dependencies, its park surrounded by walls, its orchard enclosed by a barrier of hedges, and the copses which guarded its approach from the south; the farm of La Haye-Sainte, a stone building flanked by a hedge-girt orchard and a terraced kitchen-garden; the hillock overlooking the excavation of a sand-pit which was protected by a hedge; the Papelotte farm; the large farmhouse of La Haye; and last of all the hamlet of Smohain—formed so many bastions, "covered lodgments and small forts," in front of the position.

The horizon was bounded on the north by the green masses of the forest of Soignes, standing out against which, the distant steeples of Mont-Saint-Jean and Braine-L'Alleud showed clearly. To the north-east extended the woods of Ohain and of Paris, and farther on the wood of Chapelle-Saint-Lambert. To the east, the woods of Vardre and Hubermont bordered the ridges which crown the ravine of the Lasne, which takes its rise near the village of Plancenoit. All the rest of the ground was exposed. On the summit of the plateau, on the slopes of the valleys . . . everywhere, masses of rye were beginning to turn yellow.

To conclude, a vast curtain (the plateau of Mont-Saint-Jean) rising above the valleys of Smohain and Braine-L'Alleud; two rows of hedges and a double bank like a parapet (the Ohain road), from which it was possible to attack from the slope of the parapet, every point of approach; six defensive works before the front (Hougoumont, La Haye-Sainte, the sand-pit, Papelotte, La Haye, Smohain); easy outlets for counter-attacks; in the rear of the parapet a steep piece of ground, masked from the enemy's view, crossed by two high-roads and well adapted for the rapid movements of reinforcing troops and of artillery reserves: such was the position selected by Wellington.

SECTION II

The English had bivouacked in some confusion over the whole of the plateau. Roused at daybreak, they began to relight their fires, to prepare their food, to clean their uniforms and their arms. Instead of unloading their muskets, most of the soldiers discharged them in the air. There was a continuous discharge of musketry, giving the impression of a fight. Napoleon's great guards were either very unwatchful, or war had made them callous, for no French account mentions any false alarm caused by this fusillade. Toward six o'clock, at the discordant call of the bugles, the pibrochs and the drums, sounding and beating from all sides at once, the troops assembled. The inspection once passed, battalions, squadrons, and batteries, led by the officers of the staff, took up their appointed places for the action.[4]

The English brigades of Byng and Maitland (Guards) and Colin Halkett, the Hanoverian brigade of Kielmansegge, and the Anglo-German brigade of Ompteda, posted themselves on the first line, along the Ohain road; the right (Byng), near the road to Nivelles; the left (Ompteda), backed by the road to Brussels. To the east of this road, also along that of Ohain, were placed the English brigades under Kempt and Pack (Picton's division), the Dutch and Belgian brigade of Bylandt, and the Hanoverian brigade of Best.

These nine brigades formed the centre, or more correctly, nearly the entire front of the Allied Army; indeed, in Wellington's order of battle there was not, properly speaking, any centre. There was a right centre and a left centre, separated by the Brussels road, and two wings. The right[5] wing, formed of the English brigades under Adam and Mitchell, the Hanoverian brigade under William Halkett, and the Anglo-German brigade under Duplat, was placed between the Nivelles road and Merbe-Braine; at the extreme right the Dutch-Belgian division of Chassé occupied the ground in front of Braine-L'Alleud. The left wing consisted only of the Nassau brigade under the Prince of Saxe-Weimar, and the Hanoverian brigade under Wincke; these troops were drawn up above Papelotte, La Haye, and Smohain, with posts inside the positions themselves. On the extreme left, Vandeleur's and Vivian's English cavalry brigades flanked the army in the direction of Ohain.

The reserve drawn up on the plateau in two lines, the second line near the farm of Mont-Saint-Jean, comprised: behind the right centre, the Nassau brigade under Kruse, the whole Brunswick corps (infantry and cavalry), the Anglo-German cavalry brigades under Grant, Dörnberg, and Arenschild, the horse-guard brigade under Somerset, the brigades of Trip and Von Merlen (Dutch-Belgian carabiniers and hussars); behind the left centre, the English brigade under Lambert, the brigade of English dragoons led by Ponsonby, and the brigade of Dutch and Belgian dragoons of Ghigny.[6]

The artillery was posted as follows: four batteries on the front of the right centre; one battery exactly in the centre of the line of battle, at the intersection of the road to Brussels and the road of Ohain; four on the front of the left centre; two with the right wing; two at the extreme right with Chassé; two foot batteries and seven horse batteries on the second line behind the right centre; three batteries in reserve near the farm of Mont-Saint-Jean.[7]

It was Wellington's wont in Spain and in Portugal, to meet the impetuous attacks of the French columns by very peculiar tactics. He would place his first line behind ridges, so as to conceal it from the sight and the shots of the enemy during the preparatory stage of the assault, and even during the assault itself. It was only when his assailants, separated during the ascent effected under the galling fire of the skirmishers and of the artillery posted above, gained the summit of the position that the hitherto unmolested English battalions would unmask, discharge their muskets point-blank, and rush forward with fixed bayonets.[8] The ground of Mont-Saint-Jean favoured these tactics. "Form in the usual way," said Wellington to his generals.[9] Accordingly, with the exception of the Belgian brigade under Bylandt and a chain of skirmishers who were posted on the slopes—so to speak in the front line—the whole of the infantry took up positions twenty, sixty, a hundred yards in rear of the Ohain road. These troops found themselves completely masked, some by the banks and hedges on the roadside, the remainder, owing to the interior declivity of the plateau. This declivity was also an advantage for the reserves, for it prevented their being perceived from the opposite heights.[10] The batteries were posted to the front, before and behind the Ohain road, according to the convenience of the ground and the greater or lesser extent of their range.[11] In the embankments and in the hedges, embrasures had been cut for the heavy guns.[12]

The farms, the accidents of the ground which formed the advanced works, had all been put in a state of defence. A barricade was formed across the road to Brussels at the height of La Haye-Sainte; abatis barred the road to Nivelles. Hougoumont was occupied by seven companies of the 1st, 2nd (Coldstream), and 3rd regiments of the English Guards, a company of the Hanoverians, and a Nassau battalion; La Haye-Sainte by five companies of the German Legion; the sand-pit and its approaches, by a battalion of the 95th; Papelotte, La Haye, and the first houses of Smohain by detachments under the Prince of Saxe-Weimar.[13]

But Wellington trusted in his English troops alone. For this reason, his own national troops were placed alternately all along the line with the various allied contingents. He desired the latter to be substantially supported everywhere.[14]

Deducting the losses incurred on the 16th and 17th of June,[15] the duke had in hand 67,700[16] men and 184 guns.[17] He could have concentrated at Mont-Saint-Jean a larger number of combatants, but, ever anxious about his lines of communication with the sea, and fearing that a French corps might turn his right, he had massed between Hal and Enghien—four miles as a bird flies from Mont-Saint-Jean—about 17,000 men and 30 pieces of cannon under Prince Frederick of the Netherlands.[18] It was a capital mistake to send such a body on the eve of a battle with no other object, but to parry an imaginary danger! As General Brialmont has very justly observed, "It is inconceivable that Wellington should have credited his adversary with a plan of operation which could only tend to hasten the junction of the Allied Armies, because from the outset of the campaign, Napoleon had been evidently manœuvring to prevent this junction." [19]

Whilst the troops were taking up their position, Wellington, accompanied by Müffling and a few officers, went over the whole line of battle. He examined in detail all the positions and went down as far as Hougoumont. He frequently directed his field-glass towards the heights occupied by the French. He rode his favourite horse "Copenhagen," a superb bay-brown thoroughbred who had been tested at Vittoria and Toulouse. Wellington was in his usual campaigning dress: breeches of white doe-skin, tasselled boots, a dark blue coat and a short cloak of the same hue, a white necktie, a small hat without feathers, but adorned with the black cockade of England and three other cockades smaller in size, of the colours of Portugal, Spain, and the Netherlands. He was very calm.

His face reflected the confidence which he felt in the promised co-operation of the Prussian Army.[20]

Section III

The orders of the Emperor directed that all the Army Corps should be in their positions of battle and ready to attack, at nine o'clock precisely.[21] But the troops which had passed the night at Genappe, Glabais, and at the farms in the vicinity, took a very long time in rallying, in cleaning their arms, and in preparing their soup. Moreover, the main road to Brussels was the only outlet through which they could debouch.[22] At nine o'clock, only Reille's corps arrived at the height of Le Caillou.[23] The foot-guard, the cuirassiers of Kellermann, Lobau's corps, and Durutte's division were far behind.[24] Wisely or not, the Emperor desired to have all his men in hand before beginning the action; besides, it did not seem as if the state of the ground would as yet allow of the artillery manœuvring. This at least was the opinion held by Napoleon himself and by Drouot.[25]

About eight o'clock the Emperor had breakfasted at the Caillou farm with Soult, the Duke of Bassano, Drouot, and several general officers. After the meal, which had been served on silver plate with the Imperial arms, the maps of Ferrari and Capitaine were spread out on the table.[26] The Emperor said: "The army of the enemy is superior to ours by more than one-fourth. We have nevertheless ninety chances in our favour, and not ten against us." Ney, who was entering, heard these words. He came from the outposts and had mistaken some movement of the English as a preparation for a retreat; he exclaimed: "Without doubt, Sire, provided Wellington be simple enough to wait for you. But I must inform you that his retreat is decided, and that if you do not hasten to attack, the enemy is about to escape from you." " You have seen wrong," replied the Emperor, " and it is too late now. Wellington would expose himself to certain loss. He has thrown the dice and they are in our favour."[27]

Soult was uneasy. He no more dreaded the arrival of the

Prussians on the field of battle than did the Emperor; he considered they were out of the game for several days. But he regretted that 33,000 men had been detached with Marshal Grouchy, when a single corps of infantry and a few thousand horse would have sufficed for the pursuit of Blücher. Half of these troops of the right wing, he thought, would have been invaluable in the great battle that was about to be fought with this English army, which was so firm, so resolute, so formidable. In his capacity as head of Lefebvre's staff, on the 9th of July 1794, Soult had taken this same plateau of Mont-Saint-Jean by storm, and had driven back the Imperials from the forest of Soignes to Brussels. But he knew that the English infantry was incomparably more determined in their resistance, than the Austrian infantry. For this reason, during the preceding evening, he had already urged the Emperor to recall part of the troops placed under Grouchy's orders. That morning he repeated his warning. Napoleon, exasperated, replied to him roughly: "Because you have been beaten by Wellington, you consider him a great general. And now I tell you that Wellington is a bad general, that the English are bad troops, and that this affair is nothing more serious than eating one's breakfast." "I earnestly hope so," said Soult.[28]

Shortly after Reille and Jérôme entered Le Caillou. The Emperor asked Reille his opinion of the English Army, which this general was in a position to give, since he had had many a contest with it in Spain. Reille answered: "Well posted, as Wellington knows how to post it, and attacked from the front, I consider the English Infantry to be impregnable, owing to its calm tenacity, and its superior aim in firing. Before attacking it with the bayonet, one may expect half the assailants to be brought to the ground. But the English Army is less agile, less supple, less expert in manœuvring than ours. If we cannot beat it by a direct attack, we may do so by manœuvring." For Napoleon, who had never personally fought a pitched battle against the English, the opinion of a veteran of the Spanish wars was worthy of consideration. But he was probably irritated with Reille for having spoken so freely, without reflecting that the generals who heard him might be discouraged, and therefore he did not appear to attach the least importance to his opinion. He broke off the conversation by an exclamation of incredulity.[29]

The weather had cleared, the sun was shining; a rather brisk wind, a drying wind as sportsmen call it, was beginning to blow.[30] Artillery officers came to report that they had inspected the ground, and that it would soon be possible to manœuvre the pieces.[31] Napoleon called for his horses. Before starting he graciously received the farmer Boucqueau, who had returned from Plancenoit with his family, upon hearing that the Emperor was at Le Caillou. The old man complained that he had been plundered the day before, by stragglers belonging to the enemy; Napoleon, with an absorbed expression on his face, seemed to be thinking of anything but the old man's grievances. He spoke at last, saying: "Do not distress yourself, you shall have a safeguard." This seemed very much to the point, for the Imperial headquarters were to leave Le Caillou in the course of the day. It was said they would sleep in Brussels.[32]

The Emperor, skirting at full trot the flank of the columns which were still debouching from Genappe, rode to the front of La Belle Alliance, in the very line of the tirailleurs, in order to observe the enemy's positions.[33] His guide was a Fleming named Decoster. This man owned a little inn on the roadside between Rossomme and La Belle Alliance; he had been taken in his own house at five o'clock in the morning and brought before the Emperor, who required some native of the country. The maps which Napoleon used in his campaigns indicated the features of the ground only in a very general and summary way, and Napoleon nearly always took a guide. Decoster had been carefully kept in sight, for he seemed anxious to escape; on departing from Le Caillou he had been hoisted on to a charger whose saddle was attached by a long strap to the saddle-bow of a chasseur of the escort. Naturally he cut a very sorry figure during the battle and amid the flying balls and bullets. He wriggled in the saddle and kept ducking his head and bending over his horse's neck. The Emperor said to him once: "Now, my friend, do not be so restless. A musket-shot may kill you just as well from behind as from the front, and will make a much worse wound." [34] According to local traditions, either through imbecility or through malice, Decoster gave false information throughout the whole day. Another guide as well, was brought to the Emperor, a certain Joseph Bourgeois, from the hamlet of Odeghien. He stuttered with fear and kept his eyes obstinately fixed on the ground; Napoleon sent him away. Whenever he was asked what the Emperor was like he would answer: "If his face had been the face of a clock, nobody would have dared to look at it, for the hour." [35]

The Emperor remained some time before La Belle Alliance. After dispatching General Haxo of the Engineers to ascertain whether the English had raised any entrenchments,[36] he took up his post about three-quarters of a mile in the rear, on a bank which rises near the Rossomme farm. From the farm were brought out a chair and a little table upon which the maps were spread. Towards two o'clock, when the action had become serious, the Emperor posted himself on another eminence nearer the line of battle, at a short distance from the Decoster Inn. General Foy, who had recognised the Emperor by his grey coat, could see him walking up and down with his hands behind his back; at times he would stop, put his elbows on the table and then resume his walk.[37]

At Le Caillou, Jérôme had acquainted his brother with a report he had heard the day before, in the Inn of the "Roi d'Espagne." The waiter who served him at supper, and who had previously waited on Wellington at breakfast, related that an aide-de-camp of the Duke had spoken of a junction agreed on between the English and Prussian Armies, at the entrance of the forest of Soignes. This Belgian, who seemed well informed, even added that the Prussians would march by Wavre. The Emperor treated this as mere nonsense. "After such a battle as Fleurus," he said, "the junction between the English and Prussians is impossible for at least two days; besides, the Prussians have Grouchy on their heels."[38] Grouchy, always Grouchy! The Emperor placed far too much confidence in the information, as well as in the promises of his lieutenant. According to the letter from the Marshal, written in Gembloux at ten o'clock in the evening, and which arrived at Le Caillou at two o'clock next morning, the Prussian Army, reduced to about 30,000 men, had divided into two columns, of which the one seemed to be proceeding toward Liège and the other toward Namur, possibly to join Wellington. Grouchy added that if the reports of his cavalry testified that the bulk of the Prussians was doubling back upon Wavre, he would follow it "in order to cut it off from Wellington."[39] All this was well calculated to reassure the Emperor. But did this Prussian force only amount to 30,000 men? Had they not divided for the sake of marching, and might they not reunite ultimately to fight? Would Grouchy, beyond whom they had advanced to a considerable distance, overtake them in time? These were so many questions which the Emperor never asked himself, or which he decided in the way which was most in accordance with his own wishes. Blinded himself, as Grouchy was, he imagined that the Prussians were going to halt at Wavre, or at any rate that they would make for Brussels and not for Mont-Saint-Jean. The Emperor contented himself with writing to Grouchy from Rossomme, to inform him that a Prussian column had passed by Saint-Géry proceeding toward Wavre, and to order him to march as quickly as possible to this point, with the object of driving the enemy before him.[40]

A few minutes later, the Emperor ordered Colonel Marbot to take up his position behind Frichermont with the 7th Hussars and send out piquets to Lasne, Couture, and the bridges of Mousty and Ottignies.[41] May we infer from this that Napoleon had a sudden intuition of the movement that was about to be suggested to Grouchy by Gérard, and that he thought that the Marshal, before receiving his despatch, might cross the Dyle at Mousty to bear on the left flank of the Prussians, instead of following them to Wavre? or may we conclude more simply, that in the Emperor's thoughts the only object of these piquets was to reconnoitre on the Army's right wing and to link together the communications with Grouchy's corps by ensuring the passage of the estafettes?[42]

Section IV

The troops took up their positions for the battle: Napoleon remounted his horse and passed them in review as they formed up on the ground. The whole plateau was furrowed by the marching columns. D'Erlon's corps closed up on its right, to allow the corps of Reille to establish itself on the left. On the flank and rear of these first lines of infantry—the infantry of battle in blue coats, white breeches and gaiters, the light infantry clad in blue coats with black gaiters—eight divisions of cavalry began to deploy, their swords and their cuirasses shining in the sun, the pennons of their lances waving in the breeze. It was a kaleidoscope of vivid hues and metallic flashes. After the chasseurs, wearing bright green jackets, with facings of purple, yellow or scarlet, and breeches of leather fastened with big buttons, came the hussars, with "dolmans," pelisses, breeches *à la hongroise*, plumes upon their shakos, all varying in colour with each regiment; some chestnut and blue, others red and sky-blue, others grey and blue, others green and scarlet. Then passed the dragoons with brass casques, over turban-helmets of tiger skin, white shoulder belts crossed over a green coat, with facings of red or yellow, long guns at their saddle bows and bumping against their stiff boots; the light-lancers in green like the chasseurs, and having like them sheep-skin shabracks, but distinguished from them, by their helmets with silken cords, and by the cut and colour of their plastrons; the cuirassiers wearing short coats with Imperial blue collars, facings, and trimmings varying from red to yellow, according to the different regiments, white breeches, top-boots, steel cuirasses and helmets, with crests of copper and floating horse-hair manes; the carabineers, giants of six feet and clad in white, with breastplates of gold and tall helmets with red cords—like those worn by the heroes of antiquity. And now the entire body of the horse guards deployed on the third line; the dragoons in green coats faced with white and with scarlet plumes on their helmets; the grenadiers in blue coats faced with scarlet and leather breeches, with aiguillettes and fringeless epaulettes of orange-yellow, and high caps of bearskin, with a plume and hanging cords; the lancers with red kurkas and blue plastrons, with light yellow aiguillettes and epaulettes, red trousers with a blue stripe, and the red shapska cap bearing a brass plate inscribed with an N and a crown, and surmounted with a white plume half a yard long; and last, the chasseurs, with green dolmans embroidered with orange braid, red pelisses edged with fur, and kolbachs (or caps) of brilliant scarlet, with great plumes of green and red upon their heads. The epaulettes, the braids, the stripes, the gimps of the officers glittered with a profuse display of gold and silver.

By the Brussels road other troops debouched. Men, horses, and cannon were coming up as far as the eye could reach; the numerous battalions of Lobau, Domon's chasseurs, Subervie's lancers, the foot artillery in its plain dark blue uniform with touches of red, the horse artillery in "dolmans," the front of them covered with scarlet braid; the Young Guard, tirailleurs with red epaulettes, voltigeurs with green epaulettes; the foot artillerymen of the guard, with bearskin helmets, marching by the side of those terrible 12-pounders which the Emperor called his "most beautiful daughters." Far in the rear advanced the dark columns of the Old Guard: chasseurs and grenadiers wore the campaigning-dress—blue trousers, long blue greatcoats with a single row of buttons, bearskin helmets without either plume or braid. Their parade uniforms for their triumphal entrance into Brussels, they carried in their knapsack, which brought the weight that each man carried, including equipment, arms and fifty cartridges, to a load, weighing sixty-five pounds! The grenadiers could only be distinguished from the chasseurs by their greater height, the brass plate on their bearskins, and their epaulettes which were entirely red, while those of their comrades were green with red fringe. Both grenadiers and chasseurs wore powdered queues and massive gold ear-rings half a crown in diameter.

The drums beat, the trumpets blew, the bands struck up, "Veillons au salut de l'Empire" (Anglicè, "Let us watch over the safety of the Empire"). Passing before Napoleon the eagle-bearers inclined their standards—the standards of the "Champ de Mai," the new standards already baptized at Ligny by fire and blood,—the horsemen brandished their sabres, the infantry waved their shakos on the points of their bayonets. The cheers overpowered and drowned the sound of the drums and trumpets. The cries "Vive l'Empereur" followed each other so lustily and so rapidly, that they prevented the words of command from being heard. "Never," says an officer of the 1st Corps, "were the words 'Vive l'Empereur' shouted with more enthusiasm; it was like frenzy. And what made this scene even more solemn and more affecting was the fact that facing us, only a thousand feet distant perhaps, stood the dark red line of the English Army, distinctly visible." [43]

The infantry of d'Erlon and the infantry of Reille deployed in the first line on the height of La Belle Alliance; the four divisions of d'Erlon, arranged two deep, the right opposite Papelotte, the left resting on the Brussels road; the three divisions of Reille in the same order, the right upon this road, the left not far from the road to Nivelles. The light cavalry of Jacquinot and the light cavalry of Piré, arranged in battle array three deep, flanked the right of d'Erlon and the left of Reille. On the second line, the infantry of Lobau posted itself in double column by divisions, along and to the left of the Brussels road, and the cavalry of Domon and Subervie were placed in compact columns by squadrons, along and to the right of the same highroad. Prolonging the second line, the cuirassiers of Milhaud and of Kellermann stood in battle order and two deep—the former to the right, the latter to the left. The Imperial Guard remained in reserve near Rossomme: the infantry (Young Guard, Middle Guard, Senior Guard) upon six lines, each of four battalions, deployed on both sides of the Brussels road; the light cavalry of Lefebvre-Desnoëttes (lancers and chasseurs) on two lines six hundred feet behind the cuirassiers of Milhaud; the reserve cavalry of Guyot (dragoons and grenadiers) also on two lines, six or seven hundred feet behind Kellermann's cuirassiers.

The artillery of d'Erlon was in the intervals between the brigades, Reille's artillery before the front, Lobau's artillery on the left flank. Each cavalry division had its battery of horse artillery by its side. The batteries of the Guard were placed quite in the rear between Rossomme and La Maison du Roi. The highroad to Brussels and the roads which crossed it, were left clear purposely, so as to allow of the rapid transit of artillery reinforcements to all points.[44]

74,000 men[45] were gathered there, with 246 guns.[46] On the other side of the valley, 1,300 yards off as a bird flies, was collected the allied host of 67,000 men. Never in the wars of the Revolution and the Empire had so many combatants occupied so contracted a space. From the farm of Mont-Saint-Jean, the position of Wellington's last reserves, to the farm of Le Caillou, where the Imperial treasure and the Service corps were stationed, under the protection of a battalion of chasseurs of the Old Guard, there was only a distance of 4,500 metres, and the front of each army did not extend over more than three-quarters of a league.[47] The ridges of the plateaux being very irregular, the two armies' parallel lines were very far from being straight. The English right wing lapped over upon the centre and the left wing receded. The French Army with its right in advance, its centre, its left in the rear, and the extremity of its left wing in an oblique line, formed a concave encircling line.

It was now nearly eleven o'clock and the troops ought by that time to have arrived in their positions.[48] The Emperor even thought he would not be able to commence the attack before one o'clock in the afternoon. Having returned to his observatory of Rossomme he dictated the following order to Soult:—"As soon as the whole army is arranged in battle order, towards one o'clock, and at the moment when the Emperor will give the order to Ney, the attack will commence by seizing the village of Mont-Saint-Jean, at the intersection of the roads. For this purpose, the batteries of the 12th and 2nd Corps and those of the 6th, will unite with those of the 1st. These twenty-four guns will fire on the troops at Mont-Saint-Jean, and Count d'Erlon will commence the attack by bringing forward his division from the left, and supporting it according to circumstances, by the other divisions of the 1st Corps. The 2nd Corps will advance accordingly to keep at the same level as Count d'Erlon. The companies of sappers of the 1st Corps are to be ready to barricade themselves immediately within Mont-Saint-Jean."[49]

This order does not leave any doubt as to the plans of the Emperor. He wished merely and simply, to pierce the centre of the English Army and drive it back behind Mont-Saint-Jean.[50] Once master of this position which commands the plateau, he would act according to circumstances against the shattered enemy; by that time victory would be virtually in his grasp. Thus the Emperor forgot or scorned the opinion expressed by Reille that, owing to the precision of its aim and the solidity of its infantry, the English Army could only be defeated by manoeuvres. Manoeuvring he considered unworthy of him. Without doubt an attack against Wellington's right, which was very numerous, and covered by the village of Braine l'Alleud and the farm of Hougoumont, and having as a redoubt the village of Merbe-Braine, would have demanded much time and great efforts; but the extremity of the enemy's left wing was very weak, quite unsupported, badly protected, and easy of attack. They might first operate by Papelotte and La Haye.[51] It seems as if at one time the Emperor had some idea of this.[52] But for Napoleon, it was a slight result indeed to inflict but a partial defeat upon the English, and to throw them back on Hal and Enghien! He longed for a conclusive battle, the *Entscheidungsschlacht*. His aim was the same as at Ligny: to pierce the enemy's army in the centre so as to throw it out and annihilate it. He would use his usual tactics: the parallel order, the direct attack, the assault by masses upon the strongest point of the English front, with no other preparation than a shower of shells.

The Emperor, it is true, could not form an accurate estimate of the number of the English nor of the strength of their positions. More than half of the allied army was concealed by the undulations of the ground, and General Haxo, of the Engineers, charged to ascertain whether there were any entrenchments on the enemy's front, had reported that he could not perceive any trace of fortifications.[53] Either Haxo's sight or his judgment was at fault, for the hollow road of Ohain, the sand-pit, the barricade on the Brussels highroad, the abatis of the road to Nivelles, the farms of Hougoumont, La Haye-Sainte, and Papelotte, might well have been reckoned most formidable entrenchments.

BOOK III CHAPTER III

THE BATTLE OF WATERLOO (*Continued*)

From half-past eleven to three o'clock

I. Attack of Hougoumont by the division of Jérôme Bonaparte of Reille's corps.
II. The apparition of Bülow's corps on the heights of Chapelle-Saint-Lambert—New despatch from Napoleon to Grouchy.
III. Attack of La Haye-Sainte and of the plateau of Mont-Saint-Jean by d'Erlon's corps.
IV. Counter-attack of Picton's English—Charge of Lord Somerset's horse-guards—The press of cuirassiers in the hollow road.
V. Charge of Ponsonby's dragoons—Rout of d'Erlon's infantry—Counter-charge of Jacquinot's lancers and Farine's cuirassiers—The conflagration of Hougoumont.

SECTION I

THE Emperor, a few minutes after dictating the order to attack, purposed preparing the assault on Mont-Saint-Jean, by a demonstration in the direction of Hougoumont. By thus arousing Wellington's anxiety for his right, he might induce him to impoverish his centre. Realising at last the value of time, Napoleon resolved to effect this movement without waiting until all his troops had taken up their positions in order of battle. About a quarter past eleven Reille received the order to occupy the approaches to Hougoumont.[1]

Reille entrusted this trifling manœuvre to Prince Jérôme, whose four regiments formed Reille's left. To cover the movement, a divisional battery of the 2nd Corps opened fire on the enemy's positions. Three English batteries, established on the edge of the plateau east of the road to Nivelles, replied.[2] When the first cannon shot was fired, some of the

English officers looked at their watches. It was exactly thirty-five minutes past eleven.[3]

During this artillery duel, in which other batteries of the English right soon joined, a portion of Reille's artillery and Kellermann's mounted batteries (the latter acting on orders from the Emperor) and the Bauduin brigade from Jérôme's division, preceded by its skirmishers, descended into the valley in columns by échelons; at the same time, Piré's lancers started a movement of their own on the road to Nivelles.[4] The 1st Light Infantry charged the wood with fixed bayonets, headed by Jérôme, and General Bauduin who was killed at the beginning of the action. In spite of the desperate defence of the battalion of Nassau and of a company of Hanoverian carabiniers, they gained a footing on the edge of the wood. They now had only to overcome about 300 yards of very dense thickets. The 3rd of the line forced its way in behind the 1st Light Infantry. The enemy fell back, but only step by step, taking shelter behind every clump, firing almost point-blank, and continually turning round and resuming the offensive. It took an hour to drive out of this wood, Nassau's battalion and the companies of English guards which had come to reinforce them.[5]

On debouching from the copse, the French found themselves thirty paces distant from the buildings of Hougoumont, a vast mass of stone, and from the wall of the park which was two yards high. Jérôme only needed to keep to the level or in the hollow behind the wood and maintain in front of him a good line of skirmishers.[6] But, whether the order was badly explained or misunderstood, or whether the Emperor's brother would not consent to play this passive rôle, or whether the excited soldiers rushed on of their own accord, they dashed forward to the assault. The wall and the enclosures were pierced with loopholes through which the English commenced a well-sustained fusilade. They were under shelter and they aimed coolly; and at so short a distance every shot told. Jérôme's infantry wasted their bullets on an invisible foe. A few among them tried to break in the great door with the butts of their muskets, but this door was placed in a recess; they were fired on from the front and from the flank. Others attempted to scale the wall of the park by climbing on each other's shoulders; through the loopholes the English pierced them with their bayonets. Dead bodies lay heaped up around Hougoumont. The assailants fell back to the shelter of the wood.[7]

General Guilleminot, head of Jérôme's staff, advised that they should not push the attack further.[8] It was enough to occupy the wood, the contest must cease. Reille, according to his own account, sent orders to the same effect.[9] Nevertheless, Jérôme persisted. He was determined to carry the position. He called up his second brigade (General Soye's) to relieve the brigade of Bauduin in the wood,[10] with the remnant of which he turned Hougoumont by the west. His column which was no longer defiling, marched at a range of 600 yards, under the fire of the English batteries. It succeeded in reaching the north façade of Hougoumont, which it proceeded to storm. Whilst Colonel de Cubières fell under his horse grievously wounded, a giant nicknamed "l'enfonceur" (the breaker-in), Lieutenant Legros from the 1st léger, seized a hatchet from a sapper and shattered a panel of the door. A handful of soldiers rushed into the court with him. The mass of the English surrounded them, shot them down, exterminated them; not a man escaped the slaughter. At this very moment four companies of the Coldstreams, the only reinforcement which Wellington, who watched the struggle from afar, but did not overrate the importance of the onslaught at Hougoumont, thought necessary to send, attacked the French column. Caught between two fires, the decimated battalions of Jérôme fell back, part into the wood, part toward the Nivelles road.[11]

Section II

During this combat, the Emperor was preparing his great attack. He reinforced the twenty-four 12-pounders, by the batteries of 8-pounders, of the 1st Corps and three batteries of the guard, though at the outset of the action, the first had been judged sufficient to cannonade the enemy's centre. Thus in front and to the right of La Belle Alliance a formidable battery of eighty guns was formed.[12] It was now close on one o'clock. Ney despatched one of his aides-de-camp to Rossomme, to inform the Emperor that all was ready, and that he awaited the order to attack. Before the smoke of all these cannon should have raised a curtain between the two hills, Napoleon determined to cast a last glance over the whole extent of the battlefield.[13]

At a distance of about two leagues to the north-east, he perceived what appeared to be a black cloud emerging from the woods of Chapelle-Saint-Lambert. Though his practised eye made it impossible for him to doubt, he hesitated at first to acknowledge these were troops. He consulted with the officers around him. All the glasses of the staff were turned upon this point. As usually occurs, opinions differed. Some officers contended that there were no troops there at all, but only a clump of trees or the shadow of a cloud; others saw a marching column, even discerned French uniforms, or Prussian uniforms. Soult said he could plainly distinguish a numerous body of troops which had piled arms.[14]

It was not long before the point was fully settled. As a detachment of cavalry galloped off to reconnoitre these troops, a subaltern of the 2nd Silesian Hussars whom Colonel Marbot's hussars had just captured near Lasne,[15] was brought before the Emperor. He was the bearer of a letter from Bülow to Wellington, announcing the arrival of the 4th Corps at Chapelle-Saint-Lambert. This hussar, who spoke French, made no difficulty about telling all he knew. "The troops just perceived," he said, "are the advanced guard of General von Bülow. Our whole army passed last night at Wavre. We have seen no French, and we suppose they have marched on Plancenoit."[16]

The presence of a Prussian corps at Chapelle-St.-Lambert which would have confounded the Emperor a few hours before, when he treated as "nonsense" the account brought by Jérôme with regard to the proposed junction of the two armies of the allies, now only surprised him in a slight degree, for during the interval he had received this letter from Grouchy, dated Gembloux, six o'clock in the morning:—

"Sire, all my reports and information confirm the fact that the enemy is retiring upon Brussels, either to concentrate there, or to give battle after uniting with Wellington. The first and the second corps under Blücher appear to be marching, the former upon Corbais and the second upon Chaumont. They must have started from Tourinnes yesterday evening at half-past eight, and have marched all night; fortunately, the weather in the night was so wretched that they cannot have advanced very far. I am going to start immediately for Sart-a-Walhain whence I shall proceed to Corbais and to Wavre." [17] This despatch was far less reassuring than the one of the previous day. Instead of the retreat of two Prussian corps in two columns, the one upon Wavre and the other upon Liège,[18] Grouchy announced that these two columns were marching concentrically upon Brussels, with the probable design of joining Wellington. He no longer spoke of preventing their junction; and though it was natural to conjecture he intended manœuvring to that effect, by marching to Wavre, he used but little haste in so doing, for at six o'clock in the morning he had not yet left Gembloux.

No doubt the Emperor might hope that the Prussians would march straight upon Brussels; but it was also very possible that they would join the English Army by a flank movement.

To parry this probable danger, the Emperor did not think of sending fresh instructions to Grouchy till very late. Except in the event of a delay, which was possible but highly improbable, the Marshal's letter ought to have reached the Imperial headquarters between ten and eleven o'clock;[19] and it was only at one o'clock, a few minutes before perceiving the Prussian corps on the heights of Chapelle-Saint-Lambert, that the following message from the Emperor was written to Grouchy: —"Your movement from Corbais to Wavre agrees with His Majesty's arrangements. Nevertheless, the Emperor requests me to tell you that you must keep manœuvring in our direction, and seek to draw nearer to the army, so as to be able to join us before any corps places itself between us. I do not indicate to you any special direction. It is for you to ascertain the point where we are, to act accordingly, and to keep up our communications, and to see that you are constantly in a position to fall upon and annihilate, any of the enemy's troops which might try to molest our right."[20]

This order had not yet been dispatched, when the Prussian columns appeared in the distance. A few minutes later the Emperor, after questioning the captive hussar, had this postscript added: "A letter which has just been intercepted tells us that General Bülow is to attack our right flank. We believe we can perceive this corps on the heights of Chapelle-Saint-Lambert. Therefore do not lose a minute to draw nearer to us and to join us and crush Bülow, whom you will catch in the very act" (*en flagrant délit*).[21]

The Emperor was then not otherwise disconcerted.[22] Though he realised that his situation had seriously altered, he did not consider it compromised. Indeed, the reinforcement that had reached Wellington, only consisted after all of a single Prussian corps, for the prisoner had not mentioned that the whole of the army was following Bülow. This army must be still at Wavre. Grouchy would either come up with it there, attack it, and consequently hold it back at a great distance from Bülow; or else, giving up the pursuit of Blücher, he was already marching on Plancenoit by Mousty, as the hussar supposed,[23] and would bring to the bulk of the French Army, a reinforcement of 33,000 bayonets. The Emperor, who easily deluded himself by his own fancies and wished above all things to impart them to others, said to Soult: "This morning we had ninety odds in our favour. We still have sixty against forty, and if Grouchy repairs the terrible fault he has made in amusing himself at Gembloux, and marches rapidly, our victory will be all the more decisive, for Bülow's corps will be completely destroyed."[24]

In any case, as Grouchy might delay, and Bülow's advanced guard was in view, the Emperor immediately took measures to protect the flank of the army. The light cavalry divisions under Domon and Subervie were detached to the right to observe the enemy, to occupy all the outlets, and to connect themselves with the heads of Marshal Grouchy's columns as soon as they appeared.[25] Count Lobau received orders to move up the 6th Corps behind this cavalry, to a good intermediate

CHAP. III   *THE BATTLE OF WATERLOO*   193

position, which would enable him to hold the Prussians in check.[26]

SECTION III

It was now about half-past one.[27] The Emperor gave Ney the orders to attack. The battery of eighty pieces began with the roar of thunder to pour forth a sudden storm of fire, which was at once answered by the English artillery. After half an hour's cannonading, the main battery suspended its fire for a minute, to allow of the passage of d'Erlon's infantry. The four divisions were marched in echelons by the left, with intervals of 400 yards between each echelon. The Allix division formed the first echelon, the Donzelot division the second, the Marcognet division the third, and the Durutte division the fourth. Ney and d'Erlon led the assault.[28]

Instead of arranging these troops in columns of attack, that is to say in columns of battalions by divisions, at half or at full distance, a manœuvre which is very favourable for rapid deployments, such as the forming of squares, each echelon had been arranged by battalion, deployed, and in close ranks. The divisions of Allix, Donzelot, and Marcognet (Durutte on his own responsibility would not consent to this manœuvre) thus presented three compact phalanxes of a front of 160 to 200 files, with a depth of twenty-four men.[29] Who had ordered such a formation, perilous under any circumstances, but specially unfortunate on this uneven ground? Ney or rather d'Erlon,[30] commander of the army corps. At any rate, it was not the Emperor, for in his general order of eleven o'clock, nothing of the sort had been specified; there was not even any question of attacking by echelons.[31] On the battlefield, Napoleon wisely left his lieutenants to take the initiative in all details of execution.[32]

Irritated at not having fought on the previous day, the soldiers were burning to attack the enemy. They rushed forward with cries of "Vive l'Empereur!" and descended into the valley under the fiery vault of French and English shells which crossed over their heads, the French batteries blazing forth anew every time our columns reached the fatal corners.[33]

The head of the Allix division (Quiot's brigade), wheeling slightly to the left, bore down upon the orchard of La Haye-Sainte, whence a well-sustained fusillade was issuing. The Bourgeois brigade, now forming alone the echelon of the left, continued its march toward the plateau. Quiot's soldiers quickly drove the German companies out of the orchard, and assailed the farm. But as at Hougoumont, they had not thought it necessary to open breaches in these buildings, with a few shells. The French again and again vainly attempted to assault the high and solid walls, under shelter of which Major Baring's Germans poured a murderous fire. One battalion turned the farm, scaled the walls of the kitchen-garden and dislodged the defenders who sought shelter in the buildings; but they could not demolish the walls with the butt ends of their muskets.[34]

Wellington stood at the foot of a great elm planted on the west of the road to Brussels, at the intersection of this highway with the Ohain road. During almost the whole of the battle he remained in this spot with his staff, whose numbers were increased by the presence of the allied commissaries, Pozzo di Borgo who received a slight bruise, Baron de Vincent, who was wounded, Müffling, General Hügel, General Alava.[35] Seeing La Haye-Sainte completely surrounded by the French, Wellington ordered Ompteda to send a battalion of the German Legion to the assistance of Baring. The Germans descended to the left of the main road, recaptured the kitchen-garden, and passing by the west side of the farm, advanced toward the orchard. At this moment they were charged by the cuirassiers of General Travers, whom the Emperor had detached from Milhaud's corps to second the attack of the infantry. The cuirassiers charged through them, and, continuing their rush, cut down the tirailleurs of the Kielmansegge brigade on the edge of the plateau.[36]

East of the road, the other columns of d'Erlon had climbed the slopes under the fire of the batteries, and the bullets of the English 95th, and the fusillade of Bylandt's brigade drawn up before the Ohain road. The charge went on with quickened pace, in spite of the tall stalks of rye which impeded the march, in spite of the soaked and slippery ground into which men sank and tottered. The cries "Vive l'Empereur!" at times drowned the roar of the cannon.[37] The Bourgeois Brigade (left echelon) drove back the skirmishers, assaulted the sand-pit, dislodged the carabiniers of the 95th and hurled them on to the plateau below the hedges, which it reached in the pursuit.[38] The Donzelot division (second echelon) was engaged with Bylandt's right, whilst the Marcognet division (third echelon) advanced towards the left of this brigade. The Netherlanders and Dutch gave way, fell back in disorder, recrossed the hedges of the Ohain road, and in their flight broke the ranks of the English 28th.[39] On his side Durutte, who commanded the fourth echelon, dislodged from the Papelotte farm the light companies of Nassau, and was already half-way up the hill, threatening Best's Hanoverians.[40]

In the Imperial staff the prevailing opinion was that "all was going marvellously,"[41] and, in fact, should the enemy retain his advanced posts of Hougoumont and La Haye-Sainte, these posts were attacked, hemmed in, and the left centre of his line of battle seriously threatened. Travers' cuirassiers and d'Erlon's skirmishers appeared to dominate the crest of the plateau, and the bulk of the infantry was following them closely, behind. Supposing these troops advanced a few steps farther, supposing they could maintain themselves long enough in these positions to allow time to the reserve cavalry to deal the finishing blow, ("le coup de massue"), victory seemed certain.

SECTION IV

The vicious arrangement of d'Erlon's columns, which had already hindered their march and doubled their losses in the ascent to the plateau, was now to occasion a disaster. After the skirmishers had overthrown Bylandt's Netherlanders, the Donzelot division advanced within thirty paces from the road. Here Donzelot halted his column to deploy it. In climbing the battalion had still more decreased their intervals. They were a mere mass now. The deployment, or rather the attempt to deploy—for it did not appear that they succeeded in executing it—took a very long time; each fresh command only increased the confusion. The enemy took advantage of this respite. When the French batteries opened fire, the division under Picton (brigades Kempt and Pack) had fallen back by Wellington's orders to a distance of 150 yards from the road. The men were all there in line, but lying flat, so as to evade the projectiles. Picton noticed that the Dutch were routed, and that the French tirailleurs were crossing the hedges and advancing boldly against a battery. He gave the order "Stand," and at a bound, Kempt's brigade stood on the road. It drove away the tirailleurs, crossed the first hedge, then, upon discovering the column of Donzelot, which was engaged in deploying, it saluted it with a fire in line at forty paces. Attacked thus unawares, surprised in the very act of forming up, the French instinctively and involuntarily made a slight retrograde movement. Picton, seizing the moment, shouted: "Charge! Charge! Hurrah!" The English rushed from the second hedge and flung themselves with their bayonets fixed upon this seething mass, which resisted from its very weight. Repulsed several times they repeated their charges unceasingly. The combatants were so close to each other that the wads of their guns adhered smoking to the cloth of their uniforms. During this hand-to-hand fight a French officer was killed as he seized the flag of the 32nd regiment, and the intrepid Picton fell dead with a bullet through his temples.[42]

At the time of the flight of the Dutch and Belgians the Marcognet column (third echelon) had arrived at about the same height as the Donzelot column. Marcognet, not thinking it possible to deploy his column, had continued his march and outdistanced Donzelot, who had halted. Then, with his leading regiment and shouting, "Victory!" he broke through the double hedge, and was advancing against a Hanoverian battery, when, to the piercing sounds of the pibrochs, the Scotch brigade of Pack moved forward by battalions, deployed in four ranks. At a distance of about twenty yards the 92nd Highlanders opened fire; shortly after, the rest of the Scotch followed them. Owing to their crowded formation, the French could only reply from the front line of a single battalion. They fired one volley and rushed forward with fixed bayonets. They attacked their foes; the first rank of each side were involved in a furious struggle. "I was thrusting a soldier forward," relates an officer of the 45th; "I saw him fall to the ground at my feet from a sabre wound. I raised my head and saw the English cavalry from every side forcing their way into our midst and hacking us to pieces."[43]

As the French were about to surmount the plateau—Travers' cuirassiers on the left of the main road and d'Erlon's columns on the east—Lord Uxbridge charged them with the *élite* of his cavalry.[44] The four regiments of Somerset's mounted guards—1st and 2nd Life Guards, the Blues, and the King's Dragoons—started off at a gallop in line. A few steps farther on, they arrived within pistol-range of the cuirassiers, who were only separated from them by the Ohain road. On the western side of the highway to Brussels, the Ohain road ran for the space of 400 yards between two very steep banks, which disappeared farther on. The left of Travers and the right of Somerset charged each other at a gallop on the level portion of the road. But the platoons of the right of the cuirassiers were met by the trench. They resolutely descended the outer slope, and were spurring on their horses to climb the opposite side, when ten yards above them flashed the line of sabres of the 2nd Life Guards charging them at full speed. In order to avoid being utterly crushed—for they had neither time nor space to attempt a charge back—the cuirassiers filed up the hollow road, jostling each other terribly, regained the main road, near Wellington's elm, and rallied in a field near the sand-pit. The Life Guards, who had pursued them along the edge of the road, charged before they had time to re-form, and, after a hand-to-hand struggle, in which, says Lord Somerset, "they hammered on the cuirasses like coppersmiths at work," they flung several into the excavation of the sand-pit. The bulk of the brigade under Travers was shattered and driven back into the valley by the other regiments of Somerset, which, besides being better mounted than the cuirassiers, were superior in numbers, and had the advantage of the ground.[45]

Section V

At the same time, the brigade of Ponsonby's dragoons—Royals, Inniskillings, and Scots Greys—had flung itself against the columns of d'Erlon. The Royals debouched from the main road of Brussels, swept aside the Bourgeois brigade as it was struggling with the 95th, who were ambushed behind the hedges, and drove it back as far as the sand-pit. The Inniskillings passed the road by the openings which had been cut in the double hedge for the firing of the cannon, and assaulted the column under Donzelot. The Scots Greys—so named after the colour of their horses—followed in the steps of Pack's battalions, which opened their ranks to allow them to pass through. Highlanders and Scots Greys greeted each other with the shout, "Scotland for ever!" and the horsemen fell impetuously on the Marcognet division.[46] Fired on from the front by the infantry, charged on either flank by the cavalry, paralysed by their own unwieldy masses, the heavy French columns could only make a faint show of resistance. The men stumbled over one another, and were huddled together in such dire confusion, that they had no room to take aim or even to use their side-arms against the horsemen, who penetrated through their bewildered ranks. Bullets were fired into the air; bayonet thrusts aimed so badly they had no effect. It was a harrowing sight to see the English breaking through and slaughtering these fine divisions as if they were flocks of sheep. Intoxicated with slaughter, inciting each other to kill, they pierced and cut down the miserable mass with glee. The columns were shattered, divided, scattered, and hurled down to the foot of the slopes by the swords of the dragoons. The Bourgeois brigade, which had rallied at the sand-pit, was thrown into disorder and swept away pell-mell by the crowd of fugitives and horsemen. The Quiot brigade abandoned the attack of La Haye-Sainte.[47] Above Papelotte, the Durutte division received on its right flank the charges of Vandeleur's dragoons—11th, 12th, and 13th regiments—seconded by the Dutch dragoons and the Belgian hussars of Ghigny. Although it had suffered a severe attack at the outset, it fell back without any very great losses and in fairly good order, and recrossed the ravine, still surrounded by the cavalry.[48] Not one single Frenchman was left upon the slopes of Mont-Saint-Jean.

Borne on by their horses, which, according to report, were

not wearing any curb-chains that day, themselves excited by the rush, the tumult, the struggle, the victory, the English crossed the valley at a furious speed and attacked the opposite slope. In vain was the retreat sounded by order of Lord Uxbridge; his horsemen neither heard nor wished to hear, and they dashed up to the French position at a gallop. They could not get a footing there. The Life Guards and the Dragoons were decimated by the fire of the Bachelu division posted near the eminence, to the west of the main road. The Scots Greys met the division batteries half-way up the hill, cut down the artillerymen and drivers, hurled the guns into a ravine, then assaulted the main battery. Thereupon the lancers of Colonel Martigue charged them in flank, and routed them, whilst the lancers of Colonel Brô disengaged the Durutte division from the murderous grip of Vaudeleur's dragoons. "Never," said Durutte, " did I realise before the great superiority of the lance over the sword."[49] It was in this struggle that the valiant General Ponsonby lost his life. Unhorsed by a subaltern of the 9th Lancers, named Urban, he had surrendered, when several of his Scots Greys returned to rescue him. Urban, fearing to lose his prisoner, had the cruel courage to plunge his lance into his chest. After which he rushed at the dragoons and brought three of them to the ground.[50]

The dashing charge of the lancers was promptly supported by General Farine's brigade of cuirassiers. The Emperor, perceiving that the Scots Greys were about to attack the main battery, had sent to General Delort, Lieutenant-General under Milhaud, the order to fling two regiments against them. Lancers and cuirassiers swept the slope of La Belle Alliance, the whole extent of the valley, and pursued the horse guards and the dragoons as far as the first slopes of Mont-Saint-Jean, beyond La Haye-Sainte. The light cavalry brigades of Vivian and von Merlen, which had followed the movement of Lord Uxbridge from a distance, did not consider it wise to attack also.[51]

A pause in the action followed. Either side was busy in returning to its positions.[52] The hill-sides, which a moment before had been covered with combatants, were now covered only by dead bodies and wounded men. "The ground," said an English officer, "was literally covered with French killed and wounded."[53] It had the heart-rending aspect of the day after a battle, and the battle was only commencing!

During this interval, a cuirassier detached himself from his regiment, which was re-forming at La Belle Alliance, and starting at a gallop, descended to the main road. They watched him cross the entire length of this valley of death where he was the only living being. The Germans posted at La Haye-Sainte took him for a deserter, and refrained from firing. When he reached the orchard at the very foot of the hedge, he straightened his gigantic body in the stirrups, raised his sword, and shouted "Vive l'Empereur!" Then, midst a shower of bullets, with a few bounds of his powerful charger, he returned to the French lines.[54]

At Hougoumont the contest waxed fiercer and fiercer. Three companies of English Guards, a battalion of Brunswickers, a battalion of Duplat's German legion, two regiments under Foy, had successively reinforced the defenders and the assailants. The French, once again masters of the wood which they had previously lost, took possession of the orchard; but the English Guards would not relinquish the garden above, which was protected by a small wall provided with a natural banquette, and held their own in the farm itself. By order of the Emperor a battery of Howitzers stormed these buildings. Fire burst forth in a barn, spread rapidly, and consumed the chateau, the farmer's house, the cattle sheds and the stables. The English took refuge within the chapel, the barn, the gardener's cottage and the adjoining hollow road, from whence they resumed their fusillade. The fire itself proved an obstacle to the French. From the burning stables, from whence the enemy's ambulances had not had time to be moved, were heard vain appeals for help, and shrieks of agony.[55]

BOOK III CHAPTER IV

THE BATTLE OF WATERLOO

From three to seven o'clock

I. Second attack of La Haye-Sainte—Ney's order to Milhaud.
II. First and second charges of Milhaud's cuirassiers, and of the Light Cavalry of the Guard—Order of the Emperor to Kellermann's cuirassiers and Guyot's cavalry.
III. Bulow's corps enters in line—Defence by Lobau—The capture and recapture of Plancenoit.
IV. Third and fourth charges of Milhaud's cuirassiers, supported by Kellermann's cuirassiers, the dragoons, and the mounted grenadiers of the Guard.
V. General attack on the plateau by Reille's and d'Erlon's infantry and the remainder of the cavalry—Storming of La Haye-Sainte—The English line shaken—Renewed struggle at Plancenoit.

Section I

THE one aim of Wellington was to retain his position until the Prussian Army should enter into line. This movement was delayed far longer than he liked. He had hoped that Blücher would commence the attack by two o'clock; it was now half-past three, and the Prussians did not seem ready to show themselves. The English staff feared that they would not be strong enough to resist a second assault.[1]

Napoleon also had grave anxieties. Major La Fresnaye had just delivered him a letter from Grouchy, written in Walhain at half-past eleven.[2] In this very confused despatch, two things especially struck the Emperor: the first was, that Grouchy had made his way very slowly, since at half-past eleven he was still three leagues distant from Wavre; the second was, that the Marshal seemed in nowise concerned as to what was happening on his left, and that he was asking for orders to manœuvre on the next day in the round-about direction of La Chyse.³ It was therefore most unlikely that Grouchy would have the happy inspiration by noon, to march to the cannon, that he might take in flank Bülow's corps, which was already in position at Chapelle-Saint-Lambert. At the best, the Marshal could fall upon the rear of this corps, or contrive by an energetic attack to keep back the other parts of the Prussian Army far from the battlefield. Can we wonder that the Emperor did not at once send back La Fresnaye with fresh instructions for Grouchy? These instructions could only have been " to draw nearer the army so as to fall upon any corps of the enemy which might attempt to harass the right." Napoleon had already sent these directions to his lieutenant at a quarter past one.⁴ He could not have done more than reiterate them, and at a very late hour.

The presence of Bülow at Chapelle-Saint-Lambert, the sanguinary check to Count d'Erlon, the absence of Grouchy, might perhaps have induced the Emperor to stop the contest, as he had done at Essling, and to take up a strong defensive position on the plateau of La Belle Alliance. But it does not seem that he thought of this expedient, which could only have served him for the day. Even if reinforced by Grouchy on the next day, the French Army would have to give battle to the united armies of Wellington and Blücher, nearly in the proportion of two to one. The Emperor preferred to take advantage of the expectant attitude which Bülow maintained, to crush the English before the Prussians came into line.⁵

As soon as d'Erlon had rallied some of his battalions, about half-past three, the Emperor ordered Ney to attack La Haye-Sainte again.⁶ He contemplated using this position as a base for a general movement with d'Erlon's corps, the corps of Reille—who would, he thought, be soon master of Hougoumont—the whole of the cavalry, and lastly the foot Guards.⁷ Ney led against La Haye-Sainte the brigade of Quiot, whilst one of Donzelot's brigades, the whole of it deployed in skirmishing order, climbed the slopes to the east of the Brussels high road and opened fire at twenty paces distance, on the English who were ambushed behind the hedges of the Ohain road. The attack was a failure. Donzelot's tirailleurs were repulsed half way up; the soldiers of Quiot, decimated by the point-blank fire of Major Baring's Germans, who had just received a reinforcement of two companies, fell back upon the orchard.[8]

To support this attack the main battery had increased the fury of its fire against the left centre of the enemy's position, while the batteries of Reille, reinforced by a portion of the Guards' guns of twelve, relentlessly cannonaded the right centre. This was the moment in the day when the artillery fire was most intense. "Never," said General Alten, "had the oldest soldiers heard such a cannonade."[9] Some battalions in the first of the English line retrograded a hundred paces back, so as to be sheltered by the edges of the plateau. At the same time, groups of wounded, convoys of prisoners, empty ammunition waggons and fugitives were streaming towards the forest of Soignes.[10] Ney, mistaking movements which he could not well distinguish through the dense smoke, took them for signs of a commencing retreat, and thought the time had come to gain a footing upon the plateau with the cavalry. He immediately applied for a brigade of cuirassiers.[11]

The aide-de-camp applied to General Farine, who sent his two regiments. But General Delort, commanding the division, arrested the movement. "We receive no orders," he said, "but from Comte Milhaud." Ney, growing impatient, hastened to Delort.[12] The Marshal was very irritated by this refusal to obey. Not only did he reiterate the order with regard to the Farine brigade, but he ordered that six other regiments of Milhaud's corps should move forward as well. Delort having objected that this manœuvre would be most imprudent on such ground, Ney appealed to the instructions of the Emperor. "Forward," he cried, "the salvation of France is at stake." Delort obeyed.[13] The two divisions of cuirassiers started at full trot, with the red lancers and the horse chasseurs of the Guard coming on behind. Did these regiments follow the movement in pursuance of an order from Lefebvre-Desnoëttes, to whom it would seem that Milhaud said, "I am going to charge, support me!" before he started? Or did they rush forward of their own accord, seized with the madness of the charge at the sight of their comrades' rush toward the enemy, whose retreat seemed commencing, and eager for their share in the slaughter of the English?[14]

From the commencement of the action, Ney was planning a great cavalry movement of which the Emperor had spoken to him, and for which he had placed under Ney's command the cuirassier's corps, and even the divisions of the Horse Guard.[15] The Prince of Moscow anticipated the most wonderful results from this charge. He rejoiced in the thought that he would lead it, for, as Foy says, he was considered one of the first cavalry officers in the army. He had discussed the matter with Drouot, assuring him that he was certain of its success.[16] At first Ney had not intended to engage the cavalry until he had received orders from the Emperor[17] to that effect; he had at that time no other wish but to obtain a footing on the plateau with a brigade of cuirassiers. Then the idea occurred to him to hasten the retreat of the English, by hurling all Milhaud's cuirassiers against them. It was for this reason that he had brought up both these divisions. Probably, however, he might have hesitated to employ them without a fresh order from Napoleon. But when he saw this multitude of cuirassed squadrons, the mounted chasseurs of the Guard and the red lancers all descending to the levels of La Haye-Sainte, he had no longer any doubt that all was taking place in accordance with the Emperor's own instructions, and that the Emperor had considered the time had come for the grand attack. Otherwise, would the light cavalry of the Guard have followed the cuirassiers? It seems almost certain, however, that Napoleon saw nothing of this movement.[18] From the dip of the ground in which they were posted, the divisions of Milhaud and Lefebvre-Desnoëttes could gain the Brussels highway, cross it close up to La Belle Alliance, and descend into the valley, without being perceived by the Emperor from his post near the "Maison Decoster."[19] But it was natural Marshal Ney should conclude that this glittering mass of 5,000 horsemen had not escaped Napoleon's notice. Hastily he drew up these magnificent squadrons in the hollow of the valley to the left of the Brussels road, and at their head, rushed forward against the English Army.[20]

Section II

The idea of a retreat was so far from Wellington's mind, that he had just reinforced his line of battle in front with several brigades of his second line and his reserve. The Brunswickers advanced to the support of Maitland's guards, the Mitchel and Adam brigades crossed the road to Nivelles to establish themselves above Hougoumont, before the Ohain road.[21] It must be said that in the allied army, there were also many misgivings. The staff anxiously scrutinised the French positions, seeking to predict what movement was in preparation by Napoleon, when the cavalry descended towards La Haye-Sainte. The surprise was extreme, and dispelled every fear.[22] Kennedy says: " To our surprise, we soon saw that it was the prelude to an attack of cavalry upon a grand scale. Such an attack we had fully anticipated would take place at some period of the day; but we had no idea that it would be made upon our line standing in its regular order of battle, and that line as yet unshaken by any previous attack by infantry." Instantly the men sprang to their feet and formed into squares. The batteries remained in front, on the very edge of the plateau. The teams of horses were sent to a distance, and the artillerymen received orders not to fire until the last moment, then, after abandoning their pieces, to take shelter within the squares.[23]

The French cavalry advanced in echelons of squadron columns, the cuirassiers on the right, the chasseurs and the " chevau-légers " on the left. They moved in a slightly oblique direction, the first echelons manœuvring so as to gain the level portion of the Ohain road, the left echelons converging toward the slopes above Hougoumont.[24] The flank was exposed to the enemy's artillery. As soon as the cuirassiers commenced to debouch from the hollows in which they had formed up, the French batteries ceased to fire, and the English batteries increased their cannonade. The pieces were loaded with a double charge: shell, grape-shot and bar-shot.[25] A hurricane of iron rent the air. At a slow canter, the horses climbed those steep slopes, over the soaked and greasy ground into which they sometimes sunk up to the knees, and through the tall stalks of rye which swept against their breasts. By accelerating their fire, the batteries were able to discharge several times. A last salvo at forty paces distance from the batteries of Lloyd and of Cleeves, which were posted at the exact spot where the "Butte du Lion" now rises, mowed down half the leading squadrons. The survivors halted for a few seconds and seemed to hesitate. The charge sounded, louder and louder; the shout arose of: "Vive l'Empereur!" The cuirassiers flung themselves on the cannon. One after the other, all the batteries were taken.[26] A superb feat of arms indeed, but a delusive capture! There were no horses to carry off the pieces, no spikes to make them useless. It was possible to throw them down into the ravine, and to drive the ramrods of their pistols instead of nails, into the touch-holes. Nothing was done, it did not even occur to a single officer to have the cannon sponges destroyed.[27]

The cannons were silenced, but the fusillade continued to roll and crackle. Between the Nivelles road and the Brussels highroad, twenty English, Hanoverian, Brunswick, and German[28] battalions were posted, formed into squares like those on a chess-board. The bullets struck and rebounded from the cuirasses with the sound of hail on a roof of slates. Cuirassiers and lancers, their ranks already shattered by the storm of bullets, by the ascent, by their very passage through that hedge of artillery, still fell upon these squares. But from the edge of the plateau, which they took at full gallop, to the first line of the infantry, the field was far too narrow. The charge was lacking in vigour and consequently in effect. The English were in squares three ranks deep, the first rank with one knee on the ground, with muskets resting on the earth, and sloping bayonets, thus forming chevaux-de-frise. In spite of vigorous spurring, and their maddened sabre cuts, in spite of their valour and their rage, the horsemen were powerless to pierce these serried walls of men.[29] They advanced obliquely to the right and to the left, and under cross firing spurred onwards, charging the squares of the second line. As one wave follows another, so did the squadrons follow each other in quick succession. The tide of cavalry flooded the whole plateau. Cuirassiers, chasseurs, red lancers surged around the squares, assaulted them on their four sides, dashed with fury against their corners, struck down the bayonets with their swords, with their spears pierced through the breasts of their foes, discharged their pistols point blank, in these furious hand-to-hand struggles, but they only succeeded in making partial breaches which were as quickly filled up again.[30]

Lord Uxbridge watched this mêlée. The two-thirds of his cavalry had not as yet been in action. He hurled against these disordered masses, Dornberg's dragoons, Arenschild's hussars, Brunswick's black lancers, Trip's Dutch carabiniers, the two Dutch-Belgian brigades of van Merlen and of Ghigny, altogether five thousand fresh horses. They had the advantage of numbers and cohesion. The French bent under the shock, were forced back into the spaces between the squares, and only escaped the sword to fall under the bullets of the foe. They abandoned the plateau. The gunners rushed back to their posts at the guns; all along the crest, the fire of the English batteries blazed out anew.[31] Scarcely had they reached the bottom of the valley, when Milhaud's and Lefebvre-Desnoëtte's valiant soldiers charged again. Once more they climbed, midst volleys of grape-shot, the muddy slopes of Mont-Saint-Jean, took possession of the cannon, crowned the heights, fell upon the infantry, and with their flashing swords made deep furrows in the whole chess-board of the squares.[32]

Many an Englishman believed then that the battle was lost. The batteries in reserve were prepared to retire at the first order. Artillery-Colonel Gould said to Mercer: "I much fear all is lost."[33] From La Belle Alliance the staff watched these magnificent cavalry charges; they saw the cannons abandoned, the horsemen galloping over the plateau, the lines of the enemy broken through, the squares surrounded; those around the Emperor declared the victory gained.[34] He was himself surprised and annoyed that his cavalry had been used without his orders against troops which were still unshaken.[35] He said to Soult: "This is a premature movement which may produce fatal results in the issue of this day."[36] The chief of the staff was loud in his condemnation of Ney: "He is compromising us as he did at Jena!" The Emperor swept a searching and prolonged glance over the battlefield, reflected for a moment, then resumed: "This has taken place an hour too soon, but we must stand by what is already done."[37] He sent off one of his aides-de-camp, General Flahaut, with an order to Kellermann to charge with the four brigades of cuirassiers and carabiniers.[38]

Like the Emperor, Kellermann considered that Milhaud's movement had been premature; he thought it would be most imprudent to engage his own cavalry. He was probably about to give his opinion on the matter to Flahaut, when General Lhéritier, who commanded his first division (cuirassiers and dragoons) set it off at full trot without waiting for any orders. Kellermann was obliged to follow with his second division, composed of the 2nd and 3rd cuirassiers, and of the 1st and 2nd carabiniers; however, not far from Hougoumont he halted the brigade of carabiniers in a dip of the ground; strictly forbidding General Blancard to stir from the spot unless he received formal orders from Kellermann himself.[39] This proved a wise precaution, for these eight hundred carabiniers were afterwards the only cavalry reserve which the Army possessed. Flahaut in pursuance with the Emperor's instructions had transmitted the order to charge, not only to Kellermann, but also to General Guyot, commander of the heavy cavalry of the Guards (dragoons and mounted Grenadiers).[40]

The Emperor had said that Milhaud's divisions must be supported, as he feared that any reverse suffered by them in the presence of the whole Army, might unnerve the men and bring about a panic and a rout.[41] Did he not hope also to crush the English under a fresh mass of cuirassed cavalry? It was necessary to hasten the action, to gain on one point, to hold firm on another, to vanquish and to triumph through sheer audacity, for matters had become terribly critical. The Emperor was in fact fighting two battles at the same time, the one parallel, the other oblique; in front he attacked the English; on his right flank, he was himself attacked by the Prussians.

Section III

Towards one o'clock Blücher had joined the main body of Bülow's corps at Chapelle-Saint-Lambert; but, eager as he was to fight, he judged it imprudent to advance in the defiles of the Lasne, before making sure he would not be caught there in the act of marching. Three quarters of an hour later, he learnt by reports from his scouts, that the French were very far off and that he ran as yet no risk.[42] He at once started his troops in the direction of Plancenoit. His object was to fall upon the right of the Imperial Army.[43] When one follows the steep and hollow road which descends from Chapelle-Saint-Lambert, crosses at Lasne the brook of that name, and remounts the no less abrupt slope of the other hill, one is amazed that the Prussian artillery could have overcome the difficulties of this defile. It required all Blücher's indomitable will. He was everywhere at once, cheering his soldiers, who were exhausted by fatigue and hunger (they had been on the march from five o'clock in the morning and had taken no food since the previous day), lavishing encouraging words on them and appeals to duty—kindly, pleasant words: "Now then, comrades," he said to some gunners who were straining at the wheels of a cannon which had sunk deep into the mire, "surely you would not have me break my word."[44]

At four o'clock the heads of his columns reached the wood of Paris (3,500 yards from Plancenoit). Here the Losthin and Hiller divisions established themselves without striking a blow, for instead of occupying the avenues of the wood, General Domon's cavalry had been content merely to watch its outlets.[45] In this new position the Prussians found themselves under cover. Before unmasking, Blücher would have preferred waiting for Bülow's two other divisions, which were still in the defiles of the Lasne. But Wellington's messages imploring him to take part in the fight, became more and more pressing; he could hear, too, the thunder of the French guns and distinguish, it is said, the movement of the cuirassiers on the heights of La Belle Alliance. He determined to act with what troops he had.[46] At half-past four [47] the Prussians debouched, Losthin's infantry to the right of the Plancenoit road, Hiller's infantry to the left, the front covered by two cavalry regiments and three light batteries. Blücher hastened to open fire with his guns on the squadrons of Domon;[48] his object, says Müffling, was to inform and to strengthen Wellington, and at the same time to prevent Napoleon from crushing the English.[49]

Domon at first met the attack by a counter-attack. He repulsed the Prussian hussars, and fell upon their batteries. Mown down by their cannonade and by the fusillade of the whole Losthin division, he slowly fell back; then passing to the reserve, he unmasked the infantry of Lobau, who had taken up position crosswise on the Lasne road, about half a league to the east of the road to Brussels. The Simmer and Janin divisions, deployed there one behind the other, were arranged in the shape of a T, nearly perpendicularly to the line of battle.[50] To supply their places on the front, the Emperor had moved his foot Guards forward near La Belle Alliance, to the right of the Brussels road, with the exception of the 1st Grenadier regiment, which remained near Rossomme, and the 1st battalion of the 1st Chasseurs posted at Le Caillou. At the same time he had given Durutte orders to assail Papelotte and La Haye, so as to support Ney's grand attack and to cut the communication between Bülow's right and the English left.[51]

Well aware that passive resistance was virtually doomed, Lobau headed straight for the Prussians, who gave way, whereupon the divisions under Ryssel and Hacke debouched from the woods. Again the Prussians resumed the offensive, 30,000 against 10,000 Frenchmen.[52] But Lobau had under him regiments of long standing and as firm as rocks. The 5th of the line, the first regiment which had gone over to Napoleon, in the Laffray defile, and the 10th of the line, the only one which had fought for the Bourbons at the bridge of Loriol,[53] vied with each other in courage and tenacity. With these fine troops, Lobau presented such a fierce front that Blücher, instead of persisting in his parallel attack, manœuvred for an assault on the right of the 6th Corps. The cavalry of Prince William of Prussia and Hiller's infantry, supported by the Ryssel divisions, bore down towards Plancenoit. Lobau, fearing he might be turned, drew back to the height of the village, where he posted a brigade. Assailed on three points, this brigade was unable to hold its ground and was driven out from Plancenoit, which was occupied and entrenched by the enemy. From his front Bülow cannonaded the other three brigades of Lobau with eight batteries, the shells from which sometimes fell on the Brussels road, amid the battalions of the Guard, and even of the Imperial staff.[54]

At the moment when his infantry was attacking Plancenoit, Blücher received one of Thielmann's aides-de-camp. The commander of the 3rd Corps announced that he was being attacked at Wavre by superior forces (these were Grouchy's 33,000 men), and that he was doubtful as to his power of resistance: "Let Thielmann defend himself as best he can," said Gneisenau. "It matters little if he be crushed at Wavre, provided we gain the victory here."[55] With the enemy in possession of Plancenoit, Napoleon was hemmed in and his line of retreat threatened. He ordered Duhesme, commanding the division of the Young Guard, to recapture this village. Its eight battalions, four of voltigeurs, four of sharpshooters, rushed to the charge. The Prussians were dislodged from the houses and from the cemetery, which they had made a redoubt.[56]

Section IV

The English still stood their ground. When the heavy cavalry of Kellermann and of Guyot had debouched in the valley between five and half-past five, Millhaud's cuirassiers, repulsed for the second time by the English dragoons, rushed to the bottom of the slopes.[57] Having promptly re-formed, they charged these three fresh divisions. The cuirassiers of Lhéritier, of Delort, of Wathier, of Roussel d'Hurbal, the chasseurs and lancers of Lefebvre - Desnoüttes, the dragoons and mounted grenadiers of Guyot—more than sixty squadrons —gained the plateau. The enemy's staff was amazed that eight or nine thousand cavalry, should offer battle on a front which afforded space for the deployment of one thousand only at the most. They covered the whole area between Hougoumont and La Haye-Sainte. Their ranks were so closely pressed that the horses were actually lifted off the ground by the pressure.[58] This mass of cuirasses, casques, and swords overflowed the uneven ground. To the English they looked like a rising tide of steel.

The enemy renewed their twice-successful manœuvre. After pouring a storm of grape-shot upon the cavalry, the gunners abandoned their pieces and took refuge within the squares. The latter, at a range of thirty paces, opened an enfilading fire, which mowed down entire ranks as with a scythe, receiving the shattered remains of the squadrons upon their triple line of bayonets. Charge after charge followed without any intermission. The squares sustained five, seven, ten, and even thirteen assaults. Several were shaken and partially broken, if not crushed and scattered altogether. A quartermaster of the 9th Cuirassiers seized an English flag. Captain Klein de Kleinenberg, of the chasseurs of the Guard, had his horse killed under him as he bore off the flag of the German Legion.[59] However, most of the squares remained impregnable. For an instant they seemed overwhelmed by the surging masses of cavalry, then they would reappear through the smoke, bristling with flashing bayonets, whilst the squadrons were scattered like breakers dashing against a sea-wall.

Lhéritier's cuirassiers pierced through a labyrinth of cross fires as far as the squares of the 2nd line, passed beyond them, and were swept down by the batteries in reserve. An entire regiment wheeled to the left, enfiladed at full gallop the Nivelles road, cutting down the sharpshooters along the road to Braine-l'Alleud, turned Hougoumont, and came back to re-form on the plateau of La Belle Alliance. The dragoons of the Guard engaged with Grant's light cavalry, which had been occupied all the afternoon in observing Piré's lancers before Monplaisir, and recognising at last that the movements of the latter were mere demonstrations, had fallen back from the right wing to the centre.[60] Mercer's battery, the only one whose gunners had remained at their guns in spite of Wellington's order, found itself slightly in the rear, its front sheltered by an embankment of the road, its flanks protected by two squares of Brunswickers. The mounted grenadiers, giants on huge steeds whose stature was augmented by their huge hairy helmets, advanced at a trot in line. They looked like a moving wall. Under Mercer's grape-shot, crossed by the enfilading fires of the two squares of Brunswickers, this wall crumbled quickly away, strewing the ground with bleeding fragments. A second charge only resulted in fresh butchery. General Jamin, colonel of the grenadiers, fell fatally wounded on a gun carriage. In front of the battery rose a rampart of corpses and mangled horses. "You have a goodly pile there," laughingly remarked Colonel Wood to Mercer. The last platoons of grenadiers leapt over the hideous obstacle, traversed the intervals between the guns, cutting down the gunners, and joined in the charges of the cuirassiers.[61] Terribly hampered by their numbers, which were far too great for the small expanse of ground, all these squadrons clashed together, broke in charging, and became inextricably confused in their ranks. Though their attacks were as eager as ever, they gradually became less and less vigorous, less and less rapid, less and less effective, owing to the disorder and the breathlessness of the horses, which at every step sank deeper into the soaked and slippery ground. The atmosphere was scorching; it was hardly possible to breathe: "It was like being at the door of a hot oven." General Donop was wounded, so also was General Delort, General Lhéritier, General Guyot, and General Roussel d'Hurbal. Edouard de Colbert charged with his arm in a sling. Generals Blancard, Dubois, Farine, Guiton, Picquet, Travers, Wathier, were also wounded. Marshal Ney, whose third horse had been killed under him, stood alone by the side of an abandoned battery, and was furiously striking with the blade of his sword at the bronze mouth of an English cannon. The whole field of battle was encumbered with non-combatants: dismounted cuirassiers walking heavily, borne down by the weight of their armour, toward the valley; wounded men crawling from under heaps of the slain; riderless horses galloping madly, terrified by the bullets whizzing past their ears. Wellington came out of the square of the 73rd, in which he had taken refuge during the hottest time of the action; he rushed to his cavalry and hurled it against the exhausted battalions, which were separated and broken by their own charges. For the third time the French surrendered the plateau.[62] For the fourth time they remounted the hill shouting "Vive l'Empereur!" Ney led the charge at the head of the carabiniers. From the distance he had distinguished their gold cuirasses; he flew to them, and in spite of General Blancard's remonstrances, who urged the precise orders of Kellermann, he hurried them away with him, to a wild race of death.[63]

The fury of Ney and his heroic horsemen, who, like him, were intoxicated with rage, verged on madness. This last charge with squadrons reduced one-half, with exhausted troops, with half-dead horses, could only result in a fresh reverse. The action of cavalry upon infantry consists entirely in its moral effect. And what hope was there of producing a moral effect on these foot soldiers, whose success in repulsing with their fire and their bayonets one charge after another, had taught them that these wild rushes of cavalry were merely a bugbear, and who through these two terrible hours, long as days, had acquired the assurance that they were utterly invincible? It was, on the contrary, the horsemen who were demoralised by the uselessness of their attacks, the vanity of their efforts. They charged with the same intrepidity, but no longer with the same confidence. Once more they traversed the line of the batteries, but after vainly urging their wearied horses against the squares, or, to speak more correctly, against the ramparts of dead men and slaughtered horses which protected each side, they fell back of their own accord, discouraged and despairing, to the bottom of the valley, followed at a distance, rather than actually repulsed by the English cavalry, which was itself completely worn out.[64]

Section V

These magnificent charges might have succeeded, had they been immediately followed up by infantry. Whilst the enemy's batteries, beyond which the cuirassiers had passed, were silent, the infantry could have climbed the slopes without either risk or loss, might have taken their positions on the edge of the plateau, and assailed the squares. The English would have been compelled either to submit to the fire and assaults of the infantry in a very disadvantageous formation, or to deploy, which would have placed them at the mercy of the horsemen. The Bachelu division and the Janin brigade (Foy division) were only 1,300 yards distant from the Allies' position, and stood there at attention for several hours watching this furious fight. They only waited for the order to go to the support of the cavalry. Ney had completely forgotten them ! Only after the repulse of the fourth charge, did he think of using these six thousand bayonets. The six regiments marched by échelons in columns of division with intervals of half a distance. It was too late. They were swept down by the batteries; and the Anglo-Allied infantry, which had extended its front towards Hougoumont in crescent shape, riddled them through and through with converging fires. "It was a hail of death," said Foy. In a few seconds 1,500 men were killed, wounded, and scattered. Nevertheless they came within pistol shot of the enemy, but the fresh brigades under Duplat and William Halkett commenced an offensive movement (Duplat was killed at this moment), whereupon the columns, cut to pieces by the shells, began to retreat. Vainly had Ney sent to their aid the carabiniers and the skeleton remains of a few other squadrons. In these partial charges, which continued till nearly the close of the fight, the horsemen could no longer pierce through the line of the English batteries as they had done.[65]

With his mind intent on the cavalry charges Ney, in the heat of this tumultuous action, had lost sight of his first intention, namely, the capture of La Haye-Sainte. Here, as at Hougoumont, though with far less ardour, the struggle continued, without any result. And yet the intrepid defenders, furnished with only sixty cartridges each, were beginning to slacken their fire. Major Baring had sent to ask for more ammunition. Wellington had none to give; he sent him a fresh reinforcement of two companies.[66]

Toward six o'clock, at the moment when the Foy and Bachelu divisions advanced toward the plateau, the Emperor went along the entire line of battle under a shower of shells and cannon balls. General Desvaux de Saint Maurice, commander-in-chief of the artillery of the Guard; General

Lallemand, commander of the batteries on foot; Bailly de Monthyon, chief of the general staff, had been struck down by his side, the first-named killed, the two others seriously wounded. Napoleon sent word to Ney that he was to take La Haye-Sainte whatever the cost.[67] This was a fresh prize offered to the Marshal, a new opportunity of meeting death. He went there instantly, hurried off the 13th léger (Donzelot's division), a detachment of the 1st regiment of Engineers, and hurled them against the farm. The bullets fired at ten yards and at five yards, point blank, soon thinned the number of assailants. Some soldiers tried to disarm the Germans by seizing the barrels of their muskets, which projected through the loopholes. In an instant seventy French fell at the foot of the eastern wall. Their comrades mounted on the heap of bodies to scale the top of the wall, whence they could shoot Major Baring's chasseurs in the court below; others pulled themselves up to the roof of the barn. Lieutenant Vieux of the engineers, who met with his death as colonel many years after at the siege of Constantine, hacked the door of the court-house with repeated blows of a hatchet. He received a bullet in his wrist, another in his shoulder. The axe passed from hand to hand; the door at last gave way and the human tide flowed into the court. Hemmed in, their backs to the wall, and with no cartridges, the Germans defended themselves with their side arms. Major Baring, with forty-two men— all that remained of his nine companies—broke through the crowd of the assailants and regained Mont-Saint-Jean.[68]

Ney immediately posted a mounted battery upon a mound near La Haye-Sainte and pushed forward a regiment to the sand-pit, which was once more abandoned by the English 95th. In these two positions the gunners fired at a distance of less than 300 yards, the tirailleurs at less than 80, upon the very centre of the enemy's line. Supported by this fire, which made a breach for them, the remainder of the divisions of Allix, Donzelot, and Marcognet ascended on either side of the farm as far as the Ohain road. The enemies shot at each other through the hedges, from the banks, and attacked with their bayonets. Ompteda meanwhile, with the 5th and 8th battalions of the German legion on the main road

CHAP. IV   *THE BATTLE OF WATERLOO*   217

delivered a counter-attack, which at first was crowned with success. A bullet brought him to the ground under his horse, mortally wounded. The 5th battalion fell back. The 8th, which was in advance of it, was exterminated by a squadron of cuirassiers. Its flag was taken; its chief, Colonel Shrader, killed; thirty men alone escaped from the sabres.[69]

The enemy's left centre (brigades Kempt, Pack, Lambert, Best, and Winke) still held firm; but on the extreme left, the Nassau troops of the Prince of Saxe-Weimar were for the second time driven out of Papelotte by the division of Durutte, and on the right centre, the Anglo-Allies were wavering and their strength almost spent. The ammunition gave out, the guns were dismounted, others were left without a gunner. The Prince of Orange and General Alten, both of them wounded, quitted the battlefield; Colonels Gordon and De Lancy-Evans, aides-de-camp to Wellington, were killed. The cavalry brigades, under Somerset and Ponsonby, were reduced together to two squadrons; the Ompteda brigade had now only a mere handful of men; the Kielmansegge brigade fell back behind Mont-Saint-Jean; the Krüse brigade gave way. In the rear, the fugitives grew more and more numerous. The whole regiment of the Cumberland Hussars wheeled round, with its colonel at its head, and at full trot rode away on the highroad to Brussels. Everywhere the ranks were thinning, the wounded were numerous, and numerous also were the men who went off with them under the pretext of carrying them to the ambulances. Disorder appeared even in the dauntless brigade of Colin Halkett, where a battalion found itself under the command of a mere lieutenant. The standards of the 30th and the 73rd were prudently sent to the rear.[70]

"The centre of the line was left open," said an aide-de-camp of General Alten. "We were in peril. At each moment the issue of the battle was more than doubtful."[71] In spite of his accustomed confidence, Wellington became uneasy. He could see plainly the black masses of Blücher's troops assaulting the flank of the French Army, but he himself was without any support. He was heard to murmur: "Night or the Prussians must arrive." He had already despatched several aides-de-camp in the direction of Ohain to hasten the march of Zieten's corps. But his resolution was in nowise daunted. Officers arrived to him from every side, describing the situation as desperate, and asking for fresh orders. There was no other order but to stand firm to the last man.[72]

The wavering and the slight move backward of the enemy's line, had not escaped the notice of Marshal Ney. But his soldiers were quite as exhausted as those of Wellington. He realised that the addition of a few fresh troops would have sufficed to give them new spirit and new courage, to overcome the last resistance of the English. He sent Colonel Heymès to the Emperor asking for a few infantry. "Troops!" cried Napoleon, "where do you expect me to get them? Do you expect me to make them?"[73]

The Emperor still had eight battalions of the Old Guard, and six battalions of the Middle Guard left. If at that very moment, he had sent but half of them to Marshal Ney we may believe, on the authority of the best informed and most impartial of the English historians, that this reinforcement might have forced the enemy's centre.[74] But Napoleon, who had no cavalry reserve, did not consider that with all his "bear skins" he had too many to preserve his own position. The situation was quite as critical for him as for Wellington. Before a third onslaught from the whole of Bülow's corps, Lobau gave way, and the Young Guard, after a stubborn resistance, allowed Plancenoit to be torn from its grasp.[75] The shells of the Prussian batteries were now ploughing up the ground around La Belle Alliance. Napoleon, already overpowered on his flank, was menaced by an irruption of the Prussians to the rear of his line of battle. He formed eleven battalions of the Guard into as many squares, and posted them opposite Plancenoit along the Brussels highroad from La Belle Alliance as far as Rossomme. The 1st battalion of the 1st Chasseurs was kept at Le Caillou. Generals Morand and Pelet received orders to recapture Plancenoit with the 1st battalion of the 2nd Grenadiers and the 1st of the 2nd Chasseurs.[76] With their drums beating, these old veterans charged forward in close columns of platoons. They outdistanced the Young Guard, which Duhesme was striving to rally, assaulted Plancenoit on two different points, forced their way in, without deigning to fire a shot, overthrew, trampled down, and drove out the mass of the Prussians. The attack was so impetuous, that in twenty minutes the whole village was swept. With their bayonets dyed with blood, these old soldiers followed on the heels of the fugitives, chased them for six hundred yards, and drove them to the opposite hill behind the batteries under Hiller, which were for the moment abandoned. The Young Guard aided in this movement and reoccupied Plancenoit. Lobau, struggling with the Hacke and Losthin divisions, also regained part of the lost ground.[77]

BOOK III CHAPTER V

THE BATTLE OF WATERLOO (*Continued*)

From seven to nine o'clock

I. Dispositions for the final attack—Strengthening of the English line—Approach of Zieten's corps.
II. Assault on the plateau of Mont-Saint-Jean by the "Middle" Guard.
III. "The Guard falls back!"—General forward movement of the English Army—Irruption of Zieten's Prussians—The panic.
IV. The squares of Christiani, of Roguet, and of Cambronne.
V. Arrival of Pirch's corps to the assistance of Bülow—Slaughter in Plancenoit—The struggle on the plateau of La Belle Alliance—The last squares of the Old Guard.

SECTION I

By a single stunning blow from his Old Guard, Napoleon had arrested the Prussians. His right flank was set free; he had recovered his liberty to act on the front line of battle. It was past seven o'clock,[1] but there were still two full hours of daylight, for the weather had cleared and the sun shone over Braine-l'Alleud. Grouchy's cannonade grew louder, came nearer and nearer, and rumbled in the direction of Limale.[2] It was taken for granted, that at last the Marshal had come up with the Prussian Army, that he was fighting with it, and, whether victor or vanquished, would hold it in check long enough to prevent its junction with the English. It seemed that Blücher was able to detach Bülow's corps only, and this could be easily reckoned with, by Lobau, Duhesme, and two battalions of the Old Guard. The Emperor turned his field-glass on the English position. The points from whence the artillery fire and the discharges of musketry proceeded, served him as land-marks. On the extreme right, the Durutte division, in possession of Papelotte and La Haye, was ascending the plateau.³ On the left, the struggle continued around Hougoumont, in flames; the position was stormed by one of Jérôme's brigades; the French sharpshooters, supported by Piré's lancers, had passed beyond the Nivelles road. In the centre, above La Haye-Sainte, from which the enemy was at last expelled, the soldiers of Donzelot, Allix, and Marcognet crowned the ridges and vigorously drove the English along the Ohain road. In the valley the six regiments of Bachelu and Foy had rallied, with the débris of the cavalry.⁴ The enemy's line seemed shaken. The Emperor presumed that Wellington had all his troops in action. He himself still had his Old Guard, his *invincibles*. The critical moment had come when victory, still undecided, would be won by the most furious and most daring. He ordered Drouot to bring forward, in the formation of squares previously adopted, nine battalions of the Guard (of the five which remained, two were to stay at Plancenoit, and three on the plateau as a last reserve). He placed himself at the head of the first square and quickly proceeded to La Haye-Sainte, to the very mouth of the furnace.⁵

According to the testimony of the enemy,⁶ this attack might have been decisive half an hour earlier, when Ney asked for reinforcements. But the time was past now. Whilst Morand had retaken Plancenoit, in the short space of time during which the Guard had been formed up and started, Wellington had quickly re-ordered his positions. To reinforce his shaken centre, which seemed on the point of giving way, he had recalled from his left, Wincke's brigade and from his right, four battalions of Brunswickers, of which he himself took the command. With the assistance of these fresh troops, the Kempt, Lambert, Pack, and Best brigades on the east of the Brussels road, and the Kruse and Halkett brigades on the west of the same road, made a vigorous counter-attack and drove back the infantry of Donzelot, Allix, and Marcognet. Whilst the latter fell back at the foot of the slopes, sharp-shooting all the way, the Anglo-Germans reoccupied the edge of the plateau, and their batteries, harassed no longer by the close fusillade, silenced the guns posted at La Haye-Sainte.⁷

At the same time the Dutch and Belgian division of Chassé arrived from Braine-l'Alleud with the six cavalry regiments under Vandeleur and Vivian, which, upon hearing of the imminent arrival of the Prussian corps of Zieten, left their position as flanking troops above Papelotte, and rode up at a gallop.[8]

The Prussian reinforcements, which were so urgently needed, and the first result of whose approach was to render Vivian's and Vandeleur's 2,600 fresh horses available, very nearly failed Wellington. After leaving Bierges at noon [9] Zieten had been compelled to halt for over two hours to allow Pirch's corps to defile on to the heights at the north-west of the Dyle; he was further delayed in his march by the steep paths in the woods of Rixensart, where the men often had to advance in single file and to force a passage for the cannons;[10] consequently Zieten only reached Ohain toward six o'clock with his advanced Guard.[11] He was joined there by Colonel Freemantle, aide-de-camp to Wellington, who laid before him the critical situation of the English Army and asked for some reinforcements, if only as few as 3,000 men, but at once. Zieten did not wish to run the risk of having his army corps beaten in detail; he replied that he would hasten to the rescue of the English as soon as the bulk of his troops had come up with the advanced Guard.[12] Meanwhile he sent a staff officer toward Mont-Saint-Jean in order to ascertain exactly how matters stood. The latter was deceived by the great number of wounded and fugitives who were flying to the rear, and, coming back, he reported that the English were in full retreat. Fearing to be dragged into a rout without any advantage to the Allied Army, he immediately headed to the left, in order to rally Bülow between Frichermont and the Paris wood. Müffling, who was then in observation above Papelotte, saw this movement. He spurred his horse to a gallop, and, joining Zieten, gave him more correct information, beseeching him to bear down to the English left. "The battle is lost," he exclaimed vehemently, "if the first corps does not go to the Duke's rescue." After much hesitation Zieten yielded to Müffling's arguments and resumed his previous direction.[13]

The head of Zieten's column debouched from Smohain as

the Guard was descending toward La Haye-Sainte. Already some of the French troops had fallen back on perceiving the Prussians. The Emperor rushed to them, and harangued them, and they marched forward to the front.[14] A fresh corps of the enemy broke into the right angle of our two lines of battle, and this gave the finishing blow. Yet it is doubtful whether the Emperor could then have stopped the battle.[15] Owing to the disorder which already prevailed among the troops, their dissemination over so wide an area, and the advanced position of Bülow's corps on their flank, a retreat would have proved terribly hazardous. Even had it been effected without great loss and confusion, and under shelter of a dyke formed at the summit of the Belle Alliance plateau, with all the battalions of the Guard, what terrible developments such a retreat meant to Napoleon! The Army reduced by one half (for Grouchy's corps, left isolated, and cut off from its line of retreat, seemed doomed to total destruction), the frontier left unprotected, France discouraged, patriotism cast down, the Chambers passing from secret hostility to open war; on every side intrigue, desertion, treason. Rather than live over again the agony of 1814, it was better to make a supreme and desperate effort to conquer rebellious fortune.

SECTION II

The approach of the Prussian corps had no other effect upon the Emperor than to precipitate the attack. Only six battalions of the Guard had arrived in the plain of La Haye-Sainte. The Emperor posted one (the 2nd of the 3rd Grenadiers) on a small eminence half-way between the farm and Hougoumont, and upon perceiving Ney, who was found wherever death had to be faced, he entrusted him with the command of the five others with which to assault the English right centre.[16] At the same time orders were sent to the batteries to increase their fire, and to d'Erlon, Reille, and the chiefs of the cavalry to second the movement of the Guard on their respective fronts. The rumours that the Prussians were debouching from Ohain might spread.

The Emperor determined to prevent any alarm. He ordered La Bedoyère and his orderlies to traverse the length of the line of battle and announce everywhere the arrival of Marshal Grouchy.[17] Ney said that he was indignant at this stratagem. As if Napoleon had any choice of means! In point of fact this false intelligence revived the confidence and rekindled the enthusiasm of the soldiers. The troops again formed up their ranks and shouted "Vive l'Empereur!" Even the wounded rose to cheer the columns as they passed by. A soldier with three stripes, a veteran of Marengo, whose legs had been crushed by a shell, sitting near the embankment of the road, repeated in a loud, firm voice: "This is nothing, comrades. Forward, and long live the Emperor!"[18]

Did Wellington detect the preparatory movements for this final attack through the ever-thickening clouds of smoke? It mattered little, for he was advised of them by a traitor. At the very moment when Drouot was mustering the Guard, a captain of the carabiniers rode across the valley at full gallop, defying the shells and the bullets which fell like hail, and with his sword in the sheath and his right hand raised in the air, he accosted the advanced skirmishers of the English 52nd. Brought before the major of this regiment, who was then talking to the commander of the light artillery, Colonel Fraser, he exclaimed, "Long live the King! Get ready. That scoundrel Napoleon will be upon you with his Guard in less than half an hour."[19] Colonel Fraser immediately went to Wellington to convey this intelligence to him. The Duke went along the battle line, from the Brussels road to that of Nivelles, issuing his final orders. The Adam brigade and the brigade of Maitland's guards, which had withdrawn to a depression of the ground to be sheltered from the shells, resumed their position. The William Halkett Hanoverian brigade and the German brigade of Duplat prolonged Adam's right towards Hougoumont. The Dutch-Belgian division of Chassé came up and posted themselves thus: the Aubremé brigade in the rear of Maitland's guards, having behind them Vandeleur's cavalry; the Dittmer brigade behind the three battalions of Brunswickers posted on the left of Colin Halkett's English brigade. Vivian's cavalry deployed on the west of the Brussels road, to support the decimated brigades of Ompteda and of Kruse, and another battalion of Brunswickers. The three batteries, until now kept in reserve, advanced to the front. The gunners were ordered not to respond to the French artillery, and to concentrate all their fire on the assaulting columns. They were to fire till they were reduced to the very last charge of shell.[20]

It appears that Ney gave an ill-advised order and a wrong direction to the Guard. Instead of forming one single column strong enough to pierce through the enemy's line, the Marshal left the battalions divided. Instead of marching straight up to the plateau from the lowlands of La Haye-Sainte by the Brussels road, over which the column had barely 400 yards to traverse and where the embankments sheltered it from the slanting fire of the artillery, he took an oblique course by the unprotected slopes which the cuirassiers had climbed in their first charge.[21]

The five battalions of the Middle Guard, formed into as many squares, advanced in echelons, the right leading. Between each echelon the mounted gunners of the Guard drew two cannons of 8; the total forming a complete battery under the orders of Colonel Duchand. During this oblique movement, almost identical with the movement known as "Towards the left, forward to battle," all the echelons did not maintain the proper interval. The fourth approached too closely to the third. Soon the five echelons were condensed into four: on the right, the 1st battalion of the 3rd Grenadiers; in the centre, the one battalion of the 4th Grenadiers; farther to the left, the 1st and 2nd battalions of the 3rd Chasseurs; on the extreme left, the 4th Chasseurs, now reduced to a single battalion.[22]

All the troops had received orders to support this attack. Already the Donzelot, Allix, and Marcognet divisions climbed to the plateau; the first along and up the left side of the Genappe road; the two others on the right of this road. But Reille's infantry and the fragments of the cavalry had scarcely commenced to move.[23] Between La Haye-Sainte and Hougoumont, the five battalions of the Guard advanced alone against the whole English Army! They marched presenting arms;

their line as perfect as if for a review at the Tuileries, superb and impassive. All their officers leading, the first to be exposed to the enemy's fire. Generals Friant and Porret du Mervan commanded the battalion of the 3rd Grenadiers; General Harlet, the battalion of the 4th Grenadiers; General Michel, the 1st battalion of the 3rd Chasseurs; Colonel Mallet, a faithful follower from Elba, the 2nd battalion; General Henrion, the battalion of the 4th Chasseurs. Ney fell heavily to the ground with his horse; it was the fifth that had been killed under him. He disentangled himself, rose, and walked on, sword in hand, by the side of Friant. The English artillery was drawn out in a semicircle from the Brussels highroad to the slopes around Hougoumont—for the previously convex line of the enemy's right wing had now become concave—and it discharged a double volley of grapeshot at a distance of 200 yards. The Guard was assailed from the front and in a slanting direction. Each volley made a breach in its ranks. The Grenadiers closed up their files, contracted their squares, and continued to ascend at an even pace, shouting, "Long live the Emperor!"[24]

The 1st battalion of the 3rd Grenadiers (right-hand echelon) repulsed a corps of Brunswickers, seized the batteries under Cleeves and Lloyd which were abandoned by their gunners, and by a slight divergence proceeded against the left of the Halkett brigade. The English 30th and 73rd fell back in disorder. Friant, wounded by a bullet, left the battlefield believing that the victory was won. But the Belgian General Chassé, one of the heroes of Arcis-sur-Aube (he actually served at that time under the French flag!), brought up to the right of the 30th and the 73rd, the battery of Van der Smissen, the fire of which mowed down the assailants. Then he deliberately brought to the left of the two English regiments, the Ditmer brigade, 3,000 strong, hurled it with fixed bayonets against the enfeebled square, crushed it under this mass of troops, and cast the miserable remnant to the bottom of the slopes.[25]

The battalion of the 4th Grenadiers (second echelon) was meanwhile engaged with the right of the Halkett brigade. Under the grapeshot of Duchand's two pieces and the fusillade of the Grenadiers, the fragments of the 33rd and of the 69th began to give way. General Halkett seized the flag of the 33rd, stood still and waved it above his head and by his example steadied his men. "Look at the General," they cried, "he is between two fires. He can't escape!" and indeed he fell grievously wounded. But the English had rallied and made a firm stand. An old soldier exclaimed, biting his cartridge, "We shall see who kills the longest." [26]

The 1st and 2nd battalions of the 3rd Chasseurs (3rd echelon) had almost reached the crest without meeting any infantry. They were still marching in the direction of the Ohain road, which was only the distance of a pistol-shot from them, when suddenly, twenty steps ahead, a red wall loomed before them. They beheld Maitland's 2,000 Guards drawn up four deep. The latter had been waiting all this time, lying hidden in the wheat. On the command of Wellington himself, "Up Guards, ready!" they sprang up as if moved by a spring, took aim, and fired. This very first fire swept down 300 men, almost one-half of the two battalions already decimated by the artillery. General Michel fell mortally wounded. The French halted, their ranks broken, their march obstructed by dead bodies. Instead of hurling them forward immediately with fixed bayonets, regardless of the disorder which prevailed, the officers strove to form them into line, to meet fire with fire. The confusion increased. The deployment was carried out badly and with much loss of time. For ten minutes the chasseurs remained on the same spot under the withering fire of Maitland's Guards, and under the fire also of the Bolton and Ramsay batteries, which took them slantingly. At last Wellington saw that the Guard was giving way; he ordered the charge. "Forward, my boys," cried Colonel Saltoun, "now is your time!" The impetuous English made a headlong rush upon this handful of soldiers, broke through them, and went down with them in a furious hand-to-hand struggle as far as the orchard of Hougoumont. "The combatants were so mingled together," says an officer of Bolton's battery, "that we had to stop firing." [27]

At the hurried commands of their leaders, the English halted abruptly. The battalion of the 4th Chasseurs (left echelon) drew near with the design of extricating the *débris* of the 3rd Chasseurs, as well as those of the 4th Grenadiers, who had also begun to retreat. Without awaiting the shock, Maitland's soldiers yielded the ground in disorder, and climbed back to their positions almost as fast as they had come down. Chasseurs and Grenadiers closely followed them, tramping up the hill under volleys of grapeshot. Just as they crossed the Ohain road, the Adam brigade (52nd, 71st, and 95th regiments), which had rapidly marched down upon their right flank, received them in flank with four lines of fire. Maitland's Guards wheeled half round, formed up again as best they could, and joined in the firing with Colin Halkett's brigade; whilst William Halkett's Hanoverians emerged from the hedges of Hougoumont, and fired on the French from the rear. On all sides rained a storm of bullets. Mallet was seriously wounded. A battalion deployed opposite Maitland; all that remained of the two others marched by the left against the Adam brigade. Colonel Colborn, whom the soldiers in Spain called the "fire eater," hurried along the 52nd. The whole brigade followed him with fixed bayonets. Already terribly shaken by the formidable fusillade they had experienced, Chasseurs and Grenadiers yielded to numbers, and withdrew in confusion.[28]

Section III

The cry "The Guard gives way!" rang out as the death-knell of the Grand Army. Every man felt that all was over. Reille's infantry, the cuirassiers, the squadrons of the Guard, which at last marched off to support Ney's attack, stopped, paralysed. The soldiers of Donzelot and Allix, struggling on the ridges above La Haye-Sainte with the brigades of Kruse, Lambert, Kempt, and Pack, saw the Guard fall back. They, too, yielded the conquered ground and came down to the foot of the hill, dragging along with them in their retreat, the Marcognet division which had attacked the extended positions of the enemy on the right. The retrograde movement spread from right to left over the entire line of battle.[29]

At the same time Durutte's infantry was attacked at Papelotte and at La Haye, by the vanguards of the Prussian columns which debouched from the Ohain road. The cry went up, "*Sauve qui peut!* We are betrayed!" This panic is easy to understand when we consider the state of mind of the soldiers, uneasy and haunted for the last three months with fears of treachery. Everything appeared to justify their suspicions. Under their very eyes a general, a colonel, officers of every grade had passed over to the enemy. Amongst their cartridges they discovered some filled with bran instead of powder. They were amazed by these badly-planned, fruitless manœuvres; they were disheartened by so many useless assaults. Finally, they were expecting Grouchy's corps, whose approach had been positively announced, and there was Zieten instead, marching to crush them. The rout began and increased. The Prussians rushed to the assault, drove from the farm buildings the few handfuls of heroes who still held on in spite of the panic, and hurled them down into the ravines. The remains of d'Erlon's four divisions ebbed back upon one another, mutually hustling, jostling, and trampling down each other. To the east of the main road, in the hollow of the valley where volleys of English grapeshot and Prussian shells crossed each other, the most lamentable confusion prevailed.[80]

Wellington was determined to finish this deadly wounded army. He spurred his horse to the edge of the plateau in front of the battle, took off his hat and waved it in the air. The signal was at once understood. Instantaneously all the troops marched off, preserving the order they happened to be in at the moment. Without even waiting to muster, the battalions, the batteries, the squadrons of the various divisions rushed on side by side,[81] passing over the dead and trampling the wounded under the hoofs of their horses and their cannon wheels. The brigades under Pack, Ompteda and Kielmansegge alone remained in their original positions, with two or three batteries which it was absolutely impossible to move on account of the tremendous number of corpses and dead horses heaped up in front of them. From right to left, English, Hanoverians, Brunswickers, Belgians, cavalry, infantry, artillery—altogether

40,000 men came pouring down in a torrent, amid the shadows of the twilight,[32] to the sound of drums, bugles and pibrochs. At this sight, terrifying to the bravest, the last echelons of the infantry wheeled half round, and with the whole of the cavalry rushed helter-skelter to climb the hill-slopes on the west of La Belle Alliance; the leading battalions, which ran the risk of being crushed the first by the descending human avalanche, disbanded altogether and fled for their lives. La Haye-Sainte was abandoned, abandoned, too, was the orchard of Hougoumont and the wood. Vivian's hussars and Vandeleur's dragoons, whose forward rush made a wide gap in the masses of the English, cut down the fugitives, shouting the fierce cry, "No quarter! no quarter!"[33]

Section IV

Whilst the Middle Guard were attacking the English positions, the 2nd battalions of the 1st Chasseurs, of the 2nd Grenadiers, and of the 2nd Chasseurs, with Generals Cambroune, Roguet, and Christiani, had returned to the spot where the Emperor stood at the foot of La Haye-Sainte. Napoleon was occupied in forming into a column of attack, one battalion deployed, and two on the flank in close columns, with the intention of leading them himself up to the plateau, where, as the wounded Friant reported to him, "Everything was going on well," when suddenly he beheld his whole line of battle falling to pieces! He, too, then realised that he was irretrievably beaten. Nevertheless he clung to the hope of organising and directing the retreat. Without losing any of his *sang froid*, he broke up the column of the Old Guard, and of its three battalions formed an equal number of squares; these he posted about a hundred yards above La Haye-Sainte—the right-hand square on the road to Brussels. He hoped and expected that under shelter of this dike, the army might rally and march away.[34]

Vivian's hussars, powerless to bite into these squares, turned them and continued to pour their red furrows through the disorderly mob of fugitives. Intoxicated with blood, they revelled in the slaughter. A subaltern of the 18th said to Vivian, "We will follow you down to hell, if you will lead us there!" In the train of the hussars galloped other horsemen of the enemy. The Emperor hurled his four service squadrons against this fresh tide of cavalry, which completely submerged them.[35]

Not far from the road, Marshal Ney stood bare-headed, unrecognisable, his face blackened with powder, his uniform in tatters, one of his epaulettes cut off, the hilt of his sword in his hand, shouting furiously to Count d'Erlon, who was being swept past, by an eddy of the drifting rout, "d'Erlon, if you and I escape, we shall both be hanged!" The Marshal's appearance was "less that of a human being than of a furious wild beast." His efforts throughout the day had exceeded human strength and energy. Never in any battle did any officer or soldier so generously sacrifice himself. Ney had surpassed Ney! Twice he had led d'Erlon's infantry to the attack, four times he had charged over the plateau with the cuirassiers, and he had conducted the last desperate assault of the grenadiers of the Guard. And now he rushed to the Brue brigade (Durutte's division), the only troops of the line which were falling back in good order, though they were reduced now to two battalions. He stopped the soldiers and once more flung them upon the enemy, crying to them, "Come and see a Marshal of France die!" When this brigade, too, was quickly broken and dispersed, Ney still clung to the fatal battlefield. Since he could not meet death there, he was determined to be the last man to leave it. He entered a square of the Guard with Major Rullière, who had taken the Eagle of the 95th from the dying hands of Lieutenant Puthod. Durutte, with his right wrist severed, his forehead cut open, and blood streaming from his wounds, was carried by his horse into the heart of a cavalry charge of the enemy. He galloped in the midst of the English as far as La Belle Alliance.[36]

The three battalions of the Guard repulsed the cavalry with ease. But their formation in squares, which they were compelled to retain in order to resist fresh charges, placed them in a position of tactical inferiority to the English infantry arranged in lines of four deep. The latter's far more extended and denser fire raked the squares in front and on the side. The musketry fire was mingled with grapeshot from the batteries under Rogers, Whyniates, and Gardiner, posted at only sixty yards distance. The masses of the enemy swarmed around the grenadiers; the brigades of Adam and William Halkett were more specially furious in their attacks upon them, so also were the brigades under Kempt, Lambert, Kruse, Wincke, Colin Halkett. The Emperor gave the order to abandon this untenable position. He reflected, probably when too late, that the wisest course to stop a rout, is not to remain in front of the yielding troops, but to go to their rear in order to rally them in a fresh position; and he accordingly galloped up to the heights of La Belle Alliance, with an escort of a few chasseurs.[37]

The three battalions—as well as the battalion of the 3rd Grenadiers posted on their left, assailed in turn by the English dragoons, the black lancers of Brunswick, the infantry under Maitland and Mitchel—fell back step by step. Reduced to too small a number of men to remain in squares three rows deep, they formed themselves into two ranks in triangles, and with bayonets crossed, slowly cut their way through the throng of fugitives and of the English. At each step, the men stumbled over dead bodies or fell down pierced by bullets. Every fifty yards they halted to re-form their ranks and repulse a fresh charge of cavalry or a new attack from the infantry.[38] During its heroic retreat the Guard, as it marched, was literally surrounded with enemies, like a wild boar at the "*hallali*" amidst the boar hounds. The foes were so close to each other that, despite the varied sounds of the combat, they could hear each other's voices. In the midst of the firing some English officers shouted to the veterans to surrender.[39] Cambronne, who was on horseback in the square of the 2nd battalion of the 1st Chasseurs, heard this. With despair in his breast, suffocated with rage, exasperated by the incessant summons of the enemy, he retorted furiously, "M . . . !"[40] A few seconds after, just as he had gained the summit of La Belle Alliance with his battalions, a ball struck him full in the face, and he fell to the ground bleeding and apparently lifeless![41]

Section V

During the last assault on Mont-Saint-Jean half the corps of Pirch (Tippelskirch and Kraft divisions and Jürgass's cavalry) had joined Bülow, whose forces were thrown into confusion.[42] Blücher immediately gave orders to renew the general attack upon the whole right flank of the French. At Plancenoit itself, the Young Guard of Duhesme and two battalions of the Old Guard of Morand and Pelet remained unshaken. But at the extension of this village, Lobau's infantry and Domon's cavalry, with the cavalry of Subervie, were giving way before 15,000 troops under Hacke, Losthin, and Prince William; they were overthrown completely when the Steinmetz division and the Röder cavalry, debouching from the Smohain road in pursuit of Durutte, attacked them in flank. The French masses, scattered a quarter of an hour before, over the road to Nivelles as far as the ravines of Papelotte and Plancenoit, swarmed back in the same time on to the plateau around La Belle Alliance. On their heels, sabring, shooting, shouting hurrahs, rushed the English from one side and the Prussians from the other. The two jaws of the vice closed on this terrified and defenceless rabble, which had once been the Imperial army![43]

In this frightful disorderly mob, every one pushed and jostled his neighbour to flee the faster. Dismounted cuirassiers threw away their cuirasses, drivers cut their horses' traces, men were trampled to death under foot. They stumbled over dead horses, overturned ammunition chests, abandoned cannons. The shades of night, which began to darken (it was nearly nine), added to the horror and confusion of the scene. The 12th and 16th English dragoons were charged by the 1st Hussars of the German Legion. The Adam brigade sustained the fire of a Prussian battery. The 71st Highlanders turned the French cannon upon the flying columns. The four battalions of the Guard, which had just regained the plateau, were the only infantry troops still in order. English and Prussians encircled each square with a ring of grapeshot, swords, and bayonets. Simultaneously charged by the infantry and the cavalry, they were shattered, demolished, and utterly crushed. Their wrecked fragments were merged in the general rout.⁴⁴

Five hundred yards farther to the rear, close to Decoster's house, waited, in squares and commanded by General Petit, the two battalions of the 1st Grenadiers. These men were the *élite* of the *élite*. Almost all of them had at least two stripes, and four in every ten of them, belonged to the Legion of Honour. On horseback, within the square of the first battalion, was the Emperor himself. With these living redoubts he still hoped to cover the retreat. He gave orders to place the 12-pounder battery, the same which had been playing for a long time upon the Prussians above Plancenoit, upon the prolongation of the squares; then he caused the Guard's call to arms to be sounded to rally all the detachments of the Guard. On either side of the squares an endless stream of fugitives kept pouring down the road, with the enemy following close behind. The battery of the Guard had but one shot left for each gun. Its last discharge thundered forth, and at close range, confounded a column of cavalry. The gunners, with their ammunition spent, stood stoically beside their guns, hoping thus to deceive their assailants. Other squadrons approached at a gallop. "Do not fire," cried a French grenadier, "they are French hussars." They were English hussars, who fell upon the batteries and cut down the disarmed artillerymen. But on the squares themselves, these obstinate charges dashed and broke like whirlwinds of sand on a block of granite. Before each battalion of the grenadiers rose a bloody heap of corpses and dead horses.⁴⁵

In Plancenoit, which the Prussian batteries had set on fire, the fight was waged by the lurid glare of the flames. The Young Guard, almost entirely recruited from among the Paris and Lyons volunteers and the 1st battalion of the 2nd Chasseurs and the 2nd Grenadiers, fought in the proportion of one against five. The combined attacks of the divisions led by Hiller, Ryssel, and Tippelskirch had failed. Gneisenau animated the spirit of his soldiers; once more they rushed to the assault and penetrated into the village. Victors and vanquished fired point-blank on each other, struggled hand-to-hand, slew with the bayonet and with the butt-ends of their guns. The gigantic drum-major, Stubert, of the 2nd Grenadiers, felled the Prussians with the heavy knob of his stick. A whole battalion of the Young Guard was cut to pieces in the cemetery, which served them as a redoubt. One by one, the houses fell into the hands of the Prussians. A fearful slaughter ensued in the rooms, in the garrets; and during these merciless struggles the thatched roofs caught fire and fell upon the combatants. "We must destroy the French," said Major von Damitz, "to take possession of Plancenoit." On their egress from the village, these heroic battalions were charged and vigorously pursued as far as the plateau. There the English cavalry put an end to them. General Pelet found himself alone for an instant in the midst of the enemy with a few men and the Eagle-bearer of the chasseurs of the Old Guard. "Follow me, chasseurs!" he shouted in vibrating tones, "let us save the Eagle or die by its side!" All who heard this desperate appeal retraced their footsteps, rushed to him, cut their way through the horses; they rallied round the flag and surrounded it with an impenetrable rampart of bayonets.[46] From Plancenoit both French and Prussians debouched pell-mell on the Brussels highroad, near the squares of the 1st Grenadiers. The fugitives pressed up to these to obtain refuge in their ranks, but they were remorselessly repulsed by sword and fire. This cruelty was necessary for the preservation of the squares. General Roguet narrowly escaped being shot point-blank by a grenadier. "We shall fire," said General Petit, "on every man that comes up, friend or foe, for fear of letting the latter enter with the former. It is an evil to ensure a benefit." The squares were attacked from the right and from the left; the English and Prussian masses grew more and more numerous, more and more compact. The Grenadiers repulsed all these assaults. Two battalions against two armies!

At last the Emperor ordered them to abandon the position. Slowly the Grenadiers began their retreat, the 1st battalion to the left of the road, the 2nd battalion on to the road itself. At every moment they halted to rectify the line of the squares and to arrest, in some degree, the pursuit of the enemy by effective enfilading fires.[47]

The Emperor proceeded at some distance in advance of the squares with Soult, Drouot, Bertrand, Lobau, and five or six mounted chasseurs of the Guard. At the farm of Le Caillou he joined the 1st battalion of unmounted chasseurs of the Old Guard. This battalion, entrusted with the care of the treasury and of the Emperor's equipages, was commanded by Duuring, a Dutchman by birth. About seven in the evening, two Prussian columns had advanced through the wood of Chantelet with the obvious intention of cutting off the retreat of the French army. Duuring at once sent the carriages on the road to Genappe, in concert with General Radet, the Grand-Provost, who had just rallied two or three hundred dismounted horsemen and infantry fugitives. He wheeled his battalion round later to face the enemy. The Prussians, greeted by a lively fusillade quickly followed by a bayonet charge, were driven back into the middle of the wood, whence they retreated toward Maransart.[48] The Emperor now halted for a few moments and questioned Duuring under the final shells from the Prussian batteries at Plancenoit. He congratulated him on the firmness and the initiative spirit he had displayed, and then ordered him to follow him. "I rely upon you," he said. The battalion having closed up their ranks, the Emperor let the reins drop on his horse's neck and rode slowly on, keeping pace with the flank of the column.[49]

BOOK III   CHAPTER VI

THE ROUT

I. Meeting between Wellington and Blücher in front of La Belle Alliance Inn (a quarter past nine)—The rout of the French.
II. Attempt to resist at Genappe (eleven o'clock).
III. Pursuit of the Prussian cavalry (night of the 18th to the 19th of June).
IV. Halt of the Emperor at Quatre-Bras—Passage of the army to Charleroi (morning of the 19th of June).
V. Retreat upon Laon—Departure of the Emperor for Paris (20th June).

Section I

About a quarter past nine o'clock,[1] while the Hiller, Ryssel, and Tippelskirch brigades were wrenching Plancenoit from the grasp of the Young Guard, and while the squares of the 1st Grenadiers still held their ground near the Maison Decoster, Blücher and Wellington met in front of La Belle Alliance. Blücher followed the portion of Bülow's troops which had repulsed Lobau. Wellington arrived from La Haye-Sainte with the last echelons of his army. The two generals advanced toward each other, and, according to Gneisenau's expression, "each greeted the other as victor." As they passed by, the bands of the Prussian cavalry struck up "God save the King;" in the distance, the noise of the fusillade grew fainter. Bülow's foot soldiers, who had stopped to reform their ranks, joined their voices in singing Luther's hymn: "Lord God, we praise Thee! Lord God, we thank Thee!" or ("Now thank we all our God.")[2]

Blücher, impressed by the fact that his meeting with Wellington should have taken place in front of La Belle Alliance, suggested giving this name to the battle in which the alliance between English and Prussians had produced such momentous results. But Wellington wished the victory—his victory—should bear the name of the village which had had the honour of being his headquarters on the previous night.[3]

It was decided that, in spite of the darkness, the remains of the Imperial Army should be pursued without mercy. The English were exhausted by ten hours' fighting, "wearied to death," said Wellington.[4] The Prussians had marched an average of five leagues over the most wretched roads, and between Frischermont and Plancenoit had fought with no less furious obstinacy than was displayed at Mont-Saint-Jean by Wellington's own soldiers. Nevertheless, Blücher volunteered that *his* troops should be entrusted with the pursuit. The offer being accepted without scruple, he summoned the commanders of each corps and ordered them to "pursue the enemy as long as they had a man and a horse able to stand." Gneisenau placed himself at the head of Count Röder's squadrons. All the remaining troops followed. Toward Rossomme they encountered other Prussian troops which were debouching from Plancenoit, and the more advanced columns of the English infantry and cavalry.[5]

Wellington's army halted. As the Prussians went by, the English soldiers saluted them with a threefold cheer of "Hip! Hip! Hurrah!" Then they proceeded to settle down in their bivouacs, despite the heaps of dead around them.[6] From the plateau of Mont-Saint-Jean to the heights of Rossomme, from Hougoumont to Plancenoit, and even as far as Smohain, the ground was covered with dead bodies and slain horses. More than 25,000 French, and 20,000 English, Belgians, and Prussians[7] lay upon the ground, in some places scattered about like fallen trees, in others, lying in long files like rows of wheat cut down by the reapers' sickles. The moon had risen and lit up distinctly their ghastly, bloodstained faces and their mud-stained uniforms smeared with red stains; the weapons that had dropped from their hands, gleaming in the moonlight. Now and again thick, dark clouds, spreading over the sky, veiled this vision, from which the least sensitive among the old warriors turned away their eyes. But soon the vision reappeared in the cold light of the moon. Amidst the agonised moans of the dying and the groans of the wounded, at short intervals, a hoarse cry went up, stifled as it were with horror and dread. It was some officer whom a vile robber of the dead was finishing with the butt-end of a gun in order to rob him of his purse or his cross of honour.[8]

The Prussians carried out their pursuit with the utmost vigour. Those among the fugitives of the right wing (Lobau and d'Erlon's corps, Young Guard, horsemen of Domon, Jacquinot, and Subervie), who, being too closely followed or cut off from their line of retreat, had been prevented from getting beyond the squares of the rearguard of the 1st Grenadiers, were cut down or taken prisoners. On the left wing, a certain number of cuirassiers whose horses were still in a condition to carry them, and Piré's lancers who had done nothing more than skirmish during the battle, reached Quatre-Bras unmolested *viâ* Neuve-Court, Malplaquet, and Vieux-Genappe. They crossed the Sambre at Marchienne. Five or six thousand foot soldiers of Reille's corps rallied at nightfall, proceeded to Genappe across country, in a parallel line about half a league distant from the highroad. A few Prussian squadrons sufficed to disperse them. With the exception of three companies of the 93rd, which wheeled around and faced the enemy, the whole of this mass were dispersed. In order to run faster, soldiers would throw away their knapsacks and their muskets, thus justifying the old saying, "French more than men in attacking, less than women in retreating." The chiefs were no longer listened to; panic prevailed throughout the army.[9]

The Old Guard alone remained worthy of itself. The chasseurs and the lancers of Lefebvre-Desnoëttes, the regiment of mounted Grenadiers, which had left the battlefield at a foot's pace, presenting so proud a front that the English cavalry had not dared to approach them, withdrew in good order to the west of the highroad, and reached Quatre-Bras without suffering fresh losses.[10] On the highroad itself, the Prussians were held in check by the two squares of the 1st Grenadiers, preceded by the 1st battalion of the 1st Chasseurs. The Grenadiers continued to march at their usual pace, defying all attacks. Unable to tackle them, the Prussian pack of hounds grew weary at last, and was content to follow them at a safe distance out of the reach of their guns. Finally, half a league from Genappe, General Petit deemed it unnecessary to preserve the order of battle longer, and, breaking up the squares, he made his men march in columns of sections. It was at this very moment that the Emperor separated himself from the 1st battalion of Chasseurs, and proceeded to Genappe, where he hoped to arrest the enemy's progress and rally the fragments of the army.[11]

Section II

Genappe was practically nothing but a long, steep, and winding street, which led to a bridge over the Dyle. It would have been possible to hold this defile for several hours, though it was commanded from the North by eminences where the Prussian batteries would have been planted. Unfortunately, such fearful crowding and such confusion reigned in the village, that a systematic plan of defence was not to be thought of, especially with soldiers who never ceased shouting, "We are betrayed, let us fly!" Overturned vehicles, forage and baggage waggons, guns, ammunition carts, abandoned by the auxiliary drivers, encumbered a very considerable extent of the approaches to the bridge, which, in 1815, was only $2\frac{1}{2}$ yards wide at its broadest part.[12] The fugitives poured by masses into the street, the farther end of which did not allow of the egress of more than three or four at a time; a horrible crush resulted. Maddened by fear, men attempted to cut their way through, by striking straight in front of them. The General of the Gendarmerie, Radet, also Grand-Provost of the army, was beaten with the butt-ends of muskets. Horsemen slashed with their swords, the infantry retaliated with their bayonets, and, at times, even fired. They killed one another without making any progress in front; the living becoming hampered by the dead.[13] The rear of the column stood in dense crowds at the entrance of Genappe. The Prussians approached nearer and nearer. The three battalions of the Old Guard, threatened with being crushed completely between the masses of the enemy and the throng of the fugitives, which could no longer advance a step, divided, and reached Charleroi by turning the village on the east. The Prussians did not pursue them, but furiously attacked the human herds before Genappe, which were powerless to move. Not until they found themselves literally under the lances of the Uhlans, did these unfortunate wretches think of escaping by the right and the left of the village, and of fording the Dyle. The little river, which at this point is hardly three yards broad and one yard deep, is impossible for vehicles only, owing to the steepness of its banks.[14]

Genappe was still crowded with French soldiers. A handful of men, who alone in the panic had preserved their resolution and courage, made an attempt to arrest the progress of the enemy. They rapidly erected a barricade of overturned carts, from behind which they opened fire. A few shells soon, however, shattered this feeble defence and its defenders. Röder's cavalry came riding down the sloping street, trampling under their horses' hoofs the inert multitude of fugitives, cutting and striking with sword and lance with no more risk to themselves than to butchers in a slaughter-house. The Emperor, who, it seems, had been over an hour forcing his way through this long street, was still on the near side of the bridge, and had just seated himself in his campaign carriage, recovered by chance among the abandoned vehicles. The horses were not yet in harness, when Napoleon, hearing the Prussian hurrahs, hastily alighted, sprang upon his horse, and succeeded in escaping with a few horsemen. The Prussians plundered his carriage, which contained a dressing-case, a sword, an iron bedstead, and an extra uniform, in the lining of which were sewn unmounted diamonds to the value of a million francs.[15]

Blücher had pushed on as far as Genappe with Bülow's corps. He halted for the night at the "Roi d'Espagne" inn. Almost immediately after, General Duhesme was brought there on an ambulance litter. In the last hour of the battle Duhesme had fallen, grievously wounded, between Plancenoit and Rossomme; a few devoted soldiers had raised him and carried him as far as Genappe, where he was taken prisoner by the Prussians. The Field-Marshal came to visit him, and recommended him to the care of the surgeon of his own staff. But the wound was a mortal one, and he died the following night.[16] Blücher, although broken with fatigue, would not retire to rest till he had written to his wife: "I have been true to my word," he wrote. "On the 16th I was compelled to withdraw before superior forces; but on the 18th, acting in concert with my friend Wellington, I have annihilated the army of Napoleon."[17] He also sent the following letter to his friend Knesebeck: "My friend, the finest of battles has been fought, the most brilliant of victories won. Details will follow. I think that Bonaparte's history is ended. I cannot write any more, for I am trembling in every limb. The strain was too great."[18]

Section III

Beyond Genappe, the pursuit grew fiercer. As there were no longer any troops in order forming the rearguard, the Prussians sabred this bewildered crowd with impunity. "It was a regular hunt," said Gneisenau, "a hunt by moonlight." The main road, the lanes, the cross-roads, the fields, as far as the eye could reach, were strewn with soldiers belonging to every arm of the service, dismounted cuirassiers, lancers riding maimed horses, infantry who had thrown away their knapsacks, wounded soldiers bleeding to death, amputated soldiers who had escaped from the ambulances ten minutes after their operations. Without any authority over their men, and no less demoralised, captains, colonels, and generals, thinking only of their own safety, were mixed up and carried along in the throng of fugitives.[19] Durutte on horseback, but blinded by the blood which flowed from his gashed forehead, was being guided by a sergeant of the cuirassiers. A corporal of the Old Guard supported Ney by the arm, until Major Schmidt of the red lancers alighted from his own horse and handed it over to the Marshal. The head-surgeon, Larrey, already wounded with two sword-cuts, was again struck by the Uhlans, who plundered him, stripped him, and led him, almost naked, with his hands tied, to a General; the latter ordered him to be shot. As they were taking aim at him, a Prussian surgeon recognised him, threw himself before him, and saved his life.[20]

Every man walked, ran, dragged himself along as best he could, and went wherever he wished; no one attempted to give orders, which none would have obeyed. And whenever the sound of the Prussian trumpets, the gallop of horses, the savage cries of the pursuers drew nearer, the terrified crowd would yell: "Here they are, here they are! Run for your life!" Under the goading spur of terror, infantry and cavalry, officers and soldiers, sound men and wounded, found new strength to run. Bands of fugitives, who had dropped down with fatigue and had stopped in the thickets, in hollows of the ground, in farm-houses, in the hamlets, were soon hunted out by the cavalry. The Prussians broke up nine bivouacs in succession. The wounded committed suicide, rather than fall alive into the enemy's hands. An officer of cuirassiers, seeing himself encircled by Uhlans, cried, "They shall have neither me nor my horse," and very coolly he fired a bullet into his horse's ear, then blew his own brains out with his second pistol.[21]

Nearly all Bülow's infantry having halted at Genappe, and the corps of Zieten and Pirch having not yet passed Le Caillou,[22] the troops under Gneisenau consisted merely of General Röder's Uhlans, a battalion of the 1st Pomeranians, and a battalion of the 15th regiment.[23] This fact seems absolutely incredible: it was before a force of 4,000 Prussians that 30,000 or 40,000 French were flying! Had only a few hundred French soldiers, overcoming their terror and recovering their presence of mind, re-formed and made a stand, their resistance might have put an end to this lamentable pursuit. The Prussian horsemen, who sabred with special fury the more terrified among the fugitives, were apparently very easy to overawe, since a handful of resolute Frenchmen sufficed to save the eagles of each regiment, as they marched grouped around them. The enemy gathered from the roads and on the battlefield more than 200 cannon that had been abandoned [24] and about 1,000 vehicles, but during the rout they could not capture a single flag.[25]

However hardened, however insensible a soldier may be from habit or his calling in life to scenes of death, the fugitives were struck with horror as they passed Quatre-Bras. The men who had fallen there in the battle of the 16th of June, had not yet been buried. Three or four thousand corpses, quite naked, for the Belgian peasants had stripped them even of their shirts, covered the whole of the area between the road and the wood of Bossu. The aspect was that of an immense *morgue*. The dead, alternately lighted up by the moonlight, then covered by shadows from the passing clouds, seemed in this rapid play of light and shade to be moving their stiffened limbs and contracting the features of their ashy pale faces. " We fancied," said a grenadier of the Guard, " that we beheld spectres beseeching us for burial." Lower down, at the brook of Gémioncourt, which the storm of the two previous days had turned into a torrent, and down which dead bodies were drifting, the soldiers quenched their thirst.[26]

With their numbers dwindling and their fatigue increasing, the Prussians continued the pursuit with undiminished ardour. Gneisenau had dropped half his men along the way. There were only with him a few squadrons and a detachment of the 15th Infantry, whose solitary drummer, perched on the back of a horse taken from one of the Imperial carriages, sturdily beat the charge.[27] By this time they had passed beyond Frasnes. Gneisenau judged that the fatigue of the men and of the horses, did not sanction his carrying on the pursuit any farther.

Accordingly he gave orders to halt in front of an inn, the sign-board of which bore the inscription " A l'Empereur." Such was the irony of fate![28]

Section IV

From Genappe, Napoleon had reached Quatre-Bras on horseback with Soult, Bertrand, Drouot, a few officers, and about ten red lancers of the chasseurs of the Guard. When he arrived there toward one o'clock in the morning,[29] he hoped to find the Gérard division, which had been left at Fleurus on the 17th of June to protect the passage of the convoys, and to which on the evening of the 18th had been sent the order to proceed to Quatre-Bras and to take up its position there.[30]

These instructions had not been carried out. No doubt Colonel Matis, who in the interim commanded the remains of this division, duly received Soult's order; but whether he considered it was too late for these instructions to be of any practical use, or whether he acted from any other motive, he broke up his camp during the night and proceeded to cross the Sambre at Charleroi.[31]

Meanwhile the Emperor was waiting for these troops at Quatre-Bras. He alighted from his horse in a glade of the Bossu wood, near a camp fire which a few grenadiers of the Guard had kindled. A wounded officer who was rushing along the road, recognised the Emperor by the light of the fire. He stood quite erect, his arms crossed on his chest, his figure motionless as a statue, his eyes fixed, and turned toward Waterloo.[32]

As there was no news from Grouchy, it was thought he must be in a very perilous situation. The Emperor directed Soult to send him a message to inform him of the retreat of the Army, and to order him to fall back on the lower Sambre.[33] Soldiers of all arms of the service were running by on the road and across the fields. Major Baudus, who was riding among the fugitives, caught sight of the small group of the Imperial staff. He drew near. The Emperor inquired whether he had not come across some corps which was not completely disorganised. At a short distance from Quatre-Bras, Baudus had passed the 5th Lancers of Colonel Jacqueminot, which were still marching in good order. He informed the Emperor of this. "Go quickly and tell them to halt at Quatre-Bras. It is already late, and upon finding this point occupied, the enemy will most likely halt." Baudus set off at a gallop, but he was saluted by shots from the houses at the crossway, and at once turned back and entreated the Emperor to withdraw, since he was no longer protected by any troops. As he spoke he watched the Emperor's face. Napoleon was silently weeping over his lost army. His face was filled with an intense sadness and was as pale as wax; life had nothing more to give him, save tears.[34] Through his deep despair, the Emperor still preserved his presence of mind. As the Girard division failed to make its appearance, he concluded that it had not received orders to that effect from the chief of the staff. In its ignorance of the defeat, this division ran the risk of being taken by surprise in camp and surrounded by the enemy. Accordingly he ordered Baudus to hasten with utmost speed to Fleurus, to call these troops to arms and to lead them back to the right bank of the Sambre. Then, yielding to necessity, he sprang on his horse and took the road to Charleroi by Gosselies and Lodelinsart.[35] At Charleroi, which the Emperor reached toward five in the morning,[36] he found the same disorderly mob, the same confusion as in the night at Genappe. Since the 15th of June, the ammunition waggons, the pontooning waggons, and the provision carts blocked up the squares and avenues. On the 17th, the wounded from Ligny and the prisoners, the twenty-seven guns and the equipages captured from the Prussians, had all been sent to Charleroi. It is true that on the evening of the 18th, when all our troops were giving way, a commissary of war had been sent there from Rossomme with instructions to move immediately all the vehicles to the other side of the Sambre. But on his arrival at Charleroi between one and two after midnight, he found the "commandant of the place" ill, or dead drunk, as some said, at any rate incapable of rendering him any assistance. The commissary of war had perforce to look up, one by one, the chiefs of the various departments of the service. They all displayed the greatest zeal, but too much time had been wasted. Already the first convoys of wounded were appearing from the Brussels road, and swarms of fugitives traversed the city, spreading the alarm by crying that the enemy were at their heels.[37]

The only bridge at Charleroi was 38 yards long and 8 wide. It was raised in the middle and its parapets were of wood. Some cuirassiers who were rushing at full speed down the steep slope of the street which led to it, struck one of the parapets with such violence that it snapped and fell to pieces. Several horsemen were drowned in the Sambre. The sentry box at the head of the bridge was thrown down; one of the waggons was turned over; the vehicles which were behind, and which came at a quick trot down the slope of the "Rue de la Montagne," were unable to stop in time and upset at the first obstacle. Soldiers were crushed to death. Sacks of flour and rice, casks of wine and brandy, hundreds of loaves rolled on the pavement. Owing to this obstruction of the bridge, the whole convoy stopped whilst the fugitives climbed over the barricade of overturned vehicles and fallen horses. Each man as he passed by thrust his bayonet into a loaf and bore it away. The contents of the casks were still more tempting; the soldiers stove them in with their muskets and drank the wine and brandy through the holes. When these barrels were half empty, others upon the carts were broken in the same way. Over the whole length of the street, red streams flowed down to the Sambre.[38] The Treasury waggon, which Grand-Provost Radet had despatched from Le Caillou at seven o'clock the evening before, found itself with its six horses, involved in the block of vehicles some 100 yards from the bridge. The Paymaster, who had all the responsibility of this precious load, despaired of ever making his way through the crowd. He therefore opened the waggon, and entrusted to his men and to the soldiers of the escort, as many bags of gold as each could carry. All these men were to meet at a given point on the other bank of the Sambre. The agent entered in a register, the names of the depositaires and the corresponding number of bags of 20,000 francs entrusted to each. But while this operation was still proceeding, the air rang with the shots fired into the wine casks at the lower portion of the street. An alarm was raised, which soon degenerated into a panic amid cries of "The Prussians! Save yourselves!" intentionally uttered by some of the natives of Charleroi, and even by the soldiers. These scoundrels quickly pounced upon the waggons. With blows from sword and bayonet they seized the bags of gold. All were plundered.[39] The halt of the head of the convoy, had blocked all vehicles as far as the entrance to the upper portion of the town. The berline which contained the portfolio of State papers, was also unable to move on the road amid the artillery trains. Sounds of a fusillade were heard in the distance. The Duke of Bassano commanded the most important papers to be torn to pieces and cast to the winds.[40]

The evacuation of Charleroi might certainly have been

effected without any disorder, for on the 19th of June the Prussians had slackened their pursuit. With the exception of a few cavalry reconnaissances, they did not approach the city before noon; it was quite late in the day when they seized the bridges of Marchienne, Charleroi, and Le Chatelet. In the evening, while Pirch, who in the previous night had been sent towards Gembloux with the 2nd Corps to cut off the retreat of Grouchy, was occupying Mellery, Zieten's and Bülow's corps bivouacked, with their front covered by the Sambre. The next day only, the Prussian army crossed the river in three columns and proceeded to Beaumont and Avesnes. The English, less ardent or slower in marching, were still between Nivelles and Binche.[41]

Section V

In vain had the Emperor endeavoured to organise resistance in the plains of La Haye-Sainte, at Rossomme, at Genappe, and at Quatre-Bras. He realised that with a disbanded army who were governed only by terror, it was best to make as prompt a retreat as possible.[42] He passed through Charleroi and halted in a meadow on the right bank of the Sambre.[43] From thence he issued a few orders, which were not carried out, with the object of rallying the fugitives and collecting the equipages.[44] An hour later, he mounted his horse and proceeded towards Philippeville, where he arrived at nine o'clock in the morning. The gates of the stronghold were locked; he had to reveal himself to the officer of the Guard.[45] With him were Bertrand, Drouot, Dejean, Flahaut, Bussy. He was soon after joined by the Duke of Bassano and Fleury de Chaboulon, then by Marshal Soult.[46] Among his most pressing preoccupations, was the rallying of his troops. Instructions were sent to the commanders of Givet, Avesnes, Maubeuge, Beaumont, and Landrecies. They were to revictual with provisions and ammunition, the detachments and isolated fugitives who might present themselves at these places, and to direct them afterwards to the mustering points; Laon for the 1st, 2nd, and 6th Infantry Corps; La Fère for the Artillery;

Marle, St. Quentin, Réthel, Vervins, and Rheims for the Cavalry; Soissons for the Guard. Of all the commanders of the army corps, Reille was the only one who had joined the Emperor at Philippeville; he was entrusted with the mission of reorganising the troops which arrived at the glacis of this fortress. A fresh despatch enjoining Marshal Grouchy to retreat, was sent to him by a spy named Cousin. The garrison commanders of the 2nd and 16th military divisions were ordered to stand on their guard.[47]

But the Emperor had not only to consider his army; he had also to think of public opinion, external enemies, and the Chambers. He wrote two letters to his brother Joseph. The first, destined to be read at the council of ministers, reported, with certain reservations, the issue of the battle; in the other, which was entirely personal, Napoleon concealed nothing of the great disaster[48] and announced his immediate return to Paris.[49] Fleury de Chaboulon, to whom both letters were dictated, asserts that the second ended thus: "All is not lost. By uniting all my forces, the depôts, the national guards, I shall still have 300,000 men to oppose to the enemy. But I must be helped, not bewildered. I think the deputies will realise it is their duty to stand by me in order to save France."[50]

The Emperor then proceeded to write with his own hand, the bulletin of the battles of Ligny and Mont-Saint-Jean, which was to appear in the *Moniteur*,[51] after which, leaving Soult at Philippeville to superintend the rallying of the Army, he went alone, as it appears, in one of the carriages of the head of the staff, Bassano, Bertrand, Drouot, and the other aides-de-camp following in two other carriages.[52]

From Philippeville to Paris, the most direct route (forty-eight posts and a half), was *via* Barbançon, Avesnes, La Capelle, Marle, and Laon. But the Emperor did not desire to run the risk of being captured, by some body of Prussian cavalry which might have crossed the Sambre at Marchienne;[53] he chose therefore a somewhat longer route (fifty-one posts), *via* Marienbourg, Rocroi, Maubert-Fontaine, La Capelle, Marle, and Laon. At sunset they halted for a few minutes in sight of Rocroi. The inhabitants knew nothing of the terrible defeat, and crowded to the ramparts in the hope of seeing the Emperor. Their cheers aroused him from his sleep in the deep cushions of his carriage.[54] For one instant he may have had a momentary illusion—events had followed each other so quickly—that he was merely awaking from a bad dream.

Probably from fear of being unable to find relays at Maubert-Fontaine (a number of horses having been put under requisition there a week earlier for the auxiliary services of Vandamme's corps), the travellers made a detour as far as Mézières. Here also, horses were not to be procured. They were sought for at a distance of a league. From half-past ten to midnight the three carriages remained with the horses in harness on the square of Des Fontaines in front of the post-house. General Dumonceau, governor of Mézières; Traullé, the commander of the garrison, and the officers of their staff surrounded the carriages. They stood there motionless and spoke in low tones "as in a day of mourning." None of the travellers alighted except Bertrand, who was summoned to the door of Napoleon's carriage by a staff officer of the hussars; this solitary officer formed the whole of the Imperial escort. The carriages drove off. As they neared the "Porte de Pierre" the sentries shouted "Long live the Emperor!" and repeated this cry, which was, said Commandant Traullé, "harrowing, under the circumstances," until the last carriage had passed the ramparts.[55]

It was only between six and seven in the evening of the next day, 20th June,[56] that they arrived at the foot of the mountain of Laon, in the suburb of Vaux. The Emperor alighted in the courtyard of the Hotel de la Poste. Through the large gate, which remained open, the people in the street, could see him pacing up and down, with his head bowed down, and arms folded on his chest. The courtyard was covered with straw from the adjoining barns and stables. One of the spectators said in a low voice, "It is Job on his dunghill." Napoleon appeared so overwhelmed, so wretched, the scene was so impressive, even to those rustic spectators, that none dared to cheer. However, a few faint, timid, stifled cries of "Vive l'Empereur!" arose from this crowd. The Emperor stopped and lifted his hat.[57] His arrival was known in the town. A detachment of the National Guard came down to form a guard of honour. Shortly after, came General Langeron, commander of the department, with the Prefect and the Municipal Council. The Grand-Provost, General Radet, and General Neigre then conferred with the Emperor. Napoleon charged the Prefect, with whom he coupled his aide-de-camp Bussy, a native of the country, to gather large stores of provisions, as the Army was to concentrate at Laon. He sent Neigre to La Fère to organise the batteries for the campaign, Dejean to Guise to examine the condition of the fortress, Flahaut to Avesnes to gather information respecting the march of the enemy.[58] Night fell. The Emperor did not wait for Marshal Soult,[59] with whom he had left ample instructions at Philippeville. Toward ten or eleven o'clock, he started for Paris.[60]

Since leaving Philippeville, and no doubt ever since his halt in the meadows of the Sambre, Napoleon had resolved to push on to Paris.[61] He remembered his deplorable lesson in 1814, that vote of deposition which had paralysed him at the head of his army. He knew that if he did not return immediately to his capital to overawe Fouché, with the conspirators of all parties, and the deputies, who were hostile or blinded, his crown was doomed, as well as the country's last chance of resistance. From a military, as well as from a political point of view, his place for at least a few days, was plainly in Paris. Without soldiers and without artillery, it was out of the question to arrest the enemy's progress on the frontier. As to the rallying of the wreck of his troops at Laon, Soult and the generals could effect it as well as himself. Genius was not necessary for that task; and during this time in Paris, the Emperor could arrange measures for the public safety, with the assistance of Davout and Carnot. He would calm the political crisis, accelerate all branches of the services, send towards Laon all the available men from the depôts, the mobilised battalions, the field batteries, the convoys of arms and ammunition; with the consent of the Chambers he would decree fresh levies of soldiers and national guards, and in four or five days he would himself resume the command of the army.[62]

It has been said that Napoleon "abandoned" his Army, as

he had done in Egypt and in Russia.[63] Alas! Napoleon had no Army left. Of Grouchy he knew nothing.[64] He was supposed to be in great peril with Vandamme's and Gérard's corps.[65] Of the 74,000 combatants of Waterloo, probably 40,000 had retired safe and sound and had recrossed the Sambre,[66] but more than three-fourths of their number were still scattered between Cambrai and Rocroi, straggling along the roads, singly or in small groups, bivouacking in the woods, taking refuge with the peasants. On the 20th of June, at the time when Napoleon left Laon for Paris, there were 2,600 soldiers assembled at Philippeville and about 6,000 at Avesnes.[67] This was the entire Army!

BOOK III   CHAPTER VII

THE ACTIONS AT WAVRE AND GROUCHY'S RETREAT

I. Grouchy marches on Wavre—Battle of La Baraque—Attack of Wavre (afternoon of the 18th of June).
II. Soult's second despatch—Renewed assaults upon Wavre and Bierges—Passage of the Dyle at Limale and battle in the night.
III. Renewal of the fight and defeat of Thielmann (morning of the 19th of June)—The news of the disaster (half-past ten in the morning)—Retreat of Grouchy (afternoon and evening of the 19th of June).
IV. Actions at La Falise and Le Boquet (morning of the 20th of June)—Defence of Namur (from three to nine at night)—Rallying of Grouchy's Army at Givet (21st of June).

Section I

It has been seen, that in the course of his discussion with Gérard at Walhain, on the 18th of June about noon, Grouchy received one of Exelmans' aides-de-camp, who informed him of the presence of the Prussian rearguard before Wavre.[1]

Between nine and ten o'clock, the two divisions of Exelmans' dragoons had arrived at La Baraque, five kilometres distant from this little town. Scouting parties, which had pushed beyond the defile of La Huzelle, notified that Prussian troops of three branches of the service, were on the heights of Wavre.[2] These proved to be the entire corps of Pirch, still on the right bank of the Dyle, and two regiments of the Landwehr cavalry, the rearguard of Bülow.[3] Although he had received the order "to follow closely upon the heels of the enemy,"[4] Exelmans feared to commence hostilities against these masses with his cavalry only, and in such a wooded region. Moreover, from fresh information or fresh indications, he knew that the Prussian Army was manœuvring to join the English. He thought that Grouchy would interrupt his march on

Wavre, which was now useless, in order to cross the Dyle at the nearest point. With the design of preparing this movement, he moved the Vincent brigade toward the Dyle, and it took up its position at the farm of La Plaquerie, within cannon range of Ottignies. Exelmans posted near Neuf-Sart, the Berton brigade to reconnoitre on the right. He left at La Baraque, an advanced guard of two squadrons, and fell back himself to about one league to the rear, near Corbais with the bulk of the Chastel division. It was during this halt, that he sent an aide-de-camp to Grouchy to inform him of the presence of the Prussians before Wavre, and of the steps he had taken.[5]

At that time Vandamme's corps had halted at Nil-Saint-Vincent, in accordance with Grouchy's orders of the previous evening. Notwithstanding all the information given him respecting the march of the Prussians towards Wavre, the Marshal was still so undecided on the evening of the 17th of June as to the direction he should take, that he had ordered Vandamme to proceed to Walhain only.[6] A little later, toward eleven o'clock or midnight, he wrote to him: "I have forgotten to tell you to push beyond Walhain, in order to allow General Gérard to take up his position in the rear. I think that we shall go farther than Walhain; therefore this will be rather a halt than a definite position."[7] When the bivouacs were raised on the morning of the 18th, there would still have been time for Grouchy, who had now determined to march upon Wavre, to order Vandamme to follow Exelmans' cavalry as rapidly as possible. It did not occur to him to do so. After passing Walhain, Vandamme halted at Nil-Saint-Vincent, where he awaited further orders.[8]

About one o'clock, Grouchy, who had been warned by Major d'Estournel, aide-de-camp to Exelmans, that the Prussian rearguard was in sight, reached Nil-Saint-Vincent. He gave to Vandamme, and dispatched to Exelmans, orders to start the troops on their march again.[9] A short time before two o'clock, as the head of the column of the dragoons approached La Baraque, the two squadrons which had been left as the advanced guard, were attacked by the 10th regiment of hussars debouching on their left flank.[10] This regiment, with two battalions and two guns, formed the detachment under Lieutenant-Colonel Ledebur, posted in observation at Mont-Saint-Guibert.

Until about one o'clock, Ledebur had not moved. Misinformed by his patrols and his vedettes, he was in complete ignorance of the approach of the French Army, as also of the ground to which they had advanced that morning at La Baraque, with the two divisions of Exelmans, and the position taken at the farm of La Plaquerie by the Vincent brigade. He was surrounded with enemies, and had not the slightest suspicion of it. Enlightened at last by the presence of the French at Nil-Saint-Vincent, and on the road to Wavre, Ledebur saw that his direct line of retreat ran the risk of being cut. He rapidly pushed his hussars across country to La Baraque, while his two battalions reached at double-quick step, through Bruyères and Bloc-Ry, the woods of La Huzelle, which bordered the road on either side to the north of La Baraque, forming a sort of defile.[11] The hussars drove back the two French squadrons on the east of the road, kept up the fight for a few minutes, then upon the approach of the bulk of the dragoons they retired through the defile which had just been occupied by Ledebur's sharpshooters."[12] Infantry were required to drive out the latter. The dragoons allowed the head of the Vandamme column to pass, and it began the attack at once. Two battalions of the Brause division, which was still with the Langen division (both of them belonging to Pirch's corps) on the right bank of the Dyle,[13] had been sent to support Ledebur.[14] The defence was most stubborn. Grouchy, without Exelmans' knowledge, had recalled the Vincent brigade from the banks of the Dyle.[15] All the dragoons were thus together. He then sent orders to Exelmans, to turn the position toward Dion le Mont with these three thousand horsemen. This well-conceived manœuvre was, however, executed too late or too slowly, and was not attended by the results that might have been expected. Before the movement of the French cavalry was completed, the Prussians had already evacuated the woods and were falling back upon Wavre.[16] Vandamme cleared the defile. He had orders from Grouchy to pursue the enemy as far as the heights which commanded this town, and to take up his position there, while awaiting further instructions.[17]

In spite of the confidence with which he had spoken to Gérard, Grouchy had many misgivings concerning the cannon which he heard thundering on his left. He galloped towards Limelette, "in order," he said, "to form a definite opinion as to the cause of this cannonade." He was finally convinced that a great battle was raging on the border of the forest of Soignes.[18] On regaining the Wavre road between half-past three and four o'clock[19] he received the letter from the Emperor, or rather from Soult, dated Le Caillou, ten o'clock in the morning.[20] This letter being addressed to Marshal Grouchy at Gembloux or beyond, the estafette, adjutant-commandant, Zenowicz, ought to have passed by Genappe, Sombreffe, and Gembloux. This was a journey of ten leagues. But Zenowicz could have covered the distance in less time.[21] Moreover, if this despatch, which enjoined Grouchy to march on Wavre, and at the same time to connect his communications with the Imperial Army, had reached him earlier, it would not have inclined him to alter his main dispositions. After reading it, he remarked to his aide-de-camp, Bella, that he "congratulated himself on having so well fulfilled the instructions of the Emperor, marching on Wavre instead of listening to General Gérard's advice."[22] And he sent a reply to Berthézène, who had sent him an aide-de-camp to inform him of the march of the Prussian columns in the direction of the firing: "Let the General's mind be at rest, we are on the right road. I have heard from the Emperor, and he commands me to march on Wavre."[23]

The Emperor ordered also, in a subsidiary manner, it is true, the linking together of the communications with the bulk of the Army. Grouchy took very tardy measures to execute these instructions. Pajol had just notified him, through an aide-de-camp, that the right column, in its march from Grand-Leez upon Tourinnes, had found no trace of the enemy. Grouchy sent back the aide-de-camp with an order to Pajol, to despatch at once the 2nd Cavalry Corps and the Teste division to Limale, and to cross the Dyle there by main force.[24] Grouchy did not realise the value of time; otherwise he would have entrusted the carrying of the bridge at Limale, not to Pajol, who from Tourinnes had three leagues and a half to march, but to General Vallin's cavalry, which was only one league distant from the Dyle, and the Hulot division of Gérard's corps, which had just reached La Baraque.[25]

The despatch once sent off to Pajol, Grouchy galloped toward Wavre, where he proposed to direct the attack in person. The eager Vandamme had not waited for him. Regardless of the Marshal's orders, and without reconnoitring the position, or preparing for the action by his artillery, he launched against the enemy, French fashion, the whole of the Habert division in assaulting columns.[26]

The second echelon of Zeiten's corps (Brause and Langen divisions and Sohr's cavalry), had crossed the Dyle after the fight in the La Huzelle defile, and was marching on Chapelle-Saint-Lambert. But nearly the whole of Thielmann's corps remained to defend Wavre and its approaches. At first, mistaking the deploying of the cavalry under Exelmans, between Sainte-Anne and Dion-Le-Mont, for a mere demonstration, Thielmann had set his troops in motion in the direction of Couture-Saint-Germain; two battalions only were ordered to remain behind to protect Wavre. Then seeing Vandamme's corps debouching before the town, he reoccupied the positions he had just evacuated. The divisions of Kempher and Lück, three battalions of the Borcke division, and Hobe's cavalry, posted themselves at Wavre, at Basse-Wavre, and on the heights over the left bank of the Dyle. The Stülpnagel division occupied Bierges, the detachment of Zieten's corps (three battalions and three squadrons under Von Stengel), appointed to guard the Limale Bridge, was retained at this post.[27]

Habert's infantry speedily drove the Prussians from the suburb of Wavre; but their furious charge was arrested at the Dyle, which separated the town from its suburbs. The two bridges were strongly barricaded, and enfiladed, by the batteries established at various altitudes up the steep streets leading down to the river; moreover, more than 1,000 sharpshooters were ambushed in the houses on the left bank. General Habert, Colonel Dubalen of the 64th, and 600 men, were disabled in a few minutes. Powerless to carry the bridges, the soldiers hesitated to fall back, through fear of exposing themselves to the terrible fire of the Prussian batteries which swept the approaches to the suburb, and the steep slopes of the right bank. They sheltered themselves in the streets parallel to the Dyle. "They were wedged," says Grouchy, "into a kind of *cul de sac*." [28]

Section II

After closely examining the position, Grouchy resolved to second the attack on Wavre, by two other attacks up the river and down the river. Reinforcements entered the suburb; a battalion under Lefol was detached to cross the Dyle at the bridge of the mill of Bierges; Exelmans, with his dragoons, advanced to the front of Basse-Wavre.[29] The Marshal had hardly made these dispositions, when he received about [30] five o'clock, the despatch which Soult had sent him at half-past one from the battlefield, and which concluded thus: "At this moment the battle is raging on the line of Waterloo, in front of the forest of Soignes. Therefore manœuvre so as to join our right. We think we can distinguish Bülow's corps on the height of Chapelle-Saint-Lambert. Therefore do not waste an instant in drawing nearer to us, so as to join us, and to crush Bülow, whom you will surprise in the very act." [31]

The Emperor's order was undoubtedly direct and urgent; it prescribed a march on Saint-Lambert to crush Bülow. Grouchy so understood it; but he showed neither resolution nor method in his arrangements. The two divisions of Vandamme were a sufficient force to keep the Prussians in check before Wavre. It seems clear that the Marshal should at once have despatched towards Limale, Vandamme's 3rd division, as well as the eight regiments of Exelmans' dragoons, whose diversion to Basse-Wavre was no longer of any use. But Grouchy, through the most extraordinary of strategic conceptions, determined at one and the same time to carry Wavre with half of his army, and to direct the other half upon Saint-Lambert, by the bridge of Limale. Accordingly, the whole of the 3rd Corps, with the cavalry of Exelmans,[32] he left in front of the Prussian positions, and sent his aide-de-camp, Pont-Bellanger, with a verbal order to Pajol, who was just starting from Tourinnes, to hasten his march on Limale. " Never has the Emperor been so great ! " said Pont-Bellanger, as he accosted Pajol. " The battle is won; they are only waiting for cavalry to complete the rout." [33]

Having despatched this order to Pajol, Grouchy galloped off with Gérard to La Baraque, to direct thence upon Limale, the 4th Corps, whose leading division (General Hulot) alone had reached the heights of Wavre. Is it true, as Grouchy states, that the two other divisions of the 4th Corps (Vichery and Pêcheux) had not reached La Baraque by six o'clock that evening; that the Marshal, tired of waiting for them, returned to the front of Wavre, leaving orders for these two divisions to proceed directly on Limale; and finally that owing to a misinterpretation of this order, Vichery and Pêcheux continued their march on Wavre ? Or must we not rather believe that Grouchy found these divisions at La Baraque, that he ordered them to march on Limale, but that the head of the column lost its way, owing to the absence of a guide, and returned towards Wavre ? It seems impossible to get at the truth in the midst of the contradictory testimonies of Gérard, General Hulot, and Grouchy himself, whose own assertions are far from agreeing with each other.[34] Certain it is that Grouchy did go to La Baraque, and afterwards returned to Wavre.[35]

The fight still waged fiercely on either side of the Dyle. The attack on the Bierges bridge by the Lefol battalion had been repulsed. Grouchy, who furiously persisted in crossing the Dyle at this spot, ordered Gérard to renew the attack, with a battalion of the Hulot division. And when Gérard remarked to Grouchy, that it would be better to support Lefol's detachment by other troops of the same army corps,[36] the Marshal took his judicious advice in very bad part. Gérard then passed on the order to Hulot, who, in person, led a battalion of the 9th Léger to the assault. To reach the bridge, they had to traverse a tract of marshy fields, furrowed with deep and very broad ditches running parallel to the Dyle. Hulot ordered the men to plunge into these ditches if they could not leap across them. The water being between four and six feet deep, the sharpshooters narrowly escaped being drowned; their comrades had to pull them out. Meanwhile the bullets fell thick around them. Discouraged, the soldiers fell back.[37] At this juncture Grouchy and Gérard, the latter leading another battalion, arrived on the border of the meadow. Gérard, who was not in the habit of sparing himself, exposed himself all the more that he had good reason to be in a very bad temper. He received a bullet full in his chest which necessitated his being carried to the rear.[38] Grouchy then requested Artillery-General Baltus to take Gérard's place at the head of the assaulting column. This the general having flatly refused, Grouchy sprang from his horse crying: "If a soldier can't make his subordinates obey, he must know how to be killed!"[39] This third assault failed, as the previous ones had done. Grouchy left the Hulot division before Bierges, as if he intended, says Hulot, to make fresh arrangements for attacking the mill; then, suddenly changing his mind, he joined Gérard's other two divisions, and with them proceeded towards Limale.[40]

During these ineffectual assaults, skirmishing continued before Basse-Wavre, while at Wavre the struggle was carried on with terrible ferocity. Vandamme made no less than thirteen attacks, without being able to wrench from the enemy this little town, which had been transformed into a fortress. At eleven o'clock that night the fight was still raging.[41]

When Marshal Grouchy reached Limale at nightfall[42] the Dyle bridge was free. Renewing the daring manœuvre of the preceding year at Montereau, Pajol had hurled General Vallin's hussars,[43] at full speed upon this bridge, though it was accessible only to four horses at a time, and was guarded by an entire battalion. The Prussians broken into and cut to pieces, Teste's infantry and the rest of the cavalry passed over to the left bank in the wake of the Hussars. Von Stengel gave up Limale after a hard struggle, and took up other positions on the heights which overlooked the village. In spite of the darkness, the assault was vigorously led by Teste, when Grouchy debouched from the Limale bridge with the Vichery and Pècheux divisions. These reinforcements had become very necessary, for Thielmann hearing the cannonade, had brought to Stengel's rescue,[44] by the left bank of the Dyle, the Stülpnagel division and Hobe's cavalry. They fought till eleven o'clock in the night for the possession of the crest of the plateau, which at last fell into the hands of the French.[45] And now the road to Mont-Saint-Jean was open; but for a long time the Emperor's cannon had ceased to be heard.

Section III

The French bivouacked in squares, and face to face with their foes, who occupied the woods of Rixensart. The outposts were so close to each other, that the balls they exchanged throughout the whole night, would often fall in the rear of the first lines.[46] At half-past eleven at night Grouchy sent Vandamme orders to join him at once at Limale with the 3rd Corps. He proposed resuming the fight very early in the morning to rally the Imperial Army at Brussels, for it was rumoured—no one could say on what grounds—that the Emperor had beaten the English.[47]

The Prussian staff were better informed. An officer of the Marwitz cavalry who had been reconnoitring, had brought back the news that the French were in full retreat.[48] Reassured for the future, Thielmann directed almost all his troops towards the plateau of Limale, in order to resume the offensive by daybreak. At three o'clock in the morning, Hobe's cavalry debouched from the woods of Rixensart with two mounted batteries which, in a moment, poured a rain of shells on the French encampments. Grouchy, hurrying with utmost speed to the first line, brought his artillery into play; then, with all his men formed in battle array, Pajol's cavalry on the extreme left, the Pêcheux and Vichery divisions in reserve at the centre, the Teste division on the right, he marched against the enemy. After holding firm for a long time, the Prussians at last yielded the wood of Rixensart. It was now about eight o'clock. Thielmann received from General Pirch positive intelligence of the defeat of the French. The despatch added that the 2nd Army Corps was going to manœuvre in order to intercept the retreat of Marshal Grouchy. The news of this great victory, which was immediately announced to the troops, put new spirit into them. Thielmann wheeled around his front, to the rear upon his left wing, which still occupied Bierges. Through this movement the Prussian right found itself deployed on a line parallel to the road from Wavre to Brussels.[49]

The fighting was resumed, not without advantage to the Prussians, until the Teste division had carried the village and the mill of Bierges. In this assault General Penne, one of Teste's brigadiers, who was himself wounded, had his head crushed by a shell. Berthezène, posted on the right bank of the Dyle, had seconded Teste's attack; both divisions now mustered together. Thielmann, seeing his left attacked, and his right on the point of being turned by Pajol's cavalry, which was manœuvring towards Rosieren to reach the Brussels road, fell back and retreated in the direction of Louvain. The four battalions left at Wavre, evacuated this position, and marched to La Bavette, from whence they were speedily dislodged by Vandamme's advanced guard.[50] Notwithstanding Grouchy's orders to join him at Limale with the 3rd Corps, Vandamme had remained the whole morning in front of Wavre. He had sent to the Marshal, Exelmans' dragoons only, with the Hulot division, which he had replaced before Bierges, by the Berthezène division.[51]

Master of the battlefield, where the Prussians had abandoned five pieces of cannon and a number of wounded, Grouchy had his right at La Bavette, his left beyond Rosieren. He was taking steps to march upon Brussels, when towards half-past ten o'clock,[52] an officer of the head of the staff rode up to him. With a visibly dejected face, with eyes staring from terror, his whole form bent, and apparently his horse broken down by exhaustion, he seemed the embodied image of defeat and ruin. Scarcely able to collect his ideas or to find his words, he related in such incoherent language the disaster of Mont-Saint-Jean, that at first the Marshal thought he had to deal with a madman or a drunkard. To Grouchy's questions whether he were the bearer of an order, or to which point they were to retreat, whether the army had crossed the Sambre, the officer instead of replying, began repeating his involved story of the battle. From the very precise details gathered from the midst of his confused ramblings, Grouchy was at last convinced.[53] This was not the time to give way to grief; it was necessary to save what remained of the army.

Grouchy assembled his general officers and held a sort of council of war. He announced to them the terrible news. It is said that, as he spoke, he had tears in his eyes.[54] His discussion with Gérard on the previous day at Walhain, was known to all the different staffs. The Marshal considered that circumstances called upon him to justify his refusal to listen to the advice of his lieutenant. "My honour," he said, "makes it a matter of duty to explain myself, in regard to my dispositions of yesterday. The instructions which I had received from the Emperor, left me free to manœuvre in no other direction than Wavre. I was obliged, therefore, to refuse the advice which Count Gérard thought he had the right to offer me. I do ample justice to General Gérard's talents and brilliant valour; but you were doubtless as surprised as I was, that a general officer, ignorant of the Emperor's orders, and the data which inspired the Marshal of France, under whose orders he was placed, should have presumed publicly to dictate to the latter, his line of conduct. The advanced hour of the day, the distance from the point where the cannonading was heard, the condition of the roads, made it impossible to arrive in time to share in the action which was taking place. At any rate, whatever the subsequent events may have been, the Emperor's orders, the substance of which I have just disclosed to you, did not permit of my acting otherwise than I have done."[55]

Having pronounced these words, which were as much of the nature of a confession as of an excuse, the Marshal expounded his plan of retreat. He had thought at first of marching upon the rear of the Anglo-Prussians, with the hope that this diversion might hamper their pursuit of the Imperial Army; but he quickly abandoned the idea, the only result of which would have been the total destruction of 30,000 men, overpowered and crushed by 50,000.[56] For similar reasons he wisely rejected the daring project of Vandamme, which consisted in marching on Brussels, where numerous prisoners might be set free, and in repairing then to the frontier, towards Valenciennes or Lille, by Enghien and Ath.[57] Vandamme surmised that, in this direction, only a few detachments of the allied army would be encountered. Grouchy wisely preferred directing his line of retreat upon Namur, Dinant and Givet.[58] It was necessary to hasten with the utmost speed, for he ran the risk not only of being harassed by Thielmann, who would undoubtedly hurry back to the front at the first retrograde movement of the French, but also there was the prospect of a flank attack at the hands of a corps of Blücher's army. Perhaps such a detachment might even arrive in time to take up its positions towards Gembloux, and cut off the retreat. Such was indeed the Prussians' main object; and at eleven o'clock, at the time when Grouchy still had his army beyond the Dyle, his front resting between Rosieren and La Bavette, Pirch, detached from Rossomme during the night, had already occupied Mellery with the 2nd Corps.[59] He was three hours ahead of Grouchy, for the distance between Mellery and Gembloux is ten kilometres, as the bird flies, and between La Bavette and Gembloux there are twenty kilometres.

The retreat commenced between eleven and midday, Exelmans' dragoons, with the exception of the 20th regiment placed under Vandamme's orders, rapidly marched to Namur to secure the bridges over the Sambre. Their advanced Guard arrived there at four o'clock.[60] The 4th Corps and Vallin's cavalry crossed the Dyle at Limale, and reached the direct road to Gembloux; during the night, these troops bivouacked at a distance of two leagues beyond this village, on the road which leads from Nivelles to Namur, between Le Mazy and Temploux. Grouchy, who was marching with this echelon of the army, established his headquarters at Tembloux.[61]

From La Bavette, Vandamme's corps fell back on Wavre, held its positions there until rather late, and then marched on by Dion-le-Mont, Tourinnes and Grand-Leez. In the evening, at about eleven o'clock, it halted on the road from Gembloux to Namur, on the height of Temploux.[62] Pajol, in charge of the rearguard composed of General Soult's cavalry and the indefatigable Teste division, kept Thielmann in check by following him as far as the vicinity of Saint-Achtenrode, where the latter took up his position. Then when the entire corps of Vandamme had crossed the bridges at Wavre, Pajol himself began his retreat, reached Gembloux by Sauvenière, and established his quarters there during the night.[63]

This perilous retreat was effected with some disorder;[64] but they had not been compelled to fire a shot. Thielmann, whose corps was now reduced to 12,500 men by the losses of the previous day and of that morning,[65] learned but very late of the retrograde movement of the French. As for the 2nd Prussian corps, though it had reached Mellery by noon, it had arrived there in the most pitiable condition, after an unbroken march of twenty-four hours. Besides, it is clear that Pirch did not feel strong enough with these forces to act singly. He had not heard from Thielmann, from whom he expected help. He did not wish, nor did he think it possible to lead his harassed soldiers[66] any farther, on that day.

Section IV

On the morrow, June 20th, Pajol and Teste left Gembloux in the morning, according to Grouchy's orders, and proceeded to Namur by Saint-Denis and Saint-Marc.[67] Towards nine o'clock, Grouchy directed upon Namur the 4th Corps, which was bringing on all the wounded and the reserved park of artillery. The Marshal hoped to send this army corps through the town, whilst Vandamme's corps remained in position till after twelve o'clock, across the Gembloux road, to cover the movement.[68] Matters did not, however, work smoothly by any means. At the moment when the head of the 4th Corps was leaving Temploux, a lively cannonade was heard from the front, to the left. Instead of bivouacking among his troops, Vandamme had gone to spend the night at Namur. He had not received the orders sent by Grouchy, to guard his position; and in the morning, Generals Lefol, Berthezène and Habert, who had been left without instructions, had set off for Namur, thus leaving unprotected the flank of the 4th Corps.[69] They were attacked near La Falise by the thirty and odd squadrons under Hobe whom Thielmann had started from Achtenrode with a mounted battery, at five o'clock in the morning, and who had marched ten leagues at a stretch, in pursuit of the French. At the same time, a large body of the enemy's troops debouching from Le Mazy, was notified to Grouchy. It was Pirch's advanced guard marching from Mellery.[70]

Grouchy now found himself in a position of great peril, for if Vandamme's infantry fell back too quickly on the other side of the Sambre, he himself would be cut off by Hobe from the road to Namur, whilst he was fighting Pirch. The troops, realising the danger, showed signs of uneasiness; the numerous wounded that were being convoyed from Limale and Wavre, expressed by murmurs, groans, and angry cries, their dread of falling alive into the hands of the Prussians. Grouchy came among the vehicles with General Vichery. He spoke in a loud voice. "Be quite easy," he said, "we swear never to abandon you. I am confident that our dispositions will save us."[71] Thereupon, with General Vallin's cavalry, he immediately fell upon those of the Prussian squadrons, which after turning the Vandamme divisions, were attacking his line of retreat, and repulsed them to the left. Then pursuing his course, he hurried to the assistance of Vandamme. During this time the 4th Corps, whose way was now free, reached Namur with the wounded and the artillery park; the rearguard, commanded by Vichery in person, checked for some time at Le Boquet, the Prussians under Pirch; then it fell back, disputing the ground inch by inch.[72]

Surprised by the sudden attack of the Prussian cavalry, the 3rd Corps was thrown into confusion. One of Lefol's squares was broken: the men only escaped the Uhlans' spears, by taking refuge in a wood. Two pieces of cannon were lost. Grouchy's approach arrested the enemy. Vallin's cavalry dashed off at a gallop. Colonel Briqueville, who charged at the head of the 20th Dragoons, overthrew the more advanced of the Prussian squadrons, recovered the two guns, and even captured another. The entire cavalry of Hobe fell back by its right upon Pirch's corps, which was just debouching from Temploux.[73]

At the sound of the combat, Vandamme had come from Namur. Grouchy reiterated his order to cover the retreat of the 4th Corps. Vandamme reformed his battalions, took up his position before the suburbs, and held the Prussians in check.[74] The cavalry, the entire 3rd Corps, the convoys, all entered Namur. The Prussians were detested there. The retreating French brought in their train, the terrible risks of war. They were nevertheless greeted as friends. The municipality distributed 100,000 rations of bread, 100,000 rations of brandy. The good citizens of Namur lent their boats for the transfer of the wounded by the Meuse, and even helped to embark them themselves. Women, even under fire, brought provisions to the soldiers, and assistance to the wounded.[75]

The army merely passed through Namur. Grouchy with the 4th Corps, then Vandamme slightly wounded, with the 3rd, crossed the Sambre, and plunged into the long defile formed by the Meuse and the forest of Marlagne. The Teste division, acting as rearguard, had been enjoined to hold the city until nightfall. For the defence of Namur, whose dilapidated fortifications were not proof against an escalade, Teste had eight field-guns and, at most, 2,000 men under his command. He scattered them about the ramparts and the three Eastern gates; the "Louvain Gate," "the Iron Gate" and the "Gate of St. Nicholas." Scarcely were his troops in position, when Pirch hurled his assaulting columns against him. Greeted by a volley of grapeshot and a rolling musketry fire, the Prussians wheeled half round, leaving on the glacis a heap of dead and wounded. A second attack, during which Colonels von Zastrow and von Bismark fell mortally wounded, failed like the preceding one. As the cartridges were giving out, each Frenchman aimed at his Prussian and brought him down. It was 8 at night. Pirch, who had lost 1,500 men and despaired of carrying the place by storm, stopped the fight. By that time General Teste, whose ammunition was almost exhausted, was already commencing his retreat. The Prussians having perceived this, burst into the city through the windows and the small door of the custom-house, and speedily made their way as far as the bridge on the Sambre. There, a detachment of Engineers posted in some houses which the sappers had found time to pierce with loopholes, arrested them for a long time, by a spirited and well-directed fusillade. This rear-guard then withdrew through the "Gate of France" where quantities of faggots and bundles of straw saturated with tar, were heaped up together. The sappers set them alight, and the Gate and the neighbouring houses caught fire, closing the access of the street to the Prussian columns.[76]

During this combat the main body of Grouchy's army had reached Dinant. The next day, June 21st, the forces passed the frontier, and on that evening, the whole army was re-assembled under the cannon of Givet.[77]

Even if this march from Wavre to the frontier is not,—we must allow,—" one of the most astonishing retreats of modern military history,"[78] for Thielmann's carelessness and Pirch's timidity, facilitated it to a most singular degree,—it nevertheless does the greatest credit to Grouchy. He did not give way to despair when, in the immensity of the disaster, all hope seemed lost. He acted with decision and rapidity. By the direction which he chose, and the steps he took, he saved his Army. One can only ask what might not have happened, if on the 17th and the 18th of June, the unfortunate Marshal had displayed the same resolution, the same activity, the same military talent, and the same comprehension of the necessities of the situation?

BOOK III CHAPTER VIII

THE CAMPAIGN OF 1815

I. The operations of the 15th of June—The battles of Ligny and of Quatre-Bras.
II. Napoleon's mistake.
III. Marshal Grouchy.
IV. Waterloo.

SECTION I

THE original plan of the campaign of 1815, and even the movements which were its development, rank amongst the finest strategical conceptions of Napoleon. Everything failed owing to defects of execution, some of which may be attributed to the Emperor, a far larger number to his lieutenants.

The very first day, Drouet d'Erlon started marching an hour and a half behind the time appointed; Gérard interpreted the instructions of the Emperor to suit his own convenience; Vandamme broke up his camps three hours after the hour fixed, halted his troops before the end of the fight, and refused to co-operate with Grouchy; Ney suddenly became cautious even to timidity, and did not dare to carry out the manœuvre with which he was charged. The service of the staff was badly performed, the transmission of orders was slow and uncertain. The chiefs were hesitating and apathetic, without zeal, without initiative, without spirit. They seemed to have lost all faith in the Napoleonic star; they only appeared to wish to advance with measured steps beyond the frontier, as if they felt the grip of the enemy's two great hosts already upon them. The all-powerful engine of war, constructed by Napoleon, was apparently worn out, or overstrained.

Thus the day of the 15th of June, did not produce the results which might have been anticipated. Had the army marched as the Emperor's orders directed, before twelve o'clock all the troops would have crossed the Sambre; by three o'clock, the Prussians under Pirch II. would have been dislodged from Gilly; in the evening, Grouchy would have occupied Sombreffe, and Ney, Quatre-Bras. The next day Blücher and Wellington, separated by this double manœuvre, and neither of them wishing to risk giving battle singly, to the whole of the French army, would have fallen back on the base of their operations, the first to the north-east of Sombreffe, the second to the west of Brussels. The effect of this divergent retreat, would have been to separate the English from the Prussians by a distance of some twenty leagues, as the bird flies. It would have required a period of several days before they would have been able to concert and operate a fresh junction. Meanwhile, Napoleon would have occupied Brussels without striking a blow, and arranged some overwhelming march, upon one or other of the two hostile armies.

On the morning of the 16th, however, in spite of Ney's mistakes, and the delays of the right wing, nothing was as yet compromised.[1] The Emperor even imagined that the Prussians and the English were in full retreat, and that he might possibly reach Brussels without meeting with any resistance. Probabilities induced him to believe this, for, as Kennedy remarks, Wellington and Blücher committed a serious mistake, considering the dispersion of their troops and the separation of their army, in giving battle on the 16th of June. Consequently the Emperor issued orders for a march on Brussels, and left Charleroi at nine o'clock. The criticism that he wasted his time in the morning, seems groundless. As the Emperor did not at all expect a battle that day, such an event seeming highly improbable, one day would suffice for his point upon Gembloux, and the night for his march on Brussels. By six o'clock in the morning, he dictated orders, with a view to the concentration of the whole right wing at Fleurus. He cannot be held responsible for the delay on the part of Gérard, who did not arrive till past one o'clock. If the Emperor failed to repeat to Ney early in the morning the order to take up his position at Quatre-Bras, it was because he was deceived by the latter's report, into believing that this post was merely occupied by a very small force, or even evacuated altogether; and he judged there would be no difficulty in taking possession of it. In point of fact, the Prince of Orange having received reinforcements only at three o'clock, it was as easy for Ney to dislodge the Perponcher division from Quatre-Bras at eleven o'clock,[2] at the moment when the instructions of the Emperor reached him, as it would have been during the first hours of the morning.

However, the "General Imprévu" (General Unforeseen) intervened in favour of Napoleon; Blücher knew that the French numbered 120,000; owing to Bülow's delay he himself had only 80,000 men. But faithful to his promises to protect the English left, impatient to fight, and trusting too much in the very problematical support of Wellington, he rashly offered battle to Napoleon, from his position at Ligny. When Napoleon saw the deployment of the Prussian Army, he congratulated himself that it was bringing itself within reach of his sword. This battle, which he in no way foresaw, or expected, gave him the opportunity of bringing to an end in one single day, as it were by a thunderbolt, the campaign which had only commenced on the previous day. He was going to exterminate the Prussian Army. He at once decided on his plan, disposed his troops, sent orders to Ney. Whilst he attacked, Marshal Ney would bear down on the Prussian rear, and when at the end of the day he made the final assault, Blücher's army broken at the centre, attacked on the right, assailed from the rear, would be almost entirely caught in a net of iron and fire.

Müffling, Rogniat, and others, contend that Napoleon should have limited himself to demonstrations toward Ligny, and have brought all his efforts to bear upon Saint-Amand, where the Prussian right was quite isolated, and incapable of making any but a feeble resistance. This is to misunderstand one of Napoleon's finest inspirations of military tactics. Assuredly, the attack on Saint-Amand would have brought about the retreat of the Prussians, in less time and with smaller casualties. But on the 16th of June the Emperor had a more decided aim in view, than to separate Blücher from Wellington, by driving back the latter toward the Meuse;

his object was no less, than to destroy the entire Prussian Army. This could only be accomplished through piercing its centre and surrounding its right wing. The left wing alone would have escaped from the general disaster.

We have seen through what a series of mistakes and blunders, this well-conceived plan came to fail,[3] and how each one contributed to bring about its failure. Flahaut, bearer of the first instructions of the Emperor, spent two hours in riding four leagues. Reille delayed a movement that had been ordered, under the pretext that a small loss of time was of no consequence; he considered, according to the extraordinary explanation of Jomini, that it was better to obey the laws of great tactics, than the orders of the head of the army. Forbin-Janson did not understand a single word of the despatch entrusted to him; he was unable to explain it, and after transmitting it to General d'Erlon, he omitted to communicate it to Marshal Ney. D'Erlon set out in the wrong direction; he had not the common sense to rectify it, and after going three-quarters of the way, he decided to retrace his footsteps to comply with the injunctions of Marshal Ney, who recalled him in spite of the formal orders of Napoleon; he did not see that by this countermarch, he was depriving the Emperor of a very efficient support, and that he could not reach Ney in time to fight. In a word, throughout this afternoon, D'Erlon neutralised his troops, marching them about with arms presented, from the left wing to the right wing, and without helping either one or the other. Vandamme, who perceived the first of d'Erlon's corps, was misinformed by his scouts, and notified this corps to the Emperor as belonging to the enemy. Napoleon disturbed by Vandamme's message, and by the direction of this column, lost his presence of mind. He either did not realise, or he refused to admit that the body of troops threatening his flank, might be the first corps which he had himself summoned to the field of battle; he neglected to enjoin on the officer, whom he sent to reconnoitre once more the supposed hostile column, to direct it on Brye, should it prove to be, contrary to his expectations, the corps under d'Erlon.

But on Marshal Ney, rests the principal responsibility for

CHAP. VIII   *THE CAMPAIGN OF* 1815   273

the incomplete results of the day. By recalling d'Erlon, against the special orders of the Emperor, he committed an act of disobedience liable to a court-martial, and which it is only possible to explain by the undisciplined spirit which then prevailed throughout every rank of the army. But this desperate act of Ney's had no serious influence on the issue, for already Count d'Erlon, in taking Saint-Amand, instead of Brye as his destination, had compromised the brilliant manœuvre conceived and ordered by the Emperor. The principal charge against Marshal Ney, consists in an initial mistake which brought about all the subsequent delays, misunderstandings, false movements, and misfortunes of this double action. Had he acted that morning as he ought to have done, in accordance with circumstances and with the principles of war, by eight or nine o'clock he would have had the 2nd Corps mustered at Frasnes and the 1st Corps concentrated at Gosselies. Thus at eleven o'clock, after receiving the order brought by Flahaut, he would have been in a position to attack Quatre-Bras with the four divisions of Reille and the Lefebvre-Desnoëttes cavalry, and to call up to Frasnes, the five divisions under d'Erlon, and Kellermann's four brigades of cuirassiers. Long before two, he would have wrested the position from the 7,500 Dutch who were its only defenders. At three, with his 43,000 men, he would easily have repulsed on the road to Brussels—granting that Wellington had dared take the offensive—the 7,000 English under Picton, and the 6,000 Brunswickers of Duke Frederick William. At four, when the despatch of the Emperor reached him, enjoining him to fall back on Brye, he could have detached, by the Namur road, more than half his forces on to the rear of the Prussian Army, and changed thereby Blücher's defeat, into a disaster.

Jomini allows that the results of the battle of Ligny might have been decisive, had Ney directed a portion of his troops upon Brye. But he objects that the Marshal could not have carried out this movement, even with the help of the corps under Reille and d'Erlon, because he would have had to deal with the 40,000 Anglo-Allies under Wellington. This argument rests on an essential error. At four o'clock

Wellington had with him only the Perponcher division, the Van Merlen cavalry, the Brunswick corps, and the Picton division, that is 22,000 men. (Moreover, presupposing the capture of Quatre-Bras by Ney, between noon and two o'clock, Perponcher's 7,200 soldiers would have been so crushed, as to be quite useless, when the English reinforcements arrived.) The Alten division (4,000 muskets) did not debouch till half-past five, and the Cooke and Kruse divisions (7,000 men) not before seven. Thus, either Wellington would have attacked at three with Perponcher, Picton, or Van Merlen, in which case these 15,000 men, struggling against 43,000, would have been exterminated; or rather, to prevent his two divisions being destroyed, one after the other, he would have waited not only for Brunswick, but for Alten as well, before taking the offensive; consequently, he would not have engaged in battle until about six o'clock. By this time, one-half of Ney's corps would already have been close on the Prussians' heels, and the Marshal would have had 20,000 men in a good position, whom he could oppose until nightfall against a force of 28,000, then of 32,000 assailants. Even if he were compelled to fall back on Frasnes, this retreat, at the approach of night, would have been without any strategical importance. Besides, it is very probable that if Wellington, on his return from the Bussy mill at about three o'clock, had found Quatre-Bras strongly occupied by the French, he would have prudently concentrated his troops on Genappe while awaiting the issue of the battle waging before Ligny. So much, at least, may be inferred from his ordinary circumspection and his British egotism.

After a long and confused argument, Clausewitz concludes that "ten thousand men on the rear of the Prussian Army would merely have rendered the issue of the battle more doubtful, by forcing Blücher to retire earlier." It proves the weakness of his case that he intentionally quotes inaccurate figures. Clausewitz knew very well that the number of cavalry and infantry, that might have attacked the Prussians on the rear, amounted not to 10,000, but to 20,000. Now, if this attack could have no other effect than to precipitate Blücher's retreat, by what miracle was Bülow's attack at

Waterloo, two days later, attended by an entirely different result? If we listened to Clausewitz we might, in fact, believe that an army is free to leave a battlefield as easily as a drilling-ground, and that a sudden retreat, in the heat of action, can be effected without disorder and without peril. As for Charras, he takes an entirely personal view of the question. "The generals," he exclaims, "were admirable. They did not fail their chief, their chief failed them." He extolls Ney, "who passed the bounds of possibility, in checking Wellington with 20,000 men." Charras does not seem aware that Wellington, until the arrival of the Cooke and Kruse divisions (at half-past six in the evening), had scarcely 26,000 men [4] to oppose to the French, who numbered more than 23,000.[5] And he wilfully omits to state that, if Ney had but one army corps to oppose to the English, it was because he had that morning neglected to concentrate the 2nd and 1st Corps between Gosselies and Frasnes. Here, and this cannot be repeated too often, lies the radical mistake which gave rise to all the others: the mistakes of Ney, those of Reille, those of d'Erlon, those of the Emperor.

Facts, written orders, time, dates, figures, all contradict the conclusions of Clausewitz and Charras. We have also the testimony of Kellermann: "Napoleon failed to accomplish his object, through the fault of Marshal Ney;" of Reille: "It would have been possible to achieve a far greater success by turning the right of the Prussian Army;" of General Delort: "Ney, with his 44,000 men, could have held the English in check and turned Blücher's army." Here is also the opinion of Ropes: "Had Ney carried out the Emperor's orders, the issue of the campaign would have been changed."[6] Here is also the opinion of Marshal Wolseley: "If all had happened as Napoleon had planned, it is hardly too much to say that Zieten and Pirch's corps would have been annihilated, and, in all probability, Blücher and Gneisenau would have been made prisoners."[7] Finally, there is the conclusive admission made by Gneisenau, chief of the staff with the Prussian Army, who wrote to the King of Prussia on the 12th of June 1817: "If General Perponcher had not made so bold a resistance, Marshal Ney, arriving at Quatre-Bras, might have turned the right and fallen on the rear of the army which was fighting at Ligny, and thus caused its total destruction." [8]

Section II

The battle that should have been won—and won even to the annihilation and dissolution of the enemy—was the battle of Ligny. On the 16th of June a complete victory gained over the Prussian Army might, at one blow, have closed the campaign of the Netherlands. Through Ney's fault, this battle was not a decisive one. The following day, another opportunity presented itself, of ending the campaign by the destruction of the entire English Army. Napoleon, through his own fault, allowed this opportunity to escape.

The Emperor had separated Wellington from Blücher, and, notwithstanding the pause in the action and the commencement of a panic caused by the approach of d'Erlon's corps, he had, in six hours, beaten 87,000 Prussians with 65,000 French, thus proving, as he often did, the folly of his own axiom, that victory was always on the side of huge battalions. There remained the English Army posted at Quatre-Bras, which had successfully resisted Marshal Ney. On the 17th of June it was in the Emperor's power to have exterminated it. Unfortunately, though such a battle was bound to be conclusive and prove a victory, though he had an intuition of it in time to be of use,[9] he did not attempt to enter on the struggle until he had lost four long hours in delays and hesitations. This was giving too long a respite to the enemy, and Wellington decamped.

Doubtless, at daybreak, the Emperor was unaware of the Prussians' line of retreat, and of the issue of the battle of Quatre-Bras. But between seven and eight o'clock, he learnt from a despatch from Pajol, that Blücher's army was falling back toward the Meuse, and from the verbal report of Flahaut, that the English were still at Quatre-Bras. Had he, then and there, taken the steps which he only resolved on between eleven and mid-day, that is to say, had he marched at once to Quatre-Bras with Lobau's corps, the Guard, and Milhaud's cuirassiers, these troops would have debouched between ten and half-past ten o'clock upon the flank of the English Army, at the precise moment when the latter was breaking up its camp. Wellington's forces, deducting the losses of the previous day and adding the five brigades of Uxbridge's cavalry which had arrived during the night and in the morning, numbered hardly 35,000 muskets and sabres. Caught in the very act of marching, and attacked simultaneously by the 30,000 soldiers under Napoleon on its left, by the 40,000 soldiers under Ney upon its front, the English Army, whether it made a stand, or whether it attempted a very hazardous retreat on Genappe or upon Nivelles, could never have avoided a disaster.

Instead of this Napoleon intended, at first, to leave his army in camp throughout that day. Then he changed his mind, matured a new scheme, issued his orders, and started on his march. But it was too late. The Emperor did not reach Quatre-Bras until two o'clock. The Anglo-Netherland division had crossed the Dyle at Genappe. Nothing was left for him, but to give chase to the horsemen of Lord Uxbridge. When he came up with the English Army, in position at Mont-Saint-Jean, night was falling. "I wish," he said, "that I had Joshua's power now to stop the sun." But the sun had been shining on the earth for fourteen hours, and Napoleon had not profited by its light.

It may be urged that the information which the Emperor received at seven o'clock in the morning, did not appear to him as sufficiently precise and reliable as to induce him to act immediately. Was it certain that the Prussians were retiring towards the Meuse, and could he start in pursuit of them, without even being certain of the direction they had taken? On the other hand, could he, in this uncertainty, march with his army toward Brussels, without exposing himself to an offensive blow from Blücher either against his right flank or on his lines of communication? As for Wellington, was it possible that, knowing of the Prussians' defeat, he had not already evacuated his position at Quatre-Bras? As far as the retreat of the Prussians and the march upon Brussels were concerned, the Emperor's hesitations were perfectly natural.

But his reasons for deferring the movement against Wellington, were by no means so judicious. This movement was calculated to produce such great results that, even at the risk of a useless march, it should have been undertaken at once with the Guard and the corps led by Lobau. Either Wellington would still have been found at Quatre-Bras, thus giving an opportunity to Napoleon and Ney to attack him in concert, under the most favourable conditions, or the English would have decamped already, in which case the Guard and the 6th Corps, could have effected their junction with the corps of d'Erlon and Reille. The march upon Quatre-Bras, which would have resulted in the extermination of the English Army, would not, in any case, have compromised anything, for, in view of the trifling distance between this point and Brye, it was quite as easy for the Emperor to concentrate his reserve upon his left wing, as to leave it with his right wing.

It has been alleged, again, that the troops needed rest, and had to be revictualled with food and ammunition. Rest? Exelmans' and Pajol's cavalry had fought the day before until nightfall, yet were on their march again by sunrise. With still more reason the Guard, which had been engaged for a very short time, and the 6th Corps, which had scarcely fired a shot, might have started at seven o'clock in the morning. Ammunition? Only the corps of Gérard and Vandamme needed a fresh supply, and this operation was certainly completed by noon. As for the 30,000 men of the 6th Corps and of the Guard who had marched on Quatre-Bras, their cartridge belts and ammunition boxes were undoubtedly well furnished.

There were other causes, therefore, for the Emperor's inaction during the morning of 17th June. Charras, General Berthaut, Ropes, and still more, General Wolseley, attribute it to his state of health. (Neither Wolseley nor Ropes specify the disease he was suffering from; Charras declares that he had every disease.)[10] It is possible, indeed, that, during the night of the battle of Ligny, Napoleon suffered from one of those attacks of ischuria to which he had been subject for the last three years, and which had become very frequent during the months of April and May 1815.[11] Grouchy incidentally mentions that the Emperor felt tired on leaving the Chateau of Fleurus on the morning of the 17th. According to General Le Sénecal and Colonel de Blocqueville—the former head of the staff, the latter aide-de-camp to Grouchy—Napoleon had been ill during the night.[12] We repeat once more this is possible. But as Thiers remarks: " Whatever may have been Napoleon's state of health in 1815, it did not in any way affect his activity."

Let us review once more these memorable days during which, if we believe Marshal Wolseley, Napoleon was " wrapped in a veil of lethargy." On the 15th of June he rose at three o'clock in the morning, went as far as Jamignon, mounted his horse, stormed Charleroi, issued orders for the movement of the left wing, superintended the storming of Gilly by the right wing, and returned to Charleroi at ten at night. On the 16th he despatched aides-de-camp, and was busy writing orders by four o'clock next morning. At nine o'clock he rode to the mill at Fleurus, engaged in battle at Ligny, and during the final assault at dusk he led the Guard in person, beyond the first Prussian lines. He retired to rest after ten o'clock. If he was ill in the night, that did not deter him from being present by ten o'clock in the morning of the next day at Brye, where he reviewed his troops and superintended the care of the wounded. Then he marched upon Quatre-Bras at the head of his troops, and, in his impatience, outdistanced them. He attacked the English cavalry, and pursued it with his advanced Guard during three hours at breakneck speed and under a tropical rain. At Le Caillou, where he took shelter after sunset, streaming with water, and as drenched as if he had come out of a bath, he dictated orders for the army, and was absorbed in the perusal of his Paris letters. He threw himself on his bed for a few moments; then at 1 A.M. he rose, and under the rain which was still falling, he made the entire round of all his outposts. When he returned at three o'clock, he listened to the reports of his scouts and spies. He dictated fresh orders. At nine o'clock he was on the battlefield again. He did not leave it until the middle of the night, with the last squares of the

Guard; and, always on horseback, he crossed the Sambre at Charleroi, eight leagues from La Belle Alliance. During these ninety-six hours, this man, who is represented as broken down, depressed by disease, lacking in energy, unable to overcome sleep, and incapable of keeping in the saddle, scarcely took twenty hours' rest; and, granting that he was on foot for three-quarters of the time that the two great battles lasted, he remained in the saddle for more than thirty-seven hours.

In 1815 Napoleon was in sufficiently good health to enable him to bear the great fatigues of war, and his brain had lost none of its power. But with him, his moral power no longer upheld his genius. Though he strove in his dictations at Saint-Helena, to prove that he had committed no faults during his last campaign, in intimate conversations, the secret of these faults would often escape him. " I had no longer within me the feeling of certain success," he would say, " I had no longer the confidence I had of yore. I felt that fortune was abandoning me. No sooner did I secure some advantage, than it was immediately followed by a reverse. None of these blows surprised me, for I instinctively felt the issue would be an unfortunate one." [13] This state of mind accounts for the hours wasted by the Emperor during the campaign, his irresolution, his confused estimate of events, the respite often left to the enemy. He no longer believed in success, his boldness gave way with his confidence. He dared not seize and force circumstances. With his faith in his destiny, he had always been a daring, audacious gambler. Now that fortune showed herself contrary, he became a timid player. He hesitated to risk the game, he no longer followed his inspiration, temporised, weighed the chances, saw the pros and cons, and would risk nothing save on a certainty.

Section III

In order to be at liberty to act against the English, the Emperor ought to have been protected against a counter-attack from Blücher. And where were the Prussians? Were they retreating toward the Meuse? or marching to join Wellington on the south of Brussels? The Emperor charged Grouchy to discover their traces and pursue them. It has been said that, in his uncertainty as to the direction taken by the Prussians in their retreat, Napoleon, by ten or eleven o'clock on the 17th of June, ought, at all risks, to have ordered Grouchy to march laterally by the left bank of the Dyle. The Emperor has himself refuted this criticisism. "If Grouchy," he says, in substance, "had by twelve o'clock on the 17th marched along the left bank of the Dyle, without knowing the direction the Prussians had taken, he would, no doubt, have covered the flank of the main column, but he would also have left our lines of communication unprotected."[14] In point of fact, if the Prussians had withdrawn towards Namur, they might have returned to Charleroi and cut off the Imperial Army from its base of operations.

It has also been asserted that, when detaching from the right only two cavalry corps, some cannon, and a division of infantry—a force sufficient to hold the Prussians in check—the Emperor ought to have retained with him a surplus of 20,000 men, who would have proved very useful at Waterloo. Certainly, in 1814, after the battle of Arcis-sur-Aube, Winzingerode had, with 10,000 horse, held for two days at bay, the whole of the French Army. But there were objections in the present instance. Although Vandamme's and Gérard's corps, with Pajol's and Exelmans' cavalry, were absent from Waterloo, the French were slightly superior in numbers to the English, and had not the approach of the Prussians paralysed a portion of the army, it is probable that the plateau of Mont-Saint-Jean would have been carried by them about five o'clock. On the other hand, Napoleon had detached 33,000 men with Grouchy, precisely for the purpose of holding the Prussians in check. It was much more important to keep Blücher away from the battlefield, than to have himself a surplus force of 20,000 men.

This division of the army into two main bodies, so much censured by the historians of the campaign of 1815, was the usual strategical device of Napoleon. It was thus that he had manœuvred at Marengo,[15] at Jéna, at Friedland, and throughout the whole French campaign, which is so justly admired. When two armies are to be reckoned with, it is plain that one must be held in check, whilst the other is made the object of a supreme effort.

But could Grouchy oppose the movements of the Prussians; were not the Emperor's orders sufficiently precise and explicit, to preclude their being misinterpreted by Grouchy, and make him see clearly that his principal aim was to be the warding off an offensive attack from Blücher on the flank or on the rear of the army? It may be assumed that in his verbal instructions Napoleon had explained this to the Marshal; but with respect to the Emperor's remarks to Grouchy, testimonies are so self-interested and contradictory, that fair criticism requires us to rely only on the written order. I have already quoted the original order. I will now recall the essential points. "Proceed to Gembloux, reconnoitre in the direction of Namur and Maestricht, pursue the enemy. It is important to ascertain whether Blücher proposes joining Wellington in order to give battle in front of Brussels."

If, in truth, this letter does not explicitly desire Grouchy to cover the army, it appears to me certain that it tacitly enjoins him to do so. "Ascertain whether Blücher proposes joining Wellington," that is the important point. Now as Grouchy had with him not only a few squadrons sufficient to reconnoitre the enemy, but an army capable of offering a serious resistance, it was his duty not only to keep the Emperor well informed, but also to protect him against an offensive attack by manœuvring in such a way as to interpose his forces between the Prussians and the Imperial Army. A man who had had a twenty years' experience of war could not be mistaken as to the object of the mission with which he was entrusted. And indeed the following words from Grouchy's letter, on the evening of the 17th of June, "I shall follow the Prussians in the direction of Wavre," prove that he had understood perfectly the implicit instructions of the Emperor.

Unfortunately Grouchy did not know how to manœuvre with sufficient rapidity, intelligence, or resolution. On the 17th his troops marched with incredible dilatoriness. Whereas Napoleon reached La Belle Alliance at seven o'clock in the evening, covering six leagues and fighting all the way, Grouchy, at the same hour, had only got as far as Gembloux, fourteen kilometres distant from Saint-Amand. And yet, owing to the length of the summer days, he might have marched two hours longer, but he ordered his troops to encamp for the night. On the next day he could make up for lost time. Well informed as he was, he could be in no doubt that the Prussians were heading on Wavre to join Wellington. The Emperor could not order the march by the left bank of the Dyle, as he was then ignorant of Blücher's line of retreat, while Grouchy, who knew this direction, ought not to have hesitated for a moment in taking it. He would have risked nothing in any case; for the Prussians would either be at Wavre, and then he could turn them by the left bank of the Dyle—a more advantageous manœuvre than to attack them from the right bank—or they would already be marching on Brussels or on Mont-Saint-Jean, in which case he could pursue them by a flank movement, or, could march to prolong the right of the Emperor. Grouchy should, therefore, on the 18th of June, have marched on Wavre, not at seven o'clock in the morning in single column by Walhain and Corbais as he did, but at daybreak in two columns and by Vilrom, Mont-Saint-Guibert, and Ottignies.[16] Starting at four o'clock in the morning, the two columns would have arrived on the banks of the Dyle at the bridges of Mousty and Ottignies (seventeen or eighteen kilometres from Gembloux) between nine and ten o'clock. Allowing an hour and a half for the defiling of the troops over the two bridges, Grouchy would have found himself at eleven o'clock, with the whole of his army on the left bank of the Dyle.

Before this, no doubt (about eight o'clock), Colonel Ledebur, on the look-out at Mont-Saint-Guibert with the 10th Hussars and two battalions, would have perceived the leading columns of Grouchy's troops. His detachment being too weak to resist, he would have retired upon Wavre, and would have sent an estafette to Gneisenau to inform him of the approach of the French. This despatch would have reached Wavre about nine o'clock, when Bülow's corps alone was on the march. In all probability Blücher, or rather Gneisenau, who practically had all the authority in his hands, would not have altered the orders informing Bülow and Pirch I. to march on

Chapelle-Saint-Lambert, but would have taken measures to defend the approaches to Wavre, with the corps under Zieten and Thielmann. While awaiting the development of the French manœuvre, would he have been content with leaving these two corps in position at Bierges and Wavre? Or, aware that Grouchy was passing on the left bank of the Dyle, would he have sent forward Zieten and Thielmann to encounter the French Army by Bierges and Limelette? Under the first hypothesis, it would have been allowable for Grouchy to start on his march, by his left, upon Ayviers or Maransart as soon as he heard the sound of the Emperor's cannon; a manœuvre which would have brought him close to the battlefield at half-past two, fully two hours before Blücher assumed the offensive. Under the second hypothesis, which I grant is the more probable of the two, Grouchy, with 33,000 men in a good position on the plateau of Mousty-Ceroux, could easily have resisted the 40,000 Prussians under Zieten and Thielmann. But would he have been able, between eleven and four o'clock, to inflict upon them so decisive a defeat as to disable them from any further contest, and leave himself free once more to march on Maransart? This is most doubtful.

By this battle Grouchy would, in any case, have succeeded in holding back from Mont-Saint-Jean the two corps under Zieten and Thielmann, which would have been of no small importance. In the first place, the panic which ensued at the close of the battle of Waterloo, when Zieten debouched on Papelotte, would have been avoided. Nor is this all. We have seen that at half-past six, when, according to the admission made by Colonel Kennedy, aide-de-camp to Alten, "the centre of the English line had been broken through," the approach of Zieten's corps allowed Generals Vandeleur and Vivian to move 2,600 fresh horses from the extreme left to the centre, and strengthened Wellington's confidence. If this support—a support both material and moral—had failed him, it is probable that he would not have been able to regain his positions, before the assault of the Middle Guard, and that under this supreme onslaught the English line must have yielded. Wellington has acknowledged that, on the 18th of June, he found himself in the greatest possible danger.

"Twice," he has said, "have I saved this day by perseverance. . . . I have never fought such a battle, and I trust I never shall fight such another!"[17] We may believe also that, if by mid-day Blücher had heard the cannonade of a great battle, two leagues distant from his left flank, and if estafettes had arrived, hour after hour, announcing the successive reverses of his lieutenants, he would himself have attacked Plancenoit with less resolution. Finally, it must not be forgotten that if the Emperor had been warned, between eight and nine in the morning, by a despatch from Gembloux, that Grouchy was going to cross the Dyle at Ottignies, he could, long before noon, have sent him fresh orders, and he would thereby have found it possible to remain the whole day in close communication with him. What consequences!

Grouchy, by marching towards the sound of the cannon at half-past eleven o'clock, in accordance with Gérard's advice, might have repaired his grave mistake of the morning in servilely following on the traces of the Prussians. At that hour, Exelmans had three brigades of dragoons between Corbais and La Baraque, and one brigade at the farm-house of La Plaquerie (1,500 yards from Ottignies); Vandamme's corps had halted at Nil-Saint-Vincent; Gérard's corps had reached Walhain; Pajol, with his cavalry and the Teste division, was marching from Grand-Leez on Tourinnes. The best course was plainly to push forward Exelmans as far as the woods of La Huzelle, and still farther towards Wavre (if he could do so without committing himself) in such a way that he might make the enemy uneasy, and mask from him the movement of the army; to send Vandamme on Ottignies by Mont-Saint-Guibert, and Gérard on Mousty by Cour-Saint-Etienne; and lastly, to recall Pajol, who would then have come up and formed the rearguard. Starting at noon, Vandamme's leading column would have reached the bridge of Ottignies (10 kilometres from Nil-Saint-Vincent) about a quarter past three, whilst Gérard's leading column, starting a quarter of an hour earlier, would have arrived at the bridge of Mousty (13 kilometres from Walhain) about four o'clock. After crossing the Dyle, and the troops having henceforth to march by one road only, Vandamme would have taken the lead, and his 1st division would have arrived at Maransart (2 leagues from Ottignies by Ceroux) about six o'clock. To effect this, no doubt, the columns would have had to march for 18 kilometres at an average rate of 3 kilometres an hour. In spite of the wretched cross-roads, the miry lanes, all of which, indeed, sloped down to the river; in spite of the time which the crossing of the bridges would have required, this pace was possible,[18] especially when we remember, that at each step the sound of the cannon would grow nearer and more intense. What a moral stimulant to the soldiers of 1815, to be marching to rescue the Emperor, to fight under his command and before his eyes!

Let us now see whether, as Charras and others contend, the Prussians could have hindered this movement. At noon Bülow was at Chapelle-Saint-Lambert with his cavalry and two divisions; his other two divisions were marching to join him. The corps of Pirch I., bivouacked at Aizemont, had scarcely begun to cross the bridge of Wavre; Zieten's corps, bivouacked at Bierges, was on the point of starting towards Ohain by Fromont. Thielmann's corps, destined to remain the last in position on the border of the Dyle, was massed between Wavre and La Bavette. Finally, Ledebur with his detachment, occupied Mont-Saint-Guibert, where he remained most tranquilly, without suspecting in the least that he was outflanked on his left.

Had Grouchy marched on Ottignies and Maransart instead of marching on Wavre, on the Prussian side, events would have happened exactly as they did, at least until three o'clock. Between one and two, Ledebur would have cut his way through Exelmans' cavalry; at two the Brauze and Lange divisions (Pirch's corps), hearing the noise of the battle raging in the wood of La Huzelle between Ledebur's sharpshooters and Exelmans' dragoons, who had two batteries, would have marched in the direction of this wood, and Thielmann would have postponed his departure until the issue of the fight. Towards three o'clock, it is true, the enemy would then have realised that Exelmans' attack, unsupported as it was by infantry, was but a mere demonstration. The Prussians would then have resumed the manœuvre that had been ordered. Pirch's second echelon (Brauze and Langen divisions) would have crossed the bridge of Wavre, and directed its march on Chapelle-Saint-Lambert. Thielmann would have left only a few battalions at Wavre, and he would have prepared to march on Couture with the bulk of his troops. But before starting from La Bavette in the direction of Couture, he could not have done otherwise than wait until the Brauze and Langen divisions, and the cavalry of Sohr (of Pirch's corps) had defiled; the latter, as seen previously, having to wait for the defiling of the whole of Zieten's corps, which had been obliged to allow the tail of Bülow's corps and the head of Pirch's corps, to pass before them. The Prussian staff had made the arrangements for the march, so badly that the intercrossing of the different columns was inevitable. The principal column (Bülow and Pirch I.), marching from Dion-le-Mont and Aizemont *viâ* Wavre on Chapelle-Saint-Lambert, was bound to intercept the route of Zieten's corps, which was striking from Bierges to Ohain by Fromont, and of Thielmann's corps which had orders to proceed from La Bavette to Couture.

In these circumstances, Thielmann could not possibly have started before four o'clock at the earliest. From La Bavette to Maransart by Couture, the distance is 14,500 yards. The 3rd Prussian corps could not, therefore, have reached Maransart before a quarter to nine, much too late in consequence to stop Grouchy. At that moment Bülow, taken in flank by Grouchy's troops while struggling against Lobau and the Young Guard, would have been for more than an hour thrown back beyond the Paris wood, or perhaps exterminated in the valley of the Lasne.

Grouchy acted blindly, but Napoleon did nothing to enlighten him. Although warned by Milhaud, on the evening of the 17th, of the retreat of a column of the enemy towards the Dyle; although advised by a despatch during the night from Grouchy, of the march of at least one Prussian corps towards Wavre; although cautioned on the morning of 18th June by Prince Jérôme, against a probable junction of the two belligerent armies on the entrance of the forest of Soignes, it was only one hour after midday, when the battle was raging, that the Emperor sent to Grouchy a formal and distinct order to cover his right. No doubt he had believed up till then, perhaps he believed still, that the Marshal was manœuvring toward this great object; no doubt Grouchy's letter, in which he was told, "I shall follow the Prussians in order to separate them from Wellington," had strengthened this delusion. But was it necessary to place so much confidence in Grouchy? Was it not most hazardous, with so bold an adversary as Blücher, to let the safety of his right flank depend on the strategic intelligence, the initiative, and the resolution of a leader who had never exercised so important a command before? At all events, the Emperor should have reiterated his instructions to him, much earlier, and with more precision than he had done the first time.

Section IV

At Waterloo Napoleon wished to begin the action in the early morning; his orders testify to this. Had the battle begun towards six or seven o'clock, neither Grouchy's great strategic blunder, nor the mistake of the Emperor himself in neglecting to repeat his orders, would have led to any serious consequences, for the English Army would have been routed before the arrival of the Prussians.[19] Undoubtedly Lobau's corps, the Young Guard, Domon's and Subervie's cavalry, which the Emperor was employing against Bülow, and the Old Guard itself, which, in his anxiety for his right, he kept in reserve till the last, would, by supporting the other troops, have decided Wellington's retreat towards twelve or one o'clock, or perhaps earlier.

The state of the ground, or if we wish to quibble, the false estimation of the state of the ground, by Drouot and the artillery officers, compelled the Emperor to alter his orders. The attack was postponed from six or seven o'clock, to nine o'clock, then once more deferred because the troops had not yet taken up their positions. This delay saved the English Army.

An attack against the enemy's left, which was weak and

quite unsupported, or even against his right, in which case a vast deployment was possible, would certainly have been easier and less murderous than the assault against the centre. But Napoleon, manœuvring between two armies found himself, so to speak, pressed between the two jaws of a vice. It was not enough to remove one of them for a day or two as he had done at Ligny: he must crush it entirely. For this purpose the Emperor had to pierce through the centre of the English army,[20] and crush its broken wings. "Napoleon," said Wellington, "has attacked me in the old-fashioned way, and I have repulsed him in the old-fashioned way." Owing to the circumstances, and in spite of the very restricted position of the enemy, the "old-fashioned way" was the best for the Emperor to adopt.

But how many blunders, negligencies, and errors were there not in the execution! As we have seen, the demonstration against Hougoumont, ordered by the Emperor, degenerated through Jérôme's eagerness, through the enthusiasm of the soldiers, through the lack of vigilance and firmness on the part of Reille, into a headlong attack in which the lives of half the 2nd Corps were uselessly sacrificed. We have also seen that the clumsy formation of the four divisions of General d'Erlon, was the virtual cause of the confusion in which these troops found themselves, when they gained the crests, and of the lamentable ruin into which they were thrown by the English cavalry.

How did it come to pass that Reille who, according to the Emperor's orders, was "to advance by degrees, to keep at the same height as Count d'Erlon," did not carry out this movement? It is true that one of his divisions (that of Jérôme) was engaged at Hougoumont, but Bachelu and Foy remained, and were at his disposal, ready to march against the right centre of the enemy.

How was it that Ney, who had under his immediate command, the first line, d'Erlon's and Reille's corps, more than 30,000 bayonets, led two ineffectual assaults against La Haye-Sainte defended by five companies. Why did he not shell the walls till he battered them down? After two successive failures in attacking this farm, why did he not renew the assault? Why did he not comply with the Emperor's order? How did he fail to understand that the position of La Haye-Sainte—" the key of the English position " as Kennedy, Alten's aide-de-camp, said—ought to be his main object?

Ney found it easier to commence by the end. Too cautious at Quatre-Bras, he proved too daring at Mont-Saint-Jean. Without preparations, without support, without orders, and before the appointed time, he deliberately risked the great cavalry movement planned by the Emperor. He imagined that he could fling down with his cavalry, a hitherto unshaken infantry, which was occupying a dominant position. He madly hurled forward to the assault, the two corps of cuirassiers, the mounted Guard and even the brigade of carabiniers, the last cavalry reserve of the army which Kellermann had kept back with strict orders not to stir. Reckless though they were, these heroic charges might have been successful had they been properly supported by infantry. Near La Belle Alliance, half of Reille's corps was posted within easy range of the cannon from the English position. These twelve battalions had not yet been engaged; they were waiting, standing at ease! Ney, who, according to Napoleon's remark, " would forget in the heat of the action any troops which were not actually under his eyes," never thought of summoning them to the plateau. It was only when the last charges had been repulsed, when it was too late for the infantry to intervene, that he launched these 6,000 men on to the slopes of Mont-Saint-Jean, where they were decimated without any useful result.

It was nearly six o'clock. La Haye-Sainte, which Ney had attempted to carry at two o'clock, and again at four o'clock, was still in the hands of the enemy. Notwithstanding this, the Emperor reiterated the order to take it at all costs. This time Ney did carry the position, and only then did Wellington consider he was in danger. Unfortunately, it was too late to turn this gain to advantage. Men and horses were exhausted. Napoleon entrusted the Marshal with the Middle Guard to make a supreme last effort; but instead of making a breach in the English line with these five battalions of heroes formed into a single column, Ney broke them up into " echelons," so that each battalion found itself, at each point, outnumbered by the enemy in the proportion of nearly three to one.

It seems that on the right wing, also, great negligence and mistakes had occurred. The cavalry under Domon and Subervie proceeded to the outlets of the wood of Paris, when they ought to have guarded its approaches. Lobau's defence was brave, but it was ill-conceived and ill-prepared. It was not at a distance of only 1,200 yards to the east of La Belle Alliance in open ground, that he ought to have taken up his position to arrest the Prussians. At half-past one, when Bülow's corps was still stationary at Chapelle-Saint-Lambert, Lobau had received from the Emperor an order to march in that direction, "and to choose a good intermediate position, where he might arrest 30,000 men with his 10,000." This "good, intermediate position" Lobau did not take the trouble to seek. It should have been on the range of steep hills which commanded the valley of the Lasne, opposite the solitary bridge of Lasne. Here, with his communications with the bulk of the army secured by the numerous squadrons under Domon and Subervie, Lobau might have resisted much longer and more efficiently than before Plancenoit. Indeed, he might have been impregnable. Clauzewitz admits that Blücher would have been compelled to turn him, by way of Couture. This would indeed have been time gained for the Emperor! In case Lobau would have hesitated to proceed so far in a slanting direction (one league from La Belle Alliance), he might at least have occupied the Paris wood.

Through the various incidents of the battle we can follow the development of the Emperor's plan as he had expounded it that morning to Prince Jérôme: Preparation by artillery, attack by d'Erlon's and Reille's corps, charges by the cavalry, final assault by Lobau's corps and the Guard on foot. But the presence of the Prussians on his right compelled the Emperor to hold them in check with the 6th Corps and the Young Guard, and to keep the Old Guard in reserve far too long. On the other hand, instead of operating against the English with method and concerted union, the forces acted spasmodically, awkwardly at first, then rashly, and at last desperately.

To judge fairly the Commander-in-chief, who was the greatest of captains, it must be remembered how his orders had been understood and executed, where they were not misinterpreted. Marshal de Saxe, in his *Reveries sur l'Art de la Guerre*, has said: "The orders of the general of an army must be correct and simple, as let us say: "Such and such a corps is to attack, and such and such a corps is to support." The generals under him would be men of very narrow minds indeed, if they did not know how to execute this order, and carry out the manœuvre he thought right. Thus the general of an army ought not to attend to this, or be anxious about it. He will see things better, preserve a clearer judgment, and be more in a condition to profit by circumstances. It is not for him to be everywhere, and play the part of a sergeant of battle" (Sergent de bataille).

From the great number of mistakes perpetrated at Waterloo, Charras, York of Wartenbourg, and Marshal Wolseley, have all concluded that the Emperor, broken down by misfortune, collapsed under the strain, that he remained inert and blinded far from the battlefield, and allowed the contest to proceed without any guidance. With regard to the physical and moral state of Napoleon on the 18th of June, testimonies are contradictory. Colonel Bandus relates that the Emperor "was plunged in a species of apathy."[21] According to oral traditions quoted by Marshal Canrobert and by General du Barail, Napoleon was asleep during the battle of Waterloo. (He also slept at Jéna and at Wagram, and directed the battle none the less victoriously notwithstanding.) But Marshal Regnault de Saint-Jean-d'Angély, who made the campaign of 1815 in the Imperial staff, relates that far from dozing, the Emperor was nervous and impatient, and was continually striking his boot with his cane. (It is thus that Coignet describes Bonaparte at Marengo, before the arrival of the Desaix division.) In his manuscript journal, General Foy writes that he could see the Emperor pacing up and down, his hands behind his back. I have not read anywhere that the guide Decoster, so loquacious and circumstantial, ever spoke of Napoleon's prostrate condition. Walter Scott, who questioned this innkeeper a few months after the battle, learnt from him, that throughout the afternoon the Emperor remained near La Belle Alliance on horseback most of the time, and paid great attention to the various phases of the action. From a remark of Ney uttered at Mézierès, where he passed the 19th of June, it appears that Napoleon had shown great bravery. Be this as it may, there are facts which testify more clearly than all this hearsay evidence: At eleven o'clock the Emperor dictated all his arrangements for the attack; at a quarter past eleven he ordered the demonstration against Hougoumont; at one o'clock he despatched a message to Grouchy; at half-past one he gave an order to Lobau to take up his position in order to arrest the Prussians, and commanded Ney to begin the attack on Mont-Saint-Jean. In the interval, he had caused Hougoumont to be shelled by a battery of howitzers; at three o'clock he hurled a brigade of cuirassiers against Uxbridge's cavalry, which was assailing the chief battery; at half-past three he ordered Ney to take possession of La Haye-Sainte; at half-past four he moved the Guard forward close to La Belle Alliance; at five o'clock he brought up the Young Guard to Lobau's rescue; at half-past five he ordered Kellermann to support Milhaud's charges; at six o'clock he repeated the order to take La Haye-Sainte. A short time after, he detached two battalions from the Old Guard to drive the Prussians from Plancenoit. At seven o'clock he led his Guard in the hollows of La Haye-Sainte for the final assault. On the way he harangued Durutte's soldiers, who were on the point of giving way, and sent them back to face the fire; he enjoined all the officers to go down the line of battle, announcing the approach of Marshal Grouchy. In the evening he formed into squares, in the valley, the 2nd echelon of the Guard, rushed to Rossomme, made a stand there with Petit's grenadiers, and ordered the last volley of grapeshot to be discharged into the English cavalry.

Napoleon never exercised the commandership more efficiently, and never was his action more direct. But in reality, forced to play the part of "sergent de bataille," so censured by Maurice de Saxe, he applied all his efforts in repairing the mistakes, the omissions, and the faults of his lieutenants. And, seeing all his combinations prove abortive, all his attacks failing, his generals frittering away his splendid troops, his last army melting through their hands, and the enemy dictating to him, he lost his resolution with his confidence, hesitated, limited himself to providing against the more pressing dangers, waited for the lucky moment, let it pass, and did not dare in time, to risk all, in order to save all.

Paris, 1894-1898.

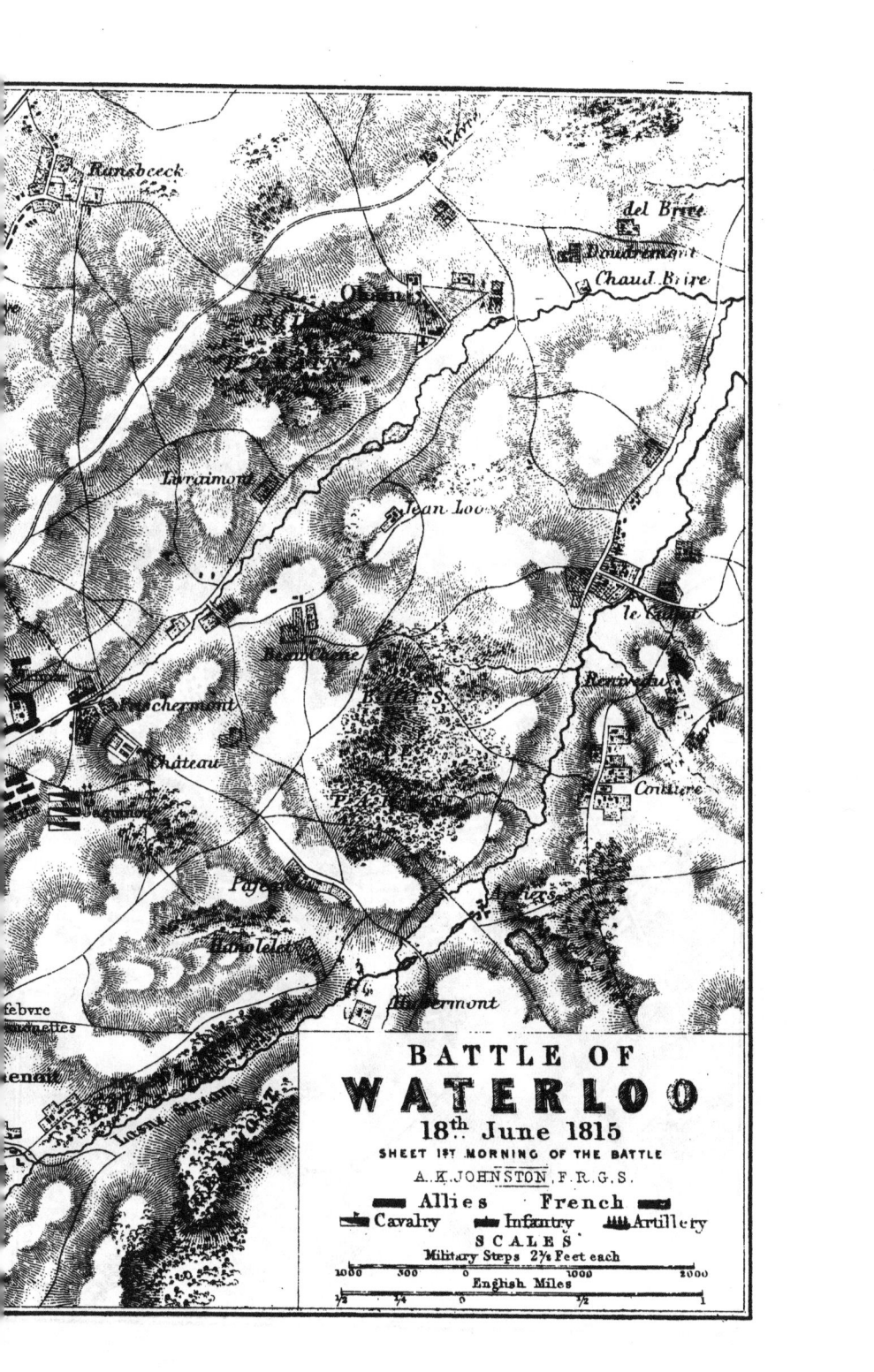

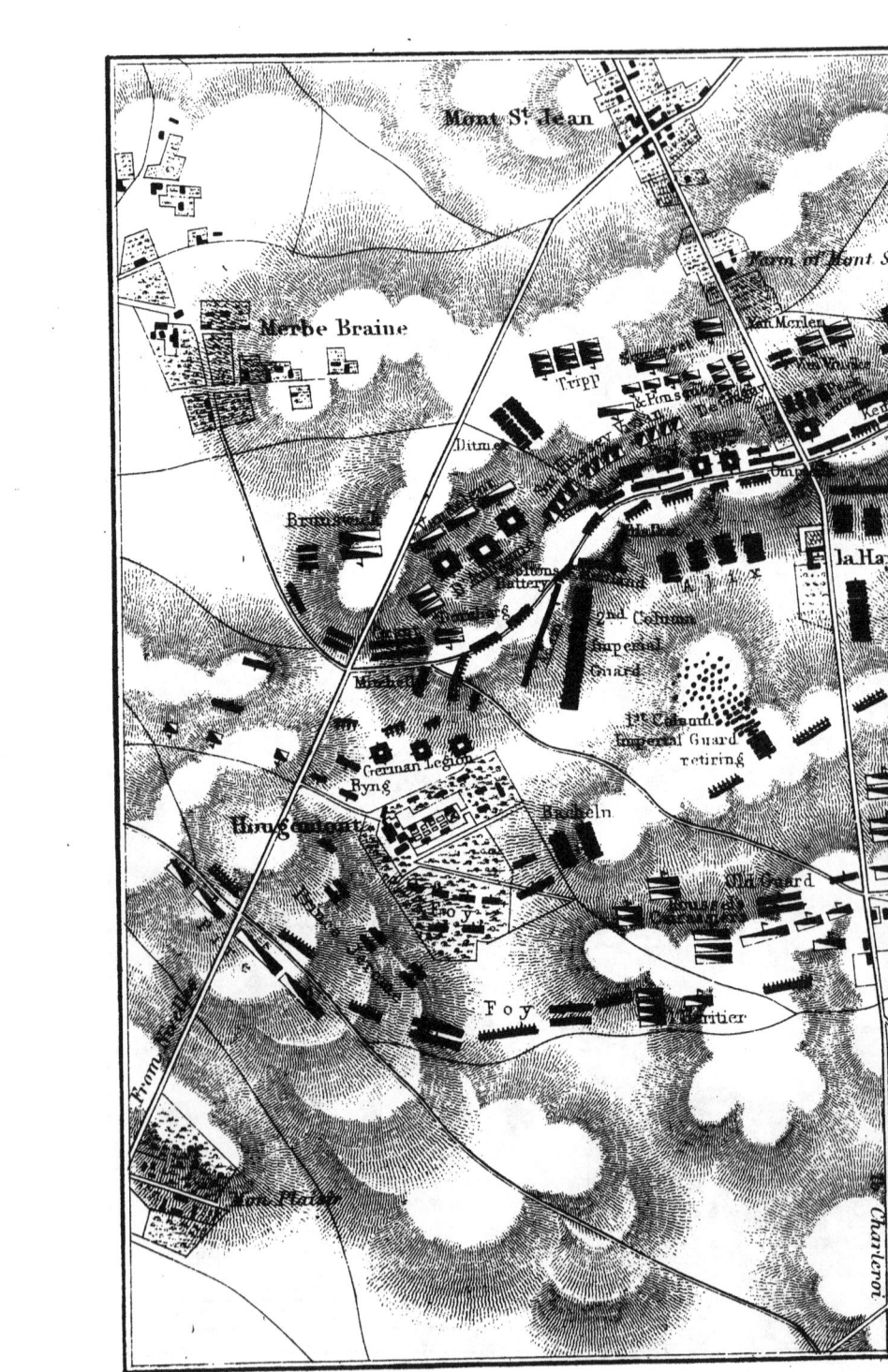

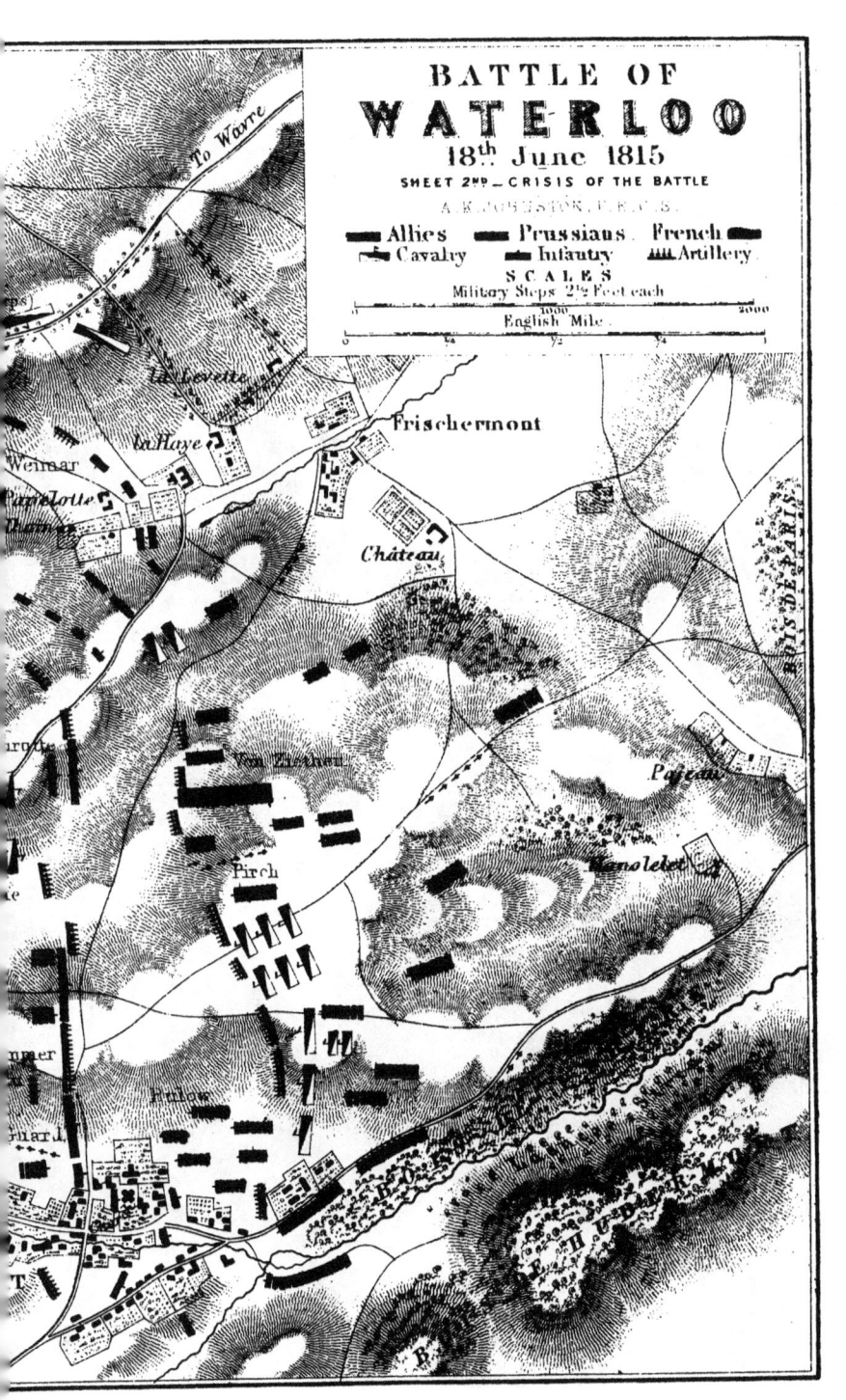

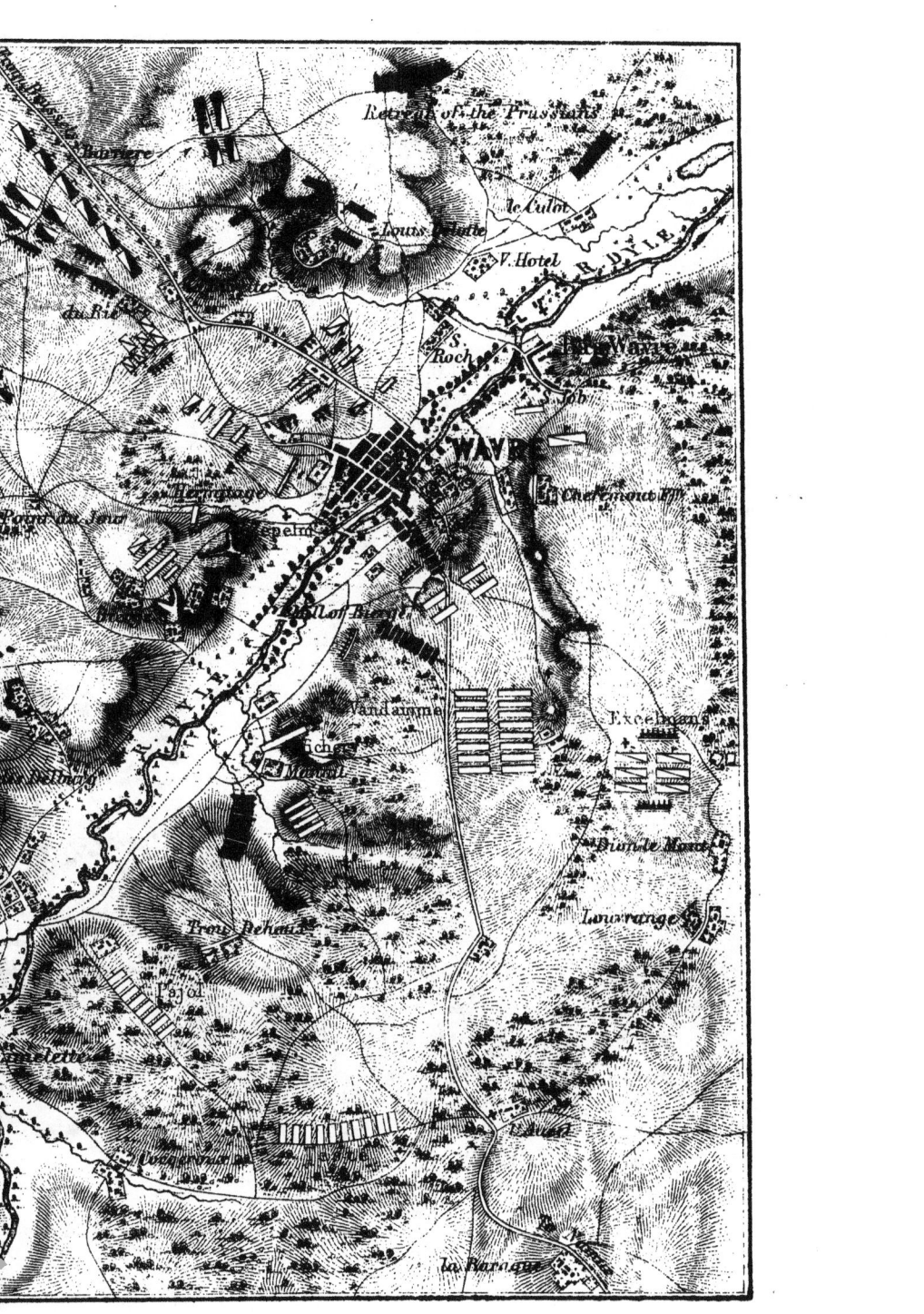

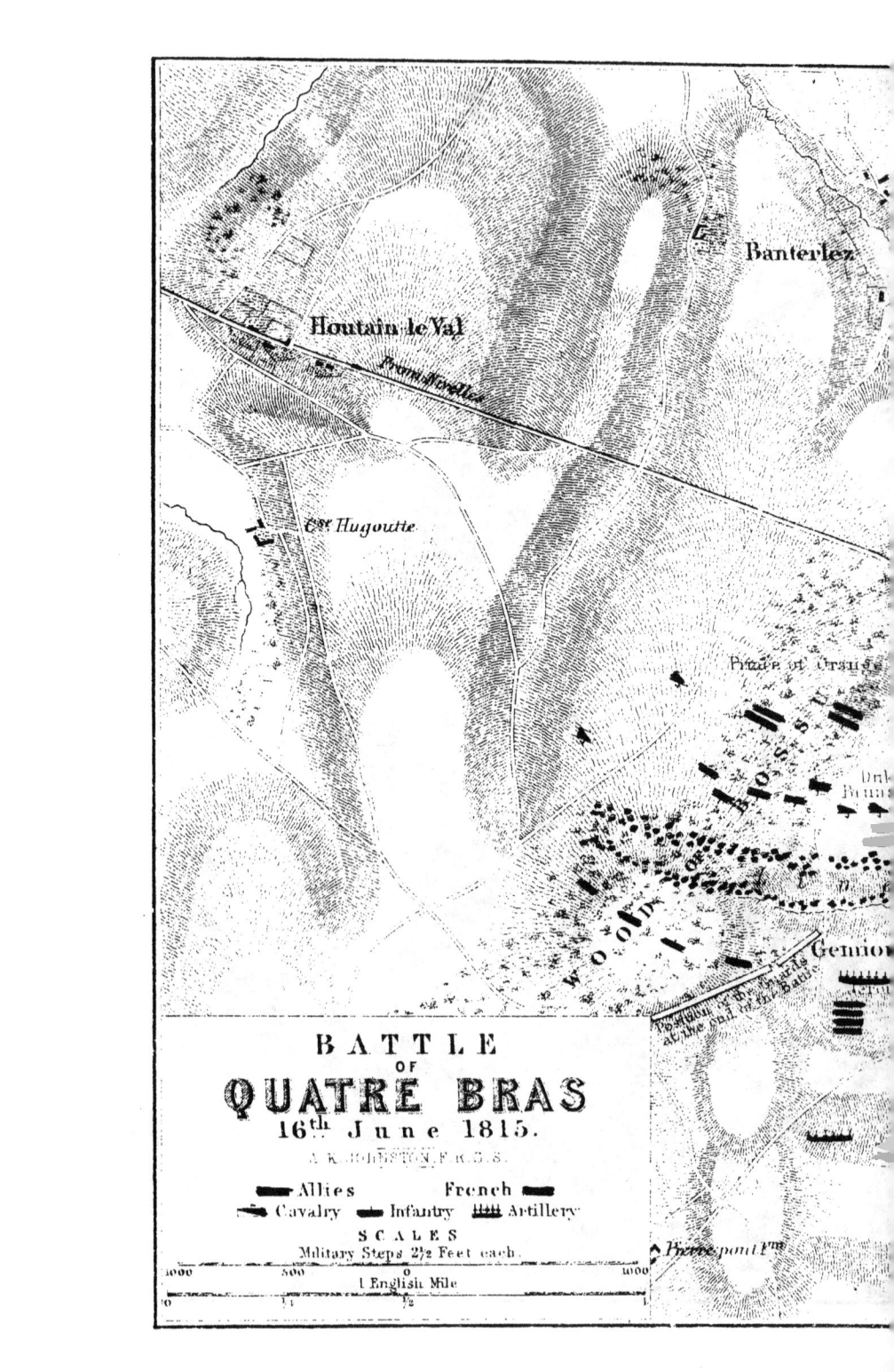

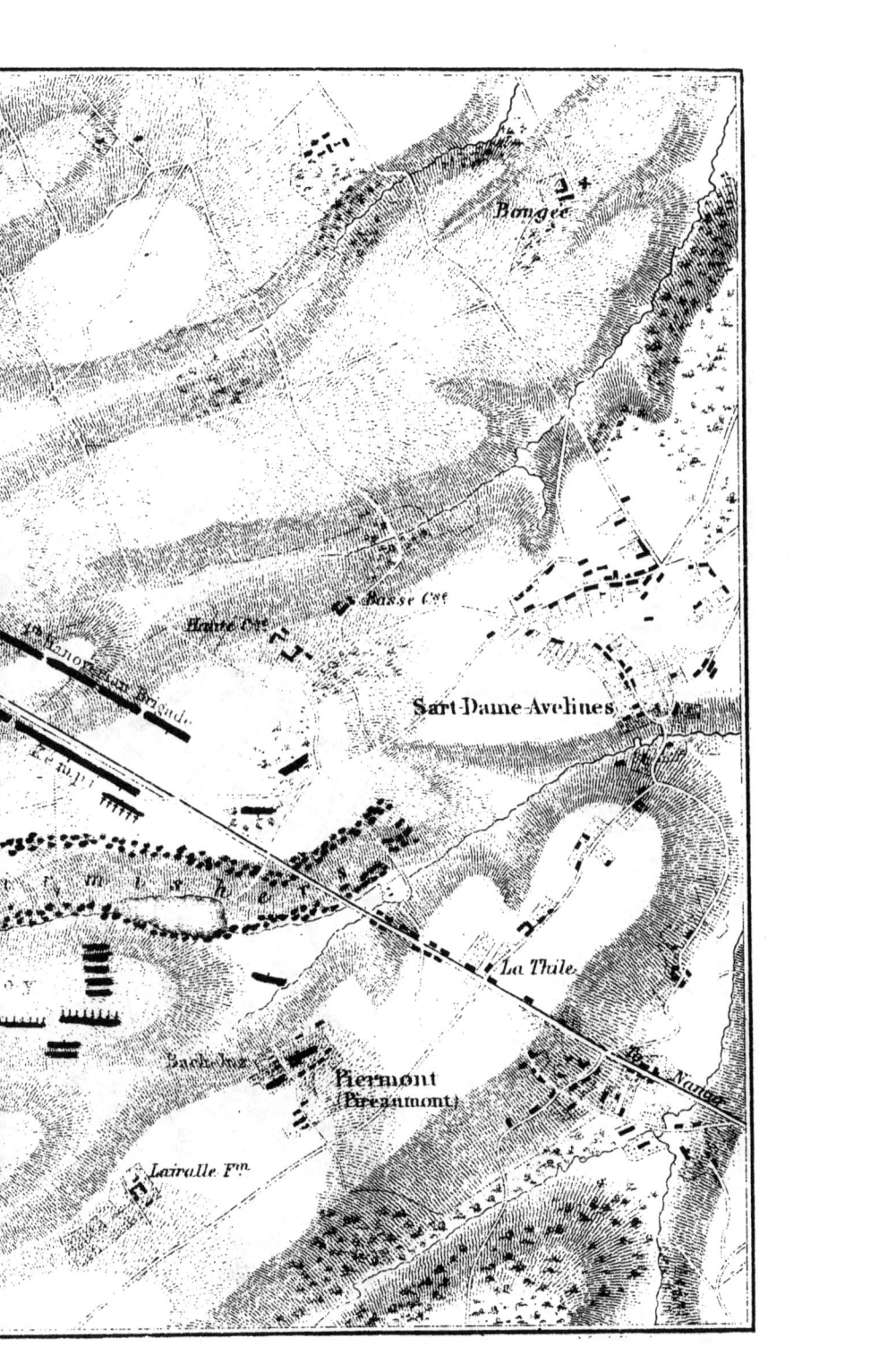

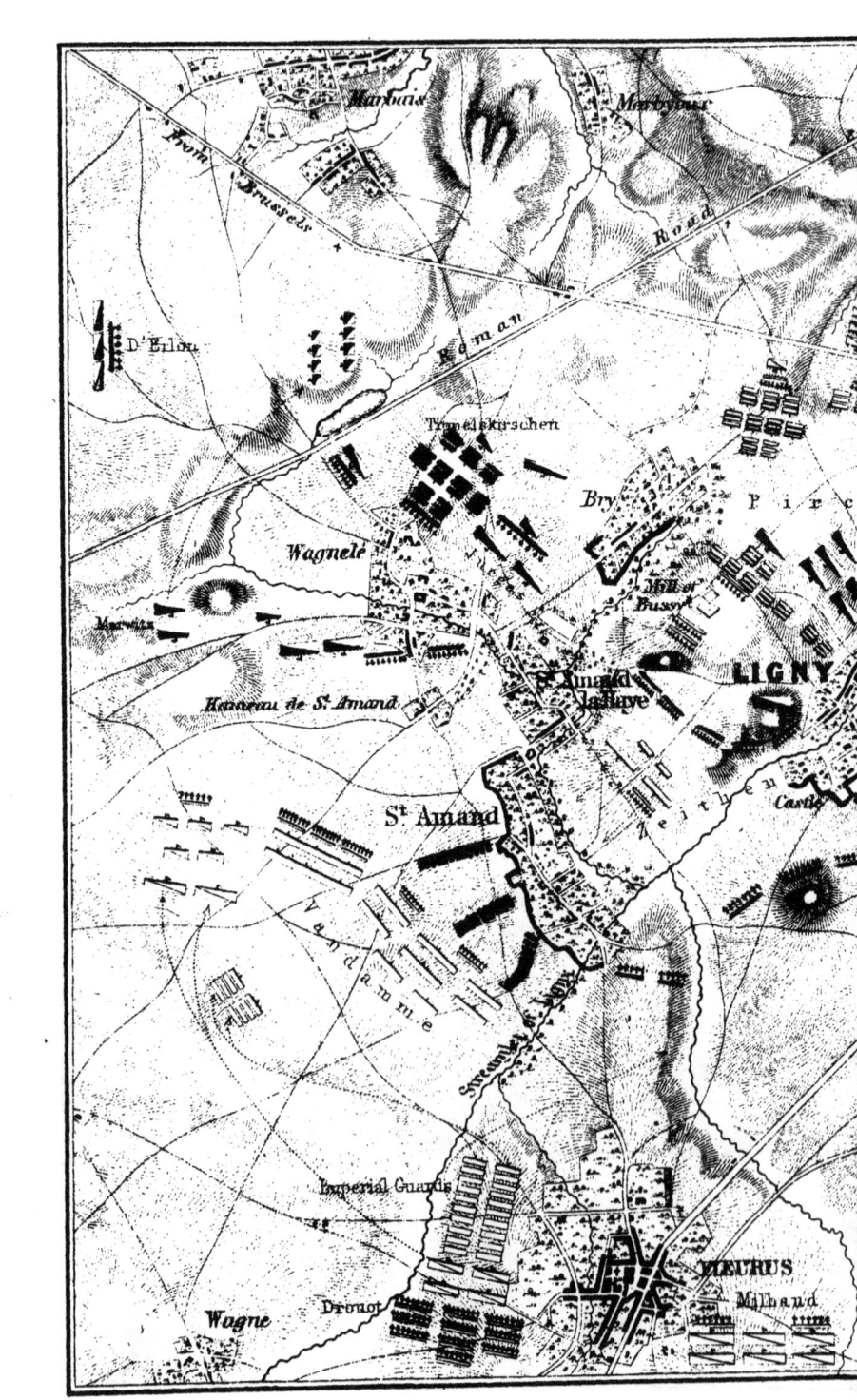

BOOK I

CHAPTER I

1. The general estimate on January 15th, 1815 (Military Archives) shows 195,883 officers and soldiers, from which number must be deducted 3,208 men of the Swiss regiments, and of the 1st foreign regiment (La Tour d'Auvergne), which Napoleon was compelled to dismiss. There remained then 192,675 men. But the Army had been increased by 7,000 to 8,000 soldiers enrolled since 15th January, in virtue of an order of recall issued in November 1814. This levy (which ought to have produced 60,000 men, and produced but 35,000) continued till February 15th (Henry Houssaye, *1815*, i. 165). As for the re-engaged men who had, on the 15th, and 20th of March, joined at the depôt centres of the departments, in conformity with the Royal rescript of 9th March (Henry Houssaye, *1815*, i. 327) their number cannot be estimated here, for, on the 20th March, they had not yet been enrolled.

The "household troops," the "gendarmerie," the veterans, etc., are not included in those 200,000 men.

I cite here the estimate of 15th January, for the excellent reason that it is, with that of 1st January, the only authentic one existing of the Royal Army of 1815. The estimate of the National Archives (AF.* iv. 1153) which is incorrectly dated 15th March, is obviously subsequent to 5th April, since the Imperial Acts of 2nd April are quoted therein, as well as the departure from Lyons of the Girard division (4th April).

Napoleon (*Memoirs to serve for French History in 1815*, 19) estimates the effective strength of the Royal Army, on 20th March, at 149,000 men, and Charras (*Campagne de 1815*, i. 40) at 224,000 men. Be it said here, once for all, that it is useless to stop and discuss the discrepancy between the estimates given by the Emperor at St. Helena, and those given by Charras, for both alternately lowered or raised the number of soldiers, the former in the interest of his memoir, and the latter in the interest of his thesis. The tables given in his *Relation*, written by Gourgaud at dictation of the Emperor, and in the *Memoirs to serve for French History in 1815*, are, as a rule, mere deceptions. As for the lists of estimates given by Charras, and taken from copies sent to him from Paris, they almost all, as I have ascertained, present notable discrepancies from the originals in the Archives. Is it the fault of the copyist, who copied them incorrectly, or that of Charras, who misinterpreted them?

2. Davout (report to the Emperor, undated, 25th or 26th of March?—Nat. Arch. AF. iv. 1936) says 26,000; the estimates show 31,469, 32,884, and even 38,233.

3. Report (mentioned above) of Davout to the Emperor. The estimates on 1st January show 101,503 deserters; but in January and February, the levy of 60,000 men, commenced in November 1814, and which reached men in that category, had continued to work efficiently. Numbers of men had rejoined the corps, others had obtained after rejoining their final dismissal at the subsequent musters.

4. The Royal rescript of the 9th March, published on the 12th March, enjoined all soldiers on leave, of every description, to present themselves, some at their corps, others at the depôt centres of the departments, to be organised into reserve battalions. The Emperor, who did not care for these reserve battalions (to Davout, 26th March, War Arch., portfolio of Napoleon's letters), issued on 28th March a decree abrogating the Royal rescript of 9th March, and ordering every soldier "who had left the Army, for whatever reason," to rejoin his corps. This decree was not published before the 9th April. Yet from March 15th to April 9th, about 4,000 soldiers on six months' leave had returned to the depôts.

5. Report above quoted of Davout to the Emperor (Nat. Arch. AF. iv. 1936).

6. Napoleon, *Corresp.* 21,737.

7. Henry Houssaye, *1815*, 435-39, 445-47, 563, and notes.

8. Caulaincourt to Napoleon, 25th March; to Cardinal Fesch, 8th April (Arch. of Foreign Affairs, 672 and 1801); F. de Chaboulon, *Mém.*, i. 330.

9. Henry Houssaye, *1815*, i. 510-11, and the notes.

10. Carnot's circular, 9th April (Nat. Arch. F.[1a] 31); Davout to Napoleon, 1st May (Nat. Arch. AF. iv. 1936).

11. Corresp. of the prefects, April-June; Reports to the Emperor and to Fouché, May-June; Davout's report, 11th May (Nat. Arch. F. 7, 3774; and AF. iv. 1934 and 1936; AF. iv. 1947; AF. 1939); General Corresp. April-June (War Arch.).

12. Davout to the prefects of Mayenne and Maine-et-Loire, 28th April; to Bigarré, 14th May (War Arch., Davout's Report to Napoleon, undated, 10th or 12th April? and 11th May; Nat. Arch. AF. iv. 1936). Those who showed themselves refractory were not prosecuted; the re-engaged men who were willing to present themselves, were authorised by certain of the prefects, to enter the departmental corps destined for home service only. After the 15th May even the reviews on reassembling were done away with.

13. "The only available resources will amount to 59,000 men," Davout had said (report to the Emperor, April, Nat. Arch. AF. iv. 1936). Davout's estimate was even increased by 25,000 men, if we add to the 76,000 men enrolled or started from 25th April to 10th

June the 4,000 men on half-year's leave, who had rejoined the corps between 15th March to 9th April, and finally a few thousand re-enlisted men who arrived at the depôt centres of departments between the 10th and the 25th June. (The recruiting operations lasted till after the abdication.)

14. Davout's report to Napoleon, 11th June (Nat. Arch. AF. iv. 1936). 82,560 re-engaged men had received their marching orders, but 6,662 had deserted. Of these 82,560 re-engaged, some belonged to the 85,000 deserters of 1814, others to the 32,000 men on leave for a limited or unlimited period, who had not rejoined their corps before 9th April.

15. Henry Houssaye, *1814*, ii. note 1.
16. Henry Houssaye, *1815*, i. note 3, 628.
17. Davout's circular, 8th May (War Arch.).
18. Napoleon to Drouot, 24th May (War Arch., Portfolio of Napoleon's Correspondence); Davout to Napoleon, 26th May (Nat. Arch. AF. iv. 1936).

19. Decrès to Napoleon, 22nd March, and state of the fleet on 23rd March (Nat. Arch. AF. iv. 1941). There were but eighty-eight armed vessels altogether, among these one man-of-war only, eleven frigates, and five "corvettes." I could not find in the Marine Archives any general estimate of the personnel; but a letter from Admiral Duperré, in command of the arrondissement of Toulon (to Decrès, 8th June, Marine Arch. BB.[3] 427) shows that the twenty-nine ships attached to this naval port—that is to say more than two-thirds of the fleet—had altogether only 2,666 men to form the united crews.

20. Napoleon, *Corresp.* 21,698, 21,783, 21,818; Decrès to Napoleon, 22nd March (Nat. Arch. AF. iv. 1941).

21. Napoleon, *Corresp.* 21,836, 21,875;. Decrès to Napoleon, 2nd May (Nat. Arch. AF. iv. 1941).

22. I vainly sought in the Archives of the Marine an estimate of those mobilised sailors. But a letter of Admiral Duperré, 8th June, gives at least an approximate result of the levy. Duperré writes that the first regiment to be formed at Toulon had but 512 officers and men, that he proposes to raise this number to 1,000, but that he does not believe it will be possible to furnish men for the second regiment. (Duperré to Decrès, Toulon, 8th June, Marine Arch. BB.[3] 427). Thus on 8th June, there was at Toulon but one battalion formed. But if the very hostile arrondissement of Dunkerque was below the mark, those of Cherbourg, Brest, Lorient, and Rochefort, where the population was more patriotic and less unwilling to serve, gave a larger number of men (see the reports on the levies for the sea, 8th, 12th, 14th, and 15th May, Nat. Arch. AF. iv. 1941). Becker, in his *Relation* (p. 98), mentions the 14th Regiment of marines. It may then be admitted that, during June, fourteen regiments of marines were in course of formation, probably amounting to a single battalion each, which gave a total of about 10,000 men.

23. The composition of garrisons (Nat. Arch. AF. iv. 1936). On

14th June, Decrès announced to the Council of Ministers that the first regiment formed at Brest would reach Paris on 18th July (Nat. Arch. AF. iv. 990 b). See with regard to the Toulon regiment the above-mentioned letter of Admiral Duperré.

24. *History of the Marine Artillery*, 135.

25. Davout to Lobau, 1st May (War Arch.); official reports of the Council of Ministers, 8th June (Nat. Arch. AF. iv. 990 b). See Napoleon, *Corresp.* 21,846; *History of the Marine Artillery*, 134-35.

26. Davout to Napoleon, 24th April (War Arch.). See Henry Houssaye, *1815*, i. 20 and 413.

27. Fririon to Davout, 21st March (War Arch.); Imperial decree, 2nd April (War Arch., Portfolio of Napoleon's Corresp.).

28. Napoleon, *Corresp.* 21,765; Davout to Durutte, 23rd March; to Napoleon, 5th and 23rd April; Derivaux to Davout, Verdun, 25th March; Lebarbier de Tinan to Davout, 12th April; Proteau to Davout, 8th April; Fririon to Davout, 16th April and 1st May; Bigarré's order, 5th June; situation of General d'Armagnac, 17th June (War Arch.); condition of the fortified posts in June (Nat. Arch. AF. iv. 1936).

29. Napoleon, *Corresp.* 21,728, 21,767, 21,775; Davout, *Corresp.* 1560, 1561; Carnot's circulars, 28th March and 12th April (Nat. Arch. F.[1 a] 31); memoirs in manuscript of Davout (furnished by General Davout, Duke of Auerstaedt).

30. Report from Carnot to the Chamber of Peers, 13th June; *Moniteur*, 15th June.

31. *Bulletins des Lois*, 13th April.

32. Decrees of 10th, 15th, 19th, 27th April, and 10th and 15th May, not recorded in the *Bulletin des Lois*, but mentioned in the estimates of the select National Guards, 3rd May (Nat. Arch. AF. iv. 1936); Carnot's circular, 13th April (Nat. Arch. F.[1 a] 31).

In his report to the Chamber of Peers, 13th June, Carnot says that orders had been issued for the formation of 417 battalions. The reason was that, during June, new battalions were levied in the departments which were not put down in the May register, namely in Basses-Alpes, Ardèche, Charente-Inférieure, Cher, Creuse, Dordogne, Gard, Indre, Lozère, Nièvre, Vaucluse, Haute-Vienne, etc. (reports from Limoges, 15th June; from Guéret, 16th June; from Poitiers, 18th June; from Perigueux, 20th June; War Arch.). Davout's report to the executive commission, 23rd June (Nat. Arch. AF. iv. 1936).

33. Carnot's circular, 18th April (Nat. Arch. F.[1 a] 31); Carnot's report to the Chamber of Peers, 13th June (*Moniteur*, 15th June).

34. Carnot's report to Napoleon, 10th April (for 10th May); estimate of the select National Guards, 31st May and 8th June (Nat. Arch. AF. iv. 1935, and AF. iv. 1936); *Corresp.* of the prefects, 1st, 4th, 15th, 16th, 17th, 22nd, and 27th May; 3rd, 4th, 6th, 8th, 9th, 11th, and 14th June (Nat. Arch. F. 7 (3044 [2]), and F. 7, 3774); General *Corresp.* from 8th April to 20th June (War Arch.); a spy's report to Clarke, Ghent, 24th April (Wellington's *Despatches, Suppl.*, x. 154). See Memoirs in manuscript of Barras (comm. by M. Georges Duruy)

"The battalions of the mobilised National Guards are most enthusiastic."

35. Henry Houssaye, *1815*, i. 628 and the notes.

36. Estimates of the select National Guards above mentioned; Corresp. of the prefects (Nat. Arch. F. 7, 3044 [2] and F. 7, 3774); Carnot's report to Napoleon, 27th May (Nat. Arch. AF. iv. 1936); General Corresp. May (War Arch.).

37. Proclamation. Amiens, printing-house of Cherche (War Arch.).

38. Delaborde to Davout, Angers, 8th May; Davout to Bigarre, 14th May; Prefect of Ile-et-Vilaine to Davout, 26th May; Charpentiue to Bigarre, Nantes, 1st June; Lamarque to Davout, 3rd June; Bigarre to Davout, Rennes, 7th and 18th June (War Arch.).

39. State of the select National Guards on 8th June (Nat. Arch. AF. iv. 1936). See Carnot's report to the Chamber of Peers, 13th June, and *1815*, i. 627, note 4.

40. Davout to Napoleon, 13th May (Nat. Arch. AF. iv. 1939); Decree respecting the National Guards, 10th April.

41. General Rouyer's reports and letters to Davout, 22nd April; others from the commissaries extraordinary, Bédoch and de Gérando, Bar-le-Duc and Nancy, 8th and 10th May; from Leclerc des Essarts, Sainte-Menehould, 18th May; from Lanusse, Metz, 21st May; from the commandant at Landrecies, 6th June; from Major Hervo, Poitiers, 18th June; from Jourdan, Besançon, 25th June; Gérard to Vandamme, Metz, 5th June; Colonel of gendarmerie at Rovigo, Nancy, 16th June (War Arch., General Corresp. and the Northern and Jura armies). Corresp. of the prefects, April-June (Nat. Arch. F. 7, 3774, and F. 7, 3040 [a]); Davout to Napoleon, 28th May (Nat. Arch. AF. iv. 1936); La Bretonnière, *Souvenirs du Quartier-Latin*, 228; Barras' Memoirs in manuscript. See Henry Houssaye, *1815*, i. 629-630.

42. Correspondence of the prefects (Nat. Arch.), and the general correspondence (War Arch.) infers that from day to day the refractory soldiers and the insubordinates came in in increasing numbers. One example amongst many; the 18 battalions to be furnished by the departments of Charente, Corrèze and Dordogne had not registered a single man in the estimates of 8th June, but on 20th June, General Lucotte writes from Perigueux to Davout: "Thanks to the mobilised columns, I have been enabled to muster 13 battalions. The others will follow" (War Arch., Army of the Western Pyrenees).

43. In his report of 13th June to the Chamber of Peers, Carnot estimated at 751,440 the National Guards, from twenty to forty years old, who were liable to be mobilised.

44. "You have done very wrong in distributing muskets to the stationary National Guards of Rethel, whatever may be their patriotism, for the mobilised Guards themselves cannot be sufficiently armed." Davout to Vandamme, 25th May (War Arch., Army of the North). The prefect of the Vosges had pikes distributed to the stationary National Guards. "Pikes are better than nothing," he said in a letter of 12th June.

45. In 1815 the reorganisation of the city and stationary National Guards, commenced by virtue of a Royal edict, on 18th July, was far from being completed; but in all the towns, and even in many of the villages, there were a certain number of National Guards provided with arms and uniforms.

46. Davout's reports to Napoleon, 11th, 20th, 22nd, and 28th May (Nat. Arch. AF. iv. 1936); Napoleon to Davout, 17th May (Nat. Arch. AF. iv. 1937).

47. Condition of the Paris National Guard on 1st June (Nat. Arch. F. 9, 760). 11,000 Fusiliers among these Guards, were not yet clothed.

48. Davout to Napoleon, 17th June (Nat. Arch. AF. iv. 1936); General Darricau to Davout, 29th June (War Arch.). On the federated sharpshooters, see Henry Houssaye, *1815*, i. 623-625 and notes.

49. Mouton to Davout, from Lyons, 12th June (Mouton's documents and papers, War Arch.); Suchet to Davout, 13th June (Nat. Arch. AF. iv. 1937).

50. Napoleon, *Corresp.* 21,861.

51. On 17th June the stationary National Guards of the Vosges started, in the ratio of one company to each battalion, to occupy the passes (Decree of the prefect, Epinal, 17th June, War Arch.).

52. Early in March the Emperor had felt it must come to this. "It is a senseless idea," he writes to Davout, "to try to convince oneself that the army can be recruited otherwise than by conscription. Besides I flatter myself I have authority enough with the nation to make them understand this" (Letter of 26th March, War Arch., Portfolio of Napoleon's Corresp.).

53. Thus the young soldiers of the class of 1815, deserters or enrolled in the corps, had been dismissed (Royal Act, 15th May 1814, *Military Journal*).

54. Davout to Napoleon, 3rd June (Nat. Arch. AF. iv. 1936).

55. Miot de Melito, *Mem.* iii. 430, 431.

56. Davout to Napoleon, 15th May (Nat. Arch. AF. iv. 1534). Cf. *1814*, 9, note 1. "The annual contingent," wrote Davout, "is 280,000 men, but there must be a deduction of more than half this number on account of undersize, infirmities, and, as enrolled in the marines, supporters of their families, etc. The levy ought to furnish 120,000 men net.

57. Napoleon to Drouot, 30th May (War Arch., Portfolio of Napoleon's Corresp.); Davout's manuscript communicated by General, the Duke of Auerstædt).

These orders were not issued till after June 3rd, since Davout's letter above cited, advising the Emperor not to use the word conscription, is dated 3rd June.

58. First and second reports from Davout to Napoleon, 11th June (Nat. Arch. AF. iv. 1936); see Davout to Caffarelli, 18th June (War Arch.).

59. Correspondence of the prefects, 5th and 22nd June (Nat. Arch. F. 7, 3774); Prefect of Seine-et-Oise to Carnot, 16th June (War Arch.).

60. Davout to Durieux, 8th May; Prefect of the Aisne to Davout, 25th May; Langeron to Lobau, Laon, 2nd June (War Arch., Army of the North); Napoleon, *Corresp.* 22,047. The following words of Carnot, in his report to the Emperor, 16th May (*Moniteur*), must also be quoted: "Citizens of all ranks, in the department of the Aisne, are giving unceasing proofs of the noblest patriotism and the most sincere loyalty to the country" (*Moniteur*).

61. General Evain's report, 21st March (Nat. Arch. AF. iv. 3940).

62. Depôts of the corps, 27,000 rifles; artillery stores, 157,000, of which 70,000 out of repair; marine arsenals, 10,990, of which 3,600 out of repair; general total, 194,990. (Drouot to Napoleon, 27th March; Davout to Napoleon, 4th April; Decrès to Napoleon, 29th March and 10th May, Nat. Arch. AF. iv. 1940 and AF. iv. 1941.)

63. Napoleon, *Corresp.* 21,755, Cf. 21,811, and Napoleon to Davout, 8th April (portfolio of Napoleon's Corresp., War Arch.).

64. *Bulletin des Lois*, 29th March.

65. Napoleon to Davout, 23rd March (War Arch., Portfolio of Napoleon's Corresp.); Davout to Napoleon, 4th April (Nat. Arch. AF. iv. 1940); Napoleon, *Corresp.* 21,755, 21,947, 21,972.

66. Davout to Napoleon, 4th, 14th, and 29th April; to Lemarois, 3rd June (Nat. Arch. AF. iv. 1940 and War Arch.); Napoleon, *Corresp.* 21,755, 21,811, 21,887; *Bulletin des Lois*, 29th March.

67. Davout to Napoleon, 4th, 14th, and 29th April (Nat. Arch. AF. iv. 1940). The rifles out of use, were in such a pitiable condition, that the Emperor's first plan was to have them taken to pieces (Napoleon to Davout, 8th April; 8th April, War Arch., Portfolio of Napoleon's Corresp.).

68. Davout to Napoleon, 3rd, 5th, 6th, and 7th of June (Nat. Arch. AF. iv. 1940); Davout, *Correspondence*, 1747. Letters from Langeron, Laon, 1st June; from Lorecez, Metz, 5th June; from the Commandant of Landrecies, 6th June; from Suchet, Chambéry, 9th and 10th June; from Bonnaire, Condé, 12th June; from Hervo, Poitiers, 18th June, etc. (War Arch., Armies of the North, of the Alps, and General Corresp.).

69. Ruty to Davout, and Davout to Ruty, 19th May (War Arch., Army of the North); Napoleon, *Corresp.* 219.

70. Davout to Napoleon, 29th April (Nat. Arch. AF. iv. 1940); Davout's circular, 22nd April; Orders of Neigre, 18th May; Reports from the colonels of the 1st and 2nd of the line, Beaumont, 22nd May; state of the artillery on 1st June (War Arch., Army of the North). A number of cartridges had been used besides for target practice. In several regiments the men had used as many as forty each.

71. Davout's report to Napoleon, 5th April (Nat. Arch. AF. iv. 1940).

In 1815 the outfit of an infantry soldier, first suit, cost 122 frs., including under-clothes and shoes; that of a cavalry soldier, 197 frs. In addition, there was a sum of 17 frs. for keeping each man's garments in repair.

72. Reports of the Councils of Ministers, 14th June 1814 (Nat. Arch. AF.* v.²); sub-prefect of St. Quentin to Clarke, 14th March 1815; Letters to Davout: from Briche, 26th March; from Vandamme, 22nd April; from Brune, 16th May; from Lobau, 12th June; from Grouchy, 14th June (War Arch. AF. iv. 1936); Davout, *Corresp.* 1661, 1664; Napoleon, *Corresp.* 21,884.

73. Davout's report, 5th and 6th April; report from Lebarbier de Tinan, 23rd June (Nat. Arch. AF. iv. 1941); C. Napoleon, *Corresp.* 21,885, 21,886, 21,891; Davout, *Corresp.* 1603; report of the Council of Ministers, 26th April (Nat. Arch. AF. iv. 990 ᵇ).

74. Davout, *Corresp.* 1590, 1603, 1667, 1678. (See in the *Corresp.* of Napoleon the above letters, in which Napoleon complains of the delays in completing the outfit and equipment.)

75. Estimates according to the tables of 1815 (War Arch.); Davout (report to Napoleon, 28th March, Nat. Arch. AF. iv. 1941) says 21,320; but he only reckons those horses fit to enter on the campaign.

76. Estimates as above. See Napoleon, *Memoirs to serve as History*, 26.

77. Napoleon, *Corresp.* 21,741, 21,756, 21,810, 21,910; report of the Council of Ministers, 17th May; Davout's reports to Napoleon, 7th and 21st April (Nat. Arch. AF. iv. 1940 and 1941); Davout's circulars 17th and 26th April; Rovigo to Davout, 27th April and 6th May (War Arch.).

78. Davout dreaded difficulties which did not arise (Letter to Napoleon, 6th May, Nat. Arch. AF. iv. 990 ᵇ and 1941). Certain departments, notably L'Aisne and the Ardennes, furnished as many as 500 horses (Letter from Langeron, 3rd June, War Arch., Army of the North).

79. On the conduct of Préval, during the campaign of France, see Henry Houssaye, *1814*, 435.

80. Napoleon, *Corresp.* 21,982; report of Bourcier, 21st June (War Arch. estimates). General Préval was restored to favour 23rd May. The Emperor appointed him director of the cavalry, at the ministry of war (Napoleon, *Corresp.* 21,961). But this measure was too late.

81. Cavalry of the line, 35,201 (general situation on 1st June, Nat. Arch. AF. iv. 1936); cavalry of the Guard, 4,958 (estimate of d'Hériot on 16th June, War Arch.); total, 40,159.

82. Artillery of the line, 13,823 (general estimate on 1st June, Nat. Arch. AF. iv. 1936). Artillery of the Old Guard. Auxiliary artillery train of the Guard, 2,851 (estimate of d'Hériot, 6th June, War Arch.); total, 16,674.

83. Napoleon, *Corresp.* 21,729, 21,733, 21,787, 21,828, 21,865; Davout to Napoleon, 11th, 13th, 19th, and 25th April (Nat. Arch. AF. iv. 1940); Davout's orders, 8th April, and various letters to Napoleon, 12th, 13th, 14th, 15th April (War Arch.).

84. Reports on the works at the fortresses, 1st, 5th, 9th, 11th, 20th, 24th, 28th of May (Nat. Arch. AF. iv. 1940). Letters to Davout, from Ruty, 7th May; from Dumonceau, 7th May; from Suchet, 21st May;

from Perrin, 26th May; Lelerc des Essarts to Lobau, 27th May. Condition of the works in various places, 15th June (War Arch.).

85. Napoleon, *Corresp.* 21,733, 21,865, 21,892; Dejean to Napoleon, 2nd May (Nat. Arch. AF. iv. 1940); General Léry's report, Lyons, 1st June (War Arch.).

86. Napoleon, *Corresp.* 21,862.

In his writings at St. Helena, Napoleon insists several times on the urgent necessity of fortifying Paris in *1815*. But neither in his correspondence, nor in any of the documents at the Archives, do we find any proof of his attending to them before 1st May. During March and April he orders a great number of towns to be placed in a state of defence; he makes no orders with regard to Paris. No special motive can be ascribed to this delay, save the fear of alarming the Parisians. It is true that in his letter of 1st May, the Emperor says, "my aim is to show that we are conscious of the danger." But if Napoleon had that aim in view on 1st May when all hopes for peace had vanished, he did not have it a month or even a fortnight previously.

87. Napoleon, *Corresp.* 21,862, 21,273. See *Memoirs to serve for History in 1815*, 45-57. Gourgaud, *Campagne of 1815*, 14-16, and the map of the defensive works planned or executed in 1815 (published about 1840).

88. Reports to Napoleon from Davout, Lannoy, and Dejean, 2nd 3rd, 8th, 20th, 24th, and 29th May. Police reports, 1st, 2nd, and 4th June (Nat. Arch. AF. iv. 1938, 1940, and F. 7, 3774); *Journal de l'Empire*, 1st June; Duponthon to Davout, 18th May (War Arch.).

89. Davout to Napoleon, 29th and 31st May, 9th June (Nat. Arch. AF. iv. 1940); Davout to Duponthon; Commandant Martin's report, June s.d.; Valence to Caffarelli, 19th June; Grenier to Davout, 20th June (War Arch.). See Davout's report to the commission of the government, 2nd July (Nat. Arch. AF. iv. 1936).

90. Napoleon, *Corresp.* 21,856, 21,867, 21,883, 21,888, 21,934, 21,973, 21,983, 21,995, 22,041, 22,048. Davout to the director of the artillery at Metz, 21st April; to Soult, 31st May. Report of the artillery, undated, Lannoy's report, Lyons, 1st June; Vallée's report, Paris, 15th and 17th June (War Arch.): Davout to Napoleon, 16th May. Decrès' report, 8th and 10th June (Nat. Arch. AF. iv. 1940 and AF. iv. 1941).

91. Davout's letters, 23rd March and 1st April; "Feuilles de travail" of the Council of Ministers, 5th April (Nat. Arch. AF. iv. 1941, and AF. iv. 990[b]). See Napoleon, *Corresp.* 21,971; Suchet to Davout, Chambéry, 21st May; La Salcette to Davout, Grenoble, 25th May (War Arch.).

92. Ordonnateur Daure's report, 16th May (War Arch.); Davout, *Corresp.* 1587, 1595, 1656, 1670, 1685, 1693; Napoleon, *Corresp.* 21,872, 21,915; Davout's manuscript souvenirs (furnished by General Davout, Duke of Auerstaedt). Draught of the Doumerc contract (Nat. Arch. AF. iv. 1941).

93. Condition of the fortified places on 15th June (War Arch.).

Napoleon, *Memoirs to serve for History in 1815*, 36-38. General-Intendant Daure's reports, 4th and 12th June (War and Nat. Arch. AF. iv. 1938).

94. Davout to Napoleon, 28th March (Nat. Arch. AF. iv. 1941); see Carnot, *Tableau of the situation of the Empire* (*Moniteur*, 15th June). Soult had deemed this budget of 200 millions to begin with (Law of 23rd September 1814) inadequate, and an increase of 98,052,000 was to be demanded from the Chambers of Louis XVIII.

95. Napoleon to Gaudin, 2nd April (*Corresp.* 21,761).

96. Las Cases, *Memoires*, vi. 418, 419; Pasquier, *Mem.* 3, 26.

97. Act of the 8th of April (*Bulletin des Lois*, 11th April).

The Emperor created besides a Fund extraordinary to receive all the casual sums not entered in the Budget; these sums to be used to indemnify the proprietors of houses destroyed during the invasion of 1814 (Act of 6th April).

98. Corresp. of the prefects, April-June (Nat. Arch. F. 7, 3774 and AF. iv. 1935).

99. 50 millions (Pasquier, *Mem.* iii. 151); 50 millions (Napoleon, *Mem. to serve for History*, 27, 28); 42 millions in bonds and 30 millions in specie (*Allgemeine Zeitung*, 16th May).

100. Vitrolles, *Mem.* ii. 339. Baron Louis' scruples, unfounded, if he believed that the royal government would establish itself at Lille, were quite legitimate, if, as may be surmised, he expected the king would pass the frontier. These funds belonged not to Louis XVIII., but to the country.

101. Corresp. of the prefects, April-May (Nat. Arch. F. 7, 3774; Lannoy's report, Lyons, 1st June (War Arch.). "The contributions are coming in well," writes the prefect of the Moselle, on 10th May. There only remain to be recovered, on the first $\frac{4}{12}$, 169,000 francs, out of 1,256,000 francs.

Needless to remark the same readiness was not manifested in all the departments. See Mollien, *Mem.* iv. 190; and Mollien to Davout, 15th June (War Arch.).

102. Napoleon, *Mem. to serve for History*, 27. (See *Corresp.* 21,761.)

103. 23,920,120 francs, Carnot, *Outline of the Situation of the Empire* (*Moniteur*, 15th June). About one-tenth of this sum was to be deducted, for the citizens who paid a minimum of 50 francs in direct taxation had to arm and clothe themselves at their own expense.

104. Carnot's circular, 29th April (Nat. Arch. F.[1 a] 31).

105. Official reports of the Council of Ministers, 1st and 24th May (Nat. Arch. AF. iv. 990[b]). Imperial act, 27th May; Carnot, *Outline of the Situation of the Empire* (*Moniteur*, 15th June). On patriotic donations amounting, it seems, to several millions, see *1815*, i. 630, 631.

These various resources were inadequate to the expenses. In the department of Yonne the prefect Gamot opened a subscription list; in the Aisne also the subscription amounted, from 8th May, to 200,000 francs. In the Ain they had recourse to a division of the contributors on account of the 13 centimes per franc paid in direct taxes; in the Ardennes, General Vandamme requested the manufacturers of Sedan to furnish cloth under guarantee of the department. By the middle of June almost all the prefects found it impossible to fulfil the engagements they had entered into with the contractors. Carnot's circular, 31st May. Letter of the prefect of the Ain, 14th May (Nat. Arch. F.¹ª 31 and F. 7, 3740); Vandamme to Davout, 1st May (War Arch.) *Moniteur*, 16th May.

106. General Corresp. between 15th May and 23rd June (War Arch.). Report on the works in the fortified places, 28th May (Nat. Arch. AF. iv. 1940).

107. Paymaster-General to Soult, 20th May; Davout to Soult, 21st May; Mollien to Davout, 28th May (War Arch., Army of the North). See Napoleon, *Corresp.* 21,960.

108. General Manager Daure's report, 12th June (Nat. Arch. AF. iv. 1935). Daure adds, "There will be 25,000 by the end of July.".

109. Piré to Davout, Laon, 13th June (War Arch.) Guilleminot to Davout, La Villette, 1st July (Nat. Arch. AF. iv. 1941). The expenses of the early part of the campaign were not paid until the army was about to retire beyond the Loire.

110. Daure's report, 12th June (Nat. Arch. AF. iv. 1938). Daure means here the pay for the Army of the North alone, and the funds belonging to this army.

111. See Napoleon, *Corresp.* 21,886, 21901, 21,960. Mollien, *Mem.* iv. 190. *Allgemeine Zeitung*, 16th May; Mollien to Davout, 28th May (War Arch.).

112. Mollien, *Mem.* iv. 192.

113. Davout's report to the Government Commission, 23rd June (Nat. Arch. AF. iv. 1941).

114. Gaudin's report to the Emperor, proposed financial bill (*Moniteur*, 20th and 21st June). A short time after the second return of the Bourbons, an absolutely similar loan, amounting, however, to 50,000,000 less, was raised or rather enforced in accordance with Baron Louis' advice.

The Imperial budget for 1815 was forecast in receipts and expenses, at the same sum, 770 millions. If one considers that the expenses of the Royal budget were estimated at 646 millions, 547,700,000 francs (*Moniteur* of 2nd July 1814) with a surplus of 98,052,000 francs for the war budgets (Davout to Napoleon, 28th March 1815. Nat. Arch. AF. iv. 1941), it seems certain that Gaudin's budget would have resulted in a deficit of some importance, though the Emperor estimated that, except in the war expenses, great saving might be effected in the budgets of all the ministries (Napoleon, *Corresp.* 21,761).

115. Henry Houssaye, *1815*, i. 342, 343.

116. Napoleon, *Corresp.* 21,723, 21,734, 21,747, 21,765. Davout *Corresp.* 1514, 1515; Lobau to Davout, 24th March; Davout to Napoleon, 31st March, 11th April (War Arch.).

The 1st Corps was formed of the garrisons of the 16th military division (Lille). The 2nd partly of the troops of the Duke de Berry's late army, partly of those who had followed the Emperor from Grenoble.

The 3rd with the garrisons in the 2nd military division (Mézières); the 4th with the garrisons of the 3rd and 4th military divisions (Metz and Nancy); the 5th with the garrisons of the 5th military division (Strasburg); the 6th with the garrisons of the 7th and 8th military divisions (Grenoble and Toulon); the 7th with the garrisons of the 9th and 10th and 11th military divisions (Montpellier, Toulouse, and Bordeaux); the 8th partly with the troops formerly under the orders of the Duke de Berry, partly with those the Emperor had brought with him.

117. Napoleon to Davout, *Corresp.* 21,749, 21,789, 21,794, 21,821, 21,822; Davout to Carnot, 11th April; Davout orders, 10th, 11th, 12th, 20th, 21st, and 27th April (War Arch.).

118. Napoleon, *Corresp.* 21,731; see 21,147, 21,810; Davout's orders, 1st April; Davout to Napoleon, 24th April (War Arch.).

119. The Guard comprised, on 20th March, 7,390 officers and soldiers (Davout's report, 21st March, Nat. Arch. AF. iv. 1940). The Emperor increased it to 28,328 officers and soldiers. (Estimates signed by d'Hériot, 16th June, War Arch., Portfolio of estimates.)

120. Napoleon to Davout, 26th March (War Arch., Portfolio of Napoleon's Correspondence); Napoleon, *Corresp.* 21,737, 21,896, 21,994; Davout to Napoleon, 22nd April, 9th and 13th May (Nat. Arch. AF. iv. 1940); d'Hériot's estimates, 16th June (War Arch., Portfolio of estimates).

Moreover, there was organised a company of foot artillery of the Young Guard, and an auxiliary artillery corps of the Guard, including horse artillery, foot artillery, and waggons.

121. Davout's circular, 14th April (War Arch.); Napoleon, *Corresp.* 21,737; Davout's reports, 22nd, 23rd, 26th April, 9th and 13th May (Nat. Arch. AF. iv. 1940).

122. See chap. ii. (pages 101-104) a complete estimate of the Army of the North on its entrance on the campaign.

123. 15th infantry division, Heudelet, then Rottenbourg; 16th division, Albert; 8th cavalry division, Merlin; division of the select National Guard, Berkheim; artillery and engineers (Estimates of the Army of the Rhine on 20th June, Nat. Arch. AF. iv. 1936).

124. 22nd infantry division, Pacthod; 23rd division, Dessaix; 15th cavalry division, Quesnel: four divisions of select National Guards under Chabert, Pannetier, Dufresse, and Morantin; artillery and engineers (Estimates of the Army of the Alps on 15th June, War Arch.).

125. 26th infantry division, Harispe; 5th Mounted Chasseurs, six battalions of select National Guards from Charente; artillery and engineers (Estimates of the corps on 8th June, War Arch.).

126. 27th infantry division, Fressinet; 15th Mounted Chasseurs, seven battalions of mobilised soldiers under the name of Chasseurs of the Pyrenees; artillery and engineers (Estimates of the corps on 1st June, War Arch.).

127. Divisions of Travot and Brayer. The general estimate on 1st June (Nat. Arch. AF. iv. 1936) places the Army of the West at 7,553

men for the infantry of the line only, that is to say leaving out the 2nd Voltigeurs, and the 2nd Light Infantry of the Young Guard, in all 2,014 bayonets.

128. 17th infantry division, Verdier; 14th Mounted Chasseurs, artillery and engineers (Estimates of the corps on 20th June). See Brune to Davout, Antibes, 16th June (War Arch., Corps of the Var).

129. 18th infantry division, Abbé; 9th cavalry division, Castex; two divisions of mobilised National Guards, artillery and engineers (condition of the corps on 15th June, War Arch.).

130. Reserve of Avesnes, 5,000 men; corps of the Argonne (at St. Ménéhould), 3,063; reserve of Colmar, 3,603; reserve of the Moselle at Nancy, 5800 (condition of the divisions of the select National Guards on 1st and 10th June, War Arch. and Nat. Arch. AF. iv. 1936).

Nine other divisions of mobilised National Guards, in all 28,437 men strong, were included, as seen before in the corps of Rapp, Suchet, Clausel, Decaen, and Lecourbe.

131. State of the garrisons on 10th, 15th, and 21st June; General Frère's report on the northern fortresses, 1st June; General d'Ambrugeac's report, Bordeaux, 17th June; estimate of the Army of the Alps, 15th June (War Arch.); Davout to Napoleon, 10th June; Davout's report to the Government Commission, 23rd June (Nat. Arch. AF. iv. 1936).

132. General estimate on 1st June (Nat. Arch. AF. iv. 1936). In this number are included the sappers, and miners, pontoonmen and artillery labourers.

133. 500 men out of these 6,000 had been attached to the flying columns of the West. See page 6.

134. General situation from the 5th to the 10th April, wrongly dated 15th March (Nat. Arch. AF.* iv. 1153).

135. The thirty fortresses from Abbeville to Metz, possessed altogether 3,236 gunners of the garrison artillery (garrisons of fortresses of the 2nd, 5th, 1st, and 16th military divisions in June. Nat. Arch. AF. iv. 1936). There is therefore no exaggeration in estimating at 3,000 the garrison artillery in the other sixty-five strongholds of France.

136. The general estimate on 1st June (Nat. Arch. AF. iv. 1936) gives 16,916 men; but according to private estimates of the army corps on 10th June, which help us to judge of the effective strength of these army corps on 10th June, 2,982 men only had joined the war battalions. On 10th June, there remained, therefore, 13,934 men on their road to join them.

137. The recapitulation of the above estimates shows for the line, only 70,792 officers and soldiers liable or not, to be employed in the depôts and in the cities of the interior. But from this total of 70,792 men must be deducted 11,233 gunners, soldiers of the engineer corps, artillery men, etc., supposed in these general estimates to be in the fortified places, and consequently already reckoned above by us.

138. Estimates of the Guard on 16th June, signed d'Hériot (War Arch.).

139. Napoleon summoned from Corsica, which he believed might defend itself with its militia only, all the troops of the line, but he sent from Toulon to Elba a battalion of the 15th of line, 700 men (Napoleon, *Corresp.* 21,698, 21,786, 21,896, 21,951).

140. Eight additional battalions of the 5th Light Infantry, 26th, 62nd, and 71st of the line. Plan of the movements of the troops, April 1814 to May 1815 (War Arch.). Trial of Admiral de Linois, 41, 44, 47.

141. General situation on 1st June (Nat. Arch. AF. iv. 1996).

142. See page 6 and the notes.

143. General situation from 5th to 10th April, falsely dated 15th March (Nat. Arch. AF. iv.* 1153).

144. Rovigo to Napoleon, 12th April (Nat. Arch. AF. iv. 1936).

145. In the only strongholds of four departments: Pas-de-Calais, Nord, les Ardennes, and Meuse, there were 3,541 custom-house officers. (Estimates of the garrisons of fortified places in June, Nat. Arch. AF. iv. 1936). In estimating three times the number of custom-house officers in all the other frontier departments, this figure is certainly below the correct one.

146. Henry Houssaye, *1815*, i. 628-629.

147. See page 7 and notes.

148.

	Officers and Men.
IMPERIAL GUARD—	
In the Army of the North	20,755
In the Army of the Loire	2,014
In the depôts : fit or unfit for service	5,559
	28,328
TROOPS OF THE LINE	
With the armies	158,174
In the fortresses : artillery, engineers, artillerymen, etc.	11,233
On the way to join the armies	13,934
In the depôts : fit or unfit for service	59,559
In the hospitals	8,162
War battalions despatched to the island of Elba, and in the Colonies	4,700
Total of the Army under Arms	284,090
AUXILIARY ARMY	
Reserve divisions of the mobilised National Guards	45,903
Mobilised National Guards (on the frontier and in the towns of the interior), about	90,000
Military pensioners on the frontier and in the towns of the interior	25,000
Marine gunners	6,000
Marine fusiliers, about	10,000
Carried forward	176,903

	Officers and Men.
Brought forward	176,903
Veteran fusiliers	5,129
Veteran gunners	2,071
Garrison artillery, about	6,000
Gendarmes	14,521
Custom-house officers (in frontier fortresses), about	12,000
Partisans and free corps, about	6,000
Total of the Auxiliary Army	222,624

(The gunners and coast-guards, the foresters, the free battalions from Corsica, and the Corsican and Elban militia, the Vendéan chasseurs, are not included in this list, neither are the federated sharpshooters from Paris, Lyons, and Toulouse, etc. (about 25,000 men), the levies *en masse*, and the garrison artillery of the National Guards.)

With regard to this table, will be given as, in some way, a mathematical proof, the list of the resources in men, which the Emperor found ready for bringing up the active strength of the army to 284,090 men.

Royal army on 15th March (troops of the line and of the ex-Imperial Guard) about	200,000
Soldiers on leave (for a limited or unlimited period) who had joined the corps on 15th March and 25th April, about	4,000
Deserters of 1814 and soldiers on leave (for a limited or unlimited period) who had joined the corps 1st May and 15th June	52,446
Men in the same categories having received their marching orders previous to 10th June, and having rejoined the depôts, 15th June, about	4,500
Foreign soldiers,—Swiss, Poles, Belgians, German, Spanish, etc., about	3,500
Troops recalled from Elba, about	1,100
Volunteers, about	15,000
Officers on half-pay re-embodied in the regiments of the New Guard, and in the new battalions, squadrons, and batteries of the line	4,506
	285,052

(The surplus of these officers was employed in the battalions of federated sharpshooters, and in the battalions of the mobilised guards.)

These two lists being a recapitulation, it seems superfluous to give again the references already quoted in the preceding pages; but it must be said that the different totals resulting, with few exceptions, from estimates made previous to 15th June, are certainly below the real total. And for this reason: During the month of June 1815, France was wholly occupied by recruiting operations. From the depôts, men were constantly starting for the army; from the chief centres of the departments, men were ceaselessly passing to the depôts; from towns and villages also men were every day sent on to the *chefs-lieux* of departments. The result was that the army daily increased, but without exhausting the depôts. Thus in a report dated 11th June (Nat. Arch. AF. iv. 1936) and necessarily compiled from previous estimates, Davout writes that there are 52,464 half-year men and re-enlisted men, enrolled, and 23,448 on their way. Now, on 15th June, not only several thousands of those 23,448 men had rejoined the depôts, but as the recruiting operations had gone on, more men than Davout had reckoned on, had left the departments. The Correspondence of the prefects (Nat. Arch. F. 7, 3044,^a and F. 7, 3774) mentions departures of re-engaged men up to 25th June.

The same applies to the mobilised National Guards. In a report of 8th June (Nat. Arch. AF. iv. 1936) Davout estimates at 108,094 the mobilised who have reached their destinations, and at 24,178 the mobilised *en route*. Now, in another report of 23rd June (Nat. Arch. AF. iv. 1936) he enumerates for each reserve division and stronghold all the mobilised men, and the total thus obtained amounts to over 140,000 men formed in battalions.

149. Davout's report to Napoleon, 11th June (Nat. Arch. AF. iv. 1936); Davout says: 23,448 from the estimates of 1st to 10th June; but as was seen in the recapitulary lists on the preceding page, one-fifth at least of those re-engaged men sent on—about 4,500—ought to have joined the depôts by 15th June.

150. See note on preceding page.

151. Davout's report to Napoleon, 11th June (Nat. Arch. AF. iv. 1936).

152. See the estimates of the National Guards on 8th June (Nat. Arch. AF. iv. 1936); review of the situation of the Empire, by Carnot on 13th June in the Chamber of Peers, and Davout's report on 23rd June to the Government Commission (Nat. Arch. AF. iv. 1936).

153. The contingent ought to have furnished 120,000 men at least, and from this number 46,419 men must be deducted who were assembled from 11th June, at the depôt centres of the departments. (Davout to Napoleon, 23rd May and 11th June, Nat. Arch. AF. iv. 1534 and 1936.)

154. The levy should have amounted to 234,720, but 150,000 only, or thereabouts, had been enrolled or sent *en route* by the beginning of June. (See Henry Houssaye, *1815*, i. 627 and note 4, also p. 8 of this vol.)

155. See p. 8 and notes 42, 43.

156. Napoleon, *Memoirs to serve for the History of 1815*, 28. At all events, if Napoleon gave a fairly accurate estimate of the French army when he computed it at 800,000 men on the 1st October, he made a radical mistake in the details he gave respecting it. His estimate (Annexe B) is in every point inaccurate. He computes the Army extraordinary, National Guards, etc., at 224,000 men only, and the army of

the line at 584,000, when the Guard and all the line together could scarcely furnish 420,000 men."

157. Henry Houssaye, *1815* i. 22.

158. Davout's circular, 28th March (War Arch.).

Moreover, a commission composed of Generals Arrighi, Girard, Berthezène, Sebastiani, Lallemand, Colonel Bernard, etc., was formed on 2nd April, to revise all promotions to the rank of superior officer and general which had been conferred on the officers of the ex-Imperial army under Louis XVIII.

(*Moniteur*, 2nd April; Davout, *Corresp.* 1617). The official reports of this commission do not exist among the War Archives (at least we have not been able to find them), and the retrogressions pronounced by it are naturally not mentioned in the record of those concerned; no more are the promotions signed during the Hundred Days. In a letter annexed to Berthezène's dossier, this general says that the work of the Commission was never completed and had no results. This assertion agrees with a report addressed from Paris to Wellington, 22nd April (*Despatches, Supplementary*, x. 163) where it is said: "The Emperor has confirmed almost all the nominations in the Army and in the 'Legion of Honour.'" We know, however, from Davout's reports, that the Commission proposed the confirmation of 36 promotions out of 66, signed by the king in the cavalry of the line, and the annulling of 30; it decided also on the retrogression to brigadier rank of several generals of division, among them Préval (Davout to Napoleon, 6th and 28th April, 26th May, 7th and 14th June, Nat. Arch. AF. iv. 1940 and 1939).

159. Lobau and Davout's circulars, 17th and 22nd April (War Arch.); Davout's report, 13th May (Nat. Arch. AF. iv. 1939). See Napoleon, *Corresp.* 21,737, and Napoleon to Davout, 26th March (War Arch., Portfolio of Napoleon's Letters).

160. *Notice on Cunéo d'Ornano, Journal de l'Institut Historique*, 1st June 1863. This appointment, unrecognised on the king's return, as well as all those made during the Hundred Days, is not mentioned in the record of Cunéo d'Ornano.

161. For the conduct, on the Emperor's return, of the 50 or 60 officers here mentioned, see Henry Houssaye, *1815*, i. 207-426.

162. Marchand's account (Marchand's documents, War Arch.).

163. Official reports of the Council of Ministers, 7th June (Nat. Arch. AF. iv. 990 [b]).

164. General Rapp, *Mem.* 342, 347.

165. Napoleon to Davout, 26th March, 10th April, 6th, 15th, and 22nd May (War Arch. Napoleon's Letters); Napoleon to Davout, 26th and 29th March, 10th and 18th April, 2nd and 28th May (Nat. Arch. AF. iv. 907); Napoleon, *Corresp.* 21,706, 21,788, 21,820, 21,964; Davout, *Corresp.* 1619, 1620, 1654, 1657, 1724; Davout to Napoleon, 26th March, 16th April (Nat. Arch. AF. iv. 1939).

I say about 100 officers, but this figure is certainly exaggerated, for the documents mention altogether only 43 dismissals, or cases of men put on the retired list, among them that of a sub-lieutenant. Of course in this number are included, neither, the officers enrolled in the army under Louis XVIII., and who left it by virtue of the Lyons decrees, nor the officers condemned for desertion by court-martial, nor the officers proposed by the Commission for retrogression, nor even the officers who passed with their rank from one regiment to another.

166. Napoleon to Davout, 18th April (Nat. Arch. AF. iv. 907). Maison was dismissed by a special decree. Beurnonville, Donnadieu, Bordessoulle, and also Clarke, lost their rank from the very fact of their emigration, by virtue of the decree of 9th May 1815, which re-enforced the laws of the Legislative Assembly against "émigrés."

167. Davout to Napoleon, 16th April (Nat. Arch. AF. iv. 1939); Napoleon, *Elba and the Hundred Days; Corresp.* xxxi. 103. These words, "What more do you want of me?" seem to confirm the assertion of Fain (Manuscript of 1814, 242) that Souham, the day before his desertion, had come to Fontainebleau to claim from the Emperor 6,000 francs, which the latter had given him.

By a chance, which gave justice fair play, Souham was replaced at Périgueux by Lucotte, the only general of the 6th Corps who remained true to his duty, in the inexpiable night of 4th April 1814.

168. In vain did Davout entreat the Emperor to maintain Moncey in his post (to Napoleon, 26th March, Nat. Arch. AF. iv. 1939).

169. Bugeaud's papers (War Arch.) and letter from Napoleon to Bugeaud, 8th May (quoted by d'Ideville, *Marshal Bugeaud*, i. 172).

170. Cross-examination of Ney. Ney's papers and documents (Archives of War); Gourgaud, *Camp of 1815*, 44, note; Montholon, *Recits.* ii. 90; MSS. Recollections of Davout, furnished by General the Duke of Auerstaedt.

Soult, when chief of the staff, requested that Bourmont should leave the Army of the North (Soult to Davout, 22nd May, Nat. Arch. AF. iv. 1949).

171. Davout to Curial, and Curial to Davout, 14th, 16th, and 17th April (Nat. Arch. AF. iv. 1940). General Girod de l'Ain, *Souvenirs*, 375, 377, 381. The Emperor rescinds Curial's commission, because that general had attempted to prevent the departure of the chasseurs. A short time after he gave him an infantry division in Suchet's army.

172. "I claim a corps in the active service, or permission to resign," Sebastiani to Davout, Amiens, 3rd May (War Arch.).

173. Colonel La Borde, *Napoleon and the Guard at Elba*, 116.

174. Napoleon to Davout, 26th March (Nat. Arch. AF. iv. 907); Napoleon, *Corresp.* 21,790.

Those strikings off the list were inserted neither in the *Moniteur* nor in the *Bulletin des Lois*, and were consequently not made public. A simple letter of notification was addressed by the Minister of War to those concerned, informing them that their names were struck off the list of marshals, and that they would be allowed a retiring pension. See on the subject Davout, *Corresp.* 1632, 1633, and Davout to Napoleon, 27th April (Nat. Arch. AF. iv. 1939).

Annulled by the mere fact of Louis XVIII.'s return, those erasures, as well as the dismissals of the Hundred Days, do not appear in the records of service of these officers.

175. Napoleon, *Corresp.* 21,790.

176. Napoleon to Davout, 26th March (Nat. Arch. AF. iv. 907), and *Corresp.* 21,790.

177. Davout, *Corresp.* 1506, 1535, 1539. Gouvion had previously been compelled to come to Paris to justify himself before the Emperor.

178. Davout, *Corresp.* 1633.

179. Out of the sixty-six senators present at the sitting of 1st April 1814, three were nevertheless created peers during the Hundred Days; they were General Valence, Pontécoulant and Roger Ducos.

180. Oudinot to Suchet and to Jacqueminot Bar-sur-Ornain, 28th March (Nat. Arch. AF. iv. 1939); Davout, *Corresp.* 1504, 1509, 1510. In his letter to Jacqueminot, Oudinot says: "Make haste and tell me that my disgrace is at an end. That is the best news you could give me."

181. Napoleon, *Elba and the Hundred Days; Corresp.* xxxi. 104. At first, Napoleon had given orders to have Oudinot's name struck out of the list of marshals (to Davout, 26th March, Nat. Arch. AF. iv. 907); but he revoked this decision (*Corresp.* 21,790).

Marshal Oudinot's wife (*Souvenirs*, 371) insists that it was at the express request of the Marshal himself that Napoleon left him unemployed. But the above-quoted letters of Oudinot (which of course the Duchess of Reggio abstained from mentioning), and his presence in the Imperial *cortège* at the ceremony of the Champ-de-Mars, testify to the weakness of his royalist scruples, and lead one strongly to infer that he might have accepted a post, had the Emperor offered him one.

182. Henry Houssaye, *1814*, 115-119.

183. Macdonald to Davout, Paris, 27th and 30th March; to Maurice Mathieu, 30th March; to his aides-de-camp, 6th April (Macdonald's ledger, War. Arch.); C. Macdonald, *Souvenirs*, 385, 387-389.

184. Napoleon, *Corresp.* 21,694. It was during the night of the 20th to the 21st March that Rovigo had been appointed inspector-general of "gendarmerie" (Rovigo, *Mém.* vii. 387).

185. Lefebvre had gone through the whole campaign of France, but on the Emperor's staff. Louis XVIII. raised him to the peerage.

186. Massena's report to the Emperor, Toulon, 14th April (Nat. Arch. AF. iv. 1938).

187. Napoleon, *Corresp.* 21,825, 22,043; Davout, *Corresp.* 1627.

188. Thus Durutte, who had the command at Metz, was appointed to the command of a division of the 1st Corps. "Although I have no cause to be displeased with Durutte, I must recall him from Metz and give him another appointment" (Napoleon to Davout, 27th March, Nat. Arch. AF. iv. 907).

189. Davout to Mortier, 22nd March; La Poype to Davout, Lille, 13th May; Lanusse to Davout, Metz, 21st May (War Arch.); Napoleon, *Corresp.* 21,852, 22,025; Davout, *Corresp.* 1657; Army Bulletin, 15th June (*Moniteur*, 18th June).

190. Napoleon, *Corresp.* 21,844; Davout, *Corresp.* 1518, 1538,

1691, 1721. The Emperor had for a moment thought of leaving Suchet at Strasburg, as commander of the Army of the Rhine; but on 30th March he had recalled him to Paris, reserving for him eventually the command of several corps (Napoleon, *Corresp.* 21,723, 21,747); then he sent him to Lyons as superior commandant of the 6th, 7th, 8th, 9th and 19th military divisions, with Grouchy under his orders (*1815*, i. 424-425). Later he gave him the Army of the Alps.

191. Davout to Napoleon, 1st and 3rd June (Nat. Arch. AF. iv. 1939).

192. Brune to Clarke, 5th January 1814 (Brune's papers, War Arch.).

193. Napoleon, *Corresp.* 21,815, 21,896, 21,952; Davout to Brune, 16th April (War Arch.).

194. Ney to Davout, Paris, 23rd March; and Lille, 28th March (War. Arch.); Ney to Napoleon, 25th, 26th, 28th and 30th March, 1st, 7th and 9th April (Nat. Arch. AF. iv. 1936); Napoleon, *Corresp.* 21,734.

195. Depositions of Captain Grison of the 37th, and of Captain Casse of the 42nd (*Ney's Trial*, ii. 163-165). See the written deposition of the justice-of-the-peace at Auxonne, 3rd November (Ney's papers and documents), who quotes these words of the marshal: "These rascally Bourbons and this cowardly nobility will have to go and spend another twenty years in England!"

196. Rousselin's notes (Bégis collection), *Aaran Gazette*, 13th May; Madame Maury's deposition (*Ney's Trial*, ii. 177, 178); Napoleon, *Elba and the Hundred Days; Corresp.* xxxi. 104; letter to the Emperor, June (Nat. Arch. AF. iv. 1934).

197. See Davout, *Corresp.* 1605.

198. Napoleon, *Elba and the Hundred Days; Corresp.* xxxi. 104.

199. *Aaran Gazette*, 13th May; *Journal Universel* (of Gand), No. 8; report to Clarke by Lieutenant Jallot, a deserter of the 11th Chasseurs, Ghent, 12th June (War Arch.).

200. Davout to Napoleon, 6th June; Napoleon to Davout, 7th June (Nat. Arch. AF. iv. 1949, and AF. iv. 907).

201. First examination of Ney (*Trial*, i. 19).

202. Peyrusse, *Memorial*, 311; letter from Ney to the Duke of Otrante (*Journal of the Empire*, 26th June).

203. First examination of Ney, before the prefect of police (War Arch., Ney's papers and documents).

204. Napoleon, *Corresp.* 22,042.

205. "The Marshal's requests were granted; he was given an army corps" (*Account of the Campaign of 1815*, by Colonel Heymès, 1st aide-de-camp to Ney, 7).

206. "I only wished for death. I was often tempted to blow my brains out" (Ney's examination, Ney's papers and documents, War Arch.).

207. Heymès, *Account*, 5, 6.

On 11th June, when the Emperor sent a warning to Ney, all the general officers had been commissioned for several weeks. It may then be surmised that Napoleon had not wished from the first to give one to the Prince of Moscow.

208. Henry Houssaye, *1815*, i. 468, 469. See Las Casas, *Memorial*, iv. 424, 425. "Murat," said the Emperor, "is one of the main causes of the misfortunes of 1814. It is difficult to conceive greater depravity, or to pursue fresh honours with greater shamelessness and vileness."

209. Las Casas, *Memorial*, ii. 276; see Montholon, *Anecdotes*, ii. 90.

210. It follows that a chief of the staff, in certain cases the real chief of the armies, should have the power of conception and direct command, of which Berthier was so lamentably deficient. In the case of Berthier, this power was not needed. It is one thing to be chief of the staff under William of Germany, like Moltke, and another to be chief of the staff under Napoleon.

211. The day before the battle of Eylau only one of those eight officers reached the headquarters of Bernadotte. This fact is related by the Intendant-General Denniée (quoted by Pierron, *Methods of War*, ii. 1551).

212. Rapp, *Mem.* 345; Mollien, *Mem.* iv. 199: "The Emperor regretted he had Berthier no longer with him." "He was," said he, "the best of staff-generals. He had a quicker perception of every thought and plan than anyone else, and explained them better to the heads of the corps." He spoke without bitterness, only saying, "I should like to see him as a captain of the body-guard."

On 10th April only (*Corresp.* 21,790), that is to say when all probability of Berthier's return to France had vanished, the Emperor ordered his name to be struck off the list of marshals. His first order of 26th March, on the striking out of names, refers only to Marmont, Augereau, Victor, Gouvion, St.-Cyr, and Oudinot (letter to Davout, 27th March, Nat. Arch. AF. iv. 907).

213. Meneval, *Napoleon and Marie-Louise*, ii. 330.

214. *Journal of Frankfort*, 4th June; *Gazette Universelle*, 5th June; *Nuremberg Gazette*, 4th June; *Journal of Cologne*, 10th June. Bamberg's correspondent of the *Journal of Cologne* gives the following details:— "For some days a change was noticed in Berthier. On 31st May he had dined at the Prince of Bavaria's palace with the Russian general, Sacken, and the latter having complimented him on his faithfulness to King Louis XVIII., he had looked extremely embarrassed and had made no reply. . . . It was from his children's apartment that he threw himself out of the window. His little boy, who caught him by the leg to save him, narrowly escaped being dragged out with him." These particulars are pure invention, for we know from the Prince of Wagram that the Princess and her children spent all the time of the interregnum at Grosbois. When the marshal fell (according to the legend, was thrown or threw himself out) there were two servants by his side.

215. The nomination of Soult is dated 9th May (Imperial Decree, Napoleon's letters, War Arch.); and on 25th April there was a rumour at Ghent (*Journal Universel*, No. 4) that this general, who for a long time had entertained the hope of succeeding Berthier, would be chief of the staff.

Soult was enough of a Gascon to persuade the Emperor he would make a first-rate chief of the staff. One must read in his *Memoirs* (ii. 206) the portrait he draws from his own model of ideal head of the staff. If it be true that, when he discharged these functions in the Lefebvre division, he was so active, so diligent, so prudent, he had somewhat altered in 1815. However, during the campaign, Soult was not as much below his task as was presumed. His greatest fault was in sometimes writing his orders without precision and clearness, and in not ensuring their rapid transmission. As for the charge of negligence and want of foresight brought against him, it is just to say that Bailly de Monthyon, who had been appointed to assist him as chief of the staff, is also responsible for these to a certain extent.

216. Soult, *Mém. Justificatif*, 24, and Soult to Davout, Villeneuve-l'Etang, 11th April (Soult's documents and papers, War Arch.).

217. Soult, *Mém. Justificatif*, 24. Soult pretends that he only came to the Tuileries because the Emperor had sent for him twice, through Clausel and Rovigo. This is doubtful. Discredited as Soult was at that time, and after the order of the day he had published against Napoleon, the latter could not be so impatient to see him, and to employ him. If Rovigo and Clausel had interfered, it was most likely at the Marshal's own request. The tone of his letters to Davout bespeaks his desire to regain lost favour. Besides, if the Emperor made any advances to Soult, Soult could have evaded them just as easily as Macdonald did.

218. *Moniteur*, 9th March.

219. Davout, *Corresp.* 1530, 1567, 1597, 1598; Soult to Davout, 11th April (Soult's documents and papers, War Arch.).

220. Soult to Davout, 11th April (Soult's documents and papers); Davout, *Corresp.* 1598.

221. Soult had been only two or three months chief of the staff in the Taponnier division, then chief of the staff in the Lefebvre division during the campaign of 1794 in the Netherlands. By the way, it would be very hazardous to conclude that Soult's participation in that campaign was one of the causes which decided the Emperor to select him as chief of the staff for a new campaign in Belgium. On the one hand, Napoleon had not (as will be seen further on) quite made up his mind on 9th May, the date of Soult's appointment, to carry the war into the Netherlands at all. On the other hand, his personal experience convinced him that, after twenty years and countless battles all over Europe, Soult could not have retained any but the vaguest recollections of the topography of the country between the Sambre and Brussels. Besides, one does not choose a chief of the staff as one chooses a guide, because he knows the country!

222. Napoleon to Davout, 30th April (*Corresp.* 21,856): "If we have war, I propose to leave you in Paris as Minister of War, Governor of Paris, and Commander-in-Chief of the National Guard of the levies "en masse" and of the troops of the line which may happen to be in the city . . ." Order for 11th June (quoted in Davout's manuscript memoirs): "Our cousin, Prince of Eckmühl, is appointed Governor of Paris." From the manuscript souvenirs of Davout and Jean de Chénier

(*History of Davoût*, 540, 541). Davout repeatedly requested a command in the army; but the Emperor invariably answered: "I can entrust Paris to no one but you."

223. Soult, who did not deceive himself as to the feeling in the Army, endeavoured to win back public opinion with an order of the day. He submitted it to the Emperor, who wrote to him: "In order that the Army should have no remarks to make, I think that you may say, without any inconsistency, that the flight of the Bourbons from French territory, their appeal to foreign powers to regain the throne, and also the wish of the entire nation, have cancelled all engagements made with them. Without this sentence, I fear this order of the day might injure you in the minds of men who take umbrage easily (Napoleon to Soult, 3rd June, Nat. Arch. AF. iv. 907). Soult added the paragraph, but he embellished it with abuse of the Bourbons and their partisans, which Napoleon had never suggested. The manifesto appeared on 4th June in the *Moniteur*.

224. Vandamme to Davout, Mézieres, 12th May (War Arch., Army of the North). Soult's appointment, signed 9th May (War Arch., Napoleon's Letters), was not officially announced until 14th May (Davout's circular, 13th May, War Arch., Army of the North).

225. Napoleon, *Corresp.* 21,723. See Davout to Lebrun, 31st March (War Arch., Army of the North); Davout to Napoleon, 19th April (Nat. Arch. AF. iv. 1939). Lebrun resumed his functions as aide-de-camp to the Emperor.

226. Vandamme to Davout, Mézières, 20th and 30th April, 9th and 14th May; Vandamme's orders, Mézières, 2nd and 7th May; report of Lieutenant Jallot of the 11th Chasseurs, deserter, to Clarke, Ghent, 12th June; Davout to Vandamme, 7th and 29th May (War Arch., Army of the North).

Before receiving his command of the 3rd Corps (20th April), Vandamme had been entrusted with the military and political inspection of all the fortresses north of Lille; he had fulfilled that mission with the utmost zeal (Vandamme to Davout, 28th March and 30th April, War Arch.).

227. Decaen's Corresp., June (War Arch., Army of the Western Pyrenees). See Villèle, *Mém.* i. 296, 297. On Clausel and Decaen, see also Henry Houssaye, *1815*, i. 398-416, 620.

228. Napoleon, *Corresp.* 21,732. Davout to Rapp, 16th April (War Arch.). See the arrest: *Ney's Trial*, and Henry Houssaye, *1815*, i. 303, 310-312, and note 3, page 314.

229. Lamarque to Gouvion Saint-Cyr, Tours, 27th July (War Arch., Army of the Loire).

See Napoleon, *Corresp.* 21,948.

230. Napoleon to Durosnel, 30th April (Nat. Arch. AF. iv. 907). See on Durosnel the "satisfecit" bestowed by Dessolles, as he resumed, in the name of the king, the command of the National Guard; supplementary order of the day, 8th July; *Moniteur*, 10th July.

231. According to one of the Emperor's letters (Napoleon, *Corresp.*

21,868), Carnot, Réal, Dubois, Regnaud were to assist Durosnel in this work, but Durosnel's correspondence indicates that he undertook it alone, or almost alone.

232. Durosnel's report to Napoleon, 30th May and 6th June; Perregaux to Napoleon, 3rd June; various letters and police notes, 28th and 31st May, 2nd June (Nat. Arch. AF. iv. 1935 and F. 7, 3774).

233. Mathieu Dumas to Napoleon, r.d. (May); Davout to Napoleon, 7th June (Nat. Arch. AF. iv. 1935 and AF. iv. 1936). On the "federated Parisians," see Henry Houssaye, *1815*, i. 623-625.

234. Napoleon, *Corresp.* 21,263, 21,960, 21,926. Davout (*Corresp.* 1740) maintains, it is true, that it was only on the verbal order of Napoleon that he appointed Chambarlhac to Dijon. But other officers, were provided by him with commissions which were never ratified by the Emperor. There is no doubt on that point.

235. Napoleon to Davout, 2nd and 16th May (Nat. Arch. AF. iv. 907, and M^{se} de Blocqueville, *Marshal Davoût*, iv. 137); Flahaut's letter to Thiers, 1st October 1861 (quoted by F. Masson, *General Flahaut*, 20, 21).

236. Moreau to Clarke, Chateauroux, 19th November 1815, and Moreau's record of service (War Arch., Moreau's documents and papers).

237. Napoleon to Flahaut, 13th April (Nat. Arch. AF. iv. 907).

238. Manuscript memoirs of Davout (furnished by General Davout, Duke of Auerstaedt. See Davout, *Corresp.* 1607; Fleury de Chaboulon, *Mem.* i. 262.

239. Napoleon to Flahaut, 18th April (Nat. Arch. AF. iv. 907). See Napoleon to Flahaut, 12th May (War Arch., Portfolio of Napoleon's Corresp.).

According to another letter from Napoleon to Flahaut, 13th April (Nat. Arch. AF. iv. 907), Lobau and Labédoyère were to share this mission with Flahaut. For some reason or other, the latter remained in sole charge of it.

240. Manuscript memoirs of Davout (above quoted); cf. I. Masson, *General Flahaut*, 21, 22; and Chenier, *History of Davoût*, ii. 503, 504.

241. Several of the unfortunate selections, quoted in the preceding page, were in fact made prior to 18th April, the day when Flahaut was ordered to overlook these propositions.

242. From 15th May, nothing in Napoleon's correspondence leads to believe that he has anything more to do with the appointments; and from several other letters, it seems that the Emperor asked Davout to select without control several of the generals.

243. Manuscript memoirs of Davout (comm. by General the Duke of Auerstaedt).

244. Pion des Loches, *My Campaigns*, 465; notes of Colonel Baudus (comm. by M. de Montenon); Ameil to Grundler, 24th April; Suchet to Davout, 21st, 22nd and 25th May; Lecourbe to Davout, 12th, 16th, and 20th June; report of Adjutant-Commandant Gordon, 20th June (War Arch.); Gourgaud, *Campaign of 1815*, 67, 68; Napoleon, *Mem.*

180; report to Wellington (*Suppl. Despatches*, x. 55, cf. Soult to Napoleon, 22nd June, War Arch.).

245. See Ney to Napoleon, Avesnes, 1st April; Davout to Napoleon, 13th, 22nd, and 26th April, 1st, 3rd, and 8th June (Nat. Arch. AF. iv. 1936, 1939, 1940 and 1949); Ameil to Grundler, Mézières, 20th April; Grundler to Davout, Amiens, 24th April; Rapp to Davout, Strasburg, 15th May (War Arch.); D'Erlon to Davout, Lille, 11th and 25th April; Vandamme to Davout, Mézières, 24th April, 6th and 12th May; Piré to Davout, 3rd June; Gressot to Soult, 8th June; confidential note to Davout's address from an officer of the Imperial Staff, 20th June (War Arch., Army of the North); Kellermann's account (War Arch.); General Delort's account; manuscript notes of Rousselin; Du Casse, *The three Marshals d'Ornano*, 105, 106; Grouchy, *Historical Fragment*, 10 (see 9) and *Short Account*, 23, Gérard, *Last Observations*, 55; D'Artez' report (*Suppl. Despatches* of Wellington, x. 250).

It is evident, that as in every generalisation of facts, one might oppose a certain number of contradictory witnesses. Gérard, Pajol, Exelmans, Vandamme, Allix, Gilly, Brayer, Michel, were, to the very last, full of enthusiasm. Foy wrote on 15th June in his diary: "No one thinks of doubting the ultimate triumph of France." Dessaix, intended first for the command of the Army of the Alps, passed without a murmur to the command of simple general of a division in that army. Travot, whose whole career had been passed in la Vendée, uttered not a word of protest when he was appointed to serve in la Vendée itself under the orders of Lamarque, a man much younger than himself, below him in military rank, and inexperienced in the wars of the Western provinces.

246. *Trial of Cambronne*, 41, 42.

247. General corresp. and the Armies of the North, the Rhine and the Jura, 25th and 28th March, 6th, 11th, 14th, 23rd, 24th, and 25th April, 3rd and 16th June (War Arch.); Letters to Napoleon, 5th and 9th May, 12th June, etc. Private letter from a soldier, Laon, 22nd June (Nat. Arch. AF. iv. 1934); Davout, *Corresp.* 1588; General Delort's account. Manuscript memoirs of the chief of the squadron Bourgeois, aide-de-camp of Hullin during the Hundred Days, and grandfather on the maternal side, of the author.

248. Davout to Napoleon, 17th May (Nat. Arch.). D'Erlon to Davout, Lille, 4th June (War Arch., Army of the North).

249. Letter of Colonel Viala de Sommières, formerly deputy-chief of the staff of the 1st Corps, published in the *Review of the Empire*, iii. 373; Colonel Taubin temporarily commanded the fortress of Condé in the absence of General Bonnaire who had come to Paris for the ceremony of the Champ-de-Mai.

250. D'Erlon to Davout, Lille, 25th April (War Arch., Army of the North); Davout, *Corresp.* 1636. It will be seen farther on that during the campaign, from the 15th to the 18th June, cartridges and cannon charges filled with bran were still distributed to certain of the corps. Soult to Davout, Laon, 21st June (War Arch., Army of the North).

251. General Saunier to Davout from Orleans, 25th March; d'Erlon

to Davout, 1st April (War Arch.); Napoleon to Davout, 25th March (Nat. Arch. AF. iv. 907); Chevalier d'Artez' report, April (*Suppl. Despatches of Wellington*, x. 250); addresses to the Emperor from the 25th, 39th, and 75th of the line, 12th of Dragoons, etc. (Nat. Arch. AF. iv. 1950).

252. This is a delusion of contemporary writers which has misled all historians. The revolution of 20th March was not a military movement submitted to by the people, but a popular movement seconded by the army. I have endeavoured to prove it (Henry Houssaye, *1815*, i. 364-369), and, judging from the opinion of most critics, I believe I have succeeded.

253. Davout's orders, 29th March (War Arch.); Drouot's report, 15th May (Nat. Arch. AF. iv. 1940).

254. La Bretonnière, *Souvenirs du Quartier Latin*, 211, 225. See the arrival of the Dragoons of the Guard at Paris, order of Davout to Pajol, 21st March (War Arch.).

255. Grouchy à le Sénécal, Aix. 15th April (War Arch., Army of the Alps). Already in July 1814, the inhabitants of Orgon had been ill-treated from the same motive by a detachment of infantry (Henry Houssaye, *1815*, i. 47).

256. Commandant of the fortress of Aire to Drouot, 8th May (War Arch.); Préfet of Les Bouches du Rhone to Carnot, 25th May (Nat. Arch. F. 7, 3774).

257. Mayor of St. Germain to Davout, 6th May; order of the day of Piré, 14th May (War Arch.); corresp. of the prefects and reports of police, April-June (Nat. Arch. F. 7, 3740 and F. 7, 3774.)

258. Order of the day, Foy, Gosselies, 11th June (registry of Foy's Corresp.); Vandamme's order of the day, Gembloux, 18th June; Radet to Soult, Charleroi, 16th June, and Fleurus, 17th June (War Arch., Army of the North).

259. Daure to Davout, Laon, 5th June; Piré to Davout, Laon, 6th June; Friant's order of the day, Charleroi, 16th June; report of the 2nd military division, 27th May (War Arch., Army of the North).

260. Lobau to Davout, 3rd and 7th April; Davout to Lobau, 5th April (War Arch.).

261. Letter quoted *in extenso* in a report from Drouot to Napoleon, 26th April (Nat. Arch. AF. iv. 1940); see Reille to Drouot, 29th April (*Ibid.*).

262. Soult to Grouchy, 5th June (War Arch., Army of the North).

263. Report of Chevalier d'Artez, April (*Suppl. Despatches of Wellington*, x. 250); La Bretonnière, *Souvenirs du Quartier Latin*, 202. See *Journal of the Empire*, 23rd March, and Alexander Roger's letter inserted in the same paper, 15th April.

264. General Hulot's report on the operations of the 3rd division of the 4th Corps (comm. by Baron Hulot); report to Wellington, May (*Suppl. Despatches*, x. 365); daily notes of General Foy (comm. by Count Foy); report of Adjutant-Commandant Gordon, Ghent, 20th June (War Arch., Army of the North); see report to Wellington, 22nd

April (*Suppl.* x. 163). "The enthusiasm of the Army is beyond all expression." Bassano to Caulaincourt, 18th June, Arch. of Foreign Affairs, 1802) ; "our Army is as good as it was in the most prosperous times."

265. Ney to Davout, 23rd and 24th March ; Colonel of the 67th to Davout, 11th May ; letter from the officers and soldiers of the 56th to Vandamme, 11th June ; Major of the 57th to Davout, Strasburg, 1st June ; Rapp to Davout, 4th June ; official reports of the restoring of eagles to the 6th, 52nd, and 101st, 24th June ; General Théry to Davout, Sarrelouis, 27th March ; the Colonel of the 106th to Napoleon, 4th June ; General de Civray to Brune, Antibes, 7th May ; Mayor of Rouen to Davout, 24th April ; Gérard to Vandamme, Metz, 2nd June ; General Hugo to Davout, Thionville, 8th April ; report of Rovigo, 17th June (War Arch., General Corresp., and the Armies of the North, the Rhine and Var); deposition of the Vendéan Major E. de Marans (Documents and Papers of Travot, War Arch.) ; La Bretonnière, *Souvenirs of the Quartier Latin*, 228, 251, 252 ; Corresp. of the prefects and report of police, April-June (Nat. Arch. F. 7, 3774 ; F. 7, 3740 ; and F. 3044[n]) ; Réal's Bulletin, 8th April ; extract of a letter from General Baraillon, Lille, 4th May ; Napoleon to Fouché, 13th May ; Mouton-Duvernet to Davout, Lyons, 12th June (Nat. Arch. F. 7, 3774 ; AF. iv. 60 and AF. iv. 1934, 1937. On the giving up of pay days, see Henry Houssaye, *1815*, i. 630.

266. The addresses of the regiments to the Emperor might also be quoted (Nat. Arch. AF. iv. 1950) if such compulsory tokens of loyalty were not generally unconvincing. These, however, have a tone of passion which seems sincere, when one knows of the soldiers' feelings for Napoleon. But do not all these protestations pale before this simple fact. The old soldiers, veterans of the Armies of the Rhine, of Sambre-et-Meuse, of Italy and Egypt, fully intending to retire or named for final dismissal, refused to leave the regiment as soon as they heard of the Emperor's return. Sixty men did so in the 42nd, and thirty in the 64th (Daumesnil's reports, Condé, 31st March ; and from Ney, Haguenau, 9th April ; Nat. Arch. AF. iv. 1950 ; and AF. iv. 1936).

BOOK I CHAPTER II

1. Letter from Kleist to the King of Prussia, Aix-la-Chapelle, 19th March (quoted by von Ollech, *Geschichte des Feldzuges von 1815*, 5). Wellington to Gneisenau, Brussels, 5th April (*Despatches*, xii. 288). See *Waterloo Campaign* (Müffling), Hist. 1, 2 ; State of the troops in the Netherlands, 23rd March (*Supplementary Despatches of Wellington*, x. 716).

Clausewitz himself (*Der Feldzug von 1815*, 16) estimates the Dutch and English forces at 20,000 men only; he gives 50,000 men to the Prussians and Saxons together. Damitz, i. 6, says that the forces of Kleist would have amounted to 50 or 60,000 men had the regiments been complete.

In the estimate (account) quoted in the *Supplementary Despatches* the Dutch-Belgian troops, quartered in Belgium on the 23rd March, are computed at 7,233 men only. Kleist writes: "The Belgians hardly deserve mention." And the fact is, if van Löben Sels (44 to 69) is to be trusted, it appears certain, that the Dutch and Belgian army, which was still being organised, could hardly muster together 10,000 bayonets and sabres by the month of March. In the middle of June the number was raised to 29,500.

2. Letter from the Minister of War to Kleist, Berlin, 13th March (quoted by von Ollech, 4). We shall see later, that a revolt of the Saxons took place at Liège, which resulted in the whole corps being sent back to Germany.

3. *Allgemeine Zeitung*, 27th March. Report from Vienna (undated, subsequent to 8th April); reports from Commandants du Quesnoy, de Maubenge, de Givet, 27th March, 7th April, 23rd and 29th May; report from Saint-Amant (a Belgian arrived from Ghent), Paris, 15th April and 29th May; report from a Belgian deserter, Mézières, 22nd April; report from a traveller, 4th June (War Arch.); reports from agents, 5th May and 3rd June (Arch. Foreign Affairs, 1802); Müffling, *Aus meinem Leben*, 193. See Wellington to Feltre (*Despatches*, xii. 389): "The fact is that these gentlemen (Blücher and Wrède) have wretchedly governed the country which fell under their government."

Napoleon, (*Mém. pour servir à l'Histoire en 1815*, 52, 57, and Gourgaud *Camp. de 1815*, 20) counted on a rising of the Belgians. His hopes, it is true, were never realised. But it must be noted that if the Emperor had occupied Brussels in the beginning of April, the policy of the French party in Belgium would have been quite different.

4. Letters from Kleist to the King of Prussia, Aix, 19th and 24th March, to Pirch, 25th March (quoted by von Ollech, 5, 6, 7).

5. Napoleon (*Mém. pour servir à l'Histoire*, 52) says 35,000 men, and Clausewitz (*Der Feldzug von 1815*, 16, 17) admits the possibility of a victory of these 35,000 Frenchmen over the Anglo-Prussian army. But the Emperor, if he had decided on weakening his garrisons in the fortresses of the North as he said, and then marching up the Paris reserve, and one-third of the troops of the 2nd division, could have formed an army of 50,000 men. According to Davout's report of the 28th March (Nat. Arch. AF. iv. 1936) at that date there were 27,949 soldiers in the 16th military division (Lille) and 10,000 in Paris. If to these 38,000 men are added, 4,000 men from the 2nd military division (Mézières) which numbered 12,340 men, the corps of Reille 15,865 men strong on 24th March (Davout to Reille, 24th March, War Arch.), and 7,390 men from the Guard (estimate of 21st March, Nat. Arch. AF. iv. 1940), a total amount is obtained of 65,204 or 50,000 men, deducting

the "incapables" from the 16th military division, from the Paris reserve, and from the Guard.

6. Kleist to the King of Prussia, Aix, 24th March and Müffling to the King of the Netherlands, Brussels, 29th March (quoted by von Ollech, 6 and 8). In point of fact the Prince of Orange had thought of giving battle between Nivelles and Braine-le-Comte on the 31st March, with the co-operation of the Prussian army (Röder to Müffling, Ath, 31st March, quoted by von Ollech, 9). But as the Prussians could not have arrived in time it is certain that the 30,000 English and Belgians, who were not yet concentrated at Ath on the 5th April, would have retired beyond Brussels without fighting.

7. Müffling to the King of the Netherlands, 30th March (quoted by von Ollech, 8); Wellington to Gneisenau in Brussels, 5th April (*Despatches*, xii. 288).

8. Napoleon, *Mém. pour servir à l'Histoire*, 52, 53. In the correspondence of Napoleon, there is no trace of any preparations for a sudden invasion of Belgium. These words of Davout, in a letter to Lobau, dated 3rd April : ". . . the possibility of the campaign beginning suddenly," can only be interpreted in the sense of a defensive campaign, in case of an attack on the part of the Allies. The proof is that Davout writes on the 9th April to Erlon : "The Emperor is only preparing for defence."

9. Clausewitz (16, 17) says "it would have been nothing but a shot in the air, without any influence on the final results of the campaign."

10. Napoleon, *Mém. pour servir à l'Histoire*, 52, 53. See Henry Houssaye, *1815*, i. 393-415.

11. Napoleon, *Mém pour servir à l'Histoire*, 52, 53. See *Corresp.* 21,756, 21,856 ; and Henry Houssaye, *1815*, i. 435-439.

12. Napoleon, *Corresp.* 21,856. See Caulaincourt to Napoleon, 25th March ; to Cardinal Fesch, 8th April (Archives of Foreign Aff. 672).

13. I say "nearly lost," for the third mission of Fleury de Chaboulon to Basle, on 29th May, was nothing but an attempt at peace (Henry Houssaye, *1815*, i. 592, note 2).

14. The correspondence of Napoleon, and that of Davout, testify that the Emperor did not decide upon his plan of campaign at the earliest before the middle of May. On the 9th May, Napoleon writes: "Vandamme ought to join the Army of the North, on the Sambre, where I shall probably be going myself, in order to act with great masses" (*Corresp.* 21,879). But "probably" suggests a doubt, and in another letter of the same day we read these words : "I am waiting till the nature of the war we are to engage in, is more clearly defined" (*Corresp.* 21,882). On his side Davout, who is acquainted with Napoleon's scheme, writes to Gérard, on 9th May : "The character of the war we are to engage in is not yet defined clearly" (*Corresp. of Davout*, 1684). On the 10th May the marshal seems to think that it is the enemy who will take the offensive, for this is his message to Vandamme : "You must render it impracticable for Wellington to force his way through the opening at Chimay" (*Corresp.* 1692). Finally,

two letters of Napoleon, dated 13th and 22nd May (*Corresp.* 21,900, 21,955), reveal that he is still hesitating on the choice of his line of operations.

The orders given by Napoleon and Davout in March and April, and in the first days of May—concentration of the army corps on the frontiers of the north, east, and south-east, armament of the fortresses, state of defence in the Vosges and the Argonne, *têtes de pont* or fortified bridges to be established on the Sambre, instructions "to be ready for any emergency,"—do not imply the existence of an offensive plan. These preparations are purely expectant.

15. Memoranda Knesebeck, 18th and 24th April (*Suppl. Despatches of Wellington*, x. 174-178).

16. Schwarzenberg's memorandum, 28th April (*Suppl. Despatches of Wellington*, x. 179-181).

17. Memorandum sent from Vienna by Gneisenau (*Suppl. Despatches of Wellington*, x. 196, 197).

18. Wellington to Clancarty, Brussels, 10th April; Wellington's memorandum, 12th April (*Despatches of Wellington*, xii. 295 *sqq.* and 304 *sqq.*).

Blücher, while he had not the same sympathy for Louis XVIII., weighed the possible influence on the campaign of the civil war in the South. He wrote to his wife on the 16th April (*Blücher in Briefen*, 138): "The French will probably destroy each other, so I don't believe we shall have much to do."

19. Baron Gay's report on his return from Vienna; Paris, 28th May (Nat. Arch. AF. iv. 1938).

20. Protocol of the sitting of the Council of War on 19th April (quoted by von Ollech, 33, 34); Wrede to Wellington, Vienna, 20th April (*Suppl. Despatches of Wellington*, x. 109).

21. On the 2nd May, the Saxon regiments stationed at Liège mutinied on the announcement they were going to be incorporated into the Prussian army. The disbanded soldiers ran through the streets, crying: "Long live the King of Saxony! long live Napoleon!" They had many sanguinary brawls with the Prussians. When night fell, the rebels made an onset on the hotel where Blücher was staying. Had it not been for the arrival of a strong Prussian detachment, the old marshal would have been in considerable danger. The next day the Prussians quelled the insurrection. Four officers were shot on the charge of inciting the movement; 2,000 soldiers were disarmed; the whole Saxon contingent was sent back to Germany and replaced by Prussian troops which were marching on the Elbe and the Rhine. General de Borstell, who on the first day had not executed Blücher's orders satisfactorily, was replaced by General Pirch I. Blücher wrote to the King of Saxony: "I am determined to restore order, if I have to shoot down the whole of your army."

Hardinge to Wellington, Liège, 4th May; Blücher to the King of Saxony, 6th May (*Suppl. Despatches*, x. 219-221, 256); Blücher to his wife, Liège, undated (*Blücher in Briefen*, 140-142); report of La

Hauvrie, Inspector of Forests, Givet, 8th May (War Arch.); report from Brussels, undated (Arch. Foreign Aff., 1802); correspondence of Liège (*Moniteur*, 9th May); Wellington to Blücher, 7th May (*Despatches*, xii. 357).

22. Wellington to Schwarzenberg, Brussels, 2nd June (*Despatches*, xii. 437); Vandamme to Davout, Chimay, 7th June (War Arch.).

23. Memorandum of Schwarzenberg, 8th June; Schwarzenberg to Wellington, Heidelberg, 10th June; protocols of the Conferences at Heidelberg, 9th and 10th June (*Suppl. Despatches of Wellington*, x. 440-448). According to Schwarzenberg's plan, the different armies should have begun to move on 27th June. But in order to march in line with the Austrians and the Russians, who had a longer way to go before reaching the Paris radius, Wellington, with the assent of Blücher, had decided that the English and the Prussian armies should not cross the frontier before the 1st July (Letter from Müffling to Blücher, Brussels, 14th June, quoted by von Ollech, 68).

24. Estimate of 6th June, quoted by van Löben Sels (82, 83), according to the Military Archives of the Netherlands. This report of the situation, apparently the only authentic one existing, computes the men present under arms at 91,228. But, on the one hand, we must deduct 2,150 men from the brigade of the Hanoverian landwehr of Beaulieu, stationed at Antwerp; and, on the other hand, we must add the strength of twelve batteries of reserve, of engineers, of transport corps, of pontonniers, etc., which are merely noted, and which may be estimated (according to Siborne's indications) at 4,000 men at the lowest : the following total is thus attained, $91,200 - 2,151 = 89,049 + 4,000 = 93,049$.

There were, moreover, stationed in Antwerp, Ostend, Ghent, etc., four brigades of the Hanoverian landwehr and a few other troops which were not to be called to enter on the campaign. These garrison troops are estimated by Siborne (i. 426) at 9,000 men, by Colonel Chesney (52, 53) at 12,000.

25. Tables given by Plotho (*Der Krieg im Yahre 1815*, 35 *sqq.*), and by Damitz (*French Translation*, i. 354 *sqq.*). In the second and third lines, the Prussians had the Royal Guard, the corps of Kleist (ultimately of Hacke), the corps of Louis of Hesse-Homburg, of York and Tauënzien, and the Rhine landwehr, which was not yet organised; altogether 124,000 men, of which 70,000 only (the Guard and the corps of Kleist and York) were successively to enter France.

26. Plotho, and Damitz, who copies him, estimate the Russian Army at 167,950 men, in addition to the battalions and the squadrons, which they compute, the first at 800 muskets, the second at 150 sabres. Now supposing, improbable as it may seem, that not a single man were missing in the corps at the time of their departure, it is impossible to believe this would still be the case when they reached the banks of the Rhine. From the confines of Poland to the French frontier, the Russians must have left about one-tenth of their effective strength on the way, at halting places and small depôts, to say nothing of the sick, the footsore

and deserters. Moreover, the 7th Corps (twenty-two infantry regiments) and the 2nd and 3rd Corps of the Reserve Cavalry (sixteen regiments) were ten marches behind. On the 8th July, they had scarcely reached the Sarre (see *Damitz*, ii. 182). According to two reports from Vienna, one dated the beginning of April (War Arch.), the other dated 28th May (Nat. Arch. AF. iv. 1938), Russia was to bring to the field only an army of 120,000 men or even of 80,000 men.

27. According to official reports quoted by Plotho (63 *sqq.*), the Army of the Upper Rhine amounted to 254,542 men. But, trusting to information given by Plotho himself, from this number must be deducted: first, 6,000 Bavarians left in the garrisons of Mayence, of Germersheim and Mannheim; second, about 15,000 men of Baden who were not to join the army till later on. It is further necessary to deduct the Saxon corps (computed by Plotho at 16,700 men) which had been sent back to Germany after the revolt at Liège, and would not have been allowed by the Allies to re-enter France on account of their French sympathies.

28. Plotho (74 *sqq.*) rates the Austrian army stationed in Upper Italy in 1815 at 48,000 men; but of these 48,000 men, Frimont leaves 10,000 in garrisons in Lombardy.

29. Plotho, *Der Krieg im Yarhe 1815*, 75.

30. Memorandum of Schwarzenberg, 6th June (*Suppl. Despatches*, xii. 440). This army, which had fought against Murat (Henry Houssaye, *1815*, i. 465-467), was reduced from about 40,000 men to 25,000 owing to losses of men killed, others left in the garrisons of Naples and the Duchies.

31. Undated reports from Vienna (previous to 8th April); from Bresson de Valensole, return to Vienna, 15th April; report from the spy Gottlieb, 3rd June; "Gendarmerie" report from Givet, 4th June, etc. etc. (War Arch.); reports from Dresden, 1st and 3rd June (Nat. Arch. AF. iv. 1936); reports from Vienna and from Brussels (undated), about 1st May, 1st and 3rd June (Arch. of Foreign Aff., 1802); *Gazette de Bade*, 27th May; *Journal de Francfort*, 22nd May.

32. In my description of these plans of campaign, I only follow the exact text of Napoleon himself (*Mém. pour servir à l'Histoire en 1815*, 51-61), although I have corrected certain estimates, with regard to dates, in accordance with documents in the archives.

33. This computation, like most of the estimates quoted in this paragraph, is necessarily only an approximate one, since the partition of troops alluded to, fits in with a plan that had not been adopted. These are the figures, the *exact* figures, which are my authority. It must be remembered (see pp. 20 and 21) that by the middle of June 135,000 mobilised National Guards had joined the armies at the frontier strongholds, and at the depôts, and that 15,000 had been sent on their road to join the points of concentration. Now, I admit that, on 1st July, two-thirds of these 150,000 National Guards had already occupied the strongholds; the last third remaining in the depôt centres of the interior, and with the armies of the Rhine, the Alps, and the Pyrenees. To these

100,000 mobilised men, I add two-thirds from the total number of pensioned soldiers, of gunners of the line, of veteran and stationary gunners, of custom-house officers, of veteran fusiliers, etc. (see p. 21), with an addition of 2,000 or 3,000 gendarmes, and 8,000 or 10,000 National Guards from the towns.

34. Napoleon goes so far as to say that the Allies could not reach Paris before the 1st August, and he did not exaggerate. No doubt after Waterloo the Prussians and the English marched to Paris from the Belgian frontier in nine days only; but, had it not been for the fact that they were advancing, so to speak, in a conquered country,—"victory giving them wings," says Grolemann,—they certainly could not have marched at the rate of 25 kilometres a day. Besides, they were bound to regulate their speed by that of the Austrians and the Russians. It was therefore the march of the Anglo-Russians which furnishes us data for computing the numbers. Now, though the Russian and Austrian armies crossed the frontier on the 23rd of June, as soon as the news reached them of the victory of Waterloo, "which electrified them," says Müffling, "up to that time, they had not stirred." On the 10th of July their vanguard had gone no further than Châlons, 43 miles from Paris. If, then, the Austrian-Russians had not crossed the frontier before the 27th of June, as they should have done according to the original plans, they could not have reached Châlons before the 14th of July. Allowing them to proceed, from that time, at the rate of 15 kilometres a day, they could not have been concentrated under Paris before the 25th or 26th of July.

35. We have seen (p. 21) that on the 15th of June, independently of the armies of operation, there were 13,900 soldiers on their way to join these armies; 65,000 at the depôts, 8,000 in the hospitals, 19,000 re-enlisted men who had received marching orders, and 46,500 conscripts of 1815 (one half of whom had taken part in the campaign of 1814) assembled in the depôt-centres of the departments; in all 152,400 men.

We must therefore admit that in six weeks' time Napoleon had been able to find in that mass of 152,400 soldiers, at least 80,000 men, 30,000 of which would form the garrison of Paris, and 50,000 reinforce the army concentrated around that city. As this army was composed of the Army of the North and the Army of the Rhine, amounting together to a total strength of 147,000 men (see p. 20), it would thus have been raised to 200,000 combatants.

36. 72,000 soldiers out of the 152,400 mentioned above, and one-third of the 25,000 pensioners, that is to say, 80,000 men or thereabouts.

37. 74,000 soldiers completing the contingent of 1815, and 84,000 men completing the levy of mobilised National Guards (see p. 21).

38. *Mém. pour servir à l'Histoire*, 55. General Berthaut (*Principes de stratégie*, 26) estimates this number at 180,000. Foreign documents inform us, in fact, that the plan of the Allies was to keep nearly all the fortresses under observation, and to invest a sufficient number of them to ensure for themselves a solid basis, *eine solide basis*. See Memorandum

of Wellington, Brussels, 12th April, and Heidelberg, 6th June; Letter of the same to Stewart, 8th May (*Despatches*, xii. 359-362, and *Suppl.* x. 440); Grolemann to Schwarzenberg, Liège, 20th May (quoted by von Olech, *Geschichte des Felzuges von, 1815*, 50).

39. During the campaign of France, Napoleon never had more than 90,000 men operating between the Aisne, the Marne, and the Aube, under his direct command or the command of his lieutenants Macdonald, Oudinot, Mortier, and Marmont. At Brienne the Emperor had 60,000 men; at Champaubert, at Montmirail, and at Vauchamps, 24,000; at Montereau, 40,000; at Craonne, 25,000; at Laon, 38,000; at Arcis sur Aube, 17,000 the first day and 28,000 the second. See Henry Houssaye, *1814*, *passim*.

40. Napoleon, *Mém.* 56, 57; Clausewitz (*Der Feldzug von 1815*, 19), and Jomini (*Précis de la Camp. de 1815*, 141) are of opinion that, from a military point of view, the defensive plan was preferable. Davout, on the contrary, thought that it was not possible to adopt any but the offensive plan. MSS. Memoirs, furnished by General the Duke d'Auerstaedt.

41. Gourgaud, *Camp. de 1815*, 30; Napoleon, *Mém.* 58.

42. Napoleon, *Mém.* 57, 58.

43. Napoleon, *Mém.* 60; Souvenirs in manuscript of Davout, quoted above.

44. Napoleon, *Mém.* 60.

45. Napoleon, *Mém.* 59. See p. 51, and note 14.

46. There are traces of this hesitation in the Correspondence, 13th May, to Davout (21,900): "How wide is the Scheldt in the neighbourhood of Mons? the Sambre by Charleroi? the Meuse by Maestricht? and how many pontoons would it require to throw a bridge across each one of these rivers?" 22nd May, to Soult (22,955): "If I took the offensive on the left. . . ."

47. Napoleon, *Corresp.* 22,004, 22,005, 22,006, 22,022. Napoleon's order, 10th June; Soult's orders and letters, 5th and 6th June (War Arch., Army of the North); Soult's report to Napoleon, Avèsnes, 12th June (Nat. Arch. AF. iv. 1938).

48. Order of the Emperor, 10th June; La Poype to Davout, Lille, 2nd June; Davout's orders, 5th and 10th June; Soult to Rouyer, 5th June; Frère to Davout, Lille, 8th June; Vandamme to Davout, 10th June (War Arch., Army of the North).

49. Grouchy, *Relation succincte*, 10, 11; Declaration of Colonel de Blocqueville; General Bonnemains' Journal (War Arch., Army of the North).

50. Order from Soult, Avèsnes, 12th June: "The Emperor commands that you should set your four corps marching on Avèsnes. . . . Your move must be completed by the 13th" (War Arch.).

51. Bonnemains' Journal; Declaration of Blocqueville; Grouchy, *Relation succincte*, 10. Bonnemains says that many horses were wounded in their withers and that all were worn out.

52. Journal des sejours de l'Empereur (Nat. Arch. AF. iv. 437).

53. Napoleon, *Corresp.* 22,049 ; Grouchy to Soult and to Kellermann, Bossus, 14th June (War Arch.).

54. Order to the Army, Avèsnes, 14th June (*Corresp.* 22,052). This proclamation was read to the troops at reveille. Order from Erlon, 14th June (War Arch.).

55. 1ST CORPS : DROUET D'ERLON—

1st Infantry Division : Allix ; Brigades—Quiot and Bourgeois ; 54th, 55th, 28th, and 105th of line.

(Allix being unable to rejoin his corps in time, the 1st Infantry Division was commanded by Quiot.)

2nd Infantry Division : Donzelot ; Brigades—Schmitz and Aulard ; 13th, 17th, 19th, and 51st Light Infantry.

3rd Infantry Division : Marcognet ; Brigades—Noguez and Grenier ; 21st, 46th, 25th, and 45th of line.

4th Infantry Division : Durutte ; Brigades—Perot and Brue ; 8th, 29th, 85th, and 95th of line.

1st Cavalry Division : Jacquinot ; Brigades—Bruno and Gobrecht ; 7th Hussars, 3rd Chasseurs, 3rd and 4th Lancers.

Artillery : de Salles ; six batteries, train.

Engineers : Garbé ; five companies.

(Estimate of the 1st Corps on 10th June, War Arch., Portfolio of the Estimates.)

56. 2ND CORPS : REILLE—

5th Infantry Division : Bachelu ; Brigades—Husson and Campy ; 2nd Light Troops, 61st, 72nd, and 108th of line.

6th Infantry Division : Prince Jérôme Bonaparte ; Brigades—Bauduin and Soye ; 1st Light Troops, 3rd, 1st, and 2nd of line.

7th Infantry Division : Girard ; Brigades—Devilliers and Piat ; 11th Light Troops, 82nd of line, 12th Light Troops, and 4th of line.

8th Infantry Division : Foy ; Brigades—Gauthier and B. Jamin ; 92nd, 93rd, 100th of line, and 4th Light Troops.

2nd Cavalry Division : Piré ; Brigades—Hubert and Vathiez ; 1st and 6th Chasseurs, 5th and 6th Lancers.

Artillery : Pelletier ; six batteries, train.

Engineers : de Richemont ; five companies.

(Estimate of the 2nd Corps on 10th June, War Arch.)

57. 3RD CORPS : VANDAMME—

9th Infantry Division : Lefol ; Brigades—Billard and Corsin ; 15th Light Troops, 23rd, 37th, and 64th of line.

10th Infantry Division : Habert ; Brigades—Gengoux and Dupeyroux ; 88th, 22nd, and 70th of line, 2nd foreign regiment (Swiss).

11th Infantry Division : Berthezène ; Brigades—Dufour and Lagarde ; 12th, 56th, 33rd, and 86th of line.

3rd Cavalry Division : Domon ; Brigades—Dommanget and Vinot ; 4th, 9th, and 12th Chasseurs.

Artillery : Doguereau ; five batteries, train.

Engineers : Nempde ; three companies.

(Estimate of the 3rd Corps on 10th June, War Arch.)

58. 6TH CORPS: MOUTON, COUNT OF LOBAU—
19th Infantry Division: Simmer; Brigades—Bellair and M. Jamin; 5th, 11th, 27th, and 84th of line.
20th Infantry Division: Jannin; Brigades—Bony and Tromelin; 5th Light Troops, 10th, 47th, and 107th of line.
21st Infantry Division: Teste; Brigades—Laffite and Penne; 8th Light Troops, 40th, 65th, and 75th of line.
Artillery: Noury; four batteries, train.
Engineers: Sabatier; three companies.
(Estimate of the 6th Corps on 10th June, War Arch.).

59. 4TH CORPS: GÉRARD—
12th Infantry Division: Pécheux; Brigades—Romme and Schoeffer; 30th, 96th, 63rd of line, and 6th Light Troops.
13th Infantry Division: Vichery; Brigades—Le Capitaine and Desprez; 59th, 76th, 48th, and 60th of line.
14th Division of Infantry: de Bourmont; Brigades—Hulot and Toussaint; 9th Light, 111th, 44th, and 50th of the line.
7th Cavalry Division: Maurin; Brigades—Vallin and Berruyer; 6th Hussars, 7th and 8th Chasseurs.
Artillery: Baltus; five batteries, train.
Engineers: Valazé; four companies.
(Estimate of the 4th Corps on 13th May and 1st June, War Arch.). From Davout's report, 23rd June, on the strength of the armies in the field (Nat. Arch. AF. iv. 1936), the 4th Corps must have been 17,303 men strong. This is not impossible, for between the 1st and the 15th of June, that corps had been reinforced. However, Gérard says (*Quelques Observations*, 45) that his infantry did not amount to 13,000 men.

60. CAVALRY RESERVE: GROUCHY—
1ST CAVALRY CORPS: PAJOL—
4th Division: Soult; Brigades—Saint-Laurent and Ameil; 1st, 4th, and 5th Hussars, one mounted battery, train.
5th Division: Subervie; Brigades—Alphonse de Colbert and Merlin; 1st and 2nd Lancers and 11th Chasseurs, one mounted battery, train.
2ND CAVALRY CORPS: EXELMANS—
9th Division: Strolz; Brigades—Burthe and Vincent; 5th, 13th, 15th, and 20th Dragoons, 8th and 11th Cuirassiers, one mounted battery, train.
10th Division: Chastel; Brigades—Bonnemains and Berton; 4th, 12th, 14th, and 17th Dragoons; one mounted battery, train.
3RD CAVALRY CORPS: KELLERMANN, COMTE DE VALMY—
11th Division: Lhéritier; Brigades—Picquet and Guiton; 2nd and 7th Dragoons, 8th and 11th Cuirassiers, one mounted battery, train.
12th Division: Roussel d'Hurbal; Brigades—Blancard and Donop; 1st and 2nd Carabiniers, 2nd and 3rd Cuirassiers, one mounted battery, train.
4TH CAVALRY CORPS: MILHAUD—
13th Division: Wathier de St. Alphonse; Brigades—Dubois and Travers; 1st, 4th, 7th, and 12th Cuirassiers, one mounted battery, train.

14th Division : Delort ; Brigades—Farine and Vial ; 5th, 10th, 6th, and 9th Cuirassiers, one mounted battery, train.

(Estimate of the corps on 1st and 15th June ; general estimate of the cavalry on 1st June, furnished by General Preval, War Arch.).

61. IMPERIAL GUARD—

Old Guard on foot ; 1st, 2nd, 3rd, and 4th Grenadiers ; first colonel, Friant ; second colonel, Roguet ; generals in command of the regiments, Petit, Christiani, Porret de Morvan, Harlet.

1st, 2nd, 3rd, 4th Chasseurs ; first colonel, Morand ; second colonel, Michel ; generals in command of the regiments, Cambronne, Pelet, Mallet, Hanrion.

(3rd and 4th Grenadiers, and 3rd and 4th Chasseurs recently formed, were in common parlance called the Middle Guard, even though they officially belonged to the Old Guard.)

Young Guard, 1st and 3rd Voltigeurs, 1st and 3rd Skirmishers Senior commandants, Duhesme and Barrois ; junior commandants, Guy and Chartran.

Light Cavalry : Lefebvre-Desnoëttes ; Chevau-légers-lancers : Edouard de Colbert ; Mounted Chasseurs : F. Lallemand.

Reserve Cavalry : Guyot ; Mounted Grenadiers : Dubois ; Dragoons : Ornano (left in Paris, wounded in a duel) ; élite gendarmes : d'Autancourt.

Artillery of the Old Guard, Auxiliary Artillery (Young Guard), train, Sappers, Marines of the Guard : Desvaux de Saint-Maurice, Artillery on foot, thirteen batteries : Dominique Lallemand ; Mounted Artillery, three batteries : Colonel Duchand.

(Estimate of the Guard, 16th June, signed d'Hériot, sub-aid-major of the Guard, War Arch.).

62. For positions : order of the day, Avèsnes, 13th June (Napoleon, *Corresp.* 22,049). Hulot's report, Soult's orders, Beaumont, 14th June ; Grouchy to Soult, to Pajol, to Kellermann, to Milhaud, Bossus, 14th and 15th June ; Reille to Soult, Solre-sur-Sambre, 14th June ; order of General Delcambre, Chief of the Staff of the 1st Corps, Avèsnes, 14th June, War Arch., Army of the North.

63. Neigre's report, 2nd June (War Arch.), Ruty's report, 13th June (Nat. Arch. AF. iv. 1938). The artillery included 35 unmounted batteries of 8 (batteries of divisions) and 12 (reserve batteries), all of them with 8 pieces, and 15 with 6 pieces.

64. 1ST CORPS : ZIETEN—

Infantry Divisions : Steinmetz, Pirch II., Jagow, and Henneckel ; Reserve Cavalry Röder : Treskow and Lützow Brigades.

12 batteries.

The Prussians called infantry brigades, the aggregation of three regiments composed each of three battalions of 730 men. In order to avoid misleading the reader, I apply the name of divisions to those brigades whose effective strength were equal and often superior to those of the French divisions.

65. 2ND CORPS : PIRCH I.—

Infantry Divisions : Tippelskirch, Krafft, Brause, and Langen.

Reserve of Cavalry: Jürgass; Thuemen, Schulenburg, and Sohr Brigades.
10 batteries.

66. 3RD CORPS: THIELMANN—
Infantry Divisions: Borcke, Kemphen, Lück, and Stülpnagel.
Reserve Cavalry: Hobe; Marwitz and Lottum Brigades.
6 batteries.

67. 4TH CORPS: BÜLOW—
Infantry Division: Hacke, Ryssel, Losthin, and Hiller.
Reserve Cavalry: Prince William of Prussia; Schwerin, Watzdorf, and Sidow.
11 batteries.

68. Plotho. Annexes viii. and xi. For the positions, Damitz, i. 35, 36, 353-364; von Ollech, 62.

69. 2ND CORPS: LORD HILL—
Clinton Division: Adam Brigade (English); Duplat Brigade (German Legion); William Halkett Brigade (Hanoverian).
Colville Division: Mitchell Brigade (English); Johnstone Brigade (English); Lyon Brigade (Hanoverian).
Estorff Brigade of Cavalry (Hanoverian).
Corps of Prince Frederick of the Netherlands; Steedmann Division (Hollando-Belgian); Anthing Brigade, surnamed Indian Brigade (Dutch).
4 batteries.

70. 1ST CORPS: PRINCE OF ORANGE—
Cooke Division: Maitland and Byng Brigades (English Guards).
Alten Division: Colin Halkett Brigade (English); Ompteda Brigade (German Legion); Kielmansegge Brigade (Hanoverian).
Perponcher Division: Bylandt Brigade (Hollando-Belgian); Prince of Saxe-Weimar Brigade (Nassau).
Chassé Division: Detmers and d'Aubremé Brigades (Hollando-Belgian).
Cavalry Division: Collaert (Dutch); Trip Brigade (Carabiniers); Ghigny and van Merlen Brigades (Hussars and Light Dragoons).
9 batteries.

71. CAVALRY CORPS: LORD UXBRIDGE—
Somerset Brigade (Life-Guards, Horse-Guards, and Dragoons of the Guard); Ponsonby Brigade (Royal Dragoons, Scots Greys, and Enniskillen Dragoons); Dornberg Brigade (Light English Dragoons and German Legion); Vandeleur Brigade (English Dragoons); Grant Brigade (English Hussars and German Legion); Vivian Brigade (English Hussars and German Legion); Arenschild Brigade (German Legion).

72. RESERVE: LORD WELLINGTON—
Picton Division: Kempt and Pack Brigades (English); Wincke Brigade (Hanoverian).
1 battery.
Cole Division: Lambert Brigade (English), and Best (Hanoverian).
1 battery.

The Duke of Brunswick corps: eight battalions, five squadrons, two batteries. Kruse Brigade (Nassau).

Reserve Artillery: 12 batteries.

Estimates of 6th June (quoted by van Löben, 82, 84, 86, after the military archives of the Netherlands). See p. 53.

There were in addition to these, as already stated (*ibid.*), 10,000 or 12,000 men of the Hanoverian garrison at Furnes, Ostend, Antwerp, Nieuport, etc. But in the hypothesis of either the Allies or Napoleon taking the offensive in the valley of the Sambre, these troops were not to take an active part in the hostilities.

For positions: Wellington to the Prince of Orange and to Lord Uxbridge, Brussels, 30th April (*Despatches*, xii. 337, 338); Siborne, *History of the War in 1815*, i. 25, 26, van Löben, 98-100.

73. Clausewitz (*Der Felzug von 1815*, 29) says that the armies could not be concentrated on their point of union in less than four or five days. This is a slight exaggeration, disproved by facts. Had not the battle of Ligny been fought, the concentration, which commenced on the 14th for the Prussians, and in the night of the 15th to the 16th for the English, would have been completed at noon on the 17th, between Sombreffe and Quatre-bras.

74. Wellington, Reply to Clausewitz (*Despatches*, xii. 523).

75. Wellington to the Czar, Brussels, 15th June (*Despatches*, xii. 470 sq.). See letter from the same to Lord Lyndoch, 13th June (*ibid.* 462): "Our strength is such that we cannot be attacked here."

76. Blücher to his wife, Namur, 3rd June (*Blücher in Briefen*, 143).

BOOK I CHAPTER III

1. Reille to Soult, Gosselies, 15th June, 9 o'clock P.M. Pajol's notes on the day's engagements, 15th June (War Arch., Army of the North).

2. Order of movement for the 15th, Beaumont, 14th June (Napoleon, *Corresp.* 22,053); Soult to Vandamme, to Grouchy, and to Gérard, Beaumont, 14th June (Register of the Chief of the Staff, *Bibliothèque Nationale*, M. Ms. F. Fr. 4366).

3. Order of movement for the 15th of June, Beaumont, 14th June (Napoleon, *Corresp.* 22,053).

4. Order from the head of the staff of the 1st Corps, Avèsnes, 14th June (War. Arch.).

5. Lobau to Soult, Jamignon (Jamioulx), 15th June, 8 P.M.; Janin, *Camp. de Waterloo*, 6, 7. The Adjutant-Commandant Janin, was deputy-chief of the staff at Lobau.

6. Hulot's report (communicated by Baron Hulot).

7. Hulot's report (communicated by Baron Hulot).

8. Hulot's report. See Mauduit, *Les Derniers Jours de la Grande Armée*, ii. 33; and *La Relation de l'Ambigu of London*, lii. 422;

Bourmont's treachery inspired the soldiers with the fear of foul play elsewhere, and predisposed them to be easily depressed by checks and hardships.

9. Hulot's report. See Clouet, *Quelques mots sur la conduite du Comte de Bourmont*, 11-22.

On the evening of the 14th Bourmont had been to supper with General Hulot, without in any way leading him to suspect his determination, says Hulot; Clouet says on the contrary that it was announced then and there. Hulot's testimony to us seems the most reliable.

10. Bourmont to Gérard, Florenne, 11th June, in the morning (War Arch., Bourmont's documents and papers); Bourmont's letter, remarks Hulot, was accompanied by another letter of Clouet to Gérard, also to be found among Bourmont's documents and papers.

In this letter he vainly attempts to vindicate his conduct. It is proved only too well (see p. 24) that, far from urging him to accept a command, the Emperor had employed him, merely at the repeated entreaties of Ney and Gérard.

Apparently, if these two generals insisted so strongly, they had only done so at the request of Bourmont himself. The letter to Gérard proves but one fact; premeditation on the part of Bourmont—premeditation which is certainly confirmed by this fact, quoted further, that Bourmont had the white cockade on his hat as soon as he stepped on the enemy's ground. It is difficult to believe that he found that cockade on the road. See concerning the disgraceful conduct of Bourmont, *Les Cent Jours en Belgique*, by an *émigré* (*Bibliothèque universelle de Genève*, July-Aug., 1857).

11. Von Ollech, *Geschichte des Feldzuges von 1815*, 100.

12. Zieten's report, on the height near Gilly, half-past one (quoted by von Ollech, 101). See von Ollech, 100, and Hooper (*Waterloo*, 68) relating, on the testimony of Sir Francis Head, who was present at the meeting of the Zieten's staff on 15th June, that Bourmont gave up the order of movement for the day, saying, "He had carried out his cherished intention of betraying Napoleon."

Not content with having *spoken* in the evening, Bourmont *wrote* from Namur to the Duke de Feltre, as if he were anxious to leave some evidence of his treachery: "Having started from Florenne this morning, I left the 4th Corps under the orders of General Gérard at Philippeville. To-day he has no doubt marched on Charleroi. The rest of the army, that is to say, three corps and the guard, were massed towards Beaumont. It is likely that the English or the Prussians will be attacked to-morrow" (Catalogue of autographs of Benjamin Fillon, No. 2840).

13. *Einerlei was das Volk für ein Zeichen ansteckt! Hundsfott bleibt Hundsfott!* Siborne, i. 56. See von Ollech, 101, who says that Blücher let Bourmont pass without asking him any question.

14. Order of Zieten, Charleroi, 9th June, and letters from Dörnberg, Zieten, Hardinge, Pirch II., and Steinmetz, 9th, 12th, 13th, and 14th June (von Ollech, 87, 88, *Suppl. Despatches of Wellington*, x. 436, 437, 454, 455, 476).

15. See p. 59.
16. Wellington to the Prince of Orange, Brussels, 2nd May (in the morning and at 9 P.M.); to Hardinge, Brussels, 5th May (*Despatches*, xii. 345, 349); Müffling, *Aus meinem Leben*, 183.
17. See Müffling, *Aus meinem Leben*, 200, 201; Siborne, *History of the War in 1815*, i. 39; Damitz, *Hist. de la Camp. de 1815* (French translation), i. 32; van Löben, *Précis de la Campagne de 1815* (translation from the Dutch), 96; Chesney, *Conférences sur Waterloo* (translation from the English), 119; von Ollech, *Geschichte des Feldzuges von 1815*, 45; Ropes, *The Campaign of Waterloo*, 71, 91, 92.

No contemporary document, except perhaps Müffling's work—which is not remarkably clear on the point—gives a detailed and specified account of the decisions taken at Tirlemont. It is very likely, as Ropes judiciously remarks, that the plan for concentration, which Müffling describes as settled between Wellington and Blücher, was conceived after the event, by Müffling himself; besides, in case of an attack towards Charleroi, the positions of the armies and the nature of the ground rendered the choice of the plan unavoidable. But Ropes goes too far in saying that offensive plans alone were discussed at Tirlemont. Wellington's letters of the 30th of April to the Prince of Orange, testify that, at that time, the Duke thought then of protecting himself against any attack, and as Müffling says (*Aus meinem Leben*, 190), he desired the Prussian army to come and prolong his left in case of need. Such was the object of the Tirlemont interview. Blücher's orders of the 5th of May, in pursuance of which the Prussians began to assemble on their right, show that defensive measures had been agreed on by the two generals on the 3rd of May. "My interview with Blücher was most satisfactory." Wellington wrote on the 4th of May to the Prince of Orange (*Despatches*, xii. 345).

18. Orders of Blücher, Liège, 5th May (quoted by von Ollech, 45, 46); Hardinge to Wellington, 5th May (*Suppl. Despatches*, x. 239). Blücher came to Namur between the 10th and 15th of May.
19. Orders of Blücher to Zieten, Liège, 5th May (quoted by von Ollech, *Geschichte des Feldzuges von 1815*, 45).
20. Wellington to the Prince of Orange, Brussels, 9th and 12th May (*Despatches*, xii. 365, 367); Prince of Orange to Wellington, Braine-le-Comte, 10th and 12th May (*Suppl. Despatches*, x. 271, 281).
21. Orders of Blücher and of Gneisenau, Namur, 14th June; Blücher to Müffling, Namur, 15th June, 9 A.M. (quoted by von Ollech, 90, 91, 96).
22. Reille to Soult, Gosselies, 15th June, 9 P.M.; Notes of Pajol, 15th June (War Arch.); Damitz, i. 62, 63; Wagner, iv. 11, 12.
23. Reille to Soult, Gosselies, 11th June, 9 P.M., Reille's Report, d'Erlon to Soult, Marchienne, 15th June, 4.30 P.M.; Notes of Pajol (War Arch.); Damitz, i. 64; Wagner, iv. 12.
24. Notes of Pajol on the engagements of 15th June (War Arch.); Gourgaud, 44; Napoleon, *Mém.* 79; Damitz, i. 63-16; Journal manuscript of Gourgaud (Papers of General G.).
25. The Notes of Pajol and the *Bulletin de l'armée* (*Moniteur*, 18th

June) both agree as to the time when Pajol, closely followed by the Emperor, passed through Charleroi, mid-day; German documents say half-past eleven.

26. Napoleon, *Corresp.* 22,055; account of the *Ambigu*, London, lii. 422. Local traditions: At Charleroi the Prussians had made themselves odious.

27. Merode, Westerloo, *Mém.* i. 348; Notes in manuscript of Colonel Baudus (commented by M. de Montenon). Local traditions. The "Belle-Vue" was pulled down about fifteen years ago. It was situated on the left of the road, about 150 metres south from the spot where the viaduct of the "Grand-Central-Belge" now stands.

28. Notes above quoted of Colonel Baudus. Baudus was then commandant attached to Soult's staff.

29. Henry Houssaye, *1815*, i. 614.

30. Manuscript journal of Gourgaud; Notes of Pajol (War Arch.); Soult to d'Erlon in front of Charleroi, 15th June, three o'clock (Major-General's Ledger); see Napoleon, *Mém.* 80, 81; Gourgaud, *Camp. de 1815*, 45, 46.

31. Numerous controversies have arisen concerning this very important question—At what time did Ney join the Emperor? Heymés (*Relation*, 6) says, seven oclock; Pajol (Notes on the events of the 15th of June, Military Arch.) says, mid-day; Gamot (rectifying letter, *Annales Militaires*, October, 1818) says, in the afternoon. All historians say, between 4 and 5 P.M.

From the general agreement of the witnesses quoted hereafter, it is beyond doubt that the interview between Ney and the Emperor took place between three or a quarter past three at the latest.

1st. Gourgaud (manuscript journal) says that Ney assumed the command before the attack of Gosselies.

2nd. Gourgaud (*Camp. de 1815*, 46) says that Ney arrived at the moment when Reille was marching from Marchienne on Gosselies.

3rd. Reille (*Relation*, War Arch.) says that Ney took the command of the 2nd Corps when this army corps was marching on Gosselies.

4th. Ney himself (letter to the Duke of Otrante, 26th June, *Journal de l'Empire* of 29th June) says that he reached Charleroi just as the enemy was falling back on Gosselies, and that soon after he pursued them and compelled them to evacuate Gosselies.

But from the little inn of Belle-Vue, the point where Ney met the Emperor, to Gosselies, the distance is about 6 kilm.; and according to the testimony of German and Dutch authors (Damitz, 67; Reiche, ii. 416; von Ollech, 101; Treuenfeld, 103, 128; van Löben, 123. See Clausewitz, 30; Plotho, 30; Wagner, iv. 14, etc.) the French attacked Gosselies at four o'clock at the latest.

One word more to prove Heymés's want of truthfulness. According to him, Ney must have left Beaumont towards eleven o'clock. If, then, he did not reach Charleroi before seven, he must have taken eight hours to accomplish 26 kilm. Is this possible with a rider like Ney, mounted on a fresh horse to boot, and with the cannon thundering in his ears?

32. Letter of Ney to the Duke of Otrante, 26th June; Heymés (*Relation*, 6). As stated (see pp. 29, 30), Ney was not called to the army before the 11th of June, the Emperor having only decided at the very last moment to give him an appointment.

33. These are the very words of Heymés (*Relation*, 6, 7), with the exception of the last sentence relating to Quatre-Bras which Ney's aide-de-camp, in a pamphlet written solely to justify the Marshal, has of course "*forgotten*" to mention. But Gourgaud (*Camp. de 1815*, 46) and Napoleon himself (*Mém.* 81) positively affirm that Ney received the order to march on Quatre-Bras, on the 15th of June. Two decisive testimonies exist to confirm on this point, the dictated accounts of St. Helena.

1st. Grouchy (*Observations sur la Camp. de 1815*, Philadelphia edition 1818, p. 32) says that the Emperor, in his presence, censured the conduct of Ney, who had stopped the movements of the troops, instead of executing his orders to march on Quatre-Bras.

2nd. The army Bulletin, dictated at Charleroi on the evening of the 15th (*Moniteur*, 18th June), states that: "The Emperor gave the command of the left wing to the Prince of Moscow who had that evening his headquarters at les Quatre-chemins (Quatre-Bras) on the road to Brussels."

This last document is conclusive and closes the discussion.

34. Grouchy says positively and repeatedly (*Relation succincte*, 12, and Appendix, iv. 32 and vii. 12: aide-de-camp Bella's declaration and notes on Jomini's letters) that Napoleon gave him not only verbal, but written orders, to pursue the enemy beyond Fleurus and Sombreffe, and even to advance to Gembloux. This assertion is confirmed by Grouchy's letter to Napoleon, Fleurus, 16th June, 5 o'clock A.M. (War Arch.): "I am now gathering my troops to effect the movement you have ordered on Sombreffe."

Thus, in spite of Napoleon's declarations to the contrary, in the 15th of his *Notes on the Art of War*, of General Rogniat, his object certainly was to occupy Sombreffe on the eve of the 15th of June.

"Had we occupied Sombreffe," says the Emperor, in his note dictated at St. Helena, "this would have involved the failure of all my manœuvres, for the battle of Ligny would not have taken place." But, as I will prove further by the letters of the Emperor himself, the possibility of this battle was absolutely overlooked, in his calculations on the eve of the 15th and even on the morning of the 16th. Consequently he could not have wished to manœuvre, so as to bring about a concentration of the Prussians at that point, as he tried to prove at St. Helena.

35. Grouchy, *Observat. sur la Camp. de 1815*, 61. See *Relation succincte*, 11, where Grouchy says that the dragoons came up before Vandamme's corps, and the Bulletin of the Army (*Moniteur*, 18th June), where it is stated that Vandamme's corps came up at three o'clock.

36. Wagner, iv. 13; Damitz, i. 69, 70; von Ollech, 103.

37. Grouchy, *Relation succincte*, 11.

38. Grouchy, *Relation succincte*, 13, and Appendix, iv. 31; declaration of aide-de-camp Bella. Napoleon, at the same time that he gave Grouchy the command of the right wing, gave also Ney the command of the left.

But written orders confirming the appointments were not addressed to the two marshals, until the morning of the 16th. (Napoleon, *Corresp.* 22,058, 22,059; Soult to Ney and to Grouchy, Charleroi, 16th June; Register of orders of the Major-General.)

39. Grouchy, *Relation succincte*, 11, 12; *Observations*, 61; Notes of Pajol (War Arch.); see Gourgaud, 82, 83; Napoleon, *Mém.* 49.

40. Grouchy, *Relation succincte*, 11. See Notes on Pajol (War Arch.).

41. Gourgaud, 49; Napoleon, *Mém.* 83; manuscript journal of Gourgaud; Damitz, ii. 70, 71; Notes of Colonel Simon-Lorière on the battles of the 15th and 16th of June (War Arch.); Grouchy (*Relation succincte*, 11 and 12, and Appendix, iv. 31) will not acknowlege that he and Vandamme had wasted time. He contends that Vandamme attacked prematurely and without waiting for his orders. But it was the Emperor himself who ordered Vandamme to attack. Grouchy, being on the left, could not exactly know what was going on in the centre.

42. Letter of Kimann, chief of the squadrons of the Night Guard, 17th June (General Gourgaud's papers); manuscript journal of Gourgaud, Army Bulletin (*Moniteur*, 18th June); Gourgaud, *Campagne de 1815*, 49, 50; Napoleon, *Mém.* 83; Damitz, 71; Wagner, iv. 15.

43. Grouchy to Napoleon, Campinaire, 15th June, 10 o'clock P.M. See Exelmans to Soult, 16th June, and Pajol to Grouchy, Lambusart, 15th June, 10 o'clock P.M. (War Arch.).

44. Wagner, iv. 16.

45. Grouchy, *Relation succincte*, 12, 13, and Appendix, iv. 32; Bella's declaration; see Pajol to Grouchy, Lambusart, 15th June, 10 o'clock P.M. (War Arch.); manuscript journal of Gourgaud. Gourgaud relates that after a long and lively discussion, Vandamme consented to give a battalion. But too much time had been wasted; it was already pitch dark.

It must be noted that on the 15th of June, Vandamme did not yet know that he was under Grouchy's orders, the Emperor having neglected to inform him of the fact, Grouchy being merely *verbally* invested with the command of the right wing. See on this subject p. 68, and note 38.

46. Grouchy to Napoleon, Campinaire, 15th June, 10 o'clock P.M.; Pajol to Grouchy, Lambusart, 10 o'clock P.M. (War Arch., Army of the North).

47. See p. 65.

48. Reille's account (War Arch.); Damitz, i. 66, 67. See Zieten's report, 11th June, half-past one (quoted by von Ollech, 100), and Soult to d'Erlon, Charleroi, 11th June (Ledger of Major-General).

As stated (p. 66), Gourgaud had carried to Reille the order to march on Gosselies from Marchienne. When Reille received this order, he had already started for Jumet on his own initiative.

49. Reille's account (War Arch.). "The divisions were marching on to the wood of Lombuc and Gosselies," says Reille. "It was at that moment that Marshal Ney came to assume the command." Nothing could be more definite. See manuscript journal of Gourgaud (General Gourgaud's papers).

50. Reille's account; manuscript journal of Gourgaud. See Wagner, iv. 14; Plotho, 30; Clausewitz, 30; Damitz, 68; Hoffmann, 28; Reiche, Reply to Hoffmann; von Ollech, 101. According to Plotho and Hoffmann, Steinmetz had recaptured and entirely reoccupied Gosselies. But Clausewitz and Reiche say that his division cut its way through with their bayonets and went on retreating. Steinmetz himself, in his official report (quoted in the *Militär Wochenblatt*, 1847), says: "I reached Gosselies and continued the retreat as far as Heppignies." There is no question here of the reoccupation of Gosselies.

Steinmetz was scarcely pursued at all. Indeed, it was only at eight o'clock in the evening when, upon the order of the Emperor to send forces towards Fleurus, the Girard division marched on Wangenies, passing through Ransart, and had a fresh struggle with the Prussians; Reille to Soult, Gosselies, 15th June (War Arch.); see Damitz, 68; Girard to Reille, Wangenies, 15th June, 11 o'clock P.M. (General Gourgaud's papers).

51. Notes of de Stuers, chief of the Red Lancers squadrons (comm. by M. de Stuers). Reille's account (War Arch., see Reille to Soult, Gosselies, 15th June, 9 P.M.) states expressly that after the attack of Gosselies, the whole of the second corps rallied and took up their positions; three divisions surrounded Gosselies—two divisions, one of which was Piré's, at Mellet, and only the cavalry of the Guard was detached to the road to Brussels. Pages 2 and 8 of Heymés's *Relation* are a tissue of intentional errors.

It may be noted also that Ney, with complete disregard of the Emperor's orders not to employ the cavalry of the Guard, sent that very corps to the front, when he had Piré within reach.

52. The Prince of Orange (Report to the King of the Netherlands, Nivelles, 17th June, 2 o'clock A.M., General Gourgaud's papers) says that the attack of Frasnes commenced about five o'clock; Prince Bernard of Saxe-Weimar, in his report of 15th June, Quatre-Bras, 9 o'clock P.M. (quoted by van Löben, 134, 135), says, at half-past six. This discrepancy between the two statements, arises no doubt from the fact that the Prince of Orange means, by the beginning of the attack, the time when the Lancers reached Frasnes, while Prince Bernard means the moment when the infantry battalion, on which they had been obliged to wait for a full hour, arrived at the village.

53. Reports above mentioned from the Prince of Orange and Prince of Saxe-Weimar; van Löben, 132-134; Notes of de Stuers, chief of the Red Lancers squadrons of the Guard (comm. by M. de Stuers). See Ney's letter to Soult, Gosselies, 16th June, 7 o'clock A.M. (General Gourgaud's papers), in which the presence at Frasnes of the battalion detached from the Ballu Division, is mentioned.

54. Colbert to the Duke d'Elchingen, 15th May 1829. This letter, the copy of which has been communicated to me by General de Colbert, was addressed to the Duke of Elchingen who collected all the testimonies of the officers who served under his father on the 15th and 16th of June, in order to insert them in his pamphlet, *Documents inédits*, etc. But

for obvious reasons this letter was not published by the Duke of Elchingen. This reconnoitring manœuvre is mentioned also by Colonel Lemonnier, Foy's aide-de-camp (*Campagnes*, 236). It is unquestionable that Colbert pushed on as far as Quatre-Bras; but the general's memory is at fault, when he asserts that he arrived there at four o'clock. He could not, at the earliest, have arrived before six, that is to say, an hour before the Prince of Saxe-Weimar himself rode in from Genappe.

55. Reports already mentioned from the Prince of Orange and the Prince of Saxe-Weimar; van Löben, 134; see 130-132; de Stuers's Notes. In his report Prince Bernard says that when he concentrated his brigade at Quatre-Bras, Normann's battalion had already taken up its position at the wood of Bossu.

56. Van Löben (130-132) expressly says that Prince Bernard began to move towards Quatre-Bras of his own accord, before receiving the order sent at about four o'clock from Nivelles, by General Perponcher; this order had been transmitted first to Houtain-le-Val. Chesney's remark (*Waterloo*, 128) is therefore absolutely erroneous.

57. 1st, 2nd, and 3rd battalions of Nassau; 1st and 2nd battalions of Orange-Nassau; a company of chasseurs on foot; a mounted battery. Altogether about 4500 men. The estimate of the 12th of June quoted by van Löben, 69, assigns only 3,821 men to that brigade; but the 2nd battalion of Orange-Nassau and the company of chasseurs are not mentioned.

58. The Lefebvre-Desnoëttes Division numbered 2,067 men (estimate of 15th June, signed d'Hériot, War Arch.), but two squadrons on duty had remained with the Emperor.

59. Notes of de Stuers, chief of the squadrons, and letter from Colbert (above mentioned); report of the Prince of Saxe-Weimar, Quatre-Bras, 9 o'clock P.M.

According to this report everything was over by eight o'clock, and the Prince feared no other attack during the evening. The Prince of Orange corroborates this in his report to the King of the Netherlands: "The skirmish," he says, "ceased at eight o'clock."

60. Reille's account (War Arch.); Stuers's Notes. See Ney's letter to the Duke of Otrante, 26th June (*Journal de l'Empire*, 29th June).

61. Heymès, *Relation*, 9.

62. In this case the other two divisions of Reille's corps would have marched on Mellet, and would have been replaced at Gosselies by the two first divisions of d'Erlon's corps. It has been asserted that d'Erlon was far in the rear. This is a mistake. His troops were close to the 2nd Corps, but seeing that the latter had halted at Gosselies, he did not push on farther than Jumet (2 kilometres from Gosselies), where he took shelter during this night of the 15th to the 16th. D'Erlon to Soult, Marchienne, 16th June, 4.30 P.M. (War Arch.).

63. Report of the Prince of Saxe-Weimar, Quatre-Bras, 9 o'clock P.M. (quoted by van Löben, 134).

BOOK II

CHAPTER I

1. Positions of the French Army during the night of the 15th to the 16th of June.

RIGHT WING—GROUCHY

Grouchy's headquarters at Campinaire.

Cavalry corps under Pajol and Exelmans, between Lambusart and Campinaire.

Milhaud's cuirassiers on the right bank of the Sambre.

3rd Corps (Vandamme): the right wing beyond Winage, the left in the wood of Soleillemont (or wood of Fleurus).

4th Corps (Gérard): Hulot's division at Chatelineau; Pécheux, Vichery, and Berthezène divisions at Châtelet; Maurin cavalry at Roussieux.

Grouchy to Soult, Campinaire, 16th June, 3 A.M.; Vandamme to Soult, La Cens de Fontenelles, 15th June, 10 P.M.; Soult to Delort, Charleroi, 15th June (P.M.), Gérard to Soult, Châtelet, 15th June (P.M.) (War Arch.).

LEFT WING—NEY

Ney's headquarters at Gosselies.

Lefebvre-Desnoëttes cavalry division of the Guard at Frasnes.

2nd Corps (Reille): Bachelu division at Mellet; Foy and Jérôme; Bonaparte divisions at Gosselies; Girard division at Wangenies; Piré division at Heppignies.

1st Corps (d'Erlon): Durutte and Donzelot between Jumet and Gosselies; Marcognet division at Marchienne; Allix division at Thuin; Jacquinot's cavalry: 1st Brigade at Jumet; 2nd Brigade at Sobray.

Kellermann's cuirassiers also with the right wing, north of Chatelineau.

Lefebvre-Desnoëttes to Ney, Frasnes, 16th June, 5.30 o'clock A.M.; Ney to Soult, Gosselies, 16th June, 7 o'clock A.M.; Girard to Reille, Wangenies, 15th June, 11 o'clock P.M. (General Gourgaud's papers); Reille's account; d'Erlon to Soult, Marchienne, 15th June, 4 o'clock P.M.; and Jumet, 15th June, evening (War Arch.).

RESERVE—THE EMPEROR

Imperial headquarters at Charleroi.

Young Guard at Gilly.

Old Foot-Guards and Guyot cavalry division of the Guard, between Gilly and Charleroi.

Grand park, back of Charleroi.

6th Corps (Lobau) on the right bank of the Sambre.

(Gourgaud, *Camp. de 1815*, 51), Lobau to Soult, on the height overlooking Jamioulx, 15th June, 8 o'clock P.M. (War Arch.) ; General Petit's manuscript account (London Morrisson Collection) ; Notes of Captain de Stuers of the unmounted chasseurs of the Guard (comm. by M. de Stuers).

2. Towards eight o'clock, seeing the enemy in full retreat, the Emperor had left the field of battle. Then he had returned to Charleroi where the Imperial headquarters were established, and there, in the house of an ironmaster of the name of Puissant, he had thrown himself on his bed for a few minutes till the reports were brought in (Napoleon, *Corresp.* 22,055 ; see Gourgaud, 50). This house, with its interior decorations of the time of the Empire, is still in existence. It is situated on the right bank of the Sambre.

3. Gourgaud, *Camp. de 1815*, 50 ; Gourgaud's manuscript journal (General Gourgaud's papers).

Grouchy's report, Campinaire, 10 o'clock P.M. (War Arch.), should have been transmitted to the Imperial headquarters towards 11 o'clock. As for Ney's, written at Frasnes, or more likely at Gosselies, between nine and ten, it must have reached the Emperor at midnight. The fact of his sending a report might seem doubtful, as there exists no trace of it. But a letter from Ney on 16th June, 7 A.M., to be found in General Gourgaud's papers, contains the following words :—"The 1st Corps is at Julmet (*sic*). My report of yesterday mentions it." Thus all doubt is dismissed.

4. See further, note 7, p. 346.

5. On the resolution taken in the afternoon of the 15th, to divide the army into three great masses, and on the distribution of troops, see p. 68, and note 38.

6. The Emperor's intentions are definitely expressed in his letters to Ney and to Grouchy (Charleroi from half-past seven to half-past eight in the morning), *Corresp.* 22,059, 22,060, and fully confirmed as to certain details in the execution, by the Major-General's orders to Ney, Grouchy, Drouot, Lobau, Gérard, and Vandamme (Charleroi, from half-past six to eight in the morning ; Soult's Register, *Bibliothèque Nat.* MSS. 4366). In the account written at St. Helena, this plan is naturally not mentioned. In the face of facts, Napoleon deemed it too chimerical to be even mentioned. He was unwilling to show to what extent he had been mistaken in the enemy's designs. But between the account written several years after the events, and the orders of battle written on the very day, the critic cannot hesitate. From Napoleon's letters we learn his real thoughts and ideas, but not from his other writings. The above quoted letters, it is evident, establish beyond a doubt that in the morning of 16th June :—

1st. The Emperor believed the Prussians were retreating, and he did not expect to find any left on the Saint-Amand-Ligny road. "Proceed to Sombreffe," he writes to Grouchy ; "Gérard has orders to proceed to Sombreffe *without passing by Fleurus.*" He even doubted whether he would find any at Sombreffe. "I shall attack the enemy *if I meet him,*" he writes to Ney ; "and I shall reconnoitre the road as far as Gembloux."

"*If the enemy be at Sombreffe,*" he writes to Grouchy, "I mean to attack him."

2nd. The Emperor was by no means certain that the Prussians, or at any rate a force of Prussians worth mentioning, were still occupying Gembloux. In this sentence of his letter to Grouchy, "If the enemy be at Sombreffe, I will attack him, I will even attack him at Gembloux," the second clause of the sentence (as may be inferred by what follows) is conditional, as the first: "I will even attack him at Gembloux, *if I find him there.*" The Emperor proceeds: " . . . my intention being, when I have studied those two positions, to go and operate with my left wing." Had the possibility of a serious battle at Sombreffe or Gembloux crossed his mind, he would not, towards evening, have been planning a night march with Ney on Brussels.

3rd. The Emperor also assumes that the English are retreating. Although he knew that Ney had not occupied Quatre-Bras the day before, he still imagined that this position had been abandoned by the Dutch and English. Otherwise he would not have written to Ney, nor would he have requested the chief of his staff to write to him: "Take up your positions at Quatre-Bras, establish a division at Genappe, and send a reconnaisance to Nivelles, from which the enemy has probably retired." Genappe is 5 kilom. further than Quatre-Bras, and Nivelles 10 kilom. to the west of this same point. Therefore it is clear that Ney was not expected to attack the cross-roads at Quatre-Bras, which Napoleon believed to be abandoned by the enemy, but to take up his positions there and to wait.

4th. The Emperor hoped to ascertain whether the Prussians had retreated beyond Gembloux, and to drive back their rearguard if he encountered it. He would then join Ney's two corps at Quatre-Bras with his Guard and the 6th Corps, and march on Brussels that same night. He writes to Grouchy: "I propose to operate to-night with my left wing. Do not use Gérard's division except in case of absolute necessity, as it has to march all night." He writes to Ney: "I propose that you should be ready to march on Brussels, where I intend to arrive to-morrow morning. . . . You realise sufficiently the importance attached to the capture of Brussels. I desire your dispositions to be so arranged, that at the first order your eight divisions may be in readiness to march rapidly, and unopposed, to Brussels."

5th. Napoleon's plan depended, moreover, on circumstances. He writes to Grouchy: "The quicker I make up my mind (that is to say, I shall make up my mind), the better it will be for the result of my operations." He writes to Ney: "There at Gembloux, according to events, I will make up my mind, perhaps at three, perhaps this evening. . . . You might be on your way this very evening, if I made up my mind in time for you to be informed of it, during the day and start for Brussels to-night. . . . It is possible I may decide to march on Brussels this evening with the Guard." The circumstances which might frustrate the Emperor's plan, was the possible presence at Sombreffe or Gembloux, of the whole or an important part of the Prussian Army. If he had merely to fight an isolated corps, it would not prevent him from marching on Brussels that same evening.

7. Register of the correspondence of the chief of the staff (*Bibliothèque Nat.* MSS. F. Fr. 4366).

These orders dated from Charleroi do not give any indication as to the hour; nevertheless they were written and forwarded before eight o'clock in the morning, since we know that Napoleon's letters to Ney and to Grouchy (*Corresp.* 22,058, 22,059), which both contain these words, "The chief of the staff has doubtless acquainted you with my intentions," started at the latest between eight and nine o'clock (Flahaut's letter to the Duke d'Elchingen, *Doc. inédits*, 63).

The letters to Ney and Grouchy having been copied on Soult's register after the orders of Kellermann, Drouot, Vandamme, Gérard, etc., it may be assumed that these orders had been dictated and despatched earlier than the letters, possibly about seven o'clock, perhaps even six in the morning. It must be noted that these orders and letters form a total of nearly 300 lines. The wording and copying of such a correspondence requires some length of time; most probably then, the Emperor had given his instructions to Soult towards 6 A.M., if not earlier still.

Moreover, as early as four o'clock, Napoleon had sent his orderly officer, Bussy, to Frasnes to learn the news (Bussy's letter to Napoleon, Frasnes, 16th June, 6 o'clock A.M.; General G.'s papers); and as early as five, Soult, in accordance with the Emperor's orders, had written to ask Ney the exact position of Reille's and d'Erlon's corps (Major-General's Register, and letter of Ney to Soult, Gosselies, 7 A.M., Gen. G.'s papers).

8. Grouchy to Napoleon, bivouac near Fleurus, 16th June, 5 o'clock A.M. (War Arch.). Pajol, who in his notes mentions this letter, says it should have reached Imperial headquarters at half-past six.

At six o'clock, Grouchy wrote again to the Emperor to inform him that General Gérard, posted at Wangenies, saw the Prussians bearing in force towards the heights which rose around the mill of Brye (War Arch. 16th June).

9. See p. 76.

10. The Emperor's letters to Ney and to Grouchy (*Corresp.* 22,058, 22,059), written (see above, p. 347, note 6) towards eight o'clock in the morning, that is to say, about two hours after receiving Grouchy's report, prove that Napoleon had attached no importance to the intelligence conveyed by the latter. Had he realised that the Prussian Army was concentrated at the entrance of Fleurus, he would not have written to Ney: "I am sending Marshal Grouchy to Sombreffe. There I will attack the enemy if I meet him, and will reconnoitre the road as far as Gembloux. Then, according to the course of events, I will make up my mind"; nor would he write to Grouchy: "The rendezvous is at Sombreffe. . . . If the enemy be at Sombreffe I mean to attack him. I should even like to attack him at Gembloux."

11. "This very instant I am gathering my troops to effect the movement you have ordered at Sombreffe" (Grouchy to Napoleon, at the bivouac near Fleurus, 16th June, 5 A.M. (War Arch.).

The day before, as the attack on Gilly was commencing, Grouchy, it will be remembered, received orders to occupy Sombreffe the same evening. He had been compelled to halt before Fleurus owing to Vandamme's refusal to second him, and also because of the lateness of the hour (see pp. 67, 69, and notes). On the morning of the 16th, he was preparing to execute the movement, which circumstances had prevented him from accomplishing on the evening of the 15th. But seeing the enemy's forces increase, he hesitated and preferred to await fresh instructions. When confirmatory orders reached him from Soult and Napoleon, towards nine or half-past nine, he was so dismayed by the display of the Prussian forces, that he limited himself to occupying Fleurus only. However, he had taken measures in the early morning to carry out the Emperor's orders, and this, as may be seen further, cannot be said of Marshal Ney.

12. Napoleon, *Corresp.* 22,058, 22,059. See Soult to Ney and to Grouchy, Charleroi, 16th June (Register of the Chief of the Staff).

13. The letter of Soult relative to that officer of lancers (to Ney, Charleroi, 16th June), bears: "The Emperor is about to proceed to Fleurus." On the other hand, Grouchy (*Relation succincte*, 14) testifies that Napoleon reached Fleurus between half-past ten o'clock and eleven. As 13 kilom. separate Fleurus from the lower portion of Charleroi, where the Imperial headquarters were (maison Puissant), the Emperor certainly left the latter before ten o'clock.

14. Soult to Ney, Charleroi, 16th June (Register of Chief of the Staff).

There has been much discussion as to who had sent that officer of lancers. It was no doubt General Reille, for he says in his account (War Arch.): "Towards nine o'clock, I received a report from General Girard informing me that from Wangenies he could perceive the Prussians massing beyond Fleurus. This intelligence was immediately conveyed to the Emperor."

15. Soult to Ney, Charleroi, 16th June (Major-General's Register).

16. Lobau to Napoleon, Charleroi, 16th June (War Arch.); Janin, *Campagne de Waterloo*, 19.

17. See pp. 76, 78, and notes.

18. Grouchy, *Relation succincte*, 14 ; see Damitz, i. 74 and 84.

19. Grouchy, *Relation succincte*, 15 ; Colonel de Blocqueville's declaration (War Arch. 18th June); Gourgaud, 54. Local traditions.

20. Damitz, i. 80. See Blücher to Müffling, Namur, 15th June, midday (quoted by von Ollech, 99).

21. "To-morrow at early dawn my army will be concentrated here," Blücher to Schwarzenburg, Sombreffe, 15th June, half-past 12 P.M. (quoted by von Ollech, 105, 106-107). See the orders for concentration of 15th and 16th June.

22. Wagner, iv. 20 ; Damitz, i. 87, note.

23. Blücher to his wife, Namur, 3rd June (*Blücher in Briefen*, 143).

24. Damitz, i. 85. See von Ollech, 104, 105.

25. Bülow to Blücher, Liège, 15th June (quoted by von Ollech, 106, 107). Bülow's delay has been almost as much criticised by the Germans as that of Ney and Grouchy was by the French. See von Ollech, 90, 91, 99, 106, 107.

26. Clausewitz, Wagner, Damitz, Delbrück assert that Blücher only decided to accept the battle after midday on the 16th of June, when he had received from Wellington a formal promise with regard to help from the English. This is one way of justifying Blücher's rashness and excusing his defeat. As may be seen further, Wellington's verbal promise was not formal, but merely conditional. Moreover, the original documents testify that long before his interview with Wellington, Blücher had resolved to maintain his position of Sombreffe. The orders of the 14th and 15th (quoted by von Ollech, 90-92, 97-99, 104-107) are conceived with a definite view to a battle at this point. At midday on the 15th of June, Blücher writes to Müffling: "I intend accepting the battle to-morrow." In the evening he writes to the King of Prussia: "I shall concentrate my army to-morrow morning. . . . I am without news from the Duke of Wellington. At any rate, to-morrow will be the decisive day" (quoted by von Ollech, 99-106). Finally his dispositions on the morning of the 16th, which were taken before the receipt of any notice from Wellington, confirm beyond any doubt, Blücher's intention of giving battle.

But all this did not prevent Blücher, in spite of Gneisenau's well-grounded mistrust of Wellington (Müffling, *Aus meinem Leben*, 184 sq.), from counting on the assistance of the English Army.

27. See pp. 63, 64, and note 17.

28. Von Ollech, *Geschichte des Feldzuges von 1815*, 80-90.

29. Müffling says expressly (190) that Wellington desired the Prussians and the English should unite, if Napoleon attacked them, that Brussels might not fall into the hands of the French till after the first battle, if things came to the worst (see Clausewitz, 31).

30. See Wellington, Memorandum (*Suppl. Despatches*, x. 513). Müffling, 191, 192, 198. See Clausewitz, 31; Siborne, i. 71; Kennedy, 171; and the letter from Paris received by Wellington on the 6th of June, where intelligence is given of Napoleon's plan of making a feigned attack on the Sambre (quoted by von Ollech, 73).

31. Letters from Dörnberg, Roisin, Uxbridge, the Prince of Orange, Hardinge (*Suppl. Despatches*, x. 451, 465, 471, 476, 478).

32. Von Ollech, 96. In his memorandum, Wellington asserts that he did not receive Zieten's letter announcing the French attack before three in the afternoon; but this assertion is discredited by the terms of Wellington's letter to Clarke, 8 P.M., 15th June: "I have received nothing since eight o'clock this morning from Charleroi" (*Despatches*, xii. 473).

33. Müffling, *Aus meinem Leben*, 198. See Wellington to the Duke de Berry and to Clarke, Brussels, 15th June, half-past 9 P.M. (*Despatches*, xii. 473).

34. Müffling, 198. See van Löben, Sels 127.

35. Order of movement, Brussels, 15th June (Wellington, *Despatches*, xii. 472).

36. Müffling, 198. Blücher's letter, or rather the letter dictated by Blücher to Gneisenau, is quoted by von Ollech, 100.

37. Müffling, 199; Letters from Dörnberg, Berkeley, de Behr, 15th June (*Suppl. Despatches*, x. 480, 481).

38. According to this order (Brussels, 15th June, 10 P.M., *Despatches*, xii. 494), the Alten division was to proceed to Nivelles, Cooke's division to Braine-le-Comte, Clinton's and Colville's divisions to Enghien. No reference was made to the two Belgian divisions, which were consequently to continue their movement on Nivelles according to the preceding order.

39. This was the last order issued in the night from the 15th to the 16th, except towards midnight, the order for Picton's division, and the Brunswick corps, to proceed at two in the morning towards Waterloo, a point which was midway between Brussels and Nivelles. At the Duchess of Richmond's ball, where Wellington gave verbal orders to the officers towards midnight, he merely spoke of a concentration at Nivelles (Letter of General Vivian, *Waterloo Letters*, 151). It was as late as six in the morning when he gave orders for a partial march towards Quatre-Bras (Dispositions of the English Army, 16th June, 7 A.M., *Suppl. Despatches*, x. 496). At the Duchess of Richmond's ball, a despatch from Constant Rebecque to the Prince of Orange, had warned him that the French had appeared at Quatre-Bras. (Braine-le-Comte, 15th June, 10 P.M., quoted by van Loben, 176.) However, when he passed at Waterloo, at about 8 A.M., Wellington was still so undecided that he commanded Picton's division to halt there till further notice.

40. Müffling, *Aus meinem Leben*, 199. Cf. Colonel Frazer, *Letters*, 535.

41. Letters from Hervey, Wellington's aide-de-camp, 3rd July 1815 (*Nineteenth Century*, March 1893); Cotton, *Voice of Waterloo*, 14, 15; Fraser, *Word on Wellington*, 283, 285, 301; Letter from General Vivian (*Waterloo Letters*, 151). See Capt. Bowles's letter (quoted by Malmesbury, *Letters*, ii. 445), in which two most inaccurate statements are made. See also on the ball of the Duchess of Richmond: Lord Byron, *Childe Harold;* Thackeray, *Vanity Fair;* William Pitt Lennox, *Percy Hamilton.*

42. List of invitations, communicated by Lady de Ros to Sir William Fraser, and reproduced in his *Word on Wellington*, 285-294.

43. Müffling, 199.

44. Lady de Ros, letters quoted by Fraser, 284, 300, 301, 305; Müffling, 199; above-quoted letters of Hervey, of Capt. Bowles, and General Vivian.

45. Gneisenau to the King of Prussia, 12th June 1817 (quoted by van Löben, 225). See van Löben, 177, note 2; Chesney, 109.

46. See pp. 70, 71.

47. Van Löben, 125.

48. Constant Rebecque's orders and letters, Braine-le-Comte, 15th June (quoted by van Löben, 128, 129, 175-178). See above-quoted letter from Gneisenau to the King of Prussia.

49. Van Löben, 142, 187. The Prince of Orange, absent from his headquarters during the day and night of the 15th, had given no orders (Berkeley to Somerset, Braine-le-Comte, 15th June, 2 o'clock P.M., *Suppl. Despatches* of Wellington, x. 480 ; and Constant Rebecque to the Prince of Orange, Braine-le-Comte, 10 P.M., quoted by van Löben, 176). All the arrangements had been made by Constant Rebecque, the Prince of Saxe-Weimar, and Perponcher.

50. It is probable that Wellington advanced as far as the hillock which rises south-east of the farm of Grand-Pierrepont, point marked 162 on the Chart of the Belgian Staff.

51. Wellington had posted Picton at Waterloo, at the branching of the roads to Nivelles and Charleroi ; although he should have made up his mind long ago, he was then still in doubt whether he should direct his troops on Nivelles or on Quatre-Bras (Siborne, i. 182).

52. Wellington (Memorandum (*Suppl. Despatches*, x. 513). Clausewitz is mistaken when he says it was past one when this order was sent. If this had been the case, Picton could not have reached Quatre-Bras at three. However, after his arrival at Quatre-Bras, Wellington again made the mistake of neglecting to call up the Chassé division and Collaert's cavalry. The latter were motionless at Nivelles all day,—excepting the 6th Hussars and the 5th Dragoons, who were led by an aide-de-camp of the Prince of Orange (van Löben, 183, 196).

53. Wellington to Blücher, on the height (north) in rear of Frasnes, 16th June, half-past ten in the morning (quoted by von Ollech, 125).

54. Müffling, *Aus meinen Leben*, 199, 202 ; Clausewitz, 67.

55. This mill, named also the mill of Winter, was pulled down in 1895. I could not find it on my second excursion to Ligny.

56. See p. 79. The altitudes are identical, about 157 metres ; but it is rather a question of the formation of the ground. Moreover, the Bussy mill was more to the centre of the positions than the Fleurus mill, which stands on the extreme west.

57. Müffling, 202 ; Damitz, i. 92. See Chesney, 145.

58. Müffling, *Aus meinen Leben*, 202-205 ; Napoleon's *Corresp.* (Müffling) 10. See Damitz, Clausewitz, 67, and Dörnberg's account, who witnessed the interview, quoted by von Ollech, 127. Von Ollech, preferring Müffling's testimony to Clausewitz's opinion,—an opinion favoured by Charras,—concludes that Wellington's promise was purely conditional.

BOOK II CHAPTER II

1. From Wagnelée to Saint-Amand, where it receives two small tributaries, that brook is called Grand-Ry, from Saint-Amand beyond Tongrinne it is called La Ligne or Le Ligny.

2. The château of Counts de Looz, no longer in existence, was already in ruins in 1815.

3. Local traditions. The Emperor then realised that the position was very strong (Gourgaud, 55).

4. Wagner, iv. 21 ; Damitz, i. 85, 90 ; von Ollech, 120.

5. "The Emperor bids me warn you that the enemy has mustered *un corps de troupes* between Sombreffe and Brye, and that at half-past two Marshal Grouchy will attack it with the 3rd and 4th Army Corps. His Majesty's intention is that you should also attack the forces in front of you, and having pressed them vigorously, that you should move back towards us to aid us in surrounding the corps I have just mentioned" (Soult to Ney, out of Fleurus, 16th June, two o'clock, Register of the Chief of the Staff).

This letter, dated two o'clock, must have been dictated by the Emperor in substance, shortly before. And at that time Napoleon had every possible reason to conclude that the Prussian forces still only amounted to a single army corps, for the 2nd and 3rd Corps only left Sombreffe and Tongrinne towards two o'clock in order to bear down on their positions.

In the accounts from St. Helena (Gourgaud 55, Napoleon 90) it is recorded—quite erroneously—that Napoleon estimated the Prussians at 80,000 men. These accounts, given on the spur of the moment, are very brief, omit many details, and take no heed of hours. The Emperor certainly *did* estimate the Prussians at 80,000 men; but that was at three o'clock, when the 2nd and 3rd Corps had already entered into line. Besides in a subsequent letter of Soult to Ney, dated a quarter past three, we read : "His Majesty bids me tell you you must manœuvre immediately; so as to surround the right of the enemy and fall on his rear at close quarters. *This army* is lost if you act vigorously." Here it is no longer a question of a *corps of troops* but of *an army*.

6. See Gourgaud, 55 ; Damitz, i. 98 ; Napoleon, *Mém.* 91. Napoleon even goes as far as to say : "Evidently Blücher did not expect to be attacked that day."

7. Grouchy, *Observations*, 43 ; *Relation succincte*, 15 ; Colonel de Blocqueville's declaration (War Arch., dated 18th of June).

8. Colonel de] Blocqueville's declaration. Gourgaud (*Campagne de 1815*, 41) relates that these words were 'spoken to Marshal Ney, another of Bourmont's patrons, on the 15th of June at Charleroi. It is possible that Napoleon spoke thus to Ney, and that he repeated these words to Gérard.

9. Gérard, *Quelques Observations*, 48 ; Colonel de Blocqueville's declaration.

10. See p. 11, and note 7.

11. According to the first order of march of the 14th of June, Gérard was to march from Philippeville to Charleroi ; but on the 15th, at half-past three, Soult had written to him to proceed forward in the direction of Lambusart (Chief of the Staff's Register). Instead of moving his whole army corps to the other bank of the Sambre, Gérard transferred the Hulot division alone to Chatelineau, and posted the three others on the right bank of the Sambre (Gérard to Soult, Châtelet, 15th June, evening, War Arch.).

Gérard (*Quelques Observations*, 48) maintains that Soult's order of 16th June only reached him at half-past nine, which seems at least strange, since this order was written between seven and eight o'clock at latest, and there is only a distance of six kilometres between Charleroi and Châtelet. He adds that in his impatience to march forward on that morning, he said to Exelmans, "whose troops were cantoned near his and who had come to talk to him, that all these delays foreboded no good."

Exelmans being at the time with his dragoons at Lambusart, two miles from Châtelet, and in presence of the enemy, how could he have come to have a chat with Gérard?

How was it that Gérard, who was always so eager to act, executed at five in the morning the Emperor's orders, which for some reason or other he had disregarded the evening before? Why had he not made his three divisions cross the Sambre, and joined them to Hulot's division at Chatelineau? Ten minutes after receiving the order he might have started all his men on their march.

12. The first order of battle for the French troops, perpendicular to the Fleurus road, is a strong presumption. See on the subject, Damitz, i. 99, 100.

13. Above-quoted letters of Napoleon and Soult (see p. 76).

14. Soult to Ney, 16th June (Major-General's Register).

Napoleon, who continues in his memoirs to confuse orders and hours, speaks as if this letter had been sent at half-past ten (that is to say, before he had arrived at Fleurus!), and as if it contained an order to Ney to march against Brye, not with all his troops, but with a single detachment. Napoleon also relates (90, 91) that he received an officer from the left, who told him that Ney hesitated to march, for fear of having his flank turned by the English and Prussians, whose junction, he was assured, had already taken place at Fleurus. This is a confusion with the report of the officer of lancers sent by Reille, of which I have spoken on a previous occasion (see p. 78). Gourgaud (56, 57) is quite as inaccurate.

15. Gourgaud, 54, 56 ; Napoleon, *Mém.* 93.

16. Gneisenau's report ; Damitz, i. 90, 95, 96, 100, 101 ; Wagner, iv. 23-25 ; von Ollech, 143-145 ; Notes of Colonel Simon-Lorière (War Arch.).

17. See p. 89, and note 5.

18. Napoleon, *Mém.* 93, 94.   See Gourgaud, 57.

19. Soult to Ney, out of Fleurus, 16th June, quarter past three (Register of the Chief of the Staff, *Bibliothèque Nationale*, MSS. F. Fr., 4365).

20. Lobau to Napoleon, before Charleroi, 16th June (War Arch., Army of the North). This letter has no indication as to time. But from what it relates concerning the state of things at the moment when Janin left Frasnes, it may be inferred that the latter started about half-past twelve in the day. At an average rate of 10 kilometres an hour he must have returned to Charleroi (at the forking of the Brussels and Fleurus roads) about two. It was therefore two o'clock or thereabouts

when Lobau sent the Emperor his letter, which must have reached Fleurus between a quarter past and half-past three in the afternoon.

On Janin's mission see p. 79. When Janin left Frasnes there were not 20,000 of the enemy at Quatre-Bras. There were hardly 7,000. The officer was misled by the great extension of the front line of the Dutch.

21. " . . . Colonel de Forbin-Janson had received the important mission of carrying the order for the marching of the 1st Corps to the rear of the right of the Prussian Army. . . . At the moment when the engagement was raging all along the line, the Emperor asked Marshal Soult for an experienced officer to carry to Marshal Ney the duplicate of the order concerning Count d'Erlon. The Major-General having summoned me, the Emperor said to me: 'I have sent Count d'Erlon the order to advance with his whole army corps to the rear of the Prussian Army's right. You will carry to Ney the duplicate of this order, although he is no doubt acquainted with it already. Tell him that whatever his own position may be, it is absolutely urgent that this order should be executed; that I do not attach very great importance to what happens to-day in his direction, but that the whole interest of the day is centred where I am, because my aim is to settle matters with the Prussian Army. As for him, if he can do nothing better, he must content himself with holding in check the English Army.'" MS. notes of Colonel Baudus, communicated by M. de Montenon, his grandson. These notes have only been partly reproduced in Colonel Baudus's *Études sur Napoléon*.

The existence of this order, implicitly denied by Napoleon, but which a letter of Soult to Ney on the 17th of June alone suffices to prove, is affirmed unanimously by all witnesses. They will be furnished further, p. 117 and the notes, where I discuss this vexed question.

22. Soult to Lobau, out of Fleurus, 16th June, quarter past three (Major-General's Ledger).

23. Pontécoulant, *Souvenirs militaires*, 92. Gneisenau, Wagner, Napoleon, Gourgaud all say three o'clock.

24. Lefol, *Souvenirs*, 61-62; Gneisenau's report, Damitz, i. 102-104; Wagner, iv. 28, 29; Gourgaud, 58; Napoleon, *Mém.* 95; von Ollech, 148, 149.

It happened that the Girard division, detached on the evening before from Ney's corps, formed the extreme left of the army then fighting at Ligny, see p. 127.

25. Journal of Captain François of the 30th of the line (*Revue Armoricaine*, 128). See Damitz, 110; Wagner, iv. 36. "At a quarter past three, the 4th Corps attacked the village of Ligny" (Napoleon, *Mém.* 91).

26. Captain François's journal; Gneisenau's report; Damitz, 110, 111; Wagner, iv. 36, 37; Gourgaud, 58; Gérard, *Quelques Observations*, 54; Simon-Lorière's account (War Arch., Army of the North).

27. Damitz, i. 112, 113; General Romme's letter to Gourgaud, Paris, 27th May, 1823 (General Gourgaud's papers; letter from Imperial headquarters at Fleurus, 17th June, Arch. of Foreign Affairs, 1802).

28. Above-quoted letter of General Romme to Gourgaud, Damitz, i. 112, 113; Wagner, 37, 38; *Relation de la dernière campagne de Bonaparte*, 51; Lefol, *Souvenirs*, 68. See official report of Gneisenau: "This battle may be considered as one of the most desperate recorded by history."

29. Napoleon's order to Grouchy, 16th June (War Arch., Army of the North); General Hulot's report; Grouchy, *Relation succincte*, 16. Wagner (iv. 41) says the action commenced only at six o'clock at Sombreffe and Balâtre; this is true, but it began much earlier at Boignée, at Tongrinelle, and at Potriaux.

30. Damitz, i. 104, 105; Wagner, iv. 29.

31. The Thuemen, Schulenburg, and Sohr brigades of Pirch's corps, and the Marwitz brigade detached from Thielmann's corps.

32. Wagner, iv. 29, 30; von Ollech, 154; Damitz, i. 104, 105. See Gneisenau's report.

33. Damitz, i. 104, 105; Wagner, iv. 30; Napoleon, *Mém.* 95; *Relation de l'Ambigû*, London, vol. liii.

34. Damitz, i. 106, 107; Wagner, iv. 32.

35. Gneisenau's report; Damitz, i. 106, 107; Wagner, 31, 33.

36. Damitz, i. 108 (see pp. 64, 65, and 67); Wagner, iv. 33.

37. Napoleon, *Mém.* 96; Gourgaud, 59. See Soult to Ney, Fleurus, 17th June (Major-General's Register).

38. Napoleon, *Mém.* 96; Gourgaud, 59. See Lefol, *Souvenirs*, 63: ". . . A false rumour that a column of the enemy had taken our left by surprise, caused a sort of panic".—Souvenirs d'un ex-officier (of the 45th, Erlon's corps), 226: "We came in sight of Saint-Amand towards five or six o'clock."

39. Napoleon, *Mém.* 96.

40. Napoleon, *Mém.* 96. According to a tradition related by Piérart (*Le Drame de Waterloo*), Vandamme's alarm may be imputed to the cowardice of the officer who was sent to reconnoitre the column. This officer dared not go within gunshot of the balls, and came back without fulfilling his mission, with the news that it was the enemy.

41. Napoleon, *Mém.* 96.

42. Napoleon, *Mém.* 96, 97; Gourgaud, 59; General Petit's account (Morrison Collection, London).

43. Lefol, *Souvenirs*, 63, 64.

44. Wagner, iv. 33, 34; see Gneisenau's report; Damitz, i. 117-121.

45. Damitz, i. 119, 120; Wagner, iv. 33.

46. *Souvenirs de 1815, les Cent Jours en Belgique* (*Bibliothèque universelle de Genève*, July 1887). The author of these souvenirs adds: "Freshly returned from the deserts of Russia and the English hulks, inspired by the recollection of their early triumphs, by the rankling shame of their recent defeats, and eager to hide under a blaze of glory their desertion of the Royal party, the French soldiers surpassed themselves."

47. General Hulot's account. See Damitz, i. 124.

48. Gneisenau's report; von Ollech, 151, 152; Gourgaud, 58, 59; Damitz, i. 122, 129, 131 (see pp. 62, 63); Wagner, iv. 38, 39.

49. Müffling, *Aus meinem Leben*, 206 ; Damitz, i. 126.
50. Wagner, iv. 39 ; Damitz, i. 126, 127.
51. Von Ollech, 154 ; Damitz, i. 127 (see 131 and 141); Wagner, iv. 33, 34.
52. Damitz, 132 and note ; Wagner, iv. 43. See von Ollech, 154 ; and Mauduit, ii. 86, 87.
53. Damitz, i. 32, Official Report from Gneisenau. See Wagner, 43.
54. Gourgaud, 59 ; Napoleon, *Mém.* 97.
55. See p. 99.
56. Napoleon, *Mém.* 97 ; Gourgaud, 59.
57. The 1st Corps ought to have gone up straight towards the north, marching 3,500 metres to the west of Wagnelée, and to have turned eastwards so as to fall back on Brye. This journey of 6 kilometres across country, required nearly an hour and a half, and another half-hour was necessary before the order to effect this movement could be sent from Fleurus, to the point occupied by Count d'Erlon. Clausewitz, more thoughtful and more just than Charras, acknowledges that it was then too late to order a turning movement upon Brye (*Der Krieg von 1815*, 84).
58. Napoleon is silent on this point (all that concerns d'Erlon's movement is intentionally left wrapt in mystery) ; but it is more than likely, for, as may be seen further (214), Delcambre, sent by Ney, and the Emperor's own aide-de-camp arrived almost simultaneously at their destination (Count d'Erlon's camp).
59. Letter from Napoleon, *Mém.* 97 ; Gourgaud, 59.
60. Letter from Imperial headquarters at Fleurus, 17th June (Arch. of Foreign Affairs, 1802); General Petit's above-quoted account. Commandant Duuring's account of the 1st Regiment of Chasseurs (comm. by M. de Stuers); Gneisenau's report to the King of Prussia, Wavre, 17th June (quoted by von Ollech, 162-165); Gneisenau's official report ; Wagner, iv. 39, 40, 43 ; Soult to Joseph, out of Fleurus, 16th June, half-past 8 P.M., and to Davout, Fleurus, 17th June (Major-General's Register).
61. Twice Damitz mentions the light which for a few seconds (i. 132, 133) succeeded the almost complete darkness caused by the storm.
62. Damitz, i. 128, 129, 133, 134. General Hulot's report (communicated by Baron Hulot) ; Wagner, iv. 42.
63. Above-quoted account of Commandant Duuring. The 4th Grenadiers, newly formed, had been clad in any kind of garments. Many of the men had shakos instead of *bonnets à poil*.
64. Gneisenau's report, Wavre, 17th June (quoted by von Ollech, 163, 164); General Petit's and Duuring's accounts ; Damitz, i. 133-135 ; Report of Kimann, captain of dragoons of the Guard, 17th June (General G.'s papers); Wagner, iv. 44.
65. Blücher to his wife, Wavre, 17th June (*Blücher in Briefen*, 146); Gneisenau's official report ; Damitz, i. 134, 135 ; Wagner, iv. 44 ; General Delort's account (General G.'s papers) ; see von Ollech, 155, 157.
66. Damitz, ii. 211. This declaration of Damitz is in direct contradiction to Gneisenau's official report, and to the accounts of the majority

of German historians, also that of Damitz himself, who affirms that the retreat was effected with perfect order at every point. A number of 8,000 or 10,000 fugitives on a field of battle points emphatically to a certain degree of confusion. Then there is the testimony of the *émigré* officer whose *Souvenirs of 1815* were published in 1857 by the *Bibliothèque universelle de Genève;* he states that very great disorder prevailed amid the greater part of the Prussians, and that everywhere there were masses of fugitives. The truth is, there was a complete rout at the centre, great confusion on the left, and a most dignified retreat on the right wing. Besides, neither Gneisenau (in his confidential report, Wavre, 17th June) nor von Ollech (157) conceal the fact that the close of the battle was marked by great disorder.

67. General Delort's account (General Gourgaud's papers). Delort's assertion is confirmed by a letter addressed from Imperial headquarters at Fleurus, 17th June, 9 A.M. (Arch. of Foreign Affairs, 1802): " . . . Had Delort been supported even in a small degree, he might have captured in less than fifteen minutes, fifty pieces of artillery."

68. The French, according to Soult (Letter to Davout, 17th June, Major-General's Register), took forty cannon and several thousand prisoners. According to Gneisenau (Report of 17th June, quoted by von Ollech), the Prussian Army lost only sixteen pieces, and left few prisoners except the wounded. Grouchy (*Relation succincte*, 17) makes a similar statement: about fifteen cannon, a few flags, and a small number of prisoners. Wagner (iv. 44) acknowledges to twenty-seven cannon lost, and this seems an accurate figure.

69. Gneisenau's report, Wavre, 17th June (quoted by von Ollech, 163, 164); Gneisenau's official report; Damitz, i. 139-142, 146; Wagner, iv. 35, 47.

From the comparison of French with German documents, the time-table of the battle can be established as follows:—

From one to three o'clock: concentration, preparatory manœuvres; skirmishing at the outposts.

From three to four: taking of Saint-Amand by the Lefol division; fruitless attacks of the Pécheux division against Ligny; Grouchy's demonstrations on Tongrinelle and Boignée.

From four to five: the Girard division takes possession of the hamlet of La Haye; counter-attack of the Prussians on these positions; Girard is killed in retaking La Haye; Tippelskirch's attack repulsed by Habert; the Pécheux division, supported by two of Vichery's regiments, occupies the upper part of Ligny.

From five to six: retaking of La Haye by Pirch II.; Napoleon prepares for the final assault; the supposed column of the enemy (d'Erlon's corps) is signalled; Napoleon stops his manœuvre and sends the Young Guard with three regiments of chasseurs of the Old Guard to reinforce Vandamme; Gérard throws his last reserve into Ligny.

From six to half-past seven: recapture of Le Hameau by the enemy; recoil of Vandamme's troops; the Young Guard comes to the front; retaking of Le Hameau by the remnant of the Girard division; Grouchy occupies Tongrinelle and attacks Potriaux; Blücher's last counter-attack on Saint-Amand; the Prussians are repulsed by the unmounted chasseurs of the Guard and by Vandamme's troops; continuation of the fight in the burning street of Ligny; Grouchy takes possession of Potriaux and drives back Lottum's cavalry; Napoleon prepares to assault the enemy's centre again.

From half-past seven to half-past nine: taking of Ligny; engagements on the north of Ligny; retreat of the Prussians.

70. Soult to Davout, Fleurus, 17th June (Chief of the Staff's Register); Notes of Captain de Stuers of the 2nd of Unmounted Chasseurs (comm. by M. de Stuers). The Imperial headquarters were established at Baron Zualart's château quite near to the mill which the Emperor had used as an observatory.

71. General Petit's account (Morrison Collection of London); above-quoted letter of Kimann of the dragoons of the Guard (Lefol, *Souvenirs*, 66, 67; Hulot's account).

72. Soult to Davout, Fleurus, 17th June (Chief of the Staff's Register); Lefol, *Souvenirs*, 69.

73. Wagner, iv. 47: 11,706 soldiers and 372 officers. Gneisenau in his report to the King of Prussia, Wavre, 17th June (quoted by von Ollech, 163, 164), says: 15,000 men, but he must include the prisoners.

Gourgaud (170) gives the number of killed and wounded for each army corps, and the total is not more than 6,800. This estimate is evidently inaccurate in many points. Thus the losses for Gérard's corps are put down to 2,170 men only, while a list quoted by Gérard in a letter to Simon-Lorière (23rd February 1820, War Arch.) brings their number to 3,686, which shows already a difference of 1,516 men. As for the Guard and the Young Guard, which were both seriously engaged in the contest, they had, according to Gourgaud, only 100 men killed or disabled. Their losses must have been at least three times that amount.

BOOK II CHAPTER III

1. 1st, letter of Soult, five o'clock; 2nd, of the same, seven or eight o'clock; 3rd, of Napoleon, half-past eight; 4th, of Soult, ten o'clock; 5th, of the same, two o'clock; 6th, of the same, a quarter past three; 7th, duplicate of the latter, half-past three; 8th, verbal order conveyed by Colonel Forbin-Janson, half-past three; 9th, verbal order conveyed by Commandant Baudus, five o'clock.

2. Gourgaud, 67, 68; Napoleon, *Mém.* 180, 181. See account of General Delort (General Gourgaud's papers) and General Kellermann's account (War Arch.).

3. Grouchy, without any fresh orders, had made his arrangements for marching at dawn upon Sombreffe, in accordance with instructions

received the day before from the Emperor (see p. 78). Ney might have done the same.

It has been urged that, during the night, Ney had another interview with the Emperor at the Imperial headquarters in Charleroi, and that the latter had undoubtedly enjoined him to await fresh orders.

But Colonel Heymès, whose testimony is suspicious, and whose pamphlet bristles with errors, is the only contemporary writer who mentions this visit of the Marshal to Napoleon. On the other hand, this nocturnal excursion seems to me at least unlikely, for several reasons :—

1st. The Marshal having sent a report to the Emperor towards nine o'clock, there was no need for him to go two hours later to report again in person.

2nd. Had Ney left his army in the night, and in the presence of the enemy, to wander about two miles away from its rear, this would have been a breach of all military rules.

3rd. From Beaumont to Charleroi, from Charleroi to the other side of Frasnes, and from Frasnes to Gosselies, Ney had already ridden thirteen leagues. It is not very likely that he would care to ride four extra leagues (there and back) in the dead of night, on an errand which was quite unnecessary, as he had already sent a report to the Emperor.

Other questions : In his letters of 16th June, why does not the Emperor blame Ney for not occupying Quatre-Bras on the 15th ? Most likely because Ney's report had alleged the darkness, the fatigue of his troops, etc., adding that Quatre-Bras might be taken at any time without difficulty, the position being weakly defended.

Why, as soon as he received the report that night, did not the Emperor write to Ney to march on Quatre-Bras as early as possible, instead of waiting till the next day to send him this order ? Undoubtedly because Ney's report had led him to think that this position was feebly defended, or perhaps already abandoned by the enemy, so that it might be considered as virtually in the hands of the French. In the first order of 16th June to Ney, Napoleon seems to consider the occupation of Quatre-Bras as a matter of course, and even overlooks the idea of a possible contest. The whole of the morning Ney himself, as will be seen further on, did not expect to meet with any resistance worth considering at Quatre-Bras. *A fortiori* he had come to this conclusion in the night, and had written his report accordingly.

4. For these estimates see p. 58.

5. Soult to Ney, Charleroi, 16th June (Major-General's Register). This letter does not bear any indication as to time, but we know that it was received by Ney towards half-past six, since his answer to that letter is dated seven o'clock.

6. Ney to Soult, Gosselies, 16th June, 7 o'clock (General G.'s papers).

7. The troops were not under arms at ten o'clock in the morning, since in his letter to Ney at a quarter past ten (War Arch.) Reille says : "I should have commenced moving on Frasnes as soon as my divisions had been under arms."

8. Reille's account (War Arch.).

9. Report of the Prince of Orange, 17th June (General G.'s papers); van Löben, 184-186.

10. Colonel Répécaud, *Napoleon at Ligny and Ney at Quatre-Bras*, 17.

Répécaud heard these words from the mouth of Ney himself, not at ten or eleven o'clock, but, stranger still, about two o'clock, at the very time of the attack.

11. Napoleon, *Corresp.* 21,058.

From Flahaut's letter to the Duke of Elchingen (*Documents inédits*, 63) we know that he left Charleroi at nine o'clock at the latest, and from Reille's letter to Ney (16th June, a quarter past ten, War Arch.) that he reached Gosselies about ten o'clock. Now Gosselies, making an allowance of 300 yards, is half-way from Charleroi (Puissant's house) to Frasnes; therefore Flahaut should have reached Frasnes towards eleven o'clock, and this is corroborated by Heymès's statement (12). It must be noted that Flahaut was in no haste; he was quietly riding a fresh horse at the rate of two leagues an hour.

12. Order of Ney, Frasnes, 16th June (between eleven and half-past eleven, War Arch., Army of the North). In this order, Ney disposes of the 7th division (Girard), for he was still unaware that the Emperor meant to employ it on the right wing. He confuses the 1st Cavalry Division with the 2nd, evidently. It was the 2nd (Piré of Reille's corps) which was to reconnoitre Reille, and the 1st (Jacquinot of d'Erlon's corps) which was to march with d'Erlon. This is how things occurred subsequently.

13. The conclusion which we gather from a perusal of this order is confirmed by the above-quoted testimony of Colonel Répécaud. Répécaud says further: "The Marshal imagined that the position was feebly occupied."

14. ". . . One division two leagues beyond Quatre-Chemins if possible; six divisions around Quatre-Chemins; one division at Marbais" (Napoleon, *Corresp.* 22,058). See almost identical letter of Soult (Major-General's Register), which Ney must have received a few moments after that from the Emperor.

15. Reille's account (War Arch.).

16. Reille to Ney, Gosselies, 16th June, a quarter past ten (War Arch., Army of the North).

Jomini, while admitting (p. 274) that this incident was a misfortune, says (p. 283): "Reille was guided by logical reasons derived from the laws of great tactics; for he would naturally suppose that the right wing would be called to that point where the enemy appeared; a disaster seemed certain if after Girard's intelligence, he were to fight on the Genappe road when he ought to fall back on Brye." This system of defence does not work:—1st, If generals under orders were "to obey the laws of great tactics" instead of obeying the orders of their chiefs, a strange confusion amongst the troops would ensue; 2nd, In fighting on the Genappe road, Reille ran only one risk, and that was precisely that of approaching Brye; 3rd, In his letter, Napoleon said that he might summon a division of the left wing, but this division was to debouch from Marbais and not from Gosselies. Now at Frasnes, to which Reille should have marched at once, he would have been far nearer Marbais than when he was at Gosselies. However, the documents must be studied minutely before forming any judgment on the matter.

That which paralysed Reille was the personal fear of the Prussian masses, that Girard announced were debouching from the Namur road. Imaginary fears and ill-founded conclusions! He knew from the Emperor's letter just communicated to him, that the latter was marching on Sombreffe through Fleurus, and this proved, evidently, that the object of the Prussians was the Emperor, not Reille at all.

17. The distance between Frasnes and Gosselies is two leagues, and Ney's order was sent at a quarter past eleven, at the earliest. Reille in his account, says that the heads of his divisions commenced the attack about two o'clock. Foy in his report of the 17th (Corresp. Register) also says that his regiment was formed in front of Frasnes at two o'clock.

18. On this letter, derived from the report of an officer of lancers, and sent by Soult towards ten o'clock, see pp. 78, 79.

19. Répécaud, 17. As already remarked, this assertion is confirmed by Ney's order of march quoted above.

20. Bylandt and Saxe-Weimar brigades. Estimates of 12th June quoted by van Löben (see note 1, p. 129). At noon, Perponcher had not even 7,000 men, for the 7th battalion of the line did not reach Nivelles before two or half-past two (van Löben, 193).

21. This wood has been cut down, as well as the wood of La Hutte, which extended 1,200 yards to the right of the road, between Frasnes and Villers-Perwin.

22. Van Löben, 185-188.

23. Diary of Foy, Frasnes, June 17 (comm. by Count Foy). See Reille's account (War Arch.) and Ney's above-quoted words to Col. Répécaud.

Reille referred to the ordinary tactics of the English in the Spanish wars, when Wellington never unmasked his forces until the moment of the enemy's decisive attack.

24. Reille's account (War Arch.); Foy's report, Frasnes, 17th June (Foy's Register of Corresp.). See Siborne i. 100: "Towards two o'clock Ney prepared for the attack." See also Ney's order above quoted, and the account of Kellermann (War Arch.), who besides confuses Frasnes with Liberchies.

25. Letter of Foy to Guilleminot, 20th October 1815 (Foy's Register of Corresp., communicated by Count Foy).

26. Reille's account; Foy's report (Register of Corresp.); van Löben, 190-196; Siborne, i. 101, 102.

Ney might have made a better distribution of his forces. The Bachelu division and Piré's cavalry would have sufficed for an attack against Gémioncourt and Piraumont; leaving Foy's 1st brigade free to march towards the wood while the 2nd formed the reserve.

27. A note of the *Suppl. to Wellington's Corresp.* (x. 525) fixes the

return of the Duke at three o'clock. Müffling (*Corresp. of Napoleon*, ii.) also says: "Towards three o'clock." Van Löben, Damitz, Siborne, Chesney agree on this point.

28. Müffling, *Aus meinem Leben*, 205. See Wellington to Lady Webster, Waterloo, 18th June, three o'clock A.M. (*Suppl. Despatches*, x. 501).

29. Wellington's report (*Despatches*, xii. 478) says that the Picton division appeared at half-past two. This is a mistake, for we know that Wellington did not return from Brye before three o'clock, and according to Müffling's testimony, *Aus meinem Leben*, 205 (see *Corresp. of Napoleon*, ii.), there is not the least doubt that the Duke's return took place before Picton's arrival. Siborne (i. 104) says on his side : "Wellington returned a short time before Picton's arrival." As for the van Merlen brigade, van Löben, whose account is based on the Dutch archives (196, 197), says that it reached Quatre-Bras at the same time as the Picton division.

30. Letters of officers of the Kempt and Pack brigades (*Waterloo Letters*, 353, 358, 373, 377); Siborne, i. 102.

31. Siborne, i. 104, 105 ; Damitz, i. 197. See van Löben, 197, 198, who says that these cannons were recaptured later.

32. Reille's account; Foy's report; *Mém du roi Jérôme*, vii. 67 ; Letters of the Prince of Saxe-Weimar, Waterloo, 19th June ; van Löben, 204.

33. See p. 90.

From the Fleurus mill to the height of Pierrepont (the point of the road to Brussels where Ney should have been posted), through Ransart and Gosselies, the distance is 20 kilometres, 500 metres ; the road is good, and slopes gently ; therefore, without pressing his horse, the officer who bore the order ought to have ridden at the rate of 10 to 11 kilometres an hour. In the *Documents inédits*, the Duke of Elchingen states that his letter arrived at four o'clock.

34. Van Löben, 203, 204 ; Reille's account, *Mémoires du roi Jérôme*, vii. 69, 75 ; Müffling, *Aus meinem Leben*, 10 ; Damitz, 198, 199 ; Siborne, 109-117. From a tradition recorded in the *Mémoires de Jérôme*, Brunswick was wounded in the act of haranguing the head of the column of the 1st Light Infantry, trying to persuade it to abandon the cause of the Emperor. This is highly improbable, considering the hatred the Duke of Brunswick had vowed to all the French in general.

35. Reille's account (War Arch.) ; Letters of officers of the Kempt and Pack Brigades (*Waterloo Letters*, 348, 353, 354, 358, 373, 374); Siborne, i. 111, 112.

These words: "Remember Egypt!" were an allusion to the battle of Ramanieh, 21st March 1801, where the English 28th resisted the desperate cavalry charges of General Roize.

36. Letters of officers of the Pack Brigade (*Waterloo Letters*, 376-379, 381); Siborne, 117, 122 ; see Damitz, i. 197, 198. In one moment the Colonel of the 42nd was killed, and 284 men were disabled. Galbois received a ball in his chest, but he remained on horseback and fought two days later at Waterloo.

37. D'Erlon to Soult, Jumet, 15th June (War Arch.). See Delcambre's

order (Marchienne, 17th June, 3 A.M.) to start the Marcognet division immediately on its march, "so that it might be at Gosselies at six o'clock in the morning at the latest" (War Arch.). Similar orders were certainly sent to the Allix division still at Thuin, and to the second Jacquinot brigade stationed at Sobray. Therefore it is likely that the entire 1st Corps was concentrated around Jumet on the morning of the 16th of June.

38. Reille to Ney, Gosselies, 16th June, a quarter-past ten (War Arch.).

39. D'Erlon to the Duke of Elchingen, 9th February 1829 (*Documents inédits*, 64).

40. We have said before that the head of the column which set out towards noon did not reach Frasnes till about half-past one, and the Jérôme division arrived towards three o'clock. Two leagues separate Gosselies from Frasnes.

41. Letter from d'Erlon to Soult, Gosselies, 16th June (without any reference to time, between one and three o'clock), (General G.'s papers).

42. See pp. 77, 78.

43. On what authority does Thiers tell us (xx. 123) that d'Erlon had directed the Durutte division on Marbais as early as eleven in the morning, but that it was recalled to Quatre-Bras an hour later by Ney? There is not a word to that effect in Durutte's account nor anywhere else.

44. See extract of the recollections of General de Salle commanding the artillery of the 1st Corps (*Nouvelle Revue*, 15th January 1895), the manuscript notes of Colonel Baudus, Durutte's account, and our note 47 of the present page.

45. See p. 92.

46. From Fleurus to the crossing of the Brussels road with the Voie romaine, there are $15\frac{1}{2}$ kilometres passing through Ransart and Gosselies; the short cut through Mellet brings this distance down to 8 kilometres.

The officer who carried Soult's order evidently took the Gosselies way, for Gamot (*Refut.* 16, 17) declares that when Ney received that order he had already been informed of d'Erlon's movement, while Kellermann says that the order did not reach the Marshal till half-past five. Apparently Forbin-Janson, who had set out half an hour after the other officer, took the short cut, and thus managed to reach d'Erlon a full hour before the other joined Ney.

Another proof lies in the fact that, if he had followed the Ransart-Gosselies road, Forbin-Janson could not have acquainted d'Erlon with the Emperor's order at the earliest before a quarter to five; yet the 1st Corps was perceived at five o'clock by Vandamme, at a league's distance, from Saint-Amand, as the crow flies.

47. Above-quoted *Souvenirs* of General de Salle, Artillery Commandant of the 1st Corps.

"While we were pressing in slowly towards the 2nd Corps, there arrived a subaltern of the Guard with the following letter from the Emperor:—

"Monsieur le Comte d'Erlon—The enemy is falling headlong into the trap I have laid for him. Proceed immediately with all your forces to the height of Ligny and fall on Saint-Amand. Monsieur le Comte d'Erlon, you are about to save France and cover yourself with glory.—NAPOLEON."

De Salle adds: "Having no map of Belgium before me, it is possible that I am transposing the names of the two villages. I rather think that it was 'at Saint-Amand,' and 'fall upon Ligny,' otherwise I am certain I make no mistake."

These last words indicate that de Salle repeated the letter from memory. Can we accept his version of the letter as authentic? At all events, there is a confusion in this sentence: "Proceed to the height of Ligny to fall on Saint-Amand." The Emperor, whose plan was to attack the Prussians on the rear of their right (see Soult's letters to Ney mentioned above), had evidently written, not, "Bear up to the height of Ligny," but rather, as corrected by de Salle, "Bear upon the height of Saint-Amand and fall on Ligny" (see Soult's letter to Ney). Except for this confusion in de Salle's quotation—a confusion which d'Erlon must have made himself, and which explains his mistaken move, it would seem that if this is not the exact text of the order, it is at least the gist of it.

The testimony of General de Salle, who affirms that the Emperor's order was addressed directly to d'Erlon, is confirmed by eleven other testimonies. I quote them in their order of date:—

1st. Soult to Ney, Fleurus, 17th June (Major-General's Register): "Had Count d'Erlon executed the movement ordered by the Emperor on Saint-Amand, the Prussians would have been totally destroyed."

2nd. Soult to Davout, Fleurus, 17th June 1815 (War Arch.): "Count d'Erlon has received wrong directions, for if he had executed the movement enjoined by the Emperor, the Prussian Army was irremediably lost.

3rd. Book of daily notes of General Foy (communicated by Count Foy). Note dated Genappe, 18th of June, morning: "The Emperor reproached Count d'Erlon because his entire corps did not bear on Marbais during the operations of the 16th."

4th. *Letter of Marshal Ney to the Duke of Otrante*, Paris, 26th June 1815 (*Journal de l'Empire*, 29th June): "I was going to send forward the 1st Corps, when I heard that the Emperor had disposed of it."

5th. Notes of Colonel Simon Lorière, deputy-chief of Gérard's staff (War. Arch.): "Orders to bear upon Brye were given to the 1st Corps."

6th. Gamot, Ney's brother-in-law, *Réfutation en ce qui concerne le maréchal Ney* (1819), p. 16: "The Marshal knew already through Colonel Laurent, bearer of the pencilled order, that he was not to count any longer on d'Erlon." P. 19: "Count d'Erlon's movement took place according to the positively expressed orders of Napoleon. I have the testimony of the bearer of these orders, Colonel Laurent."

7th. Fleury de Chaboulon present at Ligny as attaché to the Emperor's cabinet, *Mémoires sur les Cent Jours* (1820), ii. 157: "The

Emperor had sent a direct order to Count d'Erlon to come and join him with the 1st Corps."

8th. Colonel Baudus of Soult's staff (notes communicated by his grandson, M. de Montenon): "At the moment when the engagement was in full swing along the entire line, the Emperor said to me: ' I have sent to Count d'Erlon an order to proceed with his whole army corps to the rear of the Prussian Army's right. You will carry to Marshal Ney the duplicate of this order, which ought to have been communicated to him by this time. You will tell him that whatever may be his position, this order must absolutely be carried out. . . .' I reached the Marshal. He was very much excited, for when he had wished to send d'Erlon forward, that general having received orders direct from Napoleon, had set out on his march to carry them out."

9th. Account of Durutte, general of one of d'Erlon's divisions (written before 1827, the year of the general's death, and published in the *Sentinelle de l'Armée*, 8th March 1838): " The Emperor sent Count d'Erlon the order to attack the left (the right) of the Prussians, and to try to take possession of Brye. The 1st Corps passed near Villers-Perwin to execute the movement.

10th. Colonel Heymès, Ney's aide-de-camp, *Relation de la Campagne de 1815* (1829), p. 14: "Colonel Laurent's despatch from the Imperial headquarters came to inform Ney that, in pursuance of an order from the Emperor which he had transmitted to d'Erlon, the 1st Corps was proceeding in the direction of Saint-Amand."

11th. Petiet of Soult's staff, *Souvenirs militaires* (1844), p. 199: "In great haste the Emperor sends for the 1st Corps, and Marshal Ney does not hear of this before it is well on its way."

To tell the truth, d'Erlon gives rather a different version. In his letter to the Duke of Elchingen (*Documents inédits*, 64), he says: "I outdistanced my column and reached Frasnes. There I was joined by General La Bédoyère, who showed a pencilled note which he was carrying to Ney, and which enjoined the Marshal to direct his corps d'armée on Ligny. La Bédoyère warned me that he had already given orders for this movement, by causing the direction of my column to be changed; he informed me where I could rejoin it. I immediately followed the road he indicated."

And in his *Vie militaire* (95) d'Erlon writes: "The Emperor sent Marshal Ney an officer to tell him to direct the 1st Corps on Ligny, so as to turn the Prussians' right wing. This officer met the vanguard of the 1st Corps before he had delivered his orders to Ney, and straightway sent this column in the direction of Ligny. Towards four o'clock I had gone forward, still completely ignorant of the direction taken by my army; later on, having indirectly heard of it, I hastened to rejoin it."

In these two accounts of d'Erlon, a flagrant inconsistency appears, yet both accounts agree on two points: first, that the 1st Corps was directed on Ligny without the knowledge of d'Erlon; second, that the Emperor's order was addressed to Ney, not to d'Erlon, and that it was only owing to an excess of zeal on the part of the officer entrusted with this order, that the 1st Corps was acquainted with it first.

All the testimonies quoted above, refute these assertions which are inspired by personal motives. It is quite obvious that d'Erlon is endeavouring to cast off his responsibility. The movement which so fatally paralysed the 1st Corps consisted in a march and a countermarch. D'Erlon attempts to prove that he is not responsible for the march, because his generals proceeded to the right without referring to him. He also pleads not guilty on the score of the countermarch which he executed later in pursuance of Ney's order. His grounds are, that as the order was addressed to Ney, not to him, the Emperor seemed to leave him implicitly under the command of the Marshal, whom d'Erlon therefore thought himself bound to continue to obey. Evidently this is the double motive of Count d'Erlon's inaccurate and embarrassed statements.

There remains to be discovered the reason, why the Emperor in his accounts of St. Helena denied, or rather completely omitted his sending this order to d'Erlon, an order whose existence is proved by two letters of Soult, 17th of June, to say nothing of the ten other testimonies. Gourgaud, or Napoleon, for it amounts to the same, says (p. 69): "Napoleon could not perceive the reason of such a movement;" and (p. 67), "The movements of the 1st Corps are not easy to explain." But on the day after the battle, could not the Emperor have sought and obtained an explanation? Baudus, Ney, d'Erlon himself were there present to enlighten him. Undoubtedly the Emperor did not wish to acknowledge, that his keen eye and quick perception had failed him on the battlefield of Ligny to such an extent, and that he was so dismayed by the false direction of d'Erlon's corps which he had himself just summoned, that he had actually mistaken it for a body of the enemy.

48. Above quoted accounts of de Salle and Durutte. See Baudus's notes.

49. Baudus's notes. Gamot and Heymès say that this officer was Colonel Laurent; de Salle says: a marshal des logis of the Guard; d'Erlon (first account): General La Bédoyère (which is impossible, for we know from Petiet (*Souvenirs militaires*, 198) that at five o'clock La Bédoyère was with the Emperor); second account: an officer of the Imperial staff.

Baudus's notes, so minute and precise on this point, show beyond a doubt that it was Forbin-Janson.

50. See order quoted after de Salle, p. 171, and note 47.

51. From Durutte's and de Salle's accounts, from the announcement sent by Vandamme to Napoleon towards a quarter-past five, "That a column of the enemy was emerging from the woods one mile off to the left, and apparently bearing on Fleurus," one must infer that d'Erlon's column first took a short cut between Villers-Perwin and the Voie romaine, then joined the Voie romaine near the road that skirts the Chassart mill, and proceeded by this road in the direction of Fleurus. From the intersection of this road with the Voie romaine, to the point

before Saint-Amand where Vandamme was posted, there is a straight line of just one league. The woods from which the column seemed to emerge were the woods of Villers-Perwin, now cleared out and cut down.

52. See pp. 98, 99, 103.

53. Manuscript notes of Baudus (communicated by M. de Montenon).

54. Manuscript notes of Baudus. D'Erlon's letter to the Duke of Elchingen (*Documents inédits*) and d'Erlon, *Vie militaire*, 295. See letter of Ney to the Duke of Otranto, 26th June : " I learnt that the Emperor had, without informing me, disposed of the 1st Corps." One cannot give credit to Gamot, who is very confused, and Heymès, who is always inaccurate, when they say that Ney was warned by Colonel Laurent of the Imperial staff, for then it would be necessary to admit that Laurent was entrusted with a duplicate. As already stated, the original pencilled note was carried by Forbin-Janson who neglected to convey it to Ney.

55. An hour later, said Baudus (above quoted notes), Ney was still in a state of most violent exasperation.

56. From Gamot's *Refutation*, it appears that Soult's despatch of a quarter-past three reached Ney when the latter already knew of the movement of the 1st Corps. Delcambre must have joined Ney towards five o'clock, and Soult's officer arrived a few minutes later.

Besides, Gamot confuses things when he says that Soult's despatch was brought by Forbin-Janson. Forbin-Janson carried not the despatch from Soult, but the pencilled order from the Emperor; and after acquainting d'Erlon with this order, he had returned directly to Fleurus. Gamot's confusion is accounted for by the fact that Forbin-Janson was seen near Ney on the battlefield of Quatre-Bras, though this was long after the charge of the cuirassiers. On his return to Fleurus, towards five, Forbin-Janson had again been sent to Ney by the Emperor, who was dissatisfied with the way in which he had discharged his mission, and entrusted him with a duplicate or rather a triplicate of the pencilled order. The Emperor even had him provided with a fresh horse, as his own charger was half spent by the first journey. In his manuscript notes, Baudus gives the most minute details on all these points.

57. Letters from officers of the Halkett brigade (*Waterloo Letters*, 320-323, 326, 333, 334), etc.; Letter of Alten to the Duke of Cambridge, Brussels, 20th June (General Gourgaud's papers). The English brigade of Colin Halkett advanced in company columns in the direction of Gémioncourt, whilst the Hanoverian brigade of Kielmansegge came to prolong Picton's left, facing Péraumont.

58. Pontécoulant, 121 ; Fleury de Chaboulon, ii. 159. Baudus (manuscript notes) relates that an hour later Ney exclaimed several times in his presence : " What, is there neither a ball nor a bullet for me ! "

59. Jomini, without entirely excusing Ney, pleads that the Marshal, having only Reille's corps at his disposal, had good ground to fear lest he might not be able to cover the entrance of the Charleroi road till night, and this was the retreating line for the whole Army. This may be true, but for all that d'Erlon could not return in time !

The Duke of Elchingen (*Documents inédits*) remarks that d'Erlon having committed himself to a false direction, his movement could not produce the great results expected by the Emperor. But it is highly improbable that Ney at that time was aware that the 1st Corps was going the wrong road; if he knew it, it was his duty to enlighten d'Erlon through Delcambre as to the right direction, instead of summoning him back to Frasnes.

60. D'Erlon, letter to the Duke of Elchingen (*Documents inédits*, 64); and *Vie militaire*, 95; Durutte's and de Salle's accounts.

Ney (in his *Letter to the Duke of Otrante*), and his apologists, Heymès and Gamot, carefully avoid mentioning this order.

61. Kellermann's account (War Arch.). On the three brigades posted at Liberchies, see Ney's order, Frasnes, 16th June, a quarter-past eleven or half-past eleven.

62. Kellermann's report to Ney, near Frasnes, 16th June, 10 P.M. Kellermann's account. Kellermann to Grouchy, 16th June, P.M. Reille's account (War Arch.); Woodberry, *Journal*, 310; letters of officers of the Halkett brigade (*Waterloo, Letters*, 318, 319, 322, 323, 324, 335, 337). See *Souvenirs d'un ex-officier* (of the 45th), 227, in which there is a statement that the day after the battle, one of the squares remained visibly marked out on the soil by the bodies of the dead.

Most English authors deny that the charge was pushed as far as Quatre-Bras, but Kellermann's testimony is confirmed by Mercer, captain of artillery. He relates (*Journal of the Waterloo Campaign*, i. 263) that, on his arrival, the night of the 16th to the 17th, he saw many bodies of dead cuirassiers lying "just opposite the large farmhouse of Quatre-Bras, on the road which skirts the farm."

63. The Duke of Elchingen says that Ney had an order from the Emperor enjoining him not to use this division. If the verbal order of the 15th was indeed to that effect (the written order enjoins merely to spare the Guard, and to employ in preference the cavalry of the line), Ney certainly acted in direct contradiction to it. On the 15th, it was the Lefebvre-Desnoëttes cavalry in preference to that of Piré, which was at his disposal, that he had directed on Frasnes, against the battalions of Nassau, without any scruple as to sparing it (see pp. 70-72). Besides, it is not absolutely certain that this division was not partially engaged on the 16th at Quatre-Bras in an early stage of the battle. Damitz (i. 197) attributes to it the charge of three o'clock against the 5th battalion of militia. In point of fact, Colbert (letter communicated by General de Colbert) says that the division of the Guard remained in reserve on the 16th; but we know that he had received a bullet wound; and, moreover, the squadron chief, de Stuers of the Red Lancers, without specifying the part taken by his division in the day's business, relates in his notes (comm. by M. de Stuers) that fifty men were disabled in the fight. The question remains therefore a doubtful one.

At all events, it would have been better to employ this division, rather than to place it in a position where it suffered a profitless loss of fifty men; it would have been better still to send it at noon to Liberchies, and to call to Frasnes the three brigades of Kellermann.

64. Kellermann is most emphatic on this point, not only in his account, but in his report to Ney, dated 10 o'clock P.M. It is therefore a grave error on the part of Charras and others, to represent the charge of cuirassiers and the charge of lancers and chasseurs as simultaneous.

65. General Guiton and Colonel Garavaque were also dismounted. Whenever they had to deal with the cavalry of the cuirassiers, the English always preferred aiming at the horses (*Waterloo Letters*, 378).

66. Kellermann's report, 16th June; Kellermann to Grouchy, 17th June; Kellermann's account; Reille's account (War Arch.); Woodberry, *Journal*, 310; Siborne, i. 144; letters of officers from the Kempt and Pack Brigades (*Waterloo Letters*, 359, 378, 386).

67. *Mémoires du roi Jérôme*, vii. 78, 79; Siborne, i. 148-150; letters of officers of the Kempt Brigade (*Waterloo Letters*, 344, 354, 359).

68. Manuscript notes of Colonel Baudus (comm. by M. de Montenon). These notes, as we have stated before, have only been partially reproduced in Colonel Baudus's *Études sur Napoléon;* but they can be trusted, so accurate and so precise are they, although they do not in some points agree with other accounts; the latter, as far as names and details are concerned, do not agree among themselves. Baudus could justly write: "Nobody knows better than myself, the circumstances which precluded the 1st Corps from being of use, either to Marshal Ney or to the Emperor on the day of the 15th."

69. Notes of Baudus. Letter of General F. (comm. by M. X.).

70. Notes of Baudus. See letter of the major of the 92nd Highlanders (*Waterloo Letters*, 387); Siborne, i. 148, 149.

71. Letters of officers of the Maitland and Byng Brigades (*Waterloo Letters*, 241, 252, 258; Letter of Hervey, aide-de-camp to Wellington (*Nineteenth Century*, March 1893); report of Alten to the Duke of Cambridge, Brussels, 20th June (General Gourgaud's papers); Siborne, i. 152.

72. Letters of officers of the Maitland, Byng, Halkett, and Pack Brigades (*Waterloo Letters*, 241, 242, 251, 270, 319, 387, 388, etc.); Siborne, i. 154-158; *Mémoires du roi Jérôme*, 79; Reille's account (War Arch.); *Souvenirs d'un vieux soldat belge*, 83; van Löben, 206.

73. Reille's account (War Arch.).

74. Anglo-Hanoverians, 2,911 (Wellington, *Despatches*, xii. 486); Brunswick, Kruse, and van Merlen, about 1,100 (estimates quoted by Charras, i. 252); Perponcher, 667 (van Löben, 207).

75. With this difference, however, that the enemy established themselves in force in the positions where there were only detachments in the morning, and also that the French kept the farmhouse of Grand Pierrepont taken from the Nassau Corps in the early part of the fight. See plan of the battle at 9 o'clock P.M. in the *Letters of Waterloo*.

76. Reille's account (War Arch.) and d'Erlon's letter to the Duke of Elchingen (*Documents inédits*, 64).

77. D'Erlon's letter to the Duke of Elchingen; Durutte's account

(*Sentinelle de l'Armée*, 1838); *Souvenirs* of General de Salle (*Nouvelle Revue*).

The 1st Corps must have been posted at about 2,000 yards to the east of Saint-Amand and 1,500 yards to the south-east of Wagnelée. This point is precisely in the direction taken by d'Erlon, who marched in accordance with Vandamme's suggestion to the Emperor, from the woods of Villers-Perwin on to Fleurus; the distance which separated him from Fleurus, about 3 kilometres, may account for the fact that the officer sent by the Emperor took a full hour to get there, to reconnoitre the column, to speak to d'Erlon or the officer in charge of the advanced guard, and to return to Napoleon.

Moreover, we know from Damitz (i. 139) that a little later the cavalry of the 1st Corps advanced between Wagnelée and Mellet. It seems then that it did come from the point indicated. This point is 11 kilometres distant from Gémioncourt. Having left Gémioncourt about a quarter past five, Delcambre must have joined d'Erlon towards six o'clock.

78. De Salle, *Souvenirs*, Durutte's account. Durutte speaks of "entreaties" from the right which embarrassed d'Erlon. Do not these "entreaties" mean the advice and requests of the officer despatched by the Emperor to reconnoitre? Surprised to meet the 1st Corps instead of the presumed English column, may he not have pressed d'Erlon to act against the Prussian Army? This is most probable. At any rate, there could not have been fresh instructions from the Emperor, for the Emperor never used "entreaties," he gave orders; and if d'Erlon had received orders from Napoleon, he certainly would have obeyed them. But no order did the Emperor send, because the column then nearing his flank had been described as that of the enemy, and he never thought it could be the 1st Corps.

79. De Salle, *Souvenirs* (*Nouvelle Revue*, 1895); *Souvenirs d'un ex-officier* (of the 45th), 277.

According to a tradition, held as authentic by several historians, the battalions of Drouet d'Erlon's corps which had advanced farthest, were able to distinguish (with a field-glass no doubt) the figures on the knapsacks of the Prussians. The Tippelskirch division was then emerging from Wagnelée, to bear down against Le Hameau and La Haye. This explains how the rear of the Prussians could be visible from the point where the Durutte column had its vanguard, 300 or 400 yards to the south of the mill at Chassart. However, it is a mistake as far as figures on the knapsacks are concerned. In the Prussian Army the knapsacks were not numbered, but their colour was different in the battalions of each regiment, so that the chiefs of the corps might recognise their own battalions at a distance; it was therefore the colour of the knapsacks, not the numbers, which were spoken of.

80. D'Erlon's letter to the Duke of Elchingen (*Documents inédits*, 64).

81. *Souvenirs d'un ex-officier* (of the 45th), 277.

82. Durutte's account. Durutte's rather confused account is elucidated by Damitz's book, i. 141, 142. Wagner (iv. 35) confirms the information of Damitz. Durutte maintains that he hurled two battalions upon Brye.

This is incorrect. As may be seen farther on, the Prussians occupied Brye the whole night.

83. General Brue's letter to Captain Chapuis, Toulouse, 3rd November 1837 (quoted in the *Journal des sciences militaires*, second half-year of 1863).

BOOK II   CHAPTER IV

1. Not only did Ney send no news to the Emperor during the afternoon of the 16th June, when at six o'clock Soult's aide-de-camp, Commander Baudus, wished to return to the Emperor to report to him on the mission he had just fulfilled, but Ney detained him, on the pretext that he needed staff officers. Baudus did not return to Fleurus till two o'clock in the morning or even later (Notes of Baudus, communicated by M. de Montenon).

We must reject the following assertion of Gourgaud (*Campagne de 1815*, 72) : " At eleven in the morning, the Emperor received at Fleurus, the report on what had occurred at Quatre-Bras. The Emperor immediately sent to Marshal Ney orders to pursue the English Army as soon as day dawned, when the latter had begun the retreat, necessitated by the losses of the battle of Ligny."

All this is incorrect.   1st. The account of Ney's sending a report on the evening of the 16th is contradicted by this letter dated from Imperial headquarters at Fleurus (17th) in the morning, and sent to Paris to the Minister of Foreign Affairs : " There is no report from Marshal Ney " (Arch. of Foreign Affairs, 1802).   2nd. The despatch by night to Ney ordering him to attack on the morning of the 17th, is contradicted by this letter of Soult, dated Fleurus, 17th June, morning (Major-General's Register) : " Gen. Flahaut just arrived intimates that : *you are in a state of uncertainty about the results* of yesterday's battle.   Yet I believe I have informed you of the victory."   If the order to attack the English on the 17th had been sent to Ney during the night, the Marshal would not have been *in a state of uncertainty* as to the results of the battle of Ligny, as Flahaut said. On the other hand, these words of Soult : " *Yet I believe* I have informed you," are an apology for a negligence, rather than a statement of a fact. In conclusion, Ney received no information during the night of the 16th to the 17th, and still less any orders.   Equal carelessness on all sides ! Ney neglects to send his report on his movements, and Soult forgets to inform Ney of the victory won at Ligny.

2. Clausewitz (*Der Feldzug von 1815*, 95) applauds the Emperor in this circumstance.

3. From the two accounts of Grouchy (*Observations*, 10, and *Relation succincte*, 17), it would seem—1st, that Grouchy saw the Emperor at Fleurus at eleven o'clock in the evening of the 16th ; 2nd, that the Emperor enjoined him to send the cavalry in pursuit of the enemy that

same night or very early the next morning. Therefore Charras has no right to accuse Napoleon of neglecting to give these orders.

According to Jomini (185, 188), who, however, is mistaken in saying that these orders to Grouchy were given only on the morning of the 17th, the Emperor had also given orders to General de Monthyon, chief of the general staff, to have the enemy pursued in the direction of Tilly and Mont-Saint-Guibert. This is possible for, if Napoleon thought of having the ground explored to his right, he must also have thought of having it explored in front of the centre and before the left. But Monthyon neglected to ensure the execution of these orders. The Prussian documents testify that no reconnaissance took place towards Tilly and Mont-Saint-Guibert during the morning of the 17th.

4. Flahaut's note (in *Le General Flahaut*, by F. Masson, 23). See Soult to Ney, Fleurus, 17th June (Major-General's Register): "General Flahaut who has just arrived. . . ." This letter bears no indication as to time, but it says: "The Emperor proceeded to the mill at Brye." Now we know from Grouchy (*Observations*, 10, and *Relation succincte*, 18), and by a letter dated Imperial headquarters at Fleurus, nine in the morning, 17th June, that Napoleon left Fleurus between eight and nine in the morning. Soult's letter, then, was written about eight in the morning, and Flahaut's assertion that he (Flahaut) left Frasnes at one o'clock in the morning is false. He only started about four, and reached Frasnes about six o'clock.

5. Pajol's despatch before Balâtre, 17th June, four in the morning (General Gourgaud's papers). This message, addressed to Grouchy, had been sent or brought by him to the Imperial headquarters. I have definite reasons for affirming this.

6. Grouchy, *Observations*, 10 ; *Relation succincte*, 18.

7. Soult to Ney, Fleurus, 17th June (Major-General's Register). As we have just seen, this letter which bears no indication as to the time, was written towards eight o'clock in the morning.

8. "I am going to march with the Teste division which His Majesty has just sent me." Pajol to Grouchy, before le Mazy, 17th June, midday (War Arch., Army of the North).

From the point where Teste had bivouacked, on the morning of the 17th, between Brye and Sombreffe to le Mazy, which he reached before noon, there is a distance of two leagues. Consequently Teste had received the order of movement about nine o'clock at the latest, so that this order must necessarily have been sent from Fleurus before nine o'clock. Moreover, a letter dated from the Imperial headquarters at Fleurus, 19th June, nine in the morning (Arch. of Foreign Affairs, 1802) reads thus: "Lobau (which means one of Lobau's divisions) is following the enemy in their flight."

9. Grouchy, *Observations*, 11, 12 ; *Relation succincte*, i. 19 ; Gourgaud, 73, 74.

10. General headquarters, Fleurus, 17th June. "It was nine in the morning. We sprang on our horses to follow the enemy on Namur and Brussels. Yesterday the whole bodyguard of the Emperor came with us to the fire. Had General Delort been only fairly supported he might

have captured fifty cannon in a quarter of an hour. But all this will be done to-day" (Arch. of Foreign Affairs, 1802).

This letter, or rather this note, without either address or signature, yet with all the marks of authenticity, was probably written to the Duke of Vicenza, either by General Fouler, equerry to the Emperor (there are in existence similar letters from Fouler), either by an officer of the Imperial staff, or by an attaché of Bassano's cabinet. It shows that from the time of his leaving Fleurus, Napoleon had conceived the double manœuvre which was carried out during that day. This is confirmed by Soult's letter to Davout, Fleurs, 17th June (Major-General's Register): "The Emperor remounts his horse to follow up the success of the battle of Ligny." This letter was written a short time after the departure of the Emperor, that is to say, between nine and ten o'clock. We know from the notes of Baudus, Soult's aide-de-camp (communicated by M. de Montenon), that the chief of the staff did not accompany the Emperor on his visit to the battlefield, but joined him later at the Bussy mill.

11. Above quoted note (Arch. of Foreign Affairs, 1802). Grouchy, *Observations*, 10; *Relation succincte*, 18; Letter of General Baudrand, quoted by Grouchy, App. viii. 63. According to local traditions, Napoleon must have left the château at eight o'clock. General von Gröben, in observation at Tilly, wrote at noon to Gneisenau: ". . . The French Army was making soup. A short time after nine o'clock a long retinue appeared in sight. The soldiers sprang to their feet shouting: 'Long live the Emperor!'" (report quoted by von Ollech, *Geschichte des Feldzuges von 1815*, 168, 169).

12. Grouchy, *Observations*, 11; *Relation succincte*, 18; Lefol, *Souvenirs*, 69; above quoted notes of Baudus.

13. Grouchy, *Observations*, 11; *Relation succincte*, 18; Report of von Gröben, Tilly, 17th June (quoted by von Ollech, 169).

14. Grouchy, *Observations*, 11; *Relation succincte*, 18.

15. Ney to Soult, 17th June, half-past six in the morning (General Gourgaud's papers). This despatch only reached Soult at Fleurus, after the Emperor's departure. Soult had it forwarded to him on the battlefield of Ligny.

16. Gourgaud, 73, 74; Grouchy, *Observations*, 11, 12; *Relation succincte*, 19. According to Gourgaud, this reconnaissance returned at ten; according to Grouchy, as late as midday. This is an intentional inaccuracy on the part of Grouchy. As may be seen further, by midday, the Marshal had quitted the Emperor, at least half an hour previously.

17. From Pajol's letter to Grouchy, le Mazy, 17th June, midday (War Arch.), it appears that he had sent to the Marshal an aide-de-camp at three o'clock, to announce that he was starting off in pursuit of the enemy; from le Mazy, between six and seven, a despatch to the effect that he had captured on the Namur road several waggons and eight cannon. Moreover, he had written from Balâtre at four o'clock to announce that he had already taken several prisoners (this letter of Balâtre is in General Gourgaud's papers).

The despatch here mentioned (between six and seven o'clock) is from le Mazy.

18. "I had the honour of acquainting you this morning with the movement I effected on Gembloux in pursuit of the enemy who is mustered there. . . ." Exelmans to Grouchy, 17th June (War. Arch.). From this despatch, which was written in front of Gembloux between noon and two o'clock, it is evident that in the course of the morning Exelmans had informed Grouchy of the movement he had effected, between eight and nine in the morning. See on this point, General Berton, *Précis des Batailles de Fleurus et de Waterloo*, 47, and General de Bonnemains' Journal (War Arch.).

19. The 6th Corps now included only the Simmer and Jannin divisions, the Teste division having been detached in the morning with Pajol.

20. Gourgaud, 75 ; see Soult's letter to Ney at the fore of Ligny, 17th June, twelve o'clock (quoted by the Duke of Elchingen, *Documents inédits*, 44) : " The Emperor has just posted in front of Marbais a body of infantry and the Guard, to second your operations ; " and von Gröben's report from Tilly, 17th June, midday (quoted by von Ollech, 168) : " Numerous troops (the 6th Corps) are moving towards Marbais. Fresh reinforcements of troops (the Guard) will follow later in the same direction." Gourgaud says that Lobau's movement commenced at ten o'clock. I believe that it began at eleven o'clock.

21. I give here the Emperor's words, in substance and not literally, as they have been reported in ten different ways.

In the first, by date of his writings (*Observations*, 12), Grouchy simply says : " The Emperor gave me the order to march in pursuit of Marshal Blücher." In his *Fragments historiques* (4), and in his *Relation succincte* (19, and Appendix, i. 17), he repeats in the following terms the Emperor's verbal order : " Set off in pursuit of the Prussians. Complete their defeat by attacking them as soon as you have come up with them, and never lose sight of them. I am going to unite with Marshal Ney in attacking the English, if they keep to this side of the forest of Soignes. You can communicate with me by the paved road (road from Namur to the Quatre-Bras)." In the same work Grouchy also quotes (Appendix, iv. and viii. 63) the testimony of de Blocqueville : " The Emperor gave Marshal Grouchy the order to pursue the enemy as far as Gembloux and Wavre," and this testimony of General Baudrand : " The Emperor says : ' You are to take the 1st and 3rd Army Corps, one division of the 6th, the cavalry, etc., and this evening you must enter Namur.' "

Naturally other versions are given in the accounts from St. Helena. Gourgaud (75) says : " The Emperor issued orders to pursue the Prussians closely, to overthrow their rearguard, not to lose sight of them, to attack their right wing, and to be always in communication with the rest of the army." In his *Mémoires pour servir à l'histoire* (107) Napoleon writes : " Grouchy ought to have followed Blücher, sword in hand, to prevent him from rallying." He had positive orders always to keep between the Charleroi road and Blücher, in order to be in constant communication with the army and in a position to join it. If the enemy fell back on the Meuse, he was to send Pajol's cavalry, to keep them under observation and occupy Wavre with the bulk of the troops.

All discussion on the purport of this verbal order is useless, for a quarter of an hour or half an hour at the most after issuing it, the Emperor sent Grouchy a written order which is quoted further. It is in this written order, not in words more or less correctly repeated, that we find Napoleon's real thought and intention.

22. From the various accounts of Grouchy (*Observations*, 12; *Rémarques*, 10; *Relation succincte*, 19, 20, 23), it appears that it was with no slight embarrassment and annoyance, that the Marshal received the mission to pursue the Prussians. This feeling on the part of Grouchy has been confirmed to me by M. G. de Molinari, formerly chief editor of the *Journal des Débats*, who knew Grouchy in 1845. The Marshal in conversing did not attempt to conceal his regret that the Emperor should have entrusted him with this command, for which he felt himself totally unfitted. Edgar Quinet (*Campagne de 1815*, 166), so to speak, has pictured this state of mind of Marshal Grouchy. Grouchy threw himself at the feet of the Emperor and said: "Sire, take me with you, and bestow this command on Marshal Ney." Such was indeed Grouchy's secret desire, but there is no evidence that he ever expressed it. Is it possible to imagine Ney being recalled from Quatre-Bras, where he was supposed to be fighting with the English? The two divisions of the army changing their heads again? The pursuit of the Prussians thus delayed three hours longer? All this to give Ney time to come to Ligny and assume the command? The idea is an absurdity.

23. Grouchy, *Observations*, 12, 13; *Relation succincte*, 19, 20.

If we are to believe Grouchy, he should have said also that the troops would be very slow in getting started; "that they had not been warned they would have to march on that day; that squads of the men were foraging for provisions; that the infantry had unscrewed their muskets to clean them; that the cavalry (Maurin division) had unsaddled their horses."

I very much doubt whether Grouchy would have dared to urge such paltry objections in the Emperor's presence. How was it that soldiers who had not stirred since *réveil*, had not commenced to clean their arms before ten o'clock? Besides, putting the muskets together was the work of a few minutes. As for the cavalry whose horses were unsaddled, five minutes would have sufficed for re-saddling them.

I also doubt whether the Marshal advised Napoleon to keep him at hand "to cover his right flank" (as he declares, *Relation succincte*, 20), by marching on the left bank of the Dyle, so as to prevent the junction of the English and the Prussians (as the aide-de-camp Bella, questioned in 1841 by Grouchy, pretends that the Marshal told him, during the evening of the 17th June, Appendix, iv. 42). These are assertions made after the event. Grouchy could not have advised the Emperor to employ him in covering the right flank of the army, for Napoleon had already precisely entrusted this very operation to him. But to carry it out, it was necessary to discover the Prussians. Grouchy himself acknowledges this (*Observations*, 12). Napoleon said to him : " It devolves upon you to discover the direction taken by the Prussians." Grouchy says also (*Fragment historiques*, 31), " When I left the Emperor *he was uncertain whether it would be on Brussels or on Namur* that I should have to march." And so from Grouchy's own confession he was in nowise bound by the Emperor's instructions. Besides, if at noon the Marshal had formed the idea of marching along the left bank of the Dyle as he pretends, why did he not do so early the next morning, when all the information gathered gave him every inducement to do so? Finally, it will be noticed that in the declarations of Colonel Baudrand and Colonel de Blocqueville, who were present at this conversation (declarations quoted by Grouchy in his voluminous appendix), it is not even hinted that Grouchy made the slightest objection to Napoleon.

24. Pajol, as I have said, note 17, had sent three despatches to Grouchy before seven in the morning. The eight Prussian cannons had arrived at Imperial headquarters before half-past eight (Grouchy, *Relation succincte*, 17).

25. Exelmans had written from Sombreffe about eight o'clock, that he was marching on Gembloux, and at nine o'clock the Berton brigade had already taken up its position before this village, opposite Thielmann's corps (Exelmans to Grouchy); Gembloux, 17th June, and General de Bonnemains' Journal (War Arch.) ; Berton, *Précis*, 47.

26. Grouchy, *Relation succincte*, 19 ; Appendix i. 18.

27. Manuscript notes of Colonel Baudus : " The chief of the staff, who had not yet finished sending off orders when Napoleon started on horseback (for Ligny), remained at Fleurus for some time longer, and only reached the battlefield at the moment when the head of Marshal Grouchy's columns was going to open the fight in the direction assigned to them."

28. Order to Grouchy, Ligny, 17th June, " dictated by the Emperor to the grand-marshal, in the absence of the chief of the staff" (War Arch.).

29. Some historians contend that it was a report from General Berton which induced Napoleon to give Grouchy fresh instructions, and the only reference they quote is the pamphlet by this general. However, in his *Précis des Batailles de Fleurus et de Waterloo*, Berton says (p. 47): " I heard there (near the Orneau) that the Prussian army was retreating by way of Wavre, and that there were still a great number at Gembloux. *I reported this*, and received orders to proceed at once to Gembloux. I arrived in front of this town at nine in the morning." *He reported this*, not to Napoleon but to Exelmans, and the effect of this report was, that Exelmans directed all his dragoons on Gembloux, and only informed Grouchy of the movement when he was executing it (above quoted letter of Exelmans to Grouchy). In his turn, Grouchy informed Napoleon of it, but not before nine or ten in the morning. Consequently the Emperor received no report at all from Berton. No mere brigade-general ever sent direct reports to the Emperor, unless they were entrusted by him with some special mission.

30. To Marshal Grouchy, Ligny, 17th June, "dictated by the Emperor to the grand-marshal, in the absence of the chief of the staff" (War Arch., Army of the North).

This letter, like the preceding one, bears no indication as to the hour; but it is easy to prove that they were both written *between half-past eleven and midday*, that is to say, between the time Grouchy left Napoleon after receiving his verbal orders, and the moment when Soult rejoined the Emperor in front of Ligny.

1st. In his answer to Grouchy's own questions, aide-de-camp Bella says (*Relation succincte*, Appendix iv. 41): "The Emperor caused a letter to be written to you *soon after you left him*, enjoining you to march on Gembloux. This letter was in General Bertrand's handwriting."

2nd. This annotation inscribed on both letters written by General Bertrand: "*In the chief of the staff's absence*" proves that, if Napoleon by derogation dictated them to the grand-marshal, it was because he could not have them written by Soult, who had not yet joined him. Colonel Baudus, aide-de-camp to Soult (Manuscript Notes, communicated by de Montenon), in fact, says: "The chief of the staff, who had not yet finished sending off orders when Napoleon mounted his horse, remained at Fleurus for some time longer."

It only remains to determine exactly at what time Grouchy left the Emperor, and at what time the latter was joined by Soult.

The report of the Prussian general, von Gröben, addressed about midday from Tilly to Wavre (quoted by von Ollech, 169) bears: "A number of troops are in motion on the Fleurus road in the direction of Gembloux. These are Grouchy's troops." General Rogniat, in command of the engineers of the army, says (*Réponse aux notes critiques de Napoléon*, 270): "The army left the battlefield of Ligny in two columns, between eleven and twelve. As an eyewitness, I can testify to the fact." Baudus (above-quoted notes) says that when Soult arrived from Fleurus at Ligny (which he reached a little before noon, as I will prove further), he saw Grouchy's columns on the march.

The conclusion is that Grouchy had received a verbal order, and had left the Emperor, to execute it between *eleven and half-past eleven*.

On the other hand, it is evident that Soult joined Napoleon at the Bussy mill *a little before noon*, since the order he wrote there, in accordance with the instructions of the Emperor to Marshal Ney, bears: Before Ligny, 17th June, midday (War Arch., Army of the North).

I will add simply, to point it out as a curiosity, that Bertrand's letter to Grouchy emphasising the verbal orders—which letter I repeat has no indication as to the hour, in the copy at the War Arch.—reads thus, "towards three o'clock," in Grouchy's *Relation succincte*. This is an interpolation which cannot be censured too severely.

It is known, moreover, that Grouchy only *recovered* this important and conclusive letter, and published it (1843) after it had been produced in the discussion by Pascallet, in his *Notice biographique sur le maréchal de Grouchy* (Paris, 1842). In 1819 Grouchy coolly wrote: "Such are word for word the only dispositions (the verbal orders) that were communicated to me, and the only orders that I received" (*Observations*, 13). And again, p. 30 : "If I refrain from publishing the orders that I received, it is because they were only transmitted to me verbally." Truly, there never was a more timely and convenient lack of memory !

31. Soult to Ney, before Ligny, 17th June, at noon (quoted by the Duke of Elchingen, *Documents inédits*, 44): "The Emperor has just posted an infantry corps and the Imperial Guard at Marbais. His Majesty charges me to tell you his intentions are that you should attack the enemy at Quatre-Bras in order to drive them from their position, and that you will be assisted in these operations by the corps now posted at Marbais. His Majesty will proceed to Marbais, where he will impatiently await your reports."

In this instance the order is formal. The course is no longer left to Ney, as had been prescribed in Soult's letter of eight o'clock that morning, *to take up positions at Quatre-Bras, should there be only a rearguard there, and to wait, while informing the Emperor if the English army be present in full numbers.* Now, whatever force he has in front of him, Ney is to attack it.

It will be seen that this letter to Ney, dated Ligny, midday, is written by Soult. It is no longer Bertrand's hand that holds the pen, as was the case with both orders to Grouchy.

32. Report of Gneisenau to the King of Prussia ; Wavre, 17th June, 2 o'clock (quoted by von Ollech, *Geschichte des Feldzuges von 1815*, i. 162 *sqq.*); Wagner, *Plan of the Battles*, iv. 46 ; Damitz, *Camp. de 1815*, i. 143 ; von Ollech, 155-157 ; Delbrück, *Das Leben des Grafen von Gneisenau*, ii. 191.

33. Report of Wellington to the King of the Netherlands (19th and 20th of June), copy of which was sent on the 24th June to the King of Würtemberg (quoted by Pfister, *Aus dem Lager der Verbündeten 1814 und 1815*, 371).

34. Even after Wellington had taken up his position at Waterloo, and had asked Blücher to assist him, Gneisenau, as will be seen farther on, hesitated for some time, before engaging the Prussian Army in this new operation. In his report to the King of Prussia, 17th June (already quoted) Gneisenau does not suggest in any way, that he prescribed the retreat upon Wavre, with a view to ultimate action in concert with Wellington.

35. Damitz, i. 210.

36. Von Ollech, 157.

37. Gneisenau's report, Wavre, 17th June, two o'clock (above quoted); Wagner, iv. 47; Damitz, i. 142, 145-147 ; ii. 206-209 ; von Ollech, 157.

38. Gneisenau's report, Wavre, 17th June, two o'clock ; Wagner, iv. 46, 54, 55 ; Damitz, ii. 207, 226 ; von Ollech, 166, 167.

39. Wagner, iv. 46, 55 ; Damitz, ii. 207-209 ; von Ollech, 167. Damitz justly blames Thielmann for his too prolonged halt at Gembloux, although he adds that Thielmann knew that Bülow, who was marching one league off, from Baudeset on Dion-le-Mont, would support him in case of attack. But it was neither for Thielmann nor for Bülow to risk an action in which they might have to contend with the whole French

Army; their object was to concentrate speedily at Wavre, while concealing from the French the direction of their retreat.

40. Bülow's report to Blücher, Dion-le-Mont, 17th June, 10 P.M. (quoted by von Ollech, 167, 168); Damitz, ii. 209, 210. From information gathered by Grouchy and recorded by him (War Arch., Army of the North, 18th June) Bülow passed through Walhain and Corroy. Indeed this is the most direct road from Baudeset to Dion-le-Mont; moreover, had Bülow passed through Corbais, he might have hampered the march of Thielmann, who was compelled to pass through that village. According to the reports of the inhabitants (Grouchy to Napoleon, Gembloux, 17th June, and Walhain, 18th June, War Arch.), Thielmann and Bülow's corps marched in several columns, for there were Prussians passing through all the villages, within an area of from ten to twelve kilometres.

41. Von Gröben's report to Gneisenau, 17th June, about noon (quoted by von Ollech, 169-379).

42. The 1st Hussars (Soult division) had not rallied yet, and the Subervie division had been detached to the left.

43. The previous day, towards the end of the battle, the mounted battery, No. 14 (Pirch's corps), having exhausted its ammunition, had fallen back to the east of Sombreffe, near one of the columns of the Grand Park, which had come from Namur and halted there. Before sunrise, battery and column, probably through fear of being cut off from Sombreffe, had taken the direction of Namur; on their way they had been joined by an isolated squadron of the 7th Uhlans. Damitz, ii. 215, 216. See Wagner, iv. 55, and von Ollech, 172.

44. Pajol to Grouchy before Mazy, 17th June, twelve o'clock (War Arch.). See Pajol, *Le Général Comte Pajol*, iii. 212, 213, 218; and Damitz, ii. 216.

45. Berton, *Précis*, 47. Berton insinuates that in following Pajol up the Namur highway, he merely complied with orders received from Exelmans or from Lieutenant-General Strols, and that he did not act on his own inspiration. He also contends that he heard from the peasants that the Prussians were falling back by Gembloux *on Wavre*, and that he warned Exelmans of this direction of their retreat. This addition of Berton is more or less involuntary. If Exelmans had known at eight in the morning that the direction of retreat was Wavre, is it possible to admit that he would not have notified this to Grouchy, either in the first letter that he sent him at the very time, or in the second written in the afternoon, or in the course of his conversation with Bella, aide-de-camp to the Marshal? (Letter of Exelmans to Grouchy, 17th June, War Arch.; and Grouchy, *Relation succincte*, App. iii. 22).

46. Had Pajol received this information, most likely he would have marched to the right of Exelmans, on the right bank of the Orneau, threatening Thielmann's flank.

47. Exelmans to Grouchy, 17th June (in front of Gembloux from twelve to two o'clock); Gen. de Bonnemains' Journal (War Arch., Army of the North); Berton, *Précis*, 48.

48. According to the above-quoted letter of Exelmans, which bears no indication as to the time, he warned Grouchy about eight o'clock that he was bearing on Gembloux, in pursuit of the enemy. But after giving this message he sent no news whatever, except in this very letter which he wrote between midday and two o'clock, and which Grouchy declares he did not receive till four o'clock (*Relation succincte*, Appendix iii. 22).

However, the intelligence sent at eight o'clock was too slight to lead the Emperor to take any decisive step, for it left him in doubt whether the enemy would still be at Gembloux when Exelmans arrived there. If, on the contrary, at half-past nine Exelmans had sent a second despatch, announcing that he had before him at Gembloux a Prussian corps of 20,000 men in camp, this announcement would very probably have induced Napoleon to make his arrangements an hour earlier.

49. In the details gathered by Grouchy at Walhain (War Arch., Army of the North, 18th June) it is mentioned that the passage of Bülow's corps at Walhain was completed by three in the afternoon of the 17th. This information agrees with the German documents which state that the head of the Bülow column did not reach Dion-le-Mont before eight in the evening.

50. See Henry Houssaye, *1815*, ii., note on page 230.

51. Grouchy, *Observations*, 13 ; Bella's and de Blocqueville's declarations (*Relation succincte*, Appendix iv. 4, 40, 41).

52. Grouchy, *Observations*, 13. See manuscript notes of Baudus (communicated by M. de Montenon).

53. Manuscript notes of Baudus. See General Pétiet, *Souvenirs*, 202.

54. Grouchy, *Relation succincte*, 22, 23. See *Fragment historique*, 9, 10.

55. Grouchy, *Relation succincte*, 22 ; Gérard, *Dernières Observations*,

56. Gérard says that it was then about one o'clock. It was certainly not so late, Grouchy having left the Emperor about half-past eleven, and having had but a short conversation with Soult.

Grouchy credits himself with the idea of the Gembloux movement, although it is obvious that he only ordered it in compliance with the instructions of Bertrand's second letter. The proof is that, on quitting the Emperor, Grouchy sent to Vandamme orders to proceed to *Point-du-Jour*, and that half an hour later, after receiving the letter in question, he ordered Gérard to go to *Gembloux*.

56. "I was indignant. Instead of ordering his horses, Gérard had given orders for his dinner to be prepared" (Grouchy, *Relation succincte*, 23. See 24, 25).

And indeed Gérard had ample time to dine, since before mounting his horse he must of necessity wait till the 3rd Corps had reached the height of Saint-Amand and defiled completely. General Hulot (Report communicated by Baron Hulot) says that, towards one, the 4th Corps received the order to prepare to march, and that the movement commenced as soon as the 3rds Corps had cleared the way.

57. I shall not attempt to explain the extraordinary dilatoriness of this march, for there are no documents whatever on the question. I

shall limit myself to proving that Vandamme, who had left Saint-Amand before noon, did not reach *Point-du-Jour* till after three.

There are ample proofs that he broke up camp before noonday. 1st. The report of von Gröben, addressed about noon from Tilly to Wavre (quoted by von Ollech, 169) : "A number of troops are moving on the Fleurus road, in the direction of Gembloux." 2nd. By the *Notes critiques* (270) of Rogniat, commander-in-chief of the engineers, the army in two columns left the battlefield between eleven and midday. 3rd. By the Manuscript Souvenirs of Baudus, who relates that when Soult went from Fleurus to the Bussy mill (where he arrived before twelve, as I have proved in the preceding pages), he saw Grouchy's columns on the march. 4th. Berthezène, lieutenant-general of Vandamme, who says in his *Souvenirs* that Grouchy's little army started about twelve.

On the other hand, General Hulot says that "the tail of the 3rd Corps had got beyond Ligny at three o'clock." Allowing an hour and a quarter for the passing of the whole army corps, it may be presumed that if the tail had passed beyond Ligny at three, the head must have arrived there at a quarter to two. The distance from Ligny to *Point-du-Jour* is one league. Therefore, even on the assumption that Vandamme's corps had marched much more rapidly on leaving Ligny than it had done previously, the head of the column could not have arrived before three at the very earliest.

58. Grouchy, *Relation succincte*, 23.

59. The Vallin division of Gérard's corps was at liberty to effect this operation.

60. Grouchy, *Observations*, 12.

61. Grouchy, *Relation succincte*, 23 ; Bella's declaration (Appendix iv. 40).

62. Exelmans to Grouchy, Gembloux, 17th June (War Arch.).

It will be remembered (see p. 136) that Exelmans' letter was written at two o'clock at the latest, that is to say, before Thielmann had resumed his march.

63. "I have just arrived with Vandamme's and Gérard's corps" (Grouchy to Exelmans, Gembloux, 17th June, seven in the evening, War. Arch.). In his various reports, Grouchy pretends that he rode at a gallop to Gembloux, leaving the infantry column behind him. His letter to Exelmans proves this assertion to be incorrect.

64. Grouchy's above-quoted letter. Having reached the *Point-du-Jour* towards three o'clock, Vandamme's infantry could not have taken four hours to traverse seven kilometres. Most likely it made a long halt at the *Point-du-Jour*.

65. Hulot's report (communicated by Baron Hulot).

66. Berton, *Précis*, 47, 48. See above-quoted letter of Exelmans.

67. Of course Exelmans with his 3,300 dragoons, even had they been assisted by the 4,500 infantry and horsemen of Pajol (granting that he had warned the latter before noon), could not have blocked the road, by Ernage or Walhain, against Thielmann's 20,000 men. Thielmann would have held him at bay with his rearguard, and continued his

march on Wavre. But while following the Prussians closely, without getting seriously engaged, Exelmans might at least have known as early as three o'clock, that they were falling back on Wavre, and this information conveyed to Grouchy would have compelled the Marshal to manœuvre in a different way.

68. Berton, 48, 49. See Wagner, iv. 35; Damitz, ii. 208; Journal of the Bonnemains brigade (War Arch., at the date 3rd June).

69. Berton, 49. See Grouchy to Napoleon, Gembloux, 17th June, a quarter past ten (War Arch.).

70. Grouchy (*Relation succincte*, 24) contends that Vandamme posted his army corps a league and a half beyond Gembloux. This is another lapse of memory. Lefol (*Souvenirs*, 75), whose testimony agrees with that of Vandamme (Letter to Grouchy, and order of the day, Gembloux, 17th June, War Arch.), expressly states that the troops of the 3rd Corps bivouacked around Gembloux, excepting the staff, who were housed in this village. The position of Gérard's bivouacks is indicated in Hulot's report (communicated by Baron Hulot).

71. Grouchy, *Relation succincte*, 25. The Marshal also pleads in excuse the darkness of the night; he forgets that Vandamme's corps halted at Gembloux at seven o'clock in the evening, and that at this time of the year, even in heavy rain, it is quite light enough to march up to half-past eight.

72. Bonnemains' Journal (War Arch.); Berton, *Précis*, 49. Grouchy says in his letter to Napoleon (Gembloux, 17th June, 10 P.M.) that Exelmans sent out these reconnaissances by his orders. This is not certain, for—1st, no such order is prescribed in Grouchy's letter to Exelmans (Gembloux, 7 P.M.); 2nd, we know by Bonnemains' letter to Exelmans (Ernage, 10 P.M.), that Bonnemains had pushed on as far as Tourinnes, had halted about an hour in front of this village, and was already retracing his steps by eight in the evening. Sauvenière being nearly two leagues distant from Tourinnes, Bonnemains must certainly have left Sauvenière before seven o'clock, that is to say, before the arrival of Grouchy at Gembloux.

73. Bonnemains to Chastel, Ernage, 17th June, a quarter past ten in the evening (War Arch.); Journal of the Bonnemains brigade; Berton, *Précis*, 49.

74. Pajol to Grouchy, before Mazy, 17th June (*Relation succincte*, 24), states that he received this letter before reaching Gembloux.

75. Information gathered at Gembloux, 17th June (War Arch.,' Army of the North). This "information," with two more of the same order, is reproduced in Grouchy's book *Relation succincte*, Appendix ii. 21, 22. There, as in the copy at the War Arch., it is described as *troisième renseignement recueilli à Gembloux*. In reality it should be entered as *premier renseignement recueilli à Gembloux*. It is obvious that this "information" of Gembloux is previous to both the others of Sart-à-Walhain dated "yesterday, 17th June." Moreover Grouchy (*Relation succincte*, 25, 27, 33) expressly says that the first piece of information was obtained at Gembloux towards seven in the evening on the 17th;

the second at Sart-à-Walhain during the night; and the third at Sart-à-Walhain on the 18th, about ten o'clock in the morning. Finally, Grouchy's three letters to the Emperor, 17th June, 10 P.M.; 18th June, 6 A.M.; and 18th June, 11 A.M. (*Relation succincte*, Appendix ii. 3-6), reproduce in part and in sequence these three pieces of information. It is easy to perceive that the first, which is erroneously numbered third, was received first; that which is numbered first was received second; and that which is numbered second was received last.

76. Grouchy might have have effected this movement without overtaxing the strength of his troops or exhausting their patience. Exelmans' dragoons alone would have had to leave their cantonment; Vandamme's corps had hardly commenced preparations for bivouacking, while Gérard's corps was still on the march.

Before arriving at Gembloux, Gérard would only have had to wheel the head of his column to the left, to gain the road leading to Saint-Géry.

77. Grouchy to Napoleon, Gembloux, 17th June, 10 P.M. (War Arch., Army of the North).

In his *Relation Succincte* (Appendix ii. 3, 4) Grouchy quotes this letter, but in slightly different terms. Instead of " . . . If the bulk of the Prussians retire upon Wavre, I will follow them in this direction in order that they may not reach Brussels, and so separate them from Wellington"; it reads: " . . . I will follow them in this direction and attack them as soon as I have come up to them." Marquis de Grouchy (*Mémoires de Grouchy*, iv. 58, 59, and 263, 264) has also quoted the letter of ten in the evening with this second wording, adding that he has the original before his eyes. He no doubt means the "rough copy," for the orginal of a letter generally remains in the hands of the recipient. However, the copy at the War Arch. bears on its margin, *after the original*, and Gérard has quoted this letter (*Dernières Observations*, 15, 16) in the first edition with this note: "Certified in conformity with the original handed to us by the Emperor Napoleon, and which is in our possession. Signed, GENERAL GOURGAUD."

Finally, I was informed of another copy belonging to the collection of St. Helena, and which agrees with the copy at the War Archives.

The two different versions of this letter have given rise to much discussion. I am inclined to believe that the copy at the War Arch. is the authentic one. But in my opinion the question is of little importance. In both texts Grouchy commences by speaking of a possible movement of the Prussians to join Wellington by Wavre. Whether he says: "I will pursue them so that they cannot reach Brussels, and I will thus separate them from Wellington," or "I shall follow them and attack them as soon as I come up to them," the meaning remains the same. Be it as it may, it is clear that Grouchy announces his intention to attack the Prussians on the march, and that the Emperor on receipt of the letter was certain that Grouchy would manœuvre, so as to prevent a flank movement of the Prussians.

78. Grouchy's orders to Exelmans, to Vandamme, to Pajol, and to Gérard, Gembloux, 17th June, in the evening, and 10 P.M. (War Arch.).

It is worthy of remark that in these various orders, Perwez is several times mentioned, whereas there is no reference to Wavre.

BOOK II CHAPTER V

1. Ney's report to Soult, Frasnes, half-past six in the morning (General Gourgaud's papers); d'Erlon's report to Ney, 17th June, in the morning (War Arch.). From five in the morning to two in the afternoon a few shots were exchanged between the outposts (Colonel Taylor's letter of the 10th Hussars, *Waterloo Letters*, 166).
2. By Marshal Soult's letter written between seven and eight in the morning (see Henry Houssaye, p. 126).
3. This despatch arrived at about eight o'clock in the evening (Letter of Hervey, aide-de-camp to Wellington, 3rd July 1815, *Nineteenth Century*, March 1893). See Damitz, ii. 206.
4. Hervey's above-quoted letter. Müffling, *Aus meinem Leben*, 206; Damitz, ii. 206, 212.
5. Hervey's above-quoted letter; Müffling, *Aus meinem Leben*, 206; Report of the Prince of Orange, 17th June, 2 A.M. (General Gourgaud's papers).
6. Wellington's orders, 16th June, in the evening (*Despatches*, xii. 474-476); Letters of Uxbridge, Kennedy, Vivian, Banner, Taylor (*Waterloo Letters*, 5, 66, 93, 148, 166); van Löben, 231, 232.
7. Above-quoted letter of Hervey, aide-de-camp to Wellington.
8. Wellington, Memorandum on the Battle of Waterloo (*Suppl. Despatches*, x. 527); Colonel Taylor's above-quoted letter; Müffling, *Aus meinem Leben*, 207, and *Histoire de la Campagne*, 16; Hervey's above-quoted letter; General von Hoffmann, *Geschichte des Feldzuges von 1815*, 67; Lord Malmesbury, after Captain Bowles's Souvenirs (*Letters*, ii. 447). Müffling and Hoffmann say that the officer in charge of this reconnaissance was the quartermaster-general of the English Army, Colonel de Lancy. I am satisfied with the English testimonies.
9. Lord Malmesbury (from the notes of Captain Bowles), *Letters*, ii. 447. See Corresp. of Wellington (Müffling), *Histoire de la Campagne*, 18, 19, 20.
10. Müffling, *Aus meinem Leben*, 207.
11. Memorandum on the defence of the Netherlands, 22nd September 1814 (*Despatches of Wellington*, xii. 129; Wagner, iv. 61).
12. Wellington to Lord Hill, 17th June (*Despatches*, xii. 475); Müffling, *Aus meinem Leben*, 208, and (Corresp. of Wellington) *Histoire de la Campagne*, 16; Letter of Vivian (*Waterloo Letters*; 166); Siborne, *History of the War in 1815*, i. 250. See Wellington's memorandum (*Suppl. Despatches*, x. 527).
13. Müffling, *Aus meinem Leben*, 208, and (Wellington's Corresp.) *Histoire de la Campagne*, 19, 20; Colonel Fraser, *Letters*, 543. Cf. von

Ollech, *Geschichte des Feldzuges von 1815*, 180, and Wellington's Memorandum (*Suppl. Despatches*, x. 527).

14. Wellington's Corresp. (Müffling), *Histoire de la Campagne*, 18, 19; Siborne, i. 252, 253. See Damitz, ii. 226; W. Gomm, *Letters*, 356; and *Waterloo Letters*, 5, 27, 66, 94, 148, 253, 366, etc.

Whilst this infantry was advancing on Mont-Saint-Jean, through Genappe and Rossomme, the troops which had concentrated at Nivelles under Lord Hill were marching from the latter town on Mont-Saint-Jean, *vià* Braine-l'Alleud. See orders from Wellington to Lord Hill (Quatre-Bras, morning of 17th June) *Despatches*, xii. 477).

15. Mercer, *Journal of the Waterloo Campaign*, i. 266. See Colonel Taylor's letter, of the 10th Hussars (*Waterloo Letters*, 166), relating that at midday he could see the French preparing their soup.

16. See pp. 129, 132; Soult's order to Ney, 17th June, midday: "His Majesty proceeds to Marbais."

17. See Soult's letters to Ney, Fleurus, 8 A.M. (Chief of the Staff's Register), and at the front of Ligny, 17th June, midday (Duke d'Elchingen, *Documents inédits*), in which he enjoins this Marshal to send reports and to attack the enemy.

We must absolutely discard the local tradition, according to which Napoleon stopped at Marbais, at the house of a certain Delestange, and slept an hour there, after taking some breakfast. (While I was in Belgium, I was shown twenty different houses where the Emperor stopped.) The Bussy mill is at a distance of 10 kilometres from Quatre-Bras. The Emperor, who had left the mill about a quarter past twelve, arrived at 1,000 or 1,500 yards' distance from Quatre-Bras about two o'clock. As he was marching with the columns, that is to say, at a foot's pace, he had only time for a short halt at Marbais. Moreover, this halt was necessary to allow the officer who carried Soult's order (sent at midday) enough time to rejoin Ney at Frasnes, by the Roman way and Villers-Perwin. The Emperor had intended at first to second Ney's attack (see the order referred to), and not to precede it. But in a fit of impatience at Marbais, he marched on Quatre-Bras without waiting till Ney had opened fire.

18. Napoleon, *Mém.* 109; Gourgaud, 76; Damitz, ii. 226.

It is expressly stated in the three accounts, that the march was reconnoitred by the hussars. But of the five regiments of hussars in the Army of the North, the 1st, 4th, and 5th were with Pajol on 17th June, on their way to Namur, and the 6th (Maurin division) was with Gérard marching to Gembloux. Therefore the regiment referred to here can only be the 7th (Colonel Marbot) of the Jacquinot division in d'Erlon's corps. On the previous day, when d'Erlon had retraced his steps towards Frasnes, he had left this division and also Durutte's division before Wagnelée. We know from Durutte's account (*Sentinelle de l'Armée*, 8th March 1836) that Jacquinot pushed on to the north-west of Wagnelée, as far as the road from Quatre-Bras to Namur, that is to say pretty near Marbais. We are also told by Durutte that on the morning of the 17th his division was recalled by d'Erlon to Villers-Perwin;

but from his account may be inferred the fact that Jacquinot's cavalry did not follow this manœuvre. It was most likely left near Marbais. The Emperor having come across it there, employed it to form his advanced guard.

19. Napoleon, *Mém.* 109.

Subervie, detached from Pajol's corps, from the afternoon of the 16th, had marched with Lobau in the morning. The preceding note explains the circumstances through which Jacquinot (of d'Erlon's corps) found himself with Napoleon. Domon (of Vandamme's corps) and Milhaud, had just joined the Emperor, who, in his letter of half-past eleven, had ordered Grouchy to send them on to him (see p. 131).

20. Gourgaud, 76, 77 ; Napoleon, *Mém.* 109, 110.

21. Pontécoulant, *Souvenirs militaires,* 180. See Mercer, *Journal of the Waterloo Campaign,* i. 269.

22. Letters of General Vivian and Colonel Taylor of the 10th Hussars (*Waterloo Letters,* 148, 154, 155, 167); Letter of Hervey, aide-de-camp to Wellington, 3rd July 1815 (*Nineteenth Century,* March 1893). See Siborne, ii. 256-258.

Taylor asserts that he heard Wellington say that the battle should begin against the cuirassiers, but that Wellington gave up this scheme upon the judicious advice of Lord Uxbridge. In any case, Wellington could never have thought of making but one single charge against his assailants, and then falling back immediately. He could never have wished to engage in battle at Quatre-Bras, with his cavalry only, against the united armies of Napoleon and of Ney.

23. Letters of Lord Uxbridge, Vivian, Taylor, Kennedy, Banner, etc. (*Waterloo Letters,* 2, 5, 66, 94, 119, 148, 167, etc.); Mercer, i. 267-278; Tomkinson, *Diary of a Cavalry Officer,* 383.

24. The approach of the Imperial army had been signalled toward one or a quarter past one, and the retreat of the English cavalry commenced about two o'clock. All the witnesses among the combatants who thought of marking the hour, agree on these points (*Waterloo Letters,* 5, 27, 94, 148, etc.).

25. Mercer, *Journal of the Campaign,* i. 269, 270. See letters of Colonel Taylor and General Vivian (*Waterloo Letters,* 154, 167).

26. Mercer, i. 269, 270; Vivian's letters (*Waterloo Letters,* 154, 167, etc.); W. Gomm, *Letters,* 356; Cotton, *A Voice of Waterloo,* 24; Gourgaud, 77; Napoleon, *Mémoires,* 110; Pontécoulant, *Souvenirs,* 180.

By his silence in regard to this cavalry manœuvre Napoleon seems to imply that he waited for d'Erlon's corps at least half-an-hour before sending his cavalry forward; but from the above-quoted English documents, it appears that the pursuit on the part of the cavalry followed immediately on Lord Uxbridge's retreat. As for the regiments employed in the first line in this pursuit, we know from the details of the fight of Genappe (see further) that they belonged, not to the Domon division, as Pontécoulant asserts, but to the divisions led by Subervie and Jacquinot.

27. Gourgaud, 77, 78; Napoleon, *Mémoires,* 110. Foreign documents (Mercer's Journal, *Waterloo Letters,* book on Damitz) confirm absolutely the assertion of Napoleon in regard to Ney's immobility.

28. Diary of General Foy, 17th June (communicated by Count de Foy); Souvenirs of General de Salle, in command of the artillery of the 1st Corps in 1815 (*Nouvelle Revue*, 15th January 1895). These impartial testimonies must take precedence over that of d'Erlon (*Notice sur ma vie*, 96), who does not mention these reproaches of the Emperor. According to him, however, it would seem that Napoleon said with deep grief, "They have ruined France!" But this appeared to refer to Marshal Ney.

29. "The Emperor has seen with deep concern that yesterday you were unsuccessful; the divisions have acted independently of each other. It is owing to this that you have suffered losses. Had the corps of Counts d'Erlon and Reille been together, not an Englishman of the corps that attacked you would have escaped; had Count d'Erlon executed the movement that the Emperor ordered, the Prussian army might have been totally destroyed and we might have taken 30,000 prisoners" (Register of the Chief of the Staff).

30. Gourgaud, 78; Napoleon, *Mémoires*, 110; Fragment of Molitor's Memoirs (War Arch., Historical Memoirs).

31. Wellington would perhaps have attempted to double back on Nivelles. But the French, finding themselves two to one, would have thrown themselves furiously in the pursuit of him, and at any rate, in taking this line of retreat, Wellington would have sacrificed Brussels, and renounced all hope of joining the Prussian Army.

32. Gourgaud, 78, 79; Napoleon, *Mémoires*, 111; Pontécoulant, 183. See Napoleon, *Mémoires*, 182; ". . . What would I not give to have Joshua's power to-day and stop the progress of the sun for two hours!"

It was Domon, not Subervie, who flanked the right (see note 26).

33. Mercer, *Journal of the Waterloo Campaign*, i. 270-274. Pontécoulant, 185: "This march resembled a steeple-chase rather than the pursuit of an enemy." Gourgaud, 79: "The enemy was hotly pursued at the point of the sword" (see *Waterloo Letters*, 167, 168). And it is of this furious pursuit that Wellington dared to write, in his report of 19th June (*Letters and Despatches*, xii. 478): "The enemy did not attempt to molest our march from the rear."

34. On old maps, the small river which passes Genappe, bears the name of Genappe river, and runs on towards the east, till its junction with the Dyle. But the map of the Belgian staff calls this river the Dyle. It is generally known as such in the country.

35. Tomkinson, *Diary of a Cavalry Officer*, 284, 285; Mercer, i. 275-278; Letter of Lord Uxbridge, Brussels, 28th June, quoted by Cotton, *A Voice of Waterloo*, 27; Letters of Evans, Grady, Vivian (*Waterloo Letters*, 37, 60, 135, 155); Siborne, i. 261-267; Pontécoulant, 186, 187; Pétiet, *Souvenirs militaires*, 205-208; Paillard, *Biographie du General Sourd*, 15.

During the skirmish at Quatre-Bras, the English lost 238 men killed, wounded, or taken prisoners (Lists of the missing, 17th June, *Despatches of Wellington*, xii. 485).

36. Pétiet, *Souvenirs*, 204, 208 ; Pontécoulant, 185, 186 ; *Souvenirs d'un ex-officier*, 281.

Pétiet was on Soult's staff. Pontécoulant, the son of the Senator, was a lieutenant in the horse artillery of the Guard, and was attached to the very battery which marched in the advanced guard on 17th June.

37. Larrey, *Relations de Campagne*, 395 ; Letter of Sourd quoted by Paillard, *Sourd*, 17 ; Pontécoulant, 186.

38. On the 26th of November 1812, a gunner, whose arm had been amputated in the open field, rose immediately after the operation, and resumed his course with a firm gait, saying, "Never mind, I have still a long way to cover before I get to Carcassonne!" (General Lejeune, *Mémoires*, ii. 275).

39. Letter of Lieutenant Grady (*Waterloo Letters*, 162) ; Mercer, i. 275 ; Cotton, *A Voice of Waterloo*, 24 ; Napoleon, *Mémoires*, 111.

40. Gourgaud, 79, says : half-past six ; Pétiet, 208 : six o'clock.

These assertions are confirmed by foreign testimonies. The Prince of Orange, in his report to the King of the Netherlands, Brussels, 22nd June (*Suppl. Despatches of Wellington*, x. 555) reports that he rejoined the rearguard of the Brunswickers near Mont-Saint-Jean, passed it, established his battery, and that, a short time after, the Brunswickers crossed the valley, followed by the French advanced guard.

The distance from Quatre-Bras to La Belle Alliance is only twelve kilometres ; but the pursuit, very brisk at the outset, considerably slackened after the struggle at Genappe, which had lasted over an hour. See Report of von Gröben (quoted by von Ollech, 179), who had heard the cannonade from Mont-Saint-Guibert.

41. *La Belle Alliance* is an inn situated on the highroad from Charleroi to Brussels, on the extreme edge of the plateau which faces the Mont-Saint-Jean plateau. The name of *Belle Alliance* was ironically intended to commemorate the marriage of the first proprietor of the inn, who was old and ugly, with a young and pretty peasant girl.

42. Gourgaud, 79 ; Napoleon, *Mémoires*, 111, 112 ; Mercer, i. 281-283 ; Pétiet, 208, 209 ; Letter of Captain Rudyart (*Waterloo Letters*, 232) ; Cotton, 27.

43. Reille's account (War Arch.) ; Daily notes of General Foy (communicated by Count de Foy) ; Notes of Duuring, chief of battalion (communicated by M. de Stuers) ; Durutte's account (*Sentinelle de l'Armée*, 8th March 1836) ; *Relation de la dernière Campagne* (by René Bourgeois, surgeon-major in the cuirassiers), 67.

44. Gourgaud, 79, 80 ; Napoleon *Mémoires*, 112 ; Pétiet, 209.

45. Mercer, i. 283.

46. D'Erlon to Ney, in camp, on the evening of 17th June (War Arch.).

47. D'Erlon to Ney, in camp, on the evening of 17th June (War Arch.) ; Reille's account ; above-quoted notes of Foy ; Notes of Captain de Stuers of the red lancers (communicated by M. de Stuers). Dupuy, *Souvenirs militaires*, 288, 289. See *Relation de la dernière Campagne*, 71.

48. General Petit's account ; above-quoted notes of Duuring, chief of battalion of the 1st Unmounted Chasseurs of the Guard. See Mauduit,

Derniers jours de la Grande Armée, ii. 230. In Petit's account, the name of the village is left blank, but it must be Glabais, the only village between Genappe and Le Caillou farm, to the east of the Brussels road. Only the 1st battalion of the 1st Chasseurs came as far as Le Caillou; it did duty as Guard at the Imperial headquarters. Duuring, who commanded this battalion, states that the next day, from Le Caillou he saw the Guard marching on the highroad.

49. René Bourgeois (surgeon-major of the cuirassiers), *Relation de la dernière Campagne,* 67, 71; Lemonnier, *Souvenirs militaires,* 375; Mauduit, ii. 231, 233; Précis des journées des 15, 16, 17, et 18 juin (*Ambigû* of London, lii. 430); *Souvenirs d'un ex-officier,* 281-283; Pétiet, *Souvenirs militaires,* 209. Gembloux was also pillaged, and the night before, Fleurus, Ligny, Saint-Amand, and Gosselies had been looted also.

See the orders of the day of Vandamme, Gembloux, 18th June (War Arch.); of Foy, Gosselies, 17th June (Register of correspondence, communicated by Count Foy); and Gen. Radet's letter to Soult, Fleurus, 17th June, in which he offers his resignation of the post of Grand Provost of the Army (War Arch.).

50. Mauduit, ii. 231; Letter of Lavoye, sub-lieutenant of the 29th of line, Soissons, 26th June (communicated by M. Piat); Lemonnier, 375; *Souvenirs d'un ex-officier* (of the 45th), 283, 284; *Relation de la dernière Campagne,* 71. Surgeon Bourgeois, the author of this report, does not attempt to conceal his ultra-royalist sentiments; therefore his testimony on this point is all the more weighty.

51. Colonel Tomkinson, *The Diary of a Cavalry Officer,* 287; Letters of Gomm, Kennedy, Taylor, Pratt, etc. (*Waterloo Letters,* 28, 67, 168, 326, and *passim.*); Cotton, *A Voice of Waterloo,* 28; *Relation anglaise de la bataille de Waterloo,* 13, 32; *Relation* (anglaise) *de la Campagne de Flandre,* 215, 223, 236, 285; Mercer, *Journal of the Campaign,* ii. 285-292; Letter of Hervey, aide-de-camp to Wellington, 3rd July 1815 (*Nineteenth Century,* March 1893).

52. Journal of the Emperor's halting-places (Nat. Arch. AF.* iv. 437).

With its two-storey front, its small proportions, and the garden that surrounds it, Le Caillou has more the appearance of a villa than of a farmhouse. It is a country villa at the present time. A barn adjoining it in 1815 was burnt down by the Prussians, during the night of the 18th of June. The room in which the Emperor slept on the 17th is on the ground floor, and looks on the road. Here his attendants had prepared his camp bed, covered with a silk counterpane with gold fringe, and hung with green satin curtains. Next to this room, and looking on the garden, was the half dining-room, half drawing-room in which he dined on the 17th and breakfasted on the 18th. Through the cordial hospitality of the present proprietors of Le Caillou, Mme. Emile Coulon and her two sons, MM. Emile and Henry Coulon, I sat at the very table—still religiously preserved—where Napoleon, so to speak, ate his last meal as Emperor. Besides M. Coulon, whom I can never sufficiently thank for the collection of local traditions and various documents he made for my benefit in that neighbourhood, I am also indebted to M. Clement Lyon of Charleroi for his very cordial reception and much valuable information. He was kind enough to act as my guide from this town to a point beyond Ligny, during one of the excursions I made to the scene of the war, with my kind colleague of "La Sabretache," M. Paul Marmottan. To MM. Gouttier, notary at Braine-l'Alleud, van Malderghem, sub-director of the Archives in Brussels, Berger, burgomaster at Genappe, Dr. Delpierre of Braine-l'Alleud, Viandier, notary at Nil-Saint-Vincent, I offer also my sincere thanks.

53. *La Belle Alliance, Ode à la Princesse d'Orange,* by Conquébau (son of the farmer of Le Caillou, Boucqueau, of which Conquébau is the anagram).

All these facts, as well as the details given in the preceding note, are recorded in the bills of sale of Le Caillou (communicated by M. Emile Coulon).

54. Napoleon, *Mém.* 114. See Soult's letter to Grouchy, Le Caillou, 18th June, 10 A.M. (Major-General's Register). See Wagner, iv. 55; Damitz, ii. 226.

It was Colonel von Sohr's brigade stationed behind Tilly to observe the movements of the French. Two or three *platoons* were detached from the bulk of the cuirassiers in order to reconnoitre the Prussian cavalry. After a slight skirmish, the latter withdrew slowly, and was followed at a respectful distance nearly as far as Mont-Saint-Guibert (nine kilometres as the crow flies). There at about four o'clock the cuirassiers moved off.

Wagner is mistaken when he says that von Sohr's cavalry only reached Mont-Saint-Guibert at dusk. We know from von Gröben's report (quoted by von Ollech, 170) that at five this cavalry was relieved at Mont-Saint-Guibert by the Ledebur detachment (Bülow's corps).

55. Napoleon (*Mém.* 115), expressly states that he sent to Grouchy, at ten at night, on the 17th, the order to despatch a detachment of 7,000 men to Saint-Lambert to unite with the Imperial Army, and to march himself with all his troops on this point, as soon as he had ascertained that Blücher had evacuated Wavre (see Gourgaud, *Campagne de 1815*, 82, where the same order is reported in slightly different words).

This assertion is obviously erroneous. If, as is probable, though not certain, the Emperor wrote to Grouchy on the evening of the 17th, it was simply to inform him of the march of a Prussian column on Wavre, and to enjoin him to march himself in that direction, "in order to draw nearer to the Imperial Army and manœuvre with it." The proof is that the very next morning at ten, Napoleon sent Grouchy instructions to that effect (Soult to Grouchy, Le Caillou, 18th June, ten o'clock, Register of Chief of the Staff). If, on the 17th, when he did not yet know whether he would fight a battle on the next day or not, Napoleon sent to Grouchy precise and formal orders to occupy Saint-Lambert, on the 18th, when the battle was on the point of commencing, there was all the more reason for giving him this same order. On the other hand, in the letter written at Le Caillou, Wavre is mentioned and not Saint-Lambert.

The statement of Baudus (Manuscript Souvenirs) to the effect that Soult advised the Emperor, on the evening of the 17th, to recall part of Grouchy's forces, and that his advice was disregarded, is another proof that the said letter was not sent.

As for the argument of many historians, that Napoleon could not have sent Grouchy this order on the evening of the 17th, because it does not appear in the Register of the Chief of the Staff, it is worthless. During this campaign several others of Napoleon's orders were not entered in this register, namely, Soult's letter to Ney, on 17th June, midday (Duke of Elchingen, *Documents inédits*), and the letter of Soult to Grouchy, 18th June, one o'clock (quoted by Grouchy, *Relat. succ.* App. i. 21).

On the testimony of a certain Letourneau, whose letter is quoted in Grouchy's *Relat. succ.* (App. iv. 21), an aide-de-camp of Blücher's asserted at Caen in 1815, that the French officer, bearer of the order of 10 P.M. in the evening, was brought to the Field-Marshal at Wavre "as a prisoner or a traitor." This fact is not mentioned in any of the German documents.

56. "We must know whether Blücher and Wellington propose uniting to cover Brussels" (Napoleon to Grouchy, Ligny, half-past 11 A.M). (I have quoted this letter *in extenso*, pp. 229, 230.)

57. Even the next morning, Napoleon still did not admit this hypothesis. It was only an hour after noon that he ordered the following message to be written to Grouchy: "Draw nearer to the army, that no body of the enemy may get between us." See Grouchy's two letters, Le Caillou, 18th June, one o'clock (quoted by Grouchy, *Relation succincte*, Appendix i. 21).

58. Napoleon, *Mém.* 119. See 193-196, 198, 199.

59. See above-quoted order of Grouchy, 17th June: "Keep me informed of the movements of the enemy, so that I may discover what they mean to do."

60. Napoleon, *Mém.* 195, 199. See Bassano's letter to Caulaincourt (Le Caillou, 18th June, in the morning, Arch. of Foreign Affairs, 1802), which reflects the Emperor's idea: "The victory of Ligny is of supreme importance. The *élite* of the Prussian Army has been crushed. The *morale* of this army will for a long time be affected." The Relation of the *Ambigu* of London (lii. 429), which Napoleon considered as very reliable: ". . . The results of the battle of Ligny were much exaggerated." Words of Soult quoted in the manuscript notes of Baudus: "The battle left the Prussian Army in such a state, that a small corps only was sufficient to watch it."

61. The letters of Wellington in which he announces that he is going to give battle are dated Waterloo, 18th June (from two to four in the morning (*Despatches*, xii. 476, 478, and *Supplementary*, 501). On this he eventually takes up his stand. He hopes to fight the next day (to Colville, 17th June, evening, *Despatches*, xii. 476): ". . . The army will probably keep its position before Waterloo to-morrow"; but he has not yet made his final decision. Moreover, Hügel, commissary to the King of Würtemberg at the English headquarters, writes to his sovereign on the evening

of the 17th: "At the news of the Prussians' retreat, Wellington retired on Waterloo, and will retain that position if Blücher keeps his promise" (Letter quoted by Pfister, *Aus dem Lager der Verbündeten*, 367).

62. Müffling, *Aus meinem Leben*, 208. See Wellington's report to Bathurst, Waterloo, 18th June (*Despatches*, xii. 479), and Memorandum of Wellington (*Supplementary Despatches*, x. 527).

63. Von Ollech, 186.

64. Von Ollech, 187.

65. Wagner, iv. 55; Damitz, ii. 145, 146, 207; von Ollech, 166, 167, 187.

66. Letter of Bülow, Dion-le-Mont, 17th June, 10 P.M. (quoted by von Ollech, 167, 168); Damitz, ii. 207-210.

67. Von Ollech, 187.

68. Hardinge's testimony, quoted by Stanhope, *Notes of Conversations with the Duke of Wellington*, 110. See Colonel Maurice's article in the *United Service Magazine*, July 1890. Hardinge, wounded at Ligny by the side of Blücher (his left hand had to be amputated), had been removed to Wavre.

69. Blücher to Müffling, Wavre, 17th June (between eleven and midnight), quoted by von Ollech, 187. Orders to Bülow and to Pirch, Wavre, 17th June (midnight), quoted by the same, 188. See Corresp. of Wellington (Müffling), 20.

70. From Wavre to Waterloo the distance, as the crow flies, is fifteen kilometres. Müffling (Corresp. of Napoleon, 20) says that this letter arrived at nine in the morning. This is a mistake, for Wellington's letters, dated three o'clock (after midnight), testify that he had already received Blücher's despatch.

71. Wellington to Sir Charles Stewart, to the Duke de Berry, to Lady Webster, Waterloo, 18th June, 3 P.M. (*Despatches*, xii. 476, and *Supplementary*, x. 501).

In these letters Wellington seems certain of the victory at Mont-Saint-Jean; but he admits the possibility of being turned by Hal. In this case he would abandon his position and leave Brussels exposed. "Hold yourself in readiness to leave Brussels for Antwerp," he writes to Lady Webster, "in case this should become necessary!"

72. Marshal Wolseley (*Decline and Fall of Napoleon*, 196) considers that Wellington's conduct is unaccountable. To explain it, he is rather inclined to admit, without, however, emphasising the idea, that, in accordance with the statements of Lockhart, Young, Colonel Maurice, and Ropes, the Duke went to Wavre in the evening, conferred with Blücher, and returned to Waterloo before midnight, with the formal assurance of Prussian co-operation.

But this visit of Wellington to the Prussian headquarters is implicitly and positively denied by Blücher's letter quoted above. Moreover, if Wellington went to Wavre, how is it that Müffling should neither know of it nor mention it, that the fact should not have been rumoured and related afterwards by German and English historians?

Since I wrote this note, Mr. Archibald Forbes has published (*Century*,

1st January 1898) an article in which he emphatically denies, and for many good reasons, the supposed visit of Wellington to Blücher at Wavre. Besides, he quotes a conversation of Wellington in the course of which the Duke said: "No; that was not so; I did not see Blücher the day before Waterloo."

73. Napoleon, *Mém.* 118. In Soult's order (18th June, War Arch.), which I will quote later, mention is made of an order of battle dictated the day before by the Emperor.

74. Davout's Reminiscences of the Hundred Days, dictated to Gordon, tutor to his son (comm. by General the Duke of Auerstaedt).

It seems to me that this assertion of Davout should not be doubted, especially as there had been at the Chambers on the 16th, a rather stormy sitting, of which Napoleon was informed. Note for the Emperor, 16th June (Arch. of Foreign Affairs, 1802), and Berlier to Bassano, 17th June (Arch. of Nat. Affairs, iv. 1933): "The proposal respecting the finances will furnish the Chambers with a subject for discussion. All the better, for when one has nothing to do, one is apt to grow excited and to act in an unfortunate manner. . . . The successes of the Army will be useful in raising the courage of the weak, and overawing the discontented."

The author of *Napoléon, sa famille et ses amis*, etc. (iv. 382, 385), assures us, from a confidential remark made by the Emperor to Regnaud de Saint-Jean-d'Angély, that into this mail of the 17th of June some treacherous hand had slipped a note, signed "*Duke d'Enghien, Ferdinand VII., Pie VII.*," in which the fall of the Emperor was prophesied in apocalyptical terms. The same author also says that on the battlefield of Ligny, the day after the action, a wounded Frenchman predicted to Napoleon treason on the part of the generals-in-chief, and that in the orchard of Le Caillou the following notice was found: "This will be the grave of the French." This seems an amazing number of prophecies for a single day!

75. Napoleon, *Mém.* 120. Napoleon's account is confirmed by the notes of Conquébau (Boucqueau, son of the farmer at Le Caillou), written in 1816 (*La Belle Alliance, Ode dediée à la Princesse d'Orange*), and by local traditions. The Emperor, in the course of his visits to the outposts, stopped at the farm of Chantelet, where Marshal Ney had taken up his abode. Soult, Bertrand, Bassano were sleeping on straw at Le Caillou, in the second-floor rooms; other officers were quartered at Plancenoit and Montplaisir.

76. Gourgaud, 82. The distance between Gembloux and Le Caillou, by Sombreffe and Quatre-Bras, is over eight leagues. It is not strange that the messenger, in the dead of night, should have spent four hours on the journey. Marmont, who is always very unreliable, contends (*Mém.* vii. 124), according to Bernard's testimony, that this letter reached the Imperial headquarters at eight in the evening, that is to say, *two hours before it was written!* Napoleon (*Mém.* 116) is quite as inaccurate when he says—1st, that this letter was dated five o'clock; 2nd, that he received it at eleven o'clock.

77. I have quoted this letter *in extenso*, pp. 141, 142.

78. Napoleon (Gourgaud, 83, and *Mém.* 117) asserts that he sent a duplicate of the order which he had despatched at nine o'clock, ordering Grouchy to send a detachment to Saint-Lambert. The arguments which I have before given against the despatch of an order from the Emperor to Grouchy to occupy Saint-Lambert, have the same weight in regard to the supposed duplicate of this supposed order.

79. Napoleon, *Mém.* 122. See Gourgaud, 84, and Drouot, Speech to the Chamber of Peers (*Moniteur*, 24th June).

80. Napoleon, *Mém.* 122.

81. Napoleon, *Mém.* 122.

82. The existence of this order of 17th June (from eight to ten in the evening), which no one had mentioned before, is proved by the words of Soult's order of the 18th of June, in the morning (War Arch., Army of the North): " . . . that in the battle each man may stand in the fighting order which the Emperor *has indicated in his order of yesterday evening.*"

It was plainly for the execution of this evening order, that Foy had ordered his division to be under arms at Genappe at half-past three in the morning, and to hold itself in readiness to follow the movement of Jérôme's division (Order, Genappe, 17th June, Register of Corresp. of Foy, comm. by Count de Foy).

83. Napoleon, *Mém.* 122 ; Drouot's Speech at the Chamber of Peers (*Moniteur*, 24th June).

84. Soult's order, general Imperial headquarters, 17th June (between 4 and 5 A.M.), (War Arch., Army of the North).

This order proves that the Emperor expected to attack at nine in the morning. It may also be concluded that, on the evening of the 17th, he had intended to attack earlier still. In short, if Napoleon had already prescribed in his order of ten in the evening, that the army should be ready for the battle at nine next morning, he would not have seen any use in reiterating this same order at daybreak. In the second order there is no mention of any new positions. The positions to be occupied, were those indicated the day before. What is the reason then for this new order, if it is not to appoint a different hour for mustering? As to the causes of this delay, as I have said before, they were the condition of the ground, and also the necessity of giving the troops, who were widely scattered, sufficient time to rally.

BOOK III

CHAPTER I

1. Blücher to Müffling, Wavre, 17th June, 11 P.M. (quoted by von Ollech, *Geschichte des Feldzuges von 1815*, 187) ; Müffling, *Aus meinem Leben*, 209.

2. Bülow's orders to Pirch, Wavre, 17th June, midnight ; Bülow's order, Dion-le-Mont, 18th June (quoted by von Ollech, 188, 191).

3. Above-quoted letter of Blücher to Müffling. See von Ollech, 188; Wagner, iv. 58.

4. Bülow's report (quoted by von Ollech, 192); Wagner, iv. 58; von Ollech, 191. See Clausewitz (126), who erroneously says that the 4th Corps only broke up their camp at seven o'clock.

The head of Bülow's corps reached Chapelle-Saint-Lambert about ten o'clock, the bulk of it after midday, and its rearguard (von Ryssel division) at three o'clock only.

5. Von Ollech, 193. See above-quoted order to Pirch I., Wavre, 17th June, midnight.

6. Von Ollech, 188, 189. See Wagner, iv. 58, and Corresp. of Wellington (Müffling), 22.

7. Blücher's letter to Müffling, Wavre, 18th June, half-past ten (quoted by von Ollech, 189). See Hugel to the King of Würtemberg (quoted by Pfister, *Aus dem Lager der Verbündeten*, 369); Müffling, *Aus meinem Leben*, 289.

8. Müffling, *Aus meinem Leben*, 184. (See p. 80, and note 26.)

9. Von Ollech, 190.

10. Nostiz to Müffling, Wavre, 18th June, half-past 10 A.M. (quoted by von Ollech, 189).

11. Damitz, ii. 248; von Ollech, 190.

12. See pp. 140, 141.

13. Letter of Bonnemains, Ernage, 17th June, a quarter past 10 P.M., and Journal of the Bonnemains brigade (War Arch., Army of the North); General Berton, *Précis*, 49.

14. Information gathered at Sart-à-Walhain in the night of the 17th of June (War Arch., Army of the North). See Grouchy's letter to Napoleon, Gembloux, 18th June (War Arch.). This information, gathered at Sart-à-Walhain, is erroneously numbered *first information*. It is in reality the second (see on this subject p. 140, and note 75). It reads as follows: "From 30,000 to 40,000 Prussians passed yesterday at Sart-à-Walhain, between nine in the morning and three in the afternoon. Three corps are supposed to have passed, the second and the third for certain, and probably the first. They are all proceeding to Wavre. They announced their intention of giving battle near Brussels, whither they are mustering."

15. "All my reports and information confirm the fact that our foes are withdrawing on Brussels" (Grouchy to Napoleon, Gembloux, 18th June, 6 o'clock A.M., War. Arch.).

16. "Having been notified by Your Majesty, when I left you at Ligny, that you were marching against the English to fight them, if they kept on this side of the forest of Soignes . . ." (Report of Grouchy to Napoleon, Rosiren, 19th June, War Arch., Army of the North).

17. See p. 142. Far from cancelling these orders, Grouchy confirmed them by a fresh despatch to Pajol. Pajol was at Le Mazy at four in the morning; from Le Mazy to Grand-Leez the distance is 10 kilometres as the crow flies; from Le Mazy to Gentinnes it is 12 kilometres. Consequently Pajol might have been at Gentinnes, to concentrate with the

army in the direction of Mont-Saint-Guibert, almost in the same time he took to reach Grand-Leez, where there was nothing for him to do, whereas there were 12 extra kilometres to travel—making a total of 22—before he could join the army from Grand-Leez to Gentinnes. This movement was therefore most eccentric; but Grouchy only thought of covering his right, neglecting altogether to protect his left. The same remark applies to the movement of the Vallin cavalry, which had spent the night at Bothey, between Le Mazy and Gembloux, and which was also sent on to Grand-Leez (Grouchy to Gérard, 17th June and at Vallin, 18th June, War Arch.).

18. Grouchy to Napoleon, Gembloux, 18th June (War Arch., Army of the North).

This letter, which I give *in extenso* further on, has no date as to the hour, but it is quoted in the *Relation succincte* of Grouchy (App. ii. 4), with the mention *three o'clock in the morning*. On the other hand, in a letter of the head of the staff to Grouchy, of the 18th June, after midday (quoted by Grouchy, App. i. 21), we read: "You wrote this morning at three o'clock." But the original of this letter of Soult's, which has been communicated to me (Arch. Guerre) reads: "You wrote this morning at *six o'clock*." It seems certain, therefore, that this letter of Grouchy's was written at six o'clock. Besides the text of Soult's letter, there are two good reasons for believing this. The first reason is, that in a letter from the head of the staff to Grouchy, ten o'clock in the morning, there is no allusion made to this letter. It follows that if it had been written at three o'clock, Napoleon would undoubtedly have received it before ten, and had he received it, he would certainly have mentioned it in his letter. The second reason is, as will be seen further, that Grouchy did not leave Gembloux before eight or nine o'clock. Consequently, he could not have written to the Emperor at three in the morning: "I am starting immediately." This would have been giving him a false impression of extreme gravity, considering the circumstances.

19. Vandamme's infantry: 13,960 men.

Gérard's infantry: 10,275 men.

Teste division (detached from Lobau's corps): 2,960 men.

Maurin's cavalry division (passed under the command of General Vallin, Maurin having been wounded at Ligny): 1,326 men.

Exelmans' cavalry: 3,250 men.

Pajol's cavalry (minus the Subervie division): 1,374 men.

Total: 33,145 men (deduction to be made of the losses at Ligny), and 96 cannons. See official returns at the outset of the campaign, to compare the strength of the corps at the opening of the campaign and the losses at Ligny (see pp. 58 and 107).

20. Grouchy to Vandamme, Gembloux, 17th June (War Arch.): "As has been agreed between us, I desire you to commence moving to-morrow by six in the morning."

Grouchy to Gérard, Gembloux, 17th June (War Arch.): "I desire that you should start on your march to-morrow, the 18th inst., at eight in the morning. You will follow General Vandamme's corps."

In his various writings (*Observations*, 15; *Fragments*, 8; *Relation succincte*, 28), Grouchy contends that, according to his orders, Vandamme ought to have started on his march at daybreak, and Gérard early in the morning. But the letters above quoted are unanswerable.

21. According to Hulot's report (comm. by Baron Hulot), all the troops had been obliged to send detachments to Gembloux for the distributions, which were not completed at eight o'clock.

22. Bonnemains in his "Journal de marche" (War Arch.) states that Exelmans' cavalry, of which he commanded a brigade, reached Walhain at seven o'clock. Now from Sauvenière to Walhain (by Baudeset) the distance is five kilometres. Exelmans (letter quoted by Gérard, *Nouvelles Observations*, 24, 25) says that he broke up his camp at half-past seven only. But Bonnemains' testimony seems the more reliable of the two.

23. Berthezène (letter quoted by Gérard, *Nouvelles Observations*, 25) says, "eight o'clock." See Hulot's report stating that about nine o'clock Vandamme's troops were still defiling through the streets of Gembloux. Grouchy, whose memory is decidedly defective, asserts that Vandamme began his march before sunrise.

24. Above-quoted report of Grouchy; Hulot's report.

25. Gérard (*Quelques Documents*, 47) complains that Grouchy made the two infantry corps march in a single column. Grouchy replied (*Relation succincte*, 28, 29) that he had ordered Gérard to take another road. But this order came far too late, for Gérard was already following Vandamme, in compliance with the order of the previous day.

26. In his various writings, Grouchy does not state the precise time of his departure. He only says that he joined the head of Vandamme's corps five or six kilometres from Gembloux (*Relation succincte*, 28), and his statement is confirmed by the testimony of his orderly-officers, la Fresnaye and Legouest (*Relation succincte*, App. iv. 13, 25). But as Vandamme's division did not commence its movement before seven in the morning, Marshal Grouchy could not have left Gembloux before eight o'clock. Moreover, as Grouchy himself tells us that he wrote to the Emperor as soon as he had reached Walhain or Sart-à-Walhain, his letter being dated eleven o'clock, and as the distance from Gembloux to Walhain or Sart-a-Walhain is less than seven kilometres, it is obvious, not only that the Marshal started very late from Gembloux, but that he must have made the journey at a foot's pace on horseback. Le Sénécal's statement (App. iv. 6) that Grouchy left before daybreak is therefore a palpable falsehood.

27. The village of Walhain and the hamlet of Sart-à-Walhain, 1,700 yards distant from each other, were united into the same commune in 1822. Four roads led from Gembloux to Corbais, the route of Grouchy's army; one of them passing through Walhain, and another, the longest of the four, through Sart-à-Walhain.

This point being settled, I shall recall the fact that all French historians, even Charras and Quinet, who resided in Belgium, say that Grouchy halted at Sart-à-Walhain on the 18th of June. In point of fact, in every one of Grouchy's orders, reports, and accounts, as well as in the written recollections of the officers of his staff, Sart-à-Walhain is constantly mentioned, and Walhain never.

But Gérard (*Quelques Documents sur la Bataille de Waterloo*, 7) says: "*Walhain* or *Sart-à-Walhain*, a small village between Gembloux and Wavre"; then in the pages which follow, and in his other writings, he alternately says *Walhain* and *Sarra-Walhain;* Colonel Simon-Lorière says *Walhain;* General Berton says *Walhain;* Berthezène says *Sarra Walhain*, but these words—"village situated slightly in front of Nil-Saint-Vincent," imply that he speaks of *Walhain;* Lefol says *Walhain* and *Sarra Walhain;* Catoire, a Belgian, says, in a letter to Gérard, *Sarra-Walhain*, which is obviously a slip, meaning *Walhain*, for he speaks of the château of notary Hollaërt (really Hollërt), who lived at *Walhain*, not at *Sart-à-Walhain*.

Must we conclude then that, like Berthezène and Catoire, Grouchy and other officers made a confusion between the hamlet and the village, writing Sart-à-Walhain for Walhain. Such an error would be all the more natural, because on the map by Ferrari, which Grouchy used, the name of Sart-à-Walhain is inscribed almost above the spires of the two villages, whilst the name of Walhain is on the left. In a rapid glance of the map one might easily be mistaken. Grouchy, besides, was rather addicted to such mistakes. As may be seen further, he wrote Dion-le-Val for Dion-le-Mont, and Temploux for Gembloux.

The following indication is of great importance in the discussion: the house of the notary Hollërt, where, according to Gérard and his officers, Grouchy stopped for breakfast, is situated not at Sart-à-Walhain, but at Walhain. And we read also in the *Histoire des Communes belges*, that the famous discussion between Grouchy and Gérard took place at Walhain, not at Sart-à-Walhain.

But everything is perplexing in this question. Neither in his letter to the Emperor nor in his *Relations* does Grouchy speak of the notary Hollërt. He says, "an old decorated officer at whose house I stopped to write to Napoleon." I thought at first that the old decorated soldier and the notary of Sart-à-Walhain might be the same person. I made inquiries and found that Hollërt *did* serve in the French army from 1792 to 1795 (*Campaign of the Netherlands*), but as a health officer, and that he was not decorated. Could Grouchy have intentionally described the ex-medical officer as an old decorated officer with the object of giving more authority to the intelligence he was conveying to the Emperor? Or rather, as Major la Fresnaye seems inclined to believe, had the Marshal, after receiving some false information from an officer, or some man claiming to be such, just entered Hollërt's house to acquaint the Emperor with what he had heard? All that is certain, according to the very minute details given by Gérard, Colonel Simon-Lorière, General Valazé, and Chief-Intendant Denniée, is that the discussion between Grouchy and Gérard took place in a private house with a large garden attached, in which there was an "arbour painted green." Now at Walhain the farm of La Marette (anciently the house or château of Longpré) answers to this description thoroughly, whereas at Sart-à-Walhain there is not a trace nor a recollection of any dwelling of this type. Moreover, Gérard and Simon-Lorière particularly mention the name of Hollërt; it is notorious in the country that Grouchy was the guest of Hollërt; at the death of the latter the circumstance was referred to, in his funeral oration (this was communicated to me by his great-grandson, M. Vianvier, notary at Nil-Saint-Vincent). And, finally, this funeral sermon records the fact that after his death, Hollërt, in accordance with his express wish, was laid on the same stretcher which, on the evening of the 18th of June 1815, had been used to carry General Gérard to his house at Walhain after he was wounded at Bierge. This stretcher had been religiously preserved by Hollërt for forty years. Now we know by a letter from the Intendant-General-Denniée that Gérard, after being wounded, was transported to the same house in which his discussion with Grouchy at noon had taken place.

To sum up, it is possible that in 1815 a decorated officer lived at Walhain or Sart-à-Walhain; but no recollection is left of him, whereas the existence of notary Hollërt is undeniable, and he in his lifetime had often asserted that Grouchy had been his guest on the morning of the 18th June.

28. Grouchy, *Observations*, 15; *Relation succincte*, 33. See note above.

29. Grouchy, *Relation succincte*, 27. See Le Sénécal's declaration and Grouchy's letters to Marbot (Appendix viii. 50, 51, 56).

The mission of Pontbellanger does not seem certain. At any rate, this officer fulfilled it badly, for he failed to inform Grouchy of the presence at Mont-Saint-Guibert of Colonel Ledebur's detachment (two battalions and four squadrons), which remained there till about one o'clock (see Ledebur's letter to Bülow, Mont-Saint-Guibert, 18th June, half-past-twelve; quoted by von Ollech, 207).

30. Grouchy, *Observations*, 15; *Fragments historiques*, 8; *Relation succincte*, 33; La Fresnaye's declaration (Appendix iv. 13).

31. Information gathered at Sart-à-Walhain (Walhain), (War Arch.). See Grouchy to Sart-à-Walhain, 18th June, eleven o'clock (War Arch.); see Declaration of La Fresnaye (*Relation succincte*, iv. 13): "A decorated officer came to you and told you that Prussian columns were marching to Wavre, although he thought that Blücher would collect his army near Louvain."

As explained above (see p. 166, note 31), this report, which is erroneously numbered second, is in reality the third received. In it La Chyse is mentioned for the first time. Also for the first time, Grouchy speaks of La Chyse in the letter written from Walhain at eleven o'clock.

Here is this third report: "The wounded proceed to Liège through Beauvale, Jodoigne, and Tirlemont. The capable, and those who have not taken part in the battle of Fleurus, march upon Wavre, and a few on Tirlemont. The bulk of the troops are camping on the plain of La Chyse, near the road from Namur to Louvain. The plain of La Chyse is two and a half leagues to the right of Wavre, close to Goddechius. The latter report is positive. It was here that they seem to have decided to mass themselves. They say they hold the field of battle (at Ligny), and that they are only retreating, to give battle again after their concerted reunion with Blücher and Wellington."

32. Grouchy to Napoleon, Sart-à-Walhain (Walhain), 18th June, 11 A.M. (War Arch.).

The first portion of this letter is not very clear. Grouchy says: "The 1st, 2nd, and 3rd Corps of Blücher are marching in the direction of Brussels. A corps arriving from Liège has effected its junction with those who fought at Fleurus. Some of the Prussians I have in front of me are proceeding towards the plain of La Chyse. It would seem that they are doing so with the object of mustering there, or of fighting the troops which may pursue them, or lastly of joining Wellington, a plan announced by the officers."

Does Grouchy really believe, then, that three Prussian corps were marching on Brussels, and that a fourth was proceeding towards La Chyse? But which could this 4th Corps be, for he says that the Liège corps joined those who fought at Fleurus? And if Grouchy supposes that the bulk of the Prussian Army is already marching on Brussels, how can he say, "I shall find myself at Wavre, between Wellington and the Prussian Army"? Also, why does he speak of going to the marshy neighbourhood of La Chyse, to overtake a mere detachment, when he thinks that the bulk of the Prussians is already near Brussels? Lastly, if he believes that three Prussian corps are marching on Brussels, why does he not speedily pursue them or draw nearer to Napoleon, why does he put off his manœuvre till the next day?

Thus, in comparing the first part of his letter with its conclusion, it is evident, that if Grouchy rightly understood the information of the "old officer," he gave a very incorrect résumé of it in his letter. Obviously, on the 18th June, at eleven in the morning, Grouchy believed that the bulk of the Prussian Army was concentrated towards La Chyse. Indeed he could not think otherwise, since he unfortunately considered, as reliable, the information he had just received to the effect that "the bulk of the Army is camping on the plain of La Chyse."

33. Grouchy to Napoleon (Walhain), 18th June, 11 A.M.; and Rosieren, 19th June (War Arch.); above-quoted declaration of Major la Fresnaye (*Relation succincte*, Appendix iv. 3).

34. Gérard to Simon-Lorière, 10th August 1819; Simon-Lorière to General Hulot, 16th August 1819 (War Arch.); Gérard to Colonel de Grouchy (*Quelques Documents*, 24). See Grouchy, *Relation succincte*, 33; Lefol, *Souvenirs*, 76.

35. Simon-Lorière to General Hulot, 16th August 1819; Gérard to Lorière, 10th August 1819; Declaration of Captain of Artillery, Thouvenin, attaché to the staff of the 4th Corps (War Arch., Army of the North, at the date of 18th June); Denniée's letter and Simon-Lorière's report (quoted by Gérard, *Dernières Observations*, 31); Gérard to Colonel de Grouchy (*Quelques Documents*, 24). See Grouchy, report to Napoleon, Rosieren, 19th June (War Arch.).

36. Letter from Valazé, quoted by Gérard (*Dernières Observations*, 31;

Quelques Documents, 24). See Grouchy, report to Napoleon, Rosiren, 19th June, and *Relation succincte*, 33.

37. List of questions to Grouchy and Bella's answers (Grouchy, *Relation succincte*, 33; Appendix iv. 43, 44, 49, 50; Grouchy, *Fragment historique*, 26).

38. Simon-Lorière's report (quoted by Gérard, *Quelques Documents*, 12, 13); above-quoted letters of Valazé and Denniée. See Grouchy's report to Napoleon, Rosiren, 19th June (War Arch.).

39. List of questions to Grouchy (Grouchy, *Relation succincte*, iv. 45).

40. Grouchy, *Relation succincte*, 33, and Colonel de Blocqueville's declaration (*ibid*. Appendix v. 5); above-quoted letter of Valazé. See Grouchy to Napoleon, Rosiren, 19th June.

41. Valazé's and Denniée's letters; Grouchy, *Relation succincte*, 33. Thouvenin, though he was in the garden, did not hear the discussion; but he asserts that Baltus repeated these words to him when they left Walhain.

42. Letter of Valazé; Grouchy, *Relation succincte*, 34.

43. Letter of Valazé.

44. Letter of Valazé; Grouchy, *Relation succincte*, 34.

45. Grouchy, *Relation succincte*, 33. See list of questions to Bella (*Relation succincte*, Appendix iv. 45).

46. Grouchy's report to Napoleon, Rosiren, 19th June (War Arch.); list of questions to Bella (*Relation succincte*, Appendix iv. 34).

47. Grouchy, *Relation succincte*, 34.

48. Exelmans's letter to Gérard, 1st February 1830 (quoted by Gérard, *Dernières Observations*, 13 and 25); Account of an officer of Grouchy's army (General Gourgaud's papers). See Grouchy's report to Napoleon, Rosiren, 19th June (War Arch.); Grouchy, *Relation succincte*, 34; le Sénécal's declaration and questions to Bella (Appendix iv. 7 and 44). As will be seen further, Exelmans, to prepare the movement on the Dyle, had already despatched a brigade of dragoons within 1500 yards of Attignies.

49. Grouchy, *Relation succincte*, 34; de Blocqueville's declaration; Simon-Lorière's report. See Gérard, *Dernières Observations*, 41.

50. Grouchy, *Relation succincte*, 34; de Blocqueville's declaration; Simon-Lorière's report.

51. Thouvenin's declaration (War Arch., Army of the North, dated 18th June).

52. Thouvenin's declaration.

BOOK III CHAPTER II

1. It has been seen that Wellington, on the evening of the 17th, had established his headquarters at Waterloo; from thence, on the 19th, he wrote the official report of his victory. For this reason, the battle

received the name of Waterloo, although the action took place one league to the south of this village.

2. I experienced this several times. Owing to the uneven surface of the ground through which it runs, the Brussels road is now on a level with the fields, now raised, now sunk between two banks. These depressions were much deeper in 1815, from La Haye-Sainte to the Ohain road.

3. I ought to use the past instead of the present tense, for Wellington said in 1825, on his return from an excursion to Mont-Saint-Jean, that his battlefield had been quite changed. Several woods, as well as the Soignes forest, which surrounded Waterloo to the north, have been cleared away. The hedges which bordered the Ohain road to the east of the Brussels highroad, have been torn up. And lastly, nothing remains of the embankments which ran along this road and to the west of the highroad, as far as the road to Merbe-Braine, but a portion of the inner embankment. The other was rased to the ground at the time of the important excavation which took place for the erection of the "Belgian Lion," on an immense artificial conical mound which is seen for miles round, and which spoils the scenery on all sides.

It has been said repeatedly that to raise this mound, two yards depth of earth were cut from the entire plateau, over a surface of 14 to 15 hectares. (A hectare in English terms amounts to over two acres.) If this is so, by what miracle does the inner embankment of the highroad still exist? It is an erroneous tradition. The surface of the plateau was never removed, and the soil of the Ohain road is the original soil. The ground was levelled only on the upper slopes of the hill, to the west of the road from the kitchen-garden of La Haye-Sainte to the present base of the "Butte-du-Lion." The outer embankment of the road was rased at the same time. This portion of the ground belonged to the Fortemps family. The bill of sale was shown to me by M. Goutier, the notary of Braine-l'Alleud.

It is admitted that the original height of the cleared ground is approximately marked to-day, by the summit of the mound which supports the monument of the English Colonel Gordon. This mound is not an artificial one, as tourists believe. The monument, erected in 1817 on the very spot where Gordon was killed, was then on a level with the top of the embankments. The ground which it covers was untouched, and when the earthworks were being made, the surrounding ground was lowered, and the tomb remained like a sort of pyramid. It would seem also, that the steep embankment which on the east bordered the road to Brussels was also rased, from the sandpit, as far as the Ohain road. The position of the high bank, which rose above the sandpit, is marked now by the sandy hillock on which stands the monument of the Hanoverians.

For the rest, to clearly understand what the Ohain road was at that time, it will be sufficient to consult the grand *Plan du Champ de Bataille de Waterloo* drawn by W. B. Craan, engineer and surveyor of Brabant, and published in Brussels in 1816. In this plan, the Ohain road is bordered with an unbroken line of hedges for a space of 700 yards to the east of the road to Brussels, and it runs between two steep banks from this road westward for about 400 yards. At this point the embankments disappear. A little farther on, facing the road of Merbe-Braine, a few hedges are indicated; also, some near the Nivelles road.

4. Mercer, *Journal of the Campaign of Waterloo*, i. 288, 292, 296; Letter of Hervey, aide-de-camp to Wellington, 3rd July 1815 (*Nineteenth Century*, March 1893); Siborne, *History of the War*, i. 325-327; Cotton, *A Voice of Waterloo*, 46, 47.

5. These expressions "right centre" and "left centre" are used by Wellington in his official report to Lord Bathurst (*Letters and Despatches*, xii. 479) and by Major Pratt of the English 27th (*Waterloo Letters*, 325).

6. Report of Wellington, Waterloo, 19th June; Report of Kempt, Genappe, 19th June (*Despatches*, xii. 479, 534); Kennedy, *Notes on the Battle of Waterloo*, 60-67; Siborne, i. 330-354; van Löben, 257-259. See Craan's chart, and Chart I. of the *Letters of Waterloo*, drawn according to the information found in numerous letters of officers who were present at the battle.

7. Siborne, i. 356, 357. See van Löben, 257-260; Kennedy, 72; and above-quoted charts.

8. See on the subject Marbot, *Mém.* ii. 391; Laurillard-Fallot, *Cours d'Art militaire*, 71; and the very learned and suggestive pamphlet of A. de Selliers de Moranville, head of the staff of the Belgian Army, *De l'Occupation des positions dans la défensive*.

9. Kennedy, 98.

10. Report of Pozzo di Borgo to Prince Wolkonsky, 19th June (General G.'s papers); Siborne, i. 328-350; Cotton, 34; Kennedy, 66; Daily Notes of Foy (comm. by Count Foy). The correctness of these assertions can be verified by walking over the plateau.

11. Craan's maps and those of the *Waterloo Letters*.

12. It was through these openings, that the squadrons of the Scots Greys passed to charge d'Erlon's infantry (Letter of Colonel Windham of the Scots Greys, *Waterloo Letters*, 78). See Kennedy, 110.

13. *Waterloo Letters*, 345, 404; Siborne, i. 131, 234, 335; van Löben, 259, 260.

Chesney (182) says that La Haye-Sainte was not fortified. This is only a figure of speech. Undoubtedly this position, as Kennedy remarks (174) was not fortified as much as it might have been, but it had nevertheless been put in a state of defence, for according to Cotton's express testimony (39) loopholes had been made in the walls and in the roof. Traces of these can still be seen on the south and west walls.

14. Above-quoted report of Pozzo di Borgo, Brussels, 19th June.

15. At Quatre-Bras, and in the pursuit of the 17th, Wellington's army had lost 4,916 men (*1815*, 213, note 3; 263, note 1).

16. Exactly: 67,661 men (Siborne, i. 460, 461). Wagner says, 69,000 men; van Löben: 66,000 men. [The estimates quoted in the

Letters and Despatches of Wellington (xii. 486) only give to the English troops and the German Legion 37,603 men.]

17. The number of pieces of artillery, 156, which is given by Siborne (i. 460) does not correspond with the number of batteries: 17 unmounted artillery of 8 pieces ; 8 horse artillery of 6. Van Löben says : 194 cannon ; Damitz, 230.

18. Wellington to Hill (Quatre-Bras), 17th June, in the morning ; to Colville (Waterloo), 17th June, in the evening ; to the Duke of Berry (Waterloo), 18th June, 3 o'clock A.M. (*Letters and Despatches*, xii. 475, 476). See Memorandum of Wellington on the Battle of Waterloo (*Suppl.* x. 530) ; Kennedy, 68, 69 ; Müffling, *Aus meinem Leben*, 210.

The troops detached between Hal and Enghien comprised the Johnstone and Lyon brigade (of the Colville division), the Steedmann division, the Indian brigade, and the Hanoverian brigade of cavalry under Estorff.

19. Brialmont, *Histoire de Wellington*, ii. 412.

Clausewitz, Kennedy, Hoffmann, Chesney are unanimous in condemning this arrangement of Wellington. Napoleon, it is true, asserts (*Mém.* 114) that on the evening of the 17th he had sent towards Hal a detachment of 2,000 horse, and that Wellington, informed of this movement, had felt afraid of being turned. But this assertion seems doubtful. The Emperor does not state the corps to which this detachment belonged, it is mentioned in no contemporary account, either French or English, and on the evening of the 17th, the cavalry were too fatigued to attempt such a vast turning movement. It seems then likely that Napoleon at St. Helena, learning from English works that Wellington had sent 17,000 men to Hal, imagined this cavalry manœuvre of his, after the event. Thus he gave himself the credit of having, through a feigned menace, paralysed a whole corps of the enemy. Be it as it may, the above-quoted letter of Wellington to Hill proves that, by an early hour of the morning, the Duke intended guarding himself in the direction of Hal ; consequently the movement of the French cavalry in this direction, whether real or imaginary, had had no influence on his determination.

20. Müffling, *Aus meinem Leben*, 208 ; Letter of Hervey, aide-de-camp to Wellington, 3rd July 1815 (*Nineteenth Century*, March 1893) ; Letter of Hügel to the King of Würtemberg, Brussels, 19th June (quoted by Pfister, *Aus dem Lager der Verbündeten*, 369) ; Cotton, 47. See Wellington to Sir Charles Stuart, Waterloo, 18th June (3 o'clock A.M.): " The Prussians will be again ready for everything this morning " (*Letters and Despatches*, xii. 476).

21. Order of Soult, Le Caillou, 18th June, from 4 to 5 A.M. (War Arch., Army of the North). Janin, deputy-chief of the staff of the 6th Corps, also says that the attack was ordered for nine o'clock (*Camp de Waterloo*, 51).

22. Account of General Petit (*Morrison Collection* of London); Janin, 51.

In the *Souvenirs d'un ex-officier* (283) it is stated that in the morning, the soldiers of the 1st Corps, who had bivouacked on the first line, became impatient at the other corps not coming up more quickly.

23. Reille's account (War Arch.). Reille says that he left Genappe

at daybreak. It may be surmised that, having on his way received Soult's order to see that the troops were fed and had cleaned their arms, Reille had made a long halt for that purpose. And indeed if he had not lingered he might have reached Le Caillou, five kilometres distant from Genappe, long before nine o'clock.

24. General Pétit (above-quoted account) says that the Guard did not break up camp till ten, and Durutte (*Sentinelle de l'Armée*, March 1838) relates that he took his post in the battle, only when the cannonade was going on along the whole line, that is to say, at about midday. The son of Boucqueau, the farmer of Le Caillou, who wrote, under the anagram of Conquébau, an ode entitled *La Belle Alliance*, also remarks, note 9, that at nine o'clock the troops were still debouching from Genappe. It is a curious fact that a writer of romances, Walter Scott, is the only historian of the battle of Waterloo, who points out that at eleven o'clock the French Army was not yet in line (*Life of Napoleon*, viii. 559).

25. Napoleon, *Mém.* 121, 122.

Jomini was the first to express this opinion (*Précis de la Campagne de 1815*, 199), confirmed by almost all military historians, that a few hours of fair weather are not sufficient to harden the ground. This is an open question. I put the question to many artillery officers, on their return from the grand manœuvres of 1897, which were specially rainy; most of them answered that, even in September, the soil dries rapidly, provided there be sun and wind. My friend Mr. Charles Malo, one of the first military critics of our time, told me that when he visited the battlefield of Bouvines, where the soil is formed of clay as it is at Waterloo, he had been surprised to find that the ground, though it had been soaked by a long and tremendous rain, had hardened in two or three hours under the combined action of sun and wind.

Jomini goes so far as to say that the condition of the ground was a bad excuse concocted at St. Helena, as an apology for the delay in the attack. But this is so far from being an invention made at St. Helena, that on 23rd July 1815, Drouot declared in the Chamber of Peers, that at daybreak the weather was so frightful that it was impossible to manœuvre with the artillery. Towards nine the weather improved and the wind dried the country a little (*Moniteur*, 24th June). According to a note of Colonel Combs-Brassard, quoted by Thiers (xx. 283, 284), Drouot in April 1816 accused himself of having involuntarily contributed to the disaster of Waterloo, by advising the postponement of the attack. Pontécoulant (*Souvenirs milit.*) bears the same testimony, and adds that the difficulties attendant on an early manœuvre had been very much exaggerated. This is very possible, but the fact remains that, rightly or wrongly, both Napoleon and Drouot dreaded these difficulties.

26. Napoleon, *Mém.* 124; *La Belle Alliance*, ode to the Princess of Orange, by Conquébau, note 9; Bill of sale of the farm of Le Caillou, (comm. by M. Emile Coulon).

I have had in my hands, copies of the two original maps which the Emperor used during this campaign. The map by Capitaine belongs to His Imperial Highness Prince Napoleon, Ferrari's map to Baron Gourgaud.

27. Gourgaud, 85 ; Napoleon, *Mém.* 124, 125.
28. Manuscript Notes of Baudus, aide-de-camp to Soult (comm. by M. de Montenon, his grandson).
29. Ségur, *Mélanges*, 273. Thiers, who no doubt, like Ségur, had this account from Reille himself, repeats the anecdote in almost similar terms (xx. 180, 181). But he adds that Napoleon replied : " I know the English are difficult to beat in position ; and that is why I am going to manœuvre." However, for some reason or other, no manœuvre took place.

The Duke d'Aumale, who had also known Reille, gave me a different version. Reille said nothing to Napoleon, but he spoke to d'Erlon of the risk there was in attacking the English in front. D'Erlon having advised him to return to the Emperor and state his opinion, Reille replied, " What is the use ? He would not listen to us."

30. Drouot, speech at the Chamber of Peers (*Moniteur*, 24th June), Manuscript Notes of Baudus ; Heymès, *Relation*, 19 ; *Souvenirs d'un ex-officier* (of the 45th), 284 ; Colonel Lemonnier, *Campagnes*, 375 ; Pétiet, *Souvenirs*, 212.

The same testimony comes from the English : " Towards seven o'clock the weather cleared up," says Hervey, aide-de-camp to Wellington (*Nineteenth Century*, March 1893). " In the morning the weather cleared up and the sun shone as if to illumine the victory of the English," says Siborne, who anticipates.

31. Napoleon, *Mém.* 125. See Gourgaud, 86 ; and Siborne, i. 384 : " By midday the ground had become practicable for artillery."
32. Couquébau (Boucqueau), *La Belle Alliance*, ode, note 9 Boucqueau says that the Emperor left Le Caillou about half-past eight ; Zenowicz (*Waterloo*, 28) says at nine o'clock, which seems more probable.
33. Boucqueau, *La Belle Alliance*, note 10 ; Napoleon, *Mém.* 125 ; Gourgaud, 86 ; Zenowicz, 28.
34. Decoster's account, in the *Relation de la Bataille de Mont-Saint-Jean*, 4th edition, 1816, pp. 249, 250-252 ; Boucqueau, note 10.

In several accounts this Decoster is called Lacoste ; his cottage still exists, and is marked on several maps as *maison d'Écosse* (a corruption of Decoster : *Decostre, d'Écosse*).

35. Local tradition.
36. Napoleon, *Mém.* 125 ; Gourgaud, 86. See Boucqueau, note 10.
37. Daily notes of Foy (comm. by Count Foy).

The map of the Belgian staff inaccurately indicates the place of Napoleon's observatory, the point *150*, as 700 yards to the west of the road. A trigonometrical observatory built of timber had been erected there in 1815, for surveying purposes (see Craan's and Maud'huy's maps, ii. 255). But Napoleon did not go there. Wagner (62) is right when he states that this observatory was not used by the French.

Napoleon at first took up his post on an eminence at the distance of a musket-shot from the road, near the farm of Rossomme (burnt down in 1895). Napoleon (*Mém.* 133) states that he first went to Rossomme.

Mauduit (ii. 214) says that the Guard was on the heights of Rossomme, below the little mound upon which the Emperor stood.

Later, Napoleon took up his post, as Gourgaud relates (91), between La Belle Alliance and Decoster's house. Foy (Daily Notes) says that the Emperor placed himself on a low eminence behind La Belle Alliance. Captain Lambert de Stuers, of the 2nd of Unmounted Chasseurs (Manuscript Notes), says that the Emperor was on the height by Decoster's house. Guided by these various documents, I went up to these two positions, and verified the fact that they command an extended view of the battlefield. From neither of them, however, is it possible to distinguish the hollows of the valley. But the Emperor knew the ground well, for he had been several times to La Belle Alliance.

38. Daily Notes of General Foy, Ham, 23rd June 1815 (comm. by Count Foy). Foy was one of the guests at the supper, in the course of which the waiter gave this information; and though he was not present at the conversation between Jérôme and the Emperor, he learnt all details from Jérôme himself. We also know from another source that Jérôme, on the morning of the 18th, had a talk with the Emperor at the farm of Le Caillou (Letter to Queen Catherine, 15th July 1815, quoted in the *Mém. du roi Jérôme*, vii. 21).

39. Grouchy to Napoleon, Gembloux, 17th June, 10 o'clock P.M. (War Arch.). I have given the text of this letter, p. 181.

40. "The Emperor has received your last report, dated from Gembloux. You speak to His Majesty of only two Prussian columns which passed at Sauvenière and at Sart-à-Walhain. However, other reports state that a third column of some importance passed through Géry and Gentinnes, making for Wavre. The Emperor bids me warn you that at this very moment he is about to attack the English Army, which has taken its position at Waterloo near the forest of Soignes. Accordingly His Majesty desires that you should direct your movements on Wavre in order to draw closer to us, so as to operate in concert with us, and to preserve our line of communications, meanwhile driving before you any corps of the Prussian Army which may have taken this direction and halted at Wavre, where you should arrive as soon as possible. You will pursue the columns of the enemy which have turned off to your right, with a few light infantry corps, that you may observe their movements and capture the stragglers. Let me know your arrangements and your line of march at once, as well as all news you may have heard regarding the enemy, and do not neglect to keep up your communication with us. The Emperor wishes to hear from you very frequently" (Soult to Grouchy, before the farm of Le Caillou, 18th June, ten o'clock in the morning, Register of the Chief of the Staff).

Ingenious efforts have been made to read more in this letter than it ever meant, namely, an order to Grouchy to manœuvre upon his left so as to draw nearer to the bulk of the French Army. Of this there is not a word. The Emperor does say: "in order that you should draw closer to us." But it is obvious that in marching from Gembloux to Wavre, Grouchy must draw nearer to the Emperor; and even admitting the

Emperor's meaning to be that Grouchy is to draw nearer still, Grouchy is not to do so until he has reached Wavre, that is rather late in the day. As for the expressions "to operate in concert, and keep up communications," they do not mean at all that Grouchy, by operating in concert, is to come and support the Emperor's right. At Wavre, whether he were fighting or driving the Prussians, he was placed in an almost parallel position to that of Napoleon, who was fighting the English, and thus Grouchy was *operating in concert*. And by sending numerous patrols and establishing piquets to ensure the service of the estafettes, he was "keeping up the line of communications." From this order it is clear that the Emperor, at ten in the morning, neither summoned Grouchy to his battlefield nor expected him to appear there.

41. The existence of this verbal order is proved not only by the *Dernières Observations* of Gérard (44) and by Marbot's letter to Grouchy, May 1830 (*Relation succinte*, App. viii. 51-54), but also by a private letter of Marbot, 26th June 1815 (Marbot, *Mém.* iii. 403).

In his letter to Grouchy, Marbot, who always blows his own trumpet, exaggerates the extent of his exploration of the 18th of June. He was able to push his reconnaissances as far as Couture, Mousty, Ottignies, on the right bank of the Lasne, and as far as Lasne on the left bank; but they certainly did not go as far as Saint-Lambert, from whence radiated by ten o'clock, the cavalry of the Losthin division of Bülow's corps (see report of Bülow, quoted by von Ollech, 192; Damitz, ii. 242, 243, and the letter of Hervey, aide-de-camp to Wellington, of 4th July 1815 (*Nineteenth Century*, March 1893).

42. According to Marbot, the object of these piquets was to send the Emperor prompt notice of Grouchy's approach; but on referring to the above-quoted letter from Soult to Grouchy, it would seem that the mission of the hussars was to keep up the communications. Moreover, it will be noticed that, even if the Emperor foresaw the arrival of Grouchy through Mousty, the order to Grouchy and the order to Marbot were not contradictory. Whilst ordering the Marshal to march to Wavre, Napoleon, admitting the possibility that Grouchy, before receiving these last instructions, might have marched to the left, sent piquets to meet him near the Dyle.

43. Gourgaud, 91; Napoleon, *Mém.* 132, 133; Pétiet, 213; Mauduit, ii. 248, 271; Pontécoulant, 261; *Souvenirs d'un ex-officier*, 284 (this testimony is all the more interesting from the fact that, this officer belonging to the 45th Line was born a Swiss. His name was Martin, and at the time of his death he was a pastor at Geneva). The English, Siborne (i. 282) and Cotton (51), also speak of tremendous acclamations.

44. Napoleon, *Mém.* 128-132. See Gourgaud, 87, 88, and the above-quoted accounts of Reille, Foy, General Petit, de Stuers, etc.

45. D'Erlon's corps: 20,531 men.

Reille's corps (minus the débris of the Girard division left at Ligny to ensure the lines of communication): 16,774 men.

Lobau's corps (minus the Teste division detached under Pajol's orders): 7,861 men.

Imperial Guard : 20,000 men.

3rd and 4th cavalry corps (Milhaud's and Kellermann's cuirassiers) : 6,500 men.

Domon's cavalry division (detached from Vandamme's corps) : 1,100 men.

Subervie cavalry division (detached from Pajol's corps) : 1,200 men.

Total, 73,935 men (deducting the losses of the 15th, 16th, and 17th of June). See the estimate at the commencement of the campaign and the returns of the losses (pp. 57, 58, 107, 123).

46. At the outset of the campaign the Army had 50 batteries of 8 pieces for the unmounted batteries, and 6 pieces for the horse batteries (see p. 58). From these 50 batteries, forming a total of 370 guns, I deduct 8 pieces in the battery of the Girard division, and the 96 pieces with the corps and divisions placed under the command of Grouchy.

47. According to the arrangement now in force, the first French line (seven infantry and two cavalry divisions) would normally have a front of four leagues.

48. The fine description by the Emperor, so often quoted (*Mém. pour servir à l'Histoire*, 127-132), of the eleven columns deploying almost simultaneously, and the whole of the army ranged in six lines in the shape of a V, long before the beginning of the battle, is perfectly inaccurate. According to the accounts of Generals Durutte and Petit already quoted, several divisions came on the field when the battle had been for some time raging with violence. The very order of Napoleon of eleven o'clock in the morning, quoted further : "By the time the whole army is in order of battle, towards one in the afternoon," proves that at eleven o'clock all the troops were not engaged in battle.

49. Order, 18th June, eleven in the morning (Napoleon, *Corresp.* 22,060).

In the copy of this order (at the War Arch.) it is mentioned that the original, written in Soult's hand, bore the following pencilled marginal note, signed Ney : "Count d'Erlon will understand that the action is to commence on the left, not on the right. Communicate this new arrangement to General Reille." It would seem, therefore, that the Emperor had previously given an order, in pursuance of which d'Erlon should have attacked with the right of the 1st Corps, either by Papelotte or La Haye.

50. This is indeed what Napoleon says in his first account, dictated to Gourgaud (*Correspondence de 1815*, 88). It is true that in the second account he is not so precise (*Mém. pour servir à l'Histoire*). He speaks first of this single attack upon the centre (133), but he contends (134, 135) that he intended at the same time to turn the enemy's left by La Haye and Papelotte. It is safer to trust the first account, which fully confirms the order of eleven o'clock in the morning.

51. No doubt on this side they would not have the main road on which the batteries could defile, but the artillery posted to the east of La Belle Alliance could none the less have crushed the enemy's masses ; and the infantry, as well as the cavalry, might have climbed the slopes without

more difficulty than at the other points. This was proved by the march of the Durutte division at half-past two, and by the fact related by Wagner (67), and by Siborne (i. 387), that a short time after midday, a body of French cavalry (very likely from the Jacquinot division) pushed forward a reconnaissance as far as the edge of the plateau, where it appeared before the Hanoverian brigade of Best, which speedily formed up into squares. I have explored this portion of the ground. The levels are not less practicable and the slopes are not more abrupt than they are around the main road. Opposite La Haye, the soil of the valley is very stiff. And further the Ohain brook is only 0·30 or 0·40 *centimetres* in breadth.

Doubtless had they attacked at first by Papelotte, Wellington would have ordered a partial change of front, and denuded his centre and his right, to reinforce his threatened left. But such a movement was exactly what Napoleon ought to have wished for, since it was his tactical interest to compel the English to manœuvre.

52. See note 49, p. 185.
53. Napoleon, *Mém.* 125.

BOOK III CHAPTER III

1. Reille's account (War Arch.).

The existence of this order,—a verbal one, no doubt,—which is not mentioned by any historian, cannot be gainsaid ; for in the general order, dictated at eleven o'clock, no mention is made of a movement upon Hougoumont, and it states that the artillery is to enter into action towards one. Now Reille, posted at about 1,000 or 1,500 yards' distance from the Emperor, would not have taken upon himself to open fire without provocation, an hour and a half before the appointed time, had he not received fresh instructions to that effect.

Napoleon also modified in other points his original order. For instance, this order enjoins that the great battery should be composed of 24 pieces, yet it was increased to 80 pieces before opening fire. Moreover, according to the order of eleven o'clock, Reille's corps was to second the movement of d'Erlon on Mont-Saint-Jean, "advancing at the same time to keep pace with the 1st Corps." These instructions were not carried out ; either Napoleon modified them, or more likely Reille, preoccupied with the diversion on Hougoumont, where one of his divisions was already fighting, neglected them completely.

With regard to Napoleon's orders concerning the movement towards Hougoumont, or at least the spirit of this order, Reille expressly says that the only direction was "to keep in the hollow behind the wood, meanwhile maintaining in front a strong line of tirailleurs." He adds that the injunction not to exceed these instructions, was repeated again and again, but in vain. Guilleminot, chief of Jérôme's staff, also states that he had attempted to put a stop to a fruitless contest at

Hougoumont (conversation reported by General Woodford, *Waterloo Letters*, 261). These testimonies are of great importance, and demonstrate that Napoleon did not propose to take Hougoumont, as its possession was of small avail to him, for the attack he had ordered on the English left centre. And indeed it may be noticed that: 1st, in the order of eleven o'clock there is no mention of an attack on Hougoumont; 2nd, in the report of the battle (*Moniteur*, 21st June) the name of Hougoumont does not even appear, and consequently the attack on the farm is not mentioned. It only says: "Prince Jérôme commanding a division of the 2nd Corps, destined to form the extreme left, attacked the wood, which was partially occupied by the enemy. At one o'clock the prince was master of the entire wood."

2. Reille's account (War Arch.); Jérôme's letter to Queen Catherine, 15th July (*Mémoires du roi Jérôme*, vii. 22); Report of the Prince of Orange (*Suppl. Despatches of Wellington*, x. 555); Letters of Captain Yalcott and of Colonel Gawler (*Waterloo Letters*, 192, 288, etc.); Kennedy, 102.

3. Kennedy (102), "half-past eleven"; *Waterloo Letters* (288, Captain Yalcott's letter), "twenty minutes past eleven"; (192, Colonel Gawler's letter), "half-past eleven"; Siborne (i. 384), "half-past eleven."

4. Reille's account (War Arch.); Report of the Prince of Orange; Napoleon, *Mém.* 136; Jérôme's letter to Queen Catherine; Kennedy, *Notes on the Battle of Waterloo*, 102, 103; Cotton, *A Voice of Waterloo*, 54, 55.

5. Jérôme's letter to Queen Catherine, 15th July (*Waterloo Letters*, 249, 259); Report of the Prince of Orange; Kennedy, 104; Cotton, 55, 56; Siborne, i. 386-389.

6. Reille's account (War. Arch.). See last paragraph of our note, p. 187.

7. Lord Saltoun's and General Woodford's letters, etc. (*Waterloo Letters*, 246, 259, 261); Cotton, 55, 56; *Mémoires du roi Jérôme*, vii. 91; Siborne, i. 389.

8. General Woodford's letter, Gibraltar, 27th January 1838 (*Waterloo Letters*, 261). Woodford, former major of the Coldstreams, had this information from Guilleminot himself, whose acquaintance he made later.

9. Reille's account (War Arch.). The order to that effect was issued several times (to keep in the level behind the wood), but other attacks were attempted in vain.

10. *Mémoires du roi Jérôme*, vii. 92. See Reille's account.

11. Kennedy, 105, 106; Letters of General Woodford, of Captain Bull, of Ensign Standen, etc. (*Waterloo Letters*, 258, 261, 264, 265, 268. See 188, 192); Letter of Hervey, aide-de-camp to Wellington (*Nineteenth Century*, March 1893); Report of Pozzo di Borgo to Wolkonsky, 19th June (General G.'s papers); *Mém. de Jérôme*, vii. 94, 95; *Mauduit*, ii. 321, note; Cotton, 57, 58; Siborne, i. 395, 396.

12. Gourgaud, 92; Pontécoulant, 263; Heymès, 19; Kennedy, 107; Marshal W. Gomm, *Letters*, 351.

13. Napoleon, *Mém.* 137.

14. Napoleon, *Mém.* 137. See Gourgaud, 89 ; Rogniat, *Réponse aux notes critiques de Napoleon*, 273 ; and Baudus, *Études sur Napoleon*, i. 225.

Baudus affirms that it was Soult who first distinguished this column. This may be, but Baudus furnishes inaccurate details :—1st. It is not true that at one o'clock Soult was nearer the enemy's line than Napoleon, since, at one o'clock, Soult was with the Emperor busily employed in writing or dictating a letter to Grouchy (quoted below) ; 2nd. It is not true that the letter aforesaid, which ordered Grouchy to join the main portion of the army, was sent because the Prussians had made their appearance, for the approach of Bülow is not hinted at, in the body of this letter, and is mentioned only in the postscript ; 3rd. It is not true that Soult was more uneasy than the Emperor about the possible arrival of the Prussians, since the letter to Grouchy expressing their anxiety was written in obedience with the instructions of the Emperor. Baudus, very royalist, and aide-de-camp to Soult, is anxious to exalt his chief at the expense of Napoleon, but he forgets what he wrote (p. 224), that Soult's advice was to recall part of Grouchy's corps, not because he feared the arrival of the Prussians, but because he desired more men to attack the English army ; and on p. 222 that Soult said : "Considering the state in which the defeat of Ligny had left the Prussian army, a small body of troops would suffice to follow it and watch it in its retreat."

Neither is Napoleon more truthful, when he says that Soult declared that the Prussian corps of Saint-Lambert was " probably a detachment from Grouchy." Soult could not really believe this, since Grouchy, in his letter written at six in the morning and received between ten and eleven, announced that he was still at Gembloux, and that he was going to follow the Prussians on to Wavre. From Gembloux to Chapelle-Saint-Lambert, through Wavre, Grouchy would have had a march of six leagues to accomplish, and a Prussian corps to put to the rout.

15. Marbot's letter to Grouchy, 1830 (quoted by Grouchy, *Relation succincte*, Appendix viii. 51 *sqq.*). Marbot asserts that this hussar was taken near Saint-Lambert ; but the French cavalry, as I have said before (187, note 1), advanced no farther than Lasne.

No mention of this intercepted letter is made in the German reports ; yet the fact cannot be doubted, since not only Napoleon, Baudus, and Marbot speak of it, but Soult refers to it as well, in a despatch to Grouchy (quoted below), dated 18th June, one o'clock in the afternoon.

Napoleon says : a black hussar. I do not know what the uniform of this sub-officer was, but he must have belonged to the 2nd Silesian Hussars forming the Prussian advanced guard, several detachments of which assaulted the height in front of Saint-Lambert as early as eleven in the morning (see Damitz, ii. 242, 243 ; and Bülow's report, quoted by von Ollech, 192).

16. Napoleon, *Mém.* 139 ; Gourgaud, 89 ; Baudus, i. 226 ; Soult to Grouchy, before Le Caillou, 18th June, one o'clock (Chief of the Staff's Register).

17. Grouchy to Napoleon, Gembloux, 18th June (War Arch., Army of the north).

As I have previously remarked (p. 165, note 18), this despatch, the different copies of which are dated some three o'clock, some six o'clock in the morning respectively, was written at six o'clock. I gave several reasons for this. I repeat here that if this despatch had been written at three o'clock, it would have reached the Imperial headquarters before ten o'clock, whereas it did not arrive till after ten. Otherwise Soult would have mentioned it in his letter to Grouchy (before Le Caillou, ten o'clock), and the instructions contained in this letter would have been quite different; they would have been the same which were written by Soult in the letter of one o'clock, reproduced further, and which obviously were the outcome of the perusal of the said despatch of Grouchy.

18. See Grouchy's letter to the Emperor, Gembloux, 17th June, 10 P.M., quoted p. 248.

19. See note 17.

20. Soult to Grouchy, 18th June, one o'clock (quoted by Grouchy, *Relation succincte*, Appendix, i. 21).

21. Soult to Grouchy, 18th June, one o'clock (quoted by Grouchy, *Relation succincte*, Appendix i. 21). See Gourgaud, *Campagne de 1815*, 89; and Napoleon, *Mémoires pour servir à l'Histoire*, 139.

It is certain, as I stated before, that the body of this letter, dated one o'clock, was written before the appearance of the Prussians, and that the postscript was added after the hussar prisoner had been examined. The interval must have been from a quarter to half an hour.

22. According to Gourgaud (118, 119), the Emperor, although immovable in his resolution to give battle, wavered for a moment whether it would be wise to carry his line of operations on to the road to Nivelles to attack the English right. By this means he might have kept his line of retreat at a greater distance from the Prussians. He gave up this plan for fear of hastening the junction of Blücher with the English, and also because he judged correctly that the right of the English was stronger than their left centre.

23. Napoleon, *Mém.* 139.

24. Napoleon, *Mém.* 142. A letter of Marbot written from Laon, 26th June 1815 (*Mém. de Marbot*, iii. 403), proves that the Emperor, in the afternoon of the 18th, hoped to see Grouchy debouch on Bülow's flank. "I was flanking the right during the battle," says Marbot. "I was assured that Marshal Grouchy would arrive at this point. Instead of the Marshal, it was Blücher's corps which appeared."

25. Gourgaud, 90; Napoleon, *Mém.* 137, 138, 140. Napoleon says that the cavalry was spread over 3,000 toises (about 5,580 yards). In this case it would have reached as far as Lasne. This is not correct, for the bulk of these divisions did not go farther than the south-eastern border of the Paris wood (see Bülow's report quoted by von Ollech, 192, and Damitz, ii. 257-260, only one of Marbot's patrols, as has been seen above, advanced beyond the Paris wood), but this was towards noon, and it did not remain there long.

26. Napoleon, *Mém.* 140, 141; Gourgaud, 90. See. 94. The two accounts from St. Helena do not tally, with regard to the execution of this manœuvre. According to the one, Lobau changed his position shortly after Domon's cavalry; according to the other Lobau merely went to reconnoitre his future position in the line of battle, and he established himself there only at half-past four. In this case, as in so many others during this campaign, the question arises whether the orders of the Emperor were faithfully executed or not?

27. Kennedy, aide-de-camp to Gen. Alten (*Notes on the Battle of Waterloo*, 166). Lieutenant Shelton's letter (*Waterloo Letters*, 349), and Siborne, ii. 3.

28. Report of Kempt, Genappe, 19th June (Wellington, *Supplementary*, x. 524); *Souvenirs d'un vieux soldat belge*, 84; *Souvenirs d'un ex-officier*, 285, 286; Mauduit, ii. 293-295; Janin, *Campagne de Waterloo*, 33; Kennedy, 107, 108; Siborne, ii. 3-5; Cotton, 62. See Gourgaud, 92; Napoleon, *Mém.* 143; Damitz, ii. 260, 261.

29. *Souvenirs d'un ex-officier*, 285, 286; Mauduit, *Derniers jours de la Grande Armée*, ii. 293; note of General Schmitz, brigadier of Donzelot (communicated by Commandant Schmitz); Durutte's account (*Sentinelle de l'Armée*, March 1838); Durutte's notes (communicated by Commandant Durutte of the Belgian army).

30. There is every presumption that this order was given by Count d'Erlon, who had the direct command.

It may be that the aide-de-camp, in transmitting the order, made a confusion between the division column (that is to say, a battalion closely massed) and the column arranged in divisions (that is to say, in united companies and marching at half distance or whole distance).

31. Order of the Emperor, before Le Caillou, 18th June, eleven o'clock (War Arch.).

32. See on the subject, Jomini, *Précis de la Campagne de 1815*, 229.

33. Siborne, *History of the War*, ii. 3, 5; Cotton, *A Voice of Waterloo*, 63.

34. *Waterloo Letters*, 404; Siborne, ii. 3, 16; Kennedy, 107, 108; Jomini, 204, 206; Cotton, 63, 73, 74.

35. Hügel to the King of Würtemberg, 19th June (quoted by Pfister, *Aus dem Lager der Verbündeten*, 69); Wellington's report, Waterloo, 19th June (*Despatches*, xii. 478).

According to the plan of Craan, this tree was planted near the southern border of the hollow road. Consequently, Wellington must therefore have stood on the road, where he was sheltered from the shells and the fusillade.

The elm tree was bought for 200 francs by a clever Englishman, who sold it in London in the shape of canes, snuff-boxes, and napkin-rings to Wellington's adorers.

36. Kennedy, 107, 108; Siborne, ii. 16, 19; Cotton, 73, 74. See *Waterloo Letters*, 38.

37. *Souvenirs d'un ex-officier*, 287; Siborne, ii. 5, 10.

38. Letter of an officer of Kempt's brigade (*Waterloo Letters*, 345,

64,363, 3367). "The French came within two yards of the hedge," says Sir Andrew Barnard, Colonel of the 95th.

39. Report of Kempt, Genappe, 19th June (*Despatches of Wellington, Suppl.* x. 534); Letters of brigade officers Pack and Kempt (*Waterloo Letters,* 349, 361, 382, etc.). See Kennedy, 109; Siborne, ii. 5-7; General Eenens, *Les troupes des Pays-Bas en 1815,* 29, 30.

Foreign writers confuse the French columns and place them incorrectly in this order, from the left to the right: Donzelot, Allix, Morcognet, Durutte. Van Löben alone (267) gives the accurate arrangement: Allix, Donzelot, Marcognet, Durutte.

40. Kennedy, 109, 111; Siborne, ii. 4. See van Löben, 267, and Durutte (*Sentinelle de l'Armée 1838*), who says that he reached the height.

It is probable that, while one or two battalions assailed Papelotte, the rest of the Durutte division, masked by this attack from its right, continued their ascent towards the plateau.

41. Letter of Jérôme to Queen Catherine, Paris, 15th July (*Mém. du roi Jérôme,* vii. 22, 23).

Shortly after two o'clock the Emperor sent Jérôme orders to come and join him: "It is impossible to fight better," he said; "since you have only two battalions left, remain ready to give help wherever there is danger." Did Napoleon wish to shield the life of his brother, who had been wounded two days before, and who had just remained for two hours and a half in the thickest of the fight? or, displeased that Jérôme had so untimely involved his whole division in the useless attack upon Hougoumont, did he recall him in order to leave the command in the hands of Guilleminot, a less ardent but far more cautious general?

42. Report of Kempt, Genappe, 19th June (*Wellington's Despatches, Suppl.* x. 534); Fraser, *Letters,* 554; Letters of officers of the Picton division, and of the Ponsonby brigade (*Waterloo Letters,* 70, 85, 89, 345, 349, 350, 356, 361, 363); Kennedy, 109; W. Gomm, *Letters,* 352; Siborne, ii. 11-14.

Siborne, carried away by his patriotism, says that the French officer was killed in attempting to recover the flag of the French 32nd. The 32nd was not in the Army of the North, whilst the 32nd English undoubtedly formed part of Kempt's brigade.

43. Letters of brigade officers Kempt, Pack, and Ponsonby (*Waterloo Letters,* 64, 69, 355, 356, 371, 374, 382, 383, etc.); Cotton, 67, 68; *Souvenirs d'un ex-officier* (of the 45th), 287, 288.

English historians refuse to confess (why should they, since Wellington's army was victorious?) that in this first attack the French reached the crest of Mont-Saint-Jean. But the *Waterloo Letters,* all of them written by officers who took part in the battle, testify that:—1st. On the English right, the cuirassiers of Travers arrived exactly on the border of the Ohain road; 2nd. On the left, the Bourgeois brigade also reached the road after dislodging from their position the defenders of the sand-pit; 3rd, Donzelot's column stopped to deploy at a distance of 40 yards from the road, and his tirailleurs pushed past the hedges; 4th. At least the battalions forming the head of the Marcognet column crossed the road, and advanced as far as the Hanoverian cannon, and attacked the Scotch under Pack on the plateau itself. In his report to Wellington, 19th June (*Suppl. Despatches*, x. 534), Kempt expressly says that Picton's charge took place as the French carried the crest of the position, and that, even a few minutes afterwards, when Picton was killed, *the situation was very critical*. In a letter of 23rd June to Hervey, aide-de-camp to Wellington (*Suppl. Despatches of Wellington*, x. 568), Colonel Clifton, who replaced General Ponsonby, who was also killed, says on his side: " The enemy (*previously successful*) was routed by our cavalry."

44. Kennedy, 110; Siborne, ii. 19; Colonel Tomkinson, *The Diary*, 300.

45. Report of Somerset to Wellington, La Forêt, 24th June (*Suppl. Despatches of Wellington*, x. 577); Letter of Hervey, aide-de-camp to Wellington; W. Gomm, *Letters*, 352; Letters of officers in the brigades of Somerset and Kempt and Lieutenant Graëme of the German Legion (*Waterloo Letters*, 41-56, 361, 406); Siborne ii. 19-24; Cotton, 74; Kennedy, 110.

It is very likely that it is this jostling and scramble of the cuirassiers between the embankments of the Ohain road, followed by the fall of some of them into the sand-pit, which gave rise to the legend of their destruction in the hollow road, and inspired Victor Hugo with the epic pages of *Les Misérables*.

46. Letters of brigade officers Ponsonby, Kempt, and Pack (*Waterloo Letters*, 63, 64, 70, 78, 349, 363, 383); Kennedy, 110; Report of Kempt, 19th June (*Despatches of Wellington, Suppl.* x. 534).

47. Somerset's report; Colonel Clifton to Hervey, Croix, 23rd June (*Supplementary Despatches of Wellington*, x. 568, 577); Letters of brigade officers Ponsonby, Kempt, and Pack (*Waterloo Letters*, 58, 61, 63, 65, 70, 72, 78, 86, 345, 367, 374, 376, 384, 404; Kennedy, 118; *Souvenirs d'un ex-officier*, 288, 290.

In this rout the English took from 2,000 to 3,000 prisoners. Ponsonby's dragoons captured the eagle of the 45th (Marcognet division) and that of the 105th (Bourgeois brigade). Another standard taken by the mounted guards under Somerset, was recovered in the fight.

48. Letters of officers in the Vandeleur brigade (*Waterloo Letters*, 103, 104, 112, 114, 115); Durutte's account; Van Löben, ii. 9. See Siborne, ii. 38, 39.

Durutte, whose account contains, however, more than one mistake, contends that he repulsed the charges of the Vandeleur brigade. He, consciously or unconsciously, confuses the first charges of this body of cavalry, which compelled him to retreat in disorder, with another charge of Vandeleur's against the 85th, left in reserve in their original position; a charge which was in fact repulsed with heavy losses. See on the subject Captain Chapuy's account (*Journal des Sciences militaires*, July 1863).

49. Above quoted reports of Somerset and of Clifton; Letters of officers of the Somerset, Ponsonby, and Vandeleur brigades (*Waterloo Letters*, 38, 62, 64, 65, 79, 86, 114, 115); above quoted accounts of

Durutte and Captain Chapuy (of the 85th); Kennedy, 110; Siborne, ii. 36-39; Cotton, 71, 72.

It has been said that the English horsemen were intoxicated. This is a bold charge to bring against such valiant soldiers.

50. Mauduit, ii. 300. See Letters of Colonels Evans and Straton (*Waterloo Letters*, 64, 85) and above quoted report of Clifton.

A relative of General Ponsonby, Lieutenant-Colonel Ed. Ponsonby (of the Vandeleur brigade), was severely wounded during the same action, and remained on the battlefield till the next morning. He has given an account of the sixteen or eighteen terrible hours which he passed there (Cotton, App. vi.). In the evening a French tirailleur crouched behind Colonel Ponsonby's body, using it as a sort of shield, under shelter of which he commenced shooting at the enemy. Whilst he was firing he conversed gaily with the English officer. When he had exhausted his stock of cartridges he went off, saying: "You will be glad to know that we are getting out of this. Good night, my friend."

51. Reports of Somerset and Clifton (*Suppl. Despatches of Wellington*, x. 568, 577). Above quoted letter of Hervey; Letters of Somerset, Kennedy etc. (*Waterloo Letters*, 38, 42, 69, 77); Kennedy, 110, 111; Siborne, ii. 39-43; Cotton, 71 72; Van Löben, 279; Gen. Delort's account (General G.'s papers); Gourgaud, 93; Napoleon, *Mém.* 144.

52. Kennedy, 111, 114 (*Waterloo Letters*, 346, 383); Siborne, ii. 43, 46.

53. *Waterloo Letters*, 406.

54. Letter of Lieutenant Graëme of the Hanoverian Legion (*Waterloo Letters*, 407).

55. Letters of officers of the 1st regiment of the Guards and the Coldstreams (*Waterloo Letters*, 246, 249, 259, 261, 264, 266); Kennedy, 106; Daily notes of Foy, and letter of the same to Guilleminot (Register of Correspondence, comm. by Count de Foy); Van Löben, 272, 273; Cotton, 85, 86.

BOOK III CHAPTER IV

1. Letter of Hervey, aide-de-camp to Wellington, 3rd July 1815 (*Nineteenth Century*, March 1893); Müffling, *Aus meinem Leben*, 209.

2. La Fresnaye's declaration, quoted by Grouchy (*Relation succincte*, Appendix iv. 13). See Napoleon, *Mém.* 146.

La Fresnaye says that he was "fully two hours and a half" on the journey, and that he found Napoleon on the battlefield. Starting from Walhain between eleven and half-past eleven, La Fresnaye must therefore have reached the Emperor about half-past two in the very heat of the action, at the moment of d'Erlon's assault.

3. Grouchy's letter to Napoleon, Gembloux, 18th of June, eleven o'clock (War Arch.). See Napoleon, *Mem.* 146.

4. Soult to Grouchy, 18th June, one o'clock (War Arch.). As previously stated, the postscript of this letter was written between one and a quarter-past one. The estafette must have left at half-past one.

5. Clausewitz (*Der Krieg von 1815*, 166) very judiciously remarks: "Turenne or Condé would have withdrawn at mid-day without giving battle, but Napoleon could not do otherwise than fight, for there was no salvation for him except in victory."

6. Gourgaud, 93. See 96. Kennedy, generally a very precise and very truthful witness, says (*Notes on the Battle of Waterloo*, 114) that a long interval elapsed between the grand assault of d'Erlon and the second attack on La Haye-Sainte. According to the *Waterloo Letters* (404) and Kempt's report (Despatches of Wellington, *Suppl.* x. 534) the second attack of La Haye-Sainte followed closely on the first. Undoubtedly, there was a pause in the fight after the cavalry engagement of Lord Uxbridge with the cuirassiers and the French Lancers, for the scattered battalions of d'Erlon had need of time to rally; but this respite was a short one. D'Erlon's assault and the cavalry engagements which followed, had lasted at least an hour, from two to three o'clock. Delort in his account expressly states that this period of the fight ceased at three o'clock. From four o'clock or a quarter-past four, the great cavalry charges commenced. In the interval, Ney's second attack against La Haye-Sainte had failed.

7. Letter of Jérôme to Queen Catherine, 15th July 1815 (*Mémoires du roi Jérôme*, vii. 23). See Gourgaud, 96: "The Emperor had ordered Marshal Ney to hold out at La Haye-Sainte, to throw up entrenchments and post several battalions there, but to keep perfectly still. . . ." Napoleon, *Mém.* 187: "The Emperor's intention had been to order this attack of cavalry, but an hour later, and to have it supported by the infantry of the Guard." Daily notes of Foy (communicated by Count de Foy): The Emperor said in the morning at Le Caillou: "I shall bring my numerous artillery into play, and charge with my cavalry, then I shall march with my Old Guard."

It will be noticed that the manœuvres spoken of by Jérôme and Foy were in fact executed, but without method, without harmony, as if at random.

8. Kempt's report to Wellington, Genappe, 19th June (*Letters and Despatches, Suppl.* x. 534); Major Baring's account (*Hanoversches militarisches Journal*, 1831); Letters from officers of the Somerset, Kempt, and Lambert brigades, and the Germanic Legion (*Waterloo Letters*, 52, 354, 391, 394, 404, 406); Siborne, ii. 62. The English brigade under Lambert, which by Wellington's order had arrived at three o'clock, and taken up its post to the east of the Brussels road, to reinforce Kempt's right, took part in this action.

9. Alten's letter to the Duke of Cambridge, Brussels, 20th June (Gen. Gourgaud's papers); Letter of Pratt of Halkett's brigade (*Waterloo Letters*, 327, 328); Notes of Gen. Foy (above quoted); Kennedy, 114; Cotton (87, 88).

10. Letter from Windham of the Scots Greys (*Waterloo Letters*, 80);

Heymès, 23, 24; *Bulletin de l'Armée* (*Moniteur*, 21st June); Kennedy, 113; Siborne, ii. 65. See *Relation* (English) *de la Campagne de Flandre*, 170.

It has been seen (page 196) that during the fire of the chief battery which preceded the attack of d'Erlon's four columns, several English and Scotch battalions had effected a similar retrograde movement.

11. Heymès, 23; General Delort's account (Gen. Gourgaud's papers). These two concordant testimonies, one of which is from the chief of Ney's staff, seem to me conclusive. It was Ney, as Gourgaud expressly says (97), who asked for cavalry; it was not the Emperor who of his own accord supplied him with it, as several historians assert; Ganiot (Ney's brother-in-law) says that the Marshal asked the Emperor for more troops, and that Milhaud's cavalry came forward (*Réfutation*, 40). Both these apologists of Ney, endeavour also to insinuate that Ney only asked for more cavalry because he had no infantry at his command. This is obviously incorrect, for, in addition to the Allix, Donzelot, and Marcognet divisions, which still amounted to 10,000 or 12,000 men, whom Ney could have employed, the whole Bachelu division and Foy's second brigade were intact and ready for work at the left of La Belle Alliance. See on this subject the daily notes of Foy and his letter to Guilleminot (already quoted). Foy expressly says that only one of his brigades and the Jérôme division were engaged at Hougoumont.

12. General Delort's account.

13. General Delort's account (Gen. G.'s papers).

14. See Bulletin of the Army (*Moniteur*, 21st June); Napoleon, *Mém.* 149; Heymès, 23; Mauduit, ii. 346-348; General Thoumas, *Les trois Colbert*, 46. In his manuscript account, which I have often quoted, Capt. de Stuers of the Red Lancers does not say that the movement was spontaneous. One may conclude therefore that it was effected by order of the chief directly in command, Lefebvre-Desnoëttes. Be this as it may, it is certain that the light cavalry of the Guard left its position, neither by Ney's orders nor by those of the Emperor.

15. See Jérôme's letter to Queen Catherine (*Mém. de Jérôme*, vii. 23): "The Emperor ordered Marshal Ney to bear upon the enemy's centre with the bulk of his cavalry, two infantry corps, and the Guard, in order to deal the final blow, and in fact the fate of the English army was as good as sealed, had the Marshal executed the Emperor's orders; but, carried away by his ardour, he attacked three quarters of an hour too soon." *Victoires et Conquêtes*, xxiv. 217, note: "It is not true that General Guyot engaged the heavy cavalry division of the Guard without orders, as is stated in the *Mémoires sur la Campagne de 1815*, attributed to Napoleon. We know from General Guyot himself that *from three o'clock in the afternoon he had been placed at Marshal Ney's disposal*." Daily notes of General Foy (already quoted); "The Emperor had said at the farm of Le Caillou, 'I will bring my numerous artillery into play, order my cavalry to charge, and march with my Old Guard.'"

16. Drouot's speech at the Chamber of Peers (*Moniteur*, 24th June).

17. From the above passage in Jérôme's letter it is evident that the

Emperor had placed the cavalry under Ney's command, but that the latter was not to use it at once, and was expected to await fresh orders. See Gourgaud, 96: "Marshal Ney, carried away by an excess of ardour, and forgetting the order received (to keep perfectly still at la Haye-Sainte), debouched on the plateau with Milhaud's cuirassiers and the light cavalry of the Guard."

This grand cavalry charge was part of the Emperor's scheme. He never said (and this should be noticed) that the charge itself was contrary to his plans. He simply said (*Mém.* 150, and Gourgaud, 97): "The movement was premature," and (*Notes sur l'Art de la Guerre, Corresp.* xxxi. 393) "the cavalry charge of four o'clock took place rather too soon." He also said (*Mém.* 189): "It was the Emperor's intention to order this movement, but an hour later."

In his letter of July 15th Jérôme does not state the reason why the Emperor wished Ney to carry out this grand charge three-quarters of an hour later. Gourgaud (96) says "that it was necessary first to ascertain the result of the Prussians' manœuvre." This cannot be the true reason. At half-past three, when the Emperor ordered Ney to occupy La Haye-Sainte—a movement preparatory to the proposed grand attack,—Bülow's advanced guard had scarcely reached the Paris wood, where its approach had not even been announced. If the smoke was not too dense, Napoleon could see, two leagues ahead, on the heights of Saint-Lambert, a portion of the Prussian troops (Hacke division). He might, therefore, suppose that Bülow was still waiting on the alert; he could not have wished to defer his great attack, at the risk of losing at least three hours, till he learnt the "result of a manœuvre" which had not yet commenced, and which was still subject to future contingencies. Besides, it stands to reason that the Emperor did not intend to await the attack of the Prussians in order to attack the English; he intended, on the contrary, to overthrow the English before the arrival of the Prussians, and this was divined by Blücher's staff. "Napoleon," says Gneisenau, "will make a supreme effort to force the English line. He will use against us the minimum of force necessary to hold us in check till he has dealt his great blow against the English" (von Ollech, 227). Thus if Napoleon commanded Ney not to hasten anything, it was probably to give the artillery time to perform its deadly work, the infantry of d'Erlon to rally completely, Reille's infantry to occupy Hougoumont, and the unmounted guard to advance: in a word to be perfectly prepared, and to support effectually the grand charge of the cavalry.

18. General Rogniat, who at Waterloo commanded the engineers, and cannot be suspected of partiality towards Napoleon, says in his *Considerations sur l'Art de la Guerre*, 235: "When the cavalry engaged with the English lines, Napoleon seemed surprised, and for a moment doubted whether these masses of cavalry which he saw in the midst of the English were his own; and when he had convinced himself that they were, he seemed displeased with this premature change." Therefore it is likely that, had the Emperor seen the cavalry start, he would have given orders to stop it.

19. This configuration of the ground is sufficient to account for the fact that the Emperor did not see the manœuvre of the cavalry. Napoleon also said in his notes (*Notes sur l'Art de la Guerre, Corresp.* xxxi. 398): "When General Milhaud was engaged on the plateau, Napoleon was busy repulsing Bülow, whose grapeshot reached as far as the causeway in front of La Belle Alliance." The Emperor confuses Milhaud's charge with that of Kellermann. Milhaud began his charges between four and a quarter-past four, at the latest. All foreign documents agree on this point (Report of the Prince of Orange, Kennedy, 115, 119, 120; *Waterloo Letters*, 54, 124, 292, etc.). In the same note the Emperor himself says: "at four o'clock." On the other hand, it is certain that Bülow unmasked only at half-past four. Up till that time he had remained ensconced and hidden in the Paris wood (Bülow's report; Gneisenau's report; Damitz, ii. 273). Napoleon says himself (Gourgaud, 94): "At half-past four General Domon reported that Bülow's corps was emerging from the wood." Therefore, at four o'clock Napoleon was not occupied with repulsing Bülow, whose approach had not even yet been signalled.

20. Kennedy (114, 117), Cotton (88), Major Lautour of the 23rd *Light Dragoons* (*Waterloo Letters*, 99), Siborne (ii. 65, 66) expressly say that this first charge was general and sudden. Their testimony is confirmed by Reille's account and the daily notes of Foy. "In a few minutes," says Foy, "the plateaux were covered, flooded with the *procella equestris.*" See Heymès, 23.

It is not true that the grand charge of Milhaud was provoked, as has been often said, by an engagement of Jacquinot's lancers with the English cavalry, or as also said, by the engagement of a brigade of cuirassiers with a Hanoverian battalion marching to the help of La Haye-Sainte. The error is due to a double confusion with the partial charges of the cuirassiers and of the lancers, between half-past two and three.

21. Letters from officers of the Adam, Maitland, Byng, Mitchell brigades (*Waterloo Letters*, 252, 270, 271, 289, 290, 316, 391). Craan, *Notice pour le Plan;* Siborne, ii. 63.

22. Kennedy, 114, 115; General Hügel to the King of Würtemberg, Brussels, 19th June (quoted by Pfister, *Aus dem Lager der Verbündeten,* 369).

The English infantry forming the left centre had suffered most severely, but on that side the plateau was inaccessible to the cavalry, on account of the high and dense hedges of the Ohain road.

23. Kennedy, 115; Letters of officers of the English artillery (*Waterloo Letters*, 186, 193); Cotton, 88; Siborne, ii. 67. See Mercer, i. 310, and Müffling (C. of W.), 27.

24. Kennedy, 116; Notes of Capt. de Stuers of the red lancers (Communicated by M. de Stuers); Siborne, ii. 66; Cotton, 88.

25. Letter of Yalcott of the *Royal Horse Artillery* (*Waterloo Letters*, 193); Kennedy, 116; Siborne, ii. 65, 66; Cotton, 88, 92; Mercer, *Journal of the Campaign*, i. 320.

26. Letters from English artillery officers (*Waterloo Letters*, 186, 193,

195, 215, 282); Letter of Hervey (*Nineteenth Century*, March 1893); Capt. Pringle, *Rémarques* (vol. viii. of *The Life of Napoleon*, by Walter Scott, 644); Kennedy, 116; Siborne, ii. 65-68; Cotton, 88; Notes of Colonel Planzeaux (War Arch.); daily notes of Foy. Foy says that all the batteries were past, and Siborne that the firing completely ceased for twenty minutes. This proves that they were in our power.

27. Colonel Baudus (account communicated by M. de Montenon) is justly surprised that the precaution was never taken, to provide a few chosen horsemen, in every regiment, with headless nails and hammers, to enable them to spike all captured guns quickly. Four times such an opportunity presented itself at Waterloo.

28. On the first and second line there was then one of Byng's battalions (the others were at Hougoumont); four of Colin Halkett's; two of Maitland's (comprising 1,000 men each); two of Adam's (the others were in reserve); two of Ompteda's (the others were at La Haye-Sainte); five of Kielmansegge's; three of Kruse's; four of the Brunswickers (the others in reserve). Later the four battalions of Duplat left their position near Merbe-Braine, and came to prolong the line of squares.

The squares were composed of one battalion, except the squares of Halkett, which were of two battalions on account of the losses suffered at Quatre-Bras. On the very minute plan of Craan, sixteen squares are indicated.

29. Letters of artillery officers of the Mitchell and Halkett brigades (*Waterloo Letters*, 193, 216, 311, 318, 320, 326, 339); Siborne, ii. 67, 68; Cotton, 88, 89; Heymès, 23; Pringle, *Rémarques*, 644; Kellermann's account (War Arch.); Notes of Foy; Notes of de Stuers.

Some squares consisted of four rows. Most of them had rounded angles.

30. Letters from artillery officers of the Maitland, Halkett, Adam, and Mitchell brigades (*Waterloo Letters*, 189, 235, 242, 252, 272, 302, 311, 320); Report of Pozzo di Borgo to Prince Wolkonsky, Nivelles, 19th June (Gen. G.'s papers); Letter of Hervey, aide-de-camp to Wellington; Kennedy, 116; Mercer, ii. 301; Siborne, ii. 69; Cotton, 89; De Brack, *Avant postes de cavalerie*, 79; Heymès, 23; Notes of Foy; Notes of de Stuers of the red lancers.

31. Letters of Lord Uxbridge, Major Lautour of the 23rd Light Dragoons (*Waterloo Letters*, 10, 99, 100); Mercer, ii. 307-309; Kennedy, 117; Siborne, ii. 70; Notes of de Stuers; Tomkinson, *Diary*, 305.

32. Letters from artillery officers of the Dörnberg, Halkett, and Adam brigades (*Waterloo Letters*, 99, 189, 193, 234, 235, 302, 328, 339); Kennedy, 117; Report of the Prince of Orange, Brussels, 22nd June (*Suppl. Despatches of Wellington*, x. 555); Siborne, ii. 71, 72; Mercer, ii. 308; Notes of Foy; Notes of de Stuers.

33. Capt. Mercer, i. 301, 307, 308: "*I fear all is over.*" See Müffling, *Aus meinem Leben*, 213.

34. Gourgaud, 97; Napoleon, *Mém.* 150.

35. Jérôme's letter to Queen Catherine, 15th July 1815; Gourgaud, 97; Napoleon, *Mém.* 150; Flahaut's letter (*Moniteur*, 9th April 1857).

See General Rogniat, *Rémarques sur l'Art de la Guerre*, 235 : " Napoleon seemed displeased with this premature charge." I have explained previously that owing to the conformation of the ground, the Milhaud and Lefebvre-Desnoëttes divisions were able to carry out their movement without the Emperor's knowledge.

36. Gourgaud, 97. Jérôme, who was at the time near the Emperor, relates (above-quoted letter) that the latter, speaking of Ney, said to him : "Unfortunate man ! it is the second time since the day before yesterday, that he has compromised the fate of France !"

At the battle of Heilsberg the Emperor, seeing that Murat's cavalry had advanced too far, before the arrival of the infantry, looked anxious and seemed to say : " A badly-managed affair" (Saint-Joseph, *Relation de la Campagne de Prusse en 1807*, 17.

37. Napoleon, *Mém.* 150. See Gourgaud, 97, and above-quoted letter of Flahaut :. "the Emperor said, 'There is Ney turning a safe affair into an uncertain one ; but now that the manœuvre has begun there is nothing to be done but to support him.'"

38. Gourgaud, 97 ; Napoleon, *Mém.* 150, 187 ; Flahaut's letter (*Moniteur*, 9th April 1857).

39. Kellermann's account (War. Arch.) ; account of Col. Planzeaux of the 2nd Dragoons (War. Arch.).

40. Napoleon contends that the Guyot division charged without orders, by a spontaneous impulse, and that he sent off Bertrand to recall this cavalry, but that it was already engaged (Gourgaud, 104 ; Napoleon, *Mém.* 151, 187, 188). This is a gross error of memory. Two formal testimonies correct it :—

1st. Flahaut, in his letter inserted in the *Moniteur* of the 9th April 1857, says : "The Emperor commanded me to convey to *all the cavalry*, the order to support and follow those who had already passed the ravine."

2nd. Montholon (*Récits de la captivité*, ii. 84) says : "17th February 1817—At dinner the Emperor discussed a few facts which his memory recalled uncertainly, and which all refer to Waterloo. He refuses to believe that he gave General Guyot the order to attack with the cavalry of the Guard. It is, notwithstanding, an indisputable fact."

41. Gourgaud, 97 ; Napoleon, *Mém.* 151.

42. Bülow's report quoted by von Ollech, 192 ; Wagner, iv. 75.

In his *Memorandum on the Battle of Waterloo* (*Despatches*, xii. 528), Wellington asserts that the advanced guard of Bülow's cavalry was on the ground in front of Ohain at daybreak on the 18th. Damitz also states (ii. 242, 243) that on the 18th, very early in the morning, a detachment of the 2nd Silesian Hussars went to reconnoitre the passes of Lasne. Both these statements are inaccurate. Hervey, aide-de-camp to Wellington (letter of 9th July 1815, in the *Nineteenth Century*, March 1893), says that it was between ten and eleven only, that the Prussian cavalry was perceived two leagues off in the direction of Ohain. We know, on the other hand, that the 2nd Hussars were still at Dion-le-Mont at four o'clock in the morning of the 18th, and that Bülow's advanced guard, of which it formed part, reached Chapelle-Saint-Lambert only about ten o'clock.

Besides, had the defiles of the Lasne been explored early in the morning, these horsemen would have given an account of their errand before two o'clock.

43. Bülow's report. See Müffling, *Aus meinem Leben*, 209, and C. of W. (Müffling), 23 ; von Ollech, 214, 215.

Müffling assures us that he submitted to Wellington, and sent off towards half-past twelve to Bülow, a plan of attack comprising three hypotheses :—

1st. If Napoleon attacked the centre or the left of the English army, the Prussians were to bear down on his right flank ; 2nd. If he attacked the English right, the Prussians were to come and reinforce it ; 3rd. If he manœuvred towards Chapelle-Saint-Lambert, the Prussians should receive the shock and the English would advance towards his right flank. The original of this disposition exists, in fact, at the War Arch. of Berlin. But from the two letters of Blücher that I have quoted at p. 163, and the report of Bülow himself, it is evident that the field-marshal, before receiving Müffling's plan of attack, had conceived the scheme which he subsequently carried out, and which consisted in attacking Napoleon's right flank, with one half of his army, and seconding the English left with another portion of his troops.

44. Varnhagen von Ense, *Biographisch Denkmalle*, Blücher, 447 ; Damitz, ii. 272 ; letter of Hervey, aide-de-camp to Wellington (*Nineteenth Century*, March 1893) ; Wagner, iv. 75.

45. Bülow's report, quoted by von Ollech, 192. Bülow and the German historians state expressly that there was not a single Frenchman in the Paris wood.

46. Bülow's report ; Wagner, iv. 75 ; Damitz, ii. 273 ; Müffling, *Aus meinem Leben*, 263 ; and C. of W. (Müffling, 31).

47. Bülow's report ; Damitz, ii. 273 ; von Ollech, 242 ; C. of W., 31 ; see Napoleon, *Mém.* 146 ; and Gourgaud, 93, 94 : "At half-past four General Domon notified the Emperor that Bülow's corps was in motion."

Clausewitz (*Der Feldzug von 1815*, 128) is guilty of a double error when he says that Bülow occupied the wood from three o'clock, and that he attacked *at half-past six*.

48. Order of Bülow, quoted by von Ollech, 242 ; Wagner, iv. 76 ; Damitz, ii. 274.

49. C. of W. (Müffling), 31 ; Damitz, ii. 274.

50. Damitz, ii. 274 ; Gourgaud, 94 ; Durutte's account.

51. General Petit's account (Morrisson Collection) ; Duuring's account (communicated by M. de Stuers) ; Gourgaud, 95 ; Letter of General Vivian (*Waterloo Letters*, 161) ; Damitz, ii. 275. See report of Prince Bernard of Saxony (quoted by Gourgaud, 227) ; Gourgaud, 95.

The Jacquinot cavalry, reduced to 900 sabres and lances,—for Marbot's 1st Hussars were detached to Domon's right,—had to remain for the time in its first position, forming the extreme right of the original line of battle.

52. At the outset of the campaign Bülow's corps consisted of 30,328 men, and it had not been engaged yet. Lobau's corps, deducting the

Teste division detached to Grouchy, numbered 7,860 muskets; the Domon and Subervie divisions comprised about 2,200 sabres, deducting the losses suffered on June 16th and 17th.

53. See Henry Houssaye, *1815*, i. 244, 254, 256 and 416, 417.

Colonel Roussille, who had refused to leave his regiment, which rebelled against him, on the entrance of the Emperor into Grenoble, was killed before Plancenoit.

54. Damitz, ii. 274, 275, 280, 281; Wagner, iv. 76; Gourgaud, 95; Mauduit, ii. 390, 391.

The attack on Plancenoit took place at six o'clock (Damitz, ii. 281); the Ryssel and Hacke divisions had emerged from the Paris wood at half-past five (Damitz, iv. 279).

55. An hour or two before, Gneisenau had already sent the same reply to a former despatch of Thielmann. Lieutenant Nüssow's account (quoted by von Ollech, 195); Wagner, iv. 77; Damitz, ii. 281.

56. Wagner, iv. 77; Damitz, ii. 280, 281; Gourgaud, 95, 96. See Napoleon, *Mém.* 159; Mauduit, ii. 385, 393, 394.

57. Letters of Colonel Lautour and artillery Major Bull (*Waterloo Letters*, 99, 189); Kennedy, 116; Mercer, i. 309; Siborne, ii. 73.

58. Kennedy, 118. Account of Capt. de Steurs of the Red Lancers (communicated by M. de Stuers, *Waterloo Letters*, 130, 235); Siborne, ii. 79.

59. Letters from artillery officers of the Maitland, Adam, and Halkett brigades (*Waterloo Letters*, 216, 242, 283, 289, 290, 304, 305, 311-316, 320, 336, 339, 342); Letter of Colonel Harris of the 73rd (quoted by Cotton, 211); Alten's report to Wellington, Brussels, 19th June; Report of the Prince of Orange to the King of the Netherlands, Brussels, 22nd June (Wellington *Suppl. Despatches*, 534, 555); Siborne, ii. 81, 86, 114; Van Löben, 291; General Delort's account, Klein de Kleinenberg's Dossier (War Arch.); Delort quotes besides the following attestation: "Received an English flag, taken at the battle of Waterloo, by the 9th regiment of cuirassiers, 16th June 1815. For Marshal Grouchy, the aide-de-camp: De Lafontaine." According to the *History of the 10th Cuirassiers*, an English flag had also been taken by le Maréchal des logis, Gautier.

The English deny the charge that any of these squares were even shaken. But General Delort expressly states that several squares were broken, and Jomini also acknowledges that three squares were broken (*Précis de la Campagne de 1815*, 210, 211). At any rate how could the flags have been captured during the charges, if breaches had not been made in the squares?

60. Daily notes of Foy (above quoted); Letters of officers of the Grant and Mitchel brigades (*Waterloo Letters*, 126, 137, 142, 144, 313, 314, 316); C. of W. (Müffling, 30).

61. Mercer, *Journal of the Campaign*, i. 311, 324; Letters of officers of the Grant and Royal Artillery brigades (*Waterloo Letters*, 144, 186, 214, 219); Note of Valery de Siriaque, aide-de-camp to Janin (War Arch., Janin's dossier).

62. Kellermann's account (War Arch.); Kennedy, 118; Mercer, i. 310; Letters of officers of the Grant, Adam, and Halkett brigades (*Waterloo Letters*, 142, 144, 302, 305, 328, 329). Colonel Laborde, *Napoléon et sa garde à l'île d'Elbe*, 117, note; Siborne, ii. 82; Cotton, 94.

63. Kellermann's account; Kennedy, 119; De Stuers's notes; Siborne, ii. 95; Letters of Capt. Rogers of the Royal Artillery, and of officers of the Halkett brigade (*Waterloo Letters*, 235, 318-342); Fraser, *Letters*, 559.

64. Kellerman's account; Note of Colonel Planzeaux (War Arch.); Notes of De Stuers; Kennedy, 119; *Journal* of Lieutenant Woodbury, 321; Letters of officers of the Royal Artillery, and the Dörnberg and Halkett brigades (*Waterloo Letters*, 100, 235, 328, 339, 342; Siborne, i. 82, 90, 97); Alten's report to Wellington, Brussels, 19th June, Somerset's report, 24th June (*Despatches of Wellington*, Suppl. x. 534, 578).

65. Daily notes of Foy and letter of the same to Guilleminot (comm. by Count de Foy); Reille's account (War Arch.) *Waterloo Letters*, 126, 128, 193, 242, 256, 305, etc.; Kennedy, 124, 125; Siborne, ii. 84.

Foy expressly says: "When our cavalry returned, we received the order to ascend to the plateau. . . . The 5th and 9th divisions did not move until our cavalry began to retire." Lieutenant-Colonel Davis of the Maitland brigade also says (*Waterloo Letters*, 256): "Towards evening, when the attacks of the cavalry had been repulsed, the infantry advanced against us, supported by the cavalry." Capt. Eeles of the 95th rifles makes a similar statement (*Waterloo Letters*, 305); "There was a pause between the charges of the cavalry, and the fresh attack from the infantry."

Ney's forgetfulness in regard to Reille's divisions confirms this remark of Napoleon (*Mém.* 182): "Ney, always the first under fire, forgot the troops which were not actually under his eyes."

66. Account of Major Baring (*Hanovérsches militärisches Journal*, 1831); *Waterloo Letters*, 404; Kennedy, 123; Siborne, ii. 74, 84, 86. See General Rogniat, *Réponse aux notes de Napoléon*, 174. "The attacks were feebly renewed. There was some skirmishing."

67. Note of Colonel Planzeaux (War Arch.); Heymès, 25, 26; Account of Delort; Napoleon (*Mém.*), 145; Kennedy, 124; Monthyon's dossier (War Arch.).

68. Account of Major Baring; Letters of Leach, of the 95th rifles, and of Graëme of the Germanic Legion (*Waterloo Letters*, 365, 404-406); Kennedy, 121-123; Cotton, 104, 105, 110, 111; Mauduit, ii. 333, 334; Siborne, ii. 62, 63; Dossier of chief of battalion Borrel-Vivier, of the 1st Engineer Regiment (War Arch.); Note of General Schmitz (communicated by Commandant Schmitz).

All the accounts of the combatants, Baring, Kennedy, Planzeaux, Heymès, and those of the *Waterloo Letters* agree on this point that La Haye-Sainte was not taken until between six and half-past six o'clock. How then, in face of the agreement of all these eye-witnesses, can the French historians, without exception, assert on the sole authority of

Gourgaud, that this position was carried at four o'clock? The historians Siborne and Chesney say that La Haye-Sainte was taken at six o'clock. True, van Löben says that *he believes* La Haye-Sainte was taken at four o'clock, or a little later, but he adds in a note that in the Dutch account from which he draws his information, the time is not specified.

Wellington, in a letter of the 17th of August 1815 (*Despatches*, xii. 619), says that La Haye-Sainte was taken at two o'clock through the negligence of the officer who commanded that post. "This is a gross error, as well as an unjust accusation. Major Baring defended it like a hero. This error of Wellington has been accounted for, by the fact that, at two o'clock, seeing the orchard in the hands of the French, he imagined that the whole farm was also in their possession. This may be. However, the "noble Duke" should have inquired more thoroughly.

69. Alten's report, Brussels, 19th June (*Despatches of Wellington, Suppl.* x. 534); Letter of Alten to the Duke of Cambridge, Brussels, 20th June (General G.'s papers); *Waterloo Letters*, 128, 330, 390, 391; Kennedy, 124; Cotton, 105, 113, 114; Siborne, ii. 113-116; *Souvenirs d'un ex-officier*, 293.

70. Report of Kempt, Genappe, 19th June; Report of Lambert, Genappe, 19th June; Reports of Alten, Brussels, 19th and 22nd June (*Despatches of Wellington, Suppl.* x. 533, 535, 537, 559); *Waterloo Letters*, 161, 179, 330, 340; Letters of Hügel to the King of Würtemberg, 19th and 25th of June (quoted by Pfister, *Aus dem Lager der Verbündeten*, 370, 390); Kennedy, 127; Müffling, *Aus meinem Leben*, 215; Cotton, 106, 119, 120, 123, 126, 127; Siborne, ii. 146, 152, 153, 156; Captain Pringle, *Remarks on the Campaign of 1815* (in vol. ix. of the *Life of Napoleon* by Walter Scott, 649).

71. Kennedy, 127. See Hügel (letter of June 19th to the King of Würtemberg): "The firing began to grow dangerous for the Duke;" Pringle, 649: "Owing to the dead, the wounded, and the fugitives, our forces were considerably diminished"; Cotton, 120: "The fight appeared to be desperate"; Siborne, ii. 121: "The situation was extremely grave."

72. Letters of Colonel Freemantle and Colonel Murray (*Waterloo Letters*, 20, 21, 22, 178); *Journal* of Lieutenant Woodberry, 313, 314; Cotton, 125; Siborne, ii. 143. See Kennedy, 128; von Ollech, 243; and Colonel Frazer, *Letters*, 560.

73. Heymès, 25-26.

74. Kennedy, *Notes on the Battle of Waterloo*, 127, 129, 130.

At Waterloo, Colonel Kennedy was captain and aide-de-camp to General Alten. Of all those who have written about the battle, no one was more observant. His opinion, therefore, has great weight. The judgment he pronounces, is besides, expressly or implicitly, confirmed by Hügel (letter to the King of Würtemberg, 19th June), Müffling (*Aus meinem Leben*, 215), by Cotton (120), by Colonel Freemantle (*Waterloo Letters*, 22), by Siborne (ii. 121), and—curiously enough—by Marmont (*Esprit des Institutions militaires*, 25).

75. Report of Colonel von Hiller, commanding the 16th Prussian

brigade (division) (quoted by von Ollech, 248); Damitz, ii. 282 ; Wagner, iv. 77, 78.

76. Account of General Petit (Morrisson Collection of London); Mauduit, ii. 394, 400.

77. Account of General Petit ; Report of Colonel von Hiller; Mauduit, ii. 400-404 ; Wagner, iv. 78 ; Damitz, ii. 282.

BOOK III CHAPTER V

1. Gourgaud, 99 : "At half-past seven, we heard at last the cannonade of Marshal Grouchy, two leagues and a half on our right. The Emperor thought that the time had come to make a decisive attack." Kennedy (140) also says, at half-past seven.

2. Gourgaud, 99 ; Napoleon, *Mém.* 153.

3. Except van Löben, who speaks from hearsay, and expresses doubts, all the witnesses agree on this point, that Durutte had taken possession of La Haye-Sainte and of Papelotte about a quarter-past seven. Müffling, *Aus meinem Leben*, 215 ; Letter of General Vivian (*Waterloo Letters*, 161); Damitz, ii. 287 ; von Ollech, 244.

4. Letters from officers of the Grant, Kempt, and Lambert brigades (*Waterloo Letters*, 128, 354, 365, 391); Reports of Kempt and Lambert, Genappe, 19th June (*Despatches of Wellington, Suppl.* x. 534, 537); Kennedy, 124, 127 ; Cotton, 118-121 ; Siborne, ii. 113-116, 121, 146, 152, 153 ; Daily notes of Foy ; Gourgaud, 99 ; Napoleon, *Mém.* 152, 153.

5. Gourgaud, 99 ; Napoleon, *Mém.* 159, 160 ; Rogniat, *Réponse aux notes de Napoleon*, 277, 278 ; Account of General Petit (Morrisson Collection of London).

In the *Relation of the Ambigû* of London, vol. lii. 434, it is stated that murmurs began to be heard in the army against the inaction of the Foot Guard.

6. Kennedy, Hügel, Freemantle, Müffling, Cotton, Siborne. See our note on page 382.

7. Kennedy, 127, 128 ; Letters from officers of the Adam, Halkett, and Lambert brigades (*Waterloo Letters*, 306, 328, 342, 391); Cotton, 119 ; Siborne, ii. 116 ; Gourgaud, 100.

8. Letters from officers of the Vivian brigade (*Waterloo Letters*, 149, 179, 180); Kennedy, 127, 128 ; Müffling, *Aus meinem Leben*, 214 ; Siborne, ii. 120.

9. Damitz, ii. 245 ; von Ollech, 193.

10. Account of Colonel von Reiche, quoted by von Ollech, 193, and von Ollech, 193.

11. Von Ollech, 194 ; Wagner, iv. 79.

12. Letters of Colonel Freemantle (*Waterloo Letters*, 21, 22).

13. Müffling, *Aus meinem Leben*, 215 ; Wagner, iv. 79 ; von Ollech, 243, 244.

According to von Ollech, Zieten hesitated all the more, because Blücher, who had made up his mind to sacrifice everything in order to take possession of Plancenoit, had sent him orders to strike in this direction.

14. Gourgaud, 100, 101; Napoleon, *Mém.* 160.

15. Rogniat himself (*Réponse aux notes critiques*, 277) says: "*Perhaps* the battalions of the Guard might have succeeded in assisting the retreat." Clausewitz (*Der Feldzug von 1815*) and York of Wartenburg (*Napoleon as Feldher*) blame the desperate resolution of Napoleon, but they are far from affirming the possibility of a retreat. There is more justice in the opinion of Ch. Malo and Arthur Chuquet. The former says (in his *Précis de la campagne de 1815*): "What else could Napoleon have done?" The latter (in the *Revue critique*, 25th October 1886) says: "The Emperor had no alternative left. He was compelled, as the Germans say, '*den grossen Trumpt ausspielen*'—'to play his highest trump.'"

16. Letter of Ney to the Duke of Otranto, 26th June (*Journal des Debats*, 29th June); Account of General Petit (Morrisson Collection of London); Drouot, Speech at the Chamber of Peers (*Moniteur*, 24th June); Gourgaud, 101; Napoleon, *Mém.* 160.

General Petit specifies that five battalions only marched on to the plateau, all belonging to the Middle Guard: the 1st of the 3rd Grenadiers; the single battalion of the 4th Grenadiers; the two battalions of the 3rd Chasseurs; the 4th Chasseurs, reduced to a single battalion, in consequence of the losses suffered at Ligny. Ney says that he led four regiments against the enemy. This is not less accurate; but of these four regiments, two consisted of a single battalion, and one battalion was detached. Therefore five battalions remained under Ney's command.

English authors are quite at fault, but it is easy to understand their motive, when they contend that eight and even twelve battalions of the Guard took part in the attack.

17. Letter from Ney to the Duke of Otranto, 26th June; Gourgaud, 101; Napoleon, *Mém.* 160; Notes of Baudus (comm. by M. de Montenon).

18. Notes of Baudus; *Souvenirs d'un ex-officier*, 296; Letter of Captain Powel (*Waterloo Letters*, 254); Letter of Hügel to the King of Würtemberg, Brussels, 19th June (quoted by Pfister, *Aus dem Lager der Verbündeten*, 390); Colonel Lemonnier, *Campagnes*, 387, 388.

19. Frazer, *Letters*, 552; Letters of General Adam, of Major Blair, and of Colonel Colborne (*Waterloo Letters*, 276, 280, 283).

Strange to say, this officer had twice gallantly charged the English. Many years after, on a visit to the field of battle, he met there the ex-sergeant of the 23rd Dragoons, Cotton, who had become guide at Waterloo. He explained to him that he had not deserted sooner, because he hoped to carry off with him several of his comrades (Cotton, *A Voice of Waterloo*, 126).

20. Letters from officers of the brigades under Vandeleur, Vivian, Maitland, Adam, and of the Royal Artillery (*Waterloo Letters*, 104, 179, 187, 194, 228, 237, 244, 276, 277, 280, 291). See Kennedy, 126, 127; van Löben, 285, 298, 301; map and notice of Craan, and letters from

Chassé to Lord Hill, and from Lord Hill to Chassé, 5th and 11th July (quoted in the *Relation belge de la Bataille de Waterloo*, 10-12).

21. This remark is by Colonel Kennedy, aide-de-camp of Alten, *Notes on the Battle of Waterloo*, 130.

22. My authority is the very precise and very minute account of General Petit (Morrisson Collection of London), who was present during the formation of these squares, saw them move off and perhaps climb the hill of Mont-Saint-Jean, and subsequently gathered supplementary information from the very lips of the surviving officers. It seems certain from this account that the battalions marched in squares. This formation, rather singular for the assault of a position, may be explained by their fear of having to parry the charges of cavalry. Strictly speaking, according to Siborne, Cotton, Kennedy, and a number of *Letters of Waterloo*, the Guard was formed in *close columns;* but at a distance, through the smoke, it was easy to confuse the squares with " columns *en masse*." " *I believe*," says Lieutenant Sharpin (229), " they were in close columns." " I was not able to make out exactly," says Colonel Gawler (292), " what the formation of the enemy was, the smoke being too thick, but I was told that it was in columns." I add that in the *English Relation of the Battle of Waterloo*, published in 1815 (32), we read that the Guard attacked in squares.

According to all French historians, the Guard attacked in a single column; according to English authorities, *in two columns*. Both statements are wrong. Had the attack taken place in *a single column*, it would have been impossible for the Guard to assail the two battalions of Brunswick and the left of the Halkett brigade and the Ditmer brigade and Halkett's right, with Maitland's guards, and finally the Adam brigade, all together, these troops being disposed, not in depth, but in a semicircle 1,000 yards wide. Had the attack been carried out *in two columns*, the Guard would have assailed only the Maitland and the Adam brigades. The battalions of Brunswickers, the Halkett and the Ditmer brigades, would not have been engaged at all. Such, however, is the contention, inspired by vain glory, of some English historians, who also pretend that the attack was effected by twelve battalions. But, as I myself prove further on, exclusively from the testimony of English combatants (letters of Lord Hill to Chassé, of Lieutenant Sharpin, of Colonel Gawler, of Major Kelly, of Captain MacReady, etc., and *The 5th Brigade at Waterloo*, account by an officer of the 30th Regiment, published in the *United Service Gazette*, October, 1845), the five battalions of the Guard attacked together, at four different points, two battalions of Brunswickers, three English brigades, and a Belgian brigade. Hügel (letter to the King of Würtemberg, Brussels, 19th June, quoted by Pfister, 370) expressly states that the " attack of the Guard was repulsed by 6,000 to 8,000 men of the English infantry." Thus the Guard was drawn up in five echelons at starting, according to General Petit, and four echelons at the attack, in consequence of the union of the third with the fourth echelon, as is indicated by the positions of the different brigades of the enemy, and as is absolutely confirmed by the account in the *United Service Gazette:* " The column of the Imperial

Guard was subdivided, and advanced towards our front in four columns, by echelons."

23. Daily notes of General Foy; Account of Reille (War Arch.); *Souvenirs d'un ex-officier* (of the Marcognet division), 296; Kennedy, 141, 147.

D'Erlon's attack was very spirited; but Foy and Reille agree in saying that, except on the east of Hougoumont, where the Jérôme division made an effort, the infantry marched slowly and languidly. As for the cavalry, it seconded the Guard with only a detachment of cuirassiers, which took possession of a battery of the enemy at the very end of the assault, and was repulsed by the 23rd Dragoons (*Waterloo Letters*, 91, 273; Siborne, ii. 175).

Ropes (*The Campaign of Waterloo*, 319) remarks, not without reason, that if the attack of the Guard was a failure, it was because it was not backed up as it should have been by the other troops.

24. Letters of officers of the Royal Artillery, and of the Adam, Maitland, and Halkett brigades (*Waterloo Letters*, 187, 194, 223, 227, 232, 237, 244, 254, 257, 292, 322, 330); Letter of Ney to the Duke of Otranto; Account of General Petit; Journal of Mackworth of Lord Hill's staff (quoted by Sidney, *Life of Lord Hill*, 309); W. Gomm, *Letters*, 361.

25. Concerning the repulse of the Brunswickers, and the capture of the battery:—Letters of Colonel Taylor and Captain MacReady (*Waterloo Letters*, 172, 330, 332); Account of General Petit; van Löben, 296, 297; Damitz, ii. 288.

Concerning the attack against Halkett's left and the reverse of the 30th and 73rd:—The note of the *Waterloo Letters*, 319; the letters of Major Luard, Colonel Gawler, Colonel Kelly, Captain MacReady (*Waterloo Letters*, 121, 291, 330, 331, 341). After speaking of the giving way of the 30th and 73rd, MacReady says: "I beg you will keep this a secret." MacReady adds: "The dead and wounded who remained before us, belonged to the Middle Guard." (In the account of the *United Service Gazette* (see note 22) it is also stated that all the dead lying in front of the Halkett brigade were grenadiers of the Guard.) Major Luard says: "For a moment I thought that the infantry was repulsed. The hill seemed to me to be on the point of being carried by the enemy."

Concerning the action of the van der Smissen battery, and the charge of the Ditmer brigade:—Letter from Chassé to Lord Hill, and answer of Lord Hill, 5th and 11th July 1815 (quoted in the *Relation belge de la Bataille de Waterloo*, 9, 11); the already quoted account of the *United Service Gazette*; and the letters of Colonel Taylor, Lieutenant Anderson, and Captain MacReady (*Waterloo Letters*, 172, 330, 338). Anderson says that there was a foreign corps behind Halkett's left, and MacReady, that the Imperial Guard attacking Halkett's infantry disappeared suddenly. The foreign corps was the Belgian brigade under Ditmer, and if the Guard disappeared suddenly, it was because it was repulsed by this foreign corps.

English historians, in their desire to spread the belief that the

English army won the battle unassisted, do not mention the charge of the Belgians. They even attempt to make a confusion between the 2nd brigade of Chassé (d'Aubremé), which was very nearly giving way, in spite of its being placed on the second line (*Waterloo Letters*, 104, 108, 118), with his first brigade (Ditmer), which repulsed the grenadiers.

26. The 5th Brigade at Waterloo (*United Service Gazette*, October 1845); Letters from Lieutenant Gawler and Colonel Kelly (*Waterloo Letters*, 291, 340); Cotton, 123, 134, 136. See the very reticent letter of Lieutenant Anderson (*Waterloo Letters*, 338).

27. Letters from officers of the Maitland and Halkett brigades and of the Royal Artillery (*Waterloo Letters*, 223, 225, 227, 228, 229, 237, 242, 244, 254, 257, 319); Kennedy, 142; Account of General Petit; *Relation of the Amlugh* of London, lii. 436; Letter of Hügel to the King of Würtemberg, Brussels, 19th June (quoted by Pfister, *Aus dem Lager der Verbünd.* 370; W. Gomm, *Letters*, 373.

28. Letters from officers of the Maitland, Adam, Mitchell, Dörnberg, and Vivian brigades, and of the Royal Artillery (*Waterloo Letters*, 91, 100, 162, 237, 242, 245, 248, 254, 276-278, 280, 284, 286, 294, 298, 308, 309, 319). See letter of Hügel to the King of Würtemberg, 19th June.

From these various incidents of the attack, it appears that each of the five battalions of the Guard, except that which was opposed to Maitland, began by repulsing the enemy, but that, one after another, they all yielded to superior forces, being scarcely 3,000 against 8,000 to 10,000 and a formidable artillery. It appears then likely, as was pointed out by a captured grenadier officer to the author of *The 5th Brigade at Waterloo*, that had the assault been directed on a single point by these five battalions together, the English line would certainly have been broken. See on this subject the remark of Colonel Kennedy, which I quoted, page 225, note 21.

29. Drouot's speech in the Chamber of Peers (*Moniteur*, 24th June); Bulletin of the Army (*Moniteur*, 21st June); Daily notes of Foy; Report of the Spanish general, Alava; Kennedy, 147; Cotton, 154; Letters from officers of the Vivian, Maitland, and Lambert brigades (*Waterloo Letters*, 149, 245, 273, 391, 400).

30. Bulletin of the Army (*Moniteur*, 21st June); Report of Colonel de Bellina to Davout, 23rd June (War Arch.); General Delort's account; Petiet, *Souvenirs*, 221, 222; Kennedy, 150; Wagner, iv. 80; Damitz, ii. 248; Müffling, *Aus meinem Leben*, 215; von Ollech, 244, 245. On the false cartridges: Soult to Napoleon and to Davout, Laon, 21st June (Major-General's Register).

In his letter to the Duke of Otranto, Ney says that there were no cries of: "Run for your life!" This may have been true on the left, where Ney stood; but on the extreme right, the fact appears certain. According to the report of Mouton-Duvernet to Davout, 28th June (Nat. Arch. AF. iv. 1938), the above-quoted letters of Soult, and many other documents, it is undeniable that the opinion prevailed in the army that they had been betrayed at Waterloo.

31. Letter from Hervey, aide-de-camp to Wellington, 3rd July 1815

(*Nineteenth Century*, March 1893); Report of General Alava; Cotton, 146; Colonel Tomkinson, *Diary of a Cavalry Officer*, 314.

32. It was then a quarter-past eight (Cotton). Colonel Gawler (*Waterloo Letters*, 295) says that the general attack took place after sunset (on the 18th of June the sun sets at three minutes past eight), and that it was dusk when his regiment crossed the Brussels road, which seems to indicate about half-past eight.

General Byng (*Waterloo Letters*, 261) gives this further information: "The general movement forward did not commence until ten or twelve minutes after the Imperial Guard had been repulsed." As this movement commenced after sunset, the Guard must have remained in the English positions until about eight o'clock.

33. Report of Wellington, Waterloo, 19th June, and note of the same, October 1836 (*Letters and Despatches*, xii. 478, and *Supplementary*, x. 513); Müffling, *Aus meinem Leben*, 216; Kennedy, 148; Letters from officers of the brigades under Somerset, Ponsonby, Dörnberg, Vandeleur, Grant, Vivian, Royal Artillery, Maitland, Adam, C. and W. Halkett, Kempt, and Lambert (*Waterloo Letters*, 42, 59, 91, 100, 101, 116, 122, 124, 149, 153, 185, 187, 201, 202, 238, 245, 257, 261, 267, 277, 306, 340, 356, 393); *English Account*, 32; Mercer, i. 232; Mauduit, ii. 462; Daily notes of Foy; Account of Reille (War Arch.).

Müffling and the German historians assert that the rout was caused by the intervention of Zieten. Captain Pringle and the other English historians claim, on the contrary, that it was caused by the general attack by Wellington. As both manœuvres took place almost simultaneously, the discussion might be carried on for ever. However, the retreat of the French army was marked by three very distinct movements, of which the first and third were due to the English alone. The check to the Middle Guard occasioned the yielding of more than two-thirds of the French line. Later on, the irruption of the Prussians provoked the panic and disorder on the right (d'Erlon's corps). Finally, the forward march of Wellington hastened the disaster to the left (Reille's corps and the remains of the cavalry).

Therefore it is false to say with Müffling: "Wellington only hurled his troops against the French, to appear as if he were winning the victory without the help of the Prussians." Had Wellington at eight o'clock retained his positions, the Prussians under Zieten would very likely have sustained a check. Had Zieten refrained from attacking, the Emperor might have resisted the English, as well at La Haye-Sainte and on the Brussels road, as on the slopes to the west of La Belle Alliance.

34. General Petit's account; Gourgaud, 102, 103; Napoleon, *Mém.* 162, 169 (there is some confusion and inaccuracy in the St. Helena account); Kennedy, 145; *Waterloo Letters*, 149, 274, 298. See Bulletin of the Army (*Moniteur*, 21st June).

35. Gourgaud, 104; Napoleon, *Mém.* 162; Letters from officers of the Vivian brigade (*Waterloo Letters*, 181, 182, 182).

36. Durutte's account; Mauduit, ii. 440-442; Recollections of Lieutenant François-Victor B. (Arch. at Mézières). Ney's apostrophe

CHAP. V NOTES 433

to d'Erlon, related elsewhere in more choice language, was told me several times by General Schmitz, who held the story from one Leblanc de Prébois, a former aide-de-camp to d'Erlon in the Army of Africa.

37. General Petit's account; Gourgaud, 105, 106; Mauduit, ii. 427, 438, 444; Letters from officers of the Royal Artillery, and of the Vivian, Adam, Kempt, and Lambert brigades (*Waterloo Letters*, 149, 185, 187, 201, 239, 273, 274, 277, 279, 297, 303, 307, 308, 356, 401). See note of Wellington, October 1836 (*Despatches, Suppl.* x. 513).

38. General Petit's account; Mauduit, ii. 444, 450. See letters of officers of the Dörnberg, Vandeleur, Grant, Maitland, and Mitchel brigades (*Waterloo Letters*, 91, 122, 140, 245, 254, 274, 313).

39. Letter of Colonel William Halkett (*Waterloo Letters*, 308); Siborne, ii. 219.

40. I have gathered and compared all the testimonies relating to Cambronne's answer. I may some day publish them under the title: "The Guard dies and does not surrender—*History of an historical phrase.*" I venture to give a summary of my conclusions:—1st, From the union of all these testimonies, it seems certain that the General uttered either the sentence or the word, or something like this: "Men like us never surrender." 2nd, Cambronne has always energetically denied having uttered the sentence, which seems to have been invented in Paris after the battle of Waterloo, by an editor of the *Journal général*. 3rd, Cambronne denied, but with some embarrassment, it is true, having ever said the *word*. But if one cannot see his motive in denying the sentence, it is easy to understand why he denied the *word*, even if he did say it. Cambronne, who had the weakness to accept from Louis XVIII. a title of Viscount, and who was married to an Englishwoman, wished to pass for "a gentleman." 4th, At Nantes, where Cambronne died in 1843, it was notorious that, spite of his repeated denials, he had said the *word*. 5th, If we picture in our minds the scene of the 18th June, and think of the probable state of mind in which Cambronne was in, the exasperation resulting from the English summons, we conclude that the *word* was the word absolutely suitable to the situation. It is psychologically true. And since Cambronne did say something, this word must be the something.

41. "I was wounded and left for dead in the battle of the 18th June" (cross-examination of Cambronne, *Case of Cambronne*, 5). "General Cambronne is wounded, thrown from his horse, and supposed to be dead" (General Petit's account). Petit specifies that Cambronne fell during the retreat, between the fields of La Belle Alliance and La Haye-Sainte. Colonel William Halkett (*Waterloo Letters*, 309) asserts that a general of the Guard, separated from a square, surrendered to him, and that this general was Cambronne. I do not know who the general taken prisoner by Halkett may be, but it was certainly not Cambronne, who at that very time lay stretched on the ground unconscious.

42. Report of Gneisenau; Wagner, iv. 78, 82; von Ollech, 193. "At half-past seven," says Gneisenau, "the issue of the battle was still uncertain."

43. Report of Gneisenau; Wagner, 82; Damitz, ii. 290, 291; von

Ollech, 245; Gourgaud, 106; Colonel Janin, 39; *Souvenirs d'un ex-officier* (of the 45th), 296, 297.

44. Account of Captain de Stuers of the Red Lancers; Account of General Petit; Letters of Colonel Freemantle, of Generals Vivian and W. Halkett, and other officers (*Waterloo Letters*, 22, 108, 117, 147, 150, 162, 176, 187, 201, 222, 274, 278, 298, 309).

45. Account of General Petit; Gourgaud, 106, 107; Mauduit, ii. 460-462; Letters of officers of the Grant, Vivian, and Adam brigades (*Waterloo Letters*, 131, 148, 149, 183, 278).

Napoleon (*Mém.* 163) says that during the last discharge of artillery the Commander-in-chief of the English artillery was seriously wounded. This is a mistake. Lord Uxbridge had his leg carried off by a shell, on the plateau of Mont-Saint-Jean, towards a quarter past eight, at the moment when he was galloping to join in the general attack.

46. Report of Colonel Hiller (quoted by von Ollech, 248, 249); Report of Gneisenau; Wagner, iv. 82, 83; Damitz, ii. 292, 293; Mauduit, ii. 403, 434-436; General Pelet's account, quoted in *Victoires et Conquêtes*, xxiv. 225, 226); Account of Commandant Heuillet (*Sentinelle de l'Armée*, 8th September 1845).

47. General Petit's account (Morrisson Collection in London); Mauduit, ii. 460-463; Letters of Colonel Murray and General W. Halkett (*Waterloo Letters*, 183, 309).

After saying that Napoleon formed the square and commanded to fire, Gourgaud adds (108, note): "He seemed to have no wish to survive this fatal day. He wished to die with his grenadiers, and was in the act of entering the square when Marshal Soult stopped him, saying, 'Oh, Sire, the enemy is too fortunate already!' And he turned the Emperor's horse towards the road." This seems somewhat contradictory, for if the Emperor gave orders to fire, apparently he was within the square. Therefore Soult did not prevent him from entering it by uttering these sentimental words, which were not at all like his character.

From the concordant accounts of the eye-witnesses Petit and Mauduit, it results that Napoleon did not leave the 1st battalion of the 1st Grenadiers until he had given Petit orders to fall back, and that he afterwards rode at a foot pace some distance ahead of the two battalions which formed his protection. He outdistanced them, as will be seen later, near Le Caillou, where he joined the 1st battalion of the 1st Chasseurs.

48. Duuring's note (comm. by M. de Stuers). See Damitz, ii. 292, 293; and Radet's report to Soult, Beaumont, 19th June (War Arch., Army of the North).

In the papers of the Secretary of State's office (Nat. Arch. AF. iv. 1940) is to be found this letter of Drouot to the Emperor, 25th April 1815: "I demand a letter of naturalisation for the commander of the battalion of the chasseurs à pied, the Dutchman Duuring. In 1814 he had asked me to allow him to accompany Your Majesty to Elba, but as I had already appointed Mallet, Duuring wept for a very long time in my room. He is a first-rate officer."

49. Notes of Commandant Duuring (comm. by M. de Stuers).

BOOK III CHAPTER VI

1. Report of Gneisenau: "It was then half-past nine." C. of W. (Müffling), *Hist.* 36 : "It was nine o'clock. It was quite dark."

2. Gneisenau's report; Müffling, *Aus meinem Leben*, 217, *Hist.* 36, 37; von Ollech, *Geschichte des Feldzuges von 1815*, 252; Letters from officers of the Adam and Maitland Brigades (*Waterloo Letters*, 245, 298). Probably in his anxiety to prove that he might have dispensed with the Prussians' help in pursuing the French, Wellington denied having seen Blücher at La Belle Alliance. "This meeting," he writes to Mudford (*Suppl. Despatches*, x. 508), only "took place at Genappe, after eleven o'clock at night." This denial cannot prevail against the testimony of Gneisenau, in a public report written the day after the battle. Moreover, there is the testimony of Müffling, who was present at the interview (*Aus meinem Leben*, 217, and *Hist.* 36, 37); of Pozzo di Borgo (report of Wolkonsky, 19th June); of General Hügel (letter to the King of Wurtemberg, 23rd June; and finally, that of General Vivian (*Waterloo Letters*, 153): "I have not the least doubt that when I saw the Duke (near Rossomme) he had met Blücher. I offered to pursue the enemy, but he said to me : "Our troops have had a severe day. The Prussians will pursue; as for you, stop your brigade." After his interview with Blücher, Wellington pushed on to Rossomme, or as far as the hamlet of the Maison du Roi (letter of Hervey, *Nineteenth Century*, March 1893; Kennedy, 151), where the head of the troops halted; but he did not go to Genappe that evening. This is quite plain from the *Memoirs* of Müffling, in which it is stated that Müffling came to Waterloo to report to the Duke what had taken place at Genappe, from Cotton's account (156), and from several passages in the *Waterloo Letters*.

3. Report of Gneisenau ; Müffling, *Aus meinem Leben*, 217; above quoted letter of Hügel, 23rd June.

4. Wellington to Lady Webster, Brussels, 19th June, half-past eight (*Despatches, Suppl.* x. 53).

5. Report of Gneisenau; Report of Wellington, Müffling, *Aus meinem Leben*, 217; Letter of Hervey (above quoted); Wagner, 84; Damitz, 296, 297; von Ollech, 252; *Waterloo Letters*, 153, 274, 309.

6. Letters from officers of the brigades under Somerset, Vivian, Maitland, Adam, and Halkett (*Waterloo Letters*, 54, 150, 245, 273, 274, 319, 341); Lieutenant Woodberry, *Journal*, 314.

7. The Anglo-Hanoverians had 9,063 killed or wounded, without including 1,623 missing (*Despatches of Wellington*, xii. 485); the Dutch-Belgians, about 3,200 (van Löben, 304, 305); the corps of Nassau and of Brünswick, 1,330 (figures given by Charras after the *Geschichte des herzogliche braunschweigschen Armée-corps* and the *History of the King's German Legion*); the Prussians, 6,999 (Wagner, iv. 85); general total, 20,592.

On the casualties of the French, see further our note 66 on page 252.

8. Mercer, *Journal of the Campaign*, 1, 333-336, 342, 347, 348; Letters from officers of the Royal Artillery, of the Maitland brigade, and of the German Legion (*Waterloo Letters*, 202, 221, 241, 406); Dumesnil's account, quoted by Mauduit, ii. 452-454; Account of the wounded English officers, quoted by Cotton, *Voice of Waterloo*, Appendix, 303-313.

The removal of the wounded, who were transferred to Brussels, to Nivelles, and to Namur, commenced on the 19th; but they were so numerous that many remained on the battlefield until the evening of the 21st.

The robbers of the dead murdered the wounded indiscriminately, without stopping to see whether they were compatriots, allies, or enemies. Several of these miserable scoundrels were shot by the English.

I have not found in any authentic document the facts related by Vaulabelle, of French and Prussian wounded continuing to fight on the straw on which they lay, and who, for want of weapons, tore at each other with their hands. However, this is not impossible. Mercer says (i. 343) that during the night of the battle, an officer of lancers, mortally wounded, whom he was trying to assist, turned on him a look of fury, and violently dashed the water he held to his lips, in his face.

9. Daily notes of Foy, and letter of Foy to Guilleminot, 20th October 1815 (comm. by Count de Foy); Reille's account (War. Arch.); *Souvenirs d'un ex-officier* (of the 45th), 297, 298. See official report of Gneisenau.

10. Account of the chief of the squadrons, de Stuers (comm. by M. de Stuers); Mauduit, ii. 451-458; *Waterloo Letters*, 104, 116.

11. Account of General Petit; Account of Duuring. See Napoleon, *Mém.* 163, 164.

According to Mauduit (ii. 443, 444), the Emperor, about eight o'clock at night, had sent for that purpose an order to Piré, whose cavalry division was almost intact, to gallop in front of Genappe, to take up his position there, and to rally the fugitives. The testimony of Mauduit, then sergeant of the 1st battalion of the 1st Grenadiers, is not without authority respecting the facts he witnessed. But how did he get knowledge of this order from the Emperor? In any case, the order did not reach Piré, who withdrew, as we have seen, and passed to the west of Genappe.

12. The bridge of Genappe is to-day three yards broad. But according to the recollections of the inhabitants and the *Histoire des Communes belges* of Tarlier and Wauters, its breadth was increased when it was rebuilt.

13. *Souvenirs d'un ex-officier* (of the 45th), 298; Letter from Brussels, 22nd June 1815 (quoted in the account of Mont-Saint-Jean, 245); Report of Bellina to Davout, 23rd June (War Arch.); Wagner, 84; Damitz, ii. 297; von Ollech, 253; Napoleon, *Mém.* 267; Radet to Soult, Saint-Germain, 22nd June; to Davout, Paris, 26th June; certificate of Radet's physician, Paris, 26th June (Radet's dossier, War Arch.).

Napoleon (167) says that this accumulation of vehicles was caused by the soldiers of the waggons, who had purposely obstructed the bridge in order to stop the Prussians. According to other and more probable versions, it arose from the natural course of events.

14. Accounts of General Pétit and Commandant Duuring ; Mauduit, ii. 478, 479 ; *Souvenirs d'un ex-officier*, 298, 299.

The dimensions of the Dyle (breadth, 3 yards, depth, 0·85 cent. or 0·15 cent. as the lock gates are raised or lowered) were given me by the burgomaster of Genappe, M. Berger.

15. Report of Gneisenau ; Letter from Blücher to his wife (*Blücher in Briefen aus den Feldzugen, 1813-1815*, 150) ; Letter of Hügel to the King of Würtemberg, 23rd June (quoted by Pfister, *Aus dem Lager der Verbündeten*, 370); Napoleon, *Mém.* 167, 168; Peyrusse, *Mémorial et Archives*, 312.

These diamonds, according to Peyrusse, had been ceded to the Emperor by Joseph. They were seized by an officer of the name of Keller, who sold them to Mawe, an English jeweller. See on this subject, in the catalogue of the Tussaud museum, the letter from Bullock, who bought the carriage from the Prince Regent, to whom it had been given, and exhibited it in the Egyptian Hall.

It is also stated that from this carriage was taken a bundle of copies of a proclamation of the Emperor: "To the Belgians and to the inhabitants of the left bank of the Rhine," bearing the anticipated date, "Brussels, Imperial Palace of Laeken."

16. Letter of Captain Marquiaud (*Spectateur militaire*, 1827); Damitz, ii. 297. Captain Marquiaud, aide-de-camp and nephew of Duhesme, remained in the inn of the *Roi-d'Espagne* until the death of the general, to whom he acted as a self-appointed nurse. His testimony destroys the odious legend, related by all French historians without an exception, that Duhesme, fatally wounded at Genappe itself, and having surrendered his sword, was assassinated in cold blood by a hussar (lancer) of Brunswick.

17. Blücher to his wife, battlefield of La Belle Alliance, undated (Genappe, 19th June, towards 1 A.M.) (*Blücher in Briefen*, 150).

18. Letter of Blücher to Knesebeck (quoted by von Ollech, 254).

19. Report of Gneisenau ; Notes of Lieutenant Julius, prisoner of the French (quoted by von Ollech, 256, 257); *Souvenirs d'un ex-officier*, 290, 300 ; Wagner, iv. 84 ; Fleury de Chaboulon, ii. 181 ; *Relation de la Bataille de Mont-Saint-Jean*, 89, 90, 94.

20. Durutte's account (*Sentinelle de l'Armée* of 8th March 1838) ; Mauduit, ii. 442, note ; Ney's letter to the Duke of Otranto (*Journal des Debats*, 29th June) ; Larrey, *Relation médicale de campagnes et de voyages*, 10, 13.

The brutalities suffered by Larrey, and the danger he ran, form a contrast with the care bestowed upon Duhesme. Larry himself seems to think that it was out of spite that the Prussian general gave the order to have him shot. Larrey bore a slight resemblance to the Emperor, and on that day was wearing a gray coat. The horsemen who took him prisoner led him to their general, saying that he was Napoleon. Exasperated with the mistake, the general sentenced to death the intruder who had so grievously disappointed his hopes.

Let us add, however, that, according to Mauduit (ii. 472, 473), General Durrien, head of the staff of the 6th Corps, who did not resemble Napoleon, came very near being shot by order of another Prussian general, and that he owed his life to the interference of Colonel Dönoesberg. F. de Chaboulon (ii. 181, 182), whose testimony is confirmed by local traditions, also speaks of wounded soldiers whose lives were taken, and of slaughtered prisoners. It is asserted that when the Prussians set the barns of Le Caillou on fire, they did not take the trouble to bring out the wounded French first. It appears probable, if not certain, that during the pursuit they were too often pitiless.

21. Gneisenau's report; above-quoted note of a captive Prussian officer; *Relation de la Bataille de Mont-Saint-Jean*, 89, 90, 94; Report of Bellina to Davout, 23rd of June (War Arch.); Damitz, ii. 298; Mauduit, ii. 472; Fleury de Chaboulon, ii. 182.

22. Except the Tippelskirch brigade (Pirch's corps), which had followed Bülow as far as Genappe, and Röder's cavalry (Zieten's corps), led by Gneisenau, with that of Prince William.

23. Von Ollech, 254. See Damitz, ii. 297, 298. The cavalry of Prince William did not join Gneisenau until early in the morning of the 19th.

24. "I have, I believe, 150 pieces of cannon, and Blücher tells me that he has got sixty more" (Wellington to Lady Webster, Brussels, 19th of June, *Despatches, Suppl.* x. 531). A list, signed Wood, mentions 122 pieces of artillery, 344 chariots, ammunition carts, etc., taken from the enemy on the battlefield itself (*Despatches, Suppl.* x. 547). Wagner (iv. 85) says 250 cannons. At any rate, the whole artillery was lost, with the exception, perhaps, of three or four batteries.

25. We read in Charras (ii. 91, 92) a paragraph on the defence of the flags; but I have found no authentic documents to confirm these details. It is, however, a positive fact that the Prussians captured no flags. The only eagles lost by the French army, those of the 45th and the 105th, were carried off by the English, about half-past two, at the time of the first assault of d'Erlon's corps (see p. 198, note 47).

26. Mauduit, ii. 480-482.

27. Damitz, ii. 298; von Ollech, 254. See Mauduit, ii. 483, who says he heard in the distance the beating of this solitary drum. Damitz thinks that the horse had been unharnessed from the Emperor's carriage, taken at Genappe. This seems hardly probable, for it is difficult to admit that from Genappe, the two infantry battalions had only one drum left between them. More likely this horse was one of those belonging to the Imperial carriage overturned by the inhabitants of Quatre-Bras, in order to plunder it at the cross roads (local traditions).

28. Von Ollech, 254; Damitz, ii. 298, 299. This inn was situated on the border of the road of Charleroi to Brussels, between the Roman way and the village of Frasnes.

29. Napoleon, *Mém.* 168.

30. "Order to the Brigadier-General, Rémond, to assume the command of the Gérard division and to proceed to Quatre-Bras to take up positions there" (order of Soult, 18th of June, in front of Le Caillou, Register of the

Chief of the Staff). This order bears no indication as to time; but we may presume that it was written between eight and nine o'clock. (Previous to this, a retreat was not contemplated; there was consequently no reason for ordering a body of troops to "take up their positions" at Quatre-Bras.) The order must have arrived at Fleurus at the earliest at eleven o'clock.

31. "On the evening of that fatal day, I received the order to support the retreat. I crossed the Sambre at Charleroi" (Manuscript Memoirs of General Matis, quoted by Edgar Quinet; *Waterloo*, 437, 438). This is rather brief for an explanation. On the other hand, it has been seen that Soult's order was addressed, not to Colonel Matis, commanding the division for the time, but to General Rémond. Several general officers, notably Curély, were in the army without holding any command. Rémond was undoubtedly one of these. Did he join Matis? Did the latter evade his orders, or did he persuade him that it was too late to carry them out? Had Soult sent a direct despatch to Matis? All remains obscure; certain it is, however, that Matis received orders to proceed to Quatre-Bras, and that he did not obey them.

32. *Souvenirs d'un ex-officier* (of the 45th), 299, 300. See Napoleon, *Mém.* 168; see manuscript notes of Colonel Baudus.

33. Napoleon, *Mém.* 168. See letter of Soult to Grouchy, Philippeville, 19th June (Register of the Chief of the Staff): ". . . I wrote to you last night to recross the Sambre"; and the letter of Soult to Napoleon, Laon, 22nd June (War Arch.): "The officer who brings me the news of Marshal Grouchy's return, is the same I sent to Quatre-Bras." As we shall see later, the officer sent by Soult joined Grouchy about half-past ten, but he did not hand him the despatch, having undoubtedly lost it in his distress; he merely announced the defeat of the army.

Napoleon says (*Mém.* 168) that he found at Quatre-Bras General Neigre with the reserve parks of artillery. This seems to be a mistake. No French or German document mentions the presence of such parks at Quatre-Bras, and we know, on the other hand, that at any rate the most important number of the artillery carriages had remained at Charleroi.

34. Manuscript notes of Colonel Baudus (communicated by his grandson, M. de Montenon).

35. Manuscript notes of Baudus. See Napoleon, *Mém.* 168, 169.

The Emperor's assertion (*Mém.* 169) that he sent Jérôme from Quatre-Bras to Marchienne, with orders to rally the army between Avesnes and Maubeuge, is not correct. According to the letter he wrote on 15th July 1815 to Queen Catherine (*Mém. du Roi Jérôme*, vii. 24), Jérôme was separated from the Emperor long before reaching Quatre-Bras (most likely in the plains of La Haye-Sainte, as the editor of the *Mémoires du Roi Jérôme* is inclined to suppose). He retreated with a battalion and a squadron which he was able to keep in order, crossed the Sambre at Marchienne, and reached Avesnes. Here, without any other mandate than his patriotism and his devotion to the Emperor, he rallied a portion of the fugitive troops and led them to Laon (22nd June), where he handed over the command to the chief of the staff.

36. Journal of the Séjours de l'Empereur (Nat. Arch. AF. * iv. 437).

37. Local traditions; Mauduit, *Derniers Jours de la Grande Armée*, ii. 484, 485; Notes of the Abbé Piérard (communicated by M. Clément Lyon of Charleroi); Report of Colonel de Bellina to Davout, 23rd June (War Arch.). It is Captain Mauduit who asserts that the officer in command of the garrison at Charleroi was intoxicated.

38. Local traditions; *Souvenirs d'un ex-officier* (of the 45th), 302; Mauduit, ii. 487-489; Notes of the Abbé Piérard.

39. Peyrusse, *Mémorial et Archives*, 312; Mauduit, ii. 488, 489; *Souvenirs d'un ex-officier*, 302; local traditions; Notes of the Abbé Piérard. Fleury de Chaboulon (ii. 184) says that the bags of gold were brought back by those who had been entrusted with them; but Peyrusse confirms the local traditions that the treasury was entirely pillaged.

It was not the army treasury, but the private treasury of the Emperor, which, on leaving Paris, amounted to one million in gold, and 200,000 francs in silver (letter of Napoleon to Peyrusse, 7th June, quoted by Peyrusse, 310).

40. Bassano to Caulaincourt, Paris, 25th June (quoted by Ernouf, *Maret Duke of Bassano*, 657, 658); Fleury de Chaboulon, ii. 183. See Las-Cases, iii. 93.

Many of the letters and reports which there was no time to destroy, were seized by a Dutch officer who, being taken prisoner on the 17th of June and confined at Charleroi, appointed himself commander of the place on the 19th, after the French had left. These papers were published under the title of *Portefeuille de Buonaparte pris à Charleroi* (in 8vo, The Hague, 1815). See on the subject of this pamphlet, erroneously treated as apocryphal by some bibliographers, Henry Houssaye, *1815*, i. 497, note.

41. Order of Blücher, Gosselies, 19th June (quoted by von Ollech, 268); C. of W. (Müffling), 41-43; Wagner, iv. 85; Damitz, ii. 318, 319, 347-350; local traditions.

42. Gourgaud, 127.

43. Local traditions; *Relation of the Ambigû* of London, lii. 441; Napoleon, *Mém.* 169.

44. Report of Colonel de Bellina to Davout, 23rd June (War Arch.); Gourgaud, 130.

45. Journal des Séjours de l'Empereur (Nat. Arch. Aff. iv. 437); Napoleon, *Mém.* 169; *Relation of the Ambigû* of London, lii. 441; *Relation de la Bataille de Mont-Saint-Jean*, 99.

46. Fleury de Chaboulon, ii. 185. See 187, and account of Trauffé, in command of the garrison at Mézières (Archives at Mézières).

47. Orders of Soult, Philippeville, 19th June (War Arch.). Four only of these orders are transcribed on the Register of the Chief of the Staff. See Gourgaud, 130; Fleury de Chaboulon, ii. 185.

According to Fleury de Chaboulon, the Emperor could not have seen Soult again at Philippeville, and the instructions relative to the orders to be drawn up and sent by the chief of the staff, were dictated to the Duke of Bassano. But why, in any case, to the Duke of Bassano, since Bertrand, who in similar circumstances always filled the place of the chief of the staff, was present? But from Gourgaud's testimony (131), implicitly confirmed by the text of certain orders from Soult, it seems clear that the Marshal did receive, at Philippeville, direct instructions from the Emperor.

Gourgaud says that the Emperor also sent to Generals Rapp, Lecourbe, and Lamarque, orders to retreat by forced, marches to Paris. There is no trace of these despatches in the Register of the Chief of the Staff in the Archives of War. Besides, Rapp wrote from Wissemburg to Davout, on 24th June, that he was awaiting orders to know whether he was to return towards Paris (War Arch., Army of the Rhine).

48. Fleury de Chaboulon, ii. 185.

49. Memoirs of Mme. de X. I am not at liberty to designate these Memoirs more precisely, one of the most precious documents in existence on the last days of the Empire.

50. Fleury de Chaboulon quotes the text of this letter, which Charras and others consider authentic. I am not so positive about it; but if these are not the very words of the letter, they probably give the drift of it. I know, on the other hand, thanks to the communication I received from Mme. X.'s manuscript Memoirs (above quoted), that Joseph knew the chief details of the battle of Waterloo, from the afternoon of the 20th of June, through the letter aforesaid.

51. The Bulletin, dated from Laon, 20th June, was published in a special supplement of the *Moniteur* of the 21st June. This supplement, covering half a printed sheet, on the first pages only, must have appeared rather late in the afternoon. According to the somewhat contradictory testimonies of Fleury de Chaboulon (ii. 192, 193), of Captain de Vatry (*Notes on the Hundred Days*, quoted in the *Mémoires du Maréchal de Grouchy*, iv. 113, 114), and the *Nuits de l'Abdication*, a copy of which exists at the Archives of Foreign Affairs (1802), it appears that this Bulletin was commenced at Philippeville on the 19th, completed at Laon on the evening of the 20th, finally re-read and modified at the Elysée, on the morning of the 21st.

52. Gourgaud, 131; Fleury de Chaboulon, ii. 187; Account of Traullé, commanding the garrison at Mézières (Archives at Mézières). Traullé saw the three carriages arrive at Mézières.

53. Rogniat, *Réponse aux Notes critiques de Napoleon*, 279.

54. *Relation de la Campagne de Mont-Saint-Jean*, 100, 101; Fleury de Chaboulon, ii. 187.

55. Account of Traullé (in command of the garrison at Mézières). See General Rogniat, *Réponse aux Notes critiques de Napoleon*, 279.

56. Radet to Soult, 22nd June (Radet's dossier, War Arch.): "I reached Laon at six o'clock, and I was beginning to rally the fugitives, when the Emperor arrived."

57. Notes of Radet for his advocate (1816), quoted by Combier, *Mémoires de Radet*, 340); Devismes, *Histoire de Laon*, ii. 240, 241; Fleury de Chaboulon, ii. 289, 290. Devismes makes a mistake when he says that the Emperor arrived by the Rheims road. He came by the Marle road, for Traullé reports that, early in the morning of the 20th, Napoleon breakfasted on two eggs, at the Hotel of the Grand-Turk at

Maubert-Fontaine, and rested there for a few hours. Now Maubert-Fontaine is on the way from Mézières to Laon, through Marce.

58. Gourgaud, 131; Napoleon, *Mém.* 169, 170; Fleury de Chaboulon, ii. 189, 190; Devismes, *Histoire de Laon*, ii. 240-242. See Soult to Davout, Laon, 21st June; Napoleon, Laon, 22nd June (Register of Major-General). From an order to Neigre, this general, after mounting all the batteries he could find at La Fère, was to go to Paris to reorganise the field artillery.

59. Soult did not reach Laon before the morning of the 21st June (Soult to Davout, 21st June, Register of the Chief of the Staff).

60. From Radet's account, it may be inferred that the Emperor left Laon between eight and nine o'clock. Devismes (ii. 244) says, at ten o'clock, the Journal des Séjours de l'Empereur (Nat. Arch. A.F. iv. 437), at eleven o'clock.

61. According to Fleury de Chaboulon (ii. 190-192), it would seem that the Emperor was very undecided on the 19th and 20th of June. He made up his mind only at Laon, and although he was inclined to remain with the army, he yielded to the advice and arguments of those around him.

It is probable that a deliberation took place at Laon, as to what steps should be taken, and that arguments were brought forward, for and against the return to Paris, since this is reported by Fleury de Chaboulon, who, as a rule, is a most reliable witness. But it seems none the less certain, that the Emperor left Philippeville with the positive intention of going to Paris. In the manuscript Memoirs of Mme. de X., an invaluable document already quoted, we read: "In the afternoon of the 20th June, I heard from Mme. de Rovigo, who called on me, that the Emperor was on his way to Paris. King Joseph was informed of this." Now, if on the 20th of June, King Joseph knew of the imminent return of the Emperor, it was through the letter written, as previously seen, at Philippeville on the 19th of June. In the relation of the *Ambigu* of London (lii. 441), which Montholon (*Récits*, ii. 84) asserts the Emperor considered as trustworthy, we are told that it was there (during the halt on the banks of the Sambre) that he debated whether he should return to Paris, and that he decided to do so in spite of the objections of several bystanders. In a report to Davout of the 23rd June (War Arch.), Colonel de Bellina says: "The Emperor took post at Philippeville, bound for Paris." Lastly, in none of his accounts from St. Helena, nor in the conversations reported by Las-Cases, Montholon, Antomarchi, does the Emperor allude to the pretended advice proffered to him, urging him to go to Paris against his will. He has on the contrary repeated again and again that, of his own accord, and without any hesitation, he had taken this step, which circumstances rendered inevitable, "his presence with the army being useless for several days, and his most dangerous enemies being in Paris." (See Napoleon, *Mém.* 171; Gourgaud, 132, 133; Montholon, i. 3, ii. 178-180; Las-Cases, i. 20.)

In conclusion, it is evident that if Napoleon had planned not to leave the army, he would most probably have remained with the chief of the staff at Philippeville until the 20th of June: at all events, upon reaching Laon, he would at once have gone up to the town, to establish himself at the Préfecture, instead of making a simple halt at the foot of the mountain, in the courtyard of the Hotel de la Poste.

62. Gourgaud, 132, 133; Napoleon, *Mém.* 171; Montholon, *Récits*, i. 3, ii. 179; Las-Cases, i. 20.

63. If Bonaparte had not abandoned his army in Egypt, he would neither have become Consul nor Emperor. If Napoleon had not abandoned his army in Russia he would not, so to speak, have caused to spring from the earth the "Grande Armée" of 1813. And lastly, if he had not abandoned his army after Waterloo, the vote for his deposition would have surprised him at Laon in the midst of this army, as had happened the year before at Fontainebleau. No doubt, in 1815, his going to Paris did not arrest the march of events, since he was compelled to abdicate there; but he hoped, and with just reason, that his presence would have had a very different effect.

64. It was not until the night of the 21st to the 22nd of June that Soult received at Laon information from General Dumonceau, in command of the 2nd military division, to the effect, that according to a despatch of General Bonnemains, dated Dinant, 20th June, Grouchy's army had recrossed the Sambre at Namur (Soult to Grouchy, 22nd of June, seven o'clock in the morning, and to Napoleon, 22nd of June, six o'clock in the morning, Register of Chief of the Staff).

65. Fleury de Chaboulon ii. 191. See report of Davout to the Commission of the Government, 23rd June (Nat. Arch. AF. iv. 1936): "We have now some grounds for hope, founded on the fact that the portion of the army acting under Marshal Grouchy, about whose fate there was such grave anxiety, is preserved to the country."

66. As no returns were drawn up of the losses of the French army at Waterloo, they can only be approximately estimated. Gourgaud (128) computes them at 26,000 men, of whom 7,500 were prisoners. From the manuscript Memoirs of Mme. de X., who received her information from Joseph, 30,000 men were left on the field of battle. A confidential report sent from Avesnes to Davout on 20th June (War Arch.) estimates the killed, wounded, and prisoners at from 30,000 to 40,000.

If we consult the lists of the army corps engaged in the battle of Waterloo, we find on the 29th of June a total of men present under arms amounting to 26,715, and on the 1st of July 32,646 (War Arch., portfolio of the situations). As the army at Waterloo numbered 74,000 men, we must have lost 41,500 men. But this calculation is incorrect: 1st. Of these 32,646 men assembled on the 1st of July, a certain number had just been drafted from the depôts to the battalions and squadrons of war. 2nd. Many able and willing men had not yet joined. 3rd. Among the soldiers who had escaped from the disaster, crowds had deserted, some because they were weary of fighting, others because they thought the war was ended, "since the Emperor had abdicated." Even among the soldiers who had joined their corps from the 19th to the 23rd of June, there were numberless desertions as soon as the abdication was known.

From the *Tableau des Officiers tués et blessés pendant les Guerres de l'Empire*, by M. Martinieu, clerk of the War Arch. (a work in the press), the officers lost at the battle of Waterloo are estimated at 720, and at the battles of Ligny and Quatre-Bras at 346. I have previously given the total number of killed and wounded at Ligny and Quatre-Bras as 13,500. Therefore, if the proportion was the same at Waterloo between officers and men, there must have been in this action at least 27,000 killed and wounded French. In conclusion, probably out of the 74,000 French who fought at Waterloo, 25,000 to 27,000 were killed or wounded, 8,000 to 10,000 taken prisoners, 30,000 rallied to their corps, and from 8,000 to 10,000 deserted.

67. Soult to Napoleon, Rocroi, 20th June (Register of Major-General); Jérôme to Napoleon, Wavre, 21st June (quoted in the *Mémoires du Roi Jérôme*, vii. 131).

We have seen in the preceding note that this nucleus of an army increased rapidly; on the 22nd of June, already 14,800 men had reassembled at Laon (Soult to Napoleon, 22nd June, War Arch.).

BOOK III CHAPTER VII

1. See pp. 168, 169.
2. Journal of the Bonnemains brigade; Report of Grouchy to Napoleon, Rosiren, 19th June (War Arch.); Letter of Exelmans (quoted by Gérard, *Dernières Observations*, 13, 24); Account of an officer of Grouchy's army (papers of General G.); Grouchy, *Relation succincte*, 34; de Blocqueville's and Bella's declarations (*Relation succincte*, Appendix iv. 5, 50). General Berton (*Précis des Batailles de Fleurus et de Waterloo*, 54-56) says that Exelmans' corps was sent first by Nil-Saint-Martin towards the road from Namur to Louvain, and that it did not get near La Baraque till about two o'clock, when he heard the roar of Vandamme's cannon. This assertion is confuted, not only by all the above-quoted witnesses, but by Reyher's report to Bülow (quoted by von Ollech, 208). What is true, however, is, as we shall see presently, that the Berton brigade (but it alone) was detached from La Baraque towards Neuf-Sart. It was from there, undoubtedly, that Berton pushed forward part of it, in the direction of the Louvain road.
3. Von Ollech, 208; Damitz, ii. 245, 247. Only at noon did Pirch's corps begin to pass through Wavre. At noon, Zieten's corps also started on its march from Bierges to Ohain.
4. Grouchy to Exelmans, Gembloux, 17th June, 7 P.M. (War Arch.).
5. Above quoted letter of Exelmans; Journal of the Bonnemains brigade; above quoted account of an officer of Grouchy's army. See Grouchy's report to the Emperor, Rosiren, 19th June, and de Blocqueville's and Bella's declarations in the *Relation succincte*. Exelmans, in his letter, does not say that he fell back with the bulk of his troops, but

this is positively stated by Bonnemains and confirmed by the details given in the report from the Prussian Rehyer on the battle of La Baraque.

6. Grouchy to Vandamme, Gembloux, 17th June, P.M. (towards ten o'clock), quoted by Grouchy, *Relation succincte*, App. iii. 20. As every indication shows that Grouchy made a confusion between Walhain and Sart-à-Walhain (see p. 126, note 27), henceforth, in order to obviate further confusion, I change Sart-à-Walhain into Walhain in the orders and letters of Grouchy.

7. Grouchy to Vandamme, Gembloux, 17th June (War Arch.).

8. On this long and useless halt at Saint-Vincent, see manuscript account of Lefol (comm. by M. Paul Marmottan); Letter of Berthezène (quoted by Gérard, *Dernières Observations*, 25); and Berthezène, *Mém.* ii. 391.

9. Manuscript account from Lefol (before quoted). See report of Grouchy to Napoleon, Rosiren, 19th June; and *Relation succincte*, 34.

10. Report of Reyher to Bülow (quoted by von Ollech, 208). According to this report, it is absolutely impossible that the battle of La Baraque should have commenced before two o'clock.

11. " . . . The enemy has not disturbed us yet. Only a few patrols are to be seen in the direction of Chastre. I have sent out three reconnaissances. None have returned. According to V. E.'s order, we shall keep our position here as long as the enemy does not press us" (Ledebur to Bülow, Mont-Saint-Guibert, 18th June, half an hour after mid-day, quoted by von Ollech, 207).

Chastre lies to the south-east of Mont-Saint-Guibert. The troops seen there by the Prussians were the advanced guard of Vallin's cavalry, which, recalled from the right to the left, was now flanking the march of Grouchy's column. As for the Vincent brigade, which Exelmans had posted at the farm of La Plaquerie, the Prussians had no intimation of its being so near to them. It is true that an hour later, Vincent proved no longer vigilant, for he allowed the whole detachment of Ledebur to pass without his perceiving it, between him and La Baraque. He did not join his corps until he had received orders from Grouchy.

12. Reyher's report (above quoted). See Wagner, iv. 58, 59; Damitz, ii. 245, 246.

13. Damitz, i. 247; von Ollech, 208, 209.

At two o'clock, one-half only of Pirch's corps (Tippelskirch and Kraft's brigades, and Thuemen's and Schülenburg's cavalry) had passed through Wavre. Pirch himself was still at Wavre.

14. Von Ollech, 209; Wagner, iv. 59; Damitz, ii. 247. Pirch, says Damitz, had been warned by the scouts of Colonel von Sohr, who was posted with his brigade in the vicinity of the bridge of Bierges, and also by a despatch from Ledebur. The estafette must have ridden at full gallop.

15. Exelmans' letters to Gérard, 1st February 1830 (quoted by Gérard, *Dernières Observations*, 13); Account from an officer of Grouchy's army (papers of General G.). Exelmans says that he sent word to Grouchy

expressing his surprise, that the latter should give this order at the very moment the Emperor's cannon commanded him to march beyond the Dyle.

We must take this opportunity of destroying a legend reported by General du Barail (*Souvenirs*, iii. 185), after a story of Marshal Canrobert, who had it from some veteran officer of the "Grande Armée." Exelmans is reported to have said to Gérard : "You are the oldest of the generals of division here present. If the Marshal should disappear, you must take the command and march to the cannonading. I am going to blow out the brains of this d—— b——!"

For two reasons these words cannot have been uttered. The first is that Exelmans and Gérard were not together at any moment of the day,—neither during the march in which Exelmans commanded the advanced guard, and Gérard the 2nd échelon ; neither at two o'clock, when Exelmans was at La Baraque, and Gérard at the head of his corps, between Nil-Saint-Vincent and Corbais ; nor at five o'clock, when Exelmans was on the right towards Basse-Wavre, and Gérard on the left at the mill of Bierges. The second reason is that Exelmans must have been aware that "if Grouchy disappeared," the command would fall to Vandamme, a general of division since 1799, and not to Gérard, promoted to that rank only in 1812.

16. Grouchy, *Relation succincte*, 34, 35 ; von Ollech, 209 ; Damitz, ii. 248. Now Grouchy confuses Dion-le-Mont with Dion-le-Val, as he confused Walhain with Sart-à-Walhain.

17. Grouchy, *Relation succincte*, 35.

18. Grouchy, *Relation succincte*, 35 ; Interrogatory of Bella, de Blocqueville's declaration (Appendix iv. 44).

19. Grouchy, *Relation succincte*, 35, 36 ; Zenowicz, *Waterloo, Deposition*, 30. Zenowicz states that he handed the despatch to Grouchy between three and four o'clock. This assertion accords with Grouchy's statement that Soult's letter reached him after the Prussians' retreat from the defile of La Huselle (at three o'clock at the earliest, according to German documents), and on the return of his reconnaissance towards the Dyle. The assertion of Le Sénécal (Grouchy, *Relation succincte*, App. iv. 8), that the despatch was handed to Grouchy towards half-past twelve, at the moment of the attack of the Prussian rear-guard in the wood of Limelette (La Huselle)—an attack which began at two at the earliest—is obviously incorrect.

20. I gave the text of this letter, p. 181, note 40.

21. In truth, Zenowicz (29, 30) declares that Soult did not hand him the despatch till a quarter past eleven, though it was dated ten o'clock. "I had been galloping for a few minutes," he says, "when I first heard the cannonade." This detail seems to confirm the correctness of Zenowicz's assertion.

Zenowicz is far from being trustworthy on all points. He reports (29) that at ten o'clock the Emperor said to him in front of Le Caillou : "You must return and rejoin me here when Grouchy arrives. I long for him to be in direct communication and in line of battle with us." The words which Zenowicz attributes to the Emperor contradict flagrantly his written order: "His Majesty requests that you should direct your movements upon Wavre, and that you should arrive as soon as possible." Grouchy could not, at the same moment, march upon Wavre, and aid in prolonging the right of the Emperor's troops.

22. Grouchy's examination of Bella; Bella's declaration; le Sénécal's declaration (Grouchy, *Relation succincte*, App. iv. 9, 45, 49, 50). See report from Grouchy to Napoleon, Rosiren, 19th June, 9 A.M. (War Arch.).

23. Letter of Berthezène, quoted by Gérard, *Dernières Observations*, 25.

In a rather confused letter, full of inaccuracies (Vandamme to Simon Lorière, Ghent, 9th February 1830, War Arch., 18th June 1815), Vandamme asserts also that Grouchy accosted him in front of Wavre, with a triumphant air saying: "I have just had an order from the Emperor to unite the whole right wing before Wavre. I am glad to say that I carried out this order two hours ago." Vandamme, according to his own testimony, viewed things quite differently, and would have given the Marshal the same advice as that given by Gérard at Walhain.

24. Order to Pajol, 18th June, road from Walhain to Wavre (quoted by Grouchy, *Relation succincte*, App. iii. 31). In a duplicate at the War Arch. we read Bielge (Bierges) instead of Limale; but in the original pencil note, Limale must have been written (since Pajol was marching on Limale). See Grouchy's report to Napoleon, Rosiren, 19th June (War Arch.); Grouchy, *Relation succincte*, 37; Pajol, *Le Général Pajol*, iii. 229.

Grouchy declares that he explained and amplified his written order, by saying to the aide-de-camp who was to convey it that the object of the occupation of Limale was to re-establish communications with the Emperor. It is possible that these supplementary instructions may have been sent an hour later, after the second despatch of Napoleon had been received.

25. Hulot's report (comm. by Baron Hulot).

26. Grouchy's report to the Emperor, Rosiren, 19th June (War Arch.); Grouchy, *Relation succincte*, and Questions to Bella and Le Sénécal and declarations of the same (App. iv.); Berthezène, *Souvenirs*, ii. 392. According to Berthezène, the Habert division was at first engaged alone. Grouchy says: "The whole of the 3rd Corps." This is less likely.

27. Damitz, ii. 302-305 (see 246-248); Wagner, iv. 86, 89; von Ollech, 209, 210.

Damitz says that, deducting the six battalions of Borke, who, in consequence of a misunderstanding, continued their march on Couture, and the losses of the 16th, Thielmann had with him only 15,000 men. To this estimate, at all events, must be added Stengel's detachment (three battalions and three squadrons of Zieten's corps), which defended Limale. Damitz says that this detachment took up its positions at Limale only at four o'clock in the afternoon. There is every reason to believe that it arrived there by noon, on the departure of Zieten's corps.

28. Grouchy's report to Napoleon, Rosiren, 19th June (War Arch.); Grouchy, *Relation succincte*, and list of questions to Bella (App. iv.);

Berthezène, ii. 393 ; Damitz, ii. 306, 308 ; Wagner, iv. 89 ; von Ollech, 210. Wagner says that the attack upon Wavre commenced at four o'clock. Von Ollech says, more correctly, between four and five o'clock.

29. Grouchy, *Fragment Historique*, 12, 12, and *Observations*, 17. See *Relation succincte*, 40, 41 ; Report of Napoleon, Rosiren, 19th June (War Arch.).

30. Grouchy contradicted himself several times with regard to the time at which he received Soult's second despatch. In the first draft of his report to the Emperor, Rosiren, 19th June (War Arch.), he says, *at five in the evening*. In this same report, reproduced in *Relation succincte* (App. ii. 7), he says, *between six and seven o'clock* ; in the examinations of Bella and Le Sénécal, *between half-past four and five o'clock* ; in the *Observations* (17), *towards seven o'clock, in front of Wavre* ; in the *Fragments historiques* (14), *between four and five, in front of Wavre* ; in the *Relation succincte* (39), *at La Baraque, after being at Wavre* (which implies six o'clock).

The officers of Grouchy's staff, Blocqueville, Le Sénécal, and Bella (*Relation succincte*, App. iv. 6, 9, 51), agree in saying, *between half-past four and five o'clock*. Their united testimony claims our belief.

The Adjutant-Commandant Zenowicz had taken five hours and a half to accomplish the journey between Rossomme and Wavre, whereas the other estafette scarcely took three hours and a half. This difference is explained by the fact that Zenowicz had passed by Genappe, Les Quatre-Bras, Sombreffe, and Gembloux, whereas the second officer had evidently gone by Ottignies or Limelette ; he had ridden about six leagues over wretched side roads, instead of ten over the main roads.

31. I have quoted this despatch *in extenso*, pp. 191, 192.

31*. If we are to believe Grouchy (*Observations*, 20, *Fragm. Hist.*, 14, *Relation succincte*, 40 ; Déclarations de Blocqueville, de le Sénécal, de Bella ; *Relation succincte*, App. iv. 6, 53), Grouchy and the officers of his staff had read on this despatch, partly erased and written in an illegible hand : *la bataille est gagnée* (the battle is won), instead of *la bataille est engagée* (the battle is proceeding).

Now the original of this despatch has been communicated to me by M. de S., related by marriage to Marshal Grouchy. The whole of the despatch is written in Soult's hand and is quite legible. It is impossible that Grouchy or anybody would have read : *la bataille est gagnée*.

32. Grouchy, *Relation succincte*, 38, 41. See Journal of the Bonnemains brigade (War Arch.). General Berton says (*Précis des Batailles de Fleurus et de Waterloo*, 65) : "Four-fifths of our infantry were debarred from the engagement in front of Wavre, and our cavalry, sent to the rear and to the right, had nothing to do, for there was no one there."

33. *Souvenirs of Commandant Biot*, aide-de-camp to Pajol (quoted by Pajol, iii. 231).

34. See report of Grouchy to Napoleon, Rosiren, 19th June (War Arch.) ; Grouchy, *Observations*, 19, 20 ; *Fragments historiques*, 15 ; *Relation succincte*, 38, 40 ; Report of General Hulot ; Gérard, *Quelques Documents*, 9, 10.

Gérard declares that his troops were not in the rear, and calls as his witness General Vichery. Hulot says that at four o'clock he was on the heights before Wavre with his division (a statement confirmed by Grouchy's own testimony, *Relation succincte*, 38), and that both the other divisions under Gérard came, and were massed half an hour later, in the rear of his own.

But if the three divisions had passed beyond La Baraque, why did Grouchy go there? If he was in a hurry to march Gérard's corps upon Limale, why did he not first make the Hulot division, which was close to Wavre, turn back? If Gérard were with him in front of Wavre, why did he not give him his orders there instead of at La Baraque? If Gérard was at La Baraque, from whence he was to lead the 4th Corps to Limale, why did Grouchy summon him back to Wavre, where there was nothing for him to do? These are amongst the questions which to me, appear impossible to solve.

35. De Blocqueville's, Le Sénécal's, and Bella's declarations (*Relation succincte*, App. iv. 6, 9, 54); Gérard, *Quelques Documents*, 10.

36. Gérard, *Quelques Documents*, 10; *Dernières Observations*, 56.

37. Hulot's report; Gerard, *Quelques Observations*, 42. On the three fruitless attacks against Bierges, occupied by the whole of Stülpnagel's division, see Wagner, iv. 80, 90; Damitz, ii. 308, 310; von Ollech, 211.

38. Hulot's report; Grouchy, report to the Emperor, Rosiren, 19th June; Gérard, *Quelques Observations*, 10, 42.

39. Grouchy, *Relation succincte* (see 40); Bella's declaration (App. iv. 55): "This refusal of General Baltus caused a scandal in the army." See report of Grouchy to the Emperor, Rosiren, 19th June.

40. Report of Hulot; Grouchy, *Relation succincte*, 41; Grouchy's report to the Emperor, Rosiren, 19th June.

41. Wagner, iv. 92; Damitz, 312, 313. Grouchy, in his reports and his pamphlets, refrains from alluding to these bitter attacks from Vandamme.

42. In his report from Rosiren, 19th June, Grouchy says that he reached Limale at eleven o'clock at night; but in another report, Dinant, 20th June (War Arch.), he says, *at the close of day*, and this is correct.

43. As he debouched from Tourinnes, Pajol had found the Vallin division (Gerard's corps) at La Baraque, and had started it towards Limale at the head of his own cavalry and of the Teste division (Pajol, iii. 230, 231).

44. The Stülpnagel division was relieved at Bierges, whence it had marched towards the heights of Limale, by three battalions of the Kemphen division.

45. Grouchy to Vandamme, height of Limale, 18th June, half-past eleven at night; Reports from Grouchy to the Emperor, Rosiren, 19th June, and Dinant, 20th June (War Arch.); Grouchy, *Relation succincte*, 42, 43; Pajol, iii. 232-234; Wagner, iv. 91, 92; Damitz, 311, 312; von Ollech, 312.

46. Grouchy's report, 19th June; Grouchy, *Relation succincte*, 42; Damitz, ii. 312.

47. Grouchy to Vandamme, height of Limale, 18th June, half-past eleven at night (War Arch.); Grouchy's reports to the Emperor, 19th and 20th June.

48. Damitz, ii. 314.

49. Wagner, iv. 94, 95; Damitz, ii. 325-327; von Ollech, 259, 260. See Grouchy's reports to Napoleon, Rosiren, 19th June, and Dinant, 20th June (War Arch.); Pajol, iii. 238, 239; Recollections of Captain François (*Revue Armoricaine*, 1826); Grouchy, *Relation succincte*, 43.

50. Wagner, iv. 95-97; Damitz, ii. 326-329; von Ollech, 261; above-quoted reports of Grouchy to the Emperor; Grouchy, *Relation succincte*, 43, 44; Berthezène, *Souvenirs*, ii. 393.

51. Letter of Grouchy to Vandamme, Limale, 18th June, half-past eleven at night; Grouchy's reports to Napoleon, Rosiren, 19th June and 20th June (War Arch.); Hulot's report; General Berton, *Précis*, 68.

The Hulot division and Exelmans' dragoons joined, rather early in the morning, the 4th Corps on the plateau of Limale; but, contrary to many accounts, they were not engaged in the action, and remained in the reserve.

52. Grouchy's declaration on the conduct of General Teste (War Arch., dated 20th June); Hulot's report.

53. Report of Grouchy to the Emperor, Rosiren, 19th June, and Dinant, 20th June (War Arch.); Report of Hulot; Grouchy, *Observations*, 22; *Fragments historiques*, 18; *Relation succincte*, 44; Pajol, iii. 239, 240; Declarations of Legouest and Bella, *Relation succincte*, App. iv. 27, 57. See p. 245.

Pajol, according to the notes of Commandant Biot, aide-de-camp to Pajol, states that this officer was Captain Dumonceau, aide-de-camp to General Gressot, deputy-chief of the general staff.

54. Vandamme's letter to Simon Lorière, 10th May 1830 (War. Arch.); Pajol, iii. 230, from the testimony of aide-de-camp Biot.

"Grouchy," spitefully remarks Vandamme, "could do nothing but weep like an old woman." Vandamme is more than unjust to Grouchy and to others. In the same letter, and in another of 9th February, he actually goes so far as to say that General le Sénécal, head of Grouchy's staff, spent the whole of the night of the 18th to the 19th June at the quarters of the Prussian headquarters staff, and that he came in the morning of the 19th to acquaint the Marshal of the success of our foes, who, "no doubt, were no foes of his." The solitary testimony of Vandamme would never make any one credit such an accusation.

55. "Address of Marshal Grouchy to some of the general officers under his orders when he learnt the Waterloo disaster," *Relation succincte* (App. iii. 35); Legouest's declaration (App. iv. 27); General Hulot's report (comm. by Baron Hulot). Hulot was present at the meeting of the generals.

56. Grouchy's report to Napoleon, 19th June (War Arch.); Grouchy, *Relation succincte*, 44.

57. Letter of Vandamme to Simon Lorière, Ghent, 10th February 1830 (War Arch.).

58. Reports of Grouchy to Napoleon, 19th and 20th June (War Arch.); *Relation Succincte*, 44.

59. Wagner, ii. 99; Damitz, ii. 336; von Ollech, 263. Pirch had not been able to muster more than three of his divisions, Kraft, Brause, and Langen, and the cavalry of Jürgass, the Tippelskirch division having pursued the fugitives of Mont-Saint-Jean as far as Genappe. Pirch marched by Maransart and Bousval.

60. Journal of the Bonnemains brigade (War Arch.); General Berton, *Précis*, 69.

61. Grouchy to Vichery, Nil-Pierreux, 19th June; Reports of Grouchy to Napoleon, Temploux, 20th June, and Dinant, 21st June (War Arch.); *Relation succincte*, 45. See Hulot's report: "I arrived at Gembloux towards nine at night, and followed the two other divisions on the Temploux road."

62. Report from Grouchy to Napoleon, 20th June (War Arch.); *Relation succincte*, 45. Berthezène (*Souvenirs*, ii. 398), declares that the 1st Corps did not leave Wavre before sunset, and only reached Gembloux at eleven o'clock at night. This means a march of 20 kilom. in three hours! On the other hand, it is a positive fact that this body of troops bivouacked far beyond Gembloux, in the direction of Namur.

63. Pajol, iii. 241. See Grouchy to Teste, Temploux, 20th June (War Arch.).

64. Grouchy to Vichery, Nil-Pierreux, 19th June (War Arch.): "The disorder now prevailing in the march, makes it necessary that you should for a short time take up a position at La Baraque with your rear-guard."

65. In the battles of the 18th and 19th, Thielmann lost 2,400 men and 76 officers (von Ollech, 264).

66. Müffling, *Hist.* 41, 42; Wagner, iv. 99, 100; Damitz, ii. 336, 337; von Ollech, 263, 264. It appears that Pirch sent towards Mont-Saint-Guibert a reconnaissance of cavalry, which found the defile occupied by the French. This reconnaissance was evidently not effected until about four o'clock. The Prussian scouts encountered Vallin's cavalry, which flanked the right of the 4th Corps.

67. Grouchy's order, Temploux, 20th June (War Arch.); Pajol, iii. 242, 243. In Grouchy's order, we must read Gembloux, not Temploux.

68. Grouchy's order to Vandamme, Temploux, 20th June; Report from Grouchy to Napoleon, Dinant, 20th June, half an hour after midnight (War Arch.).

69. Grouchy's reports to Napoleon, Dinant, 20th June (War Arch.); Grouchy, *Observations*, 23; *Relation succincte*, 45, 46; Hulot's account. See Berthezène, *Souvenirs*, ii. 398, 399; Lefol, *Souvenirs*, 82.

70. Clausewitz, 140, 142; Wagner, iv. 98-100; Damitz, ii. 338, 340 (see 333); Hulot's account; Wedel, *Geschichte eines Offiziers*, 254.

Thielmann followed with his infantry, but at a very great distance. His cavalry, which was originally composed of twenty-four squadrons under Hobe, had been reinforced during the night of the 19th to the 20th June by nine perfectly fresh squadrons.

71. Grouchy, *Relation succincte*, 46, 47.

72. Reports of Grouchy, 19th and 20th June (War Arch.); *Relation succincte*, 47; Hulot's account. See Damitz, ii. 339, 340; Wagner, iv. 100.

73. Above-quoted reports of Grouchy to Napoleon; *Relation succincte*, 47; Clausewitz, 141; Wedel, 254; Lefol, *Souvenirs*, 82, 83; Berthezène, *Souvenirs*, ii. 298, 299.

74. Above-quoted reports of Grouchy; *Relation succincte*, 47.

75. Journal of the Bonnemains brigade (War Arch.); Berthezène, *Souvenirs*, ii. 29; Lefol, *Souvenirs*, 84, note. See Grouchy to Vandamme, Temploux, 20th June (War Arch.).

76. Report of Teste to Grouchy, Profondeville, 21st June (War Arch.); above-quoted reports of Grouchy; Berthezène, iv. 400; Wagner, iv. 100; Clausewitz, 142; Damitz, ii. 342-345; von Ollech, 273, 274.

Teste says in his report that he defended Namur from the afternoon of the 19th to the evening of the 20th. This is an error in editing, for in the afternoon of the 19th Teste was still at Wavre.

77. Grouchy's report to Napoleon, Dinant, 20th June, half an hour after midnight; Grouchy to Vandamme, Givet, 21st June (War Arch.).

78. Colonel Chesney, *Lectures on Waterloo*, 236. This professor of military science forgets that Grouchy's retreat was less perilous than it appeared to be. Undoubtedly, the Marshal might have feared, at the outset of his march, that he would be pursued by Thielmann and attacked on his flank by the half of Blücher's army; but these fears were only partly realised. Thielmann allowed him a fifteen hours' start, and Pirch did not begin to operate against him until Grouchy had already filed off. And even had Pirch (Clausewitz extols him for so doing) marched in time to bar the road to Namur, Grouchy, who had still 30,000 men under his command, could have easily forced his way through these 20,000 Prussians. He had more than sufficient men for this purpose.

BOOK III CHAPTER VIII

1. Colonel Chesney, always so unfair to Napoleon, acknowledges that the balance of strategy was in favour of the French.

2. Kellerman in his account states the fact (War Arch.).

3. The risks of war! After all, it might have been in the power of an obscure French cuirassier to bring about, as a result of the battle of Ligny, the decisive separation of the two allied armies. Imagine Blücher taken prisoner, at the moment when he had been thrown under his horse, by a charge from one of Milhaud's brigades. Doubtless the retreat on Wavre would have taken place notwithstanding, since it was Gneisenau and not Blücher who had given the order for it. But it has been seen that at Wavre, the entreaties of the eager Blücher were necessary to induce his all-powerful chief of the staff to march on Mont-Saint-Jean. Would Gneisenau of his own accord have decided on this flank movement? Without laying more stress than need be on this

supposition, I must, however, recall the words of Damitz: "Let us picture to ourselves Blücher prisoner to Napoleon—what impression would this not have made on the morale of the French army, of the Prussian army, and of the allied nations!" and the conclusion of Charles Malo: "Who would dare to assert that the captivity of the undaunted Blücher would in no way have influenced the result of the following days?"

4. Perponcher division, 7,500; Picton division, 7,158; van Merlen's cavalry, 1,200; Alten division (minus the Ompteda division), 4,000; Brünswick corps, 6,300; total, 26,158.

5. Reille's corps (minus the Gérard division), 21,074; Lefebvre-Desnoëttes division (minus the two squadrons of service which had remained near the Emperor), 1,800; Guiton brigade of cuirassiers, 777; total, 23,651.

6. Ropes, *The Campaign of Waterloo*, 343.

7. Marshal Wolseley, *Decline and Fall of Napoleon*, 184.

8. Letter quoted by van Löben, 225, note.

9. "... If this were so (if the English army had remained at Quatre-Bras), the Emperor would march directly upon it by the Quatre-Bras road, whilst you would attack it in front... and this army would be destroyed in a moment" (Soult to Ney, Fleurus, 17th June, between seven and eight in the morning, Register of the Head of the Staff).

10. This pathological enumeration, suppressed in the Paris edition, is to be found, pages 512-514, in the one-volume edition published in Brussels in 1863. Charras expresses himself there without any reticence.

11. Henry Houssaye, *1815*, i. 613, 615, and the notes.

12. Grouchy, *Relation succincte*, 18, and App. iv. 5, declaration of Le Sénécal; Declaration of de Blocqueville (War Arch., Army of the North, dated 18th of June).

13. Las-Cases, vii. 179-183. See Mollien, *Mém.* iv. 198; Lavallette, *Mém.* ii. 170-176; Fragments of de Molé's Memoirs (*Revue de la Révolution*, xi. 96); Notes of Lucien (Arch. of Foreign Affairs, 1815).

14. Napoleon, *Notes sur l'Art de la Guerre*, of General Rogniat (*Corresp.* xxxi. 400).

15. "Napoleon deserved to be beaten at Marengo, and we perhaps find in this unjust victory the source of the reverses which subsequently ruined the Napoleonic edifice" (York of Wartenbourg, *Napoleon als Feldherr*, i. 57).

At all events, it is curious to quote this opinion. There are other and still more curious opinions in the book by York of Wartenbourg. He admires unreservedly only two campaigns: that of 1796, and that of 1814. In 1805, in 1806, in 1807, in 1808, in Spain, he already detects in Napoleon, numberless faults, a "giving way of the mainsprings," "symptoms of decline." At Wagram, Napoleon did not know to turn the victory to good account; in Russia he was contemptible. He rises almost to his former self in the campaign of 1813, surpasses himself in 1814, and subsides into insignificance during the campaign of 1815.

York asserts, but does not prove. It would indeed be very difficult to explain how, after 1796, the military genius of Napoleon underwent an eclipse of sixteen years, shone brilliantly for one year, and then disappeared.

16. Vandamme, who had bivouacked at Gembloux, to the north of Gembloux, would have gone by Cortil, Alerne, Hévillers, and Mont-Saint-Guibert; Gérard, who had passed the night south of Gembloux, would have gone by Saint-Géry, Vilroux, and Court-Saint-Etienne (see map II. at the end of the volume).

17. Colonel Frazer, *Letters*, 560.

18. Theoretically, the average marching speed of a column of the three services, is 4 kilometres an hour, including the hourly halt. But in practice it may be more, it may be less, according to the condition of the roads, the length of the stages, the temperature, the physical training, and the morale of the troops.

I shall quote two instances which are decisive, in regard to this question. The first applies to the march of Grouchy's own troops, on June 19th; the other to a movement similar to that which Grouchy ought to have undertaken on the 18th June, and which was executed with great success in 1870 by General Voigts-Rhetz, commanding the 10th Prussian corps.

On the 19th of June 1815, as I have previously related, the corps of Gérard and Vandamme found themselves by mid-day in line between Rosiren and La Bavette; the former had marched and fought since three o'clock in the morning, the other since seven o'clock. At twelve o'clock, Gérard's corps retreated by the bridge of Limale, La Baraque, Corbais, and Gembloux, upon Temploux, where the head of the column arrived towards nine o'clock at night. Thus it accomplished 9 leagues in nine hours, which is very different from marching 19 kilometres in five hours. Vandamme's corps drew back on Wavre, where it remained in position till six o'clock. It then marched on Rhisnes by Dion-le-Mont, Tourinnes, and Grand-Leez. It reached Rhisnes at midnight, after accomplishing more than 8 leagues in six hours.

On the 16th of August 1870, General Voigts-Rhetz was marching with the 10th Prussian corps from Pont-à-Mousson to Saint-Hilaire, passing through Thiaucourt. Near Thiaucourt, he heard the cannon of Rézonville. Far from imitating Grouchy's example, he wheeled the head of his column to the right, to bring his troops to the spot where the battle was raging. The 20th division (Kraatz), which marched ahead with two batteries, left Thiaucourt at half-past eleven. It proceeded by Chambley, and at half-past three it engaged in the action in the wood of Trouville against the French, who till then were victorious. Now from Thiaucourt to Trouville the distance is over 20 kilometres. Thus in four hours the Kraatz division (twelve battalions strong), had marched 5 leagues, after having done 4 in the morning (from Pont-à-Mousson to Thiaucourt).

On this movement of the 10th Prussian corps, in every point similar to that which Grouchy ought to have undertaken, the *Account of the General Prussian Staff* says (i. 570): "On account of the evident numerical superiority of the French, the situation was very critical when the 20th division appeared on the field of battle." And Alfred Duquet (*Les Grandes Batailles de Metz*, 154) concludes: "We may say that on that day General Voigts-Rhetz saved the Prussian army."

19. Clausewitz supposes quite gratuitously that if the battle had commenced earlier, the Prussians would also have attacked earlier. He forgets that at eleven in the morning, Bülow had only at Chapelle-Saint-Lambert Prince William's cavalry and the Losthin division, in all 9,000 sabres and muskets, and that 7 kilometres of wretched roads and the rough passes of the Lasne, separated him from the battlefield. It is difficult to believe that he would have ventured to the rescue of the English, at the almost certain risk of sharing in their defeat. The Prussian generals were ardent but circumspect. We have seen that Blücher hesitated a whole hour before undertaking the defiles of the Lasne, and that he did not unmask until half-past four. It has also been seen that Zieten, at half-past six o'clock, absolutely refused Wellington's aide-de-camp to march on Papelotte, so long as the bulk of his army had not come up close to his advanced guard; that he even retraced his steps, fearing to commit himself, and that he yielded only to the entreaties and remonstrances of Müffling, who had galloped at full speed to make him turn back. There is no doubt that Bülow would have shown himself as prudent as Zieten. At all events his intervention would have come too late.

20. Clausewitz, while he extols (wrongly from a strategic point of view) an attack on the right wing, admits finally that only an attack upon the left centre, hazardous as it would have been, might have produced a decisive result.

21. "Apathy exactly similar to that which he experienced at Moscow." If it is certain that on the day of Moscow the Emperor suffered from an attack of ischuria, it is not at all proved that he kept away from the field of battle, and that he was so cast down that he took no interest in what went on around him. The testimonies of Gourgaud and General Pelet, the reports of Prince Eugene, of Ney, and of Murat, do not agree with the story of the eloquent General de Ségur. Clausewitz has said: "Circumstances fully explain and justify, to my mind, the manner in which Napoleon acted at Moscow."

THE END

GENERAL MAP OF T

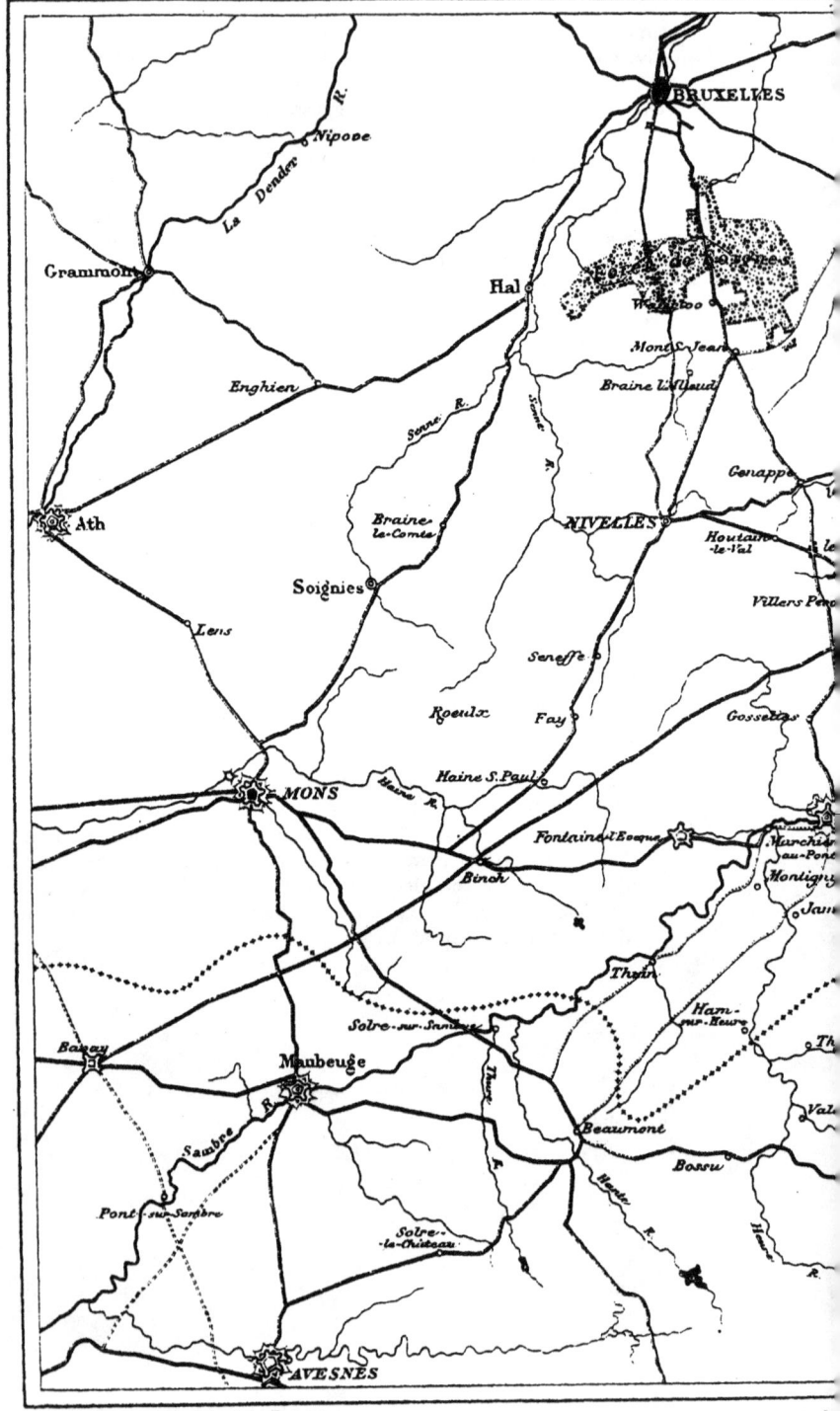

Illustrating "1815 Waterloo," by Henry Houssaye.

CAMPAIGN OF 1815

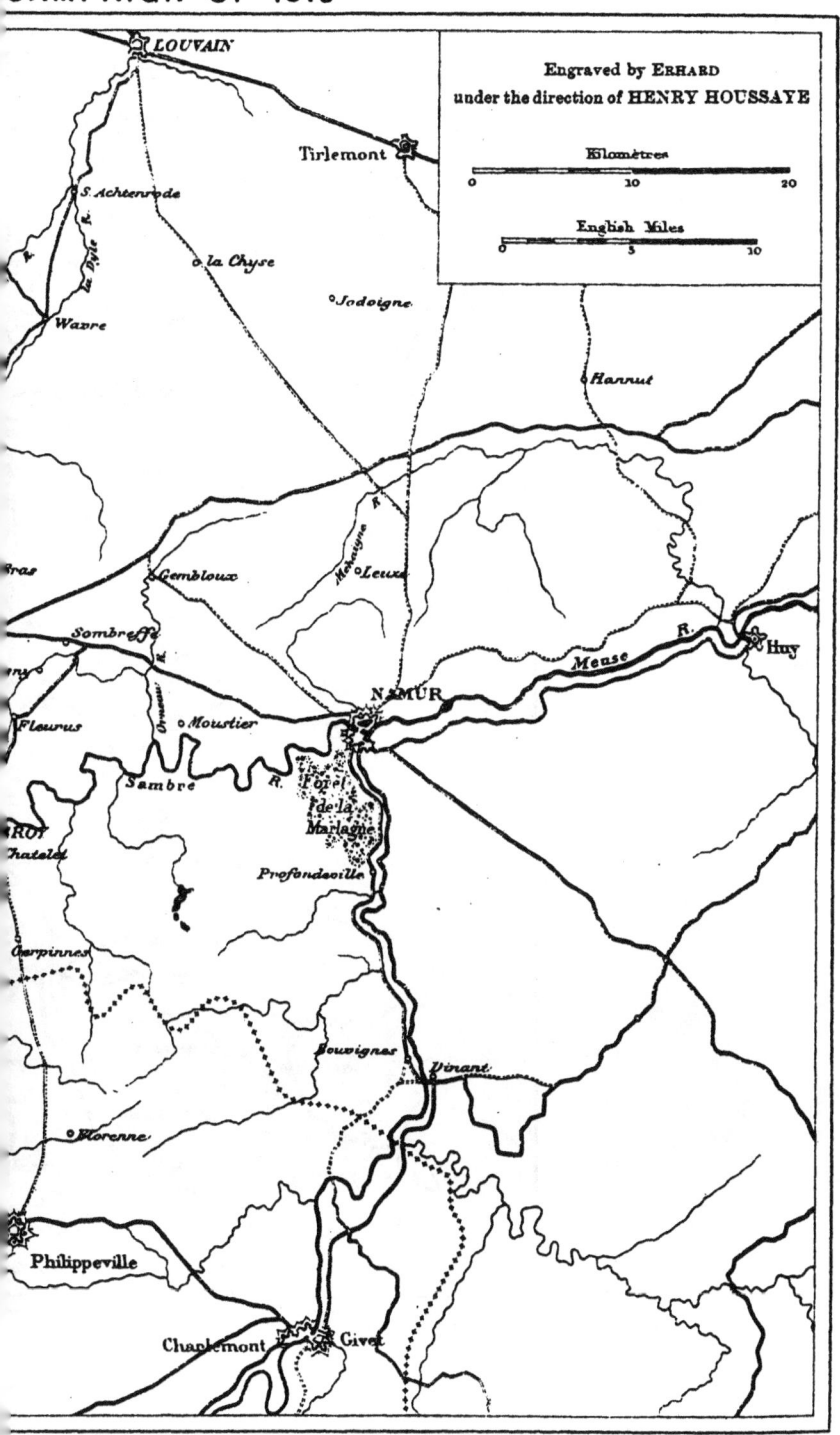

MAP OF THE MILITARY OPERATIO

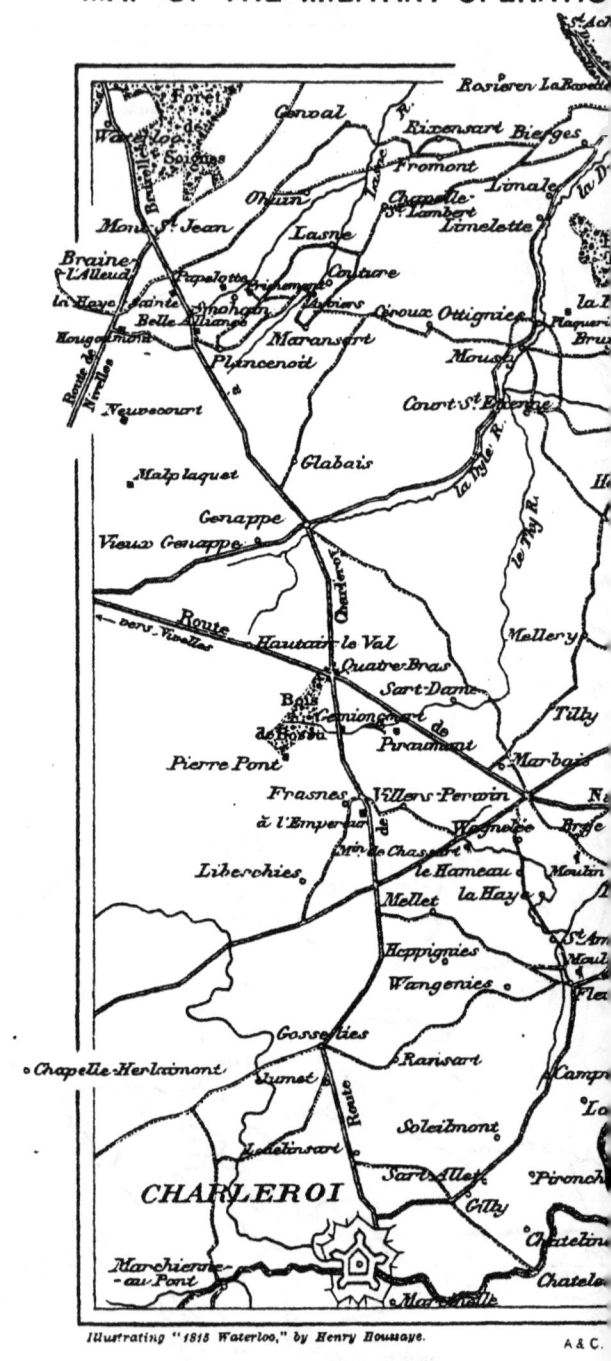

Illustrating "1815 Waterloo," by Henry Houssaye.

FROM THE 15th TO 20th JUNE 1815.

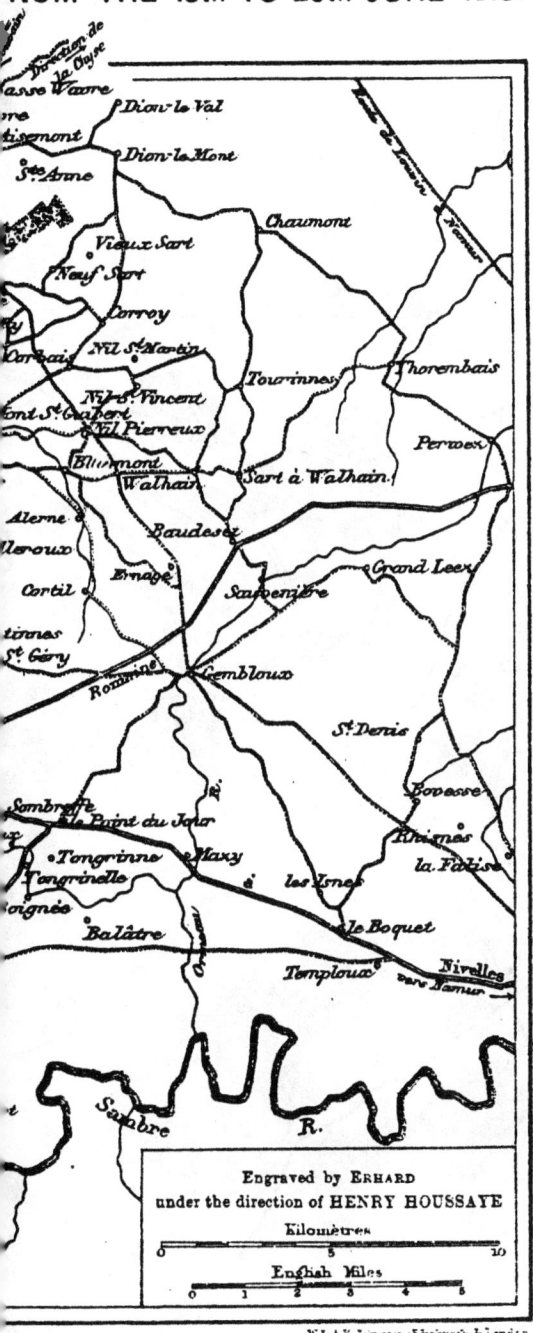

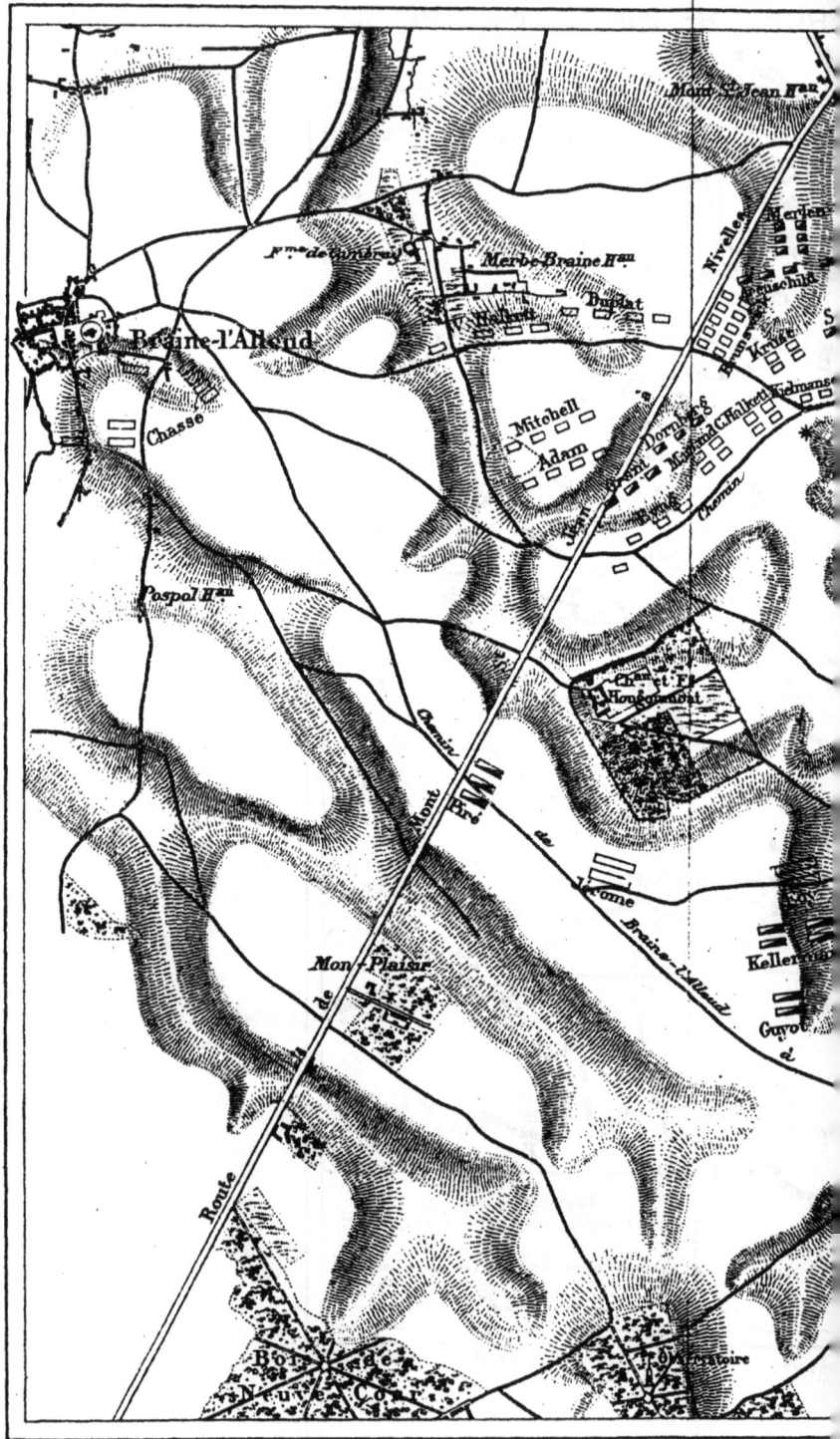

Illustrating "1815 Waterloo," by Henry Houssaye.

WATERLOO.

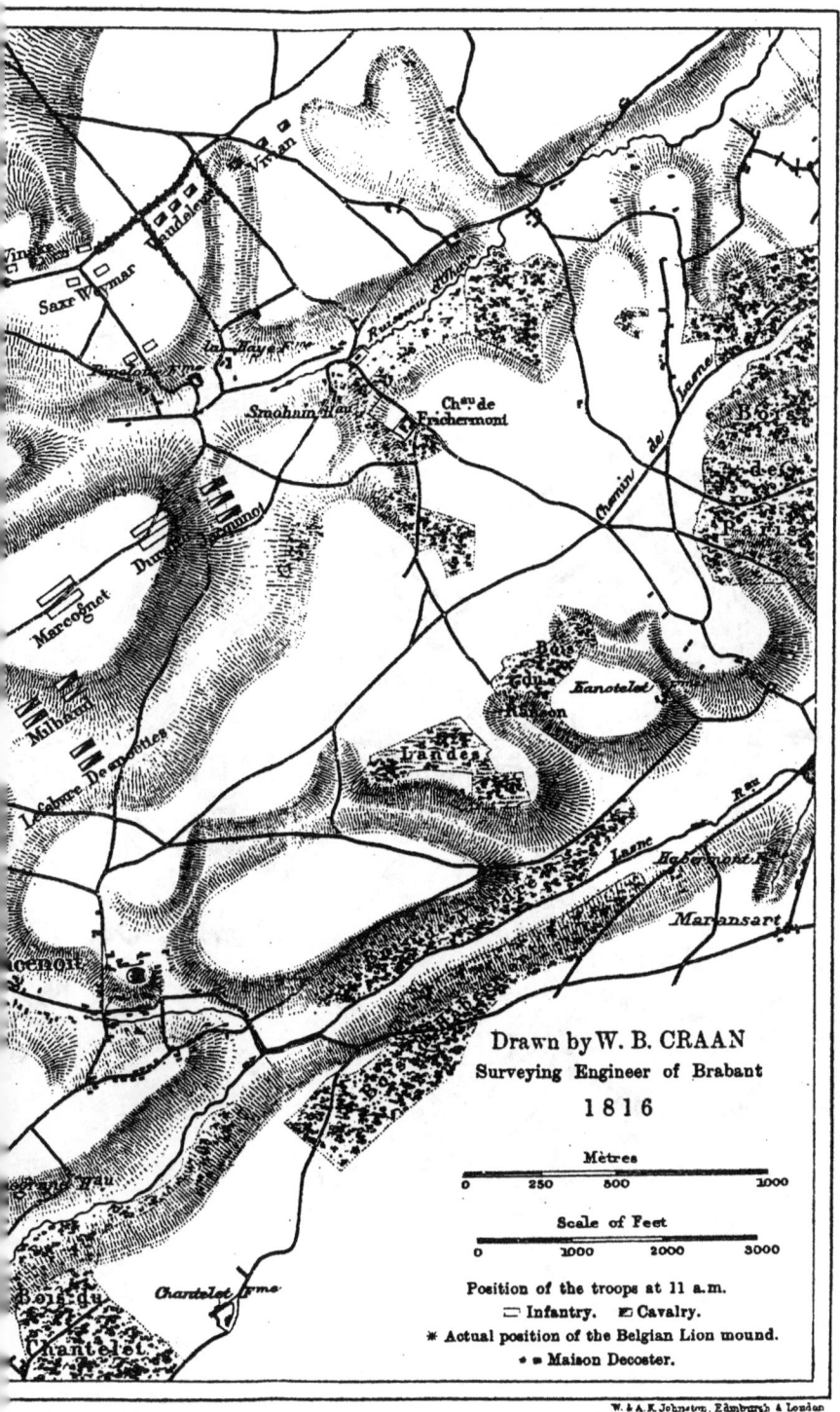

Drawn by W. B. CRAAN
Surveying Engineer of Brabant
1816

Position of the troops at 11 a.m.
⎓ Infantry. ▭ Cavalry.
* Actual position of the Belgian Lion mound.
♦ = Maison Decoster.

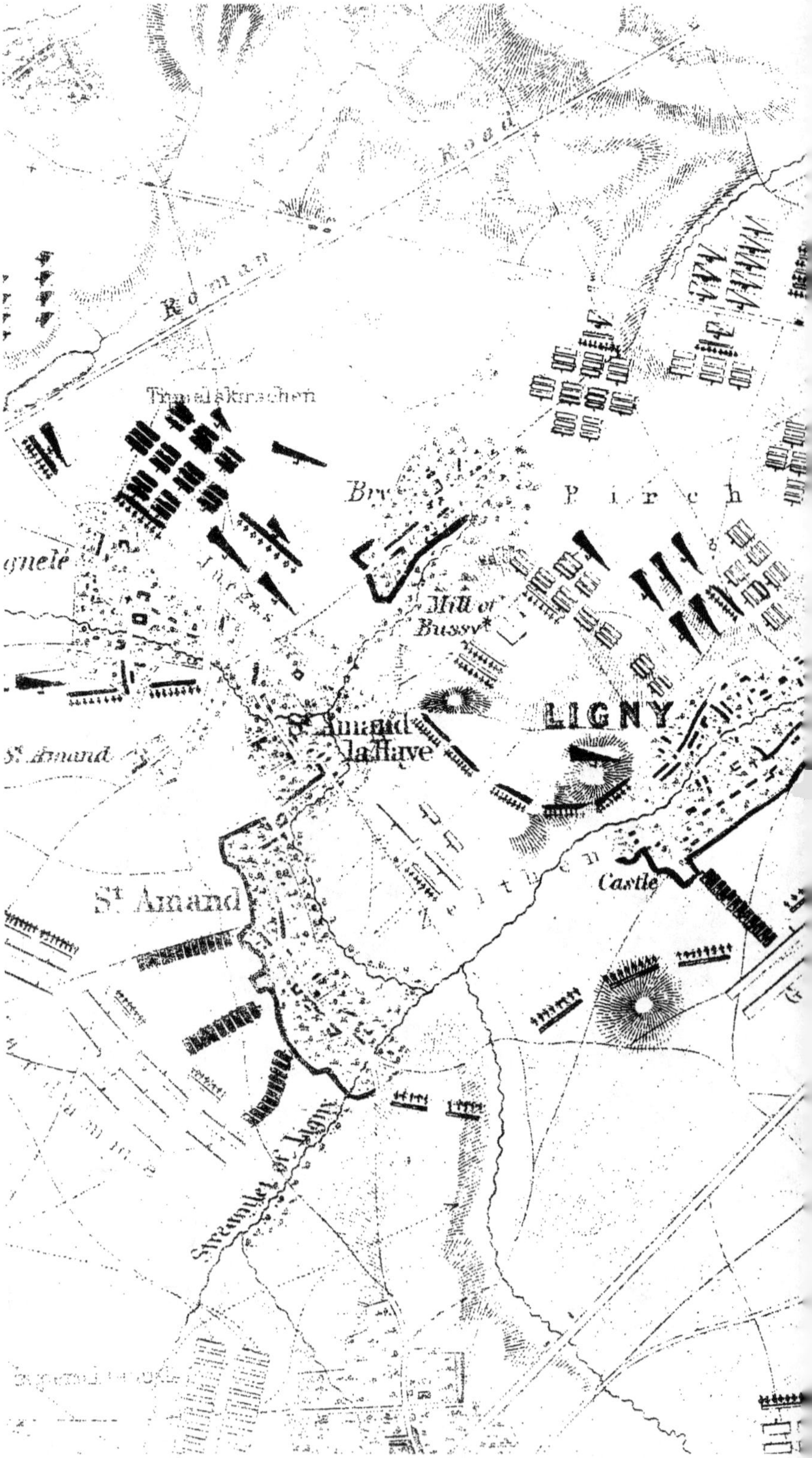
Roman Road
Tumelskirachen
Bry
Pirch
Mill of Bussy
LIGNY
St Amand la Haye
St Amand
Castle
Streamlet of Ligny

www.ingramcontent.com/pod-product-compliance
Lightning Source LLC
Chambersburg PA
CBHW070713160426
43192CB00009B/1179